COUNSELING TREATMENT FOR CHILDREN AND ADOLESCENTS WITH *DSM-IV-TR* DISORDERS

Second Edition

ROBERT R. ERK
University of Tennessee at Martin

PEARSON

Merrill
Prentice Hall

Upper Saddle River, New Jersey
Columbus, Ohio

Library of Congress Cataloging-in-Publication Data

Counseling treatment for children and adolescents with DSM-IV-TR disorders /
[edited by] Robert R. Erk. — 2nd ed.
    p. ; cm.
  Includes bibliographical references and index.
  ISBN-10: 0-13-230262-4
  ISBN-13: 978-0-13-230262-3
  1. Mentally ill children—Counseling of. I. Erk, Robert R.
   [DNLM: 1. Mental Disorders—therapy. 2. Adolescent. 3. Child
Development. 4. Child. 5. Counseling–methods. WS 350.2 C856 2008]
  RJ504.C66 2008
  618.92'89142—dc22

                                                    2007013933

Vice President and Executive Publisher: Jeffery W. Johnston
Publisher: Kevin M. Davis
Editor: Meredith D. Fossel
Senior Editorial Assistant: Kathleen S. Burk
Project Manager: Mary Harlan
Production Coordination: Pine Tree Composition, Inc.
Design Coordinator: Diane C. Lorenzo
Cover Design: Bryan Huber
Cover Image: Super Stock
Production Manager: Susan W. Hannahs
Director of Marketing: David Gesell
Marketing Manager: Autumn Purdy
Marketing Coordinator: Brian Mounts

This book was set in New Baskerville by Laserwords Private Limited, Chennai. It was printed and bound by Courier/Westford. The cover was printed by Coral Graphics.

Pearson Education Ltd.
Pearson Education Singapore Pte. Ltd.
Pearson Education Canada, Ltd.
Pearson Education–Japan

Pearson Education Australia Pty. Limited
Pearson Education North Asia Ltd.
Pearson Educación de Mexico, S.A. de C.V.
Pearson Education Malaysia Pte. Ltd.

10 9 8 7 6 5 4 3 2 1
ISBN-13: 978-0-13-230262-3
ISBN-10:   0-13-230262-4

To my parents,
Marian Yarbrough Erk
and
Ralph Adam Erk

In memory of
my beloved son,
Robert Adam Erk

PREFACE

Counseling Treatment for Children and Adolescents Diagnosed with DSM-IV-TR *Disorders* is designed to enable counselors to better understand the needs of children and adolescents who might be diagnosed with a *DSM-IV-TR* disorder. This book focuses on providing clinical information and data on behavioral disorders to people who are preparing to become counselors in mental health centers, community clinics, public schools, college counseling centers, hospital settings, government agencies, juvenile correction facilities, or private practice. Counselors from the beginning student to the more experienced counselor can learn more about the field of behavioral disorders from this book. However, it is important for readers to recognize that the broader or overarching concept of the book is to emphasize that *DSM-IV-TR* disorders are most often the result of a multifactorial causative process.

It is increasingly the message of clinical research that we need to redirect our thinking from a unitary or single cause model for disordered behavior to the consideration of multiple variables or factors. For example, important factors that counselors must carefully consider are developmental stages, environmental influences, biological or genetic contributions, socioeconomic influences, and culture. Each of these has an interwoven and causative part to play in every individual's life. Ultimately, the reasoning that all psychological or psychiatric diagnoses are the result of what can be described as a multifactorial causative process should become our guide. It is widely recognized, for example, that a comprehensive or holistic view of childhood disorders must involve a careful consideration of developmental factors. Researchers consider development and the timing of environmental events (e.g., positive, negative) in the lives of individuals to be inseparable and that they might have consequences across the individual's life span. Therefore, the issue of development is important to consider with respect to all the "factors" that are involved in the development of child psychopathology.

Inherent in a multifactorial causative process are three overriding propositions for counselors who recognize the importance of the developmental perspective. First is the conviction that *DSM-IV-TR* disorders, conditions, or problematic behaviors are connected to and best conceptualized within a "developmental" context. Accumulating knowledge tends to support this belief; however, there is much more to be known or discovered. Second, there can be no doubt about the strong "interactional and reciprocal" causes involved in both positive and maladaptive behavior. A large number of variables, such as family, school, social status, and culture, often operate as profound influences and cannot be discounted. Third, "empirical approaches" to the study and understanding of psychopathology in children or adolescents demand that we know more about the complexity of human behavior in the clients we serve.

It is beyond the scope of this book to cover all the disorders or conditions found in each of the respective sections of the *DSM-IV-TR*. Instead, the most common ones (e.g., those most often discussed in research literature and diagnosed in children or adolescents) were chosen for discussion. Still, readers will come away with a clear, concise, systematic, and up-to-date understanding of what is known about these disorders or conditions.

PURPOSE OF THIS BOOK

The interest in mental disorders or psychopathology in children and adolescents has steadily grown. New findings from the clinical literature have challenged older theoretical or conceptual models of mental disorders. We can surely say we know more today about mental disorders and psychopathology than just a decade ago. The overriding purpose of the book is to capture the interest in this rapidly evolving state of affairs for counseling students and instructors alike. Whether mental disorders are considered individually or collectively, there is a wide and extensive audience of counseling students and practicing counselors who need more education and training in this area.

This textbook can fulfill this need because it brings the counselor pertinent clinical research information describing each disorder or condition, shows how to proceed in making an appropriate diagnosis, and demonstrates how to construct appropriate treatment regimens for clients. This book is designed to address these important considerations as fully as possible.

IMPORTANT ASSUMPTIONS IN THIS BOOK

Guiding the conceptualization and crafting of the book were certain "assumptions" that were forged into the design of the book. It makes the following assumptions about students and instructors who will use the text.

1. Readers should be reasonably familiar with the diagnostic format of the *DSM-IV-TR*. Although this is not critical to have in one's educational background, it would be helpful.

2. The reader has had sufficient counseling or psychological coursework to make the material presented in this book practicable or meaningful. This will also lessen any possible misunderstanding of material that the reader might otherwise have.

3. The style or format of the book is intended primarily for individuals who are receiving education and training in counselor education or psychology programs. This book can stand alone as a source of counselor instruction. However, it can also be adapted (e.g., mated to existing coursework) for use in counseling or psychology curriculums if desired.

4. The book's comprehensiveness rests in its description of the specific disorders and therapeutic modalities that are most useful to counselors. It makes no attempt to present a complete discussion of each disorder or all of the specific treatment techniques that might be available. For the most part, the treatment paradigms recommended assume a setting in which appropriate monitoring can be accomplished, on-site care is available, if needed, and follow-up care can be arranged.

5. The links to the *DSM-IV-TR* in the book are housed in the extremely simple stance that the disorder or condition discussed, in order to be treated appropriately, has to be accurately diagnosed. Furthermore, the *DSM-IV-TR* criteria are clinically adequate as much as clinical trials and the research literature can indicate. Also, it is vitally important to recognize that the *DSM-IV-TR* is not the last or only word in our understanding of serious emotional or behavioral disorders (i.e., mental disorders). Diagnosis and treatment for behavioral disorders are dynamic, multifaceted, and evolving.

6. The book represents guidelines for the practice of counseling clients who might have a *DSM-IV-TR* diagnosis. It should not be viewed as establishing a standard of care for any specific disorder, client, or counselor, regardless of the treatment setting. The professional counselor is expected to remain ever vigilant for new information and developments in the field.

7. The book strives to be realistic in its approach to how important appropriate diagnosis and treatment are to the concept that all clients are treatable and can make improvements in their disorders or conditions. In other words, few helping professions call for outright cures.

8. A counselor with the authority to diagnose and treat disorders must take that professional responsibility very seriously. It is the counselor who is charged in our society with recording diagnoses and prescribing treatment. This fact alone presses home the need for professional counselors who are ethical and have knowledgeable information about what they can provide.

9. Finally, children and adolescents who have serious emotional and behavioral disorders often have time as their ultimate enemy, especially if the child has not been provided with an appropriate diagnosis or treatment has remained absent. This book is intended to have as much impact in this area as it can possibly impart to practicing counselors.

ORGANIZATION AND FEATURES

The organization of this book differs from that of most other texts in counseling or psychology. It integrates and presents an understandable format for the education and preparation of counselors about mental or behavioral disorders. Each chapter presents major sections on understanding how the disorder is defined, its diagnostic or clinical features, causal factors and prevention, assessment methods or procedures, comorbid conditions, implications for practice or treatment, school and family perspectives, a case illustration, summary or closing remarks, and where to go for more information.

The editor conceptualized the content and wrote three of its chapters, and 10 authors selected for their expertise in behavioral disorders wrote the remaining chapters. By having chapters in the book authored by different counselor educators or psychologists who directly teach, practice, and focus on the areas contained in this book, it means that an expert is there as a direct resource to you. Moreover, you will be able to learn what the professionals in our field are teaching students and practicing with their clients who have these disorders. The chapters were written by interested authors, who follow the research literature; they view it as a wonderful opportunity to assimilate and interpret the current state of understanding.

Furthermore, a sample treatment plan from the authors is included in every chapter that deals with *DSM-IV-TR* disorders. Whereas some chapters have similar formats for writing a treatment plan, other chapters have a different format for providing treatment. This is particularly helpful for counselors because it provides different models for viewing and constructing treatment. In summary, readers should clearly understand that there are different approaches or ways to construct or implement treatment. Currently, there are no research data to conclusively indicate that there is one way to address treatment planning and/or interventions. Chapters 10 and 11, which specifically deal with treatment planning, reinforce to readers this point as well.

The book contains three important parts to its organization. Instructors have their own preferences for the order in which they present topics or chapters in their classes. The chapters in this book can be covered in any order the instructor prefers. The chapters, however, are grouped logically to include topics that are most closely related.

Part One provides an overview of developmental issues applicable to children and adolescents. Chapter 1 begins with how to view assessment and diagnosis from a developmental perspective. Chapter 2 provides a developmental systems perspective for understanding the development of emotional and behavioral disorders in children and adolescents. It cannot be overemphasized that Chapter 2 applies to all the chapters where emotional and behavioral disorders are discussed.

Part Two deals with classifications of emotional and behavioral disorders in children and adolescents. Chapter 3 looks at the adjustment disorders; Chapter 4 examines the most prevalent childhood disorder in our society, Attention-Deficit/Hyperactivity Disorder; Chapter 5 investigates the disruptive behavior disorders: conduct disorder and oppositional defiant disorder; Chapter 6 details the spectrum of anxiety disorders; Chapter 7 discusses the mood and depressive disorders; Chapter 8 takes up the pervasive problem of substance-related disorders; and Chapter 9 stresses the seriousness and consequences of eating disorders.

Part Three brings much needed attention to the importance of treatment planning. Chapter 10 deals with the guidelines for effective treatment planning; and Chapter 11 provides case studies in treatment planning.

Finally, through its organizational structure, this book encourages counselors to become more critical thinkers and better problem solvers when they encounter clients who have developed emotional or behavioral disorders. It incorporates what every counselor wants to learn to do well: gather information, assess what is going on, hypothesize about relational patterns in the information, think outside the traditional box or lines, and develop a creative approach to problem-solving regarding the issues at hand. It is hoped that for clients and their families who come into your care, this book can make your decisions more reflective and thoughtful.

NEW TO THIS EDITION

The second edition of *Counseling Treatment for Children and Adolescents with* DSM-IV-TR *Disorders* has been thoroughly updated with new and relevant sources from the research literature. In addition, there are new sections in the chapters that expand and strengthen its appeal to students. We have been fortunate to be joined again by highly regarded experts; these contributors have continued to construct scholarly and practical information on the disorders discussed in this text.

We were especially interested in expanding for our readers both the science and art of treatment. The treatment of social, emotional, and behavioral problems of children and adolescents continues to develop. Perhaps, the main development we have seen pertains to the **effectiveness of treatment** (i.e., evidence-based, empirically supported, outcome research). Broadly conceived, these terms refer to those interventions that have evidence in their behalf. Reviews of the evidence-based treatment literature have consistently found that many treatments for children and adolescents can produce therapeutic change. Therefore, contributors were asked to provide a review of research to convey the status of treatments, in a concise way. Thus, the chapters are unique in providing readers a statement of the evidence in behalf of the treatments. Readers should realize that it is beyond the work of this book to address the complete body of evidence-based research or the questions that exist surrounding the methodologies of empirical or outcome research. This type of research is still developing and there is much about treatment efficacy that we have yet to learn.

Another unique feature to each chapter is information on where readers can go to obtain **best practice guidelines** for use with clients. These guidelines provide practitioners with the best available treatment recommendations (i.e., supported by the best available evidence from research and consensus). Practice guidelines have clear relevance when implementing treatment. Practitioners need to be aware that practice guidelines should be evaluated for their use on an individual basis (i.e., case by case).

In the treatment planning section of the book, two new cases have been added for our readers. Having an enhanced understanding of treatment planning can only increase our effectiveness with clients.

The contributors believe that in the not too distant future, the "future" for children and adolescents with social, emotional, and behavioral disorders will be even brighter. We hope you will join us in making this a reality.

ACKNOWLEDGMENTS

Consistent with writing is the acknowledgment of persons who contributed to the success of the finished work. I wish to extend heartfelt appreciation to Kevin Davis, Publisher at Merrill/Prentice Hall, for his patience and steady encouragement. Meredith Fossel, Editor, and Kathy Burk, Senior Editorial Assistant, are thanked for their kind assistance. Samuel Gladding, Professor of Counseling at Wake Forest University, contributed support and valuable assistance from the very beginning. Gary Gintner, Associate Professor of Counselor Education at Louisiana State University, and Earl Ginter, Professor, Division of Academic Enhancement at the University of Georgia, provided the editor with sound and practical advice. All the authors were always willing to go the extra mile to make their chapters better. For this, enough appreciation can never be extended. It is the support of those who trust you to create something good that is never forgotten.

A critical part of writing this textbook involved feedback from the expert reviewers. They are dedicated professionals and scholars. I thank and appreciate the reviewers for offering detailed comments and perceptive suggestions that were extremely useful in shaping the direction of the final manuscript. These reviewers are Joseph M. Cervantes, California State University, Fullerton; Daisy B. Ellington, Wayne State University; and Carolyn Stone, University of North Florida.

Robert R. Erk

MEET THE AUTHORS

MEET THE EDITOR

Robert R. Erk, Ed.D., is a past president of the Southern Association for Counselor Education and Supervision. Dr. Erk is a professor of counselor education and educational psychology in the College of Education and Behavioral Sciences at the University of Tennessee–Martin. His service includes over 30 years of teaching in the school and mental health counseling programs. He is licensed as a school counselor, a school psychologist, and a professional counselor and marital and family therapist. He received his doctorate in counselor education from Mississippi State University.

His professional work history includes public school teaching, serving as a high school counselor, and serving as head of a junior high school guidance office. He is a presenter of state, regional, and national workshops on Attention-Deficit/Hyperactivity Disorder (AD/HD), conducts national learning institutes on AD/HD for the American Counseling Association, and has authored articles for a number of American Counseling Association journals. Dr. Erk wrote the statement on AD/HD for the *ERIC/Clearinghouse on Counseling and Student Services Digest,* wrote the position statement on AD/HD adopted by the American School Counselor Association, and founded the American School Counselor Association professional interest network for children with AD/HD.

Within a counseling framework, his current research and teaching interests are centered on bringing to professional counselors a better understanding of the development of emotional and behavioral disorders in the clients and families they serve.

MEET THE CONTRIBUTORS

Annette Albrecht, Ph.D., received her doctorate in counseling from Marquette University. Dr. Albrecht is a licensed professional counselor in Texas and professor at Tarleton State University, where she has taught graduate counseling courses for the past 15 years. Dr. Albrecht teaches in both the school and mental health counseling specializations, and currently serves on the editorial board of the *Journal of Mental Health Counseling.* Dr. Albrecht has co-authored *High Tech, High Touch: Distance Learning in Counselor Preparation,* and presents extensively at regional and national counseling conferences.

Lynn F. Field, Ph.D., received her doctoral degree in counseling from George Mason University. Dr. Field is in private practice as a Licensed Professional Counselor in Northern Virginia, working at the Women's Center. She specializes in working with people with eating disorders and is a member of the Academy for Eating Disorders. Her clinical work has included supervision, administering grant programs, and providing training for clinicians who work with people with eating disorders. She also teaches graduate courses at George Mason University.

Earl J. Ginter, Ph.D., holds licenses as a professional counselor and as a marriage and family therapist. In addition to serving as a counselor, teacher, and professor at the University of Georgia, he maintains a private practice in Athens, Georgia. He is a past editor of the *Journal of Counseling and Development* and the *Journal of Mental Health Counseling.* Dr. Ginter has authored and co-authored numerous publications in journals and books pertaining to counseling and has presented at state, regional, national, and international conferences. Dr. Ginter is serving as Interim Director of the Division of Academic Enhancement at the University of Georgia.

Gary G. Gintner, Ph.D., is an associate professor and coordinator of the counselor education program at Louisiana State University. Dr. Gintner received a doctorate in counseling psychology from the University of Southern Mississippi. He has published numerous articles and book chapters on topics such as differential diagnosis, conduct disorders, mood disorders, and treatment planning.

Dr. Gintner presents national workshops and learning institutes on the *DSM-IV-TR* and treatment planning for the American Counseling Association. He is one of the most knowledgeable individuals about treatment planning in the counseling field. Dr. Gintner has clinical work experience in outpatient mental health, inpatient psychiatric care, chemical dependency, and employee assistance programs. He consults with national managed-care companies and is on the leading edge concerning mental health counseling in the managed-care environment. Dr. Gintner is President of the American Mental Health Counselors Association (2007–2008).

Ann Shanks Glauser, Ph.D., is a licensed professional counselor and assistant professor at the University of Georgia, where she has been teaching and counseling undergraduate and graduate-level students for the past 17 years. She specializes in theory, research, and the practice of humanistic counseling. She holds a doctoral degree in counselor education from the University of Georgia.

J. Scott Hinkle, Ph.D., is a National Certified Counselor, Certified Clinical Mental Health Counselor, and Approved Clinical Supervisor. Dr. Hinkle received his doctorate in clinical psychology from Florida State University. He is a licensed psychologist and has 24 years of mental health counseling experience. Dr. Hinkle served as a full-time graduate professor of counselor education for 13 years, teaching psychodiagnosis, clinical assessment, and marriage and family counseling. In addition to private practice, Dr. Hinkle serves as a national consultant for mental health treatment facilities and corporate organizations, where he provides clinical training. Dr. Hinkle specializes in providing clinical workshops and institutes on the diagnosis and treatment of *DSM-IV-TR* disorders in children and adolescents. Dr. Hinkle is the clinical training coordinator for the Center for Credentialing and Education, Inc., a corporate affiliate of the National Board for Certified Counselors, Inc. (NBCC). He also teaches online counseling courses for several universities and volunteers as an American Red Cross Disaster Mental Health Counselor. Dr. Hinkle has a private practice in Greensboro, North Carolina, where he enjoys working with children, adolescents, couples, and families.

Kathleen Maloney, M.A., received her bachelor's degree in psychology and communications from Sonoma State University, and a master's degree in clinical psychology from the University of Albany, SUNY. She maintains a private practice working with children, adolescents, and families. In addition, she teaches psychology at Regis University.

Nick J. Piazza, Ph.D., is a licensed professional clinical counselor and a licensed psychologist, and served as chairman of the Department of Counseling and Mental Health Services at the University of Toledo. Dr. Piazza received his doctorate in counselor education and supervision at Southern Illinois University, Carbondale. Dr. Piazza has worked in the mental health and substance abuse fields since 1975. He holds national certification as a Clinical Mental Health Counselor and as a Master Addictions Counselor from the National Board of Certified Counselors. Dr. Piazza is nationally recognized as a lecturer on psychopharmacology and serves on the boards of three hospitals. He has numerous publications and presents frequently at the American Counseling Association and American Psychological Association national conventions. Dr. Piazza has served on the editorial board of the *Journal of Mental Health Counseling* and *Counseling and Values,* and is presently serving on the editorial board of *Essential Psychopharmacology.* Dr. Piazza is the Director of Behavioral Sciences for the Flower Hospital Family Physician Residency Training Program.

Patricia J. Polanski, Ph.D., is an assistant professor in the Department of Counselor Education and Human Services at the University of Dayton, Ohio. Dr. Polanski teaches in the community, school, and clinical counseling tracks. She is the coordinator of the school counseling program. Dr. Polanski earned a doctorate degree in counseling and counselor education from the University of North Carolina–Greensboro. Dr. Polanski has 14 years of professional experience working with children and adolescents in residential treatment settings as a child care worker, activity therapist, and clinical counselor.

Gina Scarano-Osika, Ph.D., received a doctorate in counseling psychology from the University of Dayton, Ohio. She spent a year in a post-doctoral fellowship studying college student mental health at the University of Rochester, Strong Memorial Hospital. She is a licensed psychologist in private practice in Glen Falls, New York, working with children, adolescents, couples, and families. Dr. Scarano-Osika specializes in working with clients with eating disorders. She volunteers time to the Capital Region Association for Eating Disorders, a nonprofit organization that provides education to individuals who have eating disorders.

Linda Seligman, Ph.D., has a doctorate in counseling psychology from Columbia University. She is a licensed psychologist and licensed professional counselor. Dr. Seligman is a professor emeritus at George Mason University, where she was a full professor and served as co-director of the doctoral program in education and coordinator of the graduate programs in counseling. Currently, Dr. Seligman is a faculty associate at Johns Hopkins University and has a faculty appointment in Health and Clinical Psychology at Walden University. In addition, she has a private practice in Fairfax, Virginia, where she works with adolescents, adults, and families.

Dr. Seligman has published 9 books and over 75 articles and chapters. Her latest books are *Systems, Strategies, and Skills of Counseling and Psychotherapy* and *Technical and Conceptual Skills for Mental Health Professionals,* both published by Merrill/Prentice Hall. Her current research interests focus on diagnosis and treatment planning and the use of the mind–body–spirit connection with both healthy people and those with chronic and life-threatening illnesses.

DISCOVER THE COMPANION WEBSITE ACCOMPANYING THIS BOOK

THE PRENTICE HALL COMPANION WEBSITE: A VIRTUAL LEARNING ENVIRONMENT

Technology is a constantly growing and changing aspect of our field that is creating a need for content and resources. To address this emerging need, Prentice Hall has developed an online learning environment for students and professors alike—Companion Websites—to support our textbooks.

In creating a Companion Website, our goal is to build on and enhance what the textbook already offers. For this reason, the content for this user-friendly website is organized by topic and provides the professor and student with a variety of meaningful resources. Features of this Companion Website include:

- **Counseling Topics**—17 core counseling topics represent the diversity and scope of today's counseling field
- **Annotated Bibliography**—includes seminal foundational works and key current works
- **Web Destinations**—lists significant and up-to-date practitioner and client sites
- **Professional Development**—provides helpful information regarding professional organizations and codes of ethics

To take advantage of these and other resources, please visit the Companion Website for *Counseling Treatment for Children and Adolescents with* DSM-IV-TR *Disorders,* Second Edition, at

www.prenhall.com/erk

BRIEF CONTENTS

CONTENTS

Chapter 4
Attention-Deficit/Hyperactivity Disorder in Children and Adolescents   114

Chapter 6
Anxiety Disorders in Children and Adolescents   216

J. Scott Hinkle

Chapter 9
Adolescents and Eating Disorders   332

Gina Scarano-Osika and Kathleen Maloney

PART THREE: EFFECTIVE TREATMENT PLANNING

NOTE: Every effort has been made to provide accurate and current Internet information in this book. However, the Internet and information posted on it are constantly changing, so it is inevitable that some of the Internet addresses listed in this textbook will change.

PART ONE

OVERVIEW OF DEVELOPMENTAL ISSUES

Chapter 1
Assessment and Diagnosis: The Developmental Perspective
and Its Implications

Chapter 2
Understanding The Development of Psychopathology
In Children and Adolescents

Chapter 1

ASSESSMENT AND DIAGNOSIS: THE DEVELOPMENTAL PERSPECTIVE AND ITS IMPLICATIONS

By

Earl J. Ginter
and
Ann Shanks Glauser

In 1840, a count of mental disturbance cases was initiated by the U.S. Bureau of the Census to determine the frequency of "mental illness" occurring throughout America. The Bureau relied on the single category of "idiocy/insanity" to achieve its goal (Ginter & Glauser, 2001). This historical effort by the U.S. government, along with other attempts since 1840 in this and other countries to expand the knowledge base comprising mental disorders, has led to what might seem for today's novice practitioner to be an overwhelming amount of information to master. Even limiting oneself to the study of conditions associated with approximately the first 2 decades of life (i.e., from infancy through adolescence), one soon discovers there are a number of age-related disorders that mark the early years of human development: Attention-Deficit/Hyperactivity Disorder, Separation Anxiety Disorder, Depressive Disorder, and many other types of disorders that fall within categories such as Disruptive Behavior Disorders, Substance-Related Disorders, and Pervasive Developmental Disorders. These disorders, along with others not mentioned, require possession of special knowledge if one hopes to accurately assess and treat such conditions (Swales, 2001). It is safe to assert that much has transpired since 1840 to alter our understanding of psychological conditions. This assertion is especially true in the case of conditions that are associated with infancy, childhood, and adolescence.

Certain age-related disorders are both disruptive and prevalent enough to deserve special attention and appear in the *Diagnostic and Statistical Manual of Mental Disorders,* Fourth Edition, Text Revision (American Psychiatric Association, 2000a) under the category of "Disorders Usually First Diagnosed in Infancy, Childhood, or Adolescence." Even a cursory inspection of these disorders reveals that certain aspects of various developmental vectors (e.g., physical, cognitive, emotional, behavioral, and social) are used to render a diagnosis. The term <u>*developmental vectors* refers to those areas in human development that have been identified as areas expected to change during the life span</u>. For example, over time one may expect the child to "move along" the social vector that enables the child to handle increasingly complex interpersonal situations. However, achieving greater developmental sophistication along the social vector does not mean the child will always operate at his or her highest level of developmental achievement in all social situations. (Consistent with other vectors, as the child develops he or she *achieves* new ranges of possibilities along the social vector, and each "possible" way to respond in a social situation can represent a different level of social "maturity.")

Although it is not the intent of the *DSM* system to denote what constitutes healthy, normal development, the diagnostic criteria listed in it do provide a means to logically infer expected healthy human development. For example, failure to display certain developmentally related changes during early childhood, such as achieving a common level of communicative speech, moving beyond a simple familiarity with the alphabet, and being able to sight-read at least some "survival words," could reflect a pattern of symptoms that indicates truncated movement along the cognitive vector, and thus could result in a diagnosis of Severe Mental Retardation (*DSM-IV-TR*, 2000a, p. 43). Reversing such *DSM* criteria (e.g., the young child achieves a level that exceeds a basic familiarity with the alphabet), one is able to isolate to a certain degree what healthy, normal cognitive development encompasses for the infant, child, and adolescent. The focus of this chapter is to impart to counselors the importance of extrapolating what effects a *DSM* disorder or crisis situation might have wrought on a particular child's development, enabling counselors to better determine how a disorder or situation might impede or thwart a child's development at a particular period or at subsequent developmental periods.

A FOUNDATION FOR ACCURATE DIAGNOSIS AND EFFECTIVE TREATMENT: KNOWLEDGE OF HUMAN DEVELOPMENT

To ascertain the actual effect of certain disorders or crisis situations (e.g., divorce) in the life of the child, the child's family, and various systems outside the family that directly involve (e.g., the school attended) or indirectly involve (e.g., the school board that sets policies) the child, <u>a counselor must understand what is developmentally expected at various times in a child's life</u>. (*Note:* Unless otherwise indicated, the terms "child" or "childhood" are used in this chapter in a generic manner to denote the developmental periods of infancy, childhood, and adolescence.) Hood and Johnson (2002) indicated that accurately gauging the severity of a client's situation, even in cases where a clinical disorder is not a contributing factor, requires a valid assessment of the situation. Nevertheless, rendering a precise diagnostic assessment can easily be affected by a number of factors, such as a counselor's preconceived notions, inadequate knowledge of certain clinical conditions, or failure to meet a certain standard of valid testing (e.g., the child culturally does not match the original populations recruited to develop and norm the assessments being used to test the child).

Hood and Johnson (2002) listed 16 basic principles of psychological assessment that if violated have the potential to corrupt the accuracy of a diagnosis. They call attention to the possibility that in some cases the main obstacle to achieving an accurate diagnosis resides within the diagnostician. We believe it is this particular category of assessment concerns that deserves diligent attention, because biases that reside within the diagnostician can be the most difficult for that person to detect. Hood and Johnson (2002) provide a specific illustration of such a bias when they link *attribution bias* to violating the principle of assessing "the situation as well as the client" (p. 9). For instance, an attribution bias appears in those cases where the professional associates a child's academic problems with low motivation for achievement, an association made simply because the referral source described the child as "a kid that constantly disturbs the class and shows zero respect for authority." The professional in this example is predisposed to believe that such a child's disruptive behavior and lack of respect must be explained in terms of internal causes (e.g., the child lacks motivation to learn necessary academic skills) and not external causes (e.g., the child's teacher treats the child differently from other students because of the child's light skin color). Sometimes more than one factor contributes to a misdiagnosis. Adding to the example presented, the professional might violate the principle of considering "alternative hypotheses" when determining a diagnosis, and as a result commits a *confirmatory bias* that strengthens the existing attribution bias. Specifically, this type of combination would result in the diagnostician focusing only on evidence that supports his or her preconceived thoughts while dismissing or downplaying the significance of any opposing evidence. Although we have found Hood and Johnson's list of principles a helpful guide for increasing assessment accuracy, we have also found it to be incomplete. One must consider safeguarding against what we have termed *developmental reference point error.* This type of error occurs when a diagnostician, practitioner, or researcher who lacks knowledge or possesses false knowledge about relevant developmental factors draws an erroneous conclusion that subsequently affects the professional's conduct (i.e., diagnosis made, treatment rendered, or data interpreted). Such an error might prove deleterious for a child who is assessed for treatment intervention because misdiagnosis and the subsequent mismatching of treatment to condition might allow symptoms to take root and become pervasive.

Certainly, a crucial factor residing within the counselor is the level of knowledge the counselor possesses concerning early human development. For instance, a child's level of impulsiveness is not only age related, but can be expected to fluctuate naturally throughout the day when the child moves through periods of being tired or rested. The necessity of understanding what is typical of early childhood is clearly indicated in *DSM-IV-TR* (2000a) statement: "In early childhood, it may be difficult to distinguish symptoms of Attention-Deficit/Hyperactivity Disorder from **age-appropriate behaviors in active children** (e.g., running around or being noisy)" (p. 91, bold type used in the *DSM*). It is the stance of the authors of this chapter that when the client is a child, a developmental assessment always precedes a clinical impression; in other words, thinking developmentally is a prerequisite for rendering a valid diagnosis. Five reasons why an understanding of human development is essential are discussed next. Each is considered primary in nature by the authors.

UNAVOIDABLE REASONS FOR THINKING DEVELOPMENTALLY

Normal Developmental Deviation

What is considered as a symptom of a disorder in the adult might fall within the expected range of a particular developmental vector for a child. Several writers (e.g., Ginter & Glauser, 2001; Ivey & Ivey, 1998) are careful to point out that what might be perceived as "abnormal" by someone who has contact with the child (e.g., a teacher, parent, school counselor, or peer's parent) might fall within the established range of what is considered normal for that child's age or situation. In fact, the *DSM* system recognizes that some "situations," which are common and do not reflect a serious disorder, still might require the attention of a mental health professional. In the life of the child, many such situations can easily be conceptualized as a "developmental crisis."

According to Gazda, Ginter, and Horne (2001), a period of developmental crisis differs from serious psychopathology in that a child (and other family members) is very likely to move through the crisis eventually, although an accurate assessment and appropriate counseling intervention would move the child and family through a crisis period more quickly and with less turmoil (counseling might even enable those involved to reframe the crisis [or alter some aspect] to achieve higher developmental levels). Typical developmental crises that are frequently identified by family members as having an adverse impact on the family's ability to function are situations such as impaired communication patterns ("I can't talk to my daughter—she believes drinking alcohol is a teenager's right. Last night we got into a shoving match that resulted in me running out of the house.") and inadequate discipline ("Nothing seems to be working—following family rules doesn't seem to matter since he entered middle school. He's driving teachers and us crazy."). Rather than a personality disorder designation or a classic clinical syndrome designation, the counselor might assess these situations (impaired communication and inadequate discipline) as situations that match a *DSM* category known as "Other Conditions That May Be a Focus of Clinical Attention." Specifically, such situations could be assigned the code of V61.20 with the accompanying descriptor "Parent-Child Relational Problem." According to the *DSM-IV-TR* (2000a):

> Relational problems include patterns of interaction between or among members of a relational unit that are associated with clinically significant impairment in functioning, or symptoms among one or more members of the relational unit, or impairment in the functioning of the relational unit itself. . . . These problems . . . may be independent of other conditions that are present, or can occur in the absence of any other condition. When these problems are the principal focus of clinical attention, they should be listed on Axis I. Otherwise, if they are present but are not the principal focus of clinical attention, they may be listed on Axis IV. The relevant category is generally applied to all members of a relational unit who are being treated for the problem. (p. 736–737) (*Note:* Axis IV is used for reporting psychosocial and environment problems that are relevant considerations in terms of diagnosis and treatment.)

Certainly, a designation of "Parent-Child Relational Problem" could reflect a normal pattern of deviation in the child's developmental journey toward adulthood.

We are discussing those types of impairment in functioning that are not associated with any true psychopathology category (e.g., Schizophrenia), but nonetheless require a counselor's intervention. Differentiating a "disorder" from a "non-disorder" requires a counselor to carefully weigh the significance of all available diagnostic and developmental information. The *DSM-IV-TR* weaves an elaborate web of psychopathological criteria that can easily entrap the unwary diagnostician. The authors of the *DSM* allude to the need to look beyond what is found in the pages of the *DSM* when they state, "specific diagnostic criteria . . . are meant to serve as guidelines to be informed by clinical judgment and are not meant to be used in a cookbook fashion" (*DSM-IV-TR*, 2000a, p. xxxii). It is our belief that informed clinical judgment requires utilitarian knowledge of human development.

Effects of Developmental Level

Seligman (1986), recognizing that many practitioners focus their efforts on rendering Axis I (and Axis II) diagnoses, stated that "providing a full diagnostic picture of a client involves diagnosing [a] client according to five axes" (p. 34). As mentioned earlier, Axis IV of the *DSM-IV-TR* calls attention to environmental and psychosocial stressors that might disrupt a child's normal progression along the various developmental vectors that constitute normal development (Ginter & Glauser, 2001). Many of the stressors identified in the *DSM-IV-TR* have important developmental implications that are readily apparent to seasoned practitioners who have encountered them repeatedly. However, reviewing the stressors associated with Axis IV provides even the novice practitioner an intuitive sense of why understanding human development plays such a pivotal role in the diagnosis and treatment of children. Simply stated, the maturity level of the child will determine to a large extent the exact impact of a stressor on the child's life. The following list represents only a portion of the types of stressors identified in the *DSM-IV-TR* (2000a) that have direct implications for working with children: discrimination; familial turbulence created by separation, divorce, or estrangement; removal from a parent's custody; remarriage of a parent; physical abuse by a parent; excessive over-protection by parents; parents neglecting basic child-care duty; excessive discord with siblings; birth or adoption of a sibling; death of a close friend or playmate; major life-cycle transition (e.g., moving to a new school); frequent clashes with teachers or classmates; exposure to an unsafe neighborhood; extreme financial poverty; and personal exposure to a natural disaster, war, or suicide attack by a terrorist. As indicated by Seligman (1986), "Axes IV and V, both viewed in relation to Axis I, can facilitate treatment planning and provide information on prognosis by enabling the counselor to compare nature and level of disturbance with level of client resources" (p. 35). Alluded to by Seligman (1986), Axis V reports the results of the Global Assessment of Functioning (GAF) Scale, which is used by the diagnostician to measure the client's level of adaptive functioning/impairment. In the case of a child, the GAF would require an assessment of the child's developmental strengths in relation to the psychological, social, and occupational (e.g., the adolescent's work history) areas of child development. The GAF does not consider "impairment in functioning due to physical (or environmental) limitations" (*DSM-IV-TR*, 2000a, p. 34).

Bacon, Collins, and Plake (2002) studied counselors who use the GAF in clinical settings and found that a GAF score is frequently arrived at using factors other than those intended by the *DSM*. For example, symptom severity was one such factor often considered by the study's participants when assigning a GAF value; and because of overreliance on this and certain other factors identified by the researchers, they concluded that approaches other than the GAF are capable of achieving a more accurate assessment of adaptive functioning/impairment. Finally, when the GAF was considered for inclusion in the *DSM-IV*, its scale was changed from 0–7 to 0–100, which seems to inject an unrealistic expectation for achieving clinical precision (Seligman, 1999), raising the question of whether this change in rating has increased or decreased the GAF's usefulness. It seems reasonable at this juncture, considering the comments of Bacon et al. and Seligman, for counselors to be cautious when determining a GAF score, or in accepting a GAF score at face value when such a score is found recorded in a client's existing record.

Isolating the Normal Problem "In" the Abnormal Condition

As pointed out in the *DSM-IV-TR* (2000a), "a common misconception is that a classification of mental disorders *classifies people* (italics added), when actually what is being classified are disorders that people have. [Because of this misconception] the text of the *DSM* . . . avoids the use of such expressions as 'a schizophrenic' . . . and instead uses the more accurate . . . 'an individual with Schizophrenia' " (p. xxxi). Beyond what is implied in terms of the harm that can result from a misused label (Ginter, 1989), this statement also implies that the sum total of symptoms does not equal the total child. The importance of this latter implication cannot be overestimated in relation to effectively working with a child. Also, the distinction being made between the label and the person indicates the importance of the diagnostic qualifiers (e.g., mild, moderate, and severe) applied to any *DSM* diagnostic category pertaining to a mental disorder. The stronger the qualifier, the greater the likelihood that the condition affects a number of developmental vectors.

At the core of the third reason is the belief that adopting a developmental perspective enables the counselor to focus on the normal concerns of children diagnosed with a disorder. A couple of brief client examples illustrate the point being made. The first author, early in his career, worked with adolescents diagnosed with mild and moderate mental retardation. As is common with most adolescents, these adolescents were confronted with developmental issues pertaining to the acquisition of social, vocational, and academic skills. Whereas academic skills ranged from about the second-grade to sixth-grade level, the motivation to attain these skills at the highest possible level resulted in a type of developmental completion in a significant developmental area that affected these adolescents' quality of life. It was the author's experience that these adolescents were just as concerned about future earnings and intimate relationships as one might expect with an adolescent not diagnosed with mental retardation. Another illustrative example is the adolescent diagnosed with Attention-Deficit/Hyperactivity Disorder. It is not uncommon for such an adolescent to develop a negative self-image, and even though it is obvious that such a self-view might occur for reasons different from other adolescents, the situation can be conceptualized as a common developmental concern that dovetails with Erik Erikson's theory of identity development.

Although presence of a particular *DSM* disorder might somewhat alter the manifestation and expression of common developmental concerns, such concerns do in fact represent developmental issues that stand on their own as worthy of a counselor's attention. To mistakenly perceive a common developmental-based client concern as nothing more than symptom expression is a gross misuse of a diagnostic label, and will result in questionable treatment planning. Finally, and probably most important, viewing such a child's concern from a developmental perspective and addressing the concern with the client as a normal developmental concern, when true, better enables the client to "see beyond" the label that has been applied to his or her condition. For the counselor to recognize the "normal" in the child's developmental world enables the child to normalize for himself or herself the concern and discover, with the counselor's assistance, the most appropriate action or means of solving the developmental-based problem or difficulty. Similar to Yalom's (1995) concept of *universality*, which he applies to a group member's realization that "I am not the only one who suffers this way," normalizing a concern for the child better enables the child to see himself or herself as a member of the larger peer group rather than an isolate who is little more than a "walking, talking label."

Knowledge of Human Development Provides the Context to Understand Important Cultural Differences

Over the last few decades, the importance of considering the role that cultural factors play in counseling can be described as incontrovertible. This is especially true in the area of assessment, where accuracy is crucial. In fact, an inaccurate diagnostic label might prove to be little more than a "scientific slur"—serving to add to the problems confronting the person. Similar to a racial/cultural slur that reflects an environment of discrimination, a scientific slur has the inherent power to negatively affect the child's social status and future opportunities in various systems (e.g., the school, the playground, the neighborhood, and a summer job).

We contend that achieving diagnostic accuracy often depends on simultaneously considering developmental and cultural factors. It is generally accepted that the range of some developmental-based behaviors for children and adults in one culture can radically differ from what is found in another culture (Koss-Chioino & Vargas, 1999; Whiting & Edwards, 1988). For example, one area that usually displays variance between cultures is type of discipline used by parents to control for inappropriate behaviors. What is an acceptable type of discipline for one cultural group might be misunderstood and even perceived as abusive by a different cultural group. The complexity involved in such situations has been discussed by Fontes (2002); her discussion provides a means for counselors to determine the difference between those situations that reflect physical abuse and those that reflect a culturally driven pattern of discipline. Fontes is careful to point out that even in those situations that do not involve abuse, the counselor might still have to intervene to help the parents find alternative ways to modify their child's behavior. Intervening in such cases, the counselor should initially focus on achieving three parental insights prior to helping the parents adopt any new strategies of discipline. The three insights to work toward are these: First, in the family's new setting, certain types of disciplinary tactics are likely to be mistaken for abuse; second, incidents mistaken for abuse can be reported by anyone, including the child being disciplined, and when reported they are investigated; and third, alternative methods to correct a child's behavior, methods that will not be mistaken for abuse and are compatible with the family's cultural values, can be adopted.

Cultural differences can become a "diagnostic cloak" with the real potential to hinder a counselor from genuinely seeing the "other." Simply stated, although there is much that is universal in human development (e.g., children from around the world display the sucking reflex after birth), not all developmental achievements (i.e., identity development) unfold in a universal manner. According to Stead (1996), "counselors from a Western background may value independence, rational decision making, and self-actualization. Such values may be at odds with those of individuals from more collectivistic backgrounds and cultures" (p. 274). We have found that answering a certain question (i.e., "Even though I do not practice the same type of child-rearing practices as this child's family, based on current information about healthy human development, is this child thriving and developing normally?") can help a counselor determine, with reasonable confidence, what constitutes an appropriate type and level of intervention.

The authors of the *DSM* recognize the importance of cultural influences and are forthright in their attempt to have diagnosticians consider the interplay of culture and the child's behavior. The *DSM* outlines "steps" to ascertain the degree that cultural factors should be weighed when rendering a diagnosis. The steps suggested in the *DSM* are these: Determine the cultural identity of the child (we believe the parents' cultural identity must also be considered when working with a child because the two perceptions of identity might diverge from one another and produce conflict); seek a cultural explanation for the child's behavior; identify cultural factors related to the child's psychosocial environment and the child's level of functioning; recognize the possible existence of cultural elements that might affect the relationship between the child and the counselor (e.g., the counselor is not well versed in the child's first language); and conclude by providing an overall evaluation of how cultural factors influence the final diagnosis and proposed treatment plan (see *DSM-IV-TR*, 2000a, pp. 897–903). The *DSM* also provides a *glossary of culture-bound syndromes* that shows how cultural influences might affect the child's intrapsychic and extrapsychic environment. According to the *DSM-IV-TR* (2000a), "culture-bound syndromes are generally limited to specific . . . culture areas and are . . . categories that frame coherent meanings for certain repetitive, patterned, and troubling sets of experiences and observations" (p. 898). For example, *mal de ojo* is Spanish for "evil eye" and reflects a prevalent belief found throughout Mediterranean cultures. The *DSM* indicates "children are especially at risk" for *mal de ojo* and offers a list of symptoms (i.e., unprovoked crying, sleep irregularities, fever, vomiting, and diarrhea) that could easily denote a viral illness such as the flu. A counselor who fails to recognize a manifestation of the "evil eye" (and that its manifestation is a way for the family to conceptualize its concerns) is very likely to inaccurately assess the situation and miss an opportunity to provide any type of meaningful intervention for the family.

Developmental-Based Treatments/Recommendations

Certainly, making a diagnosis does not represent the end of the counseling process because treatment (or some type of intervention) is the flip side of the "diagnostic coin." Once the counselor has determined that a disorder does or does not exist, the counselor is still left with the responsibility of planning for an appropriate treatment or a recommendation. The developmental level of intellectual, emotional, behavioral, interpersonal, and physical maturity that the child has achieved will provide an indication of what level of communicative sophistication should be used with the child as well as the reasonableness of any therapeutic goal or recommendation the counselor establishes with the child. The level of developmental sophistication possessed by all clients can be thought of as an omnipresent consideration to guide counseling interactions with clients (Gazda et al., 2001; Ginter, 1999; Ivey & Ivey, 1998), but careful consideration of the client's developmental sophistication seems especially important when working with children. (Play therapy's effectiveness resides in a developmental-based appreciation that therapy must "speak" and use the "language" of the child to help the child—in this instance the language is play.) Setting specific counseling goals (e.g., learning appropriate interpersonal behaviors for various settings) with a 7-year-old child will differ markedly from those set with a 13-year-old. And as previously pointed out, the same approach holds true in cases where a *DSM* disorder is present (e.g., the developmental sophistication of the adolescent diagnosed with mild mental retardation will differ markedly from the 13-year-old diagnosed with Oppositional Defiant Disorder).

The importance of possessing the co-requisites of applicable *DSM* knowledge and human development knowledge is captured in the following remarks by Prout (1999), who wrote:

> Children are not simply "little adults." Their treatment cannot be viewed as scaled-down adult therapy; their developmental stages, environments, reasons for entering therapy . . . necessitate a different, if not creative, approach to therapy. The child/adolescent therapist must have an expanded knowledge base of the human condition and a different perspective of what constitutes therapy or counseling. (p. 1)

THE DEVELOPMENTAL MATRIX: THEORY AND RESEARCH

The aim of this section is not to provide an exhaustive review of developmental theory, or research, which would require an encyclopedic approach that easily exceeds the limits of a chapter; rather, the aim of this section is to highlight some of the most salient information related to child development procured during the previous and current century.

Because theory and research are time-bound, if one traces the history of developmental psychology, one finds that subsequent conclusions, compared to earlier conclusions, represent further clarifications and significant modifications, and in some cases result in a particular theory or research finding being abandoned. An example of this ongoing process of knowledge refinement is the changes that have occurred in psychoanalytic-based developmental theory. Psychoanalytic theory moved from Freud's drive theory to ego theory, which evolved into object relations theory and eventually took on the form of self-psychology (Gazda et al., 2001; Ginter & Bonney, 1993). Throughout these changes in psychoanalytic theory, several theoretical conceptualizations have been retained and modified in light of our current knowledge about human development. One such psychoanalytic concept that has been modified over time is the concept of defense mechanisms. To fully appreciate the persistent contribution that defense mechanisms have made to counseling requires a brief discussion of their past and current role.

Anna Freud's *The Ego and the Mechanisms of Defense* (1937/1966) provided a detailed description of the psychoanalytic conceptualization of psychological defenses. In this seminal work, she provided a tentative chronological classification of several defense mechanisms, but concluded that it would "probably be best to abandon the attempt to so classify them" (p. 53) in such a manner. Anna Freud believed it would be too difficult to ascertain, with reasonable certainty, the actual order in which common defense mechanisms appear. Although we agree with Anna Freud's assertion concerning the difficulty of determining their order of developmental appearance in a child's life, we disagree that this type of difficulty creates any obstacle to increasing the utility of defense mechanisms for counselors. For us the question is not when does a defense mechanism appear in the life of a child, rather it is what does a particular defense mechanism tell us about the developmental sophistication possessed by the child in terms of problem-solving (and decision-making)?

Information about defense mechanisms appears in the *DSM IV TR*, and it serves a useful purpose when distinguishing between healthy developmental-based behaviors and mental disorders or the type of stress-related conditions associated with Axis IV. Furthermore, whereas "Axis II is for reporting Personality Disorders and Mental Retardation, it may also be used for noting prominent maladaptive personality features and defense mechanisms" (*DSM-IV-TR*, 2000a, p. 28). According to the *DSM* system, identifying which defense mechanisms are prominent in the life of the child is an important clinical consideration and we believe, as touched upon earlier, it can be used to gauge the child's level of developmental sophistication.

In relation to assessing the child's level of problem-solving skills, the authors have found it helpful to reframe the *DSM* categories of defense mechanisms in terms of a *high, low-minor,* and *low-major level* of problem-solving effectiveness. A counselor could use our approach to defense mechanisms or another developmental-based approach (e.g., Gemelli, 1996; Vaillant, 1977) to achieve a better understanding of a child's ability cognitively and emotionally to process information pertaining to a doubtful or difficult situation confronting the child. Although it is beyond the scope of this chapter to provide a detailed explanation for why the authors placed each defense mechanism in a certain category, a general explanation is that placement was based on the following: consideration of various theoretical conceptualizations (i.e., drive, ego, object-relations, and self) of defense mechanisms found in the literature (e.g., Clark, 1991; Clark, 2002), research pertaining to defense mechanisms (e.g., Vaillant, 1977), our own counseling experiences, and the specific psychoanalytic position espoused by Ginter (Ginter & Bonney, 1993; see also Gazda et al., 2001). Finally, although our scheme of categorizing defense mechanisms is focused on the level of problem-solving sophistication, the scheme is not to be interpreted (of course) as age-independent. Specifically, the system's validity is dependent on the counselor's ability to make suitable adjustments to the general categorization scheme we propose. These adjustments are essentially tied to obvious chronological considerations (e.g., a 5-year-old's reliance on "acting out" might be relatively appropriate when one considers the specific problem confronting the child and the developmental maturity typically achieved by 5-year-olds, but the same type of acting-out behavior is almost certain to be viewed as inappropriate for a 13-year-old, regardless of the situation).

The following lists provide examples for each category of defense mechanisms.

High Level of Developmental Sophistication

- Sublimation
- Humor
- Anticipation
- Self-observation
- Self-assertion
- Affiliation
- Altruism

Low-Minor Level of Developmental Sophistication

- Intellectualization
- Rationalization
- Help-rejecting complaining
- Passive aggression
- Reaction formation
- Undoing
- Apathetic withdrawal
- Acting out
- Displacement
- Projection
- Repression

Low-Major Level of Developmental Sophistication

- Denial
- Splitting of self-image or image of others
- Idealization
- Devaluation
- Omnipotence
- Delusional projection
- Autistic fantasy
- Psychotic distortion
- Psychotic denial

At the *high level* of developmental sophistication, the reactions reflect both an adequate awareness of consensus-based reality (i.e., others could validate the individual's perception) and reliance on appropriate problem-solving approaches. In this latter aspect, the specific approach taken is congruent with the child's developmental-based skill level. The *low-major level* of developmental sophistication encompasses reactions that show an obvious disregard for obtainable facts. In this case, problem-solving becomes fantasy driven and is incongruent with the child's expected level of skills based on what is known about human development. Compared to the *low-major level,* a defense mechanism falling at the *low-minor level* might initially be difficult to detect. The reason for this difficulty is that elements of reality and fantasy are fused to create the defense mechanism. It is the fusing of reality and fantasy that instills in this type of defense mechanism a superficial plausibility not found in the *low-major level* of defense mechanisms. Despite the difficulty sometimes encountered in identifying the presence of a *low-minor* defense mechanism, such a defense will make itself known because this type of defense has a repetitive nature, and because this level of defense is an ineffective problem-solving approach that nets only temporary relief from an ongoing problem.

Viable Theories of Human Development Mutate Over Time

In addition to specific theoretical changes (e.g., defense mechanisms) that have occurred to psychoanalytic-based theories or other theories such as existential-humanistic and cognitive-behavioral theories (Gazda et al. 2001), there have been changes to several early general assumptions that defined the field of developmental psychology. For example, the field of human development moved from proposing universal, sequential-stage theories that typically described a series of occurrences that were intrinsic in nature and linear in movement, to proposing models of human development that relied more upon interaction types of explanations and developmental changes that incorporated notions described by terms such as nonlinear, contextual, and systemic (Thomas, 1996). This last aspect of human development, the systemic aspect, recognizes that various internal and external elements of a child's existence coalesce to help create an influential system (and set of systems). Contemporary developmental-based counseling requires the counselor to be aware of the influence that individual systems and conglomerations of systems have on a child.

Bronfenbrenner (1979) has grouped systems into categories (microsystem, mesosystem, exosystem, and macrosystem) that provide counselors with a meaningful method to sort out the combination of influences wielded by various types of systems. A *microsystem* refers to things such as the child's home environment and school environment. Microsystems are settings that the child typically experiences on a day-to-day, face-to-face basis. Each setting can be identified by its own set of unique activities, roles, and interpersonal relationships. When individuals comprising these settings are unresponsive to the child's developmental needs, there is a disruption of the child's normal development. The *mesosystem* category is used to refer to the "linkages between settings." The mesosystem is what essentially constitutes the social mode of life; in Bronfenbrenner's view, it is made up of all those societal elements functioning interdependently. The child and these settings interact in ways that have the potential to positively or negatively affect the child's development (e.g., conflicting interactions among teachers, parents, and the child can "place the child in the middle of a no-win situation"). An *exosystem* is a set of systems that do not have direct contact with the child when the systems are interacting, but still affect the child as a result of their interactions (e.g., a textile plant and the child's mother who works at the plant [she and other employees are affected by what happens at the plant]). A timeless example is the parent who experiences great amounts of work-related stress, and as a result interacts with family members in ways that do not support normal developmental gains in the child, or actually hinder such gains (e.g., the parent physically abuses her child). A *macrosystem* is the system created by the sum of commonalities found in all the other systems making up the child's world. Simply stated, the macrosystem represents the child's culture. Obviously, a wide range of cultural factors such as cultural traditions and cultural beliefs, especially about "mental illnesses," can have a profound effect on the child.

Bronfenbrenner (1979) indicated that a systemic approach, used to understand general human behavior and specific developmental-based behavior, must also account for a number of factors that can influence various systems. One such factor is time. In fact, some changes in systems can be appreciated only if one adopts a chronological perspective. Different forms of feminism, appearing at different historical points, had different effects on the various systems conceptualized by Bronfenbrenner. For example, child-rearing responsibilities have changed over the last 30 years in the United States because of contemporary feminism's influence. Another example of time's influence pertains to Bronfenbrenner's view concerning which conceptual elements are required to define the word "development." According to Bronfenbrenner, it is simplistic to think that only the child is affected by various systems; the child's own ability to influence a more encompassing circle of systems grows substantially over time because of time-bound developmental changes occurring in the child. Bronfenbrenner (1979) even paraphrased a widely known Freudian phrase (i.e., "where id was, there shall ego be") to express his view that a time-related definition of human development is a necessity. Specifically, Bronfenbrenner coined the phrase "where exo- is, there shall meso- be" (p. 289).

To summarize, the net result of developmental psychology's long history of theory and research-driven effort is that developmental psychology has amassed a wealth of information concerning what constitutes healthy human development, especially in terms of how different developmental elements influence one another. Developmental psychology clearly provides counselors with an indispensable toolbox to accurately diagnose the child's "condition" and develop the most effective approach to intervening in the life of the child.

PHYSICAL, INTELLECTUAL, EMOTIONAL, BEHAVIORAL, AND SOCIAL ASPECTS OF THE DEVELOPMENTAL MATRIX

An array of theorists and researchers, has offered numerous developmental maps or conceptual representations but each map by itself at best provides a "flat" representation of the child's growth. To obtain a true multidimensional topography of the child requires combining the developmental features offered by each map (e.g., considering the contributions of both Jean Piaget's and Albert Bandura's theories enables the counselor to have a more complete understanding of a child's learning process). Superimposing the various maps allows the diagnostician to concentrate available information in such a way as to accurately ascertain the problem situation and determine the child's needs. To differing degrees, the *DSM* system focuses attention on the various physical, intellectual, emotional, social, and behavioral maps related to each disorder or situation by isolating and listing pertinent diagnostic criteria.

Each subsection that follows is intended to provide a developmental map of a certain area of human development, but, as with any map, it is important to keep in mind that other maps of the same developmental region are available that provide a much more thorough review of the territory (e.g., a book written by Piaget provides a much more thorough map than what is provided in this chapter concerning cognitive development).

Physical Maps of Development: Contributions of Arnold Gesell, Louise Bates Ames, and Frances L. Ilg

At birth the infant's activities (such as reflexes, breathing, and heartbeat) are regulated by rudimentary structures of the developing brain, while the cortex portion of the developing brain, which is associated with higher functions, is far from its full potential. Although many early developmentalists recognized the central role the physical aspect of human development played as a structural support for psychological changes (e.g., Alfred Adler's early notion of perceived "physical inferiority" and the child's attempt at compensation that governed subsequent personality development), few of the original theorists or researchers spent time identifying and arranging in order of time the physical changes that occurred in the infant, child, and adolescent. Others soon rectified this lack of attention, such as Arnold Gesell, who paid close attention to physical growth and other areas of development. Having knowledge of the sequential physical changes that occur early in life is a prerequisite to differentiating healthy and unhealthy development in the child. For example, during the first year of life, one can expect to find fundamental reflexes to characterize much of the newborn's existence. These reflexes provide the newborn a ready-made manner to interact with the environment and can be seen as essentially "programmed" responses. Whereas some of these ready-made responses (sneezing, eye blink) will continue until the end of life, others can be expected to diminish in frequency or even vanish. For example, the following ready-made infant behaviors can be expected to essentially disappear at different points during infancy (Corsini, 2002; Karmiloff & Karmiloff-Smith, 1999):

- Moro or Startle Reflex—remove support from the infant's head and neck (or create a loud noise), and the arms of the infant will thrust outward followed by an embracing type of movement and fingers clutching.
- Sucking Reflex—automatic sucking motions occur when something (nipple, finger) is placed in the infant's mouth.
- Stepping Reflex—when held and slowly lowered toward a flat surface, such as a floor, the infant will place one foot in front of the other as if he or she were starting to walk or step.

- Placing Reflex—the infant's foot automatically lifts up when contact is made with the top of the foot.
- Babinski Sign—when the infant is positioned on his or her back and a person gently strokes the bottom of a foot, the toes will extend and then curl.
- Rooting Reflex—touching the infant's cheek will result in the infant's head turning to that side.
- Swimming Reaction—submersion of the infant in water results in the infant displaying leg and arm motions that are similar to swimming.
- Palmar Grasp—touching the inside part of the infant's hand results in fingers closing and clutching.

Motor development follows a sequence that moves the neonate from essentially a bundle of identifiable reflex actions to an increasing number of intentional actions that are associated with an observable increase in fine motor ability. Specifically, during the first month most actions seem be involuntary reactions to some internal or external stimulus. These early reactions are analogous to starting a motor that sputters into action—the reactions of the newborn often seem to reflect movements that are jerky and denote a poor ability to follow through from beginning to end in a smooth manner. By 12 months, one will notice that the achieved "smoothness" of the child's movements provides a stark contrast to the movements of the newborn. During the period spanning 12 to 15 months, the child walks by using surrounding objects for support; and around the same period of time, the child displays an ability to pick up tiny objects and to stack objects on top of one another. More fluid and purposeful behaviors are becoming evident.

Interestingly, forcing oneself to look beyond the obvious "jerky" movements of the neonate, one discovers an array of surprisingly sophisticated abilities (admittedly, this knowledge has been acquired as a result of new technologies that were not available to early developmentalists). Counter to earlier beliefs held about the infant, it appears that the infant's senses are well developed. For example, the infant displays a preference for sweet flavors and odors, soft fabrics, gentle forms of contact (rocking), and its mother's odor over the odor of others. The newborn is very capable of recognizing repetitive sounds, including the voices of those encountered frequently (e.g., at birth the child can distinguish the mother's voice from others, and by month 3 the child prefers mother's voice over others).

Even the preceding truncated review of physical changes clearly indicates that remarkable developmental changes occur in a relatively short period of developmental time. As mentioned already, Arnold Gesell deserves special recognition for placing physical changes into a meaningful developmental context. Gesell and his associates at the Yale Clinic of Child Development (later the Gesell Institute) mapped much of what we have come to accept as milestones in physical development. Over time the efforts of these researchers (e.g., Ames, Gillespie, Haines, & Ilg, 1979; Gesell, Halverson, Thompson, Ilg, Castner, Ames, & Amatruda, 1940; Ilg & Ames, 1972) produced many relevant findings for diagnosticians and practitioners. Even though these researchers devoted a great deal of attention to biological changes (in fact, they were criticized by some developmentalists for what was perceived to be an overemphasis on the biological), in truth, the discoveries of this group extended beyond the biological.

Muro and Kottman (1995) summarized some of the psychological implications of the developmental profiles completed by Arnold Gesell et al. (e.g., Ames, Hober, Ilg). A few examples of what Muro and Kottman believe to be relevant considerations for a counselor are presented for illustrative purposes. The 5-year-old child's attention span is of such a nature that the child is frequently described as restless and reaches his or her limit at about 25 minutes. The need to be a recipient of loving attention and to be perceived as a being of worth is very evident in the 5-year-old child's actions and comments. This child thrives on support and adult efforts to promote self-optimism. In contrast to the 5-year-old, the 8-year-old is critical of others and might also be very critical of the self. By age 11, the child's emotional world is frequently in flux, but it is a world of fluctuating affective elements that the child is capable of identifying upon reflection.

The findings of Gesell et al. strongly suggest that physiological developments define the limits of what a child is capable of at various points in the child's life; these findings suggest that for one to impose undue stress on the child's structural capacity is to contribute to a failure (or setback) in the developing system. Simply stated, in addition to the developmental "norms" established by Gesell, he also advocated the importance of *readiness*. Gesell's concept of readiness was established via his belief that innately driven processes can be a primary contributor to determining a maturing child's capabilities. Readiness implies that the physical structure (e.g., the nervous system) has to be mature enough to accommodate a certain behavior. For example, a child must obtain a certain "mental age" to profit from reading instruction. Ilg and Ames (1972) added to our understanding of the readiness concept when they reported findings that indicated that the lack of success some children encountered in school could be associated with adult expectations (the parent's and the educator's) that exceeded what these children could achieve based on their developmental levels. Ilg and Ames made a number of specific recommendations in 1972 for parents and educators to follow concerning "school readiness." Interestingly, even with the wealth of gathered data—amassed over several decades—the exact role of physiology's effect on behavior is still hotly debated and far from settled. The pivotal concerns of this area are too often reduced to the all-too-familiar phrase "nature versus nurture."

The term *maturation* has been used to refer to developmental characteristics or sequences of events that follow a linear timetable and have an obvious heredity component. Whereas the term maturation was "borrowed" from biology by early psychologists to differentiate between learned and unlearned behaviors, in truth even learned behaviors ultimately are dependent on heredity to varying degrees. Certainly, heredity can be a forceful influence in "healthy" and "unhealthy" outcomes (e.g., evidence exists for a genetic link for Bipolar I Disorder; see *DSM-IV-TR*, 2000a). As the knowledge base grows about such physiologically embedded influences, professionals are increasingly provided a means to reinsert normal development in those situations where inherent biological influences have gone awry, such as a widely known genetic-related metabolic disorder (i.e., phenylketonuria) that can lead to mental retardation. This particular developmental misstep can be corrected via a special diet that overcomes the failure to metabolize in the normal fashion. Of course, biological factors are not a "one-way street" of influence because outside influences such as infections, accidents, and poisonings (such as mercury and lead) can alter physiology and thus the psychology of the child. Checking for such possible outside influences can sometimes reveal the most salient contributors to a child's current problems. Clearly, the potential for outside influences to impact the child is present even from the earliest stages of life. For example, not only is an in utero baby susceptible to outside sounds, detecting and responding to sounds as early as 28 weeks in the womb, the uterine environment is also susceptible to injurious influences (e.g., Fetal Alcohol Syndrome). The ability of a woman's placenta to filter out harmful influences is not a safeguard against some medications, controlled substances, and viruses (such as rubella and congenital syphilis), which can affect length of gestation, birth weight, sight, and intellectual ability.

In part due to completion of the Human Genome Project (Ridley, 1999) and the advances made in *evolutionary psychology* (Crawford & Krebs, 1998; Gaulin & McBurney, 2001; Weinert & Weinert, 1998), the theory of hereditarianism is enjoying resurgence as a potential explanation for individual differences among children. Terms such as gene-splicing, genetic code, genetic engineering, genetic error, genetic mapping, genetic marker, and genetic psychology are just a few examples of words that are finding a niche in everyday language. These terms reveal the prominent position the word "genetic" has assumed in contemporary life. But as indicated earlier, it is evident that a persuasive argument can be made that hereditary factors do not exist in an "environmental vacuum," meaning that heredity and environmental influences are partners in the dance of life. A reasonable argument countering extreme hereditarianism is that external influences have been found to have profound influences on innate potentialities (Demetriou, Doise, & Van Lieshout, 1998; Newcombe, 1996). As stated by Rak and Patterson (1996), "It has become commonplace to identify that certain children in this modern, complex society are 'at risk' of failing to succeed in life because of the adversities of their young lives. Poverty, family discord, violence, substance abuse, and illness are among the hazards" (p. 368). Finally, Stephen Wolfram (2002) has questioned, based on approximately 2 decades of research, several basic assumptions relevant to both sides of the "nature vs. nurture" argument. If Wolfram's assertions (e.g., the limited explanatory power of concepts such as adaptation and natural selection) are supported by the findings of other researchers, counselors will have to rethink their views about the causes for complex human behavior (see Wolfram's *A New Kind of Science*).

Despite the importance of considering the interplay of genetic and environmental factors as explanations for human behavior, we have entered a period during which hereditary factors have taken center stage. The authors of this chapter believe that obtaining the genetic blueprint for humans near the start of this century pushed genetic engineering to a new level of potentiality—a potentiality far beyond what has already been achieved in genetic technology. Although any prediction is likely to be less than perfect, the authors are willing to assert that the 21st century will be remembered as the epoch of medical advances that moved genetic counseling from being essentially providing information and support to individuals and couples concerned about inherited diseases or birth defects, to an endeavor that considers issues surrounding what might be termed *developmental enhancement of genes* through genetically engineered conception. One central issue will be the extent to which parents (and others) are allowed to design a child. The change in focus for genetic counseling promises to have profound ethical and philosophical implications for humanity, and these implications will ultimately affect the views society holds concerning the value of human diversity.

The Cognitive Maps of Development: Contributions of Jean Piaget, Lawrence Kohlberg, and Carol Gilligan

Cognitive development is dependent on certain types of experiential events (e.g., hearing a spoken language and other types of stimuli such as variegated images) that help foster the growth of links between brain cells. During the first 24 months, the child can be expected to experience rapid brain growth that is marked by building connections between major regions of the brain and among neurons in the cortex. This type of growth is associated with an increase in the efficiency and speed of neurological messages (Newcombe, 1996). As the brain develops, so does the type of thinking that becomes evident, which at the earliest period of development is distinguished by a type of egocentric processing or focusing.

Jean Piaget completed one of the most impressive surveys of the cognitive territory by mapping its features via a combination of intuitively inspired data-collection tactics and a profound speculative genius. He organized his theory and findings in terms of stages that start at birth and conclude after entering the period of adolescence (Lee, 2000). The qualitative changes delineated by Piaget (1970/2000) are directly tied to thinking, memory, and language development.

According to Piaget the stages are

- *Sensorimotor* (birth–2 years): Knowledge is dependent on sensory perception and motor activity. The taking in of information and the subsequent creation of some type of organized pattern or *schema* (i.e., a type of knowledge pattern) is the key activity that defines this stage. *Assimilation* is the process of adding "information" to an existing pattern, but it also represents the process of interpreting the world through existing knowledge patterns. (That is why a child with knowledge of a dog might call a cat, seen for the first time, a dog. New information [the cat] is incorporated but is understood in terms of what is already known [a small animal is a dog].) *Accommodation* was the term Piaget used to refer to changes in established knowledge patterns and can be viewed as a consequence of encountering certain experiences that do not match existing knowledge patterns. In a sense, this is the reverse of assimilation because the experience alters the knowledge pattern. The creation of a new schema or schemas reestablishes the balance that had been upset by certain experiences. According to Piaget, when such changes lead to a significant "jump" in the child's cognitive world, the child has in essence "climbed" to a new cognitive plane from which to view the world. Such jumps to new cognitive planes represent new stages in cognitive functioning and are labeled **preoperational**, **concrete operational**, and **formal operational**. Finally, a cognitive-altering achievement is reached when the infant obtains an understanding of what was termed *object permanence*, the understanding that a person or object not "seen" continues to exist.

- *Preoperational* (2–7 years): For this child, the acquisition of knowledge involves the use of symbols (e.g., words). Interestingly, even though the use of symbols reflects a new level of cognitive complexity (use of mental images increases), the child's approach to the world is qualitatively different from the adult's and tends to operate at an intuitive level. It is an approach that lacks the type of logic found in later stages (e.g., imaginary playmates and magical explanations for events are found at the preoperational stage). Some of the explanations or conclusions offered by a child operating at this cognitive stage are surprising to the adult-level thinker. For instance, the child will perceive a tall glass of milk as having more milk (when it does not) than a shorter and wider glass of milk, even if the child sees the milk poured from a shorter container into an empty, taller container.

- *Concrete Operational* (7–11 years): The child moves from his or her intuitive approach to interacting with the world to an approach that builds more elaborate knowledge structures, both symbolically and logically. But the child's interactions are such that the child is focused on the specific or particular situation rather than the general or abstract. In a sense, the child's thinking capabilities are "earth bound." A literal quality permeates much of what occurs in the child's pattern of thinking and responding.

- *Formal Operational* (11 years and up): In addition to symbolic and logical structuring of knowledge, the child becomes a true cognitive "philosopher." It is at this stage of thinking that the child can "soar," breaking free of the somewhat prosaic restraints of the prior stage. Abstraction is now a possibility, which enables the child to adopt a hypothetical approach to the world that allows the generation of possibilities and contingencies that can then be applied to anticipated situations when they happen.

Much has been added since Piaget's early efforts at mapping cognitive development, especially in relation to what occurs at Piaget's sensorimotor stage. Examples of what can be expected to occur at that age follow (Baby Center, 1997–2000; Hendrix & Morrison, 2000; Karmiloff & Karmiloff-Smith, 1999):

- 1–3 months: The infant displays evidence of recalling feeding times and begins to react to these and other rudimentary memories, such as responding to voices associated with prior encounters (e.g., a parent's voice). The infant begins to communicate by crying, but also makes cooing and gurgling sounds while interacting with others.

- 4–6 months: Examples of memories being used are behaviors such as differentiating the mother's features from those of others and "expecting" to see the whole object if part of the object appears first. Language development involves laughter that often manifests itself as a squeal. Babbling occurs and the infant starts to vocalize using vowel-consonant combinations such as "ah-goo." While several theories have been offered about language development (e.g., Burrhus F. Skinner's conditioning explanation and Noam Chomsky's inner predisposing aspects), it is clear that maturation of the brain is associated with language development. In fact, this particular physiological link is strong enough to cut across cultures; infants in different cultures (with different languages) mouth similar sounds and combinations of sounds (e.g., dada, bababa, deedee, tata). After this initial start with its universal aspects, the infant begins to mimic the sounds made by others in his or her own particular culture.

- 10–12 months: Random use of "mama" and "dada" fades into purposeful use of these words. The child clearly begins to assemble a repertoire of words. Memory and "stored" language mingle in the sense that names are recognized as belonging to certain people. Also, acts of denial, expressed as "no," are recognized for what they are—restrictions—restrictions that might even elicit a frustration response in the child.

- 13–24 months: At this age, the child combines gestures and sounds to express thoughts (e.g., points with index finger to an empty dish and says "all gone"). The number of gestures and words continuously builds up. At one point, the child might understand a greater vocabulary than what the child can call upon. Use of words is clearly tied to need satisfaction. The child's own name, in the child's mind, becomes "connected" to self ("Me Mark.") Near the end of this period, the child's vocabulary grows rapidly and the child soon is able to express thoughts by using more than one sentence. Memory functions during this period enable the infant to crudely understand differences in time ("sooner," "later," "in a minute"). Finally, the child might understand imposed restrictions ("Don't touch—it will burn you!"), but might not follow the restriction just heard. The frequency of such "disobedience," along with other behaviors, has resulted in a common descriptive label for children at this stage of development—the "terrible twos."

One outcome of studies conducted subsequent to Piaget's claims is that the lockstep, seemingly fixed stages described by Piaget were discovered to be much more fluid than initially thought. Accumulated evidence indicates that Piaget's theory as first presented underestimated the ability of infants and overestimated the ability of adolescents to reach the highest stage of cognitive development and to consistently remain at the higher stage. Furthermore, similar to Piaget's focus on cognitive development, another area in the social sciences, known as *information processing*, has focused on how children and adults process information, and how children and adults use symbols and other means to process information at different points during their development (e.g., Miller [1956] found that for most individuals, the span of immediate memory appears to be fixed close to seven "chunks" of information). As a result of the information-processing research conducted, several theorists have suggested that cognitive development actually represents a continuous process of achieving greater cognitive sophistication, rather than a series of dramatic stage-related changes as proposed by Piaget (Demetriou, Doise,

& van Lieshout, 1998; Newcombe, 1996). It appears, from an information-processing perspective, that cognitive skills are much more fluid, reversible, and specific to situational demands than suggested by stage theorists such as Piaget.

The position taken by some information-processing theorists has important implications for understanding what a child is capable of implementing. For instance, a child is viewed as capable of transcending the type of egocentric perspective believed by stage theorists to limit the preschooler's ability to effectively communicate with others. According to advocates of information processing, preschool children are able to make appropriate changes when they communicate with younger children; preschoolers will speak more slowly and use a simplified vocabulary to communicate with younger children (Demetriou et al., 1998).

Even though not all developmentalists have accepted certain aspects of Piaget's work, Piaget's theory is recognized as a major contribution to developmental psychology. Furth and Wachs (1975, pp. 11–30) indicated that several key points could be abstracted from Piaget's work and the related work of others following in his footsteps.

1. The general development of what is termed intelligence, in the broadest sense of the word, is the foundation for all specific learning (e.g., memorizing facts).
2. Maturation and heredity come together to interact with the environment to contribute to the development of intelligence.
3. Intellectual growth results from "application of thinking at a high level." (Teaching [formal and informal forms] that is "a step" ahead of the child can facilitate movement to a higher level of thinking when certain conditions are met. This view is consistent with Piaget's "factor of equilibration," which means that a child's array of abilities, including cognitive ability, possesses an inner, dynamic tendency to develop to a higher level of functioning. Interestingly, equilibration can also be used to explain individual differences because this inner push to develop is likely to take a somewhat different form in all children—it is expected, from a Piagetian frame of reference, that this push to develop will manifest itself somewhat differently in two children even if they experience environment exactness.)
4. Language development does not precede thinking; thinking regulates itself during development and actually begins to occur before recognizable language acquisition (according to a Piagetian perspective, language can even hinder thinking).
5. Intrinsic motivation is the driving force rather than extrinsic motivation. Simply stated, the child or adolescent has inner forces or influences that result in actively seeking to obtain from the surrounding environment what is needed for cognitive development.
6. The sum total of the child's or adolescent's mechanisms of thinking constitutes intelligence. In fact, any emphasis placed on different aspects of intelligence (e.g., motor skill, general word knowledge, memory, comprehension, etc., were used by Binet and Simon [1905/1916] to conceptualize and create a measure of intelligence) imposes an artificial quality on intelligence that

distorts intelligence's real nature, according to Piagetian theory. Piaget viewed intelligence as a general ability by which the child and adolescent "make sense" of the environment. According to Furth and Wachs (1975), Piaget's theoretical formulation of intelligence is consistent with the finding that children born sightless, lacking the sense of hearing, or who are unable to move can test at normal levels of intelligence.

7. A child moving through Piaget's stages experiences changes in the structure of how he or she thinks.

Importantly, the stages proposed by Piaget are not to be equated with simple increases in the amount of knowledge the developing person possesses.

A significant branch of Piaget's work consisted of how a child's moral understanding unfolds. In real-life terms, it is not unusual for caregivers to express to the child that certain behaviors are acceptable and others are not. Aggression, which can take several forms, is a good example of what is usually perceived to be unacceptable. Whereas the child whose toy is taken by another child is likely to engage in some sort of struggle to regain the toy (instrumental aggression), this child's aggression is not likely to be viewed exactly the same as the unprovoked child who hits another child to inflict injury (hostile aggression). Certainly there are cases where one child inadvertently harms another or an animal due to a lack of cognitive maturity (e.g., pulling the dog's fur as a gesture of exploration). Furthermore, similar to other types of social interactions, aggressive behavior changes over time and the child's repertoire of aggressive actions and reactions grows in number and complexity. Past age 4, aggression can be expected to move from behavioral forms to verbal forms and is much more likely to involve a retaliative quality where the child "reaps in kind." Around age 6 or 7, greater variation and alternative reactions are evident (Newcombe, 1996). Also, in general, male children, for a number of reasons, can be expected to be more physically expressive in terms of aggression (females are also physical, but to a lesser degree).

Piaget's contribution to our understanding of how the child perceives the "rightness" or "wrongness" of aggressive behavior (and other behaviors such as stealing) is that evaluation of the moral nature of the behavior varies according to the child's general level of cognitive sophistication. Piaget assumed young children, after moving through a premoral stage, operate at a level of conceptualizing that is termed *moral realism*. Egocentric in nature and prelogical in approach, the child is focused on rules. The child equates "goodness" with "obedience" and obedience is tied to rules established and policed by adults. "Wrongness" simply means a rule has been broken. Interestingly, the magnitude of rule-breaking is considered by the child, but not in the way an adult would. For example, a child at this level of thinking is likely to assert that any child "who breaks 15 dishes by accident" deserves to be punished more than the child "who smashed 1 dish out of anger." Also, at this stage, the connection between similar rules often eludes the child (e.g., a child might say it is wrong to lie to a parent, yet the same child might not perceive this to imply that he or she should not lie to a friend). *Moral relativism* is the stage that comes next, and it represents flexibility in thinking. A central quality of this stage is that the child now considers intentions and extenuating circumstances to determine the "rightness" or "wrongness" of actions. Lawrence Kohlberg (see Kohlberg, 1994) later extended Piaget's foundational work in the area of moral development and proposed six stages, with two stages each for preconventional, conventional, and postconventional levels of judgment.

Finally, consistent with other areas of development, Carol Gilligan injected a gender modifier into the moral equation established by Kohlberg and others who built upon Piaget's early conceptualizations (Gilligan, 1993). For example, Kohlberg's finding that girls differed from males was found to be less dependent on naturally unfolding maturational processes and more dependent on cultural influences that taught different values as a result of one's gender (e.g., if one gender is typically socialized to develop a strong ethic of care, that particular gender, compared to the other gender, is likely to respond differently to some moral dilemmas). Therefore, different solutions for moral dilemmas offered by the sexes had less to do with functioning at different levels of moral reasoning or cognitive complexity and more to do with certain experiences or cultural factors that are gender related.

In addition to the gender-related expectations that permeate a culture, other factors can influence a response to moral dilemmas. Individuals experiencing a real-life moral dilemma find the difficulty level of making a decision to be much greater than the difficulty level encountered in research studies. As a research participant, they are confronted with hypothetical moral dilemmas to solve. Also, certain real-life moral dilemmas, once a decision is made, simply have the potential to affect males and females differently. For example, it seems appropriate to assume that an unwanted pregnancy and the decision to have an abortion will carry a different meaning (not exact, and possibly very different) for the male and female involved, and it is probable that the situational factors represent a better means to account for gender differences found in how the two people seek a solution, than are explanations based solely on cognitive sophistication (see Gilligan & Belenky, 1994). Simply stated, it appears that to fully understand what has contributed to a child making a certain type of decision (moral judgment) requires the counselor to be knowledgeable about both cognitive theories of development and various factors that can alter the general explanations offered by these theories.

The Social, Emotional and Behavioral Maps of Development: Contributions of Erik H. Erikson, John Bowlby, Mary D. Salter Ainsworth, and Albert Bandura

Even at an early stage of development, infants display consistent patterns of responding to their internal and external environments. In many cases these patterns become obvious to one or both parents, and as a result the child is referred to by a familial descriptor that is intended to summarize the child's typical emotional, social, or behavioral pattern (i.e., anxious, calm, fussy, difficulty sleeping, or easily startled). Such patterns have been referred to as constituting the infant's habitual inclination of responding, or simply as the infant's *temperament.*

Existent literature supports the general conclusion that temperament can play an important role in the way the child will respond emotionally, behaviorally, or socially in future situations (Carey & McDevitt, 1989; Kagan, Snidman, Arcus, & Reznick, 1994; Kohnstamm, Bates, & Rothbart, 1989; Plomin & Dunn, 1986; Shick, 1998). This body of work has allowed for the creation of various temperament profiles that provide a scheme to help identify and assess the degree to which various temperament traits combine to define a child's unique personality. Specifically, when one reviews the temperament literature, one finds that certain descriptors (or their derivations) are commonly used to identify various patterns believed to represent typical temperament traits (e.g., activity level, adaptability, intensity, approach response, shyness, distractibility, emotional response, sensitivity to environment, sensitivity to others, sensitivity to self, persistence, regularity of physiological functions, sensory awareness, and mood). According to Kagan et al. (1994) "every temperamental concept implies an actualizing environment that permits the defining behavior to appear" (p. 36). One may infer from Kagan et al.'s remark that temperament theory adds significantly to our understanding of developmental theory's position on maturational forces; specifically, temperament theory helps to explain how the unique aspects of a child's personality are established by an interaction of predispositions and environmental influences.

It is around the early part of the second year of development that the child's personality starts to obviously emerge, at which time temperament can play a measurable role. Once a child's unique traits of temperament emerge, one can expect those traits to set in motion a familial cycle in which a parent or both parents, and possibly siblings, respond to the child's temperament pattern with essentially a consistent corresponding pattern of behavior that is likely to affect the way the child interacts with others in the future. (Adolescents who remember that they were "always" told that they were anxious might respond in a manner that lives up to what they had been told—countless times.) But as Kagan et al. (1994) point out, human development is sometimes an elusive process that is rarely determined by a single factor, and temperament has been found to be an imperfect predictor of the infant's future emotional, social, and behavioral responses. In fact, it is possible for parents to misread the meaning behind an infant's behavior and respond in the same manner to two very different types of infant behavioral intentions (seeking contact versus avoiding contact). For instance, a common parental assumption is that all infants (especially infants who are crying) require and enjoy spending a lot of time being held in the arms of a parent. This commonly held assumption overlooks the reality that some infants are hypersensitive to stimulation.

In sum, it appears that although temperament is an important consideration, it is not the only consideration. Social development, and its accompanying emotions and behaviors, is also governed by common patterns of infant–parent interactions that cut across many different cultures. One illustration of this type of infant–parent interaction is found in the chain of events that follows birth and leads to what might be called the "social smile." The awareness of emotional expression's link to social interactions begins in the first few months of life when the infant starts to discover the effects of grins and facial expressions on others. During the first few months of infancy, the infant will make eye contact, express preferences for caretakers, and display smiles. Not only is there evidence that indicates displayed smiles increase in frequency during the beginning period of infancy, there is also evidence that the very nature of the displayed smile is changing (developmental and environmental elements are coming together to alter the essence of the smile).

Smiles appearing soon after birth seem to be a reaction to a stimulus that might or might not have anything to do with people (e.g., internal physiological state), but these "spontaneous smiles" soon change to something else. After a brief period of development, smiling is more likely to be displayed in concert with the occurrence of social stimuli (e.g., human faces), but soon this changes to specific social stimuli (e.g., familiar faces, such as a parent's). Once this form of the social smile is in place, the child is very unlikely to smile at a stranger's face and typically cries instead. Finally, additional evidence that supports the conclusion that infant smiling has a strong social component is that the frequency of smiling can be manipulated through a social means. The frequency of smiles goes up if parents increase the level of interaction by talking "baby talk" to the child. Also, unresponsiveness from parents appears to decrease the frequency of smiles. It appears that a number of factors emerge and contribute to a child's set of interpersonal skills developing over a short period of time.

One of the most influential developmental theorists was Erik Erikson (1968), who proposed an elaborate theory of *psychosocial development* that has been widely used (as presented by Erikson and in modified versions, e.g., to account for various multicultural aspects) to understand the child and adolescent. Although Erikson's theory covered the entire life span of humans (Corsini, 2002), only those aspects pertaining to infancy through adolescence are presented here. At the end of each stage description, appearing in brackets, are the strengths that Erikson believed emerged when the child successfully navigated the developmental currents comprising a stage (Erikson, 1963).

- *Basic Trust Versus Basic Mistrust* (birth–1 year): The child must obtain a sense of whether the world (i.e., responses of others and the child's own body) is trustworthy at a very basic, immediate level. Unless the child experiences others and his or her own bodily actions as reliable sources of satisfaction, the child will develop a sense of mistrust that has far-reaching consequences for future development. [Strengths associated with this stage are "drive" and "hope."]
- *Autonomy Versus Shame, Doubt* (1 year–3 years): At this point in time, the child is working to establish self-control and abilities related to self-sufficiency. Changes related to language acquisition, self-locomotion, cognitive abilities, and a host of other changes and experiences (e.g., toilet training) allow for the child to become more independent and less reliant on others for "everything." Failure to achieve the necessary level of autonomy and self-satisfaction will result in a general sense of doubting one's abilities and a painful feeling that others do not hold one in high esteem. [Strengths associated with this stage are "self-control" and "willpower."]
- *Initiative Versus Guilt* (3–5 years): This is the age marked by abundant play, increased levels of initiating actions, and a sense of responsibility for actions taken. Life is instilled with a purposeful quality and a rudimentary inner system to judge "right from wrong." Psychosocial failure at this stage results in

a strong self-perception of being unworthy and deserving of self-reproachment. [Strengths associated with this stage are "direction" and "purpose."]

- *Industry Versus Inferiority* (6–12 years): Formal education starts a new beginning and new challenges for the child. Developing competency takes an uppermost position at this stage because at this point in the child's development there is no guarantee that an action taken by the child will be met with unconditional acceptance of its importance. The child must now learn to "work" for recognition. This type of recognition is conditional in nature and largely dependent on the quality of the child's approach to work and the quality of the products produced (e.g., grades, chores, art projects). The child who fails to bridge the two worlds of unconditional and conditional acceptance of the value of efforts is left with a persistent and troublesome self-view that embraces the belief that one is inferior. [Strengths associated with this stage are "method" and "competence."]

- *Identity Versus Role Confusion* (adolescence): Bodily changes that mark this period of development and their sexual nature, as well as significant increases in cognitive sophistication, "push" the child to find and establish an identity. Establishing an identity leads to a strong sense of personal and interpersonal "connectedness" (leading to true intimacy), but failure at this major, pivotal task in a person's life results in a sense of isolation that taints the adolescent's view of self and relationships. [Strengths associated with this stage are "devotion" and "fidelity."]

In addition to Erikson's theory, several other theories exist to explain many of the social, emotional, and behavioral elements of a child's development. One of the most important research-based theories of human development that has profound implications not only for the infant, child, and adolescent but also the adult is referred to as *attachment* (i.e., attachment, in its elemental form, is the type of emotional bond established with another that creates a secure condition, feeling, or both).

General developmental theory would suggest that over time, the child increasingly perceives himself or herself as separate from others, a view that provides an opportunity to move beyond the early, primitive self-centered state associated with infancy (Goldberg, 2000). Around 8 months of age, the child recognizes the "self" reflected in mirrors and acts in ways that indicate self-awareness. Around 9 months, the infant shows "stranger anxiety" around unfamiliar people. The clingy type of response that immediately follows encountering a stranger is viewed as evidence of this anxiety's manifestation. Fear of separation from the nurturing other also implies that the child is continuing to move away from the type of self-centeredness in which the child is connected to everything as if the child were the hub of the universe (i.e., fear reflects a realization that the parent [or a surrogate] is a separate entity). The inverse of this developed fear of potential separateness is the delight a child displays in connection with rejoining a parent or surrogate. It is evident that children at this stage experience great pleasure in expressing affection for this important other, such as giving a series of hugs to a parent. In light of these developments, it is not surprising that the word "no" from others is understood (and is bothersome to the child) and that the child actively seeks approval from significant others.

Attachment theory rests upon the position that healthy development depends on a secure, warm relationship that has a continuous quality (Ainsworth, Blehar, Waters, & Wall, 1978). Removal of this intimate, ongoing relationship can have profound effects. According to John Bowlby (1973), the abandoned infant-child:

> At first [. . .] *protests* vigorously and tries by all the means available to him to recover his mother. Later he seems to *despair* of recovering her but none the less remains preoccupied with her and vigilant for her return. Later still he seems to lose his interest in his mother and to become emotionally *detached* from her. [Italics appear in original source.] Nevertheless, provided the period of separation is not too prolonged, a child does not remain detached indefinitely. Sooner or later after being reunited with his mother his attachment to her emerges afresh. Thenceforward, for days or weeks, and sometimes for much longer, he insists on staying close to her. Furthermore, whenever he suspects he will lose her again he exhibits acute anxiety. (pp. 26–27)

John Bowlby, earlier in the same work, writes "There is reason to believe that after a very prolonged or repeated separation during the first three years of life detachment can persist indefinitely" (p. 12). Therefore, detachment appears not only to be extremely upsetting, but also, if it is of long enough duration, an early period of detachment can affect future interpersonal relationships and linger, in some form, throughout one's lifetime. For example, many future relationships or encounters can be placed in categories of "responding strategies" such as secure, preoccupied, fearful, or dismissing; in each of these categories the person holds a certain view (positive or negative) about the self and about others (Bartholomew, Henderson, & Dutton, 2001). For example, the *preoccupied* interpersonal pattern reflects a style that results in the person evaluating others in a positive manner and evaluating the self in a negative manner. Bartholomew et al. indicate that this person will focus on establishing a very close relationship that can frighten the other away. The preoccupied style reflects an interaction approach that is overdependent on the other to meet excessive self-esteem and support needs, and the other person targeted for such a relationship soon becomes overwhelmed.

Finally, whereas *learning theory* has contributed to a greater understanding of all the maps that cover human development, learning theory has especially provided important information concerning how certain behaviors and emotional reactions come about. While early learning theorists/behaviorists such as Ivan P. Pavlov, Edward L. Thorndike, John B. Watson, Burrhus F. Skinner, and many others introduced a number of key explanatory constructs (e.g., classical conditioning, law of effect, conditioned fear, operant conditioning, shaping, and extinction), of special importance were the contributions made by Albert Bandura and later cognitive behaviorists such as Beck and Meichenbaum (Gazda et al., 2001). Albert Bandura's early form of *social learning theory* (socio-behavioristic approach) suggests that behavior (and an emotional reaction) is best understood as an interaction of the inner world of the child and the environmental situation (Bandura & Walters, 1963). Bandura emphasized that it was important to consider how the child was processing the available information (the child's values, expectations, interpretation, etc.) and not just focus on elements of the environment as "classic" behaviorism would have one do when working with a child. Bandura has long been identified with his views on vicarious or *observational learning*, which essentially means that a child can learn—when certain conditions are met—a novel response by seeing the action performed and imitating what was performed. With the introduction of new visual technologies over the last couple of decades (e.g., video games, DVDs, Internet sites), the possible avenues for the child to observe a wide array of pro-social and antisocial behaviors has been greatly expanded. As a result, Bandura's theory might be even more relevant today than when it was first presented.

THE CULMINATION OF EARLY DEVELOPMENTAL GAINS: ADOLESCENCE AS THE DEVELOPMENTAL GATEWAY TO ADULTHOOD

Unlike infancy and childhood, the span of time referred to as adolescence lacks the type of sequential markers present during the earlier years of development. Adolescence is a stage unto itself, representing a distinct stage in a process of change started prior to birth that leads to adulthood. The period of adolescence requires the adolescent to endure various tasks that can take on a Herculean form of intimidation. Havighurst's (1972) insight was that this particular developmental period could be understood as a situation in which the adolescent was "called to duty" to handle various challenges before the adolescent could ever hope to effectively tackle the next set of tasks found upon entry into adulthood. According to Havighurst (1972; see pp. 45–82), the following tasks defined his conceptualization of the period known as adolescence:

- Accepting the uniqueness of one's body and using the body effectively;
- Achieving a meaningful pattern of behavior in relation to masculine or feminine social roles;
- Obtaining relationships with peers of both sexes that reflect greater maturity;
- Achieving emotional independence from parents or caregivers (while still loving them); preparing for the future in relation to work; preparing for an intimate relationship that reflects commitment; developing a higher level of social and community responsibility; establishing a value system that includes ethical considerations that are reliable guides to behavior; and achieving a level of physical maturity consistent with what is expected for adolescent maturation.

Others have built upon Havighurst's unique understanding of adolescence's burdens. Adrian Copeland is one such example. According to Copeland (1974, as cited in Prout, 1999), the adolescent can be described as a person with a heightened sensitivity who can be expected to respond to social situations in a manner that is much more forceful than one would predict. This affective quality of adolescence might find expression in mood swings and cycles of acting out followed by behaviors denoting inhibition. According to Copeland, this developmental period is also distinguished by a number of preoccupations. There is preoccupation with self, fantasy, sexuality, and self-expression (and the need to withdraw). Unlike the type of self-centeredness found in the inner world of the infant or the young child, it is not unusual for the adolescent to be plagued by low self-esteem and mistrust in his or her ability to handle personal matters. Although sexuality is a dominant force in the life of the adolescent and accounts for certain behaviors and preferences related to grooming and dress, preoccupation with fantasy can serve to reign in both intense emotions and sexual urges. Thus, while involvement in fantasy activities might be disconcerting to a parent, these activities, unless excessive, might be providing a means to "handle" certain adolescent concerns.

Consistent with Erikson's theory of identity formation, Copeland indicated that the adolescent period is often recognized as a time of paradoxical behavior in that the adolescent frequently establishes self-expression and independence via conformity to some group, which results in the adolescent taking on the mannerisms, speech, and dress of the group embraced. Finally, one task presented to the adolescent to solve is to establish a philosophy of life, a philosophy that provides meaning and direction (e.g., vocational goals [Osborne, Brown, Niles, & Miner, 1997]). According to Copeland, each adolescent philosopher can travel a number of widely divergent pathways, e.g., the Hedonist who believes in pleasure as the proper aim of being a human being or the Ascetic who believes in abstaining from pleasure.

Developmental Models Specific to Diagnosis and Treatment

According to Paisley and Hubbard (1994):

> The professional literature provides us with a great deal of knowledge concerning how individuals develop . . . and how we can facilitate that development. The time has come . . . to take advantage of what we know and begin to implement truly comprehensive developmental programs based on solid and theoretical foundations. As this focus is appropriately utilized, the need for crisis intervention and remediation is likely to be significantly reduced. (p. xix)

We entirely agree with the comments made by Paisley and Hubbard, which point to the existence of a wealth of information that can be used to understand normal developmental deviation, determine how certain psychosocial and environmental factors are likely to affect a child's development, recognize the intertwining nature of developmental changes and cultural diversity, perceive a normal developmental concern in children diagnosed with a mental disorder, and, finally, determine the most appropriate treatment approach to take. The counselor should keep in mind that the various available models provide a scheme for asking questions to obtain a developmental history pertinent to diagnostic and treatment considerations. Several authors (e.g., Ginter, 1999; Hatfield & Hatfield, 1992; Ivey & Ivey, 1998; McAuliffe & Eriksen, 1999; Myers, 1992) have developed counseling models that incorporate a developmental aspect that serves as a major contributing factor leading to client change and growth.

McAuliffe and Eriksen (1999) outlined a developmentally based approach that focuses on four dimensions that hinge upon a consideration of constructivistic and developmental elements (i.e., social context, life phase, constructive stage, and personality style). The constructivist-developmental model advocated by McAuliffe and Eriksen proposes that the *locus of the problem* is to be perceived as not only involving the individual but also the family and the culture of the individual; *causes of the problem* are to be understood in terms of a multisystemic approach; *human development* and *family* serve as pivotal points of consideration in the model; *pathology* is seen as a "logical response to developmental history" (p. 269); *cultural influences* are assessed not only in terms of culture, but in terms of gender and other types of "frames"; and *treatment planning and implementation* relies upon network interventions and an egalitarian approach that provides opportunities for all directly involved in counseling to share responsibility for co-constructing events. Similar to McAuliffe and Eriksen (1999), Ivey and Ivey (1998) provide a model of counseling that is infused with a strong developmental and wellness focus. Ivey and Ivey's approach is known as *Developmental Counseling and Therapy,* and in their 1998 article they provide a clear example of how a developmental approach enables one to reframe common psychological conditions in a manner to bring positive, health-promoting factors to the forefront of diagnosis and treatment. Specifically, Ivey and Ivey list 11 personality styles that correspond to *DSM* personality disorders (see Ivey & Ivey, 1998, p. 338). These authors offer an insightful means to reconceptualize these disorders in terms of latent positive features (positive features that are not apparent from the pathologizing descriptors used in the *DSM* for each of these personality styles). Ivey and Ivey explore each of the personality styles in relation to how early family history might have contributed to formation of the style as well as an appropriate counter style that the counselor can use to work with the client. These counter styles are intended to reinstate growth in the client. Although it is well beyond the scope of this chapter to mention all the relevant information contained in the Ivey and Ivey article, it should be pointed out that their treatment model details intervention strategies that are labeled **sensorimotor**, **concrete**, **formal**, and **dialectic/systemic**, and represent therapeutic strategies that can easily be traced back to Piagetian theory.

The Life-Skills Model: A Developmental-Based Approach to Assessment and Treatment

The Life-Skills Model (LSM) rests on a foundation of theory and research that has accumulated over several decades. LSM has been used with a wide range of clients where the primary aim of counseling is prevention, enhancement, and remediation (Kadish, Glaser, Calhoun, & Ginter, 2001). In cases of remediation when a *DSM* diagnosis has been rendered, the counselor would conduct an additional life-skills assessment (Ginter [1999, 2003] reports that measures have been developed for three age groups, i.e., child, adolescent, and adult, and specifically for two groups associated with unique age-related environments, i.e., adults in college and adolescents incarcerated at a youth detention center). The assessment process provides a measure of the child's standing on four dimensions (Darden, Gazda, & Ginter, 1996, pp. 136–138):

1. *Interpersonal Communications/Human Relations Skills (IC/HR)* are those skills necessary for effective communication at different developmental levels, leading to ease in establishing relationships, small and large group and community membership and participation (e.g., school), and management of close and/or intimate relationships.

2. *Problem-Solving/Decision-Making Skills (PS/DM)* are those skills necessary for information seeking, assessing, and identifying the relevant parts of problem situations, problem identification, solution implementation and evaluation of the solution, goal setting, time management, critical thinking, and conflict-resolution skills.

3. *Physical Fitness/Health Maintenance Skills (PF/HM)* are those skills necessary for motor development and coordination, information acquisition related to health concerns, nutritional maintenance, weight control, physical fitness, athletic participation, physiological aspects of sexuality, stress management, and leisure activity selection.

4. *Identity Development/Purpose-in-Life Skills (ID/PIL)* are those skills necessary for ongoing development of personal identity and emotional awareness, including self-monitoring, maintenance of self-esteem (belief in oneself), manipulating and accommodating one's environment, clarifying values, sex-role development, making meaning, morals/values, and certain dimensions of sexuality (e.g., the person's goal is to start a family after graduating from college).

These four dimensions were derived from the combined efforts of George Gazda and David Brooks via a Delphi study that required developmental experts to identify and agree upon developmental descriptors that defined the age periods known as child, adolescent, and adult. The roles that these four dimensions play in an individual's life is made clear by Brooks (1984), who stated that *life-skills* are the "learned behaviors that are necessary for *effective living* (italics added), including requisite knowledge or conditions for the development or acquisition of such behavior" (p. 6). Simply stated, life-skills are basic, developmental building blocks of human existence. Finally, the life-skills model proposed by Darden, Gazda, and Ginter (1996) rests upon a foundation of 10 assumptions. The 10 assumptions reflect the essential nature of life-skills and suggest why knowledge of life-skills is vitally important if one hopes to understand the contribution made by developmental factors. The assumptions are as follows (Darden, Gazda, & Ginter, 1996):

1. There are several well-defined areas of human development: psychosocial, physical-sexual, vocational, cognitive, ego, moral, and affective.
2. Coping behaviors that are appropriate to age and stage can be determined from these areas.
3. Each area comprises identifiable stages [or sequences] requiring mastery in order to progress from lower to advanced stages [or sequences].
4. Accomplishment of developmental tasks is dependent on mastery of life-skills.
5. Generally, certain life-skills are optimally learned within given age ranges.
6. Individuals achieve optimal functioning when they attain operational mastery of fundamental life-skills.
7. Neuroses and functional psychoses frequently result from failure to develop certain life-skills.
8. Instruction and training in life-skills serve a role of preventive mental health when introduced at an appropriate developmental time.

9. [Counseling] or life-skills training serves the role of remediation when introduced during a time of emotional or mental disturbance of a functional nature.
10. The greater the degree of functional disturbance, the greater the likelihood that the individual will suffer from multiple life-skills deficits. (p. 136)

Serving as a theoretical infrastructure, the 10 theoretical assumptions provide a systemic set of fundamental features that can be relied on to guide both assessment and treatment from beginning to end.

The next section provides examples concerning how the four life-skills dimensions intersect with client and treatment concerns. Specifically, brief examples are provided in terms of different ages and the four life-skills dimensions. The following case illustration is not intended to be an exhaustive illustration of the life-skills approach; it is primarily intended to provide an illustration of the types of considerations made by a counselor relying upon the LSM to structure interventions.

Examples of Counseling Based on a Life-Skills Approach

Ginter (2001) discussed various practice considerations and specifically illustrates how the LSM could be used to comprehend the concerns of a client diagnosed with a Depressive Disorder and how the LSM treatment approach could be fitted to developmental needs to increase effectiveness. For this chapter, a case that does not involve a client diagnosed with a mental disorder is used to depict at what point the four life-skills dimensions converge with the concerns of a child. Specifically, the situation selected to illustrate various applications involves a child whose family member is experiencing a life-threatening form of cancer. Of course, a developmental assessment of the child's concerns and needs would be conducted prior to using any developmental-based interventions. One outcome of depending on the LSM is that the model provides an overarching structure for treatment planning, which *prevents overlooking relevant developmental issues while working with a client.*

According to Johnson (1997), "by understanding the profile of well children and the common emotional and behavioral response patterns found among this population, the counselor will be in a better position proactively to identify and address their needs" (p. 418). Johnson reviewed important developmental considerations in a case in which a child's parent or sibling develops cancer. According to Johnson, one may anticipate that:

> During the preschool and primary school years, children perceive their world as though they were the center. . . . Young children, when not otherwise informed, can hold private irrational views of how the patient's illness was caused or what will happen to the patient. . . . Children 6 through 12 years of age tend to engage in "hands-on thinking" and have an ability to realize that things can be changed while still conserving many of their original characteristics. . . . Developmentally, adolescents tend to be egocentric in their thinking and believe that no one can possibly understand their situation. . . . During adolescence, the search for identity unfolds as the child seeks to move toward independence from the family, typically through identification with one's peers. . . . Normally, the well adolescent would be moving away from the family but now must face demands to remain attached and may experience embarrassment about his or her parent or sibling looking or seeming different from others. (p. 420–421)

In addition to the various developmental factors mentioned by Johnson (1997), Lewis (1996) reports research findings that identify various developmental points of vulnerability for young children and adolescents. Lewis reports that when a parent suffers from a serious illness such as cancer, young children can be expected to be at risk for a decrease in global self-worth, quality of peer relations, ability to cope, and level of academic performance, and an increase in behavioral problems; adolescents can be expected to be at risk for a decrease in perceived self-worth, quality of peer relationships, and quality of parent relationships, and an increase in behavioral problems. Weihs and Reiss (1996) and Siegel, Raveis, and Karus (1996) call attention to using appropriate communication of information as one means to help counteract some of the problems experienced by the child or adolescent. A general goal is to communicate relevant information about the illness that both addresses the child's concerns and matches the level of cognitive sophistication the child has achieved.

Considering the comments of authors delineating the developmental effects of illness on a family system (e.g., Baider, Cooper, & De-Nour, 1996), and various aspects of the LSM, it appears that the PF/HM dimension (specifically, information acquisition) would be an area of concern for a counselor working with young children because they will harbor gross distortions of what it means for a parent or sibling to be seriously ill. The child who is close to 6 years of age possesses a limited understanding of illness. The child at this developmental point in time might misunderstand the true significance of the illness largely due to lingering egocentric thinking. The level of egocentric thinking that lingers from an earlier period is still powerful enough to cause the child to blame himself or herself for the cancer ("Daddy says mommy is real sick. I should not have made mommy mad. She screamed at me when I broke grandma's picture—mommy's sick now."), or even believe he or she might "catch the cancer" if he or she has direct contact with the ill person or touches something the ill person has handled. Counselors who possess a meaningful knowledge of human development are not as likely to overlook the true meaning of a child's behaviors, subtle concerns, or quietness. Anticipating and confronting the child's cognitive distortions concerning illness and wellness (PF/HM dimension) are necessary and can be accomplished by offering the child an appropriate level of reassurance and correct information in a manner attuned to the young child's level of cognitive development.

The 6-year-old to 12-year-old child is likely to have a difficult time communicating his or her concerns. These difficulties can be seen as an aspect of the IC/HR dimension (specifically, skills related to identifying personal feelings related to the illness, and skills related to effective communication) in that this child, according to Johnson (1997), requires assistance to think in flexible ways—not becoming trapped by absolutes concerning the illness ("Mom has cancer and cancer kills everyone."). The lack of flexible thinking tends to prevent the child from discussing his or her concerns with others. Because of this child's developmental achievements, the older child will require more information and greater details than the younger child. Specifically, the child requires information concerning what treatments are being administered and why these treatments are being done. Because of the absolute type of thinking that is common among this age group, it is important to emphasize that cancer does not always result in death, and that cancer is often treatable. The 6-year-old to 12-year-old child may also require skill building to help the child obtain the ability to gather information, that is, teaching the child how to ask (giving concrete examples) and when to ask for information (e.g., the counselor can help establish a "special sharing time" for the child and the well parent, a time when the parent is available for answers if the child has questions).

For the adolescent, the counselor should expect issues pertaining to the ID/PIL dimension to surface. Wellisch, Hoffman, and Gritz (1996) mention how the adolescent's task of identity development is complicated when a parent becomes ill. These authors illustrate the complexity of the situation by providing the example of the adolescent daughter, who is developing sexually, whose ill mother sees herself as losing her sexuality because of breast cancer. Wellisch et al. suggest that the adolescent's sexual identity might be affected by a sense of guilt or conflict over her developing sexuality. It appears that while identity development and the need to break away from parents are central tasks for the adolescent, achieving these tasks is likely to be profoundly affected by a long illness in the family.

The adolescent could, as pointed out by Johnson (1997) in her article, benefit from efforts to enhance the adolescent's level of empathy by having him or her adopt the psychological perspective of other family members (IC/HR dimension). Instilling empathy can be achieved via role-playing techniques. Also, even though the adolescent has achieved greater levels of independence, he or she will probably experience identity-formation conflict in ways other than the one mentioned by Wellisch et al. (1996). For instance, the adolescent's greater level of independence compared to a younger child (e.g., the adolescent can drive a car) might be depended on to a degree never before experienced by the adolescent (e.g., due to one parent's work schedule, the adolescent might be depended on to drive the ill parent to a clinic for chemotherapy). Such reliance (or overreliance) on the adolescent might tax his or her ability to juggle everything (school, part-time job, after-school activities, sibling care) and might require the counselor to help the adolescent build upon existing problem-solving and decision-making skills, and learn relaxation skills (PS/DM and PF/HM dimensions). Focusing on these issues will better enable the adolescent to handle various demands and maintain stress at an acceptable level. Potentially troublesome and conflicting situations can be discussed with the adolescent and prepared for before they become overwhelming.

Finally, as discussed earlier in this chapter, the counselor utilizing the LSM must also consider any intervention planned in relation to relevant cultural factors. Gotay (1996) recommends that seven illness-related dimensions be considered when working with a child whose parent or sibling has been diagnosed with cancer. Specifically, Gotay advocates that the counselor consider how cultural factors impact the familial system in relation to overall attitude toward cancer, general attitude toward autonomy, desire for medical-related communication, belief concerning the origin of the disease, norms related to responding to pain, preferred coping style to deal with stress, and "death customs" adhered to (p. 37). For example, concerning death customs, Gotay advocates taking a different approach, and we agree, with an adolescent from a culture that embraces the death custom that a disease is something to fight against even when one enters the final stage of dying; compared to the counseling approach one would take with the adolescent whose culture embraces the position that illness is part of the universal cycle of life, and that death is to be accepted as a necessary part of existence.

RESEARCH SUPPORT

Since their introduction decades ago the various development theories (i.e., maps) have continued to amass research evidence supporting the soundness of their basic premises. Taken collectively, these studies make it possible to assert that the developmental maps covered in this chapter are based on a foundation of facts and sound reasoning. Because of these qualities, knowledge of human development informs accurate diagnosis of *DSM* disorders. Essentially, the general validity of various developmental maps cannot be denied without contradicting actual events occurring in the life of children around the world, events that exists somewhat independently of ideas concerning them. While it is important to recognize that our current conceptualization of human development is incomplete, this lack of conceptual understanding should not prevent us from incorporating well-supported aspects of developmental maps into diagnosis and subsequent treatment planning.

In fact, it is because certain developmental theories have received wide acceptance, that many contemporary researchers are focused on refining current developmental theories rather than searching for new theories to replace them. For example, since Piaget's original formulation of cognitive development, researchers have discovered reasons to modify some aspects of Piaget's claims. Piaget overemphasized the magnitude of the relationship between object concept construction and the development of specific motor skills such as the ability to grasp objects (see Creasey, 2006). It appears that humans possess a better sense of when something is or is not present at an earlier age than what was formerly thought. Similarly, other researchers have reported research findings that serve to further validate theories while refining key elements of the various developmental maps.

The mountain of empirical research found in the professional literature suggests the importance of considering developmental maps when one wants to genuinely empathize with a child or accurately diagnose the child's actions, but this vast array of published research does not answer an essential question. Do counseling approaches, those that specifically incorporate developmental theory, represent an effective means to treat children? The answer to this question is the province of outcome studies.

Outcomes Studies: Developmentally Based Approaches and Revived Growth

Several counseling approaches have relied extensively on developmental theories to determine how the counseling process should be structured, and it is reasonable to assume that it is these types of approaches that would provide the best means to test the assertion that developmentally based treatments are effective. While there is still much to be researched in this area, the literature cited below represents a sample of what is available to support the above assertion.

Forms of counseling that require consideration of pertinent development factors (e.g., Activity-Interview Group Counseling, Developmental Group Counseling, Life-Skills [Training] Model, Parent Management Training, and Wellness Counseling) have proven to achieve desired results (Barker, 2004; Gazda, Ginter, & Horne, 2001; Ginter, 2005). Specifically, such developmentally sensitive interventions have been shown to provide the necessary knowledge, understanding, and practice of certain skills for children and/or parents to achieve positive change in the areas of mild oppositional behavior, effects of divorce, excessive stress, conduct disorders, anxiety disorders, poor communication skills, effects of sexual abuse, social-skills deficits, learning problems, and severe behavioral problems. Furthermore, it has been found that careful consideration of certain specific developmental factors can positively affect outcomes. For example, when a counselor increases the effectiveness of a counseling group for adolescents by using narrow age ranges (e.g., 12–14, 14–16, and 16–18) or by restricting membership to a single-sex (Gazda, Ginter, & Horne, 2001). Finally, there is also support for the claim that some types of treatments that recognize the importance of certain developmental dynamics (e.g., parent–child relationship) are more effective than other forms of treatment. For example, empirical findings from different studies provide strong support for concluding that family-based treatments are the most effective form of counseling for adolescent drug abuse (Barker, 2004).

There is an important distinction that should be made between outcome studies in general and outcomes associated with developmentally based approaches or techniques. This distinction is hinted at by Barker (2004), who used the term *outcome frame*. According to Barker an outcome frame:

> Is a description, in positive terms, of how things will be after treatment has been successfully completed. Rather than saying that a child's temper tantrums will have ceased, it is better to describe how that child will behave in situations in which tantrums used to occur. (pp. 191–192)

Barker's point is congruent with a basic and widely held notion in the field of counseling which can be expressed as follows: Wellness is not to be equated with the absence of illness (Ginter, 2005). Barker's comments suggest that counselors who rely on developmental-based treatments should know what indicators of wellness would fill the void left by symptom removal. The extent to which a counselor can accurately state what these wellness indicators are for each client depends on the counselor's knowledge of human development.

Finally, to be consistent with the reason for using a developmentally based counseling approach or technique, the counselor is required to move beyond simply measuring client change in terms of *DSM* symptoms. When counseling's defining features are considered (see Ginter 2002), it is logical to infer that the final and utmost measure of success would be revival of wide-based growth in the child. We have termed this type of result a *renascent outcome*. To qualify for a renascent outcome there must be evidence of three overlapping events: *meaningful change in symptoms, manifestation of wellness indicators,* and *reinstatement of multifaceted developmental growth in the child.*

CLOSING REMARKS

The primary aim of this chapter was to provide an overview of why knowledge of developmental theory and research is an indispensable component of working with children. It is important to emphasize again that the various aspects of human development (i.e., physical, intellectual, emotional, behavioral, social) are not independent entities. Understanding the connectedness of these various aspects helps to guard against the type of fragmenting, reductive, compartmentalizing approach that hinders obtaining a valid diagnosis and developing the most effective treatment plan for the child. Also, the various maps (and models) reviewed in this chapter are just that—maps. The ultimate destination of the counselor is to meet the child on his or her own territory, and such a meeting can take place only if the counselor understands what has been discovered about child development.

Chapter 2

UNDERSTANDING THE DEVELOPMENT OF PSYCHOPATHOLOGY IN CHILDREN AND ADOLESCENTS

By

Robert R. Erk
University of Tennessee–Martin

A DEVELOPMENTAL-SYSTEMS PERSPECTIVE ON THE SIGNIFICANCE OF CHILD PSYCHOPATHOLOGY

Our knowledge base for understanding the development of psychopathology in children and adolescents has grown exponentially over the past 2 decades (see Cicchetti & Cohen, 1995; Hersen & Ammerman, 1995; Goldstein & Reynolds, 1999; Mash & Barkley, 1996; Mash & Dozois, 1996; and Mash & Terdal, 1997). However, Mash and Dozois (1996) believed that the knowledge base is compromised by atheoretical, unsystematic, and somewhat fragmented information with regard to the research findings in child psychopathology. In addition, issues such as how psychopathology should be conceptualized and defined are areas that sparked rigorous debate. To better unify what has been learned from research in child psychopathology, Mash and Dozois (1996) proposed a "developmental-systems perspective" that addresses themes and issues related to conceptualizing childhood dysfunction and its determinants. The developmental-systems perspective specifically emphasizes the role for developmental processes, the importance of multiple contexts, and the influence of multiple and interacting events and processes in shaping adaptive and maladaptive development. For example, clinical and research advances in childhood psychopathology have provided ample clinical proof that many disorders diagnosed in adults had their genesis or developed in the childhood years (Goldstein & Reynolds, 1999; Rapoport, 2000).

Mash and Dozois (1996) believed that adopting the developmental-systems perspective provides a better understanding of childhood psychopathology. In turn, the developmental-systems perspective might provide the basis for designing more effective interventions or treatments. To gain a better understanding of the development of psychopathology in children (e.g., child-focused models; Mash & Dozois, 1996), different models or perspectives are often useful and informative. It is increasingly evident from clinical research and field studies that the occurrence of psychopathology cannot be attributed to a "single" or "primary" cause (Mash & Dozois, 1996; Mash & Wolfe, 2002; Sue, Sue, & Sue, 2000). For example, life events (e.g., a chaotic family environment, divorce, moving to a new school) have the potential to shape both adaptive and maladaptive behaviors. A child's response to these types of events can be conceptualized as his or her attempt to adapt to the type of life changes. For example, a common theme in defining child psychopathology is that of adaptational difficulty or failure (see Garber, 1984; Mash, 1998; Mash & Wolfe, 2002; Sroufe & Rutter, 1984). Whether particular patterns of adaptational responses are to a greater or lesser extent influenced by internal processes (e.g., temperament, personality characteristics) or experiences that occur early in the child's life, they nonetheless remain patterns of adaptation (Sroufe & Rutter, 1984). Therefore, problems or disordered behavior are more likely to occur when the child fails to adapt successfully.

Having models or perspectives available that seek to account for the development of disordered or dysfunctional behavior in children is advantageous. In essence, a model is one way to explain a phenomenon or process in a child or adolescent that cannot always be directly observed. Importantly, models assist counselors in conceptualizing the "causes" for psychopathology in individual children and adolescents. Many of the "causes" for the development of adaptive or maladaptive behavior (e.g., psychopathology) in children can be categorized into models or perspectives. For example, Mash and Wolfe (2002) and Sue, Sue, and Sue (2000) have advocated thinking in a more "integrated" way about models (e.g., there is likely to be an interplay between biological, psychosocial, and multicultural explanations in every child). Each of the models, therefore, can be expected to contribute "viable" viewpoints or perspectives that are applicable to the development of psychopathology. Likewise, each model and its explanations can also account for positive development in each child. In many instances, it might be more in the "twists and turns" of the individual's environment that emotional and behavioral disorders are shaped and reinforced.

Overall, the pressing need is to discover more about how psychopathology might develop in children because this understanding will help develop more effective treatments. Although on the surface this appears straightforward, the literature suggests that multiple causal factors for the development of emotional and behavioral disorders must be considered. As a result, counselors should think in terms of how multiple causes contributed to the client's risk or vulnerability. This knowledge should help counselors select the best treatments to target the causes. With this in mind, the purposes of this chapter are to provide a selective overview and discussion of the significance of child psychopathology, to provide models for the development of emotional and behavioral disorders, to suggest an integrative approach to understanding psychopathology, to apply the integrative approach to psychopathology through a case illustration, and to summarize in closing remarks. In particular, I tend to use the terms **model**, **theory**, **viewpoint**, and **perspective** somewhat interchangeably, and because of the complexity of human behavior and the limited understanding surrounding each model, there cannot be a definitive or all-encompassing model. Models, for example, are best utilized when you can visualize psychopathology as if it truly worked in the manner described by the models.

Common Misconceptions

Much misinformation about children with serious emotional and behavioral disorders surrounds child psychopathology. For example, misconceptions about child psychopathology have ranged from faulty conclusions such as autism being caused by poor parenting (e.g., cold mothering) (Bettelheim, 1967) to popular folklore (e.g., head size is reflective of defective intellect or morals; Gould, 1981). Descriptions of bizarre and aberrant behavior in children have existed for millennia; however, the formal or scientific study of such behavior is relatively new (Mash & Dozois, 1996). Much of the misunderstanding about child psychopathology originated from "inadequate" or what might be better termed "ungrounded" scientific, medical, psychological, and educational information (e.g., about children who exhibited seriously disordered behavior). For counseling to be more effective with these children, there needs to be a better understanding of how emotional and behavioral disorders (e.g., psychopathology) can be better conceptualized (Kauffman, 2005; Loeber, Burke, Lahey, Winters, & Zera, 2000; Wicks-Nelson & Israel, 2005).

The Prevalence of Psychopathology in Children

Psychopathology in children is relatively prevalent (Mash & Dozois, 1996). For example, according to the *Diagnostic and Statistical Manual of Mental Disorders, fourth edition, text revision* (*DSM-IV-TR;* American Psychiatric Association, 2000a), the prevalence rate for AD/HD is 3% to 7% of all school-age children in North America, whereas 1% to more than 10% of children have Conduct Disorder (CD). Overall estimates for all developmental, emotional, and behavioral disorders in children have ranged from 14% to 22% (Brandenburg, Friedman, & Silver, 1990). In the largest epidemiologic investigation on the rate and distribution of disorders ever conducted in this country, Robins, Locke, and Regier (1991) found the "lifetime" prevalence rate for phobia, alcohol abuse-dependence, generalized anxiety disorder, major depressive disorder, drug abuse-dependence, dysthymia, antisocial personality disorder, obsessive-compulsive disorder, panic disorder, schizophrenia, and manic-depressive disorder to range from 8% to 1%, respectively. What we can take from prevalence rates is that childhood problems are generally high, but that rates are likely to vary with the disorder, age, sex, social class, ethnicity, and criteria used to define the problem (Mash & Dozois, 1996).

Importantly, a significant proportion of children do not "outgrow" their childhood difficulties (Mash & Dozois, 1996; Rapoport, 2000). Moreover, sociocultural and/or environmental factors in all cultural groups (e.g., poverty, family dissolution, single parenting, use of illegal substances, abuse, and neglect) contribute to a greater number of children or youth showing serious behavioral problems and/or mental illness (Kauffman, 2005; Mash & Dozois, 1996; Mash & Wolfe, 2002; Sue, Sue, & Sue, 2000).

Mental Illness Begins Early in Life

Kessler et al. (2005a) and Kessler et al. (2005b) reported that half of all lifetime cases of mental illness begin by age 14; and, despite effective treatments being available, there are long delays, sometimes decades, between first onset of symptoms and when people seek and receive treatment. When this occurs, an untreated mental disorder might lead to a more severe, more difficult to treat illness, and to the development of co-occurring mental illnesses. With regard to the prevalence and age of onset of "mental disorders," it was found that mental illness, in contrast to physical diseases (e.g., heart disease or most cancers), begins very early in life—*half of all lifetime cases begin by age 14; three quarters have begun by age 24.* Thus, mental disorders are really the chronic diseases of the young. For example, anxiety disorders often begin in late childhood, mood disorders in late adolescence, and substance abuse in the early 20s. Therefore, young people with mental disorders suffer disability when they are in the prime of life, when they would normally be the most productive. These researchers confirmed a growing understanding about the nature of mental illness across the lifespan and there are many important findings. Conceivably, the important one is the recognition that mental disorders are the chronic disorders of young people in our country.

Terminology Used in Childhood Psychopathology

The terms **emotional disorder** and **behavioral disorder** are "labels" used to classify certain behaviors as abnormal, atypical, or dysfunctional (Newcomer, 2000). These terms are a way of comparing the normal behaviors exhibited by the majority of individuals to the "abnormal" or "dysfunctional" behaviors evidenced by individuals who are usually in a small minority. Terms also used in the research literature and by professionals include **mental disorder**, **psychosocial disorder**, and **mental illness**. In children, however, the designation **emotional** or **behavior disorder** is often viewed as more encompassing, implying developmental and learning problems (Mash & Dozois, 1996).

DEVELOPMENTAL THEORY APPLIED TO CHILD PSYCHOPATHOLOGY

A central tenet of developmental psychopathology is that "maladaptive" behavior cannot be viewed adequately unless there is the ability to view it in relation to what is "normative" behavior for a given period of development (Cicchetti & Sroufe, 2000). For example, theories of child development and how they account for the "healthy" or "normal" development of children provide counselors with central concepts and guiding assumptions (e.g., for how children's mental health should develop).

Generally, development in children is recognized as a "lifelong" process of growth and maturation. Changes are likely to unfold due to a combination of internal states and environmental conditions that might impinge on the child. These changes can often occur rapidly in the lives of many children and adolescents.

Therefore, an understanding of and appreciation for the normal development of children is considered essential. Also, an appreciation for the possible "risks" children can face in their developmental sequences is equally essential. For example, risks or discontinuities due either to the conditions operating in the child's settings (e.g., living in a high-crime neighborhood) or to some change in an internal state in the child (e.g., divorce) or both, can lead to distortions in the process we term as "normal" child development. If there are significant or serious distortions in the child's development, there may be increased risk for development of an emotional or behavioral disorder.

Moreover, it is not a question of whether the theories that address the normal development of children are incorrect; for the most part, they have accomplished much of their mission. However, the majority of developmental theories available (e.g., excepting behaviorism) have seemingly not been able to achieve the broader objective of explaining how children can grow into unhealthy adults. Perhaps new theories or understandings are needed to better understand how psychopathology develops.

Important Premises for Children's Mental Health

A number of central concepts or guiding assumptions that seem to underpin our current understanding of children's mental health and mental illness have been variously defined by different researchers (see Sroufe & Rutter, 1984; Cicchetti & Tucker, 1994; Cicchetti & Cohen, 1995). When you view the development of serious emotional and behavioral disorders in children, there are "premises" that go hand-in-hand with the development of psychopathology. The following important premises were put forward in *Children and Mental Health: A Report of the Surgeon General* (2000).

The first premise is that where there are developmental risks or discontinuities, there is the accompanying assumption that "early experiences" are capable of having an important influence on "current behavior." This implies that events that occur earlier in the child's life become part of an individual's later development. It is important to locate events associated with changes in a particular child's biological, psychological, educational, and social capacities; these are the likely determining events that interventions need to address.

The second premise is that all children to some extent have innate psychological resources (e.g., personality structure, temperament, and resilience). These and other resources are important factors for "adaptation" to their environments. This premise incorporates adaptation and acknowledges that many children do possess "self-righting" and "self-organizing" tendencies. Adaptation portends that a child within a given environmental niche modifies that niche to get needs met (e.g., positively or negatively). This would imply that where the environment is highly disorganized (e.g., socially aggressive) or chaotic, the child's psychological reaction to such a setting can be considered a **pathologic adaptation**. This is apparent when you compare this type of setting (e.g., chaotic) and the child's adaptations to it. This has particular importance, for example, when you compare the adaptations that a child from a healthy family structure makes. The resultant outcomes are simply different, qualitatively and quantitatively. An important point here is where the adaptations are in a "self-righting" direction (e.g., the individual is able to use his or her resources to make an adaptation to a particular environmental stressor), you would expect that there would be intact capacities for positive neurobehavioral adaptations. Where this is not the case in a particular individual, assessment and intervention are more likely to be indicated.

The third premise is that understanding the child's mental health or psychopathology concerns the factors of "age" and "timing." For example, crying and being difficult to soothe in a particular child at a certain age might be normal. However, these same symptoms in a child of greater age and development should warrant investigation (e.g., as an indicator of a possible disorder). In an allied example, symptoms of inattention in an infant or young child are to be expected. However, the persistence of recognizable symptoms of inattention in the first years of formal schooling should be investigated.

The fourth premise concerns the importance of the child's **context**. For most children in our society, the home or family environment is the primary setting for caretaking. The importance of the child's family environment should be considered a prime factor where a mental disorder might exist. The family can be the context where many types and varieties of early dysfunctional behaviors have been seeded or acquired. The family tends to remain (e.g., if it remains untreated) the catalyst for many of the "dysfunctional behaviors" that the child or adolescent continues to demonstrate. A catalyst promotes reactions (e.g., aggressive behaviors), but it does not change in the process. Furthermore, behaviors acquired in one context, such as the family, can also affect other important context factors, such as the school and peer relations. Thus, the tendency to fight as a way of dealing with conflict might also be played out with friends and school personnel.

The fifth and last premise is that what we term as "normal" and "abnormal" developmental factors varies across children and who is doing the reporting. What overwhelms and disables one child in any given developmental stage might be relatively innocuous to another child at the same developmental stage. There might also be differences in definition (e.g., about what is normal or abnormal) between one person and another. For example, what is defined by a parent or teacher to be too much for that child to endure, may not be the agreed-up on definition supplied by another parent or teacher who observed the same child at the same time. Although there is no clear definition of what constitutes normality, an accurate assessment entails assessing how the child is functioning in different life areas such as the family, school, and peers. Because behavior can vary across these contexts, assessment of child and adolescent problems requires integrating information provided by different sources (e.g., parent, teacher) to adequately determine the extent of "abnormality."

Models of childhood psychopathology have attempted to explain how various causal factors contributed to the development of emotional and behavioral disorders. In the next section, an overview of these models is presented.

Viewing emotional and behavioral disorders from different perspectives allows the counselor to find the best "fit" of factors for the case at hand. Using different models to describe and study how psychopathology might develop in childhood or adolescence is easily integrated with the developmental perspective of psychopathology (e.g., normal development can inform abnormal development; Lewis, 2000; Rutter & Sroufe, 2000). The intention is to focus on how each model (e.g., including many of its factors or perspectives) could be "integrated" into and account for the development of psychopathology in a particular child or adolescent. This integrative perspective is intended to sharpen the counselor's awareness of the connections that can exist between the various models.

Throughout this book, it is presumed that the "developmental" perspective of psychopathology adds developmental relevance to categorically based disorders that are contained in the *Diagnostic and Statistical Manual of Mental Disorders,* Fourth Edition, Text Revision (*DSM-IV-TR;* American Psychiatric Association, 2000a). This allows the counselor to acquire a panoramic view of how disorders might have been "seeded and developed."

Biological Models

Biological models are potentially the "all-in-one" packaged answer for the development of emotional and behavioral disorders. This thinking alone makes this model immediately attractive to most who view it. However, counselors should realize that although it is a logical starting point, it is certainly not the place where "all" of the answers to mental disorders can be found. Biological models or biological factors as causal agents in the development of emotional and behavioral disorders in children and adolescents immediately bring back the age-old question of "nature versus nurture."

It is becoming apparent that nature and nurture do not have to be pitted against each other. Instead, we should seek to learn how both work together to cause mental health and mental illness. Other important questions that fit the nature versus nurture issue are "What is the extent to which nature needs nurture?" and "What is the extent to which nurture can assist nature?" These questions have yet to be answered in a firm, scientific way. There is certainly an intricate biological and environmental dance, for example, taking place in all individuals (e.g., in constituting the mental conditions [positive-negative] that can affect individuals). By chance alone, some individuals will have primarily genetic disorders and others will have primarily environmental disorders, but most are likely to have a "mix" of both types of causes (Faraone, Tsuang, & Tsuang, 1999). In this section, we look at a number of biological models or perspectives including the brain, neurotransmitters, brain organicity or neuroanatomy, neural plasticity, genetic contributions, genes and destiny, genes and environment, and visible causes.

The Brain   The study of psychopathology requires a working familiarity with the brain. In essence, the brain is charged with receiving, deciphering, and interpreting the vast amount of information it collects. From the complex processing that takes place, the brain takes the responsibility for directing the individual's behavior. For example, Cottone (1992) emphasized that brain-based explanations for the direction of behavior (e.g., adaptive, maladaptive) share common assumptions about the internal functions of the brain. First, human thoughts, emotions, and behaviors are associated with nerve-cell activities of the brain and central nervous system. Second, any change in thoughts, emotions, or behaviors will be associated with an accompanying change in activity, structure, or both in the brain. Third, a mental disorder is highly correlated with some form of brain dysfunction, which may or may not be strictly biological in origin. It could evolve, for example, from experiences in the environment (e.g., lead or chemical exposure). Fourth, and last, mental disorders are amenable to interventions or treatments (e.g., medication, behavioral interventions, cognitive restructuring).

The brain has a critical role in mental health and in the direction and quality of our lives. For example, the frontal lobes are considered by researchers to be the area of the brain that manages the executive functions such as attention, memory, organization, planning, initiation of activity, self-inhibition, and self-monitoring (Nadeau, 1995). The frontal lobes contain the functions underlying our thinking and reasoning abilities, memory, self-control, judgment, and emotional regulation. All of these functions continue to mature late (e.g., well into late adolescence and early adulthood). Therefore, the brain you had when you reached adolescence is fortunately not the brain that you have now (Mash & Wolfe, 2002). Across the life span, the brain must rely on its maturation or development, its experiences, and its own neurobiology and neurochemistry to direct and fuel itself.

Finally, the brain is viewed increasingly by medical science as shaped by the contribution of our "genes" and the "experience" provided by the environment. These should be seen as working together rather than separately. For example, visual motor ability is enhanced if the child is exposed to environments that require the child to develop this ability (e.g., art classes). This strengthens the developmental view that mental disorders are caused and can be treated by biological and experiential processes working together. Furthermore, having a better understanding of this brain–experience transaction strengthens the developmental position that biological, psychological, and sociological models or factors "meld" in mental health as well as in mental illness.

Neurotransmitters   Neurotransmitters are minute chemical molecules that act like biochemical currents in the brain. These currents develop in an organized manner to make meaningful connections. Neurons that are more sensitive to one type of neurotransmitter, such as serotonin or dopamine, are capable of finding each other and clustering together to make a connection. Genetics can influence the chemicals that an individual has available, thereby influencing neurotransmitter activity and making the individual more or less likely to exhibit certain types of behavior (Mash & Wolfe, 2002).

The brain has billions of specialized neurons that will continue to differentiate and grow axons and dendritic connections (e.g., from infancy thorough adolescence and into adulthood) (Mash & Wolfe, 2002). These connections form the complex neural networks that support human existence and behavior (Ingalls & Goldstein, 1999). Neurons are genetically designed to be distinct in terms of their chemistry, shape, and connections. It is the neurons that conduct matching electrochemical impulses by which communication occurs. Before communication can occur, all of the connections or messages must cross the gap between neurons (e.g., the synaptic gap or cleft). When an impulse reaches the end of the axon, neurotransmitters are released that cross the **synaptic gap** and communicate with other cells through **receptor cells** on those cells. Therefore, communication in the brain is dependent on the ability of the nerve cells to communicate with each other. Neurotransmitter chemicals or molecules must "match" for connections to be made (e.g., for communication to occur).

Neurotransmitters are the all-important biochemical currents (e.g., the biochemical messengers) that inhibit or enhance our brain functioning. These biochemical molecules, for example, empower the brain to make meaningful connections. These connections are so vital that without them, important larger functions (e.g., feeling and thinking) would be impaired or not permitted (Mash & Wolfe, 2002). Proper functioning of the neurotransmitters is crucial to our behavioral repertoire. The neurotransmitter serotonin is designed to modulate or control behavior, whereas releases of the neurotransmitter dopamine are associated with experiencing pleasure and novelty seeking. Neurotransmitter dysfunction (e.g., serotonin) can lead to behavior being "unregulated" or "unmodulated" (e.g., aggressive behavior, sexual acting out).

Recently, scientists have learned that the neurotransmitters serotonin and norepinephrin are decreased in people with severe eating disorders, as they are in those with depression. In addition, people with anorexia or depression also tend to have higher than normal levels of a brain chemical named cortisol that is released in stressful situations. However, the exact meaning and implications of these brain-chemical imbalances remain under investigation (Herzog, Nussbaum, & Marmot, 1996).

In essence, neurotransmitters are neurobiological control systems that people depend upon. Their importance should not be underemphasized. There are four neurotransmitter systems that are mentioned most in the research literature in connection with psychiatric or psychological disorders. See Table 2.1 for a description of the major neurotransmitter systems and their related roles in psychopathology.

Ultimately, the pattern of synaptic connections gives rise to what are known as large arrays (e.g., tens of thousands) of "circuits" in the brain or gray matter. All areas of the brain (e.g., parietal lobes, frontal lobes, corpus callous, temporal lobes) are served by specialized brain circuitry (e.g., including many feedback loops that can aid in reality testing). Circuits in the brain are considered by scientists to be the major substrates or enablers of human behavior (Mash & Wolf, 2002). Scientists are still attempting to discover how neuronal activity within all of these small and large circuits gives rise to the complex concepts we know as consciousness, behavioral repertoires, mental health, and mental illness.

TABLE 2.1   Major Neurotransmitters, Normal Role-Function, Implications for Psychopathology

Neurotransmitter	Normal Role	Implications for Psychopathology
Serotonin	Created in the brain. Appears to be involved in some fundamental aspects of physiology(e.g., control of body temperature, cardiovascularactivity, respiration, sex drive) and in a range of behavior (e.g., anger control, aggression, eating, moderating anger, and sleeping). Serotonin neurons project into the central nervous system down to the tip of the spinal cord.	Linked with anxiety disorders, mood disorders, obsessive-compulsive disorder, eating disorders, and Schizophrenia (Jacobs, 1994; Mash & Wolfe, 2002; Sue, Sue, & Sue, 2000).
Dopamine	Concentrated in small areas of the brain. May act as a switch that turns on various circuits in the brain to facilitate and/or inhibit emotions and behavior.	Schizophrenia, mood disorders, AD/HD (Mash & Wolfe, 2002). In excess, may cause hallucinations (Sue, Sue, & Sue, 2000).
Gamma-aminobutyric acid/ Benzodiazepine- GABA	Widely distributed in the brain. Works against other neurotransmitters, particularly dopamine. Acts to inhibit arousal and to moderate emotional responses (e.g., anger, hostility, aggression) and is linked to feelings of anxiety.	Anxiety disorder (Mash & Wolfe, 2002).
Norepinephine	Facilitates or controls emergency and alarm reactions. Plays a role in emotional and behavioral regulation.	Not directly involved in specific disorders but acts to generally regulate or moderate behavioral tendencies (Mash & Wolfe, 2002).
Acetylcholine	Widespread and occurs in systems that control muscles and brain circuits related to attention and memory.	Related to Alzheimer's disease (Sue, Sue, & Sue, 2000).

Adapted by permission from Mash & Wolfe (2002) and Sue, Sue, & Sue, (2000).
Note: Jacobs (1994) pointed out that while the brain uses a surprisingly large number of chemical neurotransmitters, perhaps as many as one hundred, the preponderance of the work in the brain is accomplished in a simple and direct way by four chemicals (e.g., glutamate and asperate [both excite neurons] and gamma-aminobutyric acid and glycine [both inhibit neurons]. Other neurotransmitters (e.g., serotonin, dopamine, and norepinephrine) act somewhat differently by producing excitation or inhibition, acting over a longer time frame, and they tend to work in concert with one of the four chemical workhorses. Hence, they are also referred to as neuromodulators in the brain (e.g., a necessary system of chemical checks and balances).

The undergirding premise for the biochemical or neurotransmitter perspective is that brain chemical imbalances underlie the development and maintenance of most, and perhaps all, mental disorders (Mash & Barkley, 1996; Mash & Wolfe, 2002; Sue, Sue, & Sue, 2000; Wicks-Nelson & Israel, 2005). This premise relies on the fact that many physiological and mental processes involve complex chemical actions within the body. Support for the neurochemical imbalance perspective as being involved in many disorders has been derived from research into physiological and mental processes (see Barkley, 1997a; Brown & Ivers, 1999; Carey & DiLalla, 1994; Faraone, Tsuang, & Tsuang, 1999; Goldstein & Reynolds, 1999; Ingalls & Goldstein, 1999; Lickey & Gordon, 1991; Pliszka, Carlson, & Swanson, 1999; Pliszka & Olvera, 1999; Plomin, Owen, & McGuffin, 1994; and Vasey, Dalieden, Williams, & Brown, 1995 for more specific information).

Brain Organicity or Neuroanatomy   Brain organicity is characterized by the "neuroanatomy" of the brain and its relationships to neural dysfunction and any accompanying behavioral manifestation. Brain organicity and its importance was only hinted at in the work of researchers in the past 3 decades (Tranel, 1992). Recent research has provided more scientific information on salient neurophysiological features that can accompany individuals with brain dysfunction. For example, Mash and Wolfe (2002) discussed the hypothalmic-pituitary axis (HPA) as receiving considerable attention from brain-behavior researchers. The HPA is a central component of the brain's neuroendocrine (e.g., chemical) response to stress. The hypothalamus, when stimulated, secretes corticotropin-releasing hormone (CRII), which, in turn, stimulates the pituitary gland to secrete andrenocorticotropic hormone (ACTH) into the bloodstream. ACTH then causes the adrenal glands to release cortisol, the familiar stress hormone that "arouses" the body to prepare for a challenging situation. This system, like many others in the brain, works on a feedback loop. The adrenergic regulation of cortisol secretion is complex; however, this hormone may act as a "modulator" of the stress response by acting on the hypothalamus to inhibit the continued release of CRH. Researchers are discovering, for example, that this important feedback loop that governs our level of arousal and apprehension can be seriously disrupted or damaged (e.g., by traumatic and uncontrollable events such as mental, physical, and sexual abuse). When these events occur, for example, they can cause a child or adolescent to maintain a state of fear or apprehension that becomes "toxic" over prolonged time periods (DeBellis, Burke, Trickett, & Putnam, 1996; Van der Kolk & Fisler, 1994). The HPA axis, for example, is implicated in several *DSM IV-TR* disorders, especially those disorders related to stress and the individual's ability to effectively regulate feeling and emotions (e.g., anxiety disorders, mood disorders [depression]) (Mash & Wolfe, 2002).

In another interesting example, in the late 1980s, it was discovered that some children with obsessive-compulsive disorder (OCD) experienced a sudden onset of symptoms soon after a streptococcal pharyngitis infection (Garvey, Giedd, & Swedo, 1998; Swedo & Pekar, 2000). The symptoms were classic for OCD (e.g., concerns about contamination, spitting compulsions, and extremely excessive hoarding). But the abrupt onset was unusual and disconcerting to medical specialists. Further study, for example, of these children, led to the identification of a new classification of OCD called PANDAS. This acronym stands for **Pediatric Autoimmune Neuropsychiatric Disorders Associated with Streptococcal Infection.** PANDAS are distinct from classic cases of OCD because of their episodic clinical course, which is marked by sudden symptom exacerbation that is linked to streptococcal infection. The exacerbation of symptoms is correlated with a rise in levels of antibodies that the child produces normally to fight the strep infection.

Consequently, researchers proposed that PANDAS are caused by antibodies fighting against the strep infection that also manage to attack the basal ganglia region of the child's brain (Garvey, Giedd, & Swedo, 1998; Swedo & Pekar, 2000). In other words, the strep infection triggers the child's immune system to develop antibodies, which, in turn, may attack the child's brain (e.g., leading to obsessive and compulsive behaviors). Under this research proposal, the strep infection does not directly induce the condition. Rather, it apparently does so indirectly by triggering antibody formation. How the antibodies are so damaging to a discrete region of the child's brain and how this attack ignites OCD-like symptoms are fundamental questions guiding this research. The availability of trait markers for susceptibility to disease (e.g., as seen in PANDAS) opens the door to the possibility that "early onset" of OCD could one day be eradicated (e.g., much like rheumatic fever is today) (Swedo & Pekar, 2000).

In a last example of neuroanatomy, Castellanos, Giedd, Marsh, Hamburger, Vaituzis, Dickstein, Saifatti, Vauss, Snell, Pajapakse, and Rapoport (1996) employed anatomic brain imaging (MRI) to study the neuroanatomy of 57 boys with AD/HD and 57 non–AD/HD matched boys in the control group, ages 5 to 18 years. For participants with AD/HD, the following are the findings of this comprehensive morphometric analysis of multiple brain regions: 1) The participants had a 5% smaller total cerebral volume ($p = .02$); 2) the analysis of covariance for the total cerebral volume demonstrated a significant loss of normal "right>left" asymmetry in the caudate ($p = .006$); 3) there was a smaller right globus pallidus ($p = .005$); 4) there was a smaller right anterior frontal region ($p = .02$); 5) there was a smaller cerebellum ($p = .05$); and 6) there was a reversal of normal lateral ventricular asymmetry ($p = .03$). (Interrater reliabilities were .82 or higher for all MRI measures.) Castellanos et al. (1996) concluded that these research findings are consistent with the hypothesized dysfunction of the right-sided perfrontal-striatal systems of the brain in people who have AD/HD. Moreover, the right prefrontal cortex is involved in functions such as editing one's behavior, resisting distractions (e.g., internally, externally), and developing an awareness of self and time (Barkley, 1998). The area of the brain known as the basal ganglia, or midbrain, houses the caudate nucleus and globus pallidus; the basal ganglia, due to its reciprocal connections to higher cortical or cerebral processes, is considered to play a critical role in higher cognitive functions (e.g., attention, working memory, rule-based learning, goal-directed behavior; Middleton & Strick, 1994). The caudate nucleus and the globus pallidus are important for switching off autonomic (e.g., impulsive) responses to allow for more careful deliberation by the cortex and for coordinating neurological input among regions in the cortex (Barkley, 2005). Furthermore, the research of Rapoport (1996), using MRI on children with AD/HD and a matched control group at the National Institutes of Mental Health, found that the frontal lobes where the anterior portion of the frontal lobes connect with the basal ganglia—particularly on the right side— were statistically or significantly smaller in children with AD/HD than they were in children in the control group. The lion's share of brain research underway today is focusing on the neuroscience of mental health (e.g., the brain and its critical role in mental health) (Mash & Wolfe, 2002).

Neural Plasticity   An important feature of the brain is neural plasticity because early neural connections are not stable; some are strengthened and become more established with use, while many regress or disappear (Mash & Wolfe, 2002). Therefore, the answer to the question about the permanence of early brain connections is that the brain shows malleability or neural plasticity throughout the course of its development (Reiss & Neiderhiser, 2000). Neural plasticity implies that the brain cannot remain the same when learning and experience (e.g., whether positive or negative) are factored into the equation. Neural plasticity or the remaking of the brain is considered to be taking place regularly (e.g., it is much like the hard drive in a computer, updating itself periodically). Moreover, neural plasticity means that the brain's anatomical differentiation is use-dependent (e.g., it works largely in service to its use or environmental conditioning). For example, nature provides the basic brain processes, whereas nurture or the environment provides the input or experiences that are needed to select the most adaptive network of brain-mind connections (Cicchetti & Cannon, 1999).

Furthermore, it is fascinating how nature and nurture work together to create highly specific and extremely adaptive brain–central nervous system functions (Mash & Wolfe, 2002). Consider the finding of resilience from a wide number of risk studies and children. A number of children who came from adverse home environments were able to exhibit what the researchers called resilience. These resilient children were exposed to chronic adversities such as poverty and disruptive family environments and were able to successfully navigate these circumstances. The existence of resilient children emphasizes the importance of "neural plasticity" to development. Especially, it emphasizes how the brain can operate (e.g., even in adverse environments) to offer at-risk children strengths and attributes (Beardslee, 2000).

For example, Beardslee (2000) described children who have developed a resilient attitude as having the following characteristics: 1) They possessed higher than normal levels of adaptive functioning (e.g., they can see positive alternatives in their environment); 2) they were thoroughly involved in school activities (e.g., curricular, extracurricular); 3) they were committed to being involved in intimate interpersonal relationships (e.g., with other potential caregivers such as relatives, teachers, neighbors); and 4) they did not see themselves as to blame for their parent's condition (e.g., they saw themselves as being free to go forward). Thatcher (1994) advocated that the brain is always a work in progress and the environment plays an essential role as supervisor of this dynamic and continual rewiring and reprogramming process.

Findings from neuroscience have demonstrated the presence of neuronal plasticity (e.g., the making of new cells and connections) within the brain and central nervous system (Kay, 2001). Around puberty, for example, the brain develops more new brain cells and once again begins to reorganize (e.g., update) and consolidate itself (e.g., including the lobes [parietal, frontal, temporal] and other brain areas) (Thompson, Giedd, Woods, MacDonald, Alan, & Toga, 2000). Changes in the brain must precede or occur simultaneously for other changes in our life to take place. It is more practical to think of the brain as our most adaptable and changing organ.

Genetic Contributions   The genetic view of how behavior develops (e.g., emotional and behavioral disorders) continues to carry an appeal for parents and teachers. There is growing awareness that developmental and psychosocial models cannot account for all the "behavioral variations" that are observed in individual children. There is also growing awareness that advances coming from the Human Genome Project (e.g., advances in deciphering genetics) and sophisticated medical technologies (e.g., positron emission tomograpy [PET]) make the appeal of genetic factors (e.g., as the basis for emotional and behavioral disorders) seem more plausible. Accumulating scientific data suggests that genetics are an important attribute to emotional or behavioral disorders.

As attractive as biological or genetic determinants may seem on the surface, the assumption that one's life is lived in what may be termed biological "fortunes or misfortunes" is misleading. This assumption is misleading because although biological forces have a pervasive influence on our lives, they affect behavior only in how they interact with environmental factors. There is strong clinical evidence from genetic studies supporting the importance of environmental factors in playing a significant role in the development of emotional and behavioral disorders (Plomin, DeFries, & McClearn, 1990). For example, parental psychopathology can often be present in children who are diagnosed with antisocial behavior (e.g., conduct disorder) and parent–child interactions in the home are usually socially aggressive and punishing (Frick, 1998; Kazdin, 1995; Loeber, Burke, Lahey, Winters, & Zera, 2000). Moffitt (1993) argued that life-course persistent antisocial behavior and early onset of conduct disorder have their earliest roots in both neurological factors and exposure to environmental risk (e.g., parental antisocial behavior, poor parenting). However, when we talk about biological or genetic influences on human behavior, we do not mean robot-like behavior that is hard-wired and follows a preordained route from conception into adult life (Plomin, DeFries, & McClearn, 1990; Plomin, Owen, & McGuffin, 1994). Instead, we are talking about indirect and complex interactions (e.g., among genes, the proteins they manufacture, and physiological systems). These systems, in turn, create predispositions (e.g., to behave in a particular way). To simplify the whole process, consider it this way: Biological factors infer that various genes and the proteins they manufacture create and interact with the neurochemical and neuroanatomical brain differences that are present in each individual. All of these components, along with environmental factors, combine to be at the "heart" of differences in what is best termed "neural sensitivity" (e.g., the variations of behavior that can be displayed within the child's environment [home, school, community]).

Genes and Destiny   So, do genes determine our destiny (e.g., the development of AD/HD, ODD, or CD)? The answer is no, genetics do not determine one's destiny. This view would be unscientific and pessimistic. Although biological factors or genetics can account for a considerable portion of individual variation in the expression of important behaviors (e.g., social compliance, academic achievement), it must not be assumed that counseling and environmental interventions would be useless (Plomin & DeFries, 1998; Plomin, DeFries, & McClearn, 1990).

However, if a new genetic treatment were to become available or if a new environmental treatment (e.g., based on a genetic intervention) were introduced, it could become feasible to expect that a behavior or a behavioral pattern could be significantly altered. Just a few years ago, this thinking was only for those who believed in science fiction; now it probably will happen one day soon. Most of the research on human behavioral genetics has analyzed behavioral differences among individuals and estimated the relative extent to which these differences are due to heredity and environment (e.g., presuming the mix of genetic and environmental influences that are at work at a particular time). The scientific thinking is that if either the genetic or environmental influences change significantly, the influence of the genes and the environment will also change.

The next milestone, it appears, is unraveling how development or experience modifies (e.g., enters the physical structure of) genes (Cook, 2000). To improve the human condition, we really need to discover how experience and learning enter or modify the physical or internal structure of the person's genes. This answer is still far off, but has immense implications for refining the field of behavioral genetics (see Mash & Wolfe, 2002). An answer to how experience and learning (e.g., adaptive, maladaptive) modify the structure of a person's genes will someday provide an enriched understanding of the conflict that is ongoing between the "nature and nurture" camps. Instead, what we might find out is how one can become an "ally" to the other.

Genes and Environment Working Together   Here is a pertinent example of how genetics and an environmental intervention can "work together" to prevent a specific condition. The best example we can consider is phenylketonuria (or PKU), which is known to be a single gene defect that formerly resulted in severe mental retardation and was responsible for about 1% of all the institutionalized retarded individuals in our country. From biochemical studies of the genetic behavioral pathway, it was discovered that the ultimate cause of the retardation was the inability to break down a particular chemical, phenyketonuria, which led to this chemical attaining high levels in the blood. This, in turn, caused severe and irreversible damage to the developing brain. PKU individuals no longer suffer brain damage or retardation if a diet low in phenyketonuria is provided during the developing years. The point is that medical science (e.g., genetics) and the environment were both successful in bypassing a genetic problem. Again, a genetically determined behavioral problem can be bypassed, or at least significantly ameliorated, by environmental interventions (Plomin, DeFries, & McClearn, 1990).

Counselors should not expect all genetic–environmental relationships to turn out to be this straightforward. It is more likely that an intricate array of genetic–environmental relationships exists for most disorders to become visible. For example, the actual interfacing of genetic and environmental influences in the life of each individual might boil down to the intensity of the neurochemical features present at any given time. And we must determine how the environmental circumstances facing that individual at that particular time come to account for the development of any lasting effects.

In the severe disorder known as Schizophrenia, there is known to be a clear genetic contribution. However, how the genetic system works (e.g., environmentally) to transmit the disorder actually remains obscure. Schizophrenia remains the most studied mental disorder in the research literature. For example, over a quarter of a century of clinical study has led to the following conclusions: 1) It is genetic in its origins (e.g., because individuals inherit a genetic liability for the illness); 2) the illness, in many instances, is set off by a traumatic event (e.g., severe brain trauma) or a significant environmental factor or occurrence (e.g., exposure to substance abuse); 3) only 10% of Schizophrenics have a parent with the disorder (i.e., it does not appear to run vertically through families); and 4) in the age-old controversy of "nature versus nurture," schizophrenia seems to take both sides (as cited from Gottesman in Kauffman, 2005).

Visible Causes   In the biological arena, there are some other important considerations for counselors to keep in mind. Counselors should not overlook that the brain and central nervous system can be damaged from a host of "visible" causes such as a brain infection in early childhood. These must be considered for any effects that they might have on the development of an emotional or behavioral disorder. Examples, include traumatic brain injury (TBI), where the cause is an external force rather than a congenital condition, autism where the major characteristic is qualitatively diminished impairment in social and mental functioning, malnutrition and allergies that may significantly reduce a child's responsiveness to stimulation and learning, and physical illness that is rarely if ever caused by psychopathology. However, where increased stress from intense emotional or behavioral disorders is sustained, it can cause significant reversals in one's physical health. On the other side of the coin, one's physical health can have a profound effect on one's emotional health and behavior.

To conclude, the most tenable view coming from the findings of medical science seems to be that emotional and behavioral disorders are the function and product of both genetics and environment. We cannot view either genetic factors or environmental factors as acting strictly alone. The appeal of biological or genetic factors is quite natural considering the attraction of all behavior emanating from neurochemical and neurological functioning. The scientific yields that can come from future medical research on the use of proactive procedures (e.g., preventative measures), early interventions (e.g., medication, behavioral strategies), and continued modifications to the environments in which the child is expected to function would seem to offer the most promise.

Criticisms of the Biological Model   At the core of the criticism about the biological model is the limited amount of verifiable scientific information available. Although the amount and validity of the scientific information coming from the Human Genome Project is growing, we have yet to see how it will all finally be connected to causality for emotional and behavioral disorders. As you have probably heard, genetic factors have been suggested as causes for nearly every mental disorder. However, when genetic or biological factors are at work, they cannot be in operation in isolation or work independently from biological, psychological, behavioral, cognitive, school, family, and multicultural models or factors.

Sue, Sue, and Sue (2000) emphasized that there are four shortcomings of the biological model as the sole explanation for emotional and mental disorders (e.g., mental illness). First, the model implies that maladaptive behavior arises from underlying biological components (e.g., brain malfunction, neurochemistries). This approach, for example, does not adequately account for maladaptive behavior for which no biological cause can be readily identified (e.g., phobias). Logic would seem to suggest that many mental disorders are probably caused by a mix of biological predisposition and environment.

Second, there needs to be further research into the often complicated and interacting roles of factors such as environmental, social, and multicultural influences. Human behavior can often be the product of "multiple causes" (e.g., interacting to play important roles in the manifestation of emotional or behavioral disorders). For example, certain environmental stressors may activate a biological predisposition that results in a particular disorder. On the other side, however, is the thinking that a nonharmful or supportive environment might ameliorate or prevent the disorder from materializing.

Third, environmental factors can cause biological dysfunction. It is widely acknowledged that high levels of stress or fear produce secretions of adrenalin and noradrenalin. Similarly, it could be the case that Schizophrenia may cause the secretion of excess amounts of chemicals (e.g., dopamine) in individuals with the disorder, rather than entirely being the result of the presence of these chemicals. One positive implication from this scientific knowledge is that eventually we may be able to discover medications that can selectively correct or more efficaciously manage these biological dysfunctions (e.g, irrespective of labeling them as emotional or behavioral disorders).

Fourth, is that wholesale adoption of the biological model might lead to fostering client helplessness by eliminating the client's role in responsibility for the disorder. For example, clients could be viewed by themselves, their families, and their counselors as unfortunate victims and passive participants captured by their biological conditions. The only valid option for these individuals would be appropriate medications and increasingly more medical attention. For example, if adopted, such an approach could only further debilitate the individual.

Psychological Models

Psychological models have looked at the contributions of psychological factors such as temperament, personality, attachment, and emotional influences. Freudian or psychodynamic perspectives dominated what we knew about the development of child psychology and psychopathology in children and adolescents well into the past century (Mash & Barkley, 1996). Many of the psychological models or theories that we use today are derivatives of earlier psychological models or approaches. Rutter (1995), for example, asserted that this early work "spawned" research and provided routes into present-day psychological models or perspectives. Bretherton (1995) believed that the emergence of attachment theory signaled a definite shifting of attention from the more psychoanalytic role of intrapersonal or inner-defensive mechanisms to that of placing more emphasis on the role of interpersonal relationships (e.g., both adaptive and maladaptive in children and adolescents).

Temperament   One of the first behavioral inclinations that the infant displays to parents or caregivers is temperament. Temperament, although inwardly driven by biological or genetic predispositions, is nonetheless "outwardly" observed from birth (Thomas & Chess, 1977). Temperament, for example, can refer to fearfulness, irritability, fussiness, or the infant being difficult to calm or soothe. Temperament refers to the young child's style of behavior, and it appears early in development (Emde & Spicer, 2000; Rothbart & Bates, 1998). For example, Rothbart and Mauro (1990) defined "three primary dimensions" of temperament that can exist in young children. These dimensions are considered to be relevant to the development of dysfunctional behavior. The first dimension is typified by the "easy child," who has a positive affect and approaches the environment with adaptive responses (e.g., this child can regulate its reactions relative to emotional experiences). The second dimension is typified by the "slow to warm up child," which describes the child who is cautious in the approach to novel or unique situations. This child is more variable in self-regulation and adaptability (e.g., the child may show distress or be negative in some situations). The third dimension is typified by the "difficult child," who is predominately irritable or negative in mood and not very adaptable. Many children with this temperament show distress when faced with novel or challenging situations or when decisions need to be made. In many children with this last temperament, a general proneness to irritability can be easily aroused when limitations (e.g., rules, time limits, demands, curfews) are imposed by parents or teachers.

Where a difficult temperament is exhibited, a "mismatch" between the child's temperament (e.g., which is a behavioral style) and the child's social environment is increased (Kauffman, 2005). Therefore, the risk for the development of an emotional or behavioral disorder might be enhanced (e.g., especially when this "mismatch" is not adequately addressed). However, a difficult temperament should not be considered destiny. The malleability of the child's environment (e.g., designing behavioral interventions) for a difficult temperament is usually the crucial consideration.

The risk factor, for example, for an emotional or behavioral disorder is substantially enhanced by the way that the parents and teachers seek to "manage" or "control" the child's temperament and behavioral style (Kochanska, 1995). Counselors must be aware that children with a difficult behavioral style must be addressed primarily through environmental modifications (e.g., changing other people's demands, behavioral expectations, and responses). There must also be sufficient time allowed for the child with a difficult temperament to respond to the environmental modifications. Often where a difficult temperament exists, the difficult child has been forced to "fit" into the family or school situation as it presently exists. For example, a high-strung child might need parent or teacher supervision that entails limits and close monitoring, whereas a child who is easygoing and compliant might need relatively little attention from parents or teachers to accomplish tasks.

Remember, the child with a difficult temperament has few choices due to its condition. Unfortunately, in many instances, this has led to increased levels of conflict with caregivers or authority figures (e.g., resulting in more nonaffirming experiences in their lives). To put attachment behavior in better perspective, it can change as circumstances in the environment change, and not all studies of it show a link between parent–child attachment and adaptive behavior (Wicks-Nelson & Israel, 2005).

Personality Structure   Freud presented a model of personality that divided the individual's personality structure into three major parts (e.g., id, ego, and superego). Each part of the personality, for example, needs to be in a state of relative equilibrium for the individual to be considered mentally healthy (e.g., adaptive to the environment). The id is considered to be the unconscious part of the individual and the originator of raw drives (e.g., sex, aggression). If these raw drives become overpowering, the individual is prone to commit actions that are detrimental to the self, others, and society. The ego is considered the rational and reasonable part of the personality. Its role is to maintain contact with the outside world (e.g., reality) and to keep the id and superego in a dynamic balance (e.g., without one or more of the parts overlapping and contaminating another one). Within this scenario, for example, the ego serves as a constant mediator between internal conflicts and external realities. When this ego mediating function breaks down, for example, psychological distress and symptoms of a mental disorder can become apparent. The superego is postulated to be the individual's conscience (e.g., rights and wrongs in our society, oughts and shoulds in our society). It is developed early in life and is learned from the teachings and observations of parents, teachers, and others in close physical proximity. It can work to overpower the ego and push the individual into a world of clear rights and clear wrongs. Such a world is not in harmony, for example, with how the world really works. Again, the ego's mediating function strives to keep the individual oriented toward reality and to prevent disruption to the individual's physical and mental health.

Symptoms of psychopathology are viewed as important only in terms of the expression of underlying conflicts between the "major parts" of the personality. Anxiety and psychopathology are important concepts in psychodynamic theory and arise from conflicts among the id, ego, and superego. Realistic anxiety occurs when there is a potentially dangerous situation in the environment. For example, you smell smoke in a building and experience realistic anxiety as your ego warns you to protect yourself from harm. Moralistic anxiety results when someone does not live up to his or her own moral standards or engages in unethical conduct. In this case, the ego warns of possible retaliation from the superego. Neurotic anxiety can result when id impulses seem to be getting out of control or will burst through ego controls. As long as these conflicts are ongoing, the individual is not unified and more mental problems or disorders are likely to develop (Sue, Sue, & Sue, 2000).

Therefore, the individual must understand and resolve these conflicts (e.g., re-experiencing the old with new insights). This permits improvement in the individual's mental condition or disorder. It is with the assistance of the counselor, for example, that the person seeks to "unearth" the secrets or denied material (e.g., inner felt anxieties, fears, traumas) that could be lodged in the unconscious mind. This remains today much of the basis for psychoanalysis or therapy (e.g., as a form of long-term treatment for mental disorders or illness). However, there are proponents of short-term psychoanalysis as being an effective treatment modality (e.g., for reintegrating the personality structure in clients) (see Corey, 2005; Schultz & Schultz, 2001; and Seligman, 2001).

Finally, Freud viewed psychosexual stages of development (e.g., oral, anal, phallic, latent, genital) as integral to the development of the individual. According to psychodynamic theory, human personality develops through these five psychosexual stages, each of which brings a unique challenge. If unfavorable circumstances happen to prevail at any stage (e.g., chaotic home environment, dysfunctional parenting), the personality structure may be drastically affected. Because Freud stressed the importance of early childhood experiences, he viewed the human personality as largely shaped in the first five years of life—during the oral stage (i.e., the first year of life), anal stage (i.e., around the second year of life), and phallic stage (i.e., beginning around the third and fourth years). The last two psychosexual stages are the latency stage (i.e., approximately 6 to 12 years of age) and the genital stage (i.e., beginning in puberty) (Sue, Sue, & Sue, 2000).

The importance of each psychosexual stage for later development of the personality lies in how much "fixation" occurs during that stage. Fixation is the arresting of emotional development at a particular psychosocial stage. Moreover, if the infant or young child is traumatized or harmed in some way during a particular stage (e.g., the oral stage), the development of the child could be arrested at that point or stage (Schultz & Schultz, 2001; Sue, Sue, & Sue, 2000). Passivity, helplessness, and substance abuse may all become characteristics of an oral personality (Sue, Sue, & Sue, 2000). Schultz and Schultz (2001) have a more detailed description of the psychosexual stages and describe how a person is sometimes reluctant or unable to move from one stage to the next. This is because a "conflict" has not been resolved or because the needs have been so supremely satisfied by an indulgent parent (e.g., excessive gratification) that the child becomes "fixated" at that stage and does not want to move on. Freud did believe that a person could transcend the various fixations that could occur at any one of the psychosexual stages and develop into a normal, healthy individual (Sue, Sue, & Sue, 2000).

Attachment   Attachment refers to the process of establishing and maintaining a parent–child bond (e.g., an emotional bond) with parents or other significant caregivers. This process can begin at birth but typically begins between 6 to 12 months of age and is ongoing (Mash & Wolfe, 2002). Four patterns or styles of infant attachment have been determined (see Ainsworth, Blehar, Waters, & Wall, 1978; Ainsworth, 1979; Lyons-Ruth, Zeanah, & Benoit, 1996):

> **Secure attachment** is characterized by the infant staying close to the caregiver, may be or may be not being distressed at separation from the caregiver, reacting positively when the caregiver returns, being open to communication and affect, and displaying few ambivalent or avoidant behaviors.
> **Ambivalent attachment** is characterized by the infant communicating distress and anger, showing anger while seeking contact with the caregiver, displaying passivity and helplessness, and not being easily soothed.

Avoidant attachment is characterized by the infant showing little affect or distress, avoiding contact with the caregiver, and attending to the environment as a way to minimize anger or interest felt toward the caregiver.

Disorganized or **disoriented attachment** is characterized by the infant displaying contradictory behaviors such as a sequence of contact seeking, anger, avoidance, and distress in the face of needs for comfort and security; showing disoriented wandering around and change in affect and appearing apprehensive regarding the caretaker.

Attachment theory provides a valuable conceptual model for understanding the role of the parent–child relationship (e.g., research on attachment indicates that it has consequences for the child's view of the social world and later behavior) (Waters, Merrick, Treboux, Crowell, & Albersheim, 2000; Wicks-Nelson & Israel, 2005). Attachment style, for example, can endure across the individual's lifespan and is thought to be rooted in the child's early rearing experience (e.g., providing the context for later emotional, behavioral, and cognitive transactions with the environment) (Finzi, Ram, Shnit, & Weizman, 2001). Attachment theory and how it can provide more understanding about the developing child and psychopathology has received increasing attention from researchers. Some studies have shown that secure attachment is associated with adaptive behavior in childhood and adolescence, such as social competence and positive peer group interactions, and that insecure attachment can place children at risk for maladaptive behaviors and problems (Dunn & McGuire, 1992; Wicks-Nelson & Israel, 2005). There is accumulating information to suggest that attachment is an important concept for more understanding on the "adaptive" and "maladaptive" ways that individuals may negotiate various developmental challenges that occur across the lifespan (Lopez, 1995; Lyddon, 1995; Lyddon & Sherry, 2001).

Bowlby (1980), for example, argued that the development of psychopathology in the child might be related to the inability of the primary caregiver (e.g., parents) to respond appropriately to the child's needs, especially if the infant or child has a difficult temperament or personality characteristics that thwart the caregiver's attempts. Sroufe (1985) questioned the role of caregiving or parental influence when the infant or child has a difficult temperament (e.g., is hard to soothe or calm). For example, the reciprocal interaction of a "difficult" temperament and the parental "response" may better account for how the parent–child relationship develops.

Not all parents, for example, can be expected to respond positively or to employ appropriate caregiving strategies if these compromising factors are at work. However, it should be pointed out that the bulk of the research evidence suggests that infants and children change their attachment relationship with different cargivers (Mash & Dozois, 1996). Moreover, it is important to recognize that we cannot assume that all children who have a mental disorder were victims of an insecure or inadequate parent–child attachment.

Attachment has an important role in focusing more attention on how adaptive and deficient attachment relationships affect individuals. Rutter (1995) asserted that key issues need to be resolved surrounding the concept of attachment. Among these issues are the following: 1) Achieving a better understanding of the relationship between difficult temperament and its effects on attachment (e.g., parent–child bonding); 2) understanding how discrepant parent–child relationships can be translated into individual personality characteristics (see Lyddon & Sherry, 2001); 3) studying attachment quality across the lifespan and whether meanings for attachment are different at different ages; and 4) determining how attachment affects relationships with others across the lifespan (e.g., subsequent personal-social functioning and parenting).

One should exercise vigilance when postulating the association that can exist between early attachment style or patterns and the development of later psychopathology in a child or adolescent. For example, there does not appear to be one specific subtype of attachment that leads to one specific childhood disorder. Moreover, attachment constitutes only one aspect of human relationships (Rutter & Sroufe, 2000), and attachment style can be more effectively conceptualized as a "trajectory" or "developmental pathway" for psychopathology (Mash & Dozois, 1996).

Emotional Influences   The effects of emotions and affective expressions are underrated core elements in the development of the infant and young child (Mash & Wolfe, 2002). For example, emotions and affective expressions are essential features or stimuli connected to parent–infant communication and activity. Moreover, emotions and affective expressions are useful as benchmarks or keys for the regulation of the infant or child (Sroufe, 1997). Throughout their lives, for example, emotions and emotional reactions help the infant and young child to gauge, measure, and change behavior accordingly (e.g., to meet the expectations of caregivers).

For example, consider the parent who continually "overreacts" to activities that the infant or child may be engaged in. Over time, these emotional messages seep into the child (e.g., they may be internalized). These emotional messages can result in the child learning to feel unsafe or anxious in that particular environment. In effect, emotions tell us what to pay attention to, what we can ignore, what to approach, and what to avoid (Mash & Wolfe, 2002). They are subtle yet direct learning connections that the child or adolescent makes. Emotions are also accompanied by individual biochemistry (e.g., hormones such as cortisol that assist in the regulation of stress). Hormones may serve to further embed particularly emotional messages in the child. Emotions, for example, are crucial components to making healthy adaptations (e.g., short-term and long-term) to the environmental influences or stressors that frequently surround us.

Interest from researchers in the emotional processes and their reciprocal relationships to child psychopathology has grown considerably (Lemerise & Arsenio, 2000). Children, for example, have a natural tendency to attend to emotional cues from others, this helps them learn to interpret and regulate their own emotions. It is easy to see how children learn from a very young age through emotional responses from others. For example, the child–caregiver relationship plays a critical developmental role in this process. It provides the basic setting for the child to express emotions safely, to have caring guidance, and to have limits put on them when their emotions are inappropriate or problematic (Bretherton, 1995). To young children, emotions are a primary form of communication that permits them to further explore their world with increasing levels of independence (LaFreniere, 1999).

Where this is not occurring or is impeded, one can expect emotional development and behavior often to be impaired.

The development of psychopathology, for example, in the child or adolescent can often be connected to emotional influences, emotional reactivity, and emotional regulation (Mash & Wolfe, 2002). Emotional reactivity, for example, refers to the child's individual threshold and the intensity of the emotional experience (e.g., the child may be overly sensitive to emotional stimuli). These emotional reactions can provide important clues to the individual's level of distress and sensitivity to the environment (Mash & Wolfe, 2002). Emotional regulation, for example, involves enhancing, maintaining, decreasing, or inhibiting emotional arousal (e.g., where parental reactions are harsh) (Rubin, Coplan, Fox, & Caukins, 1995).

There is an important distinction between emotional reactivity and emotional regulation. For example, regulation problems with emotions involve weak or absent control structures. Dysregulation problems with emotions involve existing control structures operating maladaptively (e.g., a greater emotional display from the person than what the stimulus provided) (Cicchetti, Ackerman, & Izard, 1995). Problems in emotional dysregulation, for example, may also present themselves in the child as due to emotional or sexual abuse (e.g., shallow emotions, numbing oneself emotionally as a protective device). Emotions typically serve as important appraisers of emotional situations; we tend to internally appraise emotional events as being beneficial or dangerous (Zahn-Waxler, Klimes-Dougan, & Slattery, 2000). Emotional events are usually set into the child's cognitive structures or schemas for future reference.

The child's emotional regulation abilities are often characterized by the child's emotional "reactivity" or "regulation"; these can be meaningful signals about normal or abnormal development. The parent–child relationship reemerges again and again as the linchpin in children's emotional development (Loeber et al., 2000; Mash & Wolfe, 2002). The child's emotional experiences, emotional expressions, and emotional regulation can be critical variables that affect the quality of social interactions and relationships across the lifespan.

Criticisms of the Psychological Model   Although the influence of the Freudian psychodynamic model has waned (e.g., particularly the Freudian view of personality structure), other contributions and modifications evolved to draw researchers' attention. For example, among the contributions that drew attention were the importance of attachment patterns (e.g., early childhood experiences, the parent–child relationship), emotional influences on children, and the effects of temperament on child raising.

The present-day psychological models have certain inherent limitations (Mash & Wolfe, 2002). These researchers, however, believe that the psychological models or perspectives have tremendous value in explaining the development of childhood psychopathology. The psychological models propose that many emotional and behavioral disorders have their roots in disturbed or dysfunctional interpersonal and intrapersonal relationships.

It therefore appears reasonable to conclude that you should view the psychological model as providing a "continuum" of psychological information for viewing emotional and behavioral development. It is extremely useful for seeing how at any point on it, things can go wrong (e.g., the degree of "fit" between the individual and environmental factors). Interest in the psychological model continues because it is a place that we can learn more about how this model affects the individual trajectories and consequences in the child or adolescent.

Behavioral Models

Behavioral or learning models stand at loggerheads with the psychodynamic or psychoanalytic position. For example, behavioral models reject the existence of internal underlying personality conflicts and the realm of the unconscious as "primary" agents for behavior. Instead, behavioral models subscribe to behavioral or learning perspectives as being responsible for "shaping" adaptive and maladaptive responses (e.g., dysfunctional behavior). Learning and the influence of the environment are seen as the "central tenets."

Behaviorists, for example, believe that all individuals make "learned adjustments" to their environments. Although biological predispositions can exist in the individual, it is the individual's learned adjustments to the environment that count. For example, fear of the physician from a painful experience of getting a shot, fear of driving after being in an automobile accident, and fear of dogs from being bitten— all of these can be learned through the classical conditioning model (Santrock, 2002). In the operant conditioning model, the consequences produce the result. For example, when a person smiles at a child after the child has done something, the child is more likely to engage in the activity again than if the person gives the child a nasty look (Santrock, 2002).

In the behavioral models, it is maintained that environmental influences are the primary agents responsible for learning. People are shaped by their environments, but behavior also affects the environment they live in or create (e.g., hostile behavior invites a hostile response from the environment). Following is an overview of some of the major behavioral models. For a more detailed explanation of these theories or models, consult Gredler (2005) and Mash and Dozois (1996).

Classical Conditioning   At first glance, classical conditioning would not seem to be sufficient to explain how a child could develop dysfunctional or disordered behavior. However, based on the work of Ivan Pavlov and John Watson (see Gredler, 2005), classical or respondent conditioning explains the acquisition of disordered or dysfunction behavior on the basis of "paired" associations (e.g., between previously neutral stimuli such as math problems and unconditioned stimuli such as criticism) (Mash & Wolfe, 2002). Any neutral event, for example, can become a "conditioned stimulus" if it is paired enough times with an event that already elicits a certain response.

For example, an infant could associate screaming with a parental figure and have a conditioned fear response. In a chaotic home environment, the infant or young child could associate frequent punishment with a fear of authority figures. Early classical conditioning could go to work on the infant or child who lives in these specific environments. Moreover, think of the number of serious adjustment problems identified in children where we do not have an idea of what the original "paired associations" might have been.

Operant Conditioning Behavior is controlled by the expected outcomes. B. F. Skinner emphasized that the challenge in understanding behavior (e.g., adaptive, maladaptive) lies in determining which changes in the independent variables (e.g., conditions or events) lead to changes in the dependent variable (e.g., the behavior) (Gredler, 2005). Skinner took a functional approach to behavioral analysis. For example, Skinner's approach to learning was to examine the relationships between the behavior (e.g., adaptive, maladaptive) and its antecedents (e.g., the events that take place prior to a response or behavior). From this behavioral analysis, one could better understand the "consequences" that were being produced. Here is a simply-put example: A child who has AD/HD is teased and taunted by school peers on the way to classes each day. The child enters the classrooms of the teachers visibly upset or angry almost every day. From a behavioral analysis, the antecedent events are shaping and setting in motion the maladaptive behavior exhibited by this child in the teachers' classrooms. In essence, the antecedent events are integrally involved in the "consequences" that take place. Realistically, before meaningful changes can occur in the classrooms for this particular student and his or her teachers, the antecedent events will need to be addressed and modified. For Skinner, this constituted a more scientific way to a better understanding of how behavior (e.g., adaptive, maladaptive) in an individual can evolve or develop. Gredler (2005) provided this example of a behavioral analysis: Parents are entertaining guests in the home; the child begins crying and whining; parents turn attention to the child to try and quiet him; the child stops crying. In this situation, the child's interruption or crying and whining is the aversive stimulus for the parents' attention; the parents giving attention terminates the interruption (e.g., there is a withdrawal of the aversive stimulus). The child's interruption serves as a negative reinforcer for the parents. It should be clear that giving attention to the child is likely to increase under similar circumstances because it terminates the crying for the parents. However, the parents' attention, particularly if prolonged, serves as a positive reinforcer for the child. The key to understanding complex behaviors is to understand the events and processes responsible (Gredler, 2005).

As a behaviorist, Skinner made no statements about "internal" mental states (e.g., underlying needs or motives) that contribute to disordered or dysfunctional behavior. Skinner found it nonrewarding to engage in the contributions of internal states because they cannot be observed or quantified as to their direct or indirect contribution to disordered behavior. Rather, Skinner would emphasize in cases of disordered behavior the need to examine the relationships between the stimuli in the environment, the behavioral responses, and the consequences. In this process, disordered or dysfunctional behavior can be more accurately ascertained prior to behavioral modifications being put into place (Gredler, 2005).

The following discussion of operant learning principles will help to explain how behaviors in the individual are acquired or changed (see Gredler, 2005 for a more full explanation). Importantly, Skinner believed that positive or negative reinforcement is any "action" that increases the target response. Reinforcers can be categorized in terms of the nature of the reinforcing consequence. Certain behaviors can be followed by the appearance of a new object or event. For example, the child responds correctly and receives a verbal or physical affirmation from the parent. Any new stimulus added to the situation that produces a positive type of reinforcement (e.g., a satisfying state of affairs) in the person can be defined as **positive reinforcement**. In contrast, consider the loud buzz in some cars when the ignition is turned on. The intent is that the driver's behavior of fastening the seat belt will increase because it removes the irritating buzzing sound. This form of reinforcement is referred to as **negative reinforcement.** In other words, a negative reinforcer is properly defined as a stimulus, the reduction or removal of which strengthens behavior. Negative reinforcement is also known as **escape conditioning** because it strengthens escape behaviors (Gredler, 2005).

Skinner, for example, cautioned that negative reinforcement to control behavior often leaves emotional by-products that accompany the individual's escape or avoidance behavior. Included in this set of emotional by-products can be increased levels of anxiety or fear, gastric changes, and possibly increased blood pressure. A child, for example, who has been repeatedly scolded or browbeaten by parents or teachers for "inattentive behavior" may develop excessive anxiety or have a stomach ache in the presence of authority figures.

Skinner believed that children can become quite accomplished, for example, at learning how to "operate" and secure what they want or need in their environment. For example, children learn quickly the contingencies that can exist between their behavior and the outcomes. Outcomes for the individual, Skinner believed, did not have to be oriented toward the positive. For example, a child's refusing to go to school can serve a number of behavioral functions (Kearney & Silverman, 1995; 1996). One function could be to avoid stimuli that provoke negative affective responses (e.g., teachers and classroom routines). A second function could be to escape from aversive social evaluations (e.g., teachers, peers). A third function could be to gain attention (e.g., through oppositional behavior, noncompliance, school vandalism). A fourth and final function could be to allow access to rewards or reinforcers (e.g., play activities, interacting with the peer group, being on the computer).

Understanding behavior through operant conditioning provides insight into the "function" (e.g., positive or negative, escape or avoidance, attention-seeking) that the behavior is serving. From this understanding, interventions or treatment can be suggested. The operant conditioning model remains influential across a variety of settings (e.g., school, home, community), and in many cases it cannot be discounted for its contribution to child psychopathology (Mash & Wolfe, 2002). It is advantageous to think in terms of both classical and operant conditioning being at work and making contributions to what the child or adolescent is learning or internalizing (Mash & Wolfe, 2002).

Criticisms of the Behavioral Model   Opponents of the behavioral orientation make the point that it often neglects or places little importance on the inner determinants that are often integral to behavior. Opponents also criticize the behaviorists' extension to human beings of results obtained from animal studies conducted in laboratory settings. Others charge that people can be regarded as "organisms" and human behavior is mechanical, insight learning is not acknowledged as productive, and there is little attention to human values in relation to behavior (Sue, Sue, & Sue, 2000).

Corey (2005) maintained that individuals and their behavioral repertoires are more than simply accounting for observable or external behaviors. For example, numerous embedded internal feelings and emotions are often played down. The personality structure also receives little or no attention as directly causing or maintaining destructive behavior patterns. The individual's inner life and what occur there is not central to the behavioral models or theories. However, a recent trend among many behaviorists is to place increasing importance on the individual's inner life or cognitive processes. This has led to the development of cognitive models that conceive of clients as "thinking beings" who can help themselves by changing their thinking (Sue, Sue, & Sue, 2000).

Cognitive Models

Considerable research has focused on the role of "cognitions" in child and adolescent psychopathology (Kendall & Dobson, 1993; Mash & Dozois, 1996). Theories or approaches that specifically focus attention on altering cognitions and emotions are usually classified as "cognitive" and "cognitive-behavioral." In essence, these theories or approaches propose that understanding how the individual thinks and processes information are sources for learning and behavior. For example, cognitive restructuring seeks to induce individuals to alter or change negative or inappropriate thought processes (e.g., which are believed to contribute to negative or disordered states of behavior) (Pliszka, Carlson, & Swanson, 1999).

Representative examples of the information-processing and cognitive-behavioral approaches and their importance are described next. These descriptions should give you a clearer picture of how they operate and how they can interface to possibly produce or enhance psychopathology in an individual.

Information Processing Theories Faulty information processing has been implicated in a number of childhood disorders (Mash & Barkley, 1996). For example, socially aggressive children often evidence negative attributional styles or biases (Dodge & Crick, 1990). Children with anxiety disorders, for example, show attentional biases (e.g., over-attend) to threatening stimuli (Vasey, Daleiden, Williams, & Brown, 1995). Faulty information processing and child psychopathology seem to emanate from at least two identifiable pathways (Mash & Dozois, 1996). One pathway is related to deficits in basic information processing that are related to attention, memory, and other cognitive functions (e.g., little or no re-evaluation of information) (Carter & Swanson, 1995). The other pathway is related to deficits in social information processing (e.g., accurately evaluating the content of social information) (Crick & Dodge, 1994).

The application of faulty information processing, for example, applied to socially aggressive boys illustrates the social information-processing approach (see Crick & Dodge, 1994; Dodge & Crick, 1990). In this model, for example, the "thinking" of socially aggressive children is characterized by deficits in one or more of the following internal processes: 1) The way in which social cues are "encoded" or deficits in the way that the child searches for and focuses attention on pertinent external stimuli; 2) the way in which the child "interprets" or derives meaning from the social cues that had previously become the focus of the child's initial attention; 3) the subsequent "response" search or the generation of "response alternatives" is not functioning to serve the child; 4) the "response decision" is not functioning to serve the child; and 5) the ability to "act or enact" the most appropriate social response is not functioning to serve the child.

These researchers have recently expanded their conceptual framework on information processing. The same steps are posited, but they have emphasized the need to understand that there is an ongoing "reciprocal interaction" between the child's information-processing abilities or skills and the child's data base (e.g., collection of memories, social knowledge, cultural values, rules). Instead of thinking in terms of a "linear" information-processing model, there is also the need to realize the importance of "cyclical" feedback loops that connect and influence all of the steps, including decision-making (see Crick & Dodge, 1994).

Additionally, there are other important contributors (e.g., temperament, age, gender, social context, school, culture) that serve to "mediate" the relationship between information-processing and social adjustment. The information-processing model asserts that parent-child interactions (e.g., from which many cognitions are derived) and the "quality" of the early parent–child attachment can also be important contributors to the ongoing formulation and reformulation of the child's data base (Mash & Dozois, 1996).

Cognitive-Behavioral Theories   Cognitive-behavioral theories reflect the importance of both behavioral and cognitive approaches to understanding and helping human beings (Kalodner, 1999). Cognitive-behavioral theories assert that maladaptive cognitive processes and behavior predispose an individual to psychopatholology (Mash & Dozois, 1996). Moreover, cognitions are considered the major player in the maintenance of psychological problems (e.g., the dysfunctional behavior patterns; Hollon & Beck, 1994). Cognitive-behavioral theories attempt to preserve the positive features of behavioral approaches while at the same time working to incorporate cognitive activity and information-processing factors of the individual (Kendall & McDonald, 1993). Cognitive-behavioral theories also stress the importance of contextual variables (e.g., family, peers, school, culture) in both the etiology and maintenance of psychopathology (Corey, 2005; Kendall & Dobson, 1993; Seligman, 2001).

Cognitive-behavioral theories or models place strong emphases on the role of cognitive distortions (e.g., all or nothing thinking, disqualifying the positive, catastrophizing); the role of insufficient cognitive mediation (e.g., not taking the time to sufficiently consider alternative behavioral actions including the feelings of others); the role of attributional styles (e.g., internal ideas that we use to explain to ourselves the cause for our failure and lack of control); and the role of expectations (e.g., I cannot succeed, I should not try, I am not liked) as crucial determinants in the development of behavioral and emotional disorders.

Together cognitive structures and their content make up what is called **schema** or **schemas** (i.e., belief systems that can be accurate or distorted; Corey, 2005). The schema, for example, stems from a child or adolescent's mental processing of life experiences. The schema comes to act as the child's core philosophy, influencing expectations and filtering information in a manner consistent with the child's core philosophy (Kendall & McDonald, 1993; Mash & Dozois, 1996). The schema can also be referred to as **cognitive filters** and **templates** that can be applied to life experiences as they confront the child or adolescent.

Beck (as cited in Corey, 2005) has written about the "cognitive triad" as a pattern of beliefs that triggers depression. In the first component of the triad, the individual holds a negative view of him- or herself (e.g., blames setbacks on personal inadequacies without considering circumstantial explanations, is convinced the personal qualities essential to bring success are lacking). The second component of the triad consists of the tendency to interpret experiences in a negative manner (e.g., selecting certain facts that conform with the negative conclusion about the self or others). The third component of the triad pertains to the individual's gloomy vision and projections about the future (e.g., expecting their present difficulties to continue, anticipating only more failure in the future). The key aspect to the therapeutic process using the cognitive-behavioral model involves the restructuring of distorted beliefs or schema (Corey, 2005).

Kendall (1993) asserted that childhood anxiety can be based on cognitive distortions. As a result, this researcher theorized that anxious children seem preoccupied with concerns about evaluations by self, evaluations from others, and the likelihood of severe negative consequences. According to Kendall, anxious children or children who are prone to anxiety disorders seem to misperceive or misjudge (e.g., cognitively) the demands of the environment. For example, many of these children routinely add increased stress to situations that they encounter in the environment. For the anxious child, changing negative cognitions (e.g., their schema) is again considered to be the key aspect for therapeutic results (e.g., decreasing anxiety, increasing the range of functioning, improving the self-concept).

It is particularly important in child psychopathology to know the distinction between cognitive deficits and cognitive distortions. Cognitive deficits refer to the absence of thinking (e.g., when it would be to the advantage of the individual). Aggressive youths, for example, frequently lack the ability to generate alternatives to problem situations, and impulsive children often fail to think before they respond (Mash & Dozois, 1996; Crick & Dodge, 1994; Loeber et al., 2000; Lochman & Dodge, 1994). Conversely, children who manifest cognitive distortions (e.g., I made a mistake, I'm stupid) have thinking that is typically described as biased, dysfunctional, or misguided (Kendall, 1993; Kendall & McDonald, 1993).

The depressed individual's private view of himself or herself, the world, and the future is an example of distorted thinking. Generally speaking, internalizing disorders are related to distortion in thinking; externalizing disorders are most often associated with cognitive deficits. However, research evidence implies that where aggression involves both physical force and social aggression, there behaviors usually involve both internal distortions and cognitive deficits (Lochman, White, & Wayland, 1991; Mash & Dozois, 1996).

Cognitive-behavioral models and the assumption that the development of maladaptive thinking leads to or causes maladaptive behavior awaits firm conclusions. For example, Tems, Stewart, Skinner, Hughes, and Emslie (1993) examined the cognitive patterns of depressed children and adolescents. Their examination revealed that while depressed children and adolescents displayed more cognitive distortion than controls, no significant differences between groups remained upon remission. Mash and Barkley (1996) confirmed that this clinical finding is unique neither to the childhood or adulthood literature. Moreover, studies of the treatment of childhood aggression have revealed, in some cases, that altering cognitive processes does not necessarily lead to changes in overt behavior. However, there is considerable support in the research literature (e.g., outcome studies) for faulty cognition as concomitant to various child and adolescent disorders (Mash & Dozois, 1996; Kalodner, 1999; Mash & Wolfe, 2002; Rapoport, 2000; Seligman, 2001; Sue, Sue, & Sue, 2000).

Social-Cognitive Theories   Social-cognitive theory, also known as **social learning theory** (see Bandura, 1977, 1986, 1995; Gredler, 2005), explains human learning as transpiring in the naturalistic setting. Social learning theory stresses that classical and operant conditioning are not the only mediators of learning. For the social learning theorists, behaviors can be acquired not only as the result of direct experience but also "indirectly" through the accumulation of observational (e.g., vicarious) learning experiences. Observational learning experiences, which can be selectively determined, are considered to be the major determiners of overt behaviors (e.g., because we live in social situations). For example, children can learn a new behavior merely by watching another person "model" the behavior (e.g., without apparent reinforcement or environmental practice).

Social-learning theory incorporates the crucial role of "social cognition" in the acquisition of both desirable and undesirable behavior. At the heart of social learning is how children come to think about themselves and others. Bandura (1977, 1986), for example, believed that "thought" about what is being observed in the child's social world is also being internalized and results in the formation of mental schemas or representations of themselves, their relationships, and their social world (Gredler, 2005; Mash & Wolfe, 2002). These internal representations are not fixed or static, but are continuously being updated on the basis of experience and maturation, including how they will come to affect future learning (Noam, Chandler, & LaLonde, 1995). Furthermore, social learning and social-cognitive viewpoints on children place importance on contextual variables (e.g., family systems, peer relationships, community) in both the origins and maintenance of psychopathology (Lemerise & Arsenio, 2000).

A central tenet of social learning theory is the concept of triadic reciprocality (see Bandura, 1986). This social-cognitive viewpoint contends that behavior, environmental influences, and personal factors (e.g., cognition, temperament, biology) all work "together" in an interactive manner. They all have the common effect of determining one another. In other words, the causes for human behavior are "reciprocally" determined by the behavior, environment, and personal factors (e.g., an interactivist perspective).

For example, Merrill (1994) used the example of the infant who happens to have a very irritable temperament (e.g., which is present at birth and probably biological in nature). The infant's irritable temperament is an example of a personal factor (e.g., biological). Due to the fact that this infant tends to cry almost constantly, is highly demanding, and sleeps for only short periods of time, it may invite more irritable responses from the parent. The parents are thereby shaped in their behavior and characteristics in the direction of being constantly tired, more irritable than normal, anxious, and perhaps mildly depressed. The behavioral responses shape the environment of the child, and the child's behavior continues to shape the environment of the parents. Should the infant persist in being irritable and demanding and the parents reinforce this with immediate attention, the child's irritable and demanding characteristics will likely be strengthened and persist. However, if the parents learn to deal with their irritable child in a quiet and relaxed manner, the child's demanding irritability may be changed.

Kauffman (2005) related the triadic-reciprocality model to an "interactionist-transactional model" of influence (e.g., children have effects on adults that are equal to adults' effects on children). Family interactions are understandable only when reciprocal influences of parent and child on each other are taken into account. From here it takes only a small leap to understand that parent–child interactions are typically shaped through complex, mutually influential interactions, whether in the family, school, or community (Merrill, 1994).

Criticisms of the Cognitive Model   Criticisms of the behavioral models can be leveled at the cognitive models according to what they both emphasize. For example, they both emphasize the altering of behavior, de-emphasizing childhood experiences as determining, and successful treatment measuring by changes in overt or observable behavior. There is also the objection that human beings cannot be reduced to the sum of their cognitive parts. Also, do thoughts and beliefs really cause behavioral disturbances, or do the disturbances themselves distort thinking (Sue, Sue, & Sue, 2000)? B. F. Skinner warned that thoughts or beliefs (e.g., cognitions) are not observable phenomena and cannot form the foundations of empiricism (Skinner, 1990).

Criticisms have been leveled at the therapeutic approach taken by cognitive therapists. For example, the nature of the approach makes the therapist a teacher, expert, and authority figure to the client. The therapist needs to be direct and confrontive in the identification and attacking of irrational cognitive beliefs and processes. Moreover, clients may readily be intimidated into acquiescing to the therapist's authority. If the counselor were to misidentify the client's problem or disorder, the clients may be hesitant to challenge the counselor's opinions (Sue, Sue, & Sue, 2000).

Finally, there is a need for more research and long-term evaluative studies on the effectiveness of the cognitive models. However, its emphasis on the powerful influence of internal mediating processes offers an exciting new direction for behavioral and cognitive approaches (Sue, Sue, & Sue, 2000).

School Models

School models focus on the importance that the school experience has to the development of children and adolescents. Like the family system, the school is a system that has the potential to foster the development of emotional and behavior disorders (Kauffman, 2005). Student–teacher relationships, classroom structure, pedagogy, school rules or standards, methods of discipline, and expectations all influence the child. Remember, the school is a system that children must encounter every day throughout their school-age years. The school is, therefore, one of the most central contexts in children's lives (e.g., next to the family). The actions taken at schools seriously affect childrens' lives and act powerfully on each child's development (Wicks-Nelson & Israel, 2005). Therefore, school is a place where intervention and prevention services can be initiated, and it is also a place that behavior disorders can be exacerbated (Durlak, 1997; Weist, 1997). The family and the educational systems in our country have a longstanding history as important influences on children and adolescents (Wicks-Nelson & Israel, 2005). Kazdin (1995), for example, stressed that the characteristics found in schools (e.g., a strong need for order and discipline) can have the effect of contributing substantially to the risk of a child developing an emotional or behavioral disorder.

Counselors should observe that the characteristics of schools and the characteristics of students and families that they seek to serve can often be incompatible. For example, in many high-poverty areas, there may be a preponderance of families and children with emotional and behavioral disorders because of the increased risk factors in these environments. Consequently, for example, success at school assumes even greater importance if a child's home and community environments are highly disadvantaged (Kauffman, 2005). For children who are at increased risk from these conditions, the school environment can inadvertently foster the very behavior that teachers and parents find objectionable. This is not to say that the family or the school is to blame for this increased risk. The conditions, for example, that the family might find itself in are often not a good fit with that particular school and its missions. For example, some children develop emotional or behavioral problems before they begin school, but even if a child already has an emotional or behavioral disorder, the school experience can ameliorate the problem or make it worse (Kauffman, 2005). Therefore, what does or does not transpire in that school cannot be discounted as a major influence on the child's life.

The School as a Contributor   The school is an important contributing factor to disruptive behavior disorders in children and adolescents (see Loeber et al., 2000). For children and adolescents, school maintains a sizable influence over their lives, especially in the domains of academic success and socialization (Sylva, 1994). Moreover, some of the schools' contributions can operate directly, whereas others operate indirectly, affecting students' motivation to learn, their self-concepts, their cognitions, and even their belief systems about school itself (Wicks-Nelson & Israel, 2005).

Schools can be associated with a number of negative events for children with emotional and behavioral disorders. Among these events are the following: 1) below-average academic functioning (e.g., academic difficulties often stem from lowered expectations for these students); 2) serious problems with rule adherence (e.g., compliance with teacher demands); 3) repeated instances of social dysfunction (e.g., resulting in teasing, shunning, and devaluation by classmates for children who do not meet social or peer-group norms); and 4) repeated negative contacts with school personnel (e.g., administrators, teachers). These experiences can reasonably be expected to impede or prevent the child from "bonding" with his or her school (e.g., teachers, classmates) (Kauffman, 2005). For children who have disordered behavior, "bonding" to one's school becomes less likely. Furthermore, as the behavior at school becomes more disordered or disruptive to school routines, it might eventually contribute to school suspension, expulsion, and failure. In reality, the demands of school and the student's behavioral and academic repertoire (e.g., which is often limited by the disorder) can be at odds (e.g., affecting each other reciprocally). Educators and classmates, for example, may become enmeshed in escalating aversive exchanges with the child.

There are two important points that need to be considered about how schools are equipped to deal with disordered or dysfunctional behavior in children and adolescents (Kauffman, 2005). First, some schools, due to their physical placement and resources, are better equipped than others to more effectively deal with children who have emotional and behavioral disorders. Second, the dysfunctional behavior usually escalates where schools are not properly equipped to deal with children who have serious emotional and behavioral disorders. In these schools, for example, one can expect that the child's subsequent emotional and behavioral development will be adversely affected (e.g., further contributing to the dysfunctional behavior style).

Peers and School Dysfunction Counselors should remember that the school, like biological and family factors, does not operate unilaterally (i.e., in a linear way) to precisely determine the child's emotional and behavioral development. The school, however, is where children spend the second largest part of their days. For 12 years, it functions as a major force in their lives. It is at school, often in kindergarten, that a child who is "different" is first detected by his or her classmates. Peers, for example, are often the first group to detect at an early age the child who comes across to them as somehow different. Therefore, for the child who is somehow different from the group norm, the message in many of their classrooms becomes that the different child is somehow unacceptable or bad. While the reason for such a message might never be clear or substantial, perception on the part of the peer group typically plays a powerful role in labeling. Moreover, peers who are observed in the company of this child often risk being socially cast out. When this peer-group treatment is prolonged, the affected child's self-esteem quickly erodes and the motivation for socializing and academic achievement is substantially weakened. Frequently, the child becomes isolated with other "identified" children.

Conditions and Internal States at School Researchers (Colvin, Greenberg, & Sherman, 1993; Gelfand, Ficula, & Zarbatany, 1986; Kasen, Johnson, & Cohen, 1990; Walker, Colvin, & Ramsey, 1995; Kauffman, 2005) have emphasized that "conditions" in classrooms and "reactions" of teachers can be a contributing factor to the occurrence of behavioral difficulties in these children. School factors that can make this more likely include the following: 1) Insensitivity to the student's individuality (e.g., administrators and teachers often seek to squelch individuality by demanding conformity); 2) inappropriate expectations for these students (e.g., using labels to identify problem children, having lowered expectations, not consulting with the student on learning objectives [these students have irregular work habits, are slow to adapt to new learning situations, and can often be negative in mood]); 3) inconsistent management of these students' behaviors (e.g., poor classroom-management skills; Hetherington & Martin, 1986); 4) ineffective instruction in critical skills (e.g., few schools teach social skills or how to make positive self-attributions [positive self-talk]); 5) using destructive contingencies of reinforcement (e.g., providing positive reinforcement for inappropriate behaviors, failing to provide positive reinforcement for desirable behaviors, providing negative reinforcement for behavior that allows students to avoid their work); and 6) undesirable models of school conduct (e.g., students are influenced for good or ill by models of conduct that are displayed by teachers and peers; Rutter, Maughan, Mortimer, Ouston, & Smith, 1979).

Schools and Intervention   Although schools (e.g., K–12) can often be considered a causal factor in the development of an emotional or behavioral disorder, the school can also be one of the best places to intervene. It is at school that risk factors for a behavior disorder can often be diagnosed and treatment administered. Moreover, the school delivers a tremendous advantage to the student in that it is at school where points of intervention can be directed at different ages (e.g., infancy, early childhood, childhood, and adolescence). For example, opportunities for intervention or treatment are not necessarily gone even if the school does not conduct the intervention at an earlier age (e.g., preschool or kindergarten).

Moreover, schools do represent places where proactive or positive measures to prevent or ameliorate a disability or disorder can be taken. For example, Kauffman (2005) considered good instruction to be the first line of defense in behavior management (e.g., a well-planned instructional program prevents many of the behavior problems from arising). It has become apparent, for example, that the antecedents of behavior problems—the events preceding an act and the context or setting in which it occurs—are strong teaching tools that have been neglected in working with problematic students (Alberto & Troutman, 1995; Mayer, 1995). Teachers should understand that the classroom conditions they create and the instructional processes they use can contribute to behavioral problems as well as their resolution. For example, given that academics and appropriate social behavior are viewed as the central role of schools, there may be less tolerance for educational programs in which the objectives are merely behavioral containment (Kauffman, 2005). Schools are also the places that licensed professionals (e.g., teachers, counselors, school psychologists, and learning disabilities specialists) work. These school personnel are best equipped to serve children who either are at risk for the development of a disruptive behavior disorder or who are already identified with one. The school is not a separate entity from the parents or family; it is an "active" partner in the family-to-school-to-community relationship. What does or does not happen in our schools ultimately happens in our communities.

Criticisms of the School Model   Criticisms of the school models are directed at how school administrators and teachers set up and operate many of their schools (e.g., often to the disadvantage of children and adolescents with emotional or behavioral disorders) (Kauffman, 2005). The following are pertinent examples of what Kauffman thinks might be happening often in our schools:

1. School administrators might be insensitive to the individual student (e.g., often a principal might see moving a student out of the school [to an alternative school] as the best solution).
2. Teachers might hold unrealistic expectations for the student (e.g., all students can sit still, learn, and behave when asked).
3. Teachers can maintain an insensitive attitude toward the student's problem (e.g., thinking that they are not expected to work with such a difficult child or their problem areas).
4. Teachers are likely to be uncertain and inconsistent in how they seek to manage the problematic student (e.g., not understanding how they might be reinforcing the problematic behaviors).
5. Teachers can have little concern that the instruction for the emotionally or behaviorally disturbed student is realistic or relevant (e.g., ineffective instruction might be offered to these students).
6. Teachers and school administrators might inadvertently arrange destructive contingencies for reinforcement (e.g., "you must do this task correctly to gain my approval or support").

Schools also come under criticism because they have not worked hard enough to develop a school–family–community relationship so that all of these systems work together (Green & Keys, 2001; Keys & Bemak, 1997; Keys, Bemak, & Lockhart, 1998). In the school-family-community framework, the programs or services could be complimentary and continuous, rather than sporadic or fragmented (Green & Keys, 2001). This framework can bring together school personnel (e.g., administrators, teachers, counselors), family members, and community resources (e.g., mental health center specialists).

Overall, schools have remained reluctant to pursue putting into place this type of a working relationship in their communities. Children and adolescents, for example, are often in need of diagnosis and treatment that the school can be ill-equipped to furnish. The 21st century is expected to see an increase in children with emotional and behavioral disorders (Osborne & Collison, 1998). Present-day school guidance programs should consider that a school–family–community approach (e.g., that encompasses community mental health services) could more aptly meet the needs of children and adolescents who might exhibit seriously disordered behavior (Green & Keys, 2001; Lockhart & Keys, 1998; Mucher, 1996; Sink & MacDonald, 1998; Keys, Bemak, & Lockhart, 1998).

Family Models

Research into the development of psychopathology in children has increasingly focused on the role of the family or family systems as determining factors (Gladding, 2007; Mash & Wolfe, 2002; Seligman, 2001; Wicks-Nelson & Israel, 2005). In this chapter, almost all of the models or theories that can be related to psychopathology have focused on the individual. The family systems model or perspective, regardless of the particular approach, holds that the individual is connected to living systems and that a change in any one part of the family unit reverberates throughout the other parts (Corey, 2005). The identified client's problem might be a symptom of how the system functions, not just a symptom of the individual's maladjustment. To focus on the internal dynamics of an individual without adequately considering interpersonal dynamics yields an incomplete picture (Corey, 2005).

Therefore, the behavior of one member directly affects the entire family system, and correspondingly, members of the family typically behave in ways that reflect family influences (Sue, Sue, & Sue, 2000). Dysfunctional behavior in the individual is usually a reflection or symptom of unhealthy family dynamics (e.g., often resulting from poor communication among family members) (Gladding, 2007; Kauffman, 2005; Sue, Sue, & Sue, 2000). All of the models or approaches to behavioral disorders acknowledge the family as having a major impact (Dykeman & Appleton, 1999; Wicks-Nelson & Israel, 2005). The reciprocal transactions and influences, for example, among family members (e.g., parent-child relationships) have become the object of increased research interest (Gladding, 2007).

Family Systems   In the family systems model, behavioral differences are conceptualized as being the result of **systemic factors** (e.g., familial interactional factors or patterns) influencing the individual. Major emphasis, for example, is given to understanding individuals in their systems (e.g., examining family relationships and interactional patterns) (Corey, 2005). The family is empowered in this model through the process of identifying and exploring interactional patterns could lie at the heart of problematic or dysfunctional behavior. In other words, the linchpin assumption is that transmission of behavioral disorders can take place from parents to offspring. This can occur directly through genetic and modeling effects, and indirectly through heightened parental distress and physical problems. Typically, there is a concomitant lack of physical and emotional closeness in many of these family situations. As a result, children in these types of family situations are thought to somehow come to act out much of their parents' distress. In all likelihood, much of the disordered behavior in these children is considered to be acting out of the dysfunctions inherent in the parents and in the family setting. There is a need to consider that distressed or dysfunctional relationships affect the mental health of both individual family members and the family as a whole.

The family systems model holds strongly that all members of a family are connected systems that can be enmeshed or disconnected (Gladding, 2007). For example, the behavior of one member can directly affect the entire family system. Moreover, family members learn to behave in ways that portray and reinforce family influences and norms. In the family system, for example, a social system is constructed from repeated interaction of family members (Dykeman & Appleton, 1999). Over time, these interactions establish learned patterns of behavior for how family members relate to each other (e.g., functionally, dysfunctionally) (Gladding, 2007; Sauber, L'Abate, Weeks, & Buchanan, 1993).

Corey (2005), Gladding (2007), and Goldenberg and Goldenberg (1994) have written extensively on the distinct characteristics of the family systems model (e.g., how it can be applied to the child or adolescent). These researchers have emphasized that in the family systems model, there are at least three guiding principles that need to be recognized. First, the family system has primary influence on the personality development of the child (e.g., the way that parents behave toward and around the child cannot be discounted). Second, dysfunction or disordered behavior in the child is usually a reflection of dysfunctional family systems (e.g., parent–child dynamics). Third, the counselor has to focus on the family system rather than solely on the child. The counselor, therefore, must strive to involve the whole family in the counseling treatment because the locus of the disorder or dysfunction is seen to reside within the family system rather than within the individual child (Corey, 2005; Gladding, 2007; Sue, Sue, & Sue, 2000).

Family Dynamics at Work   In families with a child who has a disruptive behavior disorder (e.g., Attention-Deficit/Hyperactivity Disorder, Oppositional Defiant Disorder, or Conduct Disorder), there is often a high frequency of disturbed and conflictual parent–child interactions. Children who have these disorders are much less compliant with parents' and teachers' instructions—cannot sustain compliance except for short time periods, find it difficult to remain on task, and display to parents and teachers high levels of negative behavior—than are their normal same-age counterparts (Wells et al., 2000a). What typically transpires here is an unending cycle of parenting and family stress. For example, parents continue to show a continuation of elevated levels of negative interactions, angry outbursts, and progressively less positive behavior toward the child and each other, relative to their normal family counterparts. Within the family domain, family life often becomes characterized by ongoing discord and disharmony (Wells et al., 2000a). What is usually at the "core" of the parent–child interactions and what can maintain the "adversity" in these families is their often elevated rates of reciprocal, highly charged "negative behaviors."

Family Dynamics: Unlearning the Negative Family Cycle   Continued negative parent–child interactions or the negative family cycle are of "etiologic" significance in the development and maintenance of a disruptive behavior disorder (Patterson, Reid, & Dishion, 1992). Counseling interventions or treatments that reduce these etiologic factors might prevent or ameliorate to a significant extent the development of the "negative behavioral repertoire" or the "negative family cycle." In essence, because of the primary symptoms connected to a disruptive behavior disorder, the responses from parents and teachers are "reactions" to the child's primary symptoms.

Therefore, treatment from counselors should stress teaching parents to modify their reactions (e.g., parental negative responses) to the child's primary symptoms, and training in how to increase their nonpunitive and positive responses to the child. An interactive or synergistic approach might suggest that combined behavioral treatment and medication (e.g., where indicated) should produce a greater impact than either treatment strategy alone. This is because combined treatment targets both of these important elements in the causal chain (Wells et al., 2000a). After all, the idea is to change the previous negative reciprocal interaction model that has existed in the family's history. To develop a new model, for example, the interactions that occur within the family's systems (e.g., parent–child, child–parent) should increasingly be based on positive sets of interactions.

The Effect of Parent Cognitions on Dysfunction   In working with the family's systems to improve their reciprocal interactions, counselors need to consider at the forefront that the cognitions (e.g., the preset thinking) of parents can act as "predictors" of a child's response. For example, Hoza et al. (2000) predicted that parents' cognitions about their children, about their parenting, and about themselves are all possible predictors of treatment response. If parents are the implementers of responses to their children, it is conceivable that the parents' thinking will influence the way in which they respond to their children. The success that these responses will have following misbehavior are thought to accrue from the "parental" cognitions. Hence, parents' cognitive beliefs about the causality of the child's misbehavior (e.g., how they view it) can be an important factor that deserves consideration.

According to Hoza et al. (2000), parents become more upset when a child misbehaves if the parents view the child's misbehavior as any combination of the following: 1) A deliberate or willful act, 2) a negative disposition (e.g., an unsettling temperament) on the part of the child, or 3) the child had prior knowledge to behave differently but did not choose to behave differently (e.g., behave compliantly). Any of these reactions, of course, can become affectively charged and form the link between the parents and their behavior toward the child (Miller, 1995). This reciprocally begins to elicit more negative affect and misbehavior from the child. Counselors should be cognizant that the parents' internal belief system about the causality of the child's misbehavior might be the determining factor, for example, influencing how these negative parental behaviors came about. In turn, interventions will need to first address how these parents' reactions will influence treatments or interventions, including as well how they might interfere with treatment compliance.

For example, parents who have cognitive beliefs that their child, with effort, can control his or her misbehavior, may be more likely to pursue a behavioral intervention involving the setting of behavioral limits and consequences in the hope that they can teach their child better self-discipline. On the other hand, parents who have cognitive beliefs that their child is completely incapable of exercising control over his or her behavior, may feel that imposing limits and consequences is fruitless (Hoza et al., 2000). In cases where dysfunctional cognitions from parents persist, these parents are likely to be more invested in the use of negative or forceful ways of controlling their child's misbehavior. Parental cognitions about themselves and their child tend to reinforce the child's behavior in a positive or negative fashion (Hoza et al., 2000).

The Role for Parenting Self-Efficacy   There can be many instances where counselors should think that parenting **self-efficacy** deserves attention. For example, parenting self-efficacy can be conceptualized as the degree to which parents perceive themselves as capable of performing the varied tasks associated with parenting highly demanding children (Coleman & Karraker, 1998; Hoza et al., 2000). Parenting self-efficacy can often be dependent on the models and experiences that were present (e.g., learned) in their family of origin. Examples include the parents' temperament and personality characteristics, comorbidities that could be at work in one or both parents, and opportunities for the parents to educate themselves about parenting children who are highly demanding. These should be assessed for any possible interference.

It would seem logical to assume that parents who are low in parenting self-efficacy would be less well-equipped to provide positive experiences for their child. For this reason, an increase in parenting self-efficacy might be expected by counselors to predict better treatment outcome. Self-efficacy for parents, for example, can be developed by watching models similar to themselves parent successfully and the parents themselves experiencing success for their parenting efforts (Bandura, 1986). Indeed, improved efficacy or personal effectiveness when dealing with serious behavior problems (e.g., any one of the disruptive behavior disorders) places effective parenting skills in a prominent position.

In addition to the parents' cognitions about their children and their parenting skills, the parents' cognitions about themselves (e.g., their self-esteem), individually and together, can have a great bearing on their level of effective participation in treatments for their child (Hoza et al., 2000). For example, parents with inadequate self-esteem may genuinely feel less confident in themselves (e.g., finding it especially hard to enforce appropriate consequences), especially when faced with continued resistance from the child. Moreover, parents themselves can manifest a **learned helplessness** style of parenting and have depressed thinking that further impedes treatments or interventions. Parents' cognitions about themselves and their negative attributional style in managing the child tends to sustain ineffective parenting (Hoza et al., 2000). It is unrealistic to expect, for example, the child who is exposed to these conditions to be better behaviorally positioned than are the parents.

For counselors working with families that have children with emotional or behavioral disorders, there might be a better treatment response where some combination of the following are present: 1) Parents' cognitions have been altered from negative to positive; 2) parents are given opportunities to experience higher self-esteem; 3) parents are provided opportunities to experience greater parenting self-efficacy; 4) parents are instructed in more adaptive discipline strategies; and 5) parents are guided to adopt more positive attributions about themselves and their child (e.g., from the positive parenting experiences that are replacing the prior ones).

Criticisms of the Family Systems Model   A major criticism of the family systems model centers on the different clinical terms that are used to describe the systems or subsystems of the family. These different terms serve to de-emphasize the individual family member and his or her respective feelings or emotions (Corey, 2005). For example, in the family systems model, there are terms that describe families and family systems as **dyads**, **triads**, **dysfunctional**, **enmeshment**, **feedback loops**, and as **stuck** and **unstuck**, which connotes an inordinate concern for how the whole family is functioning. It seems as if the family needs to function like a well-oiled machine. When it does not, the individuals need to be thoroughly examined (e.g., rather than the biases that can be produced by the family-systems language) (Corey, 2005; Mash & Wolfe, 2002).

A second criticism is that the family cannot be considered apart from being a culturally defined or determined institution (Dykeman & Appleton, 1999). However, the dominant definition of family in this country has been the one connected to "white" or Anglo-Saxon Protestant (WASP) values that focuses on an intact, well-functioning, nuclear family unit. In different cultural groups (e.g., African American), the definition refers to a wide network of relatives or kin and community (Kaslow, Celano, & Dreelin, 1995). For many Italian Americans, family implies a strong, tightly knit three–four-generation unit including godparents and old friends. In many Eastern families (e.g., Japanese, Chinese, Korean), by definition and influence the family includes all ancestors (e.g., decedents) (Dykeman & Appleton, 1999). Clients, for example, are served well when the counselor remembers that the proper application of the family model always involves a careful consideration of cross-cultural factors and limitations.

A third criticism comes from the feminist perspective, which takes issue with the language and mainly the assumptions of the family systems approach (Corey, 2005). For example, sexual and physical abuse could serve a functional role in the family systems model to highlight its dysfunction. Moreover, all members are considered to be more or less responsible for dysfunction (e.g., the abused wife or daughter may come to be viewed as a symptom of family dysfunction) (Cottone, 1992; Sue, Sue, & Sue, 2000). The family systems model may indirectly and in unintended ways (e.g., with its emphasis on the interrelationship of its parts to the whole) not put the proper emphasis on family violence (e.g., physical, sexual) that is required (Sue, Sue, & Sue, 2000). Corey (2005) emphasized that in the family or family systems model, there needs to be more attention placed on the mental health of each individual. The family systems researchers could retort that where family systems counseling or therapy is practiced correctly, this is among the major objectives.

Multicultural Models

Culture and its components "construct" our personal identity and outlook (e.g., as individuals, as family members). Each of us, for example, cannot be identified as distinct or apart from our cultural presence and its influences (e.g., culture shapes and reinforces behavior in all humans). Multiculturalism (e.g., multicultural behavior), for example, cannot be unaccounted for because it is a fact of life (Ivey, D'Andrea, Ivey & Simek-Morgan, 2002). Multicultural behavior creates norms, values, and expectations that might contribute to the problems that individuals may experience (Sue & Sue, 2003). Moreover, special problems may also arise because of racism, discrimination, social stratification, and inequities of power and access to power. These problems could portend the development of emotional or behavioral problems (Sue & Sue, 2003; Sue, Sue, & Sue, 2000). Therefore, it is the responsibility of counselors to increase their multicultural awareness and their competence in working with clients from ethnic minorities (Arrendondo & Arciniega, 2001).

Psychopathology and Multicultural Models   Multicultural awareness and competence should begin with the examination of the counselor's views on psychopathology in ethnic-minority clients (Sue & Sue, 2003; Sue, Sue, & Sue, 2000). Minority groups in this country have expressed increased dissatisfaction for the European-American or "Westernized" concepts of mental health or mental illness. Multicultural groups maintain that counselors cannot simply "superimpose" existing models for emotional and behavioral disorders (e.g., psychopathology) onto the various ethnic groups or minorities (Sue, Sue, and Sue, 2000). This approach has come under criticism from people from ethnic minorities themselves who are engaged in the counseling profession (Ivey, D'Andrea, Ivey, & Simek-Morgan, 2002; Sue & Sue, 2003; Sue, Sue, & Sue, 2000). Moreover, the "diversification" of this country means that multicultural counseling encompasses more than just the issues related to racial and ethnic minorities.

For this reason, multicultural counseling cannot neglect to focus on issues concerning gender, sexual orientation, religious preference, socioeconomic status, physical and mental disabilities, and social justice (e.g., social justice is more than talking; it is taking action). How counselors can go about ameliorating their own thinking or viewpoints about psychopathology among ethnic minorities is also an important ingredient of multicultural counseling. Vontress (1996) addressed this area succinctly when he noted that cross-cultural counseling does not intend to teach specific interventions or treatments for each culture. Rather, the overarching goal is to "infuse" each counselor with a cultural sensitivity and a tolerant philosophical outlook that benefits all cultures.

Often from their philosophical outlook, European-American viewpoints on psychopathology place the emphasis for locating the problem behaviors within the individual (e.g., intrapsychic) (Sue and Sue, 2003). These researchers acknowledge that European-American viewpoints do not deny that problematic behavior might emanate from outside the individual. However, Sue and Sue (2003) voiced their concern with Western viewpoints appraising external forces as equally important for all individuals, regardless of the ethnic group. In the multicultural model for behavior, there is the inherent belief that problems are more likely to be located in the social system rather than just inside the person (see developmental counseling and therapy; Ivey, D'Andrea, Ivey, & Simek-Morgan, 2002). Minority-group members, for example, may have to live with greater and more unique stressors than those encountered by many of their Caucasian counterparts. Specifically, racism, bias, discrimination, economic hardships, and culture conflicts are sociopolitical realities with which ethnic minority groups must often contend (Sue, Sue, & Sue, 2000).

Sue and Sue (2003), for example, have strived to bring attention to what is termed the **culturally different** model. This model advocates that the counselor view and interact with clients as culturally different. The culturally different model, for example, emphasizes that being culturally different does not automatically equal deviancy, inferiority, inability, or psychopathology. Sue, Sue, and Sue (2000) suggested that individuals from a European-American background (e.g., a white cultural background) have tended to adopt two models that attempt to explain the differences between various minority groups. The first model, the **inferiority model**, contends that racial and ethnic minorities are inferior in many respects to the majority population. Among African Americans and Latinos, for example, low intelligence, lower academic achievement, and high unemployment rates (e.g., essentially heredity explanations) can account for the lion's share of their inferiority. The second model, the **deficits model**, explains differences as the result of "cultural deprivation" (e.g., essentially blaming the culture itself for how its people developed). Inherent in the deficits model is the thinking that minority groups lack the "right culture" or base from which to move forward. Samuda (1998) contended that both of these models are inaccurate and biased, and potentially contribute to biased assessments or judgments that are unsupported in the research or scientific literature.

Culture, Human Interaction, and Counseling   All human interaction has to be rooted in cultural contexts. For example, cultural factors influence all social–cultural interactions, but they assume greater significance where there are cross-cultural situations (e.g., with principals, teachers, classmates, and peers). Because the majority of all interactions are social–cultural, these can be exponentially affected by other variables in operation. Where biological variables are present (e.g., with a significant genetic component such as intellectual ability, expressiveness, or emotionality), these variables may be incompatible with the individual's cultural group. In such cases, the problems for that individual might become culturally multiplied (e.g., affecting not only the individual, but also group identification or membership) (Sue, Sue, & Sue, 2000).

Consider as well the presence of gender variables (e.g., definition of male and female roles in each cultural group), the age of the individual, and the various personality types that individuals can exhibit in any culture. From these variables or any combination, there can be more problems (e.g., social, emotional) that may arise (Sue & Sue, 2003). Counselors, therefore, are always working with individuals whose cultural composition, lives, and experiences are likely to be much different than their own. To have little or no appreciation for these facts in the individual's life is to be unaware of what the individual might be experiencing and feeling (Corey, 2005).

Counselors need to be just as aware of how cultural factors might be contributing to the child or adolescent's emotional or behavioral disorder (e.g., many Asian American students may choose to keep their emotional difficulties to themselves; Constantine, 2001). Counselors should also strive to be mindful of the possibility of cultural bias being at work when they are evaluating dysfunctional behavior. Culture, for example, might not often enough be considered as a primary or concomitant cause in emotional and behavioral disorders. Culture or ethnic origin, however, is difficult to separate from other causal factors (e.g., poverty, family, social class, neighborhood, peer relations) that might operate on the behalf of disordered or dysfunctional behavior (Kauffman, 2005).

Nonetheless, one cannot separate the child or adolescent with a disruptive behavior disorder or any other type of disorder in the *DSM-IV-TR* as unaffected by cultural considerations or contexts. For example, the attitudes of the child gravitate toward the cultural expectations or norms of his or her families, schools, peer associations, and communities. Counselors cannot separate the individual from the cultural considerations that are inherently present and must be considered (Arrendondo, 1999; Sue & Sue, 2003).

Culture Should Not Confound Counseling   Culture should not be allowed to confound the counselor. For example, culture can confound the counseling only where the counselor does not acknowledge that an emotional or behavioral disorder can have its origin in repeated exposure to a particular cultural situation (e.g., poverty, family violence, or substance abuse). The counselor should view all of the individuals who come for counseling as potentially having been exposed to culturally sensitive conditions or factors. Moreover, any specific cultural factors to which any individual is exposed might have contributed to the onset of the disorder. At the least, cultural conditions or factors might be responsible for the maintenance of the disorder. To do otherwise could be considered "culturally insensitive." For example, as far as making an accurate diagnosis and devising appropriate interventions, these are basically housed in the counselor's cultural sensitivity and knowledges. Counselors, regardless of their work setting, must develop a critical awareness that every diagnosis always occurs in the intimate company of broad sociocultural, linguistic, political, and economic contexts (Smart & Smart, 1997).

Cultural Contexts and Counseling   Counselors, for example, are not operating in compliance with their ethical training and codes when they seek to diagnose a case only on the merits of the symptoms or characteristics present in the *DSM-IV-TR*. In competent counseling practice, counselors must be knowledgeable about the information that goes toward making a diagnosis. This includes examining your own attitudes and values, and recognizing whether these will adversely affect your work with clients (Arrendondo, 1999). Although a diagnosis in isolation by a licensed professional can probably be advanced, there is growing feeling among counselors, ethnic minorities, and the public that research should go beyond the mere explanation of human behavior (e.g., the diagnosis) (Sue & Sue, 2003).

Moreover, counselors engaged in psychological assessment and diagnosis must consider the culture and context for each individual that they accept as a client (Swartz-Kulstad & Martin, 1999). The cultural, sociological, and psychological underpinnings (e.g., contexts or factors) that surround individuals with a diagnosable condition provide an important lens through which practitioners can evaluate the reasons clients might have a mental disorder (Arrendondo, 1999). The counseling profession can receive, for example, more acceptance from the different multicultural groups that comprise our society when counselors demonstrate that they have the ability to contribute to the betterment of their lives (Sue & Sue, 2003).

In the final analysis, there is a tangled and complicated web of causal and contextual influences in the development and maintenance of emotional and behavioral disorders (Kauffman, 2005; Lee, 2001). When you think about the causes for behavior or mental disorders, you do not want to oversimplify and overgeneralize as to their cause or maintenance. You can, for example, be inclined to assume that disordered or dysfunctional behavior is simply the inadequate management of cultural factors. Nested tightly within all of the models or factors that seek to account for the development of child psychopathology, for example, is the child that is extremely difficult to live with or be around. This child is apparently highly effective in frustrating caregivers (e.g., parents, teachers, counselors). Moreover, the child seems to specialize in bringing out the worst in others. This problematic child can be a member of and live among any cultural group.

Causal factors, for example, are not easy to untangle and more research will be required to effect changes in the behavioral repertoires of children with emotional and behavioral disorders. Das (1995) recommended that research needed to concentrate on the role of "specific cultural factors" in the development and expression of mental disorders.

The Multicultural Counseling Commitment   Research in the area of multicultural counseling and how it can make positive contributions to the assessment, diagnosis, and treatment of children and adolescents with *DSM-IV-TR* disorders has only begun. However, counselors who have a multicultural commitment (e.g., that they institute and administer faithfully) will be providing a marked increase in the level of service to children and adolescents referred for an emotional or behavioral disorder. Many counseling researchers (Arrendondo & Arciniega, 2001; Arrendondo, 1998; Arrendondo, Toporek, Brown, Jones, Locke, Sanchez, & Stadler, 1996; D'Andrea & Daniels, 1995; Herring, 1997; Lee, 2001; Locke, 1992; Pedersen, 1994; Sue, Arrendondo, & McDaniels, 1992; Sue and Sue, 2003) have provided counselors with the essential groundwork. These researchers have provided ideas, knowledges, and specific competencies (see Arrendondo & Arciniega, 2001) that are identified in the counseling profession as multicultural counseling. As multicultural counseling proceeds to become the norm for the counseling profession and it is included in the actual practice of each counselor, an evolution in the practice of counseling will have occurred. This evolutionary step will forever bond multiculturalism into the mechanisms of competent counseling, assessment, diagnosis, and treatment.

Criticisms of the Multicultural Model

There are professionals (e.g., psychiatrists, psychologists, counselors, and educators) who assert that a disorder is a disorder, regardless of the multicultural model (e.g., in which a specific disorder may be considered or diagnosed). For example, a person who has manic-depressive disorder is suffering from a serious form of depression and there is often a lack of contact with reality. Even though the manic-depression can be caused by biological and environmental factors, it nevertheless does represent a "recognizable" disorder. The multicultural model, however, could argue that the ethnic group from which the individual emanates can be expected to have another world viewpoint. For example, what leads to psychopathology is one world view that would not necessarily be the view of another culture or ethnic minority (Sue, Sue, & Sue, 2000). Given such different experiences and values, unaware counselors might be prone to make errors that could affect judgments of normality and abnormality among various racial and ethic minorities (Arrendondo & Arciniega, 2001; Constantine, 2001; Herring, 1997; Sue & Sue, 2003; Sue, Sue, & Sue, 2000).

Another criticism is leveled at the lack of empirical evidence from longitudinal research studies concerning the key concepts and assumptions contained in the multicultural model. For example, the multicultural writers or researchers who write about the underlying concepts (e.g., conceptual formulations for each ethnic or minority group) have not had the majority of their work subjected to scientific or rigorous clinical studies. There is also not an apparent large-scale research attempt to have ethnic-minority groups themselves validate these key concepts and assumptions. Apparently, there remains a strong reliance on the case-study method, ethnic-group analysis, and a broad-based approach to investigations that are qualitative in nature. Modern multiculturalists respond to such criticisms by pointing out that the Western world's viewpoint insists on scientific investigation, statistical precision, and empirically derived models and definitions. Moreover, other information that is collected by multicultural researchers is deemed to be equally important and equally capable of answering questions about the human condition (Kiselica & Robinson, 2001; Sue, Sue, & Sue, 2000).

AN INTEGRATIVE APPROACH TO UNDERSTANDING PSYCHOPATHOLOGY

Practicing counselors typically work with individuals who are experiencing emotional or behavioral dysfunctions. At the onset of providing service to these clients, one of the most important tasks for counselors is how they are going to "think" about the various models or factors that might have contributed to the development of psychopathology. For example, each of the models or factors discussed in this chapter represents different views or perspectives for the development of psychopathology. There might also be other models out there that are not in this chapter but could be useful in further conceptualizing the development of psychopathology.

As counselors, each of us should seek to carve out and detail from each different model or perspective a way to interpret reality, the nature of people (e.g., considering their contexts), the origin for disorders, the standards for judging normalcy or abnormality, and what should constitute appropriate interventions or treatment. Each model can be expected to have strong supporters and detractors. In turn, each counselor can be expected to be influenced by the model or factors that seem to be the most important. Even though we might see different theoretical models or factors as important, it seems evident that counselors can best understand the development of psychopathology by integrating the various approaches.

What we can say with assurance is that these approaches are in reality describing the same phenomena (e.g., psychopathology), but from different orientations or perspectives. Furthermore, each of the models or approaches to understanding psychopathology in a person focuses on several of its aspects to the exclusion of most or all of the others. Sue, Sue, and Sue (2000) have advised caution when this occurs because the person as a "total package" can then be overlooked by the counselor (e.g., resulting in a distorted view).

A truly comprehensive model of human behavior (e.g., normal and abnormal) and how psychopathology might develop must address the possibility that people are all of the models or factors in this chapter and more. People are also products of their psychodynamic makeup, the quality of their attachment relationships, how they were reinforced or punished (e.g., their learning histories), their opportunities for engaging in positive social learning situations, their level of cognitive skills, how they have interpreted their inter- and intrapersonal feeling states, and how other factors (e.g., life events) might have helped shape their lives at developmentally crucial periods.

An Integrative Approach in Counseling Practice

An emerging force in counseling is the **integrative approach**. For example, the various elements or factors that are used in models to explain how the client acquires maladaptive behaviors can certainly compliment one another to more fully explain a client's condition. In fact, counselors should seek the best ideas and base their counseling interventions from knowledge about all the different approaches (Corey, 2005; Goldfried & Castonguay, 1992; Sue, Sue, & Sue, 2000).

From recent writings in research publications, it is becoming evident that there is a major evolution taking place in the counseling field. This evolutionary movement, for example, can lead counselors to an integration or "convergence" of thinking about the currently contrasting views of factors involved in psychopathology (Corey, 2005; Norcross & Newman, 1992; Sue, Sue, & Sue, 2000; Young, 1992). This convergence can be described as being in harmony with what constitutes an eclectic approach to counseling clients. Whatever form this ultimately takes, convergence or integration must be holistic, capable of addressing both the multiple levels and contexts of human development and the multiple perspectives inherent in our current models of psychopathology (Mash & Wolfe, 2002; Sue, Sue, & Sue, 2000).

Other researchers (see Masten & Coatsworth, 1998; Mash & Dozois, 1996; Mash & Wolf, 2002) have advocated that the development of children (e.g., positive developmental outcomes) can be achieved in both favorable and unfavorable environments where there is an integrative approach (e.g., to understanding the child and for planning treatment). These researchers also postulate that adopting the goal of prevention in the development of psychopathology offers the greatest potential for directing the odds in favor of the child developing normally. For example, mental disorders in this country collectively account for 15 to 20% of the overall burden of disease for all causes (e.g., clinic-level problems) (Wicks-Nelson & Israel, 2005). This data underscores the importance of preventing mental disorders. Overall, this is an optimal time with regard to prevention (see Durlak & Wells, 1997; Munoz, Mrazek, & Haggerty, 1996).

At this time, however, prevention might not be a fully attainable goal for our society. Although the prevention of psychopathology should be our ultimate goal, it is the adoption of an "integrative" approach by counselors that might be the best vehicle for delivering us to that ultimate result. Integrated approaches are viewed as vital for tackling the monumental complexity of mental function and dysfunction. It is also in the integrated approach that specific interventions from a broad array of models or perspectives can be more efficaciously matched to the array of problems that many clients tend to exhibit.

A useful learning experience is presented for you to evaluate what you think and decide is important in this case illustration of Calvin (adapted from Sue, Sue, & Sue, 2000). You are invited to try your hand at explaining the behavior of a client named Calvin, using the models or perspectives expressed in this chapter. Be sure to review the material presented in the chapter and in Table 2.2, located at the end of this section. You might want to consult other literature on the development of psychopatholgy to assist you in this exercise. The following are some "guidelines" that might be helpful as you begin this exercise; they might also be useful to remember when you are working with a client as well.

TABLE 2.2   General Models for Conceptualizing Child Psychopathology

Biological Models—General Causal Factors

The brain as the seat of constitutional or neurobiological health (e.g., physical, mental). The brain and its neurotransmitters, neuroanatomy, neural plasticity, and genetic predispositions are integrally involved in all forms of human behavior.

Psychological Models—General Causal Factors

Inborn drives, temperament, view of personality structure or intrapsychic mechanisms, attachment relationships, and emotional influences (e.g., including dysfunctional emotion-regulation mechanisms) have important roles to play. Defense mechanisms, psychosexual stages, fixation, and regression, which are more connected to the psychodynamic view, can also be factors.

Behavioral Models—General Causal Factors

Externally influenced and are the result of learning maladaptive responses or not acquiring appropriate responses. Excessive, inadequate, or maladaptive reinforcement is involved in the learning history.

Cognitive Models—General Causal Factors

Interaction of external and cognitive influences. Internally, there is a learned pattern of irrational or negative self-statements. Vicarious and observational experience including reciprocal parent-child interactions are important. There can be distorted or deficient cognitive structures and processes (e.g., that often misdirect thinking and feeling states). These all assist in explanations for learning experiences that can be largely pessimistic and nonaffirming.

School Models—General Causal Factors

The school and conditions at school operate as a social system in and of themselves. The school is a contributor to the effects that can accrue from teacher-student relationships, peer relationships at school, and conditions and internal states at school. These can foster the development of maladaptive behaviors.

Family Models—General Causal Factors

Family systems, family dynamics, negative family cycles, effect of parent cognitions on dysfunction, and parenting self-efficacy. Many of the intra- and intergenerational family systems that include the structural or functional elements within families are not functioning to serve the best interests of all family members.

TABLE 2.2   (continued)

Multicultural Models—General Causal Factors

Culture and its integral components (e.g., race, ethnicity, gender, sexual orientation, religious preference, socioeconomic status, physical and mental disabilities) are strong influences in determining how
specific cultural groups will manifest disorders, how their disorders will be viewed, and how their disorders will be treated.

Adapted by permission from Mash & Dozois (1996).
Note: These general models are not presented with any hierarchical emphasis. There is also no intention (in
this chapter) to have covered all the causal factors that may emanate or operate from these models. Most
models and their perspectives are considered overlapping and recognize the role of multiple influences as
contributors to child psychopathology.

1. Consider what each model or perspective proposes. What are the major fac-
    tors or elements proposed as the basis for the development of the client's be-
    havior? In the beginning, it is often not useful to look for all the causative
    factors or agents of change, but rather those that seem to be most directly in-
    volved in the development of the client's dysfunctional behavior or mental
    disorder.
2. Consider the type of information or data that each model or perspective
    deems to be "most important." How will it fit with your client's background
    and current problematic behavior or dysfunctions?
3. Compare and contrast what each model or perspective has to say about how
    the client has developed seriously disordered behavior (e.g., an emotional or
    behavioral disorder).
4. Because there are numerous models or perspectives presented for the devel-
    opment of psychopathology, you might want to do a comparison between only
    the models you select to use. At this time in your education, you are not ex-
    pected to be proficient in using and integrating all the models, approaches,
    or perspectives. What counts in this practice case, for example, is that you have
    the opportunity to realize how adopting an integrative approach can lead to
    the improvement of your counseling and treatment skills.
5. As you attempt to understand and explain the development of Calvin's be-
    havior, notice closely how your adoption of particular models or perspectives
    influences the type of information or data you (e.g., the counselor) consider
    important. Now you can begin to understand and appreciate that all the mod-
    els or perspectives hold some important sources of truth for your client. Fur-
    thermore, are the different perspectives necessarily contradictory, or are they
    actually useful to some degree in completing a fuller clinical picture of the
    client? Can the different models or perspectives and the elements or factors
    that they emphasize be integrated into a fairly unified explanation for the
    client's behaviors? Again, consult all the perspectives as you move through this
    learning experience.

Do not be concerned with trying to demonstrate to yourself a particular level of skill or "expertness." That is not the goal here. Simply put, the goal here is to help you see more clearly how the adoption of an "integrative approach" enables you to be of more counseling service to your clients. Last, do not be all that concerned about making a *DSM-IV-TR* diagnosis; we are not doing that in this particular experience.

Calvin: Lashing Out; Why?

Calvin was a 15-year-old African American student in the ninth grade when he was referred for counseling services. Mr. L., his father, reported that he brought Calvin in for academic and social problems at the school. The father, to use his language, indicated that Calvin was verbally "lashing out" at his peers. This lashing-out type of activity was leading to more and more confrontations with other students. On one or two occasions, there were physical altercations with other students at school. The school principal was concerned and requested a conference with Mr. L. At the conference, Mr. L. was presented with a letter requesting that Calvin see a professional counselor. In fact, it was a condition for Calvin not being suspended or possibly sent to the alternative school for what were described as "serious behavior problems at school." It seemed, however, that the school was genuinely trying to find out why this new student was having so much difficulty.

Calvin's prior academic performance ranged from below average to barely average in his previous schooling. Calvin lived in another state with his single mother until the start of the ninth grade. The teachers at Calvin's new school reported that since his arrival at their school, his academic work was consistently below average. On many occasions, he spent little time on-task, and could not be depended on to return homework assignments. The teachers also reported that Calvin was often a sullen and sad-looking young man. Several teachers reported that on more than one occasion, "Calvin was observed to be staring out into space and seemed oblivious to those around him." There were also several times when Calvin and another boy had apparently skipped school; presumably, to roam around the town. Additionally, Calvin and his friend were suspected by the school of minor vandalism in one of the washrooms. These behaviors added further concern from the school authorities.

Upon meeting with Calvin, the counselor heard his version; it was rather clear and to the point! "It is the teachers and students at school who do not like me because I am different. How am I going to be able to go to school here if the kids are always teasing me? It seems like everyone here is angry at me and I do not know why. I know that I am not a very smart person, but I have always been that way. Every time that I do something at school that should be right, it is wrong. The teachers do not seem to like me and they think that I do not try hard enough. I decided to quit trying to do the work at school and to quit trying to get along with others. I just want to be myself now. I no longer really care whether anybody likes me or not! I have been feeling very moody and out of sorts with myself and others around me." The last two comments in the session were "I need to live with my dad but that may not work out either" and "Why can't anyone understand me?" Calvin left the session seemingly agitated about what was happening to him in his new school.

Calvin's father met with the counselor separately. Mr. L. offered the following opinions about why his son was doing poorly in school. Mr. L. explained that Calvin had been living with his mother in another state. It seemed that Calvin showed up "out of the blue" (at the start of the school year) and asked to live with his father. Mr. L. thinks that his son now needs to live with him. Mr. L. reported that he did not have legal custody of Calvin, however, he was planning to file for it. Mr. L. also reported that the relationship with his former spouse had remained largely acrimonious for years. Mr. L. doubted that his former spouse would legally agree to having Calvin come to live with him. Throughout their relational history, it was apparent that Mr. L. and his former spouse could never seem to reach a consensus on what would be in Calvin's best interests.

Mr. L. thinks that as Calvin grew in age, he was experiencing emotional trauma. The father believed that the trauma was due in part to his son's blended African American/Causcasian family background. Mr. L. thought that his son was becoming increasingly disturbed about having to make a choice of which "world" to live in. Mr. L. described his son as probably "acting out" many of his inner-felt problems and frustrations. Mr. L. further felt that his son would be able to resolve many of his problems in counseling and things would get better.

Mr. L. did volunteer that he had been diagnosed with learning disabilities and Attention-Deficit/Hyperactivity Disorder when he was in school. He acknowledged that his disabilities posed significant problems as he matriculated through high school and college. The father wondered aloud if there was any possibility of these disorders also being connected to Calvin's history of poor school achievement and peer dysfunctions.

Needing to hear both sides (and with the permission of Mr. L. and Calvin), the counselor initiated a telephone interview with the former spouse. The mother voluntarily reported the following information: Calvin was coming home late (e.g., staying out past his curfew) and was having similar run-ins with the teachers and students at his former school. Moreover, the school had expressed concern that Calvin was displaying a conduct disorder with overlapping anxiety and depression. The mother and the school had decided to have Calvin undergo a complete psychoeducational evaluation. The mother expressed concern about her son's ability to adapt and function satisfactorily in the new setting. The mother indicated that she had asked her former husband to send Calvin home.

Between the divorced parents there seemed to remain longstanding unresolved familial issues that centered on their only child Calvin. It appeared, however, that both parents loved their child and were genuinely concerned about the condition of Calvin's life.

What Caused Calvin's Problems?

Suppose you were asked to state the problems that you think Calvin is experiencing. What problem areas, for example, are apparently impinging on Calvin? Here are some problem areas that you might consider identifying for Calvin's parents or teachers. First, frustrated parental relationships exist (e.g., successful adaptation of children depends largely on relationships). Second, poor academic performance is occurring (e.g., low school achievement). Third, there are increased difficulties at school with peers and teachers (e.g., social relationships with classmates, compliance with authority figures' instructions). Fourth, low self-esteem (e.g., a negative self-evaluation) is taking its toll. Fifth and last, mounting anxiety and worry about his functioning (e.g., stress-related disorders) may abound where a reliable attachment figure cannot be accessed.

Would you see other factors or influences at work here? If so, what would they be? Increasingly, you should be able to see that the development of Calvin's problematic behaviors is likely the product of many of the models, factors, or elements contained in this chapter. Now as you recognize this, do you feel comfortable making tentative hypotheses about which models or factors seem to be most pertinent?

Would you feel comfortable exploring Calvin's problems in more depth for the purpose of counseling treatment? If the answer is yes, you would likely expand your counseling to become more detailed. This will allow you to probe particular questions with greater precision. Most counseling activity begins with the counselor developing a theoretical formulation for guidance and information. The knowledge, skill, and experience of the counselor are then added to bring the theoretical clues or formations to life.

Congratulations on your progress! You are on your way to further information about Calvin. As you have proceeded to learn more, you have at the same time acquired a greater understanding of Calvin and his development. In turn, this will empower you to further organize and integrate your thinking about Calvin. For your review, here is an overview of what seem to be some of the pertinent points related to Calvin's case.

An Overview of Calvin's Case

1. Calvin's case exemplifies many of the interconnected models or factors that can cause or contribute to the development of psychopathology (e.g., emotional and behavioral disorders) in a child or adolescent.
2. Calvin's case appears to involve some factors contained in the models in this chapter (e.g., biological, psychological, behavioral, cognitive, family, school, and cultural). Of course, you have to decide which models or factors need attention now and which you think can be scheduled for addressment a little later.
3. Calvin's case involves the need to consider contexts in determining the expression and outcome of any emotional or behavioral disorders.
4. Cavin's case involves family patterns of behavior and cultural norms that should be more fully comprehended for any negative effect on members of the family unit.
5. Calvin's case shares common ground with all the other cases that involve psychopathology; there has been "adaptational failure" in one or more developmental areas (Rutter & Sroufe, 2000).

CLOSING REMARKS

The theoretical models and factors presented in this chapter were intended to provide a bridge between the normal development of children and how children and adolescents may come to develop emotional and behavioral disorders. If one considers the concept of normal development in children with a serious eye, often only the concept of what normal should be is visible. Knowing this lies at the heart of the need for more discussion and study of models and perspectives that attempt to explain how children might develop maladaptive or disordered behavior. The models or causal factors discussed in this chapter are important because we must consider how emotional and behavioral problems or psychopathology develops in our society.

In reviewing the models and perspectives on how seriously disordered behavior occurs, it is easy to draw the conclusion that each model and its perspectives resembles a piece of the puzzle. Perhaps this is the best way to conceive of it because there seems to be so much interest in studying the "multifactorial or multicomponent model" for seriously disordered behavior. Each model presents a perspective and makes a valid contribution to our understanding; it is correct to say that each model provides some answers but not the one answer that we all seem to seek. The models presented here are not exhaustive. Whatever the inherent difficulties, when we discover how to successfully prevent psychopathology in childhood, we could markedly reduce mental disorders in one generation.

In all likelihood, the causes of emotional and behavioral disorders are myriad. It will take more research and time to tease out all the factors, and in which combinations they pose the greatest developmental threats. For example, there may be specific "life spaces" or "microenvironments" in which dramatic events occur in the life of a child that can "jump-start" the development of disordered or dysfunctional behavior. They can be subsequently reinforced with enough frequency, for example, to maintain dysfunctional thinking or cognitions that enable a particular maladaptive pattern of behavior to form or sustain itself. There might even be some individuals who are more biologically prone to such a negative developmental sequence. Other arenas pertinent to the child's development such as availability of assistance (e.g., relationships with caring adults), cognitive skills (e.g., intellectual factors, academic achievement), coping strategies (e.g., self-regulation), social competence (e.g., socially appropriate conduct), and resilience, that while crucial, await clearer answers from research (see Masten & Coatsworth, 1998).

In general, the recent results of research (e.g., medical, psychological) communicate to us that some disordered states of behavior are probably due to biological or genetic deficits. Others, however, are considered by many researchers to be linked to maladaptive experiences that have been "learned" in the home, in the school, and in our communities (e.g., a sociocultural perspective). There is also strong reason to suspect that there must be an interplay occurring. In the main, the downfall for many children is probably precipitated by the overwhelming sociocultural forces to which some children are relentlessly exposed. Many children, for example, have little recourse or ways of evading these forces. We could, in most instances, consider these individuals to be the "products or outcomes" of these sociocultural forces. Consciousness and free will, for example, would be presumed to play the role of enhancing these dysfunctions rather than obviating them.

Counselors should not find and hold onto one model for how children and adolescents have come to develop or exhibit psychopathology (e.g., emotional and behavioral disorders). To do so can simplify the complexity of child and adolescent problems. Human development and identity are far too complex to believe in a single cause and a single treatment for every individual.

PART TWO
CLASSIFICATION OF EMOTIONAL AND BEHAVIORAL DISORDERS

Chapter 3
Adjustment Disorders In Children and Adolescents

Chapter 4
Attention-Deficit/Hyperactivity Disorder In Children and Adolescents

Chapter 5
Disruptive Behavior Disorders: Conduct Disorder and Oppositional Defiant Disorder In Children and Adolescents

Chapter 6
Anxiety Disorders In Children and Adolescents

Chapter 7
Mood and Depressive Disorders In Children and Adolescents

Chapter 8
Substance-Related Disorders In Children and Adolescents

Chapter 9
Adolescents And Eating Disorders

Chapter 3

ADJUSTMENT DISORDERS IN CHILDREN AND ADOLESCENTS

By

Patricia J. Polanski
University of Dayton

DEFINITION, DIAGNOSTIC FEATURES, AND PREVALENCE

Adjustment Disorder involves the emergence of clinically significant emotional and behavioral maladaptive responses to an identifiable psychosocial stressor or stressors (American Psychiatric Association [APA], 2000a). As a stress-related phenomenon, the maladaptation and symptoms associated with Adjustment Disorders are time-limited in relation to the removal of the stressor(s) or the acquisition of adaptive coping skills. Adjustment Disorder also has been characterized as a subthreshold diagnostic category (Strain, Newcorn, Wolf, & Fulop, 1994) and is considered by some to be a "wastebasket" or transitional diagnostic category (Despland, Monod, & Ferrero, 1995). Subthreshold disorders fall somewhere between normal behaviors on the one hand and major disorders on the other and are thus often unclearly defined and overlap with other diagnostic categories. However, it is this indefiniteness that makes the Adjustment Disorder label useful, in that it permits the classification of early or temporary states when the clinical picture is inconclusive, but the presenting symptoms represent more than an expected normal reaction (Strain et al., 1994). Although Adjustment Disorder is considered a subthreshold diagnosis, that does not imply that its associated symptoms (e.g., suicidal behaviors) are not regarded as part of a major mental disorder and, therefore, in need of treatment. Thus, Adjustment Disorder serves as an adequate diagnosis that can be modified or changed with ongoing assessment and treatment.

The occurrence of Adjustment Disorder seems relatively common, with the percentage of individuals (of all ages) in outpatient mental health treatment with a primary diagnosis of Adjustment Disorder ranging from approximately 10% to 30% (APA, 2000a). In community samples of children, adolescents, and the elderly, the prevalence of Adjustment Disorder is reportedly between 2% and 8% (APA, 2000a). Adjustment Disorder also has been reported as a frequent inpatient admission diagnosis, especially in adolescents (Greenberg, Rosenfeld, & Ortega, 1995). At the same time, research on Adjustment Disorder raises some questions about the prevalence of this diagnosis among children and youth by virtue of the possible inaccuracies in the application of this diagnostic label (Kovacs, Gatsonis, Pollock, & Parrone, 1994). For instance, it has been asserted that Adjustment Disorder might be overdiagnosed in youth because even when criteria for other major disorders exist, practitioners are more likely to diagnose Adjustment Disorder given the relatively benign nature of this diagnostic category (Kovacs et al., 1994). Such "diagnostic hedging" is thought to involve the clinician's preference for linking symptoms to external circumstances and avoiding stigmatizing the client with a more serious diagnosis (Kranzler, 1988). Such stigmatization is further complicated by increasing demands from third-party payers, for documentation and accountability. A diagnosis of Adjustment Disorder allows the clinician to comply with the client's desire to be reimbursed without disclosing meaningful information to an insurance or managed-care company whose intent and confidentiality, both to client and counselor, are cautiously contemplated (Kranzler, 1988). At the same time, Seligman (1990) has speculated that because many individuals with Adjustment Disorders recover without seeking treatment, the incidence of these disorders is difficult to assess. Regardless of the variability in the application of this diagnosis, the existing research on Adjustment Disorder supports its validity (Despland et al., 1995). Additionally, Newcorn and Strain (1992) have asserted the importance of Adjustment Disorder as a clinical entity in children and adolescents based on 1) the significant number of cases in all treatment settings; 2) the considerable morbidity and even mortality in a significant number of individuals; and 3) the large number of children and adolescents with Adjustment Disorders who go on to develop other, more serious disorders.

The diagnosis for Adjustment Disorder in children and adolescents requires emotional or behavioral symptoms in response to an identifiable stressor no more than 3 months following the onset of the stressor. Adjustment Disorders, according to the *DSM-IV-TR*, are manifested as impairment in functioning or subjective distress associated with decreased performance at school and temporary changes in interpersonal relationships (APA, 2000a). The essential conditions for all types of Adjustment Disorders include the following: 1) A defined, identifiable psychosocial stressor 2) observed within 3 months of the appearance of symptoms; 3) an overreaction to 1) as determined according to cultural norms and 4) affecting usual social and/or academic functioning; 5) the disturbance has manifested itself in more than one instance, but 6) it has lasted less than 6 months (Araoz & Carrese, 1997). Other diagnoses should be considered if the symptoms persist for more than 6 months following the termination of the stressor or its consequences (e.g., Mood or Anxiety Disorders). As with many other diagnoses throughout the *DSM-IV-TR*, Adjustment Disorder should not be considered if the presenting problem can be better explained by another Axis I disorder or is simply a magnification of a preexisting disorder. Adjustment Disorders can be included with other Axis I disorders if the symptoms are separate from the Axis I symptoms (APA, 2000a). For example, a child with a learning disorder could simultaneously experience an Adjustment Disorder with disturbance of conduct.

One change from the *DSM-III-R* to the *DSM-IV* (and now the *DSM-IV-TR*) was the addition of specifiers for Adjustment Disorder diagnoses in order to further describe the relationship between the duration of symptoms and the nature of the stressor(s). *Acute* is specified to indicate persistence of symptoms for less than 6 months and *chronic* applies to cases in which the duration of the disturbance is longer than 6 months in response to a stressor that is chronic or has enduring consequences (APA, 1994). Stressors can be single events (i.e., the death of a friend) or continuous circumstances (i.e., chronic illness), but they are deemed to be within the parameters of normal life experience (Seligman, 1990). Stressors may affect an individual, a family, or a larger group (e.g., a student's suicide impacting a number of students in the school), and some stressors might occur congruently with specific developmental events (e.g., leaving home to go to college). It is important to keep in mind that the presence of stressors does not automatically signify a diagnosis of Adjustment Disorder, and conversely, a diagnosis of a specific disorder does not imply the absence of causal stressful events (Kovacs et al., 1994b). Adjustment Disorders are further categorized into six subtypes according to the nature of the symptoms being presented. The *DSM-IV-TR* diagnostic criteria for Adjustment Disorders are listed in Table 3.1.

TABLE 3.1   Diagnostic Criteria for Adjustment Disorders

A. The development of emotional or behavioral symptoms in response to an identifiable stressor(s) occurring within 3 months of the onset of the stressor(s).

B. These symptoms or behaviors are clinically significant as evidenced by either of the following:

1. marked distress that is in excess of what would be expected from exposure to the stressor
2. significant impairment in social or occupational (academic) functioning

C. The stress-related disturbance does not meet the criteria for another specific Axis I disorder and is not merely an exacerbation of a preexisting Axis I or Axis II disorder.

D. The symptoms do not represent bereavement.

E. Once the stressor (or its consequences) has terminated, the symptoms do not persist for more than an additional 6 months.

Specify if:

Acute: if the disturbance lasts less than 6 months
Chronic: if the disturbance lasts for 6 months or longer

Adjustment Disorders are coded based on the subtype, which is selected according to the predominant symptoms. The specific stressor(s) can be specified on Axis IV.

309.0	**With Depressed Mood**
309.24	**With Anxiety**
309.28	**With Mixed Anxiety and Depressed Mood**
309.3	**With Disturbance of Conduct**
309.4	**With Mixed Disturbance of Emotions and Conduct**
309.9	**Unspecified**

Reprinted with permission from the *Diagnostic and Statistical Manual of Mental Disorders,* Fourth Edition, Text Revision. Copyright 2000, American Psychiatric Association.

Although the diagnostic criteria for Adjustment Disorder are generally written for and applicable to children and adults, there are no specific recommendations regarding the application of these criteria to children and adolescents at varying ages. Such lack of specificity is likely to contribute to artificially inflated diagnostic rates and difficulties in accurately subtyping the various Adjustment Disorder diagnoses (Overstreet, Nelson, & Holden, 1999). Regarding the *DSM-IV-TR*'s subtype differentiation, the level of symptom presentation, as well as developmental considerations, is not clarified. The frequent presence of emotionally based behavior symptoms in adolescents (Weiner, 1992) and the general difficulty in differentiating depressive mood from anxiety in children (Reed, Carter, & Miller, 1992) are examples of symptom presentations linked to specific developmental levels. Such developmental factors, along with unspecified subtyping criteria, can interfere with the reliable subtyping of Adjustment Disorder in children and adolescents. At this time, research has yet to clarify where along the developmental continuum Adjustment Disorder is most likely to occur. However, one might speculate that some behaviorally and emotionally vulnerable developmental target points would include initial entry into preschool or school, early adolescence, and leaving home after high school.

Although adult women are diagnosed with Adjustment Disorder twice as often as men, in clinical samples of children and adolescents, boys and girls are equally likely to receive this diagnosis (APA, 2000a). At the same time, in one study of individuals admitted to a county hospital with Adjustment Disorder, adolescents showed gender-related subtype variability in that girls tended to present with depressed mood whereas boys showed more disturbance of emotions and conduct (Greenberg et al., 1995). Adolescents tend to show more acting out and behavioral symptoms than adults, but the occurrence of Adjustment Disorders with anxiety symptoms is relatively frequent at all ages (Strain et al., 1994).

Insomnia as well as other vegetative symptoms, social withdrawal, and suicidal behaviors have been observed frequently in children and adolescents with Adjustment Disorder. In a clinically referred sample of 8–13-year-olds diagnosed with Adjustment Disorder with depressed mood, Kovacs et al. (1994a) found the most common symptoms were feeling sad (95%), suicidal ideation (58%), reduced ability to experience pleasure (42%), self-deprecation (42%), and irritability (32%). For the other types of Adjustment Disorder examined in this study, the most common symptoms were disobedience (55%), irritability (45%), feeling sad (45%), anger, physical fighting, and anxiety (36% for each). Suicidality has been significantly associated with both inpatient and outpatient cases of adolescents and young adults with Adjustment Disorders (APA, 2000a; Greenberg et al., 1995; Newcorn & Strain, 1992; Seligman, 1990). In addition, one study of adolescent suicide found that most victims with noncomorbid Adjustment Disorder or no diagnosis had experienced a precipitant within 1 day of the suicide (Marttunen, Hillevi, Henriksson, & Lonnqvist, 1994).

CAUSAL FACTORS AND PREVENTION

The characteristics of Adjustment Disorder vary over the lifespan (Strain et al., 1994), and particularly in relation to the nature of the stressors that precipitate the disturbance. Andreasen and Wasek (1980) have reported that stressors are more likely to be chronic (i.e., over 1 year) in adolescents than in adults. Various studies on stress and coping in adolescence have indicated that there tends to be an increase of stress in early adolescence, compared to younger ages, and continuous high levels of stress during adolescence (Seiffge-Krenke, 2000). Also, the influence of gender on the effects of stress varies with age. Most studies find that boys are more vulnerable than girls to stressful life events such as divorce in early and middle childhood; however, in adolescence the reverse is true (Smith & Carlson, 1997). In adolescence, girls report more adverse life events than boys, appraise these events as being more stressful, and react to them more negatively (Compas & Bond, 1989).

Some of the stressors identified in children and adolescents with Adjustment Disorder include the following: new school year/new school, disrupted/changed family situation, peer rejection/dislike/loss, parental illness, death of a parent/grandparent, and moving to a new community (Kovacs et al., 1994b). There is a widely held belief that grief reactions in most children are brief, however, some children have chronic adjustment problems associated with bereavement (Newcorn & Strain, 1992). Abrupt and traumatic shifts in the social support system (losses in particular) can be extremely difficult for young adolescents, and loss of membership in cliques is particularly difficult for girls (Maguire, 1993). One study has found that if a psychiatric disorder develops in response to the stress of a major change in health status among youths, it is most likely to be Adjustment Disorder (Kovacs, Ho, & Pollock, 1995).

The conceptual model of Adjustment Disorder presented by Woolston (1988) discusses the concept of causality as a foundation for the disorder. The author describes four types of causation: 1) Point causality, 2) linear causality, 3) circular causality, and 4) helical causality. *Point causality* may occur when sudden stressors are faced by children and adolescents, who tend to rely on magical thinking and do not separate cause and effect in a rational way. A child attempting to generate an explanation for parents divorcing might mistakenly identify him- or herself as the cause. With *linear causality*, there is one cause and one effect and the Adjustment Disorder is likely to be self-extinguishing, with the individual returning to a previous level of functioning when the stressor has ceased or effective coping is restored. For example, school failure might be a cause with a resulting effect of loss of self-esteem. More sophisticated than linear causality is the concept of *circular causality*, which involves the processes of "feedback" and "feedforward." Through feedforward, a cause produces an effect, which in turn produces another similar cause through feedback. Expounding on the previous example, the loss of self-esteem can become a cause that results in the effect of anxiousness and inattentiveness, which in turn results in more school failure. In other words, the stressor triggers a maladaptive response that uses feedback to sustain the disturbed response, and the result is a self-generating Adjustment Disorder. Finally, *helical causality* expands on the concept of circular causality in recognizing that the feedback that influences the cause in turn changes the effect in some way. The features of Adjustment Disorder related to helical causality include several intermediate links between the initial stressor and the final disturbance. For example, maladaptive adjustment to school failure might result in future anxiety when confronting difficult tasks in school, which might result in more school failure along with additional anxiety and further loss of self-esteem.

Diagnostically, persons receiving Adjustment Disorder diagnoses tend to have a history of coping reasonably well in the past, but are not coping well with present challenges. A study examining the links between stress, coping styles, and adolescent symptomatology revealed that withdrawal, or avoidant coping, proved to be a significant predictor of adolescent symptomatology (Seiffge-Krenke, 2000). Although stress has been described as the etiological agent for Adjustment Disorder, diverse variables and modifiers (i.e., ego strengths, support systems, prior mastery) are involved regarding who will experience an Adjustment Disorder following a stressor (Strain et al., 1994). In a study of youths with new-onset insulin-dependent diabetes mellitus, the findings suggested that the duration of Adjustment Disorder appeared to be less influenced by the acute versus chronic nature of the stressor than by the attributes of the patient and the milieu (Kovacs et al., 1995). Thus, while the type of stress might affect whether an Adjustment Disorder develops, there are likely individual and familial risk or protective factors that affect whether children and adolescents can cope.

Adjustment Disorders, while occurring in response to identifiable psychosocial stressors, represent nonspecific, individual reactions determined by constitutional, developmental, and environmental influences. As previously noted, certain protective factors residing in the individual or within the individual's ecosystem can play a significant role in mediating the effects of psychosocial stressors in children and adolescents. An ecosystemic perspective suggests that individual, family, and community change is inevitable and continuous, and that protective influences can be introduced into an individual's life through any relationship in any part of the ecosystem (Waller, 2001). Current research has yet to clarify the mechanisms involved with such mediation. However, the literature on risk and resilience might hold some wisdom regarding ways to shore up resources important to helping children and youths manage stressors in their lives. For example, the ability to connect with and rely upon adults outside the family has been identified as a protective factor related to resilience (Werner & Smith, 1982, 1992). School, church, and community programs that include opportunities for youth to experience support and connections with caring adults can provide help with sorting through independence and identity issues, social relationship issues, and other factors that may prove to be stressful for children and adolescents. School climate, parental involvement, and peer support have been shown to positively influence the school engagement of eighth and tenth graders who are at risk of dropping out of school (Polanski, 1998). Thus attending to students' sense of safety and security in schools, along with providing for the support that is developmentally appropriate to their social-emotional needs, can facilitate adjustment in spite of the stressors experienced during the school years.

Given our understanding of some of the precipitants of Adjustment Disorder in children and adolescents, such as parental divorce, a significant change in health status, and loss of a friend, prevention would involve providing education and support prior to the onset of any symptoms. For example, it has been reported that there is no evidence to support the hypothesis that the negative effects for adolescents traditionally associated with divorce already exist prior to the divorce (Forehand, Armistead, & David, 1997). Instead, divorce and its accompanying disruption of family processes are associated with adolescent adjustment difficulties. It is likely that in the case of a divorce, proactive interventions such as education and family counseling, to address the disrupted family processes, may help prevent Adjustment Disorder. In cases of physical illness, effective communication and education with the child and family members regarding the nature of the medical condition is essential to managing the condition itself, as well as preventing additional behavioral and emotional responses to the change in health status. Another example of Adjustment Disorder prevention is the concerted response of counselors to a crisis in a school such as the unexpected death of a student. Helping students adopt effective coping strategies for dealing with loss and grief can prevent the occurrence of symptoms associated with Adjustment Disorder.

METHODS OR PROCEDURES OF ASSESSMENT

It has been noted that although Adjustment Disorder appears to be widespread, it has not been significantly investigated due to the difficulty in defining a valid and reliable diagnostic tool. This diagnostic category's establishment basically depends on clinical judgment (Despland et al., 1995). Unlike other diagnoses in *DSM-IV*, Adjustment Disorder is not defined by specific problematic behaviors, but by a process of elimination (Beiser, Jenkins, Kinzie, & Spiegel, 1996). It has been suggested that if instruments capable of assessing Adjustment Disorder according to *DSM-IV* guidelines were available, some of the high prevalence figures for disorders such as Depressive and Anxiety Disorders might be attenuated by reclassifying them to Adjustment Disorder (Beiser et al., 1996). Indeed, beyond establishing the time parameters that designate a diagnosis of Adjustment Disorder, the counselor must rely on clinical judgment to understand and discern the subjective link that the child or adolescent maintains with the circumstances and events of his or her life.

Although qualitative assessment tools tend to be subjective and ambiguous, they provide important information that cannot be obtained in any other way. Interviews are likely the most important qualitative approach, and a well structured and purposeful intake interview marks the beginning of most effective clinical assessment processes (Seligman, 1986). During the intake interview, the counselor begins to contemplate a possible diagnosis of Adjustment Disorder, and some of the following considerations should be made. First, it is necessary to establish whether the presenting symptoms are in fact maladaptive and not an expected reaction to an identifiable stressor(s). Again, the characteristics of Adjustment Disorder vary over the lifespan and thus assessment of functioning must be considered with regard to the demands of particular developmental stages (Strain et al., 1994). A thorough psychosocial history will allow the counselor to determine the span of time between the appearance of the stressor(s) and the onset of symptoms and whether the presenting symptoms reflect a change from previous levels of functioning. Cultural context also is an important consideration when determining the expected reaction to a given stressor(s).

Second, given the significance of the interface between the individual and an identified stressor(s), the vulnerability of the individual needs to be assessed to ascertain the import of the situation on the individual (Strain et al., 1994). Complete information regarding the individual and family history of Anxiety or Mood Disorders, mental health treatment, and reactivity to stressors, can hold clues about the vulnerability or predisposition of the client to experience increasingly more severe behavioral and emotional symptoms over time. Clarifying the meaning of the stressor for the client and obtaining information about current coping strategies also might illuminate the vulnerability of the client regarding severe symptoms. Should the client express feelings of depressive mood, discouragement, or any self-destructive intentions, a thorough suicide assessment should be made. Finally, an assessment of the individual's social and family systems is important for detecting any recent abrupt or traumatic shifts that might be a precipitant of Adjustment Disorder (Maguire, 1993). Such an assessment may need to include interviewing significant members of the individual's ecology such as parents, teachers, coaches, or friends.

It has been suggested that the current descriptive classification systems (*DSM-IV-TR*) by and large ignore the contribution of psychosocial triggers, sociodemographic characteristics, and life conditions in the development of mental disorders (Barnow, Linden Lucht, & Freyberger, 2002). For example, an individual who develops a subthreshold depression after experiencing psychosocial stress would be diagnosed with an adjustment disorder, whereas an individual developing a more severe depressive syndrome would be diagnosed with a depressive disorder. This practice reflects an underlying assumption that mental disorders arise on the basis of different levels of individual vulnerability, independent of life circumstances and social conditions. One study of adult psychiatric inpatients found that for females, the severity of a depressive syndrome depends on sociodemographic factors such as marital status, education and having children at home along with the interaction of education with marital status and children in the household (Barnow et al., 2002). These results suggest that adequate assessment of children and adolescents take into account the "interaction" between the individual and his or her current family life situation as well as social and school life, as the nature of these interactions stand to influence the degree of symptom severity shown by the individual.

In addition to qualitative assessment strategies, objective measures also might be useful in the assessment of Adjustment Disorders. One study reported the use of the Children's Diagnostic Drawing Series as a potential instrument for diagnosing Adjustment Disorder (Neale, 1994). The Life Event Scale (Coddington, 1981a, 1981b) is useful in identifying the stressor(s) that preceded the presenting symptoms, as well as revealing relevant information overlooked in the intake interview and initiating discussions about sensitive or painful topics. In order to determine the clinical significance of the presenting symptoms, behavior checklists and self-report instruments can be used to assess behavioral and emotional symptoms across age ranges. The Child Behavior Checklist (CBCL; Achenbach, 1991a), the Youth Self-Report (YSR; Achenbach, 1991b), the Adjustment Scales for Children and Adolescents (ASCA; McDermott, Marston, & Stott, 1993), the Children's Depression Inventory (Kovacs, 1992), and the Revised Children's Manifest Anxiety Scale (Reynolds & Richmond, 1978) are useful in identifying areas of functioning in which the child is experiencing significant disturbances. A recent study using the ASCA developed a normative typology of behavior styles that defines distinct variations of healthy, marginal, at-risk, and clinical behavior (McDermott & Weiss, 1995). When considering the question of the subthreshold nature of a particular clinical presentation, such distinctions could be helpful in distinguishing the behavioral and emotional disturbances associated with Adjustment Disorder from those of normal and specific clinical populations. To adequately assess the client's ecology, the *ecomap* provides a visual overview of the organizational patterns and relationships within the family and between the family and their surrounding environment. The ecomap is an assessment tool developed by Hartman (1979) to help public child-welfare workers examine the needs of families in cases of adoption and has been shown to be useful in determining the needs of families in counseling (Hinkle & Wells, 1995).

Needless to say, the assessment process in counseling continues well beyond the intake interview. In children and adolescents, the persistence of Adjustment Disorder or its progression to other, more severe mental disorders may be more likely than in adults (APA, 2000a). When not a subthreshold clinical syndrome, Adjustment Disorders may represent a precursor to a major psychiatric disorder or a clinical picture of a specific disorder brought on by an event that had a traumatic value for the individual (Despland et al., 1995). Very often the only way to sort out these questions is to observe the client over time in relation to his or her responses to treatment (Araoz & Carrese, 1997), the stability of the diagnosis over the course of treatment (Greenberg et al., 1995), and the identification of comorbid disorders (Kovacs et al., 1994b).

DIFFERENTIAL DIAGNOSIS AND COMORBIDITY

Given the paucity of research and the inaccuracies involved with the assessment and diagnosis of Adjustment Disorders, the existence of comorbidity and co-occurring conditions has not been clearly established in the literature. Questions have arisen particularly regarding the reported prognosis for treatment of Adjustment Disorders. It has been suggested that even if properly diagnosed, the negative prognosis regarding Adjustment Disorders could have been due to comorbid disorders that were not recognized such as depressive, anxiety, personality, and conduct disorders, which then would account for the eventual poor treatment outcomes (Kovacs et al., 1994b). In their study, Kovacs et al. (1994b) found that Adjustment Disorders often present in the context of specific, comorbid psychiatric disorders, and that when controlling for comorbidity, early onset Adjustment Disorder made no discernable contribution to later psychiatric morbidity. Thus, it would appear that clues about co-occurring conditions might be found in the specific subtype of Adjustment Disorder designated in a particular case or in the detection of specific disorders during follow-up or subsequent treatment. In one sample of adolescents with Adjustment Disorder, Bipolar Disorder, Schizophrenia, Major Depression, Substance Related Disorders, and Antisocial Personality Disorder were the most common diagnoses at a 5-year re-evaluation (Andreasen & Hoenk, 1982). Based on a 4-year reassessment of mostly young children with Adjustment Disorder, Cantwell and Baker (1989) found the most frequently reported problems to be Attention-Deficit Disorder, Overanxious Disorder, Oppositional Defiant Disorder, and Avoidant Disorder.

Given similarities in the diagnostic features to Adjustment Disorder, other conditions to be considered when making the differential diagnosis include Post Traumatic Stress Disorder, Major Depression, Generalized Anxiety Disorder, Separation Anxiety Disorder, Disruptive Behavior Disorders, and Psychological Factors Affecting Physical Condition (Overstreet, Nelson, & Holden, 1999). A diagnostic feature that is common to both Adjustment Disorder and Post Traumatic Stress Disorder (PTSD) is the presence of a psychosocial stressor. However, the nature of the stressor in each of these disorders is quite different. In PTSD, symptoms arise in response to an extreme traumatic stressor. With Adjustment Disorder, the identifiable stressor tends to be characterized as more within the realm of normal experience. The nature of the reaction to the stressor in each of these disorders also differs. With PTSD, the reaction is a well-defined constellation of emotional and autonomic symptoms such as reexperiencing the traumatic event, emotional numbing, and physiological arousal. In Adjustment Disorder, the reactions to the stressor are less clearly defined and include a wide range of emotional and behavioral responses.

Differentiating between Adjustment Disorder with Depressed Mood and Major Depression may be perplexing when a child or adolescent presents with depressive symptoms in response to an identifiable stressor. For one, the presentation of depressive symptomatology tends to be more diverse among children and adolescents than adults. When the symptoms are extreme and clearly meet the criteria for a major depressive episode, the diagnosis of Major Depression must be made. Other distinguishing features include clinical presentation and the course and prognosis of the condition.

When considering the subtype of Adjustment Disorder with Disturbance of Conduct, it is important to rule out Conduct Disorder and Oppositional Defiant Disorder. Although each of these conditions involves a disturbance in conduct in which there is a violation of the rights of others or of major age-appropriate norms and rules, three factors differentiate Adjustment Disorder with Disturbance of Conduct from Conduct Disorder and Oppositional Defiant Disorder: 1) The course of the disorder or pattern of conduct problems, 2) the age at which onset occurs, and 3) the severity and persistence of conduct problems. In the cases of Conduct Disorder and Oppositional Defiant Disorder, onset is typically gradual, and there is a persistent pattern of inappropriate behaviors occurring over the course of months or years. In Adjustment Disorder with Disturbance of Conduct, conduct problems develop rather suddenly in association with the onset of a psychosocial stressor and cease with the termination of the stressor or its consequences. Both Conduct Disorder and Oppositional Defiant Disorder usually occur in late childhood or early adolescence, while the occurrence of conduct problems associated with Adjustment Disorder does not vary with age, but rather with exposure to a stressor(s). Last, the persistence and severity of conduct problems associated with Adjustment Disorder are not as extreme as in the case of Conduct Disorder or Oppositional Defiant Disorder.

Differentiating the clinical subtype of Adjustment Disorder with Anxiety from Generalized Anxiety Disorder and Separation Anxiety Disorder largely depends on the intensity and pervasiveness of the anxiety symptoms presented. Although each of these conditions may occur in response to stressors such as the death of a parent or divorce, the manifestations of fears and anxiety (e.g., refusal to go to school or elsewhere, worry about possible harm befalling other caregivers) persisting for more than 6 months after the termination of the stressor or its consequences warrants a diagnosis other than Adjustment Disorder with Anxiety.

Finally, the difference between Adjustment Disorder and the diagnosis of Psychological Factors Affecting Medical Condition rests in the reversed relationship between the psychological and medical features in these two conditions. In Adjustment Disorder, psychological symptoms develop in response to the stress of having or being diagnosed with a medical condition. When a medical condition is exacerbated by psychological symptoms, the alternate diagnosis is applied. In some cases, it is possible for both conditions to be present.

In summary, the research literature on Adjustment Disorder, albeit lean, indicates some variability in the application of this diagnosis for a variety of reasons. As a result, the presence of comorbid disorders might be explained as a misdiagnosis from the start or as emerging from an untreated Adjustment Disorder. It is not the author's intention to suggest rendering an Adjustment Disorder diagnosis as a "holding" diagnosis until a better diagnostic possibility appears. Instead, counselors are encouraged to 1) complete a thorough intake assessment including information regarding the onset and duration of symptoms in relation to stressor(s), 2) carefully and methodically apply the diagnostic criteria found in the *DSM-IV-TR*, and 3) use their best clinical judgment to arrive at the most appropriate diagnosis.

TREATMENT OUTCOME RESEARCH

Despite the estimated incidence of Adjustment Disorder in psychiatric consultation services for adults that ranges from 5 to 21% (Andreasen & Wasek, 1980; Despland et al., 1995; Jones, Yates, Williams, Zhou, & Hardman, 1999) and the estimated incidence rate in psychiatric hospital admissions of 7.1% (Greenberg et al., 1995), this diagnostic category continues to receive little attention in the research literature. While there is less research or information about the estimated incidence of Adjustment Disorder in children and adolescents, there are reports indicating that Adjustment Disorder is more often found in young people (Despland et al., 1995).

Some of the available research on Adjustment Disorders has addressed questions about the construct validity of this diagnostic category. Some studies have relied on "treatment outcome" data to establish construct validity. Jones and colleagues (1999), for example, examined baseline and 6-month follow-up responses to a health functioning survey by adult psychiatric outpatients. Patients diagnosed with Adjustment Disorders reported significantly different levels of physical and mental well-being in comparison to patients with other affective diagnoses, at both baseline and follow-up. Using inpatient readmission rate as a form of treatment outcome, one study found that patients with Adjustment Disorders had significantly fewer readmissions than patients with other mood and anxiety disorders (Jones, Yates, and Zhou, 2002). Another study utilizing treatment outcomes found that in comparison with individuals with other mood disorders, patients experiencing an Adjustment Disorder tend to require less treatment and are less likely to manifest a recurrence of the disorder (Greenberg et al., 1995). This same study also revealed that about half of the 54 adolescents in the sample were discharged with a different diagnosis, indicating that the Adjustment Disorder diagnosis is rather unstable over the course of one admission. While there appears to be some evidence to support the construct validity of this category, more research on samples diagnosed on the basis of structured assessment protocols is recommended (Jones, et al., 2002)

Compared to other psychiatric disorders, Adjustment Disorders are typically associated with *less severe symptoms* and *a lower level of impairment.* However, there is a significant association between Adjustment Disorders and suicidal behavior that practitioners are advised to take into account. A retrospective study of 119 patients with Adjustment Disorders revealed that 72 patients had documented suicide attempts in the past, with 96% having been suicidal during their admission to the hospital, and 50% attempting suicide before their hospitalization (Kryshanovaskaya & Canterbury, 2001). In this clinical study, a high level of suicidality at admission, involuntary hospitalization, and substance abuse disorders were associated with the Adjustment Disorder diagnosis. Moreover, suicidal ideation and suicide attempts in this study were associated with impaired psychosocial adjustment and specific personality disorders. A study of 89 adolescents with Adjustment Disorder diagnoses at an outpatient psychiatric clinic in Finland, included 25% of individuals who showed suicide attempts, suicidal threats or ideation (Pelkonen, Marttunen, Henriksson, & Lonnqvist, 2005). Compared with non-suicidal patients, the suicidal patients with Adjustment Disorders were characterized by the following: previous psychiatric treatment, poor psychosocial functioning at treatment entry, suicide as a stressor, dysphoric mood, and psychomotor restlessness. These findings indicate the importance of a thorough assessment of internalizing and externalizing symptoms and identification of any previous exposure to suicide of a significant other. A psychological autopsy study of 19 adolescent suicide victims in Belgium examined the differences in duration of the suicidal process between suicide victims diagnosed with Adjustment Disorder and suicide cases with other psychiatric disorders (Portzky, Audenaert, & van Heeringen, 2005). In this study, one-fifth of the sample was diagnosed with adjustment disorder with depressed mood and these cases showed a much shorter time interval between the first communication and their suicide compared to those with other diagnoses. Although Adjustment Disorders are often associated with less severe psychiatric symptoms and a reasonably good short-term prognosis when compared to other psychiatric disorders, currently available outcome research indicates that a thorough assessment of suicidal ideations is needed in relation to this diagnosis. It is recommended that such an assessment be completed at intake and throughout the course of treatment.

IMPLICATIONS FOR PRACTICE/TREATMENT

There is little empirical research regarding the treatment of Adjustment Disorders. The following suggestions and recommendations for counseling practice and treatment have been generated on the basis of general principles of sound counseling practice with children and adolescents, including key diagnostic features of Adjustment

Disorders. Treatment of Adjustment Disorders rests primarily upon interventions that enable the reduction of the impact of the stressor(s), enhance coping skills, and establish a support system to maximize adaptation (Strain et al., 1994). The goals of counseling include exposing the concerns and conflicts that the client is experiencing, identifying the means to reduce the stressor(s), enhancing coping skills, and helping the client gain perspective on the adversity and establish relationships to assist in the management of the stressor(s) and the self (Strain et al., 1994). The counselor needs to express to the client an attitude of confidence that with support and guidance, the client will be able to resolve the problem with personal psychological and emotional resources. Counseling should center on relieving acute symptoms by supporting the client's strengths and offering psychoeducation so that the client can gain a different perspective regarding the problem. It is recommended that the counseling approach be directive and strategic (Araoz & Carrese, 1997). Although primarily noted regarding the treatment of adults with Adjustment Disorder, environmental manipulations (e.g., change of residence), bibliotherapy (Seligman, 1990), biofeedback, and hypnosis (Desland, 1995), also may be helpful interventions with children and adolescents. Psychotropic medication is rarely needed as an intervention with Adjustment Disorders. It is considered contraindicated by some who believe that medication may interfere with the individual's motivation to make constructive changes needed to enhance coping (Araoz & Carrese, 1997). In some cases, brief pharmacological interventions may help symptom relief to facilitate addressing other issues involved in adjustment (Enzer & Cunningham, 1991).

One way to conceptualize the appropriate utilization of different treatment approaches for Adjustment Disorder is through consideration of the causal nature of the stressor(s) (Overstreet, Nelson, & Holden, 1999). For example, individual counseling is best suited for Adjustment Disorders involving stressors such as peer rejection or adjustment to a new school, which tend to activate intrapersonal issues around feelings of self-worth and self-esteem. Group counseling can help address clients' feelings of isolation and heightened sense of uniqueness regarding chronic illness or disfigurement. Group counseling also can be an appropriate intervention when the impact of a stressor is experienced by a collective, such as in the case of the unexpected death of a school student or a natural disaster.

Clients with Adjustment Disorders may require different interventions depending on how the adjustment problem is being manifested. For example, clients with Depressive Mood will respond to interpersonal support and cognitive therapies, whereas those with Anxious Mood may require relaxation programs and stress management (Seligman, 1990). Individuals with disturbances in conduct may need behavioral interventions geared toward clarifying limits and boundaries and establishing daily routines.

Woolston's (1988) theoretical model also holds implications for the treatment of Adjustment Disorder. This model explains that the interaction among the stressor, the individual's coping mechanisms, and the individual's inherent vulnerabilities underlies the stability of the maladaptive response. A treatment intervention may be effective only when the nature of the interaction of these elements is appropriately taken into account. For example, a child with learning disabilities may become anxious in the face of new learning situations and experience school failures as a result. Simply addressing the anxiety by teaching the child how to relax might not be completely effective without addressing the child's tendency to be self-critical in response to the anxiety. In addition to the relaxation instructions, the child also will need to be helped to recognize the anxiety as a useful signal to ask for help with unfamiliar learning tasks.

Woolston further explains the importance of a continuum of system responses in the treatment of Adjustment Disorder. It appears that the right combination of protective influences can outweigh the negative impact of exposure to even multiple risks (Werner & Smith, 1992). For example, having special talents, having parents who are effective advocates, and attending a school with adequate resources and flexibility can mediate the risk associated with a child's learning disability (Katz, 1997).

One's personal social network constitutes a key repository of identity and well-being (Sluzki, 1998). Adolescents are still struggling to define their values, goals, and self-concepts and the social system serves to provide feedback to the adolescent concerning these issues (Maguire, 1993). To intervene appropriately with adolescents, counselors need to be sensitive to the young client's social system. Brief intervention with adolescents who are suffering from Adjustment Disorders can and must involve an understanding of how the social system (family and friends) was relevant in the etiology of the presenting problems as well as how to involve the social system in the amelioration of that problem. This social system orientation to intervention with adolescent Adjustment Disorders is particularly salient for four reasons: 1) As part of this developmental stage, adolescents are moving from family to peers as a means of support; 2) the events that take place outside of the counseling session are very important; 3) maintenance of positive clinical outcomes can be enhanced by including the social system; and 4) social systems can be successfully utilized to become therapeutic aspects of the treatment plan (Maguire, 1993). Additionally, brief social support system intervention is ideally suited to adolescents because it helps to develop five resources that are particularly helpful at this life stage, namely, 1) sense of self; 2) encouragement and positive feedback from family and friends; 3) protection against stress; 4) knowledge, skills, and resources, and 5) socialization opportunities (Maguire, 1993).

In the case of Adjustment Disorders, overall treatment goals should include relief as soon as possible, development of more effective coping strategies in response to the current stressor(s), and preparation for coping in the future (Araoz & Carrese, 1997). Given the reports suggesting negative prognosis (Kovacs et al., 1994b) and the occurrence of subsequent treatment (Seligman, 1990), it may be useful to think in terms of relapse prevention as part of the treatment process. Thus, in addition to returning the child or adolescent to the previous or higher level of functioning, treatment also should seek to reduce the chances that the next stage in life development will not result in the same adverse reaction (Seligman, 1990).

Table 3.2 contains a summary of treatment considerations and strategies in relation to each Adjustment Disorder subtype. How the adjustment problem is being manifested, as well as the causal nature of the stressor and the interaction between

TABLE 3.2 Adjustment Disorder (AD) Subtypes and Treatment Foci and Interventions

AD with Depressed Mood	Clarify meaning of the stressor and the interaction between that meaning and the client's view of self, others, and the world; monitor feelings of hopelessness and self-destructive thoughts and/or behaviors; reinforce social support network; individual and group counseling may be indicated, as well as including members of the client's ecosystem (systemic interventions) in treatment.
AD with Anxiety	Clarify meaning of the stressor and client's self-assessment of his or her ability to manage the impact of the stressor; provide relaxation training and other skill building as appropriate; individual and group counseling may be indicated along with systemic interventions.
AD with Mixed Anxiety and Depressed Mood	Use a combination of supportive, psychoeducational, skill-building, and insight-oriented counseling to help client understand how the stressor is impacting him or her and to develop skills to manage the various emotional and physical responses; individual and group counseling and systemic interventions may be used.
AD with Disturbance of Conduct	Clarify meaning of the stressor and interaction of meaning with sense of self; help client examine connections among thoughts, feelings, and behavior to facilitate mastery and self-management skills; work with parents and other significant adults toward providing clear limits and behavioral expectations; individual, group, and systemic interventions may be needed.
AD with Mixed Disturbance of Emotions and Conduct	Clarify meaning of the stressor and help client examine his or her responses to its impact; skill building and increasing self-understanding and self-management help to restore a sense of mastery and provide effective coping in the future; individual, group, and systemic interventions may be useful.

the stressor and the individual's coping abilities, impact the selection and subsequent effectiveness of treatment interventions.

BEST PRACTICE GUIDELINES

Currently, there are not practice guidelines for children and adolescents with Adjustment Disorders. Therefore, it is recommended that the way to approach this area would be to indicate that Adjustment Disorders can be considered subclinical forms of some of the major disorders such as major depression, but clearly triggered by a stressor event. As a result, while there are no specific practice guidelines for these conditions, current consensus would recommend treatments that are indicated for treatment of their more serious versions (e.g., cognitive-behavioral therapy for adjustment disorder with depressed mood). In actuality, the empirically supported treatments have been shown to reduce certain sets of symptoms that are part of a disorder's characteristic cluster.

As previously noted, the child or adolescent's social and family systems are important aspects to consider in the assessment and treatment of Adjustment Disorders. It is sometimes the case that the precipitant to the disorder, as well as the resources for recovery, can be found within the context of these systems. Additionally, the stressor(s) involved may be impacting not only the individual who is presenting as symptomatic, but also the family of that individual (Hinkle & Wells, 1995; Sluzki, 1998). Obviously, a stressor such as moving to a new place can impact the entire family. But seemingly individualized stressors, such as the onset of a medical condition in a child, also can impact the family system.

A well-functioning family can serve as a protective and supportive factor for the child or adolescent encountering a stressor. Therefore, family counseling may be crucial to effectively addressing the impact of a stressor in order to restore the family system to its previous level of functioning. For example, the recent onset of juvenile diabetes in a child is a stressor that can result in the subsequent occurrence of behavioral problems at home and in school. In addition to impacting the child, this stressor can affect the family by creating, for instance, a breakdown in parental hierarchies, resulting in a lack of consistency in child care and limit-setting. Family counseling can address the meaning of the stressor for each member and facilitate reinforcing the structure and stability of the family system. This restoration to stability helps the child cope more effectively.

Assessment and treatment with children and adolescents is most effective when approached from an ecological frame of reference in which all aspects of the ecosystem are considered to be "part of the problem and part of the solution" (Hobbs, 1982). Again, the ecomap can serve as an optimal assessment tool for understanding the interrelationships among the family members and community agencies and subsystems (Hinkle & Wells, 1995). A community mental health counselor treating a child or adolescent with Adjustment Disorder will find that in some cases it is useful to consult with teachers or other school personnel (e.g., the school counselor) about a client's presenting problems. This enables the counselor to obtain a more clear clinical picture and to access resources to support treatment interventions (e.g., referring the student to a support group at school for children of divorce). Likewise, a school counselor with appropriate training might be able to treat a student with an Adjustment Disorder through a combination of family counseling (Hinkle & Wells, 1995), individual counseling, and group counseling.

Classroom guidance efforts can be instrumental in helping all students to develop coping skills that will enable them to effectively confront stressors and prevent Adjustment Disorders altogether. After identifying the particular needs of students (e.g., children of divorce, or children dealing with a parent's recent unemployment due to changes in local industries), school counselors can develop curricula to assist students with developing coping strategies and problem-solving skills. The teacher advisory programs, often a part of middle school organizations (Ziegler, 1993), also represent a useful strategy for providing students and teachers with an opportunity to connect and develop relationships that can provide support when students are under stress.

MULTICULTURAL CONSIDERATIONS

Cultural context must be considered when determining the nature, meaning, and experience of stressors and whether the individual's response to a stressor is maladaptive (APA, 2000a). As noted earlier, a key component to identifying accurately an Adjustment Disorder involves the counselor's ability to understand and discern the subjective link that the child or adolescent maintains with the circumstances and events of his or her life. Minority status itself has been described as a stressor because it is often associated with hostility and prejudice (Tharp, 1991). The development of effective coping styles and access to adequate social support also have been shown to be associated with minority status (Moritsugu & Sue, 1983). Given the unchanging nature of such a stressor, the minority status of a child or adolescent might act as a chronic stressor with enduring consequences. Thus in the case of Adjustment Disorder, adequate understanding of the nature of the stressor(s) and the response of the individual can be best derived from a treatment approach that is contextualized in the family's and community's structure of meanings, relationships, and language (Tharp, 1991).

Also of particular note in the most recent literature on Adjustment Disorders is the mention of cultural considerations regarding the increasing mobilization of societies (Barrett, 1997; Beiser et al., 1996; Sluzki, 1998). More and more, relocation (within countries) and migration (between countries) are frequent and thus may be perceived as normal while having the potential to be quite disruptive to the social niches of families and individuals (Sluzki, 1998). Some research suggests that during the first 2 years of resettlement, migrants have an elevated risk of developing emotional distress (Beiser et al., 1996). It is important for counselors to recognize the effects such a disruption is likely to have and actively to seek out resources for enhancing one's understanding of culturally relevant information regarding the meaning of stressors and symptoms (Barrett, 1997), as well as the workings of the client's social network. This dynamic network is sensitive to culture and gender variables in that cultures have different norms and expectations of behavior in everyday life, and males and females show marked differences in network development, maintenance, and utilization skills (Sluzki, 1998).

CASE ILLUSTRATION AND SAMPLE TREATMENT PLAN

The following case illustration and sample treatment plan represent one way to approach treatment planning and intervention with this client. The treatment objectives and interventions that have been applied in this example relate to previous discussion of the importance of acute symptom relief and the involvement of family members and school personnel in the treatment of Adjustment Disorders.

Stella

Stella is a 15-year-old high school sophomore who was brought to the mental health center for counseling by her mother. Stella's mother was concerned that over the past several months, her daughter had become increasingly withdrawn and noticeably moody. Furthermore, Stella had apparently not been eating and sleeping very well. Stella had recently failed math and science examinations; her grades in the other courses were faring no better. The school year was only a few months old. This was atypical behavior for Stella; her academic record indicated an "A" average throughout her schooling. Upon interviewing Stella, the counselor learned that at the start of the school year, she had tried out for the cheerleading squad and did not make it. However, during her middle school years, Stella was a regular on the cheerleading squad. Stella reported feeling badly about missing opportunities to spend time with her usual circle of friends. Stella admitted to not wanting to go to school on many days, and further reported she had been feeling anxious and even tense when she was called upon in any of her classrooms. Moreover, the nervousness was excessive when it came time to actually take examinations. Stella was open in her admission that making the move from middle school to high school worried her; it seemed to be the only thing that occupied her mind on many days. From the information collected, it seems that many of Stella's high school experiences might have reinforced her concerns. Stella denied having any suicidal ideation.

Diagnosis

Axis I: 309.28 Adjustment Disorder with Mixed Anxiety and Depressed Mood, Acute.
Axis II: V71.09 No Diagnosis on Axis II.
Axis III: No General Medical Conditions Reported.
Axis IV: Psychosocial and Environmental Problem:
           Problems related to the social environment (e.g., adjusting to the transition from middle to high school, changes in peer group affiliation).
Axis V: Global Assessment of Functioning (at intake): 60.

Objectives:
Short Term

1. Reduce Stella's present level of anxiety through individual and family counseling. Sessions with Stella will focus on communicating how stress is commonly involved in developmental transitions. Stella will report improvements in eating and sleeping and decreased anxiety around school.
2. Reduce the mother's concerns about Stella's present behavioral state by providing her (and the father) with information on how developmental transitions throughout the teenage years can produce affects that are, to parents, sometimes alarming, but they are considered normal and treatable.
3. Obtain (with the permission of the client and parent) additional information from school personnel (e.g., counselor, teachers) about Stella's academic functioning and peer relationships. By Stella's and the school personnel's reports, Stella will demonstrate improved academic functioning and more satisfying peer interactions.

Note: Medium or long-term goals could be established if they become necessary.

Assessment: Standardized inventories can be administered to further understand levels of stress and the severity of depressive symptoms.

Counselor/Clinician: Semi-structured, supportive, encouraging, and focused on current life situations.

Location: Outpatient.

Interventions:

1. A cognitive-behavioral approach (CBT) designed to foster rational thinking about Stella's current life situations and the transitions that need to be accomplished. This approach will also contain specific treatment planning for restoring Stella's usual eating and sleeping habits.
2. Analysis and practice in modifying negative or dysfunctional self-talk; the client will receive self-instructional training (e.g., in positive self-talk).
3. Social-skills training (e.g., mobilization of successful coping skills in social group settings appropriate to her grade level).
4. Relaxation training (e.g., breathing, deep muscle relaxation, mental imagery that can be employed when feelings of anxiety are emerging).
5. Homework assignments (e.g., practice in using newly acquired skills in a range of real-life environmental situations).

Emphasis: Highly supportive and moderately directive; the goal is to provide relief in Stella's stress levels while working to enhance the client's coping skills (e.g., modifying her internal beliefs so that she can more skillfully manage her new environment).

Numbers: Individual counseling sessions with Stella; family counseling with Stella and her parents.

Timing: Weekly sessions; short-term treatment is envisioned.

Medication: Not indicated at this time.

Adjunct Services: Assess for participation in peer support groups at school or in the community; seek additional opportunities for positive peer affiliation.

Prognosis: Very good

CLOSING REMARKS

Adjustment Disorder, although lacking in satisfying theoretical rigor, remains popular with clinicians seeking a temporary, mild, or nonstigmatizing diagnostic label (Greenberg et al., 1995). It is important to keep in mind that although Adjustment Disorder is considered a subthreshold diagnostic category, the clinical presentation of this condition often involves significant symptomatology, including suicidal behaviors. Although some questions remain about the actual prognosis for this condition, there is some evidence that a brief, directive, and supportive counseling approach can be very effective in the treatment of Adjustment Disorder. With children and adolescents, it is particularly recommended that a systems approach be undertaken, in which the school and family are involved in assessment and treatment.

FOR MORE INFORMATION

As noted earlier, some common problems of childhood and adolescence (i.e., peer relationships, dating, sexual identity, failing in school) can manifest as Adjustment Disorder. For this reason, it is important for counselors to help address these issues in a direct, timely, and even proactive manner. The following resources provide educational materials that might be used in the prevention of Adjustment Disorder.

KidSafety of America

4750 Chino Ave., Ste. D
Chino, CA 91710
1(800)524-1156
www.kidsafetystore.com

Gay, Lesbian & Straight Education Network

121 West 27th Street, Ste. 804
New York, NY 10001
(212) 727-0135
www.glsen.org

Family Education Network

20 Park Plaza, Ste. 1215
Boston, MA 02116
(617) 542-6500
www.familyeducation.com

National Education Service

1252 Loesch Rd.
Bloomington, IN 47401
1(800)733-6786
www.nesonline.com

Websites for parents and professionals

EARLY WARNING/TIMELY RESPONSE—A
Safety Guide to Schools
http://www.fape.org/topics/warning.htm

KIDSPEACE—Making kids feel competent to manage crisis.
http://www.kidspeace.org

American Counseling Association—Crisis Fact Sheet for parents.
http://www.counseling.org/consumers_media/facts_childtrauma.htm

National Institutes of Mental Health—Helping Children and Adolescents Cope with Violence and Disaster.
http://www.nimh.nih.gov/publicat/violence.cfm

The American Red Cross—Fact sheet for parents to help children cope with disaster.
http://www.redcross.org/services/disaster/keepsafe/childtrauma.html

Article on coping with national tragedy with translations to different languages.
http://www.nasponline.org/NEAT/crisis_0911.html

Chapter 4

ATTENTION-DEFICIT/HYPERACTIVITY DISORDER IN CHILDREN AND ADOLESCENTS

By

Robert R. Erk

University of Tennessee–Martin

HISTORICAL DEVELOPMENT

It is meaningful for counselors to know that the diagnosis Attention-Deficit/Hyperactivity Disorder (AD/HD) is a relatively recent addition to the *Diagnostic and Statistical Manual of Mental Disorders,* Fourth Edition, Text Revision (*DSM-IV-TR;* American Psychiatric Association, 2000a). For example, it was only with the *DSM-III* (APA, 1980) that Attention-Deficit Disorder With Hyperactivity and Attention-Deficit Disorder Without Hyperactivity could be "formally" diagnosed. Before 1980, there was not a formal or standardized classification system available for evaluating and better understanding individuals who might qualify for the diagnosis of AD/HD. Before a diagnostic system was in place, many individuals in the population affected by the disorder were overlooked, mislabeled, or not understood. It is important for counselors to have a historical overview of the "Attention-Deficit Disorder" terminology that has evolved to describe the disorder (Erk, 1995c). See Table 4.1 for the evolutionary history of Attention Deficit Disorder terminology.

As early as 1902, a physician named George Still published an article in the medical journal *Lancet.* It was a description of approximately 20 children referred by their parents for symptoms that are largely categorized in the *DSM-IV-TR* as inattention, hyperactivity, and impulsivity (Barkley, 1996). Still (1902) claimed that he knew his patients' families and did not blame any of the parents for their children's condition. From this observation, Still suspected that the children's problems could be related to genetics and neurobiological development. It was serious deficiencies in the volitional inhibition of their behavior that genuinely concerned this early physician. Moreover, he felt strongly that when behavioral defects in children are seen to the severe degree observed by the parents, they are most often the result of biological factors (i.e., not a lack of adequate parenting or child-raising). Since the observations of Still in 1902, the history or evolution of the term Attention-Deficit Disorder has unfortunately run the gamut of blaming parents for their child's problems to simply calling it "hyperkinesis" or other outright mislabeling of these children. The diagnositic criteria that we use today to categorize and diagnose the disorder was far from being developed.

To illustrate, in 1917–18, there was an outbreak of encephalitis in America. This encephalitis outbreak left many affected children with some degree of brain damage. Children surviving these brain infections were noted to have hyperactivity, inattention, impulsivity, and disorganization. Medical practitioners, therefore, came to the conclusion that if hyperactivity, inattention, and impulsivity could arise from brain damage, all children manifesting such behaviors must have some degree of brain damage (e.g., even where the history to make such a conclusion was lacking) (Barkley, 1996). For many years to come, an inaccurate but convenient label was often attached to many children with Attention-Deficit Disorder (Erk, 1995c). It is, however, crucial that people not think of Attention-Deficit Disorder as brain damage, but rather as a condition that can be treated (Copeland & Love, 1991; Schweibert, Sealander, & Dennison, 2002).

In 1960, the term Minimal Brain Dysfunction (MBD) was adopted as more descriptive of Attention-Deficit Disorder (Copeland & Love, 1991). Again, the primary symptom that characterized many of these children was "hyperkinesis" or "hyperactivity." In the *DSM-II* (APA, 1968), the term Hyperkinetic Reaction of Childhood was

TABLE 4.1　**History or Evolution of Attention-Deficit/Hyperactivity Disorder (AD/HD) Terminology**

Date	Terms
1917–18	Brain Damage
1960	Minimal Brain Dysfunction (MBD) where prominent symptom was hyperactivity
DSM II 1968	Hyperkinetic Reaction of Childhood where prominent symptom was hyperactivity or excessive body movement
DSM-III 1980	Attention Deficit Disorder With Hyperacitivity and Attention Deficit Disorder Without Hyperactivity (ADD/WO)
DSM-III-R 1987	Attention Deficit Hyperactivity Disorder (ADHD) and Undifferentiated Attention Deficit Disorder (UADD) or ADD/WO
DSM-IV 1994	Attention-Deficit/Hyperactivity Disorder, Combined Type; Attention-Deficit/Hyperactivity Disorder, Predominantly Inattentive Type; Attention-Deficit/Hyperactivity Disorder, Predominantly Hyperactive-Impulsive Type
DSM-IV-TR 2000	Attention-Deficit/Hyperactivity Disorder, Combined Type; Attention-Deficit/Hyperactivity Disorder, Predominantly Inattentive Type; Attention-Deficit/Hyperactivity Disorder, Predominantly Hyperactive-Impulsive Type

Counselors should consult the *DSM-IV-TR* (APA, 2000) for the predominating symptom pattern or type that applies *to individuals diagnosed with AD/HD*. *DSM*=Diagnostic and Statistical Manual of Mental Disorders. Adapted by permission from Erk (1995c).

put into place. Hyperactivity or excessive bodily movement was again considered the primary deficit of children with AD/HD. In the 1970s, clinical research focused on the importance of problems with sustained attention and impulse control (i.e., not just the hyperactivity component) (Barkley, 1996). Increasingly, scientists viewed the brain and its functioning as needing more scientific attention to determine how they contributed to the disorder.

In the *DSM-III* (APA, 1980), Attention-Deficit Disorder With Hyperactivity and Attention-Deficit Disorder Without Hyperactivity (ADD/WO) were adopted. The hallmark features of the disorder were clinically designated as inattention, impulsivity, and hyperactivity. Actually, this was the first time that the disorder could be clinically diagnosed without hyperactivity being present. It became clinically possible in the *DSM-III* to diagnose a client as experiencing an impairment of attention without heightened activity level having to be present (Goodyear & Hynd, 1992).

In the *DSM-III-R* (APA, 1987), ADHD and Undifferentiated Attention-Deficit Disorder (UADD) were listed. Attention-Deficit Disorder Without Hyperactivity (ADD/WO) became UADD. Barkley (2005) and Jordan (1992) maintained that individuals with passive Attention-Deficit Disorder, or ADD/WO, were often overlooked. Shaywitz and Shaywitz (1988, 1992) maintained that children, adolescents, and adults with UADD (e.g., where inattentiveness was the predominant characteristic), represented the larger percentage of the population with the disorder. Moreover, Shaywitz and Shaywitz (1992) asserted that a higher percentage of girls or females with the disorder had the predominant characteristic of inattentiveness. In the *DSM-IV* (APA, 1994), for example, the category of Attention-Deficit/Hyperactivity Disorder, Predominantly Inattentive Type was first used. It described children, adolescents, and adults with the predominant characteristic of inattentiveness rather than hyperactivity.

The increased population of individuals who are referred to as having AD/HD are of great concern to parents and professionals (e.g., school and mental health counselors, physicians, psychologists, teachers). The disorder made many aware that there was a serious need for more updated clincial information. For example, the information contained in the *DSM-IV* (APA, 1994) was based on the clinical research literature dating up to 1992. The new material in the *DSM-IV-TR* was developed by the American Psychiatric Association Workgroups during what is commonly known as "the decade of the brain." Therefore, the clinical information on AD/HD in the *DSM-IV-TR* was upgraded to remain current and relevant for counselors (Bell, 2001).

The *DSM-IV-TR* should enable counselors to have a more clear diagnostic picture and a more full understanding of individuals with AD/HD. For example, they should be able to comprehend the child's predicament and realize that the child or adolescent is experiencing difficulties (e.g., academic, social, behavioral, emotional) that are most often "linked" to the disorder (Erk, 1995c). In recent decades, the clinical knowledge base on AD/HD has evolved extensively in the research literature. This empowers counselors who diagnose and treat AD/HD with the latest clinical information (Willcutt, Pennington, Chhabildas, Friedman, & Alexander, 1999).

This chapter on AD/HD is divided into sections that provide information on definition, prevalence, diagnostic features, causal factors and prevention, methods of assessment, implications for practice or treatment, school and family perspectives, case illustration, sample treatment plan, and closing remarks. Each section focuses on information and research that can significantly enhance the ability of counselors to be of increased assistance to clients who have AD/HD.

Definition, Prevalence, and Diagnostic Features

Definition

The *DSM-IV-TR* lists Attention-Deficit/Hyperactivity Disorder (AD/HD) as among the Disorders Usually First Diagnosed in Infancy, Childhood, or Adolescence. Historically, it has been included under the broader rubric of behavior problems; however, the *DSM-IV-TR* differentiates disruptive behavior disorders (e.g., Oppositional Defiant Disorder, Conduct Disorder) from problems with attention and overactivity. AD/HD is characterized by prominent symptoms of inattention, hyperactivity-impulsivity, or a combination. In the *DSM-IV-TR*, the subtypes of AD/HD (e.g., Predominantly Inattentive Type [AD/HD-PI], Predominantly Hyperactive-Impulsive Type [AD/HD-PHI], Combined Type [AD/HD-C]) are provided by specifying or defining the prominent symptom presentation.

By definition in the *DSM-IV-TR*, AD/HD is characterized by persistent and developmentally inappropriate problems with attention, impulsivity, and hyperactivity. The presence, absence, or combination of these symptoms or problems reflects the severity and subtype of the AD/HD. Moreover, recent research findings indicate that AD/HD should not be considered as just a developmental disorder (e.g., affecting childhood). Rather, it should be viewed as a disorder that can attack and disrupt developmental stages throughout the individual's life (e.g., a longitudinal disorder).

AD/HD is the most frequently studied *DSM-IV-TR* disorder of childhood (Barkley, 1996; Goldstein, 1999). Volumes of scientific evidence exist that define the disorder and document its prevalence and diagnostic features. Long-term or longitudinal research studies have found that children, adolescents, and adults with AD/HD (e.g., compared to controls without the disorder) remain at significantly higher risk for academic, behavioral, and social problems across the lifespan (Barkley, 1996, 1997a; Goldstein, 1999; Weyandt, 2001).

Prevalence

AD/HD is now recognized as the most prevalent or common neurological disorder of childhood, affecting children from earliest infancy through school and into adult life (Epstein, Shaywitz, Shaywitz, & Woolston, 1991; Shaywitz & Shaywitz, 1991; Barkley, 1996; Goldstein, 1999). The *DSM-IV-TR* cites a prevalence rate of 3 to 7% for school-age children with AD/HD. These rates vary depending on the nature of the population sampled and the method of ascertainment. Male children are on the average six times more frequently identified with AD/HD than female children, depending on the referral setting (e.g., clinic versus community) (Barkley, 1996).

For example, a substantial discrepancy exists in the male-to-female ratio between clinic-referred (e.g., 10 to 1) and community samples (e.g., 3 to 1) of children who have AD/HD (Arnold, 1996; Gaub & Carlson, 1997). There is a dearth of clinical research comparing boys and girls with AD/HD, but the prevalence rate remains driven in the direction of more referrals for boys. It is thought that females are simply underidentified because they tend not to cause regular or overt disruptions in the family or at school (Erk, 1995a).

In the beginning of diagnosing the disorder, for example, many parents and professionals considered AD/HD to be primarily a male-oriented disorder (Erk, 1995b). Gender differences in the phenotypic expression of AD/HD (e.g., males are more aggressive and oppositional; Barkley, 1996) often provide the best rationale for the referral of more boys than girls (Gaub & Carlson, 1997). Females, for example, are only now receiving increased evaluation for the AD/HD diagnosis and how gender affects the development and course of the disorder (Biederman et al., 2002; Nadeau, 1995).

Counselors should be aware that other prevalence rates exist for the occurrence of AD/HD. Popper (1988), for example, estimated the general prevalence rate of AD/HD to range between 3 and 10% of the total school-age population. Hosie and Erk (1993) estimated that AD/HD affects 5 to 10% of the nation's children. Shaywitz and Shaywitz (1992) estimated that AD/HD affects perhaps as much as 20% of the school-age population, and it might be only the tip of the iceberg for the number of children with some degree of the disorder. Goodman and Poillion (1992) cautioned that the accepted prevalence rate and the identification of the causes for AD/HD could vary according to the counselor's professional training or beliefs. What cannot be disputed, however, is that AD/HD accounts for half of all referrals to mental health professionals (Barkley, 1996, 2005). The disorder is one of the most common reasons children and adolescents are referred to counselors, and AD/HD remains one of the most prevalent childhood disorders in our society (Barkley, 1997a, 1997b; Learner, 1993).

Diagnostic Features

Researchers have long considered the major diagnostic features of AD/HD to be inattention, hyperactivity, and impulsivity. Although many individuals present symptoms of both inattention and hyperactivity-impulsivity, there are individuals in whom one symptom pattern is predominant (*DSM-IV-TR*). See Table 4.2 for the *DSM-IV-TR* diagnostic criteria for AD/HD.

Counselors are advised to be cognizant that the "hyperactivity" component of AD/HD is not always readily observable or present. In many individuals with AD/HD, it is not uncommon for the hyperactivity component to subside with the aging process. For example, a child of 7 years who has AD/HD-PHI typically has a detectable but consistent level of hyperactivity. At age 17 however, the hyperactivity might no longer be prominent and only occasionally noticeable. Barkley (1997a) cautioned that hyperactivity should not be considered permanent in all cases of AD/HD. Hyperactivity, for example, frequently collapses into the AD/HD-C subtype (Barkley, 1997a).

TABLE 4.2   Diagnostic Criteria for Attention-Deficit/Hyperactivity Disorder (AD/HD)

A. Either (1) or (2):

1. six (or more) of the following symptoms of **inattention** have persisted for at least 6 months to a degree that is maladaptive and inconsistent with developmental level:

    Inattention

    a. often fails to give close attention to details or makes careless mistakes in school work, work, or other activities
    b. often has difficulty sustaining attention in tasks or play activities
    c. often does not seem to listen when spoken to directly
    d. often does not follow through on instructions and fails to finish schoolwork, chores, or duties in the workplace (not due to oppositional behavior or failure to understand instructions)
    e. often has difficulty organizing tasks and activities
    f. often avoids, dislikes, or is reluctant to engage in tasks that require sustained mental effort (such as schoolwork or homework)
    g. often loses things necessary for tasks or activities (e.g., toys, school assignments, pencils, books, tools)
    h. is often easily distracted by extraneous stimuli
    i. is often forgetful in daily activities

2. six (or more) of the following symptoms of **hyperactivity-impulsivity** have persisted for at least 6 months to a degree that is maladaptive and inconsistent with developmental level:

    Hyperactivity

    a. often fidgets with hands or feet or squirms in seat
    b. often leaves seat in classroom or in other situations in which remaining seated is expected
    c. often runs about or climbs excessively in situations in which it is inappropriate (in adolescents or adults, may be limited to subjective feelings of restlessness)

    d. often has difficulty playing or engaging in leisure activities quietly
    e. is often "on the go" or often acts as if "driven by a motor"
    f. often talks excessively

    Impulsivity

    g. often blurts out answers to questions before the questions have been completed
    h. often has difficulty waiting turn
    i. often interrupts or intrudes on others (e.g., butts into conversation or games)

B. Some hyperactive-impulsive or inattentive symptoms that caused impairment were present before age 7 years.

C. Some impairment from the symptoms must be present in two or more situations (e.g., at school [or work] and at home).

D. There must be clear evidence of clinically significant impairment in social, academic, or occupational functioning.

E. The symptoms do not occur exclusively during the course of a Pervasive Developmental Disorder, Schizophrenia, or other Psychotic Disorder, and is not better accounted for by another disorder (e.g., Mood Disorder, Anxiety Disorder, Dissociative Disorder, or a Personality Disorder).

Code based on type:

314.01 Attention-Deficit/Hyperactivity Disorder, Combined Type: If both criteria A1 and A2 are met for the past 6 months [or this subtype should be used if six (or more) symptoms of inattention and six (or more) symptoms of hyperactivity-impulsivity have persisted for at least 6 months].

314.00 Attention-Deficit/Hyperactivity Disorder, Predominantly Inattentive Type: If Criterion A1 is met but Criterion A2 is not met for the past 6 months [or this subtype should be used if six (or more) symptoms of inattention (but fewer than six symptoms of hyperactivity-impulsivity) have persisted for at least 6 months].

314.01 Attention-Deficit/Hyperactivity Disorder, Predominantly Hyperactive-Impulsive Type: If Criterion A2 is met but Criterion A1 is not met for the past 6 months [or this subtype should be used if 6 (or more) symptoms of hyperactivity-impulsivity (but fewer than six symptoms of inattention) have persisted for at least 6 months].

Reprinted with permission from the *Diagnostic and Statistical Manual of Mental Disorders,* Fourth Edition, Text Revision. Copyright 2000, American Psychiatric Association.

There is also the possibility that the hyperactivity might dissipate altogether in adolescence or young adulthood. However, problems with attention and impulse control might remain prominent and ongoing from childhood into adulthood, (e.g., regardless of subtype or gender) (Barkley, 2005; Biederman et al., 2002).

It is not uncommon for children who are being initially examined for diagnostic features of AD/HD (e.g., in the counselor's office) to have no readily observable or overt diagnostic criteria. For example, in one-to-one situations that are unique, novel, and in which the counselor continually focuses attention on the child or adolescent, the disorder achieves what it seems to need, "one-to-one" attention (*DSM-IV-TR*). Watching television or interacting with a video game produces much the same effect (e.g., one-to-one attention). When parents observe this type of intense attention (e.g., that video games often require), they cannot understand why the child cannot seem to function normally at school or in other social settings (e.g., these are other types of activities that require another host of skills; Barkley, 2005). To these parents, the diagnosis of AD/HD seems unlikely or improbable. However, in large part, this is why the disorder is often considered to be elusive and silent in how it affects the individual.

The examining counselor is advised that one cannot always detect the AD/HD on just one office visit. It is often recommended that the counselor arrange to have the child and parent wait in the reception area for a period of time (e.g., prior to interviewing the child or parent). By permitting some time to elapse, the disorder is often more likely to begin to diagnostically disclose itself. However, where the inattentive subtype is suspected, this procedure might not be practicable. Many children with the inattentive type of the disorder, for example, could mistakenly evoke in the counselor a search for other causes for the child's difficulties (see Erk, 2000).

It should also be observed by the counselor that the severity (e.g., mild, moderate, severe) of the AD/HD symptoms across different settings (e.g., home, school, community) might not be the same. Clinical research indicates that situational and contextual variables can often account for great variation in the severity of these diagnostic features (Barkley, 1996). In cases of AD/HD, severity can usually be measured or gauged by the frequency, duration, and intensity of the diagnostic symptoms. Severity includes as well the degree to which the symptoms impair or impede the child's attention or performance. In cases of AD/HD where the severity is "mild," it might not be detectable using the *DSM* criteria. In these cases, there might be only minimal or nondetectable effects on academic and social functioning. In the final analysis, severity can be analogous to how significant, pervasive, and disruptive the symptoms are to the child's or adolescent's ability to function (e.g., how they affect appropriate age and/or grade behaviors).

To illustrate further, AD/HD can be conceptualized diagnostically as a condition that entails inappropriate age and/or grade development. It can often center on the following areas or a combination of these areas: 1) inattention (e.g., consistently drifts off-task, cannot focus for the length of time necessary, distractible or paying attention to everything nearby); 2) impulsivity (e.g., seemingly acts with no forethought to consequences; impulsive behavior can take the form of thrill-seeking); 3) overreactivity (e.g., the child is overreactive to the level of the stimulus intended, reacts as if the stimulus is personally aimed); 4) noncompliance (e.g., refusal to obey instructions, commands, or requests); 5) self-management deficits (e.g., chronic disorganization, management of self or environment is not occurring, deficits in executive brain functioning; Barkley, 1997a); 6) academic deficits (e.g., learning problems, academic underachievement, school failure); 7) social-skill deficits (e.g., lack of peer acceptance, cannot resist peer pressure, cannot use covert and overt language skills competently in social settings); and 8) self-esteem problems (e.g., low self-worth, negative self-evaluation, and esteem problems may precede depression).

CAUSAL FACTORS AND PREVENTION

Parents and teachers often request counselors to explain how a child or adolescent has come to have AD/HD. Therefore, it is important for the counselor to be knowledgeable about the probable causes for the disorder. Since around the turn of the century, researchers have generally believed that AD/HD involves some degree of brain dysfunction, not brain damage (Riccio, Hynd, Cohen, & Gonzalez, 1993). The lines of research evidence support the claim that AD/HD is inherited and caused by physical differences that reside in the brain (Anastopoulous & Barkley, 1991). Heredity represents one of the most common identifiable factors, and a growing body of research indicates that there is a genetic risk factor for any family in which a case of AD/HD is reported (Biederman, Faraone, Keenan, Knee, & Tsuang, 1990; Faraone, Tsuang, & Tsuang, 1999; Goldstein & Goldstein, 1998).

Neurobiology and AD/HD

In a landmark study, Zemetkin et al. (1990) discovered that the brain activity of hyperactive adults was significantly lower compared to individuals without AD/HD. Using brain scans trained on two sites of the brain—while AD/HD individuals focused attention and kept still—researchers found the premotor and superior prefrontal regions of the brain were much less active in AD/HD cases, as measured by rates of glucose metabolism, (e.g., the brain's source of energy). It now appears that the irregular metabolism of brain chemicals contributes directly to AD/HD behavior patterns. These patterns of behavior frequently interfere with classroom performance, acquisition of social skills, and work-related activities. The general view, for example, is that this imbalance of the neurochemicals that act as triggers, transmitters, and receptors within the brain, serves to create many of the problem behaviors confronting children and adolescents with AD/HD.

Fundamentally, AD/HD can be thought of as a neurobiological or neurobehavioral disorder. For example, Barkley (1997a) postulated that individuals with AD/HD probably have an impairment to key neurobiological areas in the brain responsible for directing "executive" control (e.g., the behavioral inhibition process). AD/HD is not a "disease" or "illness"; it is a condition that reflects the physiology and biochemistry of the individual's nervous system, and consequently how the individual processes thought and behaves (Friedman & Doyal, 1992).

Denckla (1991) reported that magnetic resonance imaging (MRI) utilized at Johns Hopkins School of Medicine on AD/HD participants with hyperactivity revealed immature and incomplete functions within the brain's cerebellum. These factors might contribute to or trigger such problems as poor organization and poor inhibition of impulses (e.g., often typical symptoms of AD/HD clients). Hynd, Semrud-Clikeman, Nieves, Huettner, & Lahey (1991) provided clinical evidence (e.g., from sophisticated brain scans) that resulted in support for the notion that slight but significant differences exist in the corpus callosum (e.g., the region that connects the two hemispheres of the brain) in children with AD/HD. This region is found to be slightly smaller in AD/HD children as compared to non-AD/HD controls. Research indications infer subtle differences in the structure and function of the brains of children with AD/HD. Brain structure or morphology (e.g., which could be the result of genetic factors) and the dysregulation of brain chemistries are presumed to play significant roles in the matrix of symptoms and behaviors exhibited in children with AD/HD.

The **severity** of AD/HD symptoms in children and adolescents appears to be mirrored or reflected in their brain structure. For example, Plessen et al. (2006) used magnetic resonance imaging (MRI) to scan 51 children and adolescents with combined-type AD/HD and 63 healthy peers (ages ranged from 6 to 18 years). These researchers found that the hippocampus was larger bilaterally in the AD/HD group than in the healthy control group ($t = 3.35$; $P < .002$), and detailed analyses of the hippocampus further localized these differences to an enlarged head of the hippocampus in the AD/HD group. While conventional measures did not detect significant differences in amygdalar volumes, surface analysis indicated the presence of reduced size bilaterally over the area of the basolateral complex. Correlations with prefrontal measures suggested there was abnormal conductivity between the amygdala and prefrontal cortex in the AD/HD group. Enlarged subregions of the hippocampus tended to accompany fewer symptoms.

Plessen et al. (2006) concluded that the enlarged hippocampus in children and adolescents with AD/HD could represent a compensatory response to the presence of disturbances in the perception of time, temporal processing (e.g., delay aversion), and stimulus-seeking or novelty-seeking behavior often associated with AD/HD. Moreover, disrupted connections between the amygdala and orbitofrontal cortex might contribute to behavioral disinhibition (e.g., poor impulse control). This study provides further clinical evidence that the pathophysiology of AD/HD involves limbic structures and limbic-prefrontal circuits in the brain.

Shaw et al. (2006) in a longitudinal clinical study of 163 children with AD/HD (mean age of entry, 8.9 years) and 166 controls assessed participants with MRI. Ninety-seven participants with AD/HD (60%) and an equal number of controls twice underwent 2 or more MRIs and baseline follow-up clinical evaluations (mean follow-up, 5.7 years). These researchers found that children with AD/HD had global thinning of the cortex (mean reduction, −0.09 mm; $P − .02$), most prominently in the medial and superior prefrontal and precentral regions. Children with worse clinical outcome had a thinner left medial prefrontal cortex at baseline than the better outcome group (−0.38 mm; $P = .003$) and controls (−0.25 mm; $P = .002$). Cortical thickness developmental trajectories did not differ significantly between the AD/HD and control groups throughout except in the right parietal cortex, where trajectories converged. This normalization of cortical thickness occurred only in the better outcome group. It was concluded that children with AD/HD show relative cortical thinning in regions important for attentional control. Children with a worse outcome have fixed cortical thinning of the left medial prefrontal cortex, which might compromise the anterior attentional network and encumber clinical improvement. Despite the promise of the new findings, MRI brain scans are still an experimental research tool and cannot yet be used to diagnose or predict outcomes for individuals with AD/HD.

Prevention

The weight of psychological and scientific evidence does not support the view that parenting, schools, allergies, diet, or specific food substances play a role in the etiology or the maintenance of the disorder. Parents are advised, however, to eliminate any possible physical, chemical, and environmental factors with a complete medical examination (Erk, 1995a). For counselors, the causal factors that have been differentiated from the medical or scientific evidence (e.g., sophisticated brain imaging) could lead us to infer that there might be little if anything that we can do to actually prevent AD/HD at present. However, when the Human Genome Project and all of its findings are completed, genetic avenues of prevention or amelioration might be available to lessen or ameliorate the disorder's effects. This could open up new options to families with significant genetic risk factors for AD/HD. It will also provide counselors with an advanced understanding of what is causing such serious disruptions in the lives of their clients. Furthermore, a medical or scientific understanding of AD/HD places management or interventions at the forefront of activities in the child's life, not finding a lasting cure. In the final analysis, and with the clinical information that we now possess on AD/HD, the best "prevention" is likely to remain an early diagnosis and appropriately matched interventions.

METHODS OR PROCEDURES FOR ASSESSMENT

The *DSM-IV TR* contains the criteria for assisting in the identification and diagnosis of children, adolescents, and adults with AD/HD. The diagnostic criteria and the components for the diagnosis of AD/HD must be established, at a minimum, through the following: 1) an interview with the suspected child or adolescent; 2) the use of parent and teacher interviews or reports; 3) the administration of AD/HD checklists (e.g., that have established reliability and validity) to parents and key teachers (e.g., homeroom, English, math); 4) observations from across multiple settings (e.g, school, home, peer associations) that describe the degree of impairment that might exist in each setting; and 5) a written report from the examining counselor. It is recommended that licensed professionals be involved who are trained to identify, assess, and diagnose a child who might have AD/HD. Moreover, it is also recommended that a written report containing the findings, including a recommended treatment plan, be provided.

The diagnosis of AD/HD for a child or adolescent should be approached as a comprehensive assessment. The assessment should "not" be viewed as a single interview with the child, parent, or teacher, the completion of one checklist, or a single office visit to a counselor or physician. The multimethod, multisource, multisetting assessment approach incorporates the components for the diagnosis that provides the most empirical support for achieving not only a differential diagnosis, but also an accurate one. This comprehensive approach can provide an overarching structure or model for the counselor who is engaged in the diagnostic evaluation of this disorder. See Table 4.3 for a listing of instruments that counselors commonly use to identify AD/HD in children, adolescents, and adults.

TABLE 4.3   Instruments Commonly Related to the Assessment of Attention-Deficit/Hyperactivity Disorder (AD/HD): A Multimethod, Multisource, Multisetting Approach

I.   Interview Schedules

Diagnostic Interview for Children and Adolescents—Revised (Reich & Welner, 1989); Diagnostic Interview Schedule for Children (DISC-2.3; Schaffer et al., 1993); National Institute of Mental Health Diagnostic Interview Schedule for Children (Fisher, Wicks, Schaffer, Piacentini, & Lapkin, 1992); Revised Behavior Problem Checklist (Quay & Peterson, 1987); Achenbach Child Behavior Checklist (Achenbach, 1991a).

II.   AD/HD Checklists or Rating Scales

Home and School Situations Questionnaire (Barkley, 1981; Barkley & Edelbrock, 1987); Attention-Deficit Disorders Evaluation Scales (ADDES) (McCartney, 1989); Yale Children's Inventory (Shaywitz & Shaywitz, 1992); Copeland Symptom Checklist for Attention-Deficit Disorders: Attention-Deficit/Hyperactivity Disorder and Undifferentiated/Inattentive Attention-Deficit Disorder (Copeland & Love, 1991); ADHD Comprehensive Teacher's Rating Scales (ACTeRs; Ullman, Sleator, & Sprague, 1988); Brown Attention-Deficit Disorder Scales (Brown, 1995); Conners Parent and Teacher Rating Scales (Conners, 1990); Adult AD/HD Questionnaire (Nadeau, 1991).

III.   Psychometric Instruments

Wechsler Intelligence Scale for Children—Revised (WISC-R; Wechsler, 1974); Wechsler Pre-School and Primary Scale of Intelligence—Revised (WPPSI; 1989); Wechsler Intelligence Scale for Children—III (WISC—III: Wechsler, 1991); Woodcock-Johnson Psycho-Educational Battery—Revised (Riverside, 1989); KeyMath—Revised: A Diagnostic Inventory of Essential Mathematics (American Guidance Service, 1988); Woodcock Reading Mastery Test—Revised (American Guidance Service, 1987); Matching Familiar Figures Test (Kagan, 1964); Children's Embedded Figures Test (Karp & Konstadt, 1969); Wisconsin Card Sort (Heaton, Chelune, Talley, Kay, & Curtiss, 1993).
Note: For a better understanding of how intellectual functioning (IQ) may or may not be related to the AD/HD itself, see Erk, 1995b; Kamphaus & Frick, 1996a; Kaplan, Crawford, Dewey, & Fisher, 2000, and Seidman, Biederman, Monuteaux, Weber, & Faraone, 2000.

IV.   Instruments for Assessing Comorbid or Co-Occurring Conditions (in Cases of AD/HD)

Beck Anxiety Inventory (Beck, 1990); Beck Depression Inventory (Beck, 1987b); Beck Hopelessness Scale (Beck, 1987c); Children's Depression Inventory (Kovacs, 1992); Schedule for Affective Disorders and Schizophrenia for School-Aged Children (Puig-Antich & Chambers, 1978); Fear Survey Schedule

TABLE 4.3 (continued)

for Children—Revised (Ollendick, 1978; 1983); Multidimensional Self-Concept Scale (Bracken, 1992); Self-Perception Profile for Children (Harter, 1985); Self-Perception Profile for Adolescents (Harter, 1988); Social Skills Rating System—Parent and Teacher Forms (Gresham & Elliott, 1990); Inventory of Parent and Peer Attachment (Armsden & Greenberg, 1987); Personality Inventory for Children (Wirt, Lachar, Klinedinst, & Seat, 1990); *Millon* Multiaxal Personality Inventory (Millon, Green, & Meager, 1982); Dyadic Parent-Child Interaction Coding System (Eyberg & Robinson, 1983).

V. Continuous Performance Tests (CPTs)

Test of Variables of Attention (Universal Attention Disorders, Inc., 1982); Conners' Continuous Performance Test (Multi-Health Systems, 1992); Gordon Diagnostic System (Gordon Systems, Inc., 1983). Note: It is recommended that readers review Stein, Szumowski, & Halperin (1994) for recommendations about the use of CPTs.

VI. Brain Imaging Techniques

Magnetic Resonance Imaging (MRI; Lavenstein, 1995); Positron-Emission Tomography (PET; Lavenstein, 1995); Single Photon Emission Computerized Tomography (SPECT; Lavenstein, 1995). Note: Brain-imaging techniques are not used except for clinical/medical research.

Note: As part of an individual assessment for AD/HD and the co-occurring conditions, a battery of instruments is usually selected for administration. In the selection process, it is best practice to select with economy the instruments that are considered to have the best fit with that individual's case. Most clinical decisions regarding the diagnosis of AD/HD are based on what are considered as ecologically valid measures; these are derived from parent, child, and teacher interviews and AD/HD checklists. This data, for example, is obtained from the best sources, naturalistic settings (e.g., home, school). Counselors should check to see whether they are using the most recent version.

Counselors should have information on some of the more commonly employed methods, techniques, or tests that can be utilized in the multimethod assessment. Instruments that can be used in a multimethod assessment can be grouped into the following five general areas:

1. There are structured/semistructured interview schedules completed by the *parents, teachers, and on the client.*
2. Parents and teachers complete AD/HD rating scales or checklists. Counselors should be aware when selecting a scale or checklist that it should have diagnostic utility (based on *DSM* criteria for AD/HD, reliability and validity are established).
3. There are psychometric techniques that might include tests of intelligence (see Erk, 1995b), tests of academic achievement, tests for specific learning disabilities, and tests for memory or central processing dysfunctions. Typically, when the rating scale indicates AD/HD, other psychological assessment tools are employed.
4. There are instruments that can be useful in evaluating the comorbidities or co-occurring conditions that can accompany many cases of AD/HD. Researchers have consistently advised that children and adolescents with AD/HD are excellent examples of where significant secondary problems (e.g., academic

under achievement, learning disabilities, oppositional defiant disorder, conduct disorder, personality, substance abuse) often exist.

5. There are machines or programmed instruments that are advertised as continuous performance tests (CPTS). Stein, Szumowski, and Halperin (1994) believed that poor performance on CPTS, for example, other than the AD/HD itself, can be caused by a misunderstanding of directions (e.g., especially in cases of AD/HD), inattentiveness, poor effort, depression, visual deficits, mental impairment, or environmental distractions.

Multisource or multidisciplinary assessment ensures that multiple sources or disciplines are involved in the assessment, diagnosis, and treatment of the disorder. It is implied, for example, that interdisciplinary collaboration and teamwork can lead to the development of an effective working relationship among those who are seeking to serve this individual (Barkley, 2005; Learner, 1989, 1993).

Multisource or multidisciplinary assessment can be obtained from the following sources: 1) the suspected child; 2) the parents; 3) the child's teachers; 4) the family physician; 5) the counselor (e.g., school, mental health, private practitioner); 6) classmates or peers; and 7) allied school personnel (e.g., school psychologist, learning disabilities specialist). The criterion for a good assessment is its authenticity and congruence from multiple sources that reflect the reality of the child's life (Wiggins, 1993). Barkley (2005) advocated that "multiple" members of an AD/HD assessment team can provide a solid foundation for the implementation of the treatment regimens.

Multisetting assessment is the direct observation of behavior obtained from natural settings (e.g., home, school or classroom, peer-group interactions, community). For example, Jill, a child displaying symptoms of AD/HD, might remain on the task of completing her math problems 20% of the time, while other girls in the same class attend to their math problems 80% of the time (e.g., during the same observation period). Meents (1989) reported that the diagnosis of AD/HD seems to rely little on sustained observations of the child or adolescent in various structured settings.

Counselors can use multiple gating as a sequential model for systematically applying the effectiveness of the multimethod, multisource, and multisetting approach to the assessment of AD/HD. Merrill (1994) explained multiple gating as a series of assessment and decision gates, through which a large population suspected to have the disorder is sequentially narrowed down to a small population of individuals that are likely to have the disorder (e.g., AD/HD). These individuals can then be gated into an appropriate treatment program. See Table 4.4 for more specific information on multiple gating.

Importantly, counselors who apply the multimethod, multisource, and multisetting approach to the assessment and diagnosis of AD/HD significantly increase the potential for a valid evaluation. Although this approach can be more challenging to the counselor, the potential reward of obtaining a diagnosis of AD/HD through the convergence or gating of diagnostic information is the opportunity to optimize the lives of children and adolescents with AD/HD.

TABLE 4.4 Multiple Gating in the Assessment of Attention-Deficit/Hyperactivity Disorder (AD/HD)

Teacher or Parent Complaint of Inattention, Hyperactivity, and/or Impulsivity

Gate 1

Teacher and Parent Ratings of the AD/HD Symptoms

Questions to be Addressed:

1. Does this child/adolescent have problems related to possible AD/HD?
2. Is further assessment of the AD/HD required?

Gate 2

Multimethod, Multisource, Multisetting Assessment of the AD/HD
Child Interview, Parent's Interview, Physician's Information, Teachers' Interviews, School Psychologist's Information, Learning Disabilities Specialist's Information, School Counselor's Information, Peer Group Information, Observations in Natural Settings, Review of School Grades/Records, Review of AD/HD Checklists/Rating Scales

Questions to be Addressed:

1. What is the extent and nature of the AD/HD–related problems?
2. What factors (e.g., neurobiological, environmental) maintain the problem behaviors?
3. What is the frequency, duration, and intensity of the problem behaviors?
4. In what settings do the antecedents of the AD/HD–related behaviors occur?

Gate 3

Interpretation of the Results
Number of AD/HD Symptoms Documented
Diagnosis of the AD/HD Subtype (DSM-IV)
Deviance from Age/Grade and Gender Norms
Age of Onset of AD/HD and Chronicity
Pervasiveness of AD/HD Symptoms Across Situations
Degree of Functional Impairment
Rule Out Masquerading Symptoms or Other Disorders

Questions to Be Addressed:

1. Does the child/adolescent exhibit a significant number of behavioral symptoms of AD/HD according to parent and teacher reports?
2. Does the child exhibit AD/HD symptoms at a frequency that is significantly greater than demonstrated by children of the same chronological age and gender?
3. At what age did the child begin demonstrating significant AD/HD-related behaviors and are these behaviors chronic and evident across many situations?
4. Is the child's functioning at school, at home, and with peers or social groups significantly impaired?
5. Are there other possible co-occurring problems (e.g., academic skill deficits, Oppositional Defiant behavior, Conduct Disorder, mood swings, depression) or other factors (e.g., teacher intolerance for active behaviors) that could account for or accompany the AD/HD?

TABLE 4.4   (continued)

Gate 4

Develop the Multidimensional Treatment Plan/Interventions

Based Upon:

Severity of the AD/HD Symptoms/Problems
Functional Analysis of Antecedent Events and Problematic Behaviors Exhibited
Presence of Accompanying or Co-Occurring Disorders
Response to a Prior or Trial Treatment
Community-Based Resources Available

Questions to Be Addressed:

1. What are the behavioral objectives (e.g., school/academic, social/emotional, familial)?
2. What are the AD/HD child's strengths and weaknesses?
3. What are the interventions or strategies available to optimize the treatment plan?
4. What additional resources (e.g., peer group) are available to address the AD/HD child or adolescent's problems?

Gate 5

Assessment and Follow-Up of the Multidimensional Treatment Plan/Interventions
Periodic Analysis and Synthesis of the Multidimensional Treatment Plan/Interventions
Periodic Revision or Adjustment of the Multidimensional Treatment Plan/Interventions

Questions to Be Addressed:

1. Has the Multidimensional Treatment Plan/Interventions (e.g., parent training, cognitive-behavioral training, social-skills training, self-esteem training, family counseling) led to valid or significant changes in behavior?
2. Are changes occurring (e.g., over time) in the target or problematic behaviors?
3. Have the problematic behaviors (e.g., over time) become more normalized?
4. Are the Multidimensional Treatment Plan/Interventions going to be ongoing or long-term in their implementation so as to enable optimum outcome?

Note: The number of people who pass through Gates 1 and 2 should be fairly small at this point. They are then assessed using more time-intensive procedures. These individuals are almost certainly considered to exhibit the disorder under study; these individuals are then often referred or gated into a program of treatment or interventions (Merrill, 1994).

Note: Adapted (and Questions to be Addressed) from *ADHD in the Schools: Assessment and Intervention Strategies* by G. J. DuPaul and G. Stoner, 1994, New York: Guilford Press. Copyright 1994 by Guilford Press. Adapted by permission.

COMORBIDITY OR CO-OCCURRING CONDITIONS

Counselors should note that many individuals diagnosed with one mental disorder also suffer from another (Sue, Sue, & Sue, 2000). For example, a child or adolescent diagnosed with AD/HD is likely to have other co-occurring disorders (i.e., comorbidity). See Table 4.5 for conditions that are frequently found in the research literature to be comorbid or co-occuring with AD/HD.

TABLE 4.5 Comorbid Conditions Often Associated with Attention-Deficit/Hyperactivity Disorder (AD/HD)

I. **Neuroanatomical/Neurochemical Abnormalities**

Neurobiological/neurochemical abnormalities (Anastopoulos & Barkley, 1991; Barkley, 1997b; Brown, 1994; Goodyear & Hynd, 1992; Nadeau, 1995; Plessen et al., 2006; Shaw et al., 2006; Quinn, 1997; Zemetkin et al., 1990)

Irregular metabolism (e.g., the metabolism of glucose and neurochemicals that fuel brain activity; Zemetkin et al., 1990)

Decreased brain metabolism and blood flow (e.g., in specific brain regions [striatal, frontal lobes]; Lou, Henriksen, & Bruhn, 1984; Zemetkin et al., 1990)

Immature/incomplete brain functions (e.g., within the cerebellum; Barkley, 1997b; Denckla, 1991)

Corpus collusum (e.g., this brain area was slightly but significantly smaller; Hynd, Semrud-Clikeman, Lorys, Novey, Eliopulos & Lyntinen (1991).

Decreased total brain volume (e.g., it was approximately 5% smaller in boys with AD/HD and mean right caudate volume slightly but significantly smaller; Castellanos et al., 1994)

Five percent smaller total cerebral volume (e.g., there was a significant loss of normal right left asymmetry in the caudate, smaller right global pallidus, smaller right anterior frontal region, smaller cerebellum, and reversal of lateral ventricular asymmetry; Castellanos et al., 1996)

Difficulty in maintaining attention (e.g., probably associated with anterior attention mechanisms in the right hemisphere; Goodyear & Hynd, 1992; Epstein, Conners, Erhardt, March, & Swanson, 1997)

The frontal lobes are smaller (e.g., where the anterior portion of the frontal lobes connect with the basal ganglia, particularly on the right side, lobes were statistically/significantly smaller; Rapoport, 1996)

Atypical frontal brain activation (Baving, Laucht, & Schmidt, 1999; Casey, Giedd, Vauss, Vaituzis, & Rapoport, 1992; Casey et al., 1997)

Tourette's Syndrome and chronic tic disorder (Pauls, Leckman, & Cohen, 1993; Alsobrook & Pauls, 1997)

II. **Psychoeducational/Psychosocial Conditions**

Motor coordination and sequencing (Barkley, 1997a, 2005; Barkley, DuPaul, & McMurray, 1990; Breen, 1989; Denkla & Rudel, 1978; Mariani & Barkley, 1997)

Working memory and mental computation (Barkley, 1997b; Mariani & Barkley, 1997; Zentall & Smith, 1993)

Planning and anticipation (Barkley, 1997b; Barkley, Guevremont, & Anastopoulos, 1992; Douglas, 1983; Grodzinsky & Diamond, 1992)

Verbal fluency and confrontational communication (Grodzinsky & Diamond, 1992; Zentall, 1988)

Allocation of effort (Douglas, 1983; Voelker, Carter, Sprague, Gdowski, & Lachar, 1989)

Application of organizational strategies (Hamlett, Pellegrini, & Conners, 1987; Voelker, Carter, Sprague, Gdowski, & Lachar, 1989; Zentall, 1988)

Internalization of self-directed speech (Barkley, 1996, 1997b; Berk & Potts, 1991; Copeland, 1979)

Adherence to restrictive instructions (Barkley, 1985; Danforth, Barkley, & Stokes, 1991; Roberts, 1990; Routh & Schroeder, 1976)

Self-regulation of emotional arousal (Barkley, 1997b; Cole, Zahrn-Waxler, & Smith, 1994; Douglas 1983; Hinshaw, Buhrmeister, & Heller, 1989)

Decreased levels of executive functioning (e.g., a low threshold for behavioral inhibition; Barkley, 1997a)

Anxiety disorders (Barkley, 2005; Klein, 1994; Tannock, 1994; Manassis & Monga, 2001; Pliszka, Carlson, & Swanson, 1999)

Conduct Disorder and Oppositional Defiant Disorder (Lahey et al., 2000; Loeber et al., 2000; Sanford et al., 1999; Speltz, McClellan, DeKlyen, & Jones, 1999)

Mood swings and/or depression (Barkley, 2005; Biederman, Faraone, & Lapey, 1992; Biederman, Newcorn, & Sprich, 1991; Pliszka, Carlson, & Swanson, 1999)

TABLE 4.5   (continued)

Family dysfunctions (Barkley, 1997a, 2005; Biederman, Faraone, & Lapey, 1992; O'Brien, 1992; Erk, 1997; Erk, 2000; Hinshaw et al., 2000)

Personality structure (Cotugno, 1995; Erk, 2000; Lufi & Parrish-Plass, 1995; Werry, 1995)

Learning disabilities (Barkley, 2005; Cantwell & Baker, 1992; Faraone et al., 1993; Pliszka, Carlson, & Swanson, 1999)

Reading disability/disorder (Barkley, 2005; Bonafina, Newcorn, McKay, Koda, & Halperin, 2000; Dykman & Ackerman, 1991; Willcutt, Pennington, & DeFries, 2000)

Academic underachievement (Barkley, 2005; Cantwell & Satterfield, 1992; Barkley, DuPaul, & McMurray, 1990; DuPaul & Stoner, 1994; Pliszka, Carlson, & Swanson, 1999)

Social dysfunctions (Barkley, 2005; Hinshaw, Zupan, Simmel, Nigg, & Melnick, 1997; Pfiffner & McBurnett, 1997; Whalen & Henker, 1991; Pliszka, Carlson, & Swanson, 1999)

Proneness to substance abuse and/or substance use disorders (Barkley, 2005; Chilcoat & Breslau, 1999, Mannuzza et al., 1991; Wilens, Biederman, Spencer, & Frances, 1994; Wilens & Biederman, 2006; Pliszka, Carlson, & Swanson, 1999)

Accident proneness (Barkley, 1996, 2005; Copeland & Love, 1991; Weiss & Hechtman, 1993)

Note: Research studies view comorbidity as a greater-than-chance association between two or more independent disorders. Comorbid or co-occurring conditions can be unique to individual cases of AD/HD. These additional areas must be taken into account for therapeutic results to be attained and/or optimized. These comorbid conditions should not be considered as representative of each case of AD/HD or exhaustive of the associated conditions that may be present.

Barkley (2005) and Goldstein and Goldstein (1998) cautioned counselors that the co-occurring conditions in AD/HD are often overlooked. The counselor should not think that co-occurring conditions are temporary and will dissipate when treatment is undertaken. It is more practical to think that comorbidity can remain within the constellation of difficulties that the individual will experience, perhaps to some degree, across the lifespan. A large-scale survey of comorbidity found that the rate of comorbidity was high; for example, 79% of those with one disorder also had another disorder (see Kessler et al., 1994).

Counselors should remember that comorbid disorders in children and adolescents with AD/HD are often predominantly silent or invisible (e.g., except for Tourette's Syndrome; Barkley, 2005). This is especially true when contrasted to the loud, noisy symptoms and problems that are typically "exhibited" by many children with AD/HD. All the while, these comorbid conditions are capable of taking a "heavy toll" (e.g., due to their often remaining undiagnosed and subsequently untreated). For example, considerable comorbidity or co-occurrence of AD/HD with Oppositional Defiant Disorder, Conduct Disorder, mood swings, difficult temperament, anxiety disorders, specific learning disabilities, substance use disorders, and depression have been sufficiently documented (Biederman, Newcorn, & Sprich, 1991; Barkley, 2005; Goldstein, 1999; Shaywitz & Shaywitz, 1988; Wilens & Biederman, 2006; Zemetkin & Ernst, 1999).

For example, areas that might not routinely be considered comorbid in cases of AD/HD are low or depreciated self-esteem, social or peer-group dysfunctioning (e.g., social isolation), and possible suicidal ideation. The clinical literature indicates that in many individuals with AD/HD, there was a predisposition to alcohol and substance abuse above and beyond what existed in the population unaffected by AD/HD (Barkley, 2005). Currently, there is increasing research interest in examining AD/HD as an "antecedent" disorder to subsequent substance use disorders (SUDs); moreover, AD/HD is associated with greater SUD severity and chronicity (Wilens & Biederman, 2006). It is important for the counselor to remember that these areas or comorbid conditions are integral to the individual's functioning and cannot go uninvestigated.

The presence, patterns, and influence of comorbidity apparent in many individuals with AD/HD have provided counselors with a better understanding of and appreciation for the accompanying neurobehavioral dysfunctions that these clients can experience. Therefore, counselors should not underestimate the often deleterious effects that co-occurring conditions can have on the child or adolescent's life. Moreover, counselors should not conceptualize co-occurring disorders as alternate causes for the AD/HD or that the coexisting disorders are solely responsible for the child's impaired attention. It is essential that in cases of AD/HD, appropriate assessment for co-occurring conditions take place. No evaluation for AD/HD can be complete without adequate screening or assessment for possible comorbidity (Brown, 1994; Ollendick & King, 1994). It is upon the multiple pillars of assessment that practice or treatment leads to the best outcomes.

IMPLICATIONS FOR PRACTICE/TREATMENT

The Collaborative Multimodal Treatment Study of Children With Attention-Deficit/Hyperactivity Disorder (MTA Study) provides counselors with a convincing rationale for the interventions or treatments (e.g., parent training and counseling, teacher education, individual counseling, group counseling, behavioral interventions, self-esteem education, social-skills education, family counseling) discussed later. In the MTA Study, counselors are presented with an overview of the largest and most comprehensive clinical research study (i.e., empirically supported/evidence-based treatment), ever undertaken in the history of the United States. It was accomplished on behalf of one group of children, those diagnosed with AD/HD.

Treatment Outcome Research: The Collaborative Multimodal Treatment Study of Children with Attention-Deficit/Hyperactivity Disorder (MTA Study)

The MTA Study constituted a landmark in the history of treatment research in child psychopathology (see Hinshaw et al., 2000; Wells et al., 2000a; and Wells et al., 2000b for an extensive review of treatment outcome for the study). It was the largest single study of its kind ever undertaken for one clinical disorder (e.g., AD/HD) (Barkley, 2000a). Because the answers to such questions can be pursued only through large-scale efforts that generate sufficient sample sizes for powerful tests of *treatment effectiveness* (e.g., so that treatment outcomes can be more properly compared and evaluated), the National Institute of Mental Health (NIMH) launched a collaborative multisite (N = 6) clinical trial of Multimodal Treatment of children diagnosed with AD/HD. The NIMH-MTA Study has been in the field since 1992. Between 1992 and 1994, 579 children (aged 7–9 years, 11 months) were recruited at participating sites in the United States and one in Canada (Montreal). All the children had primary diagnoses of AD/HD, Combined Type, using *DSM-IV* (APA, 1994) criteria.

In addition, comorbid or co-occurring aggressive-spectrum disorders (e.g., Oppositional Defiant Disorder [ODD], Conduct Disorder [CD]), anxiety disorders, and affective disorders) occurred in the MTA sample at these respective prevalence rates—54%, 34%, and 4%. The subjects in the sample were 61% Caucasian, 20% African American, and 8% Hispanic; males constituted 80% and females 20% of the sample.

Children were randomly assigned to one of four experimental groups: (1) an intensive, multifaceted behavior therapy program (BEH) comprised of three integrated components (Parent Training, School Intervention, and Child Treatment anchored in a Summer Treatment Program)—this program can be referred to as "psychosocial treatment" because of its largely behavioral procedures; (2) a dose-adjusted and carefully monitored medication-management program consisting of methylphenidate and other stimulants (MED-MGT); (3) a careful and well-integrated combination of the preceding two (COMB); and (4) a community comparison group (CC). The CC group allowed for a comparison of the three intensive manual-based treatments to the treatment delivered in the community (e.g., local community care resources). Treatment occurred over 14 months, and assessments were taken at baselines of 3, 9, and 14 months.

The global effects of the treatment for the MTA Study of BEH, MED, COMB, and CC groups are summarized below. Keep in mind that the MTA Study was indeed large; many of the variables contained in the study are yet to be fully scrutinized for their specific roles. Nonetheless, here are some of the essential findings gleaned from the study.

First, there were generally superior effects for COMB and MED-MGT, compared to BEH or CC, on the primary characteristics of AD/HD, including some comorbid conditions. This is not unexpected because an array of interventions (e.g., a multidimensional approach) to treatment has long been advocated in the management of this disorder (Barkley, 1995, 2005; Erk, 1997, 2000).

Second, the BEH or psychosocial treatment approach alone did produce some effects despite its limitation. The amount of gain here probably occurred because the study was heavily weighted toward the BEH or psychosocial treatment approach. However, Barkley (2000b) questioned whether such an extensive BEH program could be justified (e.g., now or ever) in homes and schools (e.g., due to its extensive scale). Relevant to the gains made in this approach, Barkley (2000b) speculated that the modest differences found between the BEH and CC groups in the MTA Study might be more due to information and therapist attention (e.g., these could have accounted for the small differences in favor of the BEH group). For example, numerous parent-education and behavioral-training programs for parents with children diagnosed with AD/HD are already in existence and might obtain much the same results when properly employed. The BEH approach to treatment means that parents are becoming involved in parent education and training on AD/HD, and they are learning and actively practicing a range of behavioral interventions designed to benefit the family and the child.

Third, the MED component, which entails no skill training for parents or teachers, achieved equal or superior effects to BEH across nearly all of the outcome domains (e.g., parent–child relations, familial and school functioning) examined in the study (Barkley, 2000b). The MTA Study coupled with the incoming lines of scientific and medical information from medical imaging studies (e.g., PET scans, the Human Genome Project) should further serve to prompt parents and counselors to be increasingly receptive to MED-MGT as one of the key players for obtaining improved therapeutic results (e.g., especially where the AD/HD is moderate to severe).

Fourth, only in COMB treatment, not in BEH alone, were there the greatest reductions in negative-ineffective discipline. This finding should be a most vital consideration when planning treatment options. For example, success for COMB treatment was evident for important school-related outcomes (e.g., reduction in teacher-reported disruptive behavior). Moreover, this finding would appear to be related to reductions in negative and ineffective parenting practices in the home (e.g., reciprocal or parent–child interactions; Erk, 1997). Therefore, the home and school environments benefited reciprocally from the COMB treatment.

Fifth, when comorbid symptomatology (e.g., ODD, CD) and functional skills (e.g., academic and social skills) were considered, the differences among all the treatment groups were smaller. For example, only the COMB treatment was consistently superior to CC when the comorbid conditions were identified. Remember that comorbid symptomatology can be a major disrupter to any treatment. What this finding reinforces, for example, is the need for careful assessment of comorbid conditions and that these conditions deserve as much attention (e.g., treatment) as the AD/HD itself. Unfortunately for the child, if the comorbid conditions remain undiagnosed and untreated, the comorbid conditions are often mistakenly identified as the primary problems. This can lead to the AD/HD remaining at the core of the person's difficulties while continuing as undiagnosed and untreated (Erk, 1997, 2000).

Sixth, COMB significantly outperformed MED-MGT with a small-to-moderate effect size (Hinshaw et al., 2000). This should not be an entirely surprising result; MED-MGT alone is not considered a prudent approach when it is used in isolation. Barkley (1995, 2005) recommended that parents should not invest in a MED-MGT–only treatment plan. This is because with a MED-MGT–only plan, the child is obviously deprived of opportunities to learn or acquire an improved behavioral repertoire (e.g., social and academic skills, enhanced self-esteem).

Seventh, although overall findings were consistent for boys versus girls, for children with and without prior medication treatment, and subjects with and without disruptive comorbidity, two baseline variables (e.g., comorbidity with anxiety disorder and socioeconomic status) had the effect of moderating some treatment outcomes.

A major limitation of the MTA Study may be the exclusive use of the AD/HD Combined Subtype. It was presumed in the study that hyperactivity, impulsivity, and inattention components are incorporated into the Combined Subtype. However, for example, in the Inattentive Subtype different findings and implications for treatment might be identified for children who are diagnosed with this specific subtype (see Erk, 2000). Future studies will need to address issues such as this one (e.g., specific subtypes), gender differences, and the comorbidities that most often are co-occurring in each gender. The specific effects of a culture and how the AD/HD manifests itself in different cultural groups will also require more information and study.

Essential Questions And Answers From The MTA Study

Concisely, what are the major findings of this study so far? The MTA results indicate that **long-term combination treatments** as well as **medication-management alone** are both significantly superior to intensive behavioral treatments and routine community treatments in reducing AD/HD symptoms. The study also shows that these differential benefits extend as long as 14 months. In other areas of functioning (specifically, anxiety symptoms, academic performance, oppositionality, parent–child relations, and social skills), the combined treatment approach was consistently superior to routine community care, whereas the single treatments (medication-only or behavioral treatment-only) were not. In addition to the advantages provided by the combined treatment for several outcomes, this form of treatment allowed children to be successfully treated over the course of the study with some what lower doses of medication, compared to the medication-only group. These same findings were replicated across all six research sites, despite substantial differences among sites in their samples' sociodemographic characteristics. Therefore, the study's overall results appear to be applicable and can be generalized to a wide range of children and families in need of treatment services for AD/HD.

Given the effectiveness of medication management, what is the role and need for behavioral therapy? Several decades of research have amply demonstrated that behavioral therapies are quite effective in treating AD/HD. What the MTA Study has demonstrated is that on average, carefully monitored medication management with monthly follow-up is more effective than intensive behavioral treatment alone for AD/HD symptoms, for periods lasting as long as 14 months. All children tended to improve over the course of the study, but they differed in the relative amount of improvement, for example, with the carefully done medication management approaches generally showing the greatest improvement. Nonetheless, children's responses varied enormously, and some children clearly did very well in each of the treatment groups. For some outcomes that are important in the daily functioning of these children (e.g., academic performance, familial relations), the **combination of behavioral therapy and medication** was necessary to produce improvements better than community care. Of note, families and teachers reported some what higher levels of consumer satisfaction for those treatments that included the behavioral therapy components. Therefore, medication alone is not necessarily the best treatment for every child, and families often need to pursue other treatments, either alone or in combination with medication.

Finally, the MTA Study and its employment of a multimodal treatment model paves the way for further research and treatment appropriate for children diagnosed with AD/HD. For example, earlier clinical research (e.g., using parent behavioral training with medication management) for children with AD/HD has yielded positive results. Barkley (2000a) believed that this was strongly reinforced by findings contained in the MTA Study. For professionals who work with these children, there is certainly much in the MTA Study that is positive and informative. Undoubtedly, more clinical results will emanate from this research for years to come. The MTA Study should be clinically, scientifically, and educationally examined for every drop of information it can eventually yield on AD/HD and its management. The MTA Study was mammoth and unparalleled in the field of child treatment. For this reason, it can be expected to take years, if not decades, to tease out all the data that it has to offer researchers and professional practitioners (e.g., mental health and school counselors, psychologists, physicians, educators). Additionally, the children involved in this study will be tracked to document and evaluate long-term outcomes.

RECOMMENDED INTERVENTIONS/TREATMENTS

Counselors recognize that an array of interventions or treatments are often necessitated by the effects AD/HD can have on the lives of children. AD/HD typically arises during the early childhood years and can be pervasive, cross-situational, and typically chronic in nature (Erk, 1999, 2000). Present scientific and/or medical knowledge strongly indicates that biological predisposition and environmental conditions acting in concert seem to play key roles in how severe or chronic the AD/HD symptoms become.

If significant improvements in the child's or adolescent's adjustment (e.g., home, school, community) are to be obtained, the large number of symptoms directly associated with AD/HD require treatment to be multidisciplinary and/or multidimensional (Barkley, 1996, 1997b; Erk, 1999, 2000). Clinical results suggest that an "individualized" program of combined treatment regimens continued for extended time periods (e.g., months to years) has the potential for producing significant improvements (Barkley, 1997b). Across the lifespan, many individuals with AD/HD will require periodic reintervention or ongoing interventions that focus on the specific problematic behaviors that are occurring in their lives. Counselors need to convey this treatment focus to parents and teachers who work with these children.

Counselors won't utilize each intervention in every case of AD/HD. For example, each child or adolescent with AD/HD can be expected to manifest a unique pattern of symptoms and problematic behaviors. The unique vulnerabilities and co-occurring conditions that are experienced by many children with AD/HD will often necessitate specific interventions in key areas.

I recommend that the counselor seek to tailor the treatments or interventions to the specific type of AD/HD and the particular problems that the child or adolescent is currently experiencing. Optimal outcomes are enhanced when interventions are used in consultation and coordination with the child, the parents, and the school personnel. Additionally, children and adolescents with AD/HD are protected by federal and state statutes requiring that appropriate treatment or services be designed and implemented (Erk, 1999).

Selection and implementation of the appropriate interventions or treatments orginates with the counselor (e.g., based on the needs of the client). The counselor might need to do more research or seek out more specific information from the AD/HD literature base (e.g., for the actual design and implementation of specific interventions or treatments). There is a sweeping AD/HD literature base on interventions or treatments readily available to counselors who need more assistance (see Barkley, 2005; Erk, 1997, 1999, 2000; Learner, Lowenthal, & Learner, 1995; Teeter, 2000).

Counselors should not consider the interventions or treatments discussed here to be exhaustive of what might be needed to serve clients with AD/HD. The following sections posit interventions or treatments for AD/HD that are often recommended in the research literature (e.g., empirically supported).

Parent Training and Counseling

Kazdin (1997) reported that there was extensive research and positive results for parent training and counseling in behavior modification. Parent training can be effective in reducing activity level, conflict, and anger intensity and in increasing on-task behavior in children with AD/HD (Fiore, Becker, & Nero, 1993). Parent training and counseling is the second most widely used intervention next to medication for children and adolescents with AD/HD (Erk, 1997). It has long been recognized that increased parental competence has a positive effect on the behavior of children with AD/HD (Goldstein & Goldstein, 1998). Parents should receive training and counseling to understand that managing the child or adolescent's AD/HD problems at home requires knowledge about the disorder and its effects (Goldstein, 1999). Parent training and counseling on AD/HD can show positive results (e.g., increased compliance with family rules); it empowers the parents to take charge of the disorder (Barkley, 1995). Parent training and counseling may be effective particularly in response to the specific needs of young children with AD/HD during the preschool and kindergarten period (e.g., when noncompliance can be acute and parental stress is often at a peak) (Pisterman, McGrath, Firestone, & Goodman, 1989).

Parent training and counseling can generally be delivered together and completed in an 8- to 12-session cognitive-behavioral treatment program that is used either with individual families or with several families in a group-therapy format (Anastopoulos, Smith, & Wien, 1998). The main therapeutic objective for parents with children or adolescents with AD/HD is to learn methods or techniques of managing and coping with this ongoing learning and behavioral disability (Shaywitz & Shaywitz, 1992). Generally, parent education and counseling that is based on the Anastopoulos, Smith, and Wien (1998) model can be delivered in 12 sessions or fewer in either an individual or multifamily format. There is no clinical evidence that one intervention or approach (e.g., individual versus multifamily) is superior. Therefore, the counselor should carefully consider and probably comply with the parents' preference (Erk, 1997).

Anastopoulos, Smith, and Wien (1998) believed that counselors should not have a specific or inflexible number of parent-training and counseling sessions in mind. Rather, the counselor should guide the parents through education and counseling, taking as many sessions as necessary to bring about the desired therapeutic change. Based on the Anastopoulos, Smith, and Wien (1998) model, the sessions should typically include the following:

Step 1: Why Children with AD/HD Misbehave. For example, teaching parents how the AD/HD is connected to the child's or adolescent's behavior and that it can be rectified in their families.

Step 2: Pay Attention. For example, teaching parents positive attending and ignoring skills, adopting a positive parenting style in the face of negative or manipulative behavior, and having special time set aside for positive parent–child interaction.

Step 3: Increasing Compliance and Independent Play. For example, teaching parents how to pay attention and reinforce appropriate independent play and compliance.

Step 4: When Praise Is Not Enough, There Is the Use of Poker Chips and Points. For example, teaching parents how to establish and use a home token system.

Step 5: Step 5: Time Out and Other Disciplinary Methods. For example, teaching parents to use time out with younger children and the mechanics of a response-cost system.

Step 6: Extending Time Out to Other Misbehavior. For example, resolving for parents any problems they might have encountered in using time out and cost-response strategies.

Step 7: Anticipating Problems and Managing Children in Public Places. For example, teaching parents how to anticipate problems that can occur in public situations, how to provide rules in advance of public outings, and how to establish plans of action if these become needed.

Step 8: Improving School Behavior from Home Using a Daily School Behavior Report Card. For example, teaching parents how valuable it is for them to work as collaboratively and cooperatively with school personnel as possible.

Step 9: Handling Future Behavior Problems. For example, teaching parents to review and fine-tune all aspects of the program so that it can serve them in response to future behavior problems that arise.

Step 10: Booster Session and Follow-Up Meetings. For example, mutually scheduling any needed booster sessions and follow-up meetings for the parents or families.

This is a broad overview of the steps involved in the parent-training and counseling program formulated by these researchers. A detailed explanation of this program can be found in Barkley (2005).

Goldstein (1999) and Barkley (1997b) believed that the following topics related to "parenting" could be helpful to the parent-training and counseling process.

1. Parents must become educated consumers (e.g., they must understand AD/HD thoroughly because it can be expected to affect their child or adolescent across his or her lifespan).

2. Parents must develop an understanding of and distinguish between problems of incompetence (e.g., nonpurposeful problems resulting from the AD/HD) and problems of noncompliance (e.g., purposeful problems that occur when the child or adolescent does not wish to do as he or she is directed).

3. Parents must be taught to tell their child or adolescent specifically what to do in a clear, concise, and direct way. (e.g., long, drawn-out directions, speeches, or lectures are not going to produce the desired results).

4. Parents must be instructed to keep a balance between positive and negative reinforcement and avoid reliance on the over-use of tangible or material reinforcers.

5. Parents must recognize that a common mistake is to think that the child or adolescent will maintain compliance strictly on his or her own initiative.

6. Parents must be helped to understand the forces at school or in the community that often affect the child or adolescent (e.g., avoiding placing the child or adolescent in situations that are quite likely to exacerbate the AD/HD problems).

7. Parents must be made aware that the family unit is going to experience substantially more stress and that the child's behavior has the potential to seriously disrupt family life (e.g., some families have the feeling that the problems are never going to end).

8. Parents must recognize that their relationship with their child or adolescent is likely to be strained much of the time (e.g., parents must take extra time to balance their thinking and actions with developing and maintaining a positive relationship).

In addition, the parents of a child or adolescent with AD/HD can be at high risk for codependence. For example, caring parents naturally feel the distress of their child who is having these severe problems. Excessive identification with the child's problems or pain is unhealthy. Parents who are consumed by caring and protection for their child may be attempting to shield themselves from the realities that are often connected to the disorder. Parents may need to receive counseling to change their perspective and make a distinction between the needs of their child and their own (Erk, 1997).

Information on the efficacy for parent training and counseling for AD/HD comes from studies in which it is one form of intervention combined with other forms of treatment. Moreover, because so few clinical studies have been conducted to date, it would be premature to discount the potential therapeutic benefits that parent training and counseling can deliver in a multidisciplinary and/or multidimensional package (Anastopolous, Smith, & Wien, 1998). When parent training and counseling is neglected, for example, the parents have no accurate idea about the complications that are occurring every day in their lives.

It is vital for parents or family members to understand that AD/HD is considered a neurobiological or neurobehavioral disorder. The disorder is not a failure of parenting or a reflection on their family. For example, the child's AD/HD problematic behaviors are not considered to be willful and deliberately delivered. The disruptive behaviors are not a way of getting even with their family or teachers for what may have transpired. Parents are usually relieved to know that although poor or distressed parental or teacher reactions to the AD/HD can exacerbate the disorder, they are not considered to be the root cause for the child's condition.

Parent training and counseling on the disorder can lead parents to be consistent, predictable, and genuinely supportive of their child or adolescent in daily interactions. Research has suggested that for children with AD/HD, the relationships developed with parents constitute a significant predictor for future outcomes (Barkley, 2005; Goldstein, 1999). Another important advantage for parent training and counseling is that it can be used to target not only the AD/HD, but also the comorbid conditions (e.g., Oppositional Defiant Disorder, Conduct Disorder) that may also be present.

Teacher Education

Teachers or educators have often been without the information that they need to work more effectively with students who have AD/HD. Educating teachers on the academic, behavioral, and personal-social problems that students with AD/HD often exhibit in their classrooms is crucial for improving the lives of these students. It can also serve to maximize the treatment or interventions used in their classrooms (e.g., to target areas of deficient academic or social functioning and compliance). Moreover, teacher education or training on AD/HD might include the use of books, workbooks, and videotapes that specifically address what we know about the disorder and how to treat it at school. (See Fowler, 1992; Reif, 1993; Lucker & Malloy, 1995; Teeter, 2000).

Teachers who are educated on the problematic behaviors of the child or adolescent with AD/HD can often serve as a buffer to the negative school experiences and personal-social struggles that occur daily in the lives of these students. Counselors, for example, are increasingly being asked by schools to be active in providing information on AD/HD. One important way to initiate this process is to educate and train teachers about AD/HD in an in-service or workshop format. Erk (1999) recommended that an in-service or workshop for teachers should minimally address the following areas: 1) what the federal and/or state laws or statutes on AH/HD require for their school or in their classrooms (e.g., accommodations, treatments); 2) what an accommodation plan for the child with AD/HD should include or address; 3) what a treatment plan for students with AD/HD should include or address (e.g., the behavioral interventions or classroom-management strategies required to enhance their academic success); and 4) who the school personnel are (e.g., superintendent, principal, district supervisors, teachers or educators, counselors) responsible for developing, implementing, monitoring, and readjusting the accommodations and/or treatment plan for the child or adolescent with AD/HD.

When teachers or educators who work with children and adolescents with AD/HD receive in-service education or training on the needs of these children, they can circumvent many difficulties for AD/HD children and their families. School then becomes a more reinforcing environment for the child or adolescent who has AD/HD. Moreover, teachers who have enjoyed success (e.g., academically, socially) in reaching and teaching the child or adolescent with AD/HD can also serve as a valuable resource to other teachers and parents.

A review of the classroom research by Barkley (1997b, 2005), Goldstein (1999), and Goldstein & Goldstein (1998) dealing with children and adolescents with AD/HD has led to a number of important conclusions:

1. Environmental and academic task modifications are critical for classroom success for the child or adolescent with AD/HD. Teachers who are reluctant to make accommodations should be counseled about how these efforts will ultimately make improvements in their classrooms.

2. The classroom itself must be organized and structured with clear rules and predictable schedules. Some students may need the rules and their daily schedules attached to a corner of the desk.

3. Reinforcers or rewards for success (e.g., for agreed-upon levels of task completion or achievement) must be dispensed with immediacy. Students with AD/HD must receive reinforcers for the work that they do complete, even if it is not the complete task. Making reinforcers contingent upon completing the whole task is not viable for these children.

4. An agreed-upon response-cost program between the teacher and student is recommended as part of every classroom (see Teeter, 2000).

5. Positive feedback delivered by teachers must be conducted in each classroom every day. Teachers who work to develop positive relationships with these students can expect to have more compliance and success.

6. Minor disruptions or disturbances in the classroom (e.g., those that do not actually disrupt others) should be ignored. Teachers should resist allowing students to report disruptions or disturbances because they think that the student with AD/HD needs to be pointed out or disciplined.

7. Academic tasks must be made as interesting or stimulating as possible, and they need to have valuable payoffs. Boring or repetitive tasks will take these students quickly off-task and in the direction of other behaviors.

8. Academic materials or work must be carefully matched to the attention span and ability level of the child. The use of color or interesting presentations will enhance motivation for these students.

9. Transition times during the day (e.g., hallway, recess, bathroom, assembly, going to the bus) have to be closely monitored.

10. Teachers and parents must devise channels or ways to remain in close communication throughout the school year (e.g., especially in the lower school grades). Regular or daily progress reports should be mutually arranged by the teachers and parents.

11. Teacher expectations must be adjusted to remain in line with the child's behavioral and academic levels. Excessive expectations can disrupt what the student is capable of delivering at that time.

12. Teachers must be educated on how to develop a repertoire of appropriate interventions to manage the AD/HD problems as effectively as possible. Teachers who have the benefit of behavioral classroom training or information on these specific areas are doing what is required for students with AD/HD to experience success (e.g., academically, socially) in their classrooms (Barkley, 2005; Teeter, 2000).

Additionally, teachers should share information on interventions that are working and for revising those presently in place (e.g., so that they can better meet the changing needs of these students). Zentall (1995), for example, suggested that students who have AD/HD need to be approached with an **active learning style** (e.g., these children often need to move, respond, question, choose, debate, inquire, and even provoke in order to learn). These characteristics should not be alarming to teachers. Rather, they can be keys to teachers and classrooms working to benefit these students and their learning styles. Thus, children with AD/HD cannot be expected to do well in sedentary or over-regulated classroom situations (Goldstein, 1999).

Individual Counseling

Counselors (e.g., school, mental health, private practice) should acknowledge at the beginning of counseling that many children and adolescents with AD/HD often represent a formidable challenge. At the onset of counseling, many children and adolescents with AD/HD engage in denial of their condition, frequently see their problems as not their own, and repeatedly blame parents, teachers, and peers for their problems or difficulties. For example, a child or adolescent maintaining a negative attitude or an ongoing grudge about the way things have gone in life is not atypical. Moreover, years of frustration, rejection, and failure have propelled many children and adolescents with AD/HD into a fantasy world or private existence (e.g., where they pretend that the world cannot reach or hurt them). Where the disorder has taken a heavy toll on the child or adolescent, this fantasy world could be how the child has chosen to deal with repeated discouragement.

The child or adolescent with AD/HD can experience or undergo pressures and stresses (e.g., academic, social, familial) that are far outside the realm of normal developmental problems (Hosie & Erk, 1993). The best practice for counselors working with children and adolescents with AD/HD may be to work empathetically with the many difficulties and pressures that they encounter. For example, the counselor's personal style (e.g., self-confidence, expectations for improvement, flexibility, lack of negative judgments, accurate empathy) may serve as an ongoing therapeutic model for children and adolescents with AD/HD. It is often recommended that counselors seek to take an individual approach with these clients. This is because an individual approach to counseling is often better positioned to address personal issues (Erk, 2000).

Resnick (2000) recommended that individual counseling with children and adolescents who have AD/HD can be more effective when the counselor and client create a **treatment menu**. The treatment menu often needs to include assistance with multiple personal issues. For example, this assistance can include 1) coming to better understand the diagnosis and how it can positively affect the child's life; 2) dealing with the initial frustration or anger over the diagnosis; 3) dealing with stress or stressors that can profoundly exacerbate the AD/HD symptoms (e.g., relieving stress is almost always a part of counseling); 4) dealing with lost opportunities and relationships; and 5) dealing with the grief and suffering that might have taken place in their lives. Family relationships and school concerns are collateral and often have to be included as well.

Where a diagnosis of co-occurring conditions such as anxiety disorders or depression are present, these must be addressed concurrently with the AD/HD.

Counselors should be cognizant that although counseling can be enormously helpful and useful to children and adolescents with AD/HD, it has the potential to be somewhat arduous to conduct. When conducting individual counseling, Resnick (2000) advised counselors to keep these important factors in mind. First, the counselor must be cognizant that the peculiarities associated with the AD/HD symptomatology cluster will result in some deviation from the traditional counselor–client relationship. For example, nondirective counseling is not in harmony with the root causes for this neurobiological and/or neurobehavioral disorder. Rather, the counselor should expect to take the lead in developing and managing the counseling sessions. For example, children and adolescents with AD/HD will experience more than average difficulty with sequencing and/or follow-through on the issues that often confront them. It is not unusual for follow-through on agreed-upon strategies or homework assignments to be lacking or only partially completed. The counselor should explain to the client that habit change and learning new strategies require ongoing practice (e.g., they are not one-trial learning experiences). This might help to keep them practicing until the skill becomes a natural part of their daily routines. It is also not unusual for many of these clients to forget or be late for counseling sessions. For example, missing appointments, forgetting what day the appointment was on, or being late to the session and wanting to see the counselor anyway are not atypical. Counselors should be ready to devise ways that assist the client with better time-management (e.g., making a written list of things to do each day, keeping a small notebook with them for important obligations). Although this might seem to be extraordinary effort for both parties, it is often intertwined with what might need to be done for many of these clients who are seeking counseling assistance.

Second, the counselor must handle problem behaviors associated with AD/HD symptomatology carefully. For example, counselors should not infer that there are transference issues, latent hostilities, personality problems, or passive-aggressive tendencies in these children. This is because the core of their symptoms and problems is often beyond their volition. To interpret or refer to their behaviors as psychologically based might significantly contribute to impairment of the therapeutic alliance and contribute further to the child's or adolescent's negative self-perception. Many of these children and adolescents with AD/HD have histories of authority figures telling them that they were psychologically abnormal.

Third, individual counseling models or the counseling process typically relies on the client's verbal and affective flow. Sessions like this are relatively unstructured and unguided, but they are usually productive with normally functioning clients. This counseling approach, however, tends to be ineffective with children and adolescents who have AD/HD. Counseling sessions that depend on a free flow of voluntary verbal exchanges cannot be relied on to be viable for children and adolescents with AD/HD. For example, the lack of structure and continuity in counseling sessions with these children tends to be counterproductive. Counseling for children and adolescents with AD/HD seems to respond best to an active and pragmatic approach. Most children and adolescents with AD/HD, for example, can benefit from organizers, prompts, and reminders provided by the counselor. In other words, counseling for these children needs structure and support systems. For example, sometimes it can be helpful for the client to keep a counseling notebook. The client can enter brief notes at the conclusion of each session. The counselor and client can review these notes at the conclusion of each session or at the beginning of the next session. In this way, the client can have some indication of what has been accomplished and the progress that has taken place with each counseling session. Counselors may also provide their clients with appropriate homework assignments.

Fourth, and last, for the client's well-being, the counselor often will need to be proactive in meeting with the client. Calling the client's home as a reminder to attend the scheduled session or having the teacher remind the student to come to the counselor's office is advised. Counselors should consider using telephone and/or e-mail contacts. These are becoming more accepted in the counseling profession (e.g., especially when some parents and teachers have almost daily concerns about the child's AD/HD behaviors). Counseling sessions might then be better planned, made more timely, and designed around many of the issues or problems that are currently revolving around the lives of these children. Parents, for example, often report that just knowing that the counselor understands what AD/HD can do to the lives of family members means a great deal. Although this is extending the counselor–client interaction beyond the confines of the office, it could be an effective way of working with these clients (e.g., especially at the start of counseling and as monitoring strategy).

Counselors need to consider that they will need to make modifications or adjustments to the traditional form of individual counseling or therapy (e.g., content and process). This can enhance counseling effectiveness with individuals who have AD/HD. Counselors not only have the opportunity to help individuals with AD/HD take charge of their AD/HD problems, but also to help instill optimism and encouragement that they can have better, happier, and more productive lives (Resnick, 2000).

Due to the numerous problematic behaviors (e.g., social dysfunctions, low academic achievement, low self-esteem) that children and adolescents with AD/HD often struggle with in the course of their young lives, counseling remains a key intervention that should not be omitted. It is important for counselors to emphasize and make explicit the positive qualities and traits the child or adolescent possesses. Individual counseling aimed at easing the negative messages from parents, teachers, and peers and replacing them with positive and optimistic messages can be of substantial benefit to children and adolescents with AD/HD (Murphy, 1998).

Group Counseling

Although there is a dearth of clinical studies or literature on group counseling or therapy with children and adolescents who have AD/HD, the efficacy of group therapy seems potentially useful for this population (Murphy, 1998). In a group approach, children or adolescents can learn a great deal from each other, feel more normal or accepted for who they are, feel less isolated, and feel less alone. Murphy (1998) described one client participating in group counseling who spoke up at the onset about not wanting to take medication for the AD/HD. After interacting with fellow group members for a few sessions and getting their input on taking medication, the individual was influenced to try the medication. This was something the counselor was not able to accomplish in individual counseling with this client. In group counseling, hearing that others out there are having similar problems and how they have learned to cope with their AD/HD symptoms provides a laboratory for sharing, support, and learning.

It is recommended that group counseling be time-limited and have a semi-structured or structured format. Goals or themes should be outlined for each session. Each session should contain didactic instruction, with some open-ended discussion allowed. Sessions that are unplanned, or where any topic is open for discussion, soon lead to diffusion and disorganization. Among group topics that can often work best are the importance of organizational skills, medication issues, interpersonal skills, anger control, stress-reduction activities, and sharing with the group successes in coping with the disorder (Murphy, 1998).

Of course, the counselor should carefully screen group membership; a workable size (e.g., no more than 10; Murphy, 1998) is important. For some groups, the counselor might need to construct membership with consideration for multicultural and gender issues, age or developmental levels, comorbidities, the severity of the AD/HD itself, and privacy concerns. Remember, for example, that group counseling can also be an important adjunct to other interventions or treatments that are put in place. Clients and their parents should be advised that Children and Adults with Attention-Deficit Disorder (CHADD) may offer groups in the area, and these are another avenue for support and education.

Behavioral Interventions

Counselors are advised that behavioral-intervention strategies and techniques for the toddler/preschool stage, middle-childhood stage, and adolescent stage that focus on the child in only one stage are rarely effective when the child moves into another stage of development. It is important for the counselor to keep in mind that although interventions or techniques initiated in the early childhood stage might have addressed the challenges of the child with AD/HD at that stage, these same interventions rarely produce effects that prevent or eliminate problems in middle childhood or adolescence (Teeter, 2000). Behavioral interventions that focus solely on the child or adolescent in isolation from other interventions or treatments (e.g., such as those contained in the treatment section of this chapter) are rarely effective. When behavioral interventions are appropriately designed and adjusted for use in the different developmental stages and settings (e.g., home, school), and combinations of interventions are employed, there can be marked improvement in the management of the AD/HD (Teeter, 2000).

Erk (1999) recommended that behavioral interventions or strategies should permit the counselor (working in concert with the child or adolescent) to accomplish the following objectives: 1) to create possibilities for new patterns of thought and behaviors to evolve or to become a part of their behavioral repertoire; 2) to create or seek to provide opportunities for repeated practice in the areas where improved behavioral performance is desired; and 3) to potentially create reinforcing effects (e.g., at school or in the home) that should accumulate and provide the encouragement or impetus for adopting more satisfying or rewarding styles of behavior.

Pfiffner and Barkley (1998) provided counselors with important intervention principles that should be observed for children and adolescents with AD/HD. The following intervention principles are applicable to behavior at school, at home, and in community settings:

1. Rules and instructions provided to children with AD/HD must be clearly delivered and brief. For example, it is wise to have the child immediately repeat the rules or instructions to make sure that there is an adequate understanding.
2. Consequences that are utilized to manage the behavior of children with AD/HD must be delivered swiftly and immediately. For example, delays in the timing or delivery of behavioral consequences seriously degrade their efficacy.
3. Consequences must be delivered more frequently, not just immediately, considering the difficulty in motivating many children with AD/HD. For example, frequent feedback or consequences for rule adherance or compliance seem helpful in maintaining appropriate rule-tracking for these children.
4. The types of consequences utilized with children with AD/HD must often be powerful or of a high magnitude. For example, children with AD/HD often have a relative insensitivity to response consequences, so a behavioral management program must have sufficient reinforcement value or magnitude to motivate these children to perform the desired behaviors.
5. Positives before negatives is the order of the day for children with AD/HD. For example, when negative reinforcement or punishers fail, parents and teachers should look to positives before instituting higher-magnitude or more frequent punishment programs.
6. Reinforcers or rewards must be changed or rotated frequently for children with AD/HD. For example, even though a particular reinforcer or reward seems effective for the moment in motivating compliance, it is likely that it will rapidly lose its effectiveness.
7. Anticipation is the key to all children with AD/HD. For example, parents and teachers must think ahead and think aloud at all times before entering any activity or situation. With the previously discussed intervention principles in mind, the challenge lies in the counselor designing interventions or programs that can easily be provided for home and/or classroom use.

Barkley (1990, 1997b, 2005); Fiore, Becker, and Nero (1993); and Goldstein and Goldstein (1998) believed that the counselor could provide the child, parents, and teachers with behavioral instruction or training in the following areas:

1. gaining information on the importance of positive praise from parents and teachers (e.g., praise must be delivered regularly for even minor successes);
2. gaining information on the importance of positive internal self-talk (e.g., training children or adolescents to reward or praise themselves [internally] for accomplishments when their efforts have resulted in their best performance possible);

3. gaining information on the importance of behavioral rehearsal (e.g., having the child or adolescent acquire prior practice or rehearsal at a task or behavior without the risk of evaluation or judgement);

4. gaining information on the importance of negative reinforcement (e.g., ignoring maladaptive behavior instead of scolding or criticizing);

5. gaining information on the importance of using time out (e.g., providing a timed period and space devoid of reinforcement for the young child; time out is usually not effective for adolescents);

6. gaining information on the importance of cost-response (e.g., having the child or adolescent immediately choose from an agreed-upon list one privilege or activity that will be forfeited for noncompliance with a rule or assignment);

7. gaining information on the importance of earning special privileges (e.g., maintaining a list of special privileges that the child or adolescent can earn for on-task behaviors at school or in the home); and

8. gaining information on the importance of mentoring (e.g., being a model for positive behavior and providing empathetic guidance despite the often high stress levels that can accompany parenting or teaching the child or adolescent with the disorder).

The counselor should be aware that behavioral interventions or strategies often need to be varied, adjusted, or changed to meet the myriad and/or unique problematic situations or behaviors that can often be endemic to most children and adolescents with AD/HD. Moreover, behavioral interventions are most useful in learning more appropriate behavior when three things occur; first, when they are put in place in natural settings where the child is expected to function; second, when they are put into place at the points of performance (where the desired behavior is to occur); third, when meaningful reinforcement parallels the attempted and/or improved performance (Barkley, 1997b).

In the delivery of interventions, the counselor should expect that the child's attention difficulties might result in not listening carefully to the instructions. Even if they get off on the right foot, many of these children and adolescents cannot sustain their attention long enough to complete the whole behavioral task (e.g., thereby missing information critical to completing their assigned tasks). Barkley (2005) asserted that in the delivery of behavioral interventions for a child with AD/HD, the child must have opportunities for repeated and/or guided practices in the desired behavior at the points of performance.

Counselors should counsel parents and teachers about not finding the child's attempts at immediate or even short-term improvement unacceptable. This is because few of these children can be expected to have the knowledge and skills necessary to bring themselves under better control. Once the counselors explain this, most parents and teachers can keep these circumstances in mind. The attitude and efforts of those around children and adolescents with AD/HD become the linchpin in their behavioral development.

Research has overwhelmingly indicated that *behavioral interventions, environmental modifications,* and *medication* significantly reduce the manipulative power of the child's AD/HD behaviors when interacting with parents, teachers, and peers (Barkley, 1997a, 2005; Goldstein, 1999). Studies have demonstrated that despite many of the positive effects that can accrue from behavioral interventions in children with AD/HD, they still have problems with internalization and generalization to other settings once the interventions and/or medication are no longer in place (Teeter, 2000). In the face of the concerns of some parents and teachers about medication, an appropriately administered and monitored medication regimen as part of the larger treatment package for the management of the AD/HD should be recommended as a mainstay of treatment (Barkley, 1997a, 1997b). Vitiello (2003) noted, for example, that the MTA Study on children with AD/HD demonstrated superiority of medication combined with behavioral interventions.

Self-Esteem Education

Low self-esteem may often precede depressed affect or depression in many children with AD/HD. Therefore, the foremost goal for many children and adolescents with AD/HD should be enhancing their self-esteem (Erk, 1995b). For example, unknowingly or without being fully aware of the consequences of their actions (e.g., criticizing, complaining, nagging), many parents and teachers have often seriously undermined the self-esteem of the child or adolescent with AD/HD. Since early childhood or kindergarten, it is likely that the child or adolescent with AD/HD has often experienced feelings of being unaccepted, unattached, helpless, worthless, and separated from others or the peer group. These effects can be cumulative and negatively affect the child's self-evaluation.

Many children and adolescents with AD/HD are likely to have low self-esteem and to be in need of self-esteem education programs (Barkley, 2005). Erk (1999) recommended that counselors who begin self-esteem education programs for children or adolescents with AD/HD attempt to emphasize and focus on the following important points with these children: 1) increasing their possibilities for developing increased self-worth or self-confidence; 2) being valued and accepted for who they are; 3) realizing that they are attached, connected, and cared for by others; and 4) providing motivation and encouragement about their possibilities for the future.

Wenar (1994) indicated that self-esteem or self-worth is affected by the child's sense of his or her own physical and mental abilities. When children or adolescents, for example, perceive of themselves as incompetent physically, socially, or academically, they might not develop the sense that they are worthwhile (e.g., to self or others). Children value themselves based in part on how parents, teachers, and peers view and evaluate them. For children or adolescents with AD/HD, their self-esteem or self-evaluations are related to their everyday performance or success. Self-esteem education programs are important for their future self-evaluations.

Social-Skills Education

It is often within the "social arena" or "peer group" entry that children with AD/HD experience the most difficulty (Barkley, 2005; Friedman & Doyal, 1992; Whalen & Henker, 1991). Many children and adolescents with AD/HD are often described by their parents, teachers, and peers as, for example, socially disruptive or demanding.

In some instances, children with AD/HD seem to be the targets or victims of social harassment from many of their classmates or peers. It is not unusual for social harassment to be pervasive (e.g., across settings). It can often be mean-spirited and highly personalized. Where this type of social harassment has occurred, these highly charged emotional experiences can result in indelible memories for the AD/HD child.

Furthermore, children and adolescents with AD/HD can seem to teachers and parents (e.g., who are unfamiliar with the disorder) to be remarkably unaware of the needs of others, self-centered, and self-absorbed. For example, many children with AD/HD seem to deliberately ignore the social rules or norms by defying teachers and parents. This is a complete misreading of these children's noncompliance. Teachers and parents need to understand that many of these children are reacting in an incompetent way. They are simply unable to distinguish between their noncompliance and more competent ways to behave in the company of others.

Obviously, many children and adolescents with AD/HD need to acquire and learn a more successful repertoire of social skills. A strong didactic component of social-skills education and training, coupled with immediate and repeated practice in the desired or targeted areas of social functioning, can be crucial for many children or adolescents with AD/HD. Erk (1999) recommended that social-skills education and training for these children with AD/HD could focus on the following: 1) basic interaction skills (such as making eye contact, using the correct voice level or tone, taking turns in the conversation, or practicing covert speech or silent responses before answering); 2) getting-along skills (such as using polite words or language, following the social rules for the classroom or group, being of assistance to others, and not violating the social space or privacy of others); 3) making-friends skills (such as learning the importance of smiling, complimenting others, and demonstrating through cooperative behaviors a genuine interest or concern for the welfare of others); and 4) social coping skills (such as learning how to react more appropriately when someone says no, coping more effectively with frustration or anger when peers engage in teasing or taunting, responding to a classmate or peer who deliberately tries to inflict hurt feelings, and understanding that not all social situations go right). At opportune points, the counselor should be alert for opportunities to actively involve members of the peer group or classmates in the program.

Interventions designed to improve social skills and social competency have been shown to reduce peer-interaction difficulties for many children and adolescents with AD/HD (Barkley, 2005; Friedman & Doyal, 1992; Dowdy, Patton, Smith, & Polloway, 1998; Teeter, 2000). When peers are included in the social-skills training program, for example, improvement in social status has been increased (Teeter, 2000). When the child or adolescent with AD/HD is left without treatment for social deficiencies or cannot secure acceptance from age-grade counterparts (e.g., those without AD/HD), these children might identify or ally themselves with other children who are also deemed as different or socially unconnected.

Family Counseling

Families with AD/HD children or adolescents encounter a variety and high number of home-management and/or behavioral problems (e.g., noncompliance with family rules; conflicts over issues such as chores, curfews, and homework). Parent–child conflicts in these families often erupt and may lead to unpleasant verbal exchanges characterized by shouting, yelling, name-calling, and other hurtful and coercive communication styles (Robin, 1998).

The normal disagreements and problems found in families, for example, are exponentially magnified by the core symptoms of AD/HD. Therefore, family counseling or therapy may often be recommended. In some cases, family counseling or therapy might be necessary for the other interventions to have the intended effects.

Families with a child or adolescent with AD/HD are usually confronted with a much larger number of developmental and behavioral problems as compared to other families (Hosie & Erk, 1993). Unfortunately, the disorder can seriously affect the fabric and functioning of the family. For example, problems that typically confront many of these families are parental burnout, marital discord, and sibling dissension. The child or adolescent with AD/HD may suffer from low academic achievement, low self-esteem, social isolation, and depression from the effects of the disorder. The child or adolescent with AD/HD often becomes embroiled in many unpleasant conflicts with family members. Moreover, if the family is known at school or in the community to be experiencing many difficulties due to the AD/HD, it can be socially shunned by other families in the neighborhood or community (Erk, 1997).

Counselors should realize that in the family with a child or adolescent with AD/HD, there is a disability or a disabling condition operating within the family (e.g., it can affect or disrupt the entire family system) (Erk, 1997). It is however, the disorder and its effects and not the person that is causing the family's dysfunctions. Family counseling can provide assistance to a family unit or system that might be dysfunctioning due to the AD/HD. Robin (1998) believed that the family counseling process should be educational about the AD/HD and have four broad stages. First, the counselor gives the family the facts about family functioning and AD/HD and states the available treatment options. Second, the counselor listens carefully and assesses the family's reactions to the presentation of the facts and treatment options. Third, the counselor corrects false beliefs and myths about AD/HD and instills positive, coping attitudes toward the disorder. Fourth, the counselor collaboratively establishes the specific goals for treatment and tailors the interventions to have the best possible fit for the family.

Erk (1997) contended that focal points of intervention in family counseling could focus, in most cases, on the following: 1) changing the faulty communication patterns that evolved within the family because of the AD/HD (e.g., parents and siblings have blamed or been angry with the child who has AD/HD for behavior that arises from the disorder); 2) establishing realistic rather than heightened behavioral, academic, and social expectations for the child with AD/HD; 3) providing the child with AD/HD–consistent parental supervision, setting behavioral boundaries that are achievable, and using immediate but fair consequences for noncompliance or misbehavior; 4) ensuring that the child with AD/HD receives heavy daily doses of positive reinforcement from parents and siblings for appropriate efforts and/or achievment of on-task behavior; 5) taking advantage of and/or actually creating opportunities to enhance the social functioning of the child with AD/HD; 6) involving peers where feasible in the family counseling program. Difficult issues for the child, such as low self-esteem and depression, may best be handled in individual counseling, unless the child feels comfortable with discussing these particular issues in the presence of parents and siblings. Finally, the unity of the nuclear family in the treatment of the child or adolescent with AD/HD remains a crucial and determining factor (Erk, 1995b).

In summary, the most important information to emerge for counselors from the clinical research literature on AD/HD is that a "multidimensional" treatment approach offers an array of interventions that can attack the AD/HD on as many fronts as are feasible. The multidimensional and/or multidisciplinary approach should not be considered curative, but rather as making it increasingly possible for the child to make improved adjustments to the disorder.

BEST PRACTICE GUIDELINES

All counselors are well served by keeping abreast of the "practice guidelines" for AD/HD in the professional literature. For example, counselors should consult the practice guidelines for AD/HD contained in *Journal of the American Academy of Child and Adolescent Psychiatry* (1997a, Volume 36, Suppl., pp. 85S–121S); *Pediatrics* (2000, Volume 105, pp. 1158–1170); *Pediatrics* (2001, Volume 105, pp. 1033–1044); *Journal of the American Academy of Child and Adolescent Psychiatry* (2002, Volume 41, Suppl., pp. 26S–49S); and *Practice Guidelines for the Treatment of Psychiatric Disorders: Compendium 2006* (American Psychiatric Association, 2006). Clinical and/or practice guidelines are recommendations that are based on limited empirical evidence and/or strong clinical consensus. The counselor should always consider practice guidelines, but there may be exceptions to their application. Practice guidelines are increasingly being used and/or required by school systems, mental health centers, and managed-care organizations.

SCHOOL AND FAMILY PERSPECTIVES

The School's Influence

The school, next to the family, is the most important institution in our society for educating and socializing children. In our society, for example, success or failure at school is tantamount to success or failure as a person. Academic and social success at school are the foundations for the development of academic performance (e.g., school achievement), social skills (e.g., acceptance by teachers and peers), adaptive behavior (e.g., coping with new situations), and later adjustment in life (e.g., occupational choice) (Kauffman, 2005). The school, therefore, imposes significant demands on the academic, social, and psychological resources of children. The happiness and success of children largely depends on their adaptive responses to the expectations of the school they attend. Formalized education imposes compliance, requires focused attention or concentration, requires a willingness to listen carefully, requires working cooperatively with classmates, and imposes consequences for the child or adolescent who cannot successfully adapt or negotiate these demands.

Yet many educators are seemingly unaware of the strong contributions the school makes toward fostering the very behavior that teachers, parents, and students in the school can find objectionable or dysfunctional. For example, schools or teachers have to be responsible for scrutinizing what they are doing to students. It is what happens to students in school over which the school (e.g., teachers and principals) have direct control. For example, conditions inside the school can influence students' experiences and in-school behavior. In turn, these experiences at school return to the home at the end of each school day. For children who come to the school with behavioral disorders, it is how the school experience "unfolds" on a day-to-day basis that has the power to either make the problems worse or to ameliorate them. In cases where the behavioral dysfunctions are continuing (e.g., not abating in the child or adolescent), the school must recognize the possibility that the school experience itself is one of the major causal factors (Kauffman, 2005).

An ecological approach to understanding behavior assumes that there is a reciprocal interconnectedness between all aspects of the child's or adolescent's environment (e.g., the school, the home, the community). Therefore, success or failure in the school, in the home, and in the community are causally based or related. The central mission of the school should be to monitor and assess how the school might be contributing to the academic and social dysfunctions that a student is experiencing. Where the school is reluctant or is not examining itself for its effects on the student, the student (e.g., with AD/HD) cannot respond appropriately to the expectations and demands of the school (Kauffman, 2005).

The Family's Influence

Families with a child or adolescent who has AD/HD are confronted with many developmental, educational, social, and behavioral challenges. Important principles need to be emphasized for counselors about the families who have a child with AD/HD. Counselors who are aware of the family's influence and the following principles place themselves in a better position to understand and plan treatment for families with an AD/HD child or adolescent (Erk, 1997).

The *first and most important principle* is that the family has probably been attempting to cope with the problems related to the AD/HD for a long time prior to seeking counseling (O'Brien, 1992). There is an obvious difficulty in raising a child that constantly manifests unpleasant behavior, feelings, and attitudes within the family. It is important to realize that the stress for all members of the family has probably been at high levels for an extended period of time. It may well be that the family has been marginally coping before seeking treatment. Often the family has been fighting a battle against a mysterious enemy that they cannot fully understand or identify

(Friedman & Doyal, 1992). For example, it is not uncommon for the AD/HD to have remained undiagnosed. It seems that many AD/HD children are diagnosed in the third grade (Copeland & Love, 1991). The diagnosis finally enables the family to place many prior familial interactions into proper perspective (Barkley, 2005; Copeland & Love, 1991).

A *second principle* is that all areas of family functioning are affected by the disorder (O'Brien, 1992). The relationships the AD/HD child has within the family (e.g., parents, siblings) may abound with stress and eventually become impaired. It typically seems to parents with an AD/HD child that they are incompetent to deal with the problems that other parents seemingly handle as routine. The family often reports feeling "overwhelmed" and "helpless" to cope with the problems (e.g., familial discord, lack of attention at school reported by teachers). Moreover, these events can occur on a daily basis with an AD/HD child. The disorder continually invades and disrupts most areas of the family's existence and interpersonal functioning.

A *third principle* is that the AD/HD child should view the family as completely understanding the problems often connected with the disorder (O'Brien, 1992). It is essential that the failures and successes of children with AD/HD are fully accepted by the family members, especially by siblings. Parent and sibling responses to the behavior of the AD/HD child can either aggravate or improve the course of the child's condition (Barkley, 2005; Popper, 1988).

A *fourth principle* is that AD/HD children exist in a synchronous and circular relationship with their families and their schools (Erk, 1997). Unfortunately for children with AD/HD, much of what they do at home and school is not acceptable (e.g., behaviorally, socially, academically) to parents or educators. Hardly a day passes that something serious does not go wrong in the life of an AD/HD child. Counselors should be aware that the problems AD/HD children experience at home and in school (e.g., with teachers and peers) are inseparable and often can have negative reciprocal effects. Often there can be a **negative feedback cycle** that develops between the school and family system (e.g., which may interrupt or impede the family's social system). For example, constructive criticism in the form of a note from the school (e.g., regarding the AD/HD child's behavior) can be perceived as an affront or injury to all members of the family. It can elicit a defensive posture instead of being perceived as a constructive comment. Parents can become reactive, emotional, and defensive in relation to even a minor problem their AD/HD child encounters. Conceptions of reciprocal causality are increasingly seen as important to many parent-child and/or family problems (Emery, Fincham, & Cummings, 1992). Furthermore, it is only a small step to understand that human behavior is shaped through complex yet mutually influential or reciprocal parent-child interactions, whether in the family, school, or community (Merrill, 1994). Counselors who embrace these principles and their operation possess a base from which to proceed with family counseling and treatment for the disorder (Erk, 1997).

The effects of AD/HD on family functioning are serious and should not be underestimated. What typically occurs is that AD/HD children often initiate a dysfunctional system of interactions within their families. Having an AD/HD child in the family predisposes all members toward a higher degree of conflict (e.g., than is found in families without AD/HD). Families with an AD/HD child or adolescent, for example, often live in a state of disarray, have accumulated layers of frustration and blame, and endure unrelieved guilt feelings. The effects of the disorder can dissolve the social ecology or connectedness of the family. The counselor should be prepared to investigate the social-familial interactions of AD/HD children with their parents/siblings, the AD/HD children's influence on parents, and the signs of family interaction problems that can be present in families with AD/HD children.

Counselors should acquire an understanding of the social-familial context in which these families usually operate. Barkley (2005) pointed out the following reasons for appreciating the social-familial context in understanding the interactions of AD/HD children with their parents and siblings. First, the social interactions of these AD/HD children and the reactions from their parents and siblings have been shown to be different from those of non–AD/HD families. These interactions are inherently more negative and stressful to all family members. Second, evidence abounds that parents and siblings of AD/HD children are more likely to be experiencing their own psychological distress and psychiatric disorders than are those of non-AD/HD children. The high level of psychological distress affects the management and rearing of AD/HD children in unique ways. For example, there could be long-lasting effects on the child or adolescent that contribute to adult outcomes (e.g., marginal adjustment to adulthood, relationship problems, frequent employment changes). Third, although many counselors endorse a "family systems" approach, a number of counselors seem to ignore the strong reciprocal effects in these family interactions. The focus, for example, is primarily on the impact of parental behavior on these children and misses the substantial effects these children produce on their parents and family life. Researchers have not found parenting behavior to be a cause of AD/HD, although some family counselors may elect to spend an inordinate amount of time exploring this possibility (Barkley, 2005). In AD/HD cases, all family problems cannot be reduced to parenting problems (Emery, Fincham, & Cummings, 1992).

The child or adolescent with AD/HD does deliver a significant amount of psychological influence onto the parents. For example, children's influence on parents has not received the full attention it deserves. What has often been overlooked is the way in which parents and other caregiving adults are themselves "molded" by the very children they are trying to rear (Bell & Harper, 1977). Children's behavior can be a cause of parenting style or can affect responses parents make to their children (Fauber & Long, 1991; Steuer, 1994). For example, the AD/HD symptoms often elicit specific behavioral responses (e.g., restriction of privileges, punishment, rejection) from parents. Henggler and Borduin (1990) think that parental rejection based on child behavior that highly displeases the parent can present one of the most serious emotional traumas a child can experience. A thorough understanding of the interactional patterns of AD/HD children and their families before the counselor forms any firm conclusions and treatment regimes is advisable.

Yet, unraveling pertinent family dynamics is far from easy. Barkley (2005) finds that the parents of an AD/HD child can be unfairly scrutinized by counselors for even the slightest flaw upon which to build a clinical case as the root cause for the problems within the family. Barkley (2005) believed that such a view by the counselor is inherently one-sided and unfair, certainly untrue, and perhaps even damaging to the adjustment of the children if counseling interventions are founded upon them. Counselors need to thoroughly understand the interaction patterns of AD/HD children and families prior to forming a conclusion and initiating treatment.

Few disorders have the potential to have such a profound effect on the parents and family functioning as AD/HD. To parents, these children often exhibit unpredictable behavior and may even, at times, be out of control (e.g., physically, emotionally). Over time, AD/HD children can easily exhaust the family's coping mechanisms. The AD/HD child's activity level (e.g. hyperactive, inattentive, or inactive), mood swings, impulsiveness, lack of organizational skills, socialization difficulties, compliance problems, and the constancy of the child's behavioral difficulties often create a volatile situation in the home.

Family discord or arguments (e.g., which can be reciprocally circular and are often negative) are common, and destructive statements related to the AD/HD child are often made out of frustration or anger. AD/HD children or adolescents and their parents are more likely to use aversive behaviors (e.g., insults, complaints, commands, defensiveness) during family discussions (Barkley, Guevremont, Anastopoulous, & Fletcher, 1992). Stimulant medication as an intervention, for example, has an established record of inducing immediate reductions in child noncompliance and negativity, with reciprocal reductions in parental negativity or discipline (Barkley & Cunningham, 1979).

There are often visible signs of family interaction problems. For example, Copeland and Love (1991) provided the following signs of family interaction problems that are often found in a family with an AD/HD child or adolescent: 1) The family has frequent or ongoing conflicts; 2) family activities and social gatherings are unpleasant; 3) parents argue over discipline and whose fault it might be because "nothing really works"; 4) parents spend "hours and hours" on homework with the AD/HD child, leaving little time for others in the family or their spousal relationship; 5) family meals are frequently unpleasant occasions; 6) family arguments frequently occur between parents and the child over responsibilities and chores; 7) family stress is continuous from the child's social and academic problems; and 8) parents often feel frustrated, angry, helpless, hopeless, guilty, disappointed, alone, fearful for the child, and sad or depressed over their family's condition.

At the heart of all this is that the parents' interaction patterns (e.g., within the family) are often faulty due to the high stress level that constantly exerts itself. To complicate the situation further, the parents might be undiagnosed AD/HD adults, and there could also be undiagnosed AD/HD siblings. Again, the entire family system must be addressed to ensure successful treatment (Barkley, 1997b; Copeland & Love, 1991). Finally, it is important for counselors to realize that parents of an AD/HD child often feel that their own physical and mental health is threatened by the flow of daily stressors and problems that accompany the disorder. The parents might even come to fear that the family's well-being (e.g., psychological health) will be harmed beyond repair by the AD/HD child. Once the influence of AD/HD on the family and its relative functioning are sufficiently understood, the value of interventions or services are exponentially increased.

MULTICULTURAL CONSIDERATIONS

Counselors should know that AD/HD is considered to be a cross-cultural disorder (Barkley, 2005; Bird, 1996; Reid, DuPaul, & Power, 1998; Samuel et al., 1998, 1999). AD/HD, for example, is not native to American culture. It is being identified in diverse cultures around the globe. For example, AD/HD was identifiable by its primary characteristics (e.g., hyperactivity, impulsivity, inattention) in a sample of children in Taiwan (Li, Copeland, & Martin, 1995; Yang, Schaller, & Parker, 2000); in Germany, Baumgaertel, Wolraich, & Dietrich (1995) identified an AD/HD prevalence rate of 11% using teacher ratings and *DSM-III-R* criteria; and in Japan, Kanbayashi, Nakata, Fujii, Kita, & Wada (1994) reported a prevalence rate of 8% in children ages 4 to 12 using parent ratings and *DSM-III-R* criteria. Moreover, in a Canadian study, Szatmari (1992) found an AD/HD prevalence rate of 9% in boys and 3% in girls. In a New Zealand study, Schaughency, McGee, Raja, Feehan, & Silva (1994) believed that AD/HD prevalence rates ranged from 2% to 6% in school-age children and 4% to 6% in adolescents.

Other cultures also contain additional evidence of AD/HD. Gallucci, Bird, Berardi, Gallai, Pfanner, & Weinberg (1993) located an AD/HD prevalence rate of approximately 4% using 232 Italian school children that were rated by their teachers for the disorder on *DSM-III-R* criteria. Rohde et al. (1999) evaluated 1,013 Brazilian adolescents aged 12 to 14 using *DSM-IV* symptoms for AD/HD; these researchers reported a prevalence rate of approximately 6%. In Norway, Gjone, Stevenson, & Sundet (1996) selected a twin sample (e.g., 526 identical and 389 fraternal) that was evaluated by parent ratings using the Child Behavior Checklist (CBC). These researchers identified significant problems on the CBC with attention span in identical and fraternal twins of both sexes. This finding was considered highly indicative of problems associated with AD/HD. Slone, Durrheim, & Kaminer (1996) identified in a multicultural clinical sample of South African children the presentation of hyperactivity, attention deficits, impulsiveness, social impairment, and disciplinary problems that are frequently associated with AD/HD.

Samuel et al. (1999) believed that little was actually known about the transmission of AD/HD in African American families. Using 37 first-degree relatives of African American children diagnosed with AD/HD and 52 first-degree relatives of non-AD/HD children matched additionally by age and gender, the results indicated that AD/HD and related disorders are familial in African Americans. Samuel et al. (1998) identified interesting results in two small samples of African American school children (e.g., 19 diagnosed with AD/HD and 24 without AD/HD). The African American children identified with AD/HD had higher levels of comorbid conditions than did the African American children who did not have AD/HD. This latter finding seems to be largely in concert with what has been the clinical course for Caucasian children diagnosed with AD/HD (e.g., they evidence comorbid conditions), and their non-AD/HD Caucasian counterparts do not. Many of these findings from diverse populations should be considered initial because more research with diverse groups (e.g., replication studies) will be needed to confirm their validity.

Clinical studies, however, have documented that AD/HD can be diagnosed across age ranges (e.g., children, adolescents, adults), and although the disorder seems to be less prevalent in girls than boys, girls and/or women are increasingly being referred and identified. Clinical samples and studies of AD/HD have been dominated by males. Consequently, AD/HD in girls and/or women has been relatively neglected in research on the disorder (Arnold, 1996). Girls and women with AD/HD are likely to be underidentified and subsequently undertreated (e.g., regardless of culture) (Biederman et al., 1999).

Counselors should be alerted that there is an increasing presence of AD/HD in adults (e.g., regardless of culture) (Resnick, 2000). Adults with AD/HD are another group that is now receiving diagnosis and treatment in our society (e.g., it is estimated that 30% to 70% of children diagnosed with AD/HD will continue to exhibit symptomatology that is disruptive throughout their adult lives; Jackson & Farrugia, 1997; Klein & Mannuzza, 1991).

From a cultural standpoint (e.g., a world view), counselors should expect that there will be diverse cultural issues in attitudes and beliefs about AD/HD (e.g., how AD/HD comes about); choices for care (e.g., family, external sources); degree of trust toward major institutions (e.g., school, mental health center, hospital) and authority figures in these settings; tolerances for certain behaviors displayed by the child; and religious issues indigenous to their cultural group. In cases of AD/HD, regardless of culture, there can be a large amount of disruptive behavior that is severe enough to disrupt the home and school environments. It is how the AD/HD will ultimately be handled in each culture that is now becoming crucial.

At this point, what now seems crucial for counselors to understand is that the individual's cultural origin and cultural views of AD/HD will determine the "threshold of deviance" that will be tolerated in the child (Barkley, 2005). With this in mind, there will certainly be implications for how the cultural group subsequently comes to "view" two important areas: first, having it diagnosed in their family unit; and second, coming to an understanding of the disorder that can provide a reasonable measure of support for the treatment options that are recommended.

What needs further research, for example, is the applicability (e.g., degree of fit) between the capacities and performances of individuals from diverse cultural groups when they are evaluated for AD/HD using the *DSM-IV-TR* criteria. In a multicultural society, diagnostic measures such as the *DSM-IV-TR* for diagnosing AD/HD need to demonstrate that they are reliable and valid for different cultural groups in the population. Their diagnostic practicality must not discriminate but identify the disorder in individuals from diverse groups.

Unfortunately, for example, there is some evidence that African American young people with AD/HD are less likely to be identified and treated for the disorder than Caucasian children of similar socioeconomic status (Zito, Safer, dos Reis, & Riddle, 1998). Diagnosis and intervention will become more effective and better accepted by ethnically different groups when counselors get better at identifying and understanding ethnocultural factors. For example, parents can be recruited as allies to help pave the way for acceptance and trust by other minority families who have children with AD/HD (Livingston, 1999).

CASE ILLUSTRATION

The First Day of Kindergarten for Joey

It was the first day of formal schooling for Joey, age 5. You can imagine the pride of the parent who was picking him up after school. The kindergarten teacher hurriedly walked over to the parent's car when it pulled up in front of the school building. Tapping on the car window, the teacher motioned excitedly for the parent to come inside. The teacher asked the parent to follow her immediately down to the classroom. As the parent followed along, there was no hint of what might have occurred. The parent entered the classroom. Sitting at his little desk was Joey, hair hanging almost into his eyes and looking very innocent.

The teacher promptly explained to the parent, in a rather upset tone, that the school had installed new carpet in each classroom. Apparently, earlier in that school day, Joey was sent back to the activity area of the room to color with a few other children. When the teacher went to check on the children, Joey had colored on the carpet. The other children had dutifully colored on the paper provided. What seemed to disturb the teacher the most about this misbehavior was the fact that Joey did not admit remorse or tell the teacher how sorry he was. The teacher reported that Joey sat silently whenever she tried to ask him why he would do such a thing.

The teacher asked the parent why Joey could not follow the rules of the classroom and why he could not sit quietly until he was called on. The teacher further informed the parent that Joey was not attentive (e.g., did not follow instructions) and impulsively got up out of his seat (e.g., without permission) on numerous occasions. The teacher showed the parent the large number of check marks on the blackboard next to Joey's name. It was if he was defying the teacher, she reported. When Joey was reseated repeatedly and asked to explain his behavior, he seemed to stare blankly out into space and did not respond. It seemed to the teacher that Joey was willfully and deliberately disobeying her. It was an eventful first day at school for Joey and his teacher.

During the school year, Joey was almost daily finding his way into difficulty or conflict with the teachers and classroom routines. There were some visits to the school principal's office. The other children observed this misbehavior in Joey. At first it was viewed as comical, interesting, and novel. However, when the children at school realized that the "problem" behaviors were aggravating the teachers, and association with Joey would bring them under the scrutiny of the school, classmates increasingly distanced themselves. This left Joey, for the most part, socially shunned and devalued. Joey was increasingly cut off from social support (e.g., peer interaction) at the school.

The parents were called in for conferences. Because the behavior was not nearly as problematic in the home, Joey's parents were not willing to accept the concerns that the school was expressing. In the home, Joey sought a great deal of attention.

However, the parents considered themselves able to supply much of what was needed. Therefore, the parents suspected the school was possibly negligent in its ability to care for and serve the needs of their child. Both parents were middle-class and well-educated, had benefited from their schooling, and could not fully accept the school as being incapable of managing Joey's education and behavior.

At the conclusion of the school year, the parents were called in for another conference. It ultimately reached the point that the school was suggesting a "developmental" or "intermediate" class placement next year (e. g., in grade 1 for Joey). This was explained as not being a pure retention. The school had developed an intermediate class for students who were not ready for a full exposure to first grade. Instead, the school could place students who were experiencing "developmental lag" in this intermediate room. The school would then recommend to the parents by the end of the first semester whether Joey would be ready to enter the first grade or whether he should spend the entire year with the intermediate class. The parents listened and decided to decline this option, asking that the child be promoted to a regular first-grade room. The parents became convinced that the school alone was not capable of diagnosing or knowing what further to recommend. It was at this point that the frustrated parents sought further professional assistance and consultation.

Sample Treatment Plan

The following treatment plan can serve as an example to counselors. The treatment plan is organized according to the 12 steps of the DO A CLIENT MAP (see Seligman, 1998 for a more detailed description).

Client: Joey is a 5-year-old Asian American male who is living with both parents. There are no siblings. Throughout the kindergarten school year, the school repeatedly expressed serious concerns about Joey's academic and social difficulties. The behavioral and social problems remained problematic and Joey's success in the upcoming first grade is an issue for the school. (A fuller explanation of Joey was provided earlier.)

Diagnosis

Axis I: 314.00 Attention-Deficit/Hyperactivity Disorder—Predominantly Inattentive Type (Moderate).
313.81 Oppositional Defiant Disorder (Moderate).
Learning Disorders (Provisional).

Axis II: V71.09 No Mental Disorder/Diagnosis on Axis II.

Axis III: No General Medical Conditions Reported.

Axis IV: Psychosocial and Environmental Problems:
Problems related to the social environment (e.g., peer shunning, and devaluing).
Problems related to the educational environment (e.g., school rules, teacher discipline, classroom attention).

Axis V: Global Assessment of Functioning: 55 (Intake).

Objectives:

Short Term

1. Reduce the family's anxiety through communication about the origin and development of Joey's disorders.
2. Reduce anxiety level by informing the parents that Joey's behaviors are not willful and deliberate (e.g., they are not aimed at the school or family).
3. Reduce self-blame (e.g., communicate to the parents and Joey that they should not engage in blame for such feelings as guilt, frustration, and anger about the school year).
4. Communicate the need to reestablish closer contact/communication with school/teachers so that a collaborative relationship can now take place or develop.

Note: Medium or long-term goals would be established later in the treatment phase.

Assessments: Instrument choices made by the counselor in consultation with the parents, school, and client.

Counselor: Counselor needs to readily build rapport and support for treatment with the parents and Joey.

Location: Home and/or family environment; school and/or in the teacher's classrooms.

Interventions: A Behavioral and Cognitive-Behavioral Approach (CBT) and Family Counseling/Therapy.

Strategies/Interventions

1. Parent education and training on the disorders (AD/HD, ODD).
2. Teacher education and training on the disorders (AD/HD, ODD).
3. Individual counseling stressing behavioral and CBT training in the sessions (e.g., role-playing, getting along with others, self-talk, stress inoculation training, identifying negative self-defeating statements, anger-management strategies, identifying positive-affirmative self-statements).
4. Social-skills training program (e.g., focusing on family, teachers, peers).
5. Self-esteem-building exercises (e.g., reconstruct Joey's evaluation of self).
6. Activity practice in real-life environmental situations (e.g., home, school, peers, community).
7. Family counseling to address how the family can learn to accept and work with Joey and his disorder and how the family unit can become more cohesive.

Note: Additional interventions or more probably the refinement of interventions would be accomplished as the counseling treatment progressed. It is anticipated that treatment would be ongoing or long-term in its application (home, school).

Emphasis: Structured but highly supportive and empathetic. Goal is to foster short- and long-term client responsibility. No emphasis on missed steps. The emphasis and reinforcement is on successful approximations to the desired behaviors.

Numbers: Individual and family counseling, including contacts with the school principal, teachers, school counselor, and school psychologist. Also, help from learning disabilities personnel at the school might be needed.

Timing: Initially, the sessions would occur twice a week. The frequency would subsequently be reduced to once per week as treatment progressed. Later, there could be sessions once per month or as needed to monitor and adjust interventions or treatment accordingly.

Medication: Parents would be informed of how medication offers the family, the child, and the school possible additional options for treatment. Potential referral to their family physician, pediatrician, or a psychiatrist.

Adjunct Services: Assessment for probable learning disorders, educational tutoring, and participation in school and/or community sports programs.

Prognosis: Very good for alleviation of the major symptoms of the AD/HD. Very good for the management of the ODD. Monitoring and follow-up are required.

CLOSING REMARKS

Because AD/HD continues to account for the largest source of referrals to counseling offices, mental health centers, and clinics (Barkley, 1995, 2005; Goldstein & Goldstein, 1998; Learner, 1993; Popper & Steingard, 1994), there can be little doubt that children and adolescents diagnosed with AD/HD will continue to represent a significant clinical challenge. It should be emphasized to counselors that the majority of children with AD/HD have the potential for delivering a strong and pervasive constellation of cognitive and behavioral difficulties into not only their "own" lives, but also into the lives of those who provide care for them. For example, it is not unusual for many children with AD/HD to consistently provoke "negative" feelings and "strong" emotions in those around them. Counselors should understand from the onset that although the child and the disorder are not actually separable, they must gain a better understanding of how the disorder and the child mutually influence each other.

For example, counselors must realize that the "effects" they experience from children with AD/HD actually emanate from the disorder. In the role of parent, teacher, or counselor, it is often difficult to remember that it is the problematic behaviors that you are responding to that cause many of your reactions. Moreover, due to the disorder and the environmental conditions (e.g., home, school) that may surround many of these children, behavioral options might be constricted or unavailable. As a result of these developmental constrictions, many children with AD/HD are likely to have developed a limited behavioral repertoire, continuing to behave, for example, in maladaptive or disruptive ways. Therefore, two important points need to be advanced for counselors. First, the parents and teachers might not have been provided with sufficient opportunities to benefit from instruction and training on the disorder. Second, the child might not have received appropriate interventions (e.g., behavioral, medication) that could have provided opportunities to learn and practice an improved behavioral repertoire.

Furthermore, counselors should be aware that in all likelihood, the display of repeated negative behaviors and disruptive events in the home or school has been attributed to the child. Consequently, parents and teacher probably delivered a barrage of negative consequences (e.g., punishments). Once this pattern began emerging, a reciprocal pattern of behavior became established between the child and caregivers (e.g., one of disruptive behaviors from the child, which brought on critical and judgmental remarks from caregivers). Once negative expectations were established for disruptive behavior from the child, an unfortunate "negative cycle" was setting itself in motion. Simply put, the child's ongoing behavioral difficulties were viewed as disruptive, unacceptable, and in need of suppression.

As this "negative cycle" continues to transpire, in the children's own eyes, and in their feeling states, they often come to regard their lives as unhappy and unsuccessful. From what the child with AD/HD can perceive, life is a place where gratification or success is extremely difficult to obtain. In essence, the children have been trained by their own disordered behavior and the reactions of others to adopt the view that they will likely fall far short of their goals or aspirations, regardless of how much they try.

We might be tempted to blame the child with AD/HD for the way that others react to him or her. In reality, however, the child's behavior teaches others how to react. These reactions often include punishing, ignoring, or excluding the child (e.g., so that the parents or teachers do not feel the effects the child with AD/HD can often generate). Undoubtedly, the pressing need for caregivers is to be patient and understanding with the child or adolescent. However, the real key is to be patient with yourself. There is, however, not much doubt in the minds of caregivers who work with these children, and even in the minds of their peers, that many of these children are disabled. In many instances, their lives in our society can be severely restricted by their disorder or disabilities. As a result of their problematic behaviors and their incompatibility with their social environments (e.g., home, school, community), their dysfunctional behaviors repeatedly cost them opportunities for gratifying social interactions and experiencing self-fulfillment (e.g., self-esteem).

Lastly, we should not say that all children with AD/HD are disabled or dysfunctional. For example, where the disorder was diagnosed early, where it may be less severe, and where support systems are working, there may be far fewer family and/or school problems. However, counselors should remain aware that each child with AD/HD can be expected to have his or her own unique developmental history and constellation of problematic behaviors that are often put into place during their formative or developmental years.

For More Information

American Counseling Association
5999 Stevenson Ave.
Alexandria, VA 22304
(703) 823-9800
http://www.counseling.org

American School Counselor Association
801 North Fairfax Street, Suite 310
Alexandria, VA 22304
(703) 683-2722/ (800) 306-4722
http://www.schoolcounselor.org

American Psychiatric Association

1000 Wilson, Blvd., Suite 1825
Arlington, VA 22209-3901
(888) 357-7924
http://www.psych.org
http://www.aacap.org/publications/factsfam/
  conduct.htm

American Psychological Association

750 1st St., NE
Washington, DC 20004-4242
(202) 336-5500
http://www.apa.org

National Institute of Mental Health

NIMH Public Inquiries
6001 Executive Blvd., Rm. 8184, MSC 9663
Bethesda, MD 20892-9663
(301) 443-4513
http://www.nimh.nih.gov
http://nimh.nih.gov/healthinformation/
adhdmenu.cfm

**Children and Adults with Attention-Deficit
  Disorders (CHADD)**

8181 Professional Place, Ste. 201
Landover, MD 20785
(301) 306-7070/ (800) 233-4050
http://chadd.org

Attention-Deficit Disorder Association

1500 Commerce Park way, Suite C
Mt. Laurel, NJ 08054
(856) 439-9099
http://www.add.org

Council for Exceptional Children

1110 North Glebe Road, Suite 300
Arlington,VA 22201
(888) 232-7733
http://www.cec.sped.org

Learning Disabilities Association of America

4156 Library Rd.
Pittsburgh, PA 15234
(412) 341-1515

National Center for Learning Disabilities

381 Park Ave. S., Suite 1402
New York, NY 10016
(212) 545-7510/ (888) 575-7373
http://www.ncld.org

Tourette Syndrome Association

42-40 Bell Bird., Suite 205
Bayside, NY 11361
(718) 224-2999
http://www.tsa-usa.org

Office of Civil Rights

U.S. Department of Education
400 Maryland Ave. SW
Washington, DC 20202-4135
(202) 401-3020
http://www.ed.gov/about/offices/list/ocr

Chapter 5

DISRUPTIVE BEHAVIOR DISORDERS: CONDUCT DISORDER AND OPPOSITIONAL DEFIANT DISORDER IN CHILDREN AND ADOLESCENTS

By

Robert R. Erk

University of Tennessee— Martin

INTRODUCTION

Conduct Disorder (CD) and Oppositional Defiant Disorder (ODD) in children and adolescents are among the most prevalent and serious disruptive behavior disorders seen in mental health centers, community clinics, and school settings (Frick, 1998; Kazdin, 1995; Loeber, Burke, Lahey, Winters, & Zera, 2000). Children and adolescents with disruptive behavioral disorders have been referred to as consistently displaying undercontrolled or acting-out behaviors, aggressive behaviors, antisocial behaviors, conduct problems, hyperactivity, and delinquency (Johnston & Ohan, 1999; Loeber, Burke, Lahey, Winters, & Zera, 2000; Mash & Wolfe, 2002). According to the *Diagnostic and Statistical Manual of Mental Disorders* (*DSM-IV-TR;* American Psychiatric Association, 2000a), children and adolescents who have these serious behavioral problems are categorized as having **disruptive behavior disorders.**

The disruptive behavior disorders (e.g., CD, ODD) are of great concern in our society because of the high degree of behavioral impairment and the poor prognosis that they often carry (Johnston & Ohan, 1999; Loeber, Burke, Lahey, Winters, & Zera, 2000). For example, when people hear about a child or adolescent's disruptive or seriously impaired behavior, they often wonder why such behavior is occurring. Next, they naturally begin to search for more understanding. In many instances, the level of understanding about disruptive behavior disorders can run the gamut from misunderstanding to not understanding or recognizing the essential features of these disorders at all.

Conduct problems in children and adolescents can be better understood and are not without cause (Hinshaw & Anderson, 1996). For example, Mash and Wolfe (2002) emphasized three ways that conduct problems can be better understood. First, conduct problems are age-inappropriate actions and attitudes that violate family expectations or rules, societal norms or rules, and the personal or property rights of others. Second, the types, causes, and outcomes of conduct problems in children and adolescents are wide-ranging, requiring that counselors consider different types and pathways for their occurrence. Third, children and adolescents with conduct problems often grow up in extremely unfortunate family and neighborhood circumstances (e.g., where poverty and/or crime might seriously disrupt any attempts at normal child-raising efforts).

There is growing agreement that when parents and/or educators view and voice concerns about what are considered conduct problems (e.g., a recurrent pattern of fighting, lying, destroying the property of others, and refusing to follow the instructions of authority figures), there should be an appropriate degree of concern and alarm. Furthermore, if the behaviors the child or adolescent exhibits are causing a significant amount of disturbance or destruction in the family or at school (e.g., going well beyond the common experiences that adults or authority figures have had with most children), then a disruptive behavioral disorder (e.g., CD, ODD) needs to be strongly suspected and the child needs to be referred for evaluation (Johnston & Ohan, 1999; Loeber, Burke, Lahey, Winters, & Zera, 2000; Wicks-Nelson & Israel, 2005).

It is usually within the major institutions of our society (e.g., the family and school) that indefatigable or ongoing disruptive behavior disorders are considered to be both threatening and important enough to warrant referral. The persistence of these disruptive behaviors over time, and the fact that they might continue from childhood into adult life, further propels us to look for ways to better understand what is occurring. Our society is increasingly interested in trying to better understand the complexity and diversity that is contained in the disruptive behaviors themselves. Despite the enormous attention and research provided to disruptive behavioral disorders (see Kazdin, 1995), substantial numbers of children and adolescents continue to display antisocial, destructive, and even violent behaviors (Mash & Wolfe, 2002). Fortunately, ongoing clinical research into disruptive behavioral disorders is providing parents, educators, and counselors an improved understanding about the development and treatment of these disorders (see Lahey et al., 2000; Lahey, Waldman, & McBurnett, 1999; and Loeber, Burke, Lahey, Winters, & Zera, 2000 for more information).

This chapter on CD and ODD is divided into sections that provide information on the definition, prevalence, classification, diagnostic features, causal factors and prevention, methods of assessment, and implications for practice or treatment of CD and ODD. It also includes a case illustration, a sample treatment plan, and closing remarks. Each section focuses on information and research that can significantly enhance counselors' ability to be of increased assistance to children and adolescents who have CD and/or ODD.

Definition of Conduct Disorder

Counselors can better understand CD and ODD in children and adolescents when these disorders have been accurately defined and described. CD describes children and/or adolescents who display severe aggressive and antisocial acts involving the infliction of pain on others or interfering with the rights of others through physical and verbal aggression, stealing, or committing acts of vandalism (Mash & Wolfe, 2002). See Table 5.1 for the *DSM-IV-TR* diagnostic criteria for CD.

Moreover, counselors should be aware that CD first appeared in the *DSM-III* (American Psychiatric Association, 1980). Prior to this date, there was not a formal classification system (e.g., research based) to provide information concerning the etiology of conduct disorder, its prognosis, and its treatment response. It was in the *DSM-IV* (APA, 1994) that age of onset of antisocial symptoms is first used to create subtypes of CD (Sanford, Boyle, Szatmari, Offord, Jamieson, & Spinner, 1999). The practice of subtyping CD is continued in the *DSM-IV-TR* (APA, 2000a). The *DSM-IV-TR* subtypes are described as the following: Childhood-Onset Type defined by the onset of at least one criterion characteristic of CD prior to 10 years of age; Adolescent-Onset Type defined by the absence of any criteria characteristic of CD prior to 10 years of age. This outcome (e.g., subtyping CD) was stimulated by clinical researchers who reported differences between "early-onset" and "adolescent-onset" cases that suggested different developmental-causal pathways (Hinshaw, Lahey, & Hart, 1993; Lahey, Hartdagen, Frick, McBurnett, Conner, & Hynd, 1988; Moffitt, 1993; Moffitt, Caspi, Dickson, Silva, & Stanton, 1996).

Evidence for the subtyping (e.g., childhood-onset type, adolescent-onset type) was supplied by the *DSM-IV* Working Group, which reported on the validity of the *DSM-IV* using cross-sectional data obtained from the *DSM-IV* Field Trials (e.g., a clinically referred sample) and from the Methods for the Epidemiology of Child and Adolescent Mental Disorders Study (e.g., a community sample), which enabled a comparison sample and replication of the findings (Sanford et al., 1999). Specific findings of the "clinic" sample were that adolescent-onset cases were less likely than early-onset cases to be male, to have Oppositional Defiant Disorder, or to have a family history of antisocial behavior. However, these findings were not replicated in the community sample. Community samples, for example, often do not contain the severe antisocial behavior pattern that is typically found in clinic-referred samples (Sanford et al., 1999).

However, in both samples (e.g., clinic, community) the early-onset cases in the *DSM-IV* Field Trials exhibited more aggressive or antisocial behaviors than adolescent-onset cases (Sanford et al., 1999). Lahey et al. (1998) observed that cases of early-onset tend to be more aggressive, and early-onset cases are considered to be more predictive of the persistence of antisocial behavior. Therefore, subtyping by age of onset or aggressiveness should be useful to counselors for making an individual prognosis. Nonetheless, although these findings are useful,

TABLE 5.1   Diagnostic Criteria for Conduct Disorder (CD)

A. A repetitive and persistent pattern of behavior in which the basic rights of others or major age-appropriate societal norms or rules are violated, as manifested by the presence of three (or more) of the following criteria in the past 12 months, with at least one criterion present in the past 6 months:

Aggression to people and animals

     (1) often bullies, threatens, or intimidates others
     (2) often initiates physical fights
     (3) has used a weapon that can cause serious physical harm to others (e.g., a bat, brick, broken bottle, knife, gun)
     (4) has been physically cruel to people
     (5) has been physically cruel to animals
     (6) has stolen while confronting a victim (e.g., mugging, purse-snatching, extortion, armed robbery)
     (7) has forced someone into sexual activity

Destruction of property

     (8) has deliberately engaged in fire-setting with the intention of causing serious damage
     (9) has deliberately destroyed others' property (other than by fire-setting)

Deceitfulness or theft

     (10) has broken into someone else's house, building, or car
     (11) often lies to obtain goods or favors or to avoid obligations (i.e., "cons" others)
     (12) has stolen items of nontrivial value without confronting a victim (e.g., shoplifting, but without breaking or entering; forgery)

Serious violations of rules

     (13) often stays out at night despite parental prohibitions, beginning before 13 years
     (14) has run away from home overnight at least twice while living in a parental or parental surrogate home (or once without returning for a lengthy period)
     (15) is often truant from school, beginning before 13 years

B. The disturbance behavior causes clinically significant impairment in social, academic, or occupational functioning.

C. If the individual is 18 years or older, criteria are not for Antisocial Personality Disorder.

Code based on age at onset:

     312.8 Conduct Disorder, Childhood-Onset Type: onset of at least one criterion characteristic of Conduct Disorder prior to age 10 years
     312.82 Conduct Disorder, Adolescent-Onset Type: absence of any criteria characteristic of Conduct Disorder prior to age 10 years
     312.89 Conduct Disorder, Unspecified Onset: age at onset is unknown

Specify severity:

     Mild: few if any conduct problems in excess of those required to make the diagnosis **and** conduct problems cause only minor harm to others
     Moderate: number of conduct problems and effect on others intermediate between "mild" and "severe"
     Severe: many conduct problems in excess of those required to make the diagnosis **or** conduct problems cause considerable harm to others

Reprinted with permission from the *Diagnostic and Statistical Manual of Mental Disorders*, Fourth Edition, Text Revision. Copyright 2000, American Psychiatric Association.

there is a need to await the evaluation of the subtyping of CD by age of onset across settings and longitudinal data to confirm the classification system (e.g., early- or adolescent-onset) now employed in the *DSM-IV-TR*. There could be an up side when early-onset cases of CD are identified; the window for treatment could also be opened at a much earlier date.

Definition of Oppositional Defiant Disorder

Children with ODD display an age-inappropriate pattern of stubborn, hostile, and defiant behaviors that is persistent and might be exhibited as early as preschool or kindergarten (Mash & Wolfe, 2002). See Table 5.2 for the *DSM-IV-TR* diagnostic criteria for ODD.

ODD behaviors have been shown to have negative and/or reciprocal effects on parent–child and teacher–student relationships (Greene & Doyle, 1999). Currently, a hotly debated issue is whether ODD can be considered a separate disorder from CD or whether the ODD is a milder, earlier version (Patterson, DeGarmo, & Knutson, 2000). For example, symptoms of ODD may emerge as early as 2 to 3 years before those of CD (Loeber, Green, Lahey, Christ, & Frick, 1992). Because they often come first, it is possible that they are precursors in some but not all children who develop CD. For example, at least 50% maintain their ODD diagnosis without progressing to CD and 25% cease to display ODD problems entirely (Hinshaw, Lahey, & Hart, 1993). ODD is considered an extreme developmental variation, but not one that invariably signals escalation to more serious conduct problems (Speltz,

---

TABLE 5.2   Diagnostic Criteria for Oppositional Defiant Disorder (ODD)

A. A pattern of negativistic, hostile, and defiant behavior lasting at least 6 months, during which four (or more) of the following are present:

    (1)   often loses temper
    (2)   often argues with adults
    (3)   often actively defies or refuses to comply with adults' requests or rules
    (4)   often deliberately annoys people
    (5)   often blames others for his mistakes or misbehavior
    (6)   is often touchy or easily annoyed by others
    (7)   is often angry and resentful
    (8)   is often spiteful or vindictive

Note: Consider a criterion met only if the behavior occurs more frequently than is typically observed in individuals of comparable age and developmental level.

B. The disturbance in behavior causes clinically significant impairment in social, academic, or occupational functioning.
C. The behaviors do not occur exclusively during the course of a Psychotic or Mood Disorder.
D. Criteria are not met for Conduct Disorder and, if the individual is 18 years or older, criteria are not met for Antisocial Personality Disorder.

McClellan, DeKlyen, & Jones, 1999). However, validated cases of CD are almost always preceded by ODD, and nearly all children and adolescents with CD continue to display ODD symptoms (Biederman, Faraone, Milberger, Jetton, Chen, Mick, Greene, & Russell, 1996; Lahey, Loeber, Quay, Frick, & Grimm, 1992; Mash & Wolfe, 2002; Wicks-Nelson & Israel, 2005).

Moreover, counselors should know that the *DSM-III* (APA, 1980) first presented a psychiatrically based definition of what was believed to be a milder variant of CD. It was termed Oppositional Disorder (OD). The intention behind this category in the *DSM-III* was to capture the early manifestations of aggressive, antisocial behavior that are exhibited in early to middle childhood (e.g., thought to be precursors to CD). The constituent symptoms comprised irritable, stubborn, and defiant behavioral features. The clinical judgment at this time was that these were displayed at rates considered developmentally deviant (Hinshaw & Anderson, 1996).

In the *DSM-III-R* (APA, 1987), the name changed to Oppositional Defiant Disorder (ODD). Included in this revision were nine behavioral symptoms, five of which were necessary for making the diagnosis (Hinshaw & Anderson, 1996). The *DSM-IV-TR* defines Oppositional Defiant Disorder (ODD) as a recurrent pattern of negativistic, defiant, disobedient, and hostile behavior toward authority figures lasting at least 6 months. Whether this definition captures a true developmental precursor to the later development of CD or fails to deserve the status of a bona fide disorder (e.g., one that masquerades as CD) is considered to rest in the "developmental factors" that often surround the child. These are the forces or trajectories, for example, that propel the child toward the development of antisocial behavior patterns or a conduct disorder.

Prevalence of Conduct Disorder and Oppositional Defiant Disorder

The prevalence of CD (e.g., childhood-onset, adolescent-onset types) in our society seems to have increased over the last decades (Mash & Wolfe, 2002). CD might be higher in urban than rural settings, particularly the childhood-onset type (Loeber, Burke, Lahey, Winters, & Zera, 2000). For example, urban conditions are viewed as more likely to "seed" many of the environmental conditions that can grow into CD in many children. Rates for CD, however, vary widely, depending on the population sampled (e.g., clinic-referred versus community sample; urban versus rural; low or high socioeconomic status; male versus female). Generally, prevalence rates for CD can run from 1% to more than 10% (Loeber, Burke, Lahey, Winters, & Zera, 2000). Hinshaw and Anderson (1996) reported that CD prevalence ranges from 2% to 6% of all school-age children in North America. Keep in mind that males are diagnosed at higher rates than females. This is primarily due to males having a preference for more confrontational or aggressive behaviors, which readily brings them into focus. Females with CD, for example, typically use more covert or nonconfrontational behaviors (e.g., relational forms of aggression such as verbal insults, gossip, ostracism, and lying). These behaviors in females are more common than fighting or physical aggression and might partly account for females being identified with CD at a lesser rate. Nonetheless, females do display antisocial behavior or conduct problems, with lifetime prevalence estimates averaging approximately 3% (Eme & Kavanaugh, 1995; Webster-Stratton, 1996).

ODD in children and adolescents has prevalence rates from 2% to 16%. The disorder usually becomes evident before 8 years of age and usually not later than adolescence (*DSM-IV-TR*). Prevalence rates for ODD in community samples (e.g., nonclinical) are between 6% and 10% (Wicks-Nelson & Israel, 2005). Rates for ODD are about twice that of CD, averaging about 12% of all children (e.g., male and female) (Nottelman & Jensen, 1995). In low-income family environments, the prevalence rate can run as high as three-quarters of clinic-referred preschoolers for meeting the *DSM* criteria for ODD (Keenan, Shaw, Walsh, Delliquardi, & Giovannelli, 1997; Keenan and Wakschlag, 2000). Of course, the prevalence rate for ODD (or any disorder) can depend on the nature of the population sampled (e.g., clinic versus community), the methods of ascertainment, socioeconomic status, and gender.

Classification of the Conduct Disorder Subtypes

Increasing clinical evidence points to the importance of age of onset in not only diagnosing CD, but also for the treatment of children who have CD (Waldman, Lilienfeld, & Lahey, 1995). The classification of CD into subtypes by age of onset (e.g., childhood-onset, adolescent-onset; *DSM-IV-TR*) offers the counselor the advantage of being able to view the CD contextually (e.g., early- or adolescent-onset). Accordingly, the counselor should be able to view more clearly how it might have developmentally evolved. Lahey et al. (1998) believed that age-of-onset subtyping can encourage counselors to think in terms of the developmental course of CD. It is equally important to think in terms of the preventative measures that could be employed to prevent, treat, or ameliorate its diagnostic features at an early stage (see Patterson, Reid, & Dishion, 1992).

CD can also be categorized as *undersocialized or overt conduct disorder* (e.g., overt acts such as hyperactivity, impulsiveness, irritability, stubbornness, demandingness, arguing, teasing, poor peer-group relations, loudness, threatening, physical fighting, cruelty, showing off, bragging, swearing, blaming others, sassiness, disobedience); *socialized or covert conduct disorder* (e.g., covert social acts, negativism, lying, destructiveness, stealing, setting fires, associations with bad company, gang affiliation, truancy, running away, abuse of alcohol and drugs); and *versatile* (e.g., shows both overt and covert forms of CD) (Kauffman, 2005; Loeber & Schmaling, 1985; Quay, 1986a, 1986b). These categorizations are not listed in the *DSM-IV-TR;* however, they might prove beneficial to counselors who are looking for additional ways to better understand or comprehend the disruptive behaviors their clients exhibit.

When viewed through these categorizations, the child or adolescent can be seen in different ways. The counselor, for example, has the option of conceptualizing the child or adolescent as "undersocialized" or "socialized" or "versatile." There is an advantage in having these additional categorizations available. It obviously lies in the fact that these categorizations offer the potential for increased understanding of the child (e.g., enabling a more complete diagnostic picture on which to develop interventions or treatments). However, counselors must keep in mind that the *DSM-IV-TR* has implemented the use of the childhood- and adolescent-onset classifications for diagnostic purposes.

DIAGNOSTIC FEATURES

The *DSM-IV* diagnoses of CD and ODD have demonstrated that the internal consistency and test-retest reliabilities of the *DSM-IV* versions are higher than those of the *DSM-III* and *DSM-III-R* versions. Therefore, diagnoses by counselors are slightly improved for *DSM-IV* ODD and CD (McMahon & Wells, 1998). Moreover, research has supported the validity of the Childhood-Onset and Adolescent-Onset Types of CD. For example, children with the Childhood-Onset Type were more likely to display more aggressive symptoms, to be boys, and to receive additional or comorbid diagnoses of ODD and AD/HD (Waldman & Lahey, 1994).

Essential Features of Conduct Disorder

The essential diagnostic features for CD are antisocial behaviors that are linked to a repetitive and persistent pattern of behavior which violates the rights of others (e.g., parents, siblings, teachers, peers, classmates, community members) and/or involves the violation of major age-appropriate societal norms or rules (*DSM-IV-TR*). These antisocial behaviors are placed into 4 main groupings that encompass 15 characteristics or criteria: **aggressive conduct** that causes physical harm to other people or animals (e.g., bullying, physical fights, use of a weapon, being physically cruel to people or animals, stealing while confronting a victim, forcing someone into sexual activity, rape or assault [Criteria A1–A7]); **nonaggressive conduct** that causes property loss or damage (e.g., fire-setting, deliberately destroying others' property in other ways [Criteria A8–A9]); **deceitfulness** or **theft** (e.g., breaking into someone else's house or car, frequently lying or breaking promises, stealing items of nontrivial value without confronting the victim [Criteria A10–A12]); and **serious violations** of the rules (e.g., staying out late despite parental prohibitions, running away from home overnight, often truant from school [Criteria A13–A15]).

The *DSM-IV-TR* notes that Conduct Disorder might be classified depending on the severity of the diagnostic criteria as mild (e.g., relatively minor harm to others); moderate (e.g., problems and their effect on others are intermediate between mild and severe); and severe (e.g., problems in excess of those required to make the diagnosis are present and cause considerable harm to others). There seems to be a consensus that children diagnosed with early- or childhood-onset CD (e.g., regardless of being classified mild, moderate, or severe) are at more risk for impairment (e.g., antisocial behavior) in society, and they can have a poorer prognosis for compliance with societal norms across the lifespan (Lahey et al., 1998; Loeber, 1982, 1988; Patterson, Reid, & Dishion, 1992). Lahey, Hart, Pliszka, Applegate, & McBurnett (1993) concluded that aggressive behavior (e.g., fighting, hitting) is more correlated with indices of autonomic and neuroendocrine functioning than is CD with nonaggressive behavior. If this conclusion is accurate, there may be reason to think that aggressive behavior patterns in the childhood-onset type could be an indicator for a larger involvement in neuroendocrine or brain dysfunction (e.g., depending on the degree of accompanying environmental stressors) than what might be true in the adolescent-onset type.

Essential Features of Oppositional Defiant Disorder

The essential diagnostic features in children with ODD are the negativistic and defiant behaviors expressed by persistent stubbornness, resistance to following directions, an unwillingness to compromise or give in, or negotiating with adults or peers (e.g., mental defiance). Defiance may include deliberate or persistent testing of limits, usually by ignoring orders, arguing, and failing to accept any part of the blame for misdeeds or misbehavior. Hostility can be directed at adults or peers and is shown by deliberately annoying others or by verbal aggression. However, there is usually not the more serious physical aggression that is often exhibited in cases of CD. ODD might be observed in the home and not be evident in the school or the community. ODD symptoms are typically more evident in interactions with adults or peers the child or adolescent knows well, and thus may not be evident during one-to-one clinical evaluations. Individuals with ODD do not regard themselves as oppositional or defiant; they tend to justify their behavior as the response needed to deal with unreasonable demands or circumstances (*DSM-IV-TR*).

ODD in males can be shown to be more correlated with those who have difficult temperaments (e.g., high reactivity, difficulty being soothed) or high motor activity (e.g., hyperactivity). There may be low self-esteem or overly inflated self-esteem, mood liability, low frustration tolerance, and the precocious use of tobacco, alcohol, or illicit drugs. There are often conflicts with parents, teachers, and peers. In this cycle, the parent and child can bring out the worst in each other (*DSM-IV-TR*).

Where Conduct Disorders or Oppositional Defiant behaviors are in operation and disrupting lives, there should be concern for more information on causal factors and prevention. Although you might be shocked by the antisocial behaviors of these children, you need to look further than just to their actions. Counselors, for example, should be concerned with these questions: "What are the possible causal factors?" and "How could these disorders possibly be prevented?"

CAUSAL FACTORS AND PREVENTION

Counselors should be vigilant in thinking that antisocial or deviant behavior is "multicausal" or "multifactorial" (Hinshaw & Anderson, 1996; Mash & Wolfe, 2002). Each of the causes or factors (e.g., directly and indirectly) affects the development and the severity of the antisocial behavior or conduct problems in the child (Wicks-Nelson & Israel, 2005). For example, counselors should be aware that there is no clear and distinct separation between cultural, environmental, or intraindividual factors in cases of CD and/or ODD (Hinshaw & Anderson, 1996).

Kazdin (1995) believed that counselors should understand that disruptive behavior disorders (e.g., CD, ODD) in children and adolescents often lead to a lifetime of social dysfunctions, antisocial behavior patterns, and poor adjustments (e.g., socially, emotionally, academically, occupationally). For example, the child or adolescent with either CD and/or ODD often demonstrates from the onset an inefficiency in reading and understanding social cues, understanding the need for emotional control, and perceiving how social and emotional factors are considered necessary for success in settings where adaptive functioning is required (e.g., home, school, community).

The maladaptive or disruptive behavior patterns for CD and/or ODD are intended to serve as benchmarks for dysfunctional mental mechanisms that can signal the need for serious interventions (Hinshaw & Anderson, 1996). It is beyond the scope of this chapter to explore all the possible sources or causal factors for CD. Rather, I will provide an overarching look at the major contexts from which seriously disordered behavior patterns can often emanate or develop. These are biological-genetic factors, neuroanatomical factors, personal factors, family factors, school factors, peer-group factors, and prevention factors.

Biological-Genetic Factors

Until recent decades, there was little or no direct scientific evidence regarding biological or genetic contributions to childhood conduct problems and little evidence regarding the role of genetics in mental disorders (Faraone, Tsuang, & Tsuang, 1999). Current thinking is that biology and genetics are not seeking to pit nature against nurture; instead, they are seeking to learn how both work together to cause mental conditions or disorders (Faraone, Tsuang, & Tsuang, 1999). Increasingly, the role of biological or genetic factors in the development of emotional and behavioral disorders in children is being explored and brought into more focus. There is accumulating scientific evidence that the biology of the person, especially neurobiology and neurochemistry, can be implicated in many mental conditions or disorders (Corey, 2005; Faraone, Tsuang, & Tsuang, 1999).

The universality of antisocial behavior or conduct problems in humans, and the fact that such behavior has been documented by researchers to run in families across generations, implies an active role for genetic influences (Mash & Wolfe, 2002). It should be remembered that genetics contain the blueprint for the construction of the whole organism (e.g., including behavioral tendencies). It is likely, for example, that genetic influences contribute to a difficult temperament, impulsivity, inattention, hyperactivity, and neuropsychological deficits (Faraone, Tsuang, & Tsuang, 1999; Mash & Wolfe, 2002). These biologically based or genetically based traits can create a higher antisocial predisposition in those who have these behavioral tendencies than in those who do not (Eme & Kavanaugh, 1995; Gottesman & Goldsmith, 1994; Loeber, Burke, Lahey, Winters, & Zera, 2000).

It is important to point out that conduct problems themselves are not inherited, but genetically based traits can predispose a child to develop conduct-disordered patterns of behavior. For example, some children are predisposed at birth to have variable moods, impulsivity, restlessness, negativity, and sensitivity to stress (Caspi, Henry, McGee, Moffitt, & Silva, 1995). Moreover, a difficult early temperament management problems in a young child, and later conduct problems, are often associated in the research literature (Sanson & Prior, 1999). At the heart of many management problems in the child or adolescent can be neuropsychological deficits (McMahon & Estes, 1997). Neuropsychological deficits include such areas as verbal and executive functions (e.g., sustaining attention, abstract reasoning, formation of goals, planning ahead, and self-awareness). These important neuropsychological areas are often negatively affected in many children with antisocial behavior patterns or conduct problems (Moffitt, 1993).

Rutter, Silberg, O'Connor, and Simonoff (1999) hypothesized that it was reasonable to assume an increased genetic component in antisocial behaviors that persist from childhood into adult life. Quay (1993) hypothesized that a biological or genetic foundation existed for early- or childhood-onset CD (e.g., because it often has a lifelong course). However, the nonpersistent adolescent-onset pattern of antisocial behavior appears to be less related to genetic contribution than does the more persistent early or child-onset pattern of antisocial behavior (Frick & Jackson, 1993). There is general scientific agreement that deficits in neuropsychological functioning can contribute to the development of antisocial behavior or conduct disorders (Wicks-Nelson & Israel, 2005).

Conclusions about the role of biology or genetics in the development of antisocial or conduct-disordered behavior have to be approached with caution. Although biological or genetic factors have a role to play, they inevitably interact in complex ways with multiple environmental influences (e.g., personality structure, family variables, school, peers, community). The precise role that biological or genetic factors play in the lives of children requires further investigation and study (Caspi & Moffitt, 1995). Generally, adoption and twin studies have suggested that genetic factors do contribute to antisocial behavior and conduct problems across the lifespan, as do environmental factors. It is fair to say that the current research does not specify the mechanisms by which the process occurs (Mash & Wolfe, 2002). More research into genetics and the other biological factors (e.g., neuroanatomical) that could account for CD and/or ODD should increase our understanding.

Neuroanatomical Factors

Gray (1987) proposed that people's behavior patterns are related to two subsystems in the neuroanatomy of the brain. Each subsystem has its distinct neuroanatomical regions and neurotransmitter pathways (see McBurnett, 1992; Quay, 1993 for a more full explanation).

For example, the **behavioral activation system** (BAS) stimulates behavior in response to signals of reward or nonpunishment. In contrast, the **behavioral inhibition system** (BIS) produces anxiety and inhibits ongoing behavior in the presence of novel or stimulating events, innate fearful stimuli, and signals of nonreward or punishment (Mash & Wolfe, 2002). For counselors, what is important to understand is that different behavioral patterns can result from the relative balance or imbalance of activity in these two neural systems. For example, think of the BAS as the gas pedal in a car and the BIS as the brakes, and that some people can ride one more heavily than the other (Mash & Wolfe, 2002).

In CD, for example, it has been proposed that antisocial patterns of behavior can result from an overactive BAS and an underactive (e.g., underregulated) BIS, a behavioral pattern that likely is determined primarily by genetic predisposition (Quay, 1993). Consistent with having an overactive BAS, children with CD show a heightened sensitivity to rewards (O'Brien & Frick, 1996). Additionally, these children fail to respond to punishment and continue to respond under conditions of no reward, behavior patterns that are consistent with an underactive BIS.

Simply put, where there is an underactive BIS, there is diminished response to warnings or reprimands and a poor response to punishment. For these children, this can lead to a failure to develop the anticipatory fear needed to avoid antisocial behavior. It can also lead to what is often termed a "lack of conscience" for their maldeeds. For example, most children respond to discipline and punishment by reducing their level of antisocial behavior. However, the opposite is often true for children who have antisocial behavior or conduct problems. When disciplined or punished, they might increase their problematic behavior and become even more defiant (e.g., an underactive BIS) (Mash & Wolfe, 2002). Low cortical arousal (e.g., an underactive BIS) may lead to diminished avoidance learning, (e.g., which can increase rule defiance and the number of conflicts with authority figures). In general, low levels of cortical arousal and autonomic reactivity (e.g., brain governance) seem to play a strong role in early- or childhood-onset CD (Mash & Wolfe, 2002). Numerous researchers have found evidence for the role of neurobiological and/or neuroanatomical factors in conduct problems (see Barkley, 1998; Lahey, Hart, Pliska, Applegate, & McBurnett, 1993; Loeber, Burke, Lahey, Winters, & Zera, 2000; McBurnett & Lahey, 1994 for a more full explanation).

Personal Factors

The leading personal factor that can raise alarm in the minds of many parents or caregivers is a difficult temperament in an infant or child. For example, temperament in a child can be viewed as individual differences in the child's emotionality, activity level, and sociability (Prior, 1992). Temperament is considered to be a personality characteristic that is influenced largely by heredity and environment (Wicks-Nelson & Israel, 2005). For example, Chess and Thomas (1977) specifically categorized temperament as being reflective of the infant or child's activity level (e.g., regularity of biological functioning [eating, sleeping]); approach or withdrawal to new stimuli (e.g., smiling, crying, indifference); adaptability to changing situations (e.g., eager, reluctant); level of stimulation necessary to evoke a response (e.g., intensity of the reaction to stimuli and mood level [pleasant, friendly, indifferent]); and the distractibility of external stimuli (e.g., attention span and persistence toward a task). Counselors should take notice that the terms "temperament" and "having a difficult temperament" are often in a state of flux or development. However, Plomin, DeFries, and McClearn (1990) viewed temperament as a relatively stable, innate personality characteristic that deserves serious consideration.

Counselors should be cognizant, for example, that children who possess a difficult or irritable temperament (e.g., hard to calm or soothe as infants) are often prone to developing disordered or antisocial behavior (Wicks-Nelson & Israel, 2005). For example, their difficult temperaments as infants can initiate negative interactions with parents or caretakers, leading to high rates of noncompliance and oppositional behavior in the early childhood years (Barkley, 1998; Kauffman, 2005). It is not difficult to understand that a biologically determined set of temperament tendencies or features and the development of CD can overlap considerably. Counselors should understand that a child's difficult temperament affects all family members and caregivers. Unfortunately, it is not unusual for a difficult temperament to be unrecognized, undiagnosed, or reacted to inappropriately (e.g., negative reactions directed back at the child; Erk, 1997).

Families that are consistently disrupted by the child's unsettling temperament rarely work well (Erk, 1997, 2000). Simply stated, the difficult temperament can cause myriad problems for both the affected child and the child's family. Children who have difficult dispositions or temperaments and do not have an understanding of their predicament may suffer countless failure experiences. Family-interaction problems accumulate and low self-esteem for the affected child can rapidly set in. These children may sense that they are different and disruptive, but their temperament often leaves them with few alternatives or options. Because personality theorists consider temperament to be a personal factor or personality characteristic, it can be expected to limit the person's behavioral options or choices (e.g., often linking the child with a repertoire of dysfunctional behavior) (Schultz & Schultz, 2001).

Moreover, personality factors can be described as psychologically or introspectively experienced by the individual (e.g., as perceptions, cognitions, emotions) and inspectively observed by others (e.g., parents, teachers, peers) as "behavior" (Ballis, 1997). Harris (1995) pointed out that the child's personality structure cannot be separated from its genetically embedded components. For example, these components are the dispositions or temperament that will be carried along into the child's environment (e.g., home, school, community), affecting the ways that significant others (e.g., parents, teachers) react to the child. Furthermore, the constancy of the child's behavioral and socialization difficulties arising from personal factors can frequently create the use of aversive behaviors (e.g., complaints, threats, commands, punishment). These are frequently used in attempts to have the child become compliant (e.g., comply more promptly with requests). These aversive actions, in turn, can often be expected to have strong or lasting reciprocal effects on the child (Erk, 1997, 2000).

Family Factors

In our society the family is considered the major arena for the socialization of children (Gladding, 2007; Maccoby, 1992). In many instances, however, families can be the places where antisocial behavior is learned and transmitted. According to Kauffman (2005), families that can be characterized by socially aggressive or antisocial behavior often exhibit many of the following characteristics: 1) There are often many children in the family and they might have come from different dyads; 2) the family is often broken by divorce or abandonment; 3) there are high levels of interpersonal conflict; 4) parental monitoring of children may be lax or nonexistent; and 5) where parental discipline is employed it is usually reactive, unpredictable, and harsh. Counselors, however, should not assume that all families are this way where a child or adolescent has a CD. Nonetheless, these are often the typical family factors that operate in the homes of many children who are characterized as being antisocial or conduct disordered.

Family factors and their influence are dominant during the childhood years when malleability is at its highest levels (Kauffman, 2005). Notable in the research literature is the finding that the family's interaction patterns are almost always coercive and are accompanied by high stress levels. Such family interactions constantly exert a threatening and ominous influence over the family. To complicate the situation further, the parents may be undiagnosed adults with CD or other disorders themselves. The influence of the family is the context from which disordered behavior can be internalized and endure in offspring (Wicks-Nelson & Israel, 2005).

Because interventions or treatment will need to include the parents, it is often warranted for counselors to seek the reasons why the parents are so disabled or dysfunctional. Barkley (2000b) cautioned counselors who work with parents of dysfunctional families that the parents are already prone to harsh, abusive, or violent interactions in their marital relations and toward children in the family. Barkley (2000b) and Ducharme, Atkinson, and Poulton (2000) advocated that any improvement in coercion in the family rests in training parents to have more effective child-management strategies. Parents often need to be instructed that the family should not expose the child to more undue harm from poorly or excessively applied behavioral punishments. Parents especially need instruction on how coercive family interactions are often at the heart of the family's continuing parent–child dysfunctions.

Kauffman (2005) suggested that there are five ways that families with antisocial behavior patterns can inculcate a negative teaching-learning process in their children. First, the social environment of the family provides aversive conditions (e.g., social disadvantage, emotional rejection by parents). Second, the children perceive the social environment of the family to be a threatening place to live and the family rewards aggressive actions. Third, the children's behavior is noxious and others in the family seek to control or punish it with increased punitive responses (e.g., often physical aggression). Fourth, the children are prone to developing a perception of themselves as inadequate and that a negative image provides a "goodness" of fit (e.g., with their family of origin). Fifth, and last, the children are repeatedly successful in overcoming the control of others by being more coercive and persistent, thereby, they are obtaining reinforcement for antisocial behavior. Taken together or in some combination, these familial antisocial behavior patterns or factors present formidable challenges. They are not unchangeable, but they will require that the counselor know of their existence and how they have operated, and plan accordingly.

Family factors, unfortunately, may provide children with vivid models of social and physical aggression. The family inadvertently supplies reinforcement to the children for aggressive behavior. For example, Bandura (1986) believed that social modeling is one of the most powerful ways that a child or adolescent receives instruction. Moreover, the rewarding consequences of behaving in the same way as other members of the family (e.g., the behavior delivers control) is likely to cement reciprocal negative patterns of behavior into the child–parent dyad. The family and its behavior patterns have provided fertile ground for the unrestrained growth of conduct problems. Before counselors can work effectively with the factors that operate in families where antisocial behavior exists, they need to understand and appreciate how these families have come to display and teach antisocial behavior.

School Factors

Schools and families are the two places where the antisocial behavior patterns of a child or adolescent with CD are most observable. These settings constitute the places where the problematic behavior and failure experiences typically begin and are often reinforced (e.g., with countercontrol measures). Schools are recognized as places where structure (e.g., rule-governing behavior) has to predominate. For example, the child or adolescent who is not a good fit for a school often becomes a candidate for a good dose of punitive measures. Although these punitive measures are intended to dissuade maladaptive behavior, the school more often than not uses them as measures to try to acquire control of difficult students. Schools, apparently, have spent little time researching how the school and school personnel might exacerbate the disorders that children bring with them into the school environment. The school, mistakenly, seems to feel that strong discipline measures work best with disruptive children and adolescents. In reality, the school is unknowingly playing into the hands of the disorders that are most disruptive to their setting.

The discipline that children with disruptive behavioral disorders experience at school is often not appreciably better than the parental discipline that they experience at home (Kauffman, 2005). Furthermore, the highly punitive and escalating discipline that they encounter in the home is about the same as what the school employs. Therefore, the child has difficulty perceiving how the home and school environments are different. Neither environment, to many of these children and adolescents, seems capable of judging them accurately, knowing what to do to assist them, or knowing how to work with them to break the cycle of low school achievement and peer rejection (Kauffman, 2005). For these children, every day at school, for example, seems to be more and more self-defeating and punishing.

To be objective, it is not fair to think that all school personnel (e.g., teachers, administrators) fail at teaching and managing "difficult" students (Kauffman, 2005). However, the typical school system has not sufficiently trained or in-serviced their educators and administrators on how to work more effectively with disruptive or antisocial students (Erk, 1999). This leaves the child or adolescent with a CD in the lurch, and often set off to the side, until someone decides what to do. There is often a large void in the training of the teachers and/or school personnel for dealing more effectively with such a student. Realistically, the student with CD is caught between the disorder and the inability of the school to respond with appropriate care and intervention. For example, the typical school experience for students with disruptive or antisocial behavior is highly negative and contributes to continued maladjustment (Kauffman, 2005).

Peer-Group Factors

In all likelihood, children and adolescents who display disruptive or antisocial behavior are the least accepted by their classmates or peers. From an early age, students can readily locate other students who are considered by the peer group to be somehow different. Normally developing children, for example, tend to shun or reject children who are highly aggressive and disruptive in play or academic activities at school (Guevremont & Dumas, 1994). In the school setting, peer rejection tends to heavily influence peer selection and socialization (Sue, Sue, & Sue, 2000). It might also be involved in how the teachers perceive such students in their classrooms. Teachers cannot be expected to be immune from what others in their social setting are perceiving.

Counselors should be aware that it is often within the social arena that children with behavioral and emotional disorders experience the most difficulty (Whalen & Henker, 1991). Children and adolescents with CD can be described as frequently being disruptive and demanding. In turn, these children often become the targets or victims of social harassment and isolation from their peers. This social harassment can be pervasive, can occur across settings, and can be mean-spirited. When this occurs, these children are then socially cut off. These emotionally charged experiences in the social arena can result in indelible memories for many of these children (Erk, 1999).

To counteract being left out or rejected by the majority of children at school, a child or adolescent with serious behavior problems (e.g., antisocial behavior) will often gravitate toward the peer group that is available or accepting (Erk, 1999). To achieve some sense of social standing and belonging, these children will seek to find acceptance with peers or students who have also been rejected or considered deviant (Barkley, 2000a; Ducharme, Atkinson, & Poulton, 2000; Farmer, Farmer, & Gut, 1999). Added to this scenario is the fact that parents or family members are usually poor at monitoring or correcting their child's behavior. It therefore often appears to outside observers that the parents are "enablers" or causative agents for the antisocial behavior in these children.

Loeber, Burke, Lahey, Winters, and Zera (2000) noted that children and adolescents who exhibit antisocial behavior are likely to identify and participate in acts of delinquency, to engage in substance abuse, and to develop increased levels of antisocial behavior from their association with deviant peers. Short (1997) pointed out that cultural factors and antisocial behavior typically coexist. For example, neighborhoods with high rates of crime, drug use, poverty, violence, unemployment, substandard housing, and other negative social conditions are players in the maintenance of aggression and antisocial behavior. The child or adolescent with disruptive or antisocial behavior is often oriented by this time in their life toward antisocial peers who usually engage in delinquency and substance abuse (Patterson, Reid, & Dishion, 1992). Frequently, the child has become enmeshed in social relationships and behavioral patterns that can lead to a high risk for incarceration or institutionalization.

Prevention Factors

Kauffman (2005) believed that prevention of disruptive behavior disorders is best served when parents, educators, and counselors in educational and mental health settings, and society as a whole, begin seriously addressing the following points or factors: 1) Provide effective consequences to deter aggression (e.g., particularly in young children); 2) teach nonaggressive responses to behavior problems (e.g., aggressive behavior is imitated or learned and so is nonaggressive behavior); 3) stop aggression before it takes root in the home and school (e.g., aggression often escalates from minor belligerence to major acts of antisocial behaviors, so we need to break this aggression chain early); 4) restrict access to instruments of aggression (e.g., aggressors use the tools that they have access to and are handiest, such as words, actions, and finally weapons); 5) restrain and reform acts of public aggression or violence (e.g., behavior that is observed affects one's own thinking and feelings); 6) seek to correct the everyday conditions of life that foster aggression (e.g., poverty and attendant deprivations); and 7) offer more effective instruction and educational options in public schools and mental health centers (e.g., highly differentiated curriculums, highly individualized counseling and treatment programs, and specific after-care programs that target these individuals).

Before counselors can effectively prevent disruptive behavior disorders, however, they must have information on what methods and procedures are available for their identification and/or assessment. Typically, as is true for the assessment of the majority of disorders, there are multiple ways to obtain reliable data or information on a client who might have a disruptive behavior disorder.

METHODS OR PROCEDURES FOR ASSESSMENT

There is no one failsafe assessment procedure available to counselors for accurately identifying antisocial behavior or conduct problems. Counselors who assess children and adolescents that are suspected of having a CD should consider adhering to an assessment that incorporates clinical interviews, behavior rating scales, and behavioral observations. Such an assessment has the ability to gather assessment information from different methods, from different sources, and from different settings. Counselors who might need to assess specific comorbid conditions that can accompany the CD are referred to McMahon and Estes (1997), Kamphaus & Frick (1996a), and Merrill (1994). This section will provide a practical overview of assessment procedures as they pertain to the assessment of children and/or adolescents suspected of having CD.

Pre-Assessment Issues

Several important issues or problems should be at the forefront of the counselor's thinking when assessing the child or adolescent for a CD. First, "client deceit" is common in a child or adolescent with CD. Children who engage in disruptive or antisocial behaviors are frequently deceitful (Frick, Lahey, Applegate, Kerdyck, Ollendick, Hynd, Garfinkel, Greenhill, Biederman, Barkley, McBurnett, Newcorn, & Waldman, 1994). The tendency to be deceitful makes it difficult for the counselor to obtain diagnostically relevant information from the child. For example, the child will often lie, deceive, minimize, or outright deny having engaged in any form of misbehavior (Sommers-Flanagan & Sommers-Flanagan, 1998).

Second, parent and teacher information should be considered potentially fallible. Unfortunately, depending on the relationship the parent or teacher has with the suspected child, the parent and teacher might not be fully informed regarding the precise nature and extent of the child's misbehavior (Sommers-Flanagan & Sommers-Flanagan, 1998). Kazdin (1995) noted that parents, teachers, and peers have often demonstrated low inter-rater reliability when identifying child-behavior problems. Moreover, the *DSM-IV-TR* cautions counselors that reports from collateral informants are often limited by inadequate supervision, lack of direct observation, and the child not having revealed them. Nonetheless, parents and teachers remain primary sources and need to be fully acknowledged for their attempts to supply diagnostically important information.

Third, counselor **countertransference** occurs where the counselor has strong personal or emotional reactions to working with a child who displayed conduct disordered behaviors. In such an instance, the counselor may inappropriately label a child with a CD when the child should have been labeled with a more appropriate or less severe and less negative diagnosis. Conversely, a counselor could, due to inexperience or other confounding factors (e.g., empathy), grossly underestimate or minimize the seriousness of the child's problems (Sommers-Flanagan & Sommers-Flanagan, 1998).

Fourth, **diagnostic comorbidity** means that many researchers consider comorbidity to be common in most children and adolescents diagnosed with CD (Harrington, 1993; Sommers-Flanagan & Sommers-Flanagan, 1998). (In a later section in this chapter, more information on the importance of comorbidity will be provided).

Fifth are confounding cultural and/or situational factors that research has demonstrated play active roles in the child's development (e.g., family conflict, dysfunctions, dissolution, school factors, peer factors, biological-genetic factors). (These factors were described in detail in an earlier section of the chapter.)

Additionally, when preparing to assess a girl for CD, counselors are advised to remember that girls are more adept at disguising their behavior, and can be prone to exhibit lying, truancy, running away, substance abuse, and prostitution (*DSM-IV-TR*). Also, in the *DSM-IV-TR*, counselors are advised that they need to determine whether the child's misbehavior is caused primarily by the underlying dysfunction or disorder or by adverse familial, social, and cultural circumstances. The next section discusses specific methods and procedures often found in the research literature.

Interviews

Interviews have the distinction of being the oldest method counselors use to detect a specific condition or disorder. They can also be used to determine the presence or absence of a disruptive behavior disorder. For example, the counselor can choose to interview the child, the parents, and the teachers. However, the counselor should recognize that children younger than 10 are not often able to reliably report their own behavioral symptomatology (McMahon & Wells, 1998). With older children, interviews can be helpful and informative in assessing the child's perceptions of their behavior. However, Sommers-Flanagan & Sommers-Flanagan (1998) cautioned counselors that interview information from the child can be untruthful and must be evaluated accordingly.

Interviews with the child and parents can be developmentally based. For example, in this type of interview, the counselor is seeking to obtain a developmental history on the child or adolescent. Developmental information can be obtained in a counselor-constructed interview (e.g., question-answer format) or by using a structured questionnaire format. Developmental information can be crucial for two reasons: 1) determining onset (e.g., child- or adolescent-onset); and 2) for confirming the presence of reactive or proactive aggressive behaviors (Dodge, Lochman, Harnish, Bates, & Pettit, 1997; Kauffman, 2005; Sommers-Flanagan & Sommers-Flanagan, 1993; Vitiello & Stoff, 1997). Treatment information then can be based accordingly on reactive aggression (e.g., characterized by frustration, self-control deficits, autonomic activation) and/or proactive aggression (e.g., characterized by emotional-autonomic control and reward expectation) (Dodge, Lochman, Harnish, Bates, & Pettit, 1997).

Structured instruments (e.g., standardized clinical interviews) that can be used are the Diagnostic Interview Schedule for Children—Revised (DISC-R; Costello, Edelbrock, Dulcan, Kales, & Klavic, 1984); the Child Assessment Schedule (CAS, Hodges, 1987); the National Institute of Mental Health Diagnostic Interview Schedule for Children Version IV (NIMH; Shaffer et al., 1996a); the Child and Adolescent Psychiatric Assessment (CAPA; Arngold & Costello, 2000); the Schedule for Affective Disorders and Schizophrenia for School-Age Children (SADS; Ambrosini, 2000); and the Diagnostic Interview for Children and Adolescents (DICA; Reich & Welner, 1989).

Counselors should be informed that although interviews develop important information, they are often time-consuming. Also, structured interviews might not always be based on or specifically target all of the *DSM-IV-TR* criteria for the disruptive disorder being assessed. Counselors are advised to study carefully, in advance, any interview (e.g., unstructured, structured) that they might seek to use. Last, several studies have examined the use of rating scales as alternatives to clinical interviews in order to assess CD and ODD (see Grayson & Carlson, 1991; Verhulst & van der Ende, 1991).

Behavior Rating Scales

Specific behavior rating scales are popular diagnostic tools for children with disruptive behavior disorders. For example, children, parents, or teachers can complete these scales (Kann & Hanna, 2000). Behavior rating scales have the advantage of permitting the counselor to assess a broad range of behaviors (e.g., known as broad-band rating scales) or to assess more specific behaviors (e.g., known as specific behavioral rating scales) (Kamphaus & Frick, 1996b; Merrill, 1994).

Broad-band behavior rating scales that can be used include the Achenbach Child Behavior Checklist (CBC) (Achenbach, 1991a; Achenbach & Edelbrock, 1983). The Achenbach instruments include the following: Child Behavior Checklist, Youth Self-Report, Teacher Report Form. These particular broad-band instruments can provide information about a broad array of problem areas (e.g., particularly from the externalizing dimension). Moreover, information from multiple sources can be compared, and access to age and gender norms is possible. The Behavior Assessment System for Children (BASC; Reynolds & Kamphaus, 1992) is another behavioral rating scale that permits assessment of a broad array of problems through reports from multiple informants (Wicks-Nelson & Israel, 2005).

Specific, often-used behavioral rating scales that the child, parents, or teachers can complete are the Eyberg Child Behavior Inventory and the Sutter-Eyberg Student Behavior Inventory (ECBI, SESBI; Eyberg, 1992). The ECBI is a parent-completed behavioral rating scale that was explicitly developed to assess disruptive behaviors in children; the SESBI is a parallel instrument designed to be completed by teachers (McMahon & Estes, 1997). The Self-Report Delinquency Scale (SRD; Elliott, Huizinga, & Ageton, 1985) and the Self-Reported Antisocial Behavior Scale (SRA; Loeber, Stouthamer-Loeber, Van Kammen, & Farrington, 1989) are self-report measures for the child (McMahon & Estes, 1997).

Numerous behavioral rating scales are published for use in the assessment of children or adolescents with disruptive or antisocial behavior. Depending on the specific purposes of the assessment, counselors should, of course, acquire testing information (e.g., data on reliability and validity, age range, behaviors targeted, norms available) that applies to any of the instruments they select.

Behavioral Observations

Actual behavioral observations have a long history as part of the assessment of disruptive behavior or CD (Wicks-Nelson & Israel, 2005). Direct behavioral observations across settings such as home, school, and clinic settings has been widely employed to assess parent–child, teacher–child, and child–peer interactions (McMahon & Estes, 1997). Behavioral observations across settings are important because they significantly aid in identifying or determining maladaptive interaction patterns between the child and the parent or teacher, and in assessing changes in these interactions as outcomes for treatment functions (McMahon & Wells, 1998). Kann and Hanna (2000) recommended that counselors often gain substantial information and insight through the use of direct observation of a child or adolescent.

The rationale for using behavioral observations is that interviews and behavior checklists may not permit the counselor to develop individual insights (e.g., into the world of the child). These individual insights could permit the construction of more individualized counseling or treatment strategies.

Behavior observation formats that might be particularly valuable to counselors because they contain psychometric properties are the Behavioral Coding System (Forehand & McMahon, 1981), the Dyadic Parent-Child Interaction Coding System II (Eyberg, Bessmer, Newcomb, Edwards, & Robinson, 1994), and the Interpersonal Process Code (Rusby, Estes, & Dishion, 1991). The Behavioral Coding System and the Interpersonal Process Code have been adapted for school use as well (Kann & Hanna, 2000). McMahon and Wells (1998) have done a through job of describing these behavioral observation formats for counselors who would like to have more information.

The counselor can use some behavioral observation instruments in the home and natural settings. An example is the Fast Track School Observation Program (Conduct Problems Prevention Research Group, 1992). However, this instrument requires observers with extensive training. The times of observation are lengthy and coordinating times of observation with relevant behaviors that occur naturally represent a significant scheduling challenge for counselors (Wicks-Nelson & Israel, 2005). An alternative is using trained observers in the home or natural environments. Adults in the child's environment are trained to observe and record behaviors that typically occur at low rates (e.g., fire-setting, stealing). These likely would be missed by trained observers making only occasional visits (Wicks-Nelson & Israel, 2005). Additionally, the home environment can be further documented by the use of the Parent Daily Report (Chamberlain & Reid, 1987) and the Daily Telephone Discipline Interview (Webster-Stratton & Spitzer, 1991).

Direct behavioral observations are desirable because reports based on interviews or questionnaires are potentially biased. If the counselor wants to make direct behavioral observations, Kann and Hanna (2000) suggested that there can be much to gain from careful observation, particularly as it relates to placing appropriate treatment regimens in place. Where counselors want to use these direct observational systems, it is suggested that they acquire more information and training in that particular instrument's usage.

COMORBIDITY OR CO-OCCURRING CONDITIONS

When working with children and adolescents diagnosed with CD and/or ODD, comorbidity should be expected (Kazdin, 1995; Mash & Wolfe, 2002; Wicks-Nelson & Israel, 2005). Counselors, therefore, should keep two points firmly in mind. First, comorbidity should not be mistaken for the primary condition. For example, the CD cannot be assumed to be the outcome of the comorbid conditions. The comorbid conditions exacerbate the child's or adolescent's attempts to function more successfully; they are not the central cause. Second, comorbidity can be developmental. For example, in early childhood the co-occurring conditions can be embryonic or minor. Then, as development proceeds, comorbid conditions are prone to becoming much more problematic.

Paternite, Loney, and Roberts (1995) believed that the emergence of comorbid conditions might indicate different levels of seriousness, with some comorbid conditions resulting in higher degrees of impairment. The importance of comorbidity in any disorder cannot be overstated (Barkley, 1998). Comorbid conditions are target areas that the counselor must address along with the primary diagnosis. Moreover, counselors should view comorbid conditions as multipliers of the effects of the original cause for the referral.

Attention-Deficit/Hyperactivity Disorder

Although AD/HD, ODD, and CD are considered by a wide body of clinical evidence to be different disorders (*DSM-IV-TR*), the overlap or comorbidity of these disorders is far above the level of chance (Hinshaw, 1987). Research studies have confirmed that the most frequently co-occurring condition with CD or ODD is AD/HD (Loeber, Burke, Lahey, Winters, & Zera, 2000). For example, almost half of all children under the age of 12 who meet criteria for a diagnosis of CD or ODD will meet criteria for AD/HD (Pliszka, Carlson, & Swanson, 1999). Indeed, Klein, Abikoff, Klass, Ganeles, Seese, and Pollack (1997), when seeking to find a group of pure CD children for a research study, found 69% of the CD sample concomitantly suffered from AD/HD. In other words, there are probably few cases of pure CD. Furthermore, these researchers (Reeves, Werry, Elkind, & Zametkin, 1987; Szatmari, Boyle, & Offord, 1989) found that more than 80% of preadolescents with CD had AD/HD. However, in adolescent populations, "pure" CD is more common. For example, Szatmari, Boyle, & Offord (1989) found that approximately one-third of adolescents with CD met the criteria for AD/HD. Therefore, counselors should be aware that the research evidence accrues toward greater impairment from the CD when AD/HD is clinically diagnosed in children. Conversely, there might be lesser impairment from the AD/HD in many adolescent-onset cases of CD.

Nonetheless, it is thought that the conjoint presence of the AD/HD serves to propel an earlier onset of the CD symptomatology. Such early onset of antisocial behavior, for example, continues to be the strongest predictor for the subsequent development of antisocial patterns of behavior in adolescence and adulthood (Hinshaw and Anderson, 1996). However, a word of caution is in order for counselors: Where there are early indices of aggression and extreme oppositionality, a critical question presents itself. Is the AD/HD symptomatology, either alone or when linked with CD, an independent predictor of subsequent antisocial behavior? Perhaps the safest conclusion for this question from the research that exists thus far is that the AD/HD clearly increases the risk for the early onset (e.g., childhood-onset) of ODD and CD. Indeed, the pairing of these disorders should be a major concern to parents, teachers, and counselors because this relationship is a key aspect not only to the symptom picture (e.g., prognosis), but also to the psychopathology that could evolve in many of these children.

For example, Pliszka, Carlson, and Swanson (1999) discovered that AD/HD/CD children, when compared to AD/HD children, alone, come from families that are more severely impaired; there are higher stress levels, substance abuse is usually present, and the parents frequently evidence a history of antisocial personality disorder (APD). Moreover, Pliszka, Carlson, and Swanson (1999) believed that AD/HD/CD children have lower verbal IQs and tend to evidence a wide range of learning disabilities and neuropsychological impairment. AD/HD continues to be the comorbid condition most commonly associated with CD, and it is considered to precede the development of CD in a majority of the cases (e.g., regardless of gender) (Hinshaw & Anderson, 1996).

For counselors, given the severity involved in their symptomatology (e.g., AD/HD, ODD, CD) and the likelihood of earlier onset, this group of children merits close scrutiny and would likely need more intense interventions (e.g., because of the comorbid conditions). Hinshaw, Lahey, and Hart (1993) believed that these children display more physical aggression, greater persistence in antisocial behavior, higher rates of peer rejection, and more severe academic underachievement.

Academic Underachievement

The academic underachievement and learning disabilities associated with CD, especially as they relate to antisocial and delinquent behavior patterns and school underachievement, are well noted by researchers (Hinshaw & Anderson, 1996). In children with CD, the acting-out behaviors (e.g., breaking school rules, physical aggression, truancy) often lead them into conflict with school authorities (e.g., school suspensions or expulsions). Coupled with classroom difficulties or learning problems, these prolonged absences from school can inevitably affect school achievement (e.g., often beginning a downward spiral). Moreover, when children have CD with AD/HD, it is likely that their cognitive and learning deficits are significantly exacerbated by the operation of this additional condition.

Hinshaw (1992) and Hinshaw and Anderson (1996) offered key conclusions for educators who work with these children. First, for child-onset CD, early development is marked by several interacting risk factors. These include behavior patterns common to the AD/HD spectrum (e.g., hyperactivity, impulsivity), family discord, neuropsychological deficits, and underachievement. Second, school or academic underachievement can be expected to predict later antisocial behavior patterns (e.g., discouragement, demoralization, frustration, anger). For example, early aggression and defiance of school authorities can precipitate poor attitudes in the classroom and learning failure. Therefore, the risk for school failure appears quite early in the development of these children. Third, the effects of underachievement and antisocial behavior are likely to become reciprocally intertwined (e.g., snowballing) across the developmental stages the child experiences.

Counselors should remember that the relationship among CD, AD/HD, and academic underachievement is laden with developmental significance. This significance, for example, when it is unidentified or mislabeled, often lies at the heart of bringing about academic underachievement in children. What needs more attention is providing early diagnoses and early interventions to children who are considered at risk for this comorbid condition. When this can be accomplished, the educational future for these children does not necessarily have to be reciprocally determined.

Oppositional Defiant Disorder

The most commonly co-occurring disorder in a child or adolescent diagnosed with CD is ODD (Kazdin, 1995). However, when the CD is prominent, the child is given only the CD diagnosis (Wicks-Nelson & Israel, 2005). The question that remains in the minds of many counselors, for example, is how these two disorders relate. Are they separate disorders, or is ODD a definite precursor to CD? Although the majority of cases of CD meet the criteria for ODD, most children with ODD do not progress, developmentally or otherwise, to having CD (Hinshaw, Lahey, & Hart, 1993). Therefore, counselors might diagnose one or the other, but be assured that ODD is not a definite trajectory for the development of a CD. For example, although there is considerable co-occurrence between children with AD/HD to have ODD and CD, for children diagnosed with AD/HD it is estimated that between 35% and 70% develop ODD, and between 30% and 50% develop CD (Johnston & Ohan, 1999). When these disorders co-occur, AD/HD seems to precede the development of the other two disorders; however, the development of a CD can be markedly less or might not appear.

Lahey and Loeber (1994), Lahey, Loeber, Frick, and Grimm (1997), Lahey, Waldman, and McBurnett (1999), and Loeber, Burke, Lahey, Winters, and Zera (2000) have all expounded a model for the relationships between AD/HD, ODD, and CD in children. These researchers have proposed that only children with preexisting AD/HD who also exhibit comorbid ODD will develop CD in childhood. Also, they proposed that a small subset of children later develop antisocial personality disorder (APD). Therefore, this model protends that there is a heterotypic developmental continuity or progression (e.g., the changing of manifestations of the same disorder) that is probable in cases of ODD, CD, and APD. The AD/HD and its severity, its early diagnosis, and its early treatment might, therefore, be the linchpin that possibly influence the developmental progression from less serious to more serious manifestations of antisocial behavior or CD. On this latter point, the research literature is generally consistent. AD/HD is often found to influence the development, course, and severity of CD (Loeber, Burke, Lahey, Winters, & Zera, 2000). For example, children with CD and comorbid AD/HD have a much earlier age of onset of disruptive or antisocial behavior than children with CD alone (Moffitt, 1990). Babinski, Hartsough, and Lambert (1999) used the *DSM-IV-TR* criteria to ascertain that the hyperactivity-impulsivity criteria contribute to risk for criminal involvement but not inattention (e.g., this might preclude the predominantly inattentive subtype). This risk was calculated over and above the risk associated with the development of early conduct problems. For example, aggressiveness (e.g., especially fighting) paired with heightened motor activity at age 13 was a stronger antecedent of adult antisocial behavior or criminality than aggressiveness only or motor restlessness only (Magnusson, 1988).

Anxiety Disorders

There is a growing body of research literature suggesting that the interplay of anxiety disorders and CD is important for outcomes in children and adolescents who have these disorders (Loeber, Burke, Lahey, Winters, & Zera, 2000). For example, some epidemiological studies have indicated that prepubertal children with anxiety disorders who do not have CD are at a reduced risk for later conduct problems in adolescence (Loeber, Burke, Lahey, Winters, & Zera, 2000). On the other hand, a substantial body of evidence suggests that CD and anxiety disorders are comorbid at substantially higher than chance rates during childhood and adolescence (Loeber, Burke, Lahey, Winters, & Zera, 2000; Loeber & Keenan, 1994; Zoccolillo, 1992). In ways not fully understood, childhood anxiety disorders may protect against future antisocial behavior or conduct problems when they occur alone; however, children and adolescents who develop CD are at increased risk for comorbid anxiety disorder (Loeber, Burke, Lahey, Winters, & Zera, 2000). It may be that the protective aspects of anxiety in childhood could emanate from behavioral inhibition rather than a lack of social interest or social contact (Wicks-Nelson & Israel, 2005).

Other findings related to the comorbid pattern of anxiety disorders and CD are that it is more likely to occur in boys during preadolescence into adolescence, but in girls from adolescence into adulthood (Lewinsohn, Rohde, & Seeley, 1995b; Zoccolillo, 1992). Young boys (e.g., prepubertal) with both anxiety and conduct disorders have been reported to be less aggressive than boys with conduct disorder alone (Hinshaw, Lahey, & Hart, 1993). Anxiety and/or depression with CD typically has a worse impact on older children or adolescents (Wicks-Nelson & Israel, 2005). For example, older boys with anxiety and conduct disorders are more antisocial or aggressive than are boys with only conduct disorder (Hinshaw, Lahey, & Hart, 1993). Children who go on to develop CD typically have the effects of the anxiety disorder compounding the effects of the CD (Loeber, Burke, Lahey, Winters, & Zera, 2000; Loeber & Keenan, 1994; Zoccolillo, 1992). There remains a complex relationship between anxiety disorders and CD; however, researchers are increasingly confident that a better understanding of these disorders and their possible outcomes is emerging (Loeber, Burke, Lahey, Winters, & Zera, 2000). Once these outcomes are better understood, important steps could be taken toward prevention or early intervention.

Mood and Depressive Disorders

Mood disorders and depressive symptoms are often comorbid, with many children and adolescents qualifying for a diagnosis of CD (Loeber, Burke, Lahey, Winters, & Zera, 2000). It is possible, for example, that CD is a precursor to depression in some children and adolescents (Capaldi, 1992; Loeber, Burke, Lahey, Winters, & Zera, 2000). Frequent failures and conflict experiences with parents, teachers, and peers from childhood would be expected to contribute to depression in many children with conduct problems (Dishion, Andrews, & Crosby, 1995; Dishion, French, & Patterson, 1995). Ultimately, it might be proven that mood disorders and depressive symptoms are concomitant disorders rather than actual precursors to CD (Capaldi, 1992; Loeber, Burke, Lahey, Winters, & Zera, 2000). In a review of the literature on this topic, Zoccolillo (1992) concluded that maintaining separate diagnoses for comorbid mood disorder from CD leaves the clear conclusion that there is a need to provide treatment to the specific emotional disorders that can coexist.

The high rate of comorbidity of depression with CD, for example, appears to increase the risk for serious outcomes such as substance abuse and suicide (Kazdin, 1995). Therefore, understanding that there is a relationship between depression and CD is an important step toward prevention and treatment of these serious, life-threatening conditions (Buydens-Branchey, Branchey, & Noumair, 1989; Loeber, Burke, Lahey, Winters, & Zera, 2000; Shaffer, 1974; Shaffi, Carrigan, Whittinghill, & Derrick, 1985). Because many adolescents, for example, have qualified for a diagnosis of mood disorder or depression along with CD (Mash & Wolfe, 2002), this tends to indicate that a relationship between the depression and the CD should not be ignored when planning assessment and/or treatment.

At present, the developmental sequencing between depression and CD is unclear. However, it is conceivable that their comorbidity might have started in preadolescence or childhood (Loeber, Burke, Lahey, Winters, & Zera, 2000). Descriptions of elated mood in the child or adolescent might warrant further investigation by the counselor (e.g., regarding the role of elated or manic mood in the etiology of the disruptive or antisocial behaviors). It is possible that, especially during elated or expansive moods, the commission of delinquent acts and criminal activity is escalated (Loeber, Burke, Lahey, Winters, & Zera, 2000). In periods of elevated mood, for example, it is likely that impulse control is minimal. Impulsivity is considered to be a correlate of conduct problems (Caspi, Henry, McGee, Moffitt, & Silva, 1995). The association that mood disorders (e.g., specifically, elevated mood) and depression have in the child, and particularly the adolescent with CD, seems little understood. Further investigation needs to occur regarding the role of elated mood and the etiology of multiproblem disruptive behavior (e.g., especially in adolescents) and in the risk for negative outcome (Loeber, Burke, Lahey, Winters, & Zera, 2000).

Substance Abuse

Research studies have documented a strong association between CD and substance abuse (Loeber, Burke, Lahey, Winters, & Zera, 2000). For example, the Ontario Child Health Study (Boyle & Offord, 1991) documented that CD was strongly associated with substance abuse. Findings in much of the research literature on this topic (see Loeber, Burke, Lahey, Winters, & Zera, 2000) has led to the following conclusions: (a) onset of CD precedes or coincides with the onset of substance abuse disorder (Huizinga, Menard, & Elliot, 1989; Mannuzza, Klein, Bonagura, Malloy, Giampino, & Alddalli, 1991); (b) early onset of substance use often serves as a predictor for later criminality; and (c) it is likely that the relationship between CD and substance use is reciprocal, with each exacerbating the expression of the other (Hovens, Cantwell, & Kiriakos, 1994). The relationship between CD and substance use in males and females is often aggravated by the co-occurring mood swings or depression (Loeber, Burke, Lahey, Winters, & Zera, 2000).

There is a strong association between illicit drug use and antisocial behavior, and adolescent substance abuse is closely related to a number of immediate dangers (e.g., accidents, violence, school suspension or expulsion, risky sexual activity) (Gilvarry, 2000). There can be little debate that conduct problems or antisocial behavior during childhood or adolescence are a risk factor for adult substance abuse. This linear relationship is seemingly mediated by the drug usage and delinquency that occurred during early and late adolescence (Brook, Whiteman, Finch, & Cohen, 1996). The prevalence of delinquent behavior varies with the severity of the substance abuse (e.g., about 10% of multiple-drug users commit more than half of all felony assaults, felony thefts, and index offenses; O'Malley, Johnston, & Bachman, 1999).

Juvenile Delinquency

Juvenile delinquent is primarily a legal term; it is not a psychological description. As a legal term, it refers to a juvenile (e.g., under 18 years of age) who has committed an index crime or status offense. An index crime is a crime that is illegal for a juvenile or adult (e.g., assault, rape, murder). A status offense is an act that is illegal for juveniles (e.g., truancy, violating curfews, incorrigibility). Delinquency can also be defined as keeping bad company, stealing in the company of others, belonging to a gang, and staying away from home or school (Wicks-Nelson & Israel, 2005).

Delinquency is a comorbid condition along with CD that can often be mistaken as a legal problem by the counselor (e.g., not amenable to counseling interventions). However, when it is viewed strictly within this venue, the child might not receive counseling services that could be beneficial. It is within the purview of the counselor to provide interventions to address not only the delinquency, but also how underlying causes (e.g., truancy, substance abuse) can contribute to its existence.

Gender Differences

Little research has been conducted on the role or mix of AD/HD, ODD, and CD in girls or women and its contribution to comorbidity. Although gender differences are evident in the expression and implication of symptoms in these disorders, there has been scant empirical investigation (Loeber, Burke, Lahey, Winters, & Zera, 2000). In their literature review, Loeber and Keenan (1994) located two themes related to girls and comorbidity. First, compared with adolescent boys, adolescent girls are apparently more at risk for anxiety and depression where symptoms for CD are present. This is in agreement with Robins (1986), who reported that disorders on the internalizing dimension (e.g., anxiety, depression) were common in women with CD, occurring twice as frequently as they did in women without CD. Second, there is reason to believe that gender and age are crucial parameters in the development of comorbid disorders. For example, where AD/HD is present in girls, it is a sign of general and specific developmental delays and impairments that can include cognitive deficits and emotional-behavioral regulation problems. Such delays, for example, can place girls at risk for continued development of disruptive behavior (Loeber, Burke, Lahey, Winters, & Zera, 2000). It is speculated that comorbidity for girls (e.g., where CD is present) may often occur at a higher rate than for many of their male counterparts.

The current evidence for gender differences and ODD is much less consistent than for the more serious CD behaviors. For example, McDermott (1996) reported higher mean teacher ratings of ODD behaviors among boys than girls (e.g., only among 5- to 8-year-olds in a nationally representative sample study of 5- to 11-year-old girls and boys). Williams, McGee, Anderson, and Silva (1989) compared 11-year-old girls and boys on a number of ODD behaviors self-reported by those youths and located no gender differences. Additionally, Bird, Gould, Yager, Staghezza, and Canino (1989), Bird, Gould, and Staghezza, (1993), and Verhulst, van der Ende, Ferdinand, and Kasius (1997) found no significant gender differences in the prevalence of *DSM-III-R* ODD among female and male adolescents.

Counselors need to remember that comorbid conditions, whether with CD or ODD, are in all likelihood going to be covert or on the internalizing dimension. This might be where girls and/or women are more adept at camouflaging them. However, the research evidence seems convincing that ODD prevalence in girls and boys is approximately equal. It is in cases of CD and gender comorbidity where research is striving to locate more information. The disruptive behavior disorders are seemingly the least researched *DSM* disorders in terms of gender differences (Kann & Hanna, 2000).

EMPIRICALLY SUPPORTED TREATMENT FOR CONDUCT DISORDER

Substantial progress has been achieved in the development of efficacious interventions for children and adolescents diagnosed with CD. Various empirically supported approaches are currently available to professionals for treatment of this disorder (McMahon, Wells, & Kotler, 2006). Moreover, professionals have widely adopted the standard of empirically supported or evidence-based practice. However, it should be mentioned that evidence-based interventions, including those presented in this chapter, might not result in the elimination of CD. Such a problem (and other concerns) remain formidable as professionals enter a new phase of deliberation regarding empirical or evidence-based practice (e.g., the nature of acceptable evidence, the sustainability of evidence-based practice) (Forness, 2005). Nonetheless, we can be encouraged that research is ongoing into the efficacy of interventions for children and adolescents with CD (McMahon, Wells, & Kotler, 2006).

Treatment Outcome Studies

To evaluate treatment outcome and therapeutic change that utilized Problem-Solving Skills Training (PSST) and Parent Management Training (PMT), Kazdin (2003) reported the following clinical studies: Kazdin, Esveldt-Dawson, and Unis (1987a) [Inpatient children ages 7–13, $n = 56$; Evaluated PSST. Relationship Therapy, and treatment-outcome control]; Kazdin, Esveldt-Dawson, and Unis (1987b) [Inpatient children ages 7–12, $n = 40$; Evaluated PSST and PMT combined and treatment-contact control]; Kazdin, Bass, Siegel, and Thomas (1989) [Inpatient and outpatient children ages 5–13, $n = 112$; Compared PSST, PSST *in vivo* practice, and Relationship Therapy]; Kazdin, Siegel, and Bass (1992) [Outpatient children ages 7–13, $n = 97$; Evaluated effects of PSST, PMT, and both combined on child and parent functioning]; Kazdin, Mazurick, and Siegel (1994) [Outpatient children ages 4–13, $n = 75$; Evaluated therapeutic change of completers and dropouts and factors that account for their different outcomes]; Kazdin (1995) [Outpatient children ages 7–13, $n = 105$; Replication of effects of combined treatment and child, parent, and family moderator of outcome]; Kazdin and Crowley (1997) [Outpatient children ages 7–13, $n = 120$; Examined relation of intellectual functioning and severity of symptoms on responsiveness to treatment]; Kazdin and Wassell (2000a) [Outpatient children ages 2–14, $n = 169$; Examined relation of parent psychopathology and quality of life as moderators of therapeutic changes in children]; Kazdin and Wassell (2000b) [Outpatient children ages 2–14, $n = 250$; Examined therapeutic changes in children, parents, and families and the predictors of these changes]; Kazdin and Whitley (2003) [Outpatient children (ages 6–14, $n = 127$; Examined the effects of addressing parental stress in treatment and the impact on perceived barriers to treatment and therapeutic change].

In general, the major findings or treatment effects that Kazdin (2003) derived from these studies can be summarized as follows:

1. PSST alone and PSST in combination with PMT produce reliable and significant declines in antisocial behavior and increases in prosocial (i.e., positive) behavior among children.
2. The combined treatment of PSST plus PMT tends to be more effective than either treatment administered singularly or in isolation.
3. Improvements in children are not credibly explained by the passage of time, repeated contact with a counselor, and the common or nonspecific treatment factors associated with participation (i.e., of the client) in treatment.
4. Children/youth referred for antisocial behavior and who do not receive PSST or PMT or who receive relationship-based treatment only usually do not change or they worsen over time in relation to their disordered conduct (i.e., problem symptoms).
5. The effects of treatment are apparent in performance at home, at school, and in the community both immediately after treatment and up to a 1-year follow-up assessment.
6. The effects of treatment have been obtained with both inpatient and outpatient clients.
7. Treatment outcome is influenced by multiple moderators such as greater severity of deviance in the child's behavior, parental psychopathology and stress, and family dysfunction at pretreatment are associated with less positive change.
8. The addition of a treatment component that addresses parent sources of stress in everyday life improves the treatment outcome for these children.
9. Treatment effects are not only obvious in child behavior but can also result in declines in stress, in maternal depression, and there is improvement of family relationships.

Problem-solving skills training (PPST) is the most rigorously investigated singular approach to the cognitive-behavior treatment of CD or serious conduct problems; the effectiveness of PPST when combined with PMT has been demonstrated in clinical research studies (Target & Fonagy, 2005). Many questions are yet to be resolved (e.g., does the impact of treatment alter the lives of children and families in palpable ways and whether or not these effects are long-term); for example, making any real difference to these individuals and to others with whom they interact. Kazdin and Wassell (2000b) believed their studies have shown that statistically significant improvements are made with treatment and that the magnitude of these changes (pre–post) is rather large (e.g., mean effect size of change >1.2). Moreover, treatment outcome studies indicate that clinically referred patients improve with PSST and PMT, and therapeutic effects (e.g., home and school) are maintained at least to the 1-year follow-up assessment (Kazdin, 2003).

IMPLICATIONS FOR PRACTICE/TREATMENT

Disruptive behavior disorders are multifaceted in the diversity of the disruptive and/or antisocial behaviors that can be manifested. In an attempt to bring structure to the implications for practice or treatment, interventions are grouped around the settings where they are most often found to be problematic. Research related to the psychosocial treatment of disruptive behavior disorders in children and adolescents has identified the family, school, and community settings as places where interventions or treatments are most needed. Counselors who work with these children, in all likelihood, will be asked to provide assistance where the disruptive behaviors usually take their heaviest toll—in one or more of these settings.

For counselors, Kazdin (1995) and Frick (1998) pointed out two important and useful findings with regard to children and adolescents who are identified with a disruptive behavior disorder. First, the onset of risk factors (e.g., genetic, socioenvironmental) in many of these children strongly suggests that there is stability and continuity for CD not only from childhood through adolescence, but often into adulthood. And second, children and adolescents with a CD are likely to experience a broad and disabling range of dysfunctions (e.g., antisocial behavior, conduct problems, impaired social and academic functioning).

In many cases, for example, it has been documented that parents and families of these children have exhibited a range of parental psychopathology (e.g., anxiety disorders, AD/HD, substance abuse, marital discord, and family aggression). Children and parents who engage in conduct disorder behaviors, particularly where aggression operates, have been found to show distortions and deficiencies in various cognitive processes (e.g., a lack of cognitive problem-solving skills). The apparent lack of cognitive problem-solving skills is not to be considered a lack of native intelligence. Kazdin (1995) and Frick (1998) believed that it is more likely to be some combination of the following psychosocial deficiencies: 1) in generating alternative solutions or different ways to handle social situations; 2) in being able to identify the means to obtain better results or consequences; 3) in being able to make attributions to others that are more accurate about the motivation for their actions (e.g., aggressive individuals usually attribute negative or hostile intent to others rather than themselves); 4) in being able to perceive how others feel (e.g., prior to or in response to their aggressive actions); and 5) in being able to have expectations for one's own actions (e.g., outcomes). Instead, relying on negative reinforcement or aggression in their human interactions to win their "points" has typically replaced rational thinking and behavior.

Counselors should know that no one treatment modality alone is going to be effective for every child or adolescent with a disruptive disorder. However, counselors should provide a multidimensional or broad spectrum of interventions so that benefits can be derived (Hanna, Hanna, & Keys, 1999). Moreover, there is no modality or intervention that will not be challenging to implement and accomplish. Successes and relapses in treatment and outcomes are to be anticipated. Opportunities for counselors to provide interventions are not necessarily lost, even if no interventions were conducted at an earlier age (Kazdin, 1995). Treatments or interventions that have been identified and shown to be clinically promising by Frick (1998), Kazdin (1995; 2003), Seligman (1998), and Wells and Forehand (1985) are detailed in the following sections.

Parent Management Training

Parent management training (PMT) refers to parents who have been instructed or trained by a counselor to alter the child's behavior in the home. In this model, the counselor serves as an educator and trainer whose prime responsibility is to effect a change in the parent's responses (e.g., thoughts, behaviors) toward a child or adolescent (Gladding, 2007). Typically, this type of training involves parents and children who are both participating (e.g., reciprocally) in negative thoughts and behaviors directed at each other. There is usually a longstanding history of such interactions. These interactions often have become tightly woven into the fabric of the family. Training generally follows the "shaping model" or systematic approximations to the desired behavior (e.g., having the parent learn to respond in more predictably positive ways).

The counselor prescribes a change in the way the parents and children think about each other; then altered behavior patterns can be established. In order for this process to occur, for example, counselors need to thoroughly analyze the antecedents (e.g., precipitating behavioral factors) and consequences (e.g., aggressive responses) that are enmeshed in the family's interactions (e.g., negative reinforcements). Because parent training is linear in its construction and application, the counselor's task is to decode what has previously occurred and teach the parents and children how to make more appropriate (e.g., positive or adaptive) responses to each other.

Parent-training procedures principally involve **verbal methods** and **performance methods** in which parents can be instructed in how to relate more appropriately to each other and their children. Verbal methods involve one-to-one instruction or teaching by the counselor. The parent, for example, is taught how to improve his or her verbal and nonverbal messages. Verbal messages influence one's perceptions, private thoughts, and covert speech, and can result in improved communication patterns. Performance methods can involve the planned use of role-playing, modeling, behavioral rehearsal, prompting, and coaching. The focus for the parents is on actual practice in behavioral settings that either approximate the environment or would occur in it. The outcomes sought are improved parent-child interactions.

Research, for example, has demonstrated that parent training in a variety of situations and tasks enhances generalizations from clinic to home (Barkley, 1998; Powers & Roberts, 1995). Parents are usually asked to keep a log or diary to chart the progress or relapses over the course of treatment. Successful efforts in achieving more positive parent–child interactions are reinforced (e.g., encouragement, compliments) by the counselor at each session. Regular telephone interviews by the counselor to determine the effects of the interventions can help to assess progress. It would not be inconceivable, for example, for all or a portion of the parent training to occur in the home or the natural environment, if possible.

Frick (1998), Kazdin, Siegel, and Bass (1992), and Kazdin (1995) featured parent training as a viable approach to reducing disruptive or antisocial behaviors in children. These researchers recommended that parent training incorporate many of the following features:

1. Treatment or interventions are primarily conducted with the parents. The counselor teaches or instructs the parents how to alter verbal and behavioral interactions with their child so as to decrease maladaptive or negative behavior. The young child or children are brought into the training sessions to train both the parents and the children in how to more appropriately interact. Adolescents participate in negotiating with their parents the development of behavior-change programs that are a better fit for their age and gender.

2. Parents and children are mutually, and as equals, taught by the counselor new ways to identify, define, and behave more accordingly across a range of behavioral situations.

3. Parents and children are instructed or taught applicable social-learning principles and procedures that are applicable to a more successful family life. For example these include how to socially reinforce each other and how to use time out and loss of privileges instead of aggression (e.g., verbal, physical) as a way of reinforcing each other.

4. Treatment sessions are opportunities for parents to view first-hand how techniques are implemented and practiced. At these sessions, the counselor and parents mutually review the behavior-change programs implemented in the home.

5. The child or children's functioning at school needs to be incorporated into parent training. Parent training should seek to include how the parents can more effectively manage school-related behavior, and how they can more effectively respond to requests from the school or teachers. Teachers should be recruited to assist in monitoring and managing behavior at the school. In this reciprocal system, parent training and teacher monitoring enables the two systems to assist and reinforce each other.

6. The counselor needs to remain vigilant about where the training might not have taken effect and where retraining may need to occur for benefits to begin accruing.

7.   Parents and their children need to be assured by the counselor that 100% behavioral compliance is not expected and that parents and children still have the right to say "no." In our society, a quiet or controlled child is not desirable (Wicks-Nelson & Israel, 2005). Moreover, it would be unethical to seek to reduce noncompliance in children for that end alone; compliance is not always a desirable trait and noncompliance might, at times, provide protection for the child. The desirable outcome is improved parenting skills. Compliance based on this context makes the family a more positive place to live.

The overview of the clinical evidence directly related to PMT is convincing. This is because PMT is probably the best researched treatment mode for children with oppositional and conduct disorders (Kazdin, 1995). The effectiveness of PMT has been evident in marked improvements in child behavior on a wide range of general measures such as post-treatment parent and teacher reports of deviant behavior, direct observations of deviant behavior at home and in the school, and institutional records (e.g., juvenile arrests) (Kazdin, 1995).

The impact of PMT is relatively broad; for example, siblings who are not the direct focus of training have reported improved parent-child interactions. The effects of treatment can also bring the problematic behaviors of treated children within the normative range of peers who are functioning at normal levels (Kazdin, 1995). There are several characteristics of treatment that Kazdin (1995) considered noteworthy; for example, brief and time-limited treatments (e.g., less than 10 hours) are less likely to show clinical benefits than are time-unlimited programs extending up to 50 to 60 hours of treatment. Therapist preparation, training, and skill were important variables related to outcomes. In families where higher-than-normal risk factors (e.g., parental psychopathologies) were operating, the treatment gains were fewer and less sustainable.

Outcome data for PMT remain on the positive side for most children and their families. However, the data are less well-defined for adolescents (e.g., more research on prevention could be the forthcoming answer for older children). A major advantage to PMT for counselors is that there are numerous written manuals and materials as well as videotaped materials available for parents and professionals (Kazdin, 1995).

Teacher Management Training

Teacher or school-based social learning interventions can include a wide range of strategies or procedures to aid in a problem student's management. It is suggested that counselors who employ these strategies consult closely with the teachers involved in the management of disruptive children in order to optimize their implementation and outcomes. Although these interventions cannot be expected to provide a cure, they are a beginning point for understanding how effective interventions for disruptive behavior may be construed and potentially better managed by teachers. Teachers, however, might need education and training in these strategies.

Walker (1995) discussed 12 intervention techniques for managing the student with disruptive behavior or aggression. Each can be used individually or in some combination by teachers in their classrooms. The following descriptions provide information for understanding how teacher-classroom interventions can be constructed:

1. *Rules* from the teacher and at the school need to be put into statements that clearly define the teacher's and the school's expectations for conduct, what is prohibited, and what the certain consequences will be. Rules should be stated as much as possible in the affirmative. Negative rules should be used only minimally, if at all. The message here is that rules can be positive conveyers of direction; they should not be phrased as "red flags" waiting to be dropped on the offender.

2. *Teacher praise,* at all times, needs to be positive and fit the child's action (e.g., behavior). False praise is not to be given just for the sake of getting some behavior going. Teachers are prompted to praise positive behaviors (e.g., catch the child being good) or when the child is within the rules for the classroom. Do not use praise sparingly or in a flattering type of way; instead, be specific and remember that praise can be the most important ingredient in a program of positive reinforcement. Rules that are combined with skillful reinforcement are much more effective.

3. *Positive reinforcement* is the presentation of a rewarding consequence that results in a satisfying state of affairs for the child. This state of affairs, in turn, increases the probability that the behavior will be strengthened. Rhode, Jenson, and Reavis (1992) believed that positive reinforcement should be given 1) immediately after the appropriate behavior, 2) frequently, 3) with enthusiasm, 4) with eye contact from the teacher, and 5) with a description of the behavior that earned the reinforcement.

4. *Verbal feedback* from teachers about the appropriateness or inappropriateness of academic or social behavior in the classroom is crucial. Teachers' responses to the student's academic performance or social behavior (e.g., the content, emotional tone, and timing of what they say and do in reaction to their own behavior or another student's behavior) are important factors in how the student learns how to behave. Giving positive yet clear feedback and steering clear of arguments requires experience and training.

5. *Stimulus change* is the alteration of antecedent events or stimuli that set the stage for disruptive or antisocial behavior. For example, teachers can frequently increase compliance by making assignments or instructions shorter and clearer. Presenting tasks or assignments in different ways can defuse resistance and decrease noncompliance. Attend to the events that have previously led to disruptive episodes in the classroom. Modification of the context is often found to lessen or reduce disruption or aggression. Teachers find new ways to present instructions or assignments that defuse rather than continue to incite.

6. *Contingency contracting* is when a written behavioral contract or performance agreement is mutually written and agreed on by the child, the parents, and the teacher or school. Factors to consider are that the contract must be simple and straightforward in what is expected, and that there will arise instances or circumstances

that require revision. All parties agree on and sign the document. Contracts should not be used as the sole strategy for improvement in the student's behavior. Contingency contracts are useful for carefully delineating acceptable and not acceptable behaviors.

7. *Modeling plus reinforcing imitation* is showing or demonstrating the desired behavior and providing positive feedback and reinforcement. It is learning through careful watching of models and imitating them. It is observational learning, which is a basic social learning process. Models can be adults or peers, but it is crucial that the student be carefully instructed in whom to watch, what to look for, and what to imitate. It is not useful to simply ask the student to go watch someone. Effective instruction in modeling and reinforcement can be done in private one-to-one sessions. Positive social interactions need to be practiced in everyday circumstances. After practices are initiated, the student needs to receive clear direction and feedback on his or her performances and what he or she might need to do to effect improvements (e.g., continued practice and reinforcement).

8. *Shaping* is the process of building new responses that successively approximate the desired or target behavior. Logically, this could be an outcome of modeling or instruction and practice in making more efficacious responses. The key to shaping is not going for the whole behavior in one practice, but rather to skillfully teach the student the successive steps (e.g., shaping) that are required to learn to make a new response. For example, a pigeon learned to identify and peck the red button to get the food pellet by first learning to turn its head in the direction of the button that would ultimately release the food pellet (the reinforcer). Although the idea is simple, the timing and implementation of new behavior, as is true of reinforcement, is where art and science must meet. The science is in the details, which take time and practice.

9. *Systematic social-skills training* is actually putting together a curriculum of social skills that are taught to the student. For a social-skills training program to be effective, it must be intensive, systematic, and aimed at the demonstration and practice of the social skills the student needs. What might be different with many children who have disruptive or antisocial behavior is the often large amount of inappropriate social behavior that already exists. It may be ingrained and require great patience to understand and ameliorate. Remember that these children do have social-skill deficits (e.g., they might not possess the necessary skills) and there can be serious performance deficiencies (e.g., they really do not know how to use the social skills appropriately). Although teachers and peers cannot seem to fathom that this could be the case, in reality, it is what is keeping many of these children socially dysfunctional. First, a strong didactic or teaching approach is often recommended, where social-skills education and training is coupled with immediate and repeated practice in one-to-one sessions. Second, social functioning or the skills that were targeted are practiced in real-life settings where reliable and constructive feedback from teachers and peers can be obtained. Third, the student needs to be taught how to react more appropriately when a teacher or another student says "no," how to cope more effectively with frustration when classmates engage in teasing or taunting, how to respond to a classmate who tries to deliberately inflict hurt feelings, and the importance of understanding that not all social situations go your way. The ultimate goal of social-skills

training should be for the student to have adequate opportunities to locate an earned sense of social connectedness.

10.   *Self-monitoring and self-control training* are often at the heart of lessening or reducing disruptive behavior. So much of the problem seems to reside in these areas. This involves procedures that actually teach the student how to achieve an increased level of self-monitoring. These procedures often require explicit training and practice. Procedures can include learning to keep track of one's own behavior (e.g., externally [daily log] and internally monitoring one's one thoughts prior to any actions). In essence, it is learning how to use self-talk or hearing your own internal dialogue to change your feeling states. This makes it more feasible for the student to behave in more positive ways. Self-monitoring may be inappropriate for students who are seriously aggressive and for students whose cognitive awareness or maturity is too impaired to carry out the procedures.

11.   *Time out* is a procedure where the student is removed for a specific amount of time and placed in a specific location where positive reinforcement is not obtainable. Time out might mean removing the student from the group or classroom. This is not always necessary because the teacher can refuse to respond by turning away and withdrawing points, tokens, or other rewards. Time out should be reserved for serious behavioral problems. Time out is also considered to be more effective with young children than adolescents. Time out that is used knowledgeably and skillfully with other positive procedures has value as a behavior-change agent. When it is overused, when the child is placed somewhere where a misbehavior can occur, or when it is purely a punitive measure, time out is not being used correctly.

12.   *Response cost* is the fine or penalty for each instance of a specific misbehavior. For example, minutes of free time, a portion of recess time, or access to a preferred activity (e.g., the snack bar) can be withdrawn for an instance of inappropriate behavior. Remember that a strong program of positive reinforcement reinforces a response-cost program. The student can understand that the cost response is not simply a mean-spirited act, but rather a way of shaping more positive behavior.

The use of one or two of these teacher management procedures is not what is intended. Counselors, teachers, or school personnel should seek to employ as many of the procedures or strategies as are feasible. It is not expected that all of these will be utilized. However, each student needs to receive those procedures that have the best fit with the array of disruptive behaviors exhibited.

Family Systems

A family counseling systems approach (e.g., functional family therapy, multisystemic family therapy) makes sense where disruptive behavior disorders are present. For example, not only is the child being affected by his or her own behaviors, but family members and peers are also being seriously affected (Kann & Hanna, 2000). To the extent that negative parent–child interactions are routinely taking place, it is reasonable to expect that the family's subsystems (e.g., husband-wife, parent-child, home-school) are seriously being challenged or disrupted. In other words, the approach taken needs to take into account how specific parental behaviors are occurring, how negative parent–child interactions are occurring, and how these behaviors and interactions from the home can be transported and occur at the school and with peers.

Family counseling, for example, that deals specifically with the patterns of disruptive behavior in the family is a relatively recent treatment methodology. Increasingly, however, families with disruptive behavior disorders are being identified and often treated with one or both of these approaches. In functional family therapy and multisystemic family therapy, the therapist or counselor identifies and focuses on the individual and familial patterns of behavior that sustain the children's and parents' actions toward each other, including the multiple effects on the family's subsystems (e.g., multisystemic therapy).

Functional Family Therapy

Functional family therapy (FFT) views behavior as "functional," or as serving a purpose (Gladding, 2007). For example, these functional behaviors represent efforts (e.g., positive or negative) to meet one's needs in personal and interpersonal relationships. Many of these needs might have been learned from previous family or interpersonal situations, or they might be the products of poor cognitive functioning. In FFT, these functional (or really dysfunctional) behaviors seem to repeatedly hinder family members and operate to achieve the following interpersonal states: 1) achieving contact or closeness (e.g., parents demonstrate concern over the delinquent behavior of a child, which brings contact or closeness depending on the parent's perceptions); 2) achieving distance or independence (e.g., parents/family members learn to stay away from each other for fear of aggression or fighting); and 3) achieving a combination of contact/closeness and distance/independence (e.g., viewed as midpointing [drawing close and repelling each other]) (Alexander & Parsons, 1982; Gladding, 2007).

Counselors who use FFT, which is behavioral and systemic, often use a three-stage process to work with these families. First, there is **assessment.** This is where the counselor's focus is on the function that the behavioral sequences and exchanges (e.g., their antecedents and consequences) between each family member serves. Specifically, the counselor seeks to discover whether the behavioral sequences promote closeness, create distances, or help the family to an outcome or task. The counselor gathers this information about the family by asking each family member questions and by observing their interactions during therapy sessions. Second, there is **change.** Change is carried out by clarifying the dynamics operating in the family's relationships; identifying and integrating thoughts, feelings, and behaviors to the family's members; explaining the functions of current family behavior; relabeling behavior so as to lift the concept of blame; discussing how the removal of negative behaviors will affect the family's functioning; and ultimately, shifting the treatment (e.g., FFT) from individuals to the entire family. Third, FFT emphasizes

maintenance. This is accomplished through educating and training the family in communication skills that are useful in maintaining progress and for dealing with future difficulties (e.g., contracting, enhancement of communication skills) (Alexander & Parsons, 1982; Gladding, 2007).

Frick (1998) recommended that there are several important variables to consider in FFT; they are the following: 1) A large number of participants or families are prone to not completing its treatment; 2) counselors should attempt to avoid conveying possible indications of a condescending attitude, blame, judgment, or insensitivity to cultural issues that might be present; 3) counselors should attempt to model positive statements and beliefs that can facilitate the use of these skills in their families; and 4) the counselor should attempt to modify or add treatments or interventions based on the individual needs of the family (e.g., often needing to be tailored to each family). In essence, for counselors, FFT is the examination of the family's transactions-behaviors and the substitution (e.g., of the unworkable behavioral repertoire) for more functional responses and behaviors. This process can attain the family's release from the disunifying or dysfunctional behaviors it was previously under, consequently empowering a more fully functioning family unit. When FFT is explicit and tailored for the individual family, it can influence the effectiveness of treatment and has proven successful in treating older children and adolescents with CD (Alexander, Holtzworth-Munroe, & Jameson, 1994).

Multisystemic Therapy

Multisystemic therapy (MST) is a family-systems–oriented approach (Henggeler & Borduin, 1990; Henggeler, Schoenwald, Borduin, Rowland, & Cunningham, 1998). MST is based on the premise that the child exists and operates in multiple systems. For example, the family, school, peers, neighborhood, and community are all systems in which the child or adolescent is more or less forced to function. A significant difference between MFT and MST is the emphasis on the various systems that impinge and operate in a mutual fashion, with respect being paid to the effects of the system on the child and the child's effects on each system. MST utilizes the counselor's knowledge and ability to provide analysis of the child's systems. Particularly, it analyzes how information about the child's interactions with these systems can effect changes in not only the child, but in the systems themselves (e.g., that surround the child and the family as a whole). Actually, the family is viewed as residing and interacting within these various systems. Escape from these systems is not possible; this would not be considered healthy for the child or family members. It is within these systems that behavioral change occurs, reinforcement comes about, and a prognosis for more healthy family functioning can be achieved.

MST addresses not only the family system but also the skills (e.g., emotional control, anger management, behavioral repertoire) of the child or adolescent, especially as these skills relate to their experiences (e.g., successes, failures) in and with each system (e.g., school, peers, neighborhood, community). The goal in MST is to preserve the family, but for this to happen, the priority is to have the child and family members understand more about how their behavior affects (e.g., reciprocally) themselves and the systems in which they must live. Therefore, MST imposes on the counselor a significant amount of responsibility for the skill the counselor exhibits in clinical decision-making (e.g., assessing and providing feedback on how the individual family member is presently functioning within each system) and devising treatment regimens for all family members in order to function more adequately in these systems. Under these conditions, treatment with MST may best be considered a comprehensive approach. Each system in which the child and family members need to function more integrally is thoroughly addressed.

Frick (1998) cautioned that MST is highly dependent on the quality of the counselor's training and willingness to perform comprehensive assessments of each system (e.g., for its two-way effects). Kazdin (1995) believed that counselors who use MST should realize that it is a "family-based" treatment approach that draws on as many techniques as the counselor deems necessary to address behavioral problems at the level of the child, family, and extra-family systems (e.g., that the family operates in and with). The focus of treatment remains on interrelated systems and how they affect the child. However, specific domains that have effects on a particular system (e.g., parent unemployment, parental substance abuse, parental stress, marital discord, ineffective discipline procedures) are often addressed.

Kazdin (1995) believed that the overview of the clinical evidence on MST revealed the following:

1.   MST showed itself to be superior in reducing delinquency, reducing emotional behavior problems, and improving family functioning (Henggeler, Rodick, Borduin, Hanson, Watson, & Urey, 1986). Moreover, follow-up studies of MST in separate samples have shown that up to 2, 4, and 5 years later MST adolescents have lower arrest rates than children who received other services (Henggeler, 1994).

2.   Parents and children have shown reductions in coalitions (e.g., less conflict, hostility) and increases in support (e.g., parents have increased verbal communication and decreased conflict) (Mann, Borduin, Henggeler, & Blaske, 1990).

3.   Overall, MST has consistently shown that treatment using this model leads to change in adolescents and that changes can be sustained. Frick (1998) considered MST to be a successful treatment because it does not select "one best" intervention such as PMT and seek to use it with all the children and family members. Moreover, MST has the large advantage of not ignoring the multidetermined nature of disruptive behavior disorders. It recognizes the fact that a multidimensional approach to treatment is needed. Acknowledging that the child and the family operate in systems verifies that treatment cannot be one-dimensional for everyone.

Cognitive-Behavioral Skills Training (Including Problem-Solving Skills Training)

Cognitive-behavioral skills training (CBST; Frick, 1998), targets specific cognitive processes that have been implicated in the development of CD. Inherent in this approach is the role that learning and self-management has played in the lives of children and families where CD has been identified. For example, two processes were identified by Frick (1998), that are considered to be within the individual (e.g., intraindividual) and are linked to conduct disorders. The first one is problems of poor or inadequate impulse control (e.g., novelty or thrill-seeking behavior, actions taken without forethought for the consequences). The second is deficits connected to poor social cognition (e.g., inadequate social forethought) that often predisposes the child to act aggressively. For example, there seems to be the tendency for the individual to attribute (e.g., cognitively) malicious intent to the actions of others, and a deficit in the ability to develop a range of nonaggressive responses to perceived provocations (e.g., from peers, parents, teachers). Where counselors used this type of intervention, Kann and Hanna (2000) recommended that it needed to contain "supportive positive reframes" whether used individually, in a group, or in family therapy. This is because the issue of self-esteem is so integrally involved in the CBST approach. So while building specific skills, for example, the counselor is also reconstructing or preserving needed self-esteem.

Moreover, CBST is explicitly a skills-building type of intervention that utilizes the teaching of specific skills to change a maladaptive interpersonal style of behaving (e.g., responding). For example, Frick (1998) believed that CBST could be taught in training programs in small groups of 3 to 5 children or adolescents in 18 to 22 sessions (booster sessions might be required in individual counseling sessions). Examples of programs that the counselor could use with children and adolescents who have conduct disorders include one or more of the following: 1) the Self-Instructional Training Program (see Kendall & Braswell, 1985); 2) the Anger Coping Program (see Lochman & Wells, 1996); and 3) the Promoting Alternative Thinking Strategies Curriculum—The Fast Track Modification (see Bierman & Greenberg, 1996). Counselors may seek to develop a program of their own from one or more of these programs.

Another example of a CBST-related program is the Families and Schools Together (FAST Track) Program developed by the Conduct Problems Prevention Research Group (CPPRG, 1992). The FAST Track program was designed to have counselors intervene early in the child's development of conduct disorders. Therefore, it is a secondary tool designed to prevent the child from developing a more severe conduct-disorder behavior.

Specific parts comprise FAST Track's implementation. First, it includes 22 sessions of enhanced PMT intervention conducted in a group format. Second, the FAST Track program involves the designation of a home-visitor-management component. A case manager visits in the homes biweekly to help parents practice skills learned in PMT. Third, it includes a strong dose of CBST that features social-skills training for family members. Fourth, the FAST Track program includes an academic tutoring component designed to promote improved reading skills to enable and encourage the parents to participate more in the child's academic progress and homework assignments. Fifth, the FAST Track program includes a universal classroom intervention (e.g., how to promote emotional awareness, self-control, and interpersonal problem-solving) that teachers are asked to implement not just for FAST Track students, but for all students in the class.

In the FAST Track program, during the first summer after the first school year of intensive interventions, case managers continue to contact and monitor families.

There are monthly home visits and weekly phone contacts; the academic tutoring is continued at the level of intensity the individual child needs so that gains made will not be forfeited.

Unfortunately, there is not an overview of evidence related to the viability of the FAST Track approach. Its salient points, however, are that it is school and community based in its intent and implementation. There are few such programs available today that specifically target the other lairs for the development or maintenance of conduct disorders, the school and community.

Another line of programmatic skills-based training heavily influenced by the cognitive-behavioral skills training model (CBST) is Problem-Solving Skills Training (PSST), which can be combined with behavioral parent training or Parent Management Training (PMT), to treat children (i.e., ages 7–13) for CD (see Kazdin, 2003 for an extensive review of PPST). Central to the treatment of CD using PPST are the use of *problem-solving steps and self-statements* designed to break down interpersonal situations into units that permit identification and use of prosocial responses.

The *first* problem-solving step and self-statement is: "What am I suppose to do?" The purpose is to require the child to identify and define the problem. The *second* problem-solving step and self-statement is: "I have to look at all my possibilities." The purpose is for the child to delineate or specify alternative solutions to the problem. The *third* problem-solving step and self-statement is: "I'd better concentrate and focus in." The purpose is for the child to concentrate and evaluate the solutions he or she generated. The *fourth* problem-solving step and self-statement is: "I need to make a choice." The purpose is for the child to choose the answer he or she thinks is correct. The *fifth*, problem-solving step and self-statement is: "I did a good job" or "Oh, I made a mistake." The purpose is verify whether the solution was the best among those available, whether the problem-solving process was correctly followed, or whether a mistake or less than desirable was selected and the steps or process should be repeated. It is important to point out that role playing is used extensively; moreover, it pairs the skills training with *in vivo* practice techniques. PPST is administered individually over 20 sessions; each training session lasts approximately 45–50 minutes (Kazdin, 2003; McMahon, Wells, & Kotler, 2006).

I contend that the implications for practice or treatment contained in this chapter could wholly or with some modifications be quite workable with children and adolescents who have a diagnosis of CD, ODD, and/or AD/HD (with or without the comorbidity of the other conditions). They can also be delivered to children and adolescents with a disruptive behavior disorder in a number of different settings (e.g., home, school, mental health center, community).

BEST PRACTICE GUIDELINES

All counselors are well served by keeping abreast of the "practice guidelines" for CD and/or ODD in the professional literature. For example, counselors should consult the practice guidelines for CD and/or ODD contained in the *Journal of the American Academy of Child and Adolescent Psychiatry* (1997c; Volume 36, Suppl., pp. 122S–139S); *Journal of the American Academy of Child and Adolescent Psychiatry*

(2007; Volume 46, pp. 126–142); and *Practice Guidelines for the Treatment of Psychiatric Disorders: Compendium 2006* (American Psychiatric Association, 2006). Clinical and/or practice guidelines are recommendations that are based on limited empirical evidence and/or strong clinical consensus. The counselor should always consider practice guidelines, but there may be exceptions to their application. Practice guidelines are increasingly being used and/or required by school systems, mental health centers, and managed-care organizations.

SCHOOL AND FAMILY PERSPECTIVES

School Factors

In schools, if children with disruptive behavior disorders are to experience success, the negative attitudes of school personnel must be overcome. Although these negative attitudes have been acquired in working with these children, they are the biggest obstacles to making changes in the lives of children with conduct disorders. School personnel must realize that along with the parents, the school is a primary player in how these children will turn out.

Schools have the prerogative for setting the stage for how these children will be treated (e.g., punitively or positively). Although there would appear to be a strong need for appropriate management of these children, the counterweight is to not make each school day a punitive or punishing one. It is at this point, for example, that the school becomes the fulcrum. School personnel (e.g., teachers, administrators) have the option of setting the stage for how these children will be treated each day. For example, teachers need to make sure that attitudes toward these children are changed throughout the school building from being one of "How can I punish or avoid you?" to one of "As your teacher, I will strive to be positive each day." The child's level of achievement (e.g., academically, socially) should not be permitted to determine the teachers' attitudes. What is meant by this change in teacher's attitudes is that teachers cannot expect that change in these children or adolescents will come about rapidly; it will have to be viewed as a long-term process. For example, a planned, stepwise approach that consistently applies a positive attitude can result in significant improvement in areas of dysfunctioning (e.g., school behavior, academic effort, social skills).

However, without a positive attitude toward children with conduct disorders, the school itself cannot be perceived by the child or adolescent to be a therapeutic place. Moreover, there is not much likelihood of an alliance between the child, their family, and the school developing. It is often true that some schools have not been sympathetic or helpful in these cases. Schools and school personnel are legally charged by federal statutes and state laws to identify, assess, and provide appropriate treatment for all children who have legally recognized medical or psychoeducational disorders (Erk, 1999). Schools cannot legally claim that they cannot handle these children or that they do not have the resources for the types of problems these children bring to school. Schools that are do likely going to be in violation of applicable legal statutes. In many schools, however, school personnel seek to be in compliance and to genuinely serve these children and their parents. We must be careful not to accuse or blame all teachers and school administrators of failing to serve or teach these students. However, the typical school day for many children with conduct disorders remains highly negative and contributes to further maladjustment (Kauffman, 2005).

Family Factors

The initiation and development of communication patterns that are carefully predicated on dealing with the parents as equals to the school are often the prelude for what might subsequently follow. For example, families of children with conduct disorders often feel that school personnel have not been positive or helpful to their children (Manassis & Monga, 2001). Parents often feel that the school did not care enough about the problems that were occurring and did not work to help their child. Instead, parents often feel that they are being accused of being the sole cause of the child's problems both in the home and at school. This thinking, whether accurate or not, is the perception of the parents and what they subsequently act on. Therefore, the school is often not viewed as a source of help or assistance, only blame and continued portrayals of the parents or the home as the center of all the problems. Although these forces may certainly be at work, parent psychiatric disorders, parent discipline practices, and parent economic disadvantage can often be the more salient factors or perspectives (Kazdin, 1995). Counselors have to assess and consider these forces for their effects. Apart from the co-occurrence of the effects of the school and family on each other, and the perspective that each has of the other, the interaction of these two entities has the potential to set the stage for the development of significant risk factors (e.g., academic, social, and behavioral dysfunction). These risk factors can substantially increase contact with school authorities, the juvenile justice system, and possible incarceration. Risk factors over time may become interrelated because the presence of one or two factors can easily augment the accumulation of other risk factors. For example, because the school and the family often place themselves in the role of disagreeing or exacerbating each other.

For counselors, two points about the school and the family seem very relevant to children with conduct disorders. First, risk factors for the school and the family are more likely to result in negative outcomes where neither system has taken the time to explore what their particular roles might be in this process. For example, because risk factors cannot be eliminated, the benefits of having integrated systems (e.g., school, family) working together has to outweigh working separately. Remember that risk factors do not determine or invariably lead to a particular result. Second, it is wise to remember that risk factors do not precisely tell us how the dysfunction actually comes about. Separate lines of research are required to focus on how certain factors operate, combine, and affect some children and not others. For counselors, identifying the risk factors, how they operate, and how they interrelate, for example, with the school and family system, are all integrally important for developing effective preventative measures and treatment interventions for conduct disorders (Kazdin, 1995).

MULTICULTURAL CONSIDERATIONS

Multicultural issues that are considered to be primary to the diagnosis of a CD are generally discussed for counselors under three areas (e.g., specific culture, age, and gender issues) in the *DSM-IV-TR*. These issues are crucial because they can relate to children and/or adolescents with CD and/or ODD. I believe, for example, that although comorbidity may be present in each case where CD and/or ODD is diagnosed, multicultural issues in CD and/ODD are always present. Thus, counselors should carefully consider them before making a diagnosis.

Both CD and ODD, for example, are considered to be more prevalent among children and adolescents from families and neighborhoods where crime rates are elevated, violence is present, traumatic stress is evident, and low socioeconomic status predominates (Hinshaw & Anderson, 1996). These conditions are often underappreciated for their contribution to the development of antisocial behavior or conduct problems. For example, CD and juvenile delinquency are more common in neighborhoods characterized by high poverty and crime rates and subsequent social disorganization (e.g., dysfunctional family structures) (Lahey, Waldman, & McBurnett, 1999; Loeber, Farrington, Stouthamer-Loeber, & Van Kammen, 1998). Therefore, researchers often hypothesize that children and/or adolescents from disadvantaged neighborhoods, which are often composed of specific or culturally mixed ethnicities, are more likely to receive the label of Conduct Disordered.

The CD diagnosis need be applied only when the behavior in question is symptomatic of an underlying dysfunction (e.g., it is intraindividual or within the child or adolescent), and not simply a judgment call in reaction to the immediate social and/or economic contexts (*DSM-IV-TR*). Moreover, the prevalence rates for CD and ODD in disadvantaged neighborhoods compared with advantaged inner city neighborhoods have not been sufficiently researched and documented. Therefore, current evidence on possible prevalence rates of CD and ODD in rural and urban environments is decidedly mixed (Lahey, Waldman, & McBurnett, 1999). The clinical realities of antisocial behavior are complex and seem to be variegated. For example, there are no clearly defined demarcations of contextual versus intraindividual variables (e.g., as to their precise location) and precisely how they have come to bear on behavior patterns (Hinshaw & Anderson, 1996).

Symptoms that classify a CD can vary with the age of the individual. For example, typically less severe behaviors (e.g., lying, shoplifting) tend to emerge first (*DSM-IV-TR*). As the boy or girl develops more physical strength, cognitive abilities, and sexual maturity, symptoms can be expected to vary with development in these domains. The more severe behaviors (e.g., theft while confronting the victim, assault, rape) tend to emerge last (*DSM-IV-TR*). Age can play a vocal part in the prognosis of CD and/or ODD. For example, in boys with early-onset or the childhood-onset type of CD (e.g., especially where physical aggression or fighting is present), the prognosis can often be diminished (Loeber, Burke, Lahey, Winters, & Zera, 2000). A negative sign in girls with CD is the presence of early and repeated sexual behavior; a diminished prognosis in these cases can also be advanced (Zoccolillo, 1993). Counselors, for example, should be alert to the possibility of a more serious course or trajectory for such children, especially where age is suspected to be a major factor in future outcomes.

Gender considerations, especially as applied in the childhood-onset type, are far more common in boys (*DSM-IV-TR*). Gender disparity in CD is marked by boys having a three to four times higher rate than girls for antisocial behavior along with a younger onset and greater persistence (Keenan, Loeber, & Green, 1999; Zoccolillo, 1993).

For example, boys who have a diagnosis of CD are frequently engaged in theft or stealing, vandalism, and school discipline problems. Girls with a diagnosis of CD are more likely to use nonconfrontational aggression (*DSM-IV-TR*). This could include such behaviors as lying, truancy, running away, substance abuse, sexual behavior, and even prostitution. Furthermore, some clinical findings are significant when counselors are treating girls and/or women. For example, it is recognized that anxiety disorders and depression in girls with CD occur at a greater than chance level (Loeber & Keenan, 1994). Moreover, internalizing disorders were found to be common in women who had a CD (e.g., occurring at a rate of 64% to 73%), and they occurred twice as frequently as in women without CD (Robins, 1986). The role that anxiety disorders and depression seem to have in the development and maintenance of CD in girls remains underresearched (Hinshaw & Anderson, 1996). What counselors should know is that gender and comorbid conditions in girls portend important considerations for treatment planning.

For counselors who work with these individuals, it is important to not allow yourself to view the client, his or her culture, and the conditions that might surround the client as dictating what should take place (e.g., a particular diagnosis). It is well substantiated that the culture of an individual often provides a ready lens for viewing what is preconceived.

CASE ILLUSTRATION

Conduct Disorder

The following case illustration, which I have modified for illustrative purposes, was adapted from Sommers-Flanagan and Sommers-Flanagan (1998). It is an example of how Jimmy, a 14-year-old boy was referred for diagnosis and the development of treatment planning.

Over the past 12 months, and beginning shortly after Jimmy's parents' stormy separation and subsequent divorce, Jimmy had been suspended and finally expelled from school. This action was due to his continued participation in fighting, continued verbal abuse of teachers, and continued misconduct. Jimmy had been rejected by the majority of his peers at the school for some time. Additionally, Jimmy was cited for possession of alcohol, for running away from school and home, and for several instances of vandalism. Jimmy also had a protracted history of problems with school authorities and the legal establishment (e.g,. juvenile court). Jimmy's academic difficulties, however, predated his recent acts of misconduct. Jimmy also threatened his mother that he would "beat the holy hell" out of his mother's live-in boyfriend. During Jimmy's initial counseling interview, and in a subsequent session, he was openly disrespectful and provocative (e.g., pulling out and playing with his knife, exposing the blade). Jimmy told the counselor that he did not believe in counseling and seemed to be disregarding any responsibility that he had for any part of his own misbehavior. It was evident to the counselor that Jimmy was clearly exhibiting and expressing his own behavioral dysfunctions.

This case example illustrates the diagnoses that the counselor ascertained. Jimmy is overtly displaying systems consistent with a diagnosis of CD. There are apparently a number of other diagnostic considerations (e.g., comorbid conditions) that require the counselor's attention.

Sample Treatment Plan

The following treatment plan can serve as an example to counseling practitioners for the diagnosis and treatment of Jimmy. The treatment plan is organized according to the 12 steps of the DO A CLIENT MAP (see Seligman, 1998 for a more detailed description).

Client: Jimmy is a 14-year-old African American male living with his mother. There are no other siblings living at home. The mother seems to not have any contact with Jimmy's father. The mother has a boyfriend. Jimmy verbally expressed the desire to physically harm this person. The mother is apparently not able to manage the serious and persistent behavioral difficulties that Jimmy exhibits in the home and at school. (A more full explanation of the client was provided previously).

Diagnosis:

Axis I:	312.82 Conduct Disorder—Adolescent-Onset Type (Severe)
	313.81 Oppositional Defiant Disorder (Severe)
	314.01 Attention-Deficit/Hyperactivity Disorder—Predominantly Hyperactive-Impulsive Type (Provisional)
	Learning Disorders (Provisional)
Axis II:	V71.09 No Mental Disorder/Diagnosis on Axis II.
Axis III:	No General Medical Conditions Reported.
Axis IV:	Psychosocial and Environmental Problems:

Problems related to the school environment (e.g., problems with school authorities and teachers, truancy, school suspension or expulsion, academic underachievement, peer rejection).

Problems related to the home environment (e.g., disregard for parental authority, consistently displays maladaptive behaviors, uses illegal substances, running away from home for protracted periods, threatening physical harm to the mother's boyfriend).

Axis V: Global Assessment of Functioning: 45 (Current)

Objectives:

Short Term

1. Reduce tension in the family by informing the mother that Jimmy's negative behaviors are connected to the Conduct and Oppositional Disorders. Emphasize that the mother and Jimmy are capable of making gradual improvements in their family's problems.

2. Reduce the family's anxiety and tension through communication about the origin and development of Jimmy's Conduct and Oppositional Disorders.
3. Reduce self-blame and guilt by communicating to the mother and Jimmy that they should not engage in blaming activities for such feelings as guilt, frustration, and anger about what has occurred at home and in the school. Stress the need for a positive attitude (e.g., positive expectations between the mother and Jimmy) as the first step.
4. Reduce family stress by communicating how achieving a better understanding of the family's communication patterns and how the family's lines of communication (e.g., parent-child and child-parent) can be improved so that all parties can more appropriately express themselves (e.g., in a nonaggressive manner).

Note: Medium or long-term goals would be established later in the treatment phase.

Assessments: Instrument choices made by the counselor or clinician in consultation with the parents, school, and client.

Counselor/Clinician: Counselor needs to readily build rapport and support for short-and/or long-term treatment.

Location: Home and/or family environment, school and/or teacher's classrooms.

Interventions: A Behavioral and Cognitive-Behavioral (CBT/CBST) Approach and Family Therapies.

Strategies/Interventions:

1. Parent education and training on the disorders (CD, ODD).
2. Teacher education and training on the disorders (CD, ODD).
3. Individual counseling sessions emphasizing behavioral techniques and CBT/CBST in the sessions (e.g., role-playing, getting along with others, the importance of self-talk, stress inoculation training, identifying negative self-statements, identifying positive self-statements, anger-management training strategies).
4. Social skills training programs (e.g., focusing on family, teachers, peers).
5. Self-esteem-building exercises (e.g., reconstruct Jimmy's evaluation of self).
6. Activity practice in real-life environmental situations (e.g., home, school, peers, neighborhood/community).
7. Family therapies (e.g., including family systems, functional family therapy, and multisystemic therapy) to achieve a more functioning family unit.

Note: Additional interventions or more probably the refining of interventions would be accomplished as the counseling treatment progressed. It is anticipated that treatment would be ongoing or long-term in its application (e.g., home, school).

Emphasis: Structured but highly supportive and empathetic. Goal is to foster client responsibility short-and long-term. No emphasis on missed steps. Emphasis and reinforcement is on successful approximations to the desired behavior (e.g., shaping).

Numbers: Individual and family counseling (e.g., including contacts with the school principal, teachers, school counselor, and school psychologist). Also, learning disabilities personnel might be needed.

Timing: Initially, the sessions would occur twice a week; the frequency would subsequently be reduced to once per week as treatment progressed. Monitoring at home and school by the counselor can be utilized. Later, there could be sessions once per month or as needed to monitor and adjust interventions or treatment accordingly.

Medication: Parents would be informed of how medication offers the family, the child, and the school possible additional options for treatment. Potential referral to the family physician, pediatrician, or psychiatrist. A referral to family services in the community for this assistance may be an option.

Adjunct Services: Assessment for probable AD/HD and learning disorders, educational tutoring, and participation in school and/or community sports activities.

Prognosis: Moderately good for alleviation/management of the major symptoms of the CD. Moderately good for the alleviation/management of the major symptoms of the ODD. Close monitoring and follow-up are required.

Oppositional Defiant Disorder

Sally, a 6-year-old female, was brought to the counselor for what her parents described as being "hard to handle, making insistent demands, and capable of throwing temper tantrums when she did not get her way." The quality of life in the home was eroding for the family; the parents further described how Sally was "ruining their marriage." The mother and father had tried bribing their daughter (e.g., with toys) to get her to behave. When that did not work, the parents went to the other extreme, frequently administering punishments. However, the parents reported that Sally often seemed "unphased" and certainly unchanged by the discipline measures they attempted. The parents feared that they were becoming mentally broken because this behavior had been ongoing for the past 3 years.

The behavior patterns Sally exhibited started almost as soon as she could walk and move about the house. The mother noted that Sally was often hard to soothe or please. When playmates were invited over to Sally's house to play, the play activities became loud and disruptive because Sally insisted on having her way. This resulted in the playmates leaving and often refusing to return to play at another time. Sally continually blamed others for not being able to get along with her. It seemed that Sally could not admit that she could be at fault in any area. It was not long until there were no more playmates willing to put up with Sally's controlling ways. Sally's mother complained that at the end of play sessions, her daughter would refuse to put away her toys, even when she was standing over her. At other times, Sally's mother reported that Sally could be a sweet and loving child when attention was delivered in a one-to-one setting.

Sally's developmental milestones were normal at school; she was very capable of doing her assignments and often performed academically at levels above many of the other children. In fact, her teachers rated her as a bright child. However, the teachers repeatedly noticed that Sally was bossy and wanted to do it her way, and the other children, more likely than not, steered clear of her. Often, Sally seemed to deliberately annoy or bother other children. On the playground, she could be an isolate on many days when the teachers did not deliberately arrange play activities that included Sally.

Both parents feared for Sally's future development. The parents were willing to admit that they were at a loss to explain or manage Sally's behavior. From a recent medical examination completed by Sally's physician, there were no physical causes located for the problem behavior. Therefore, from the information supplied by the parents and by contacting Sally's teachers, the counselor was able to diagnose Sally's condition. The counselor recommended treatment planning that included the parents and the school (e.g., Sally's teachers).

Sample Treatment Plan

The following treatment plan can serve as an example to counselors for Sally's diagnosis and treatment. The treatment plan is organized according to the 12 steps of the DO A CLIENT MAP (see Seligman, 1998 for a more detailed description).

Client: Sally is 6-year-old Caucasian female who is in the first grade of school. Sally is the only child. The parents are college educated and have achieved a middle-class socioeconomic status. The mother and father are apparently not equipped to manage Sally's persistently difficult behavior. (A more full explanation of the client was provided previously.)

Diagnosis:

Axis I: 313.81 Oppositional Defiant Disorder
Axis II: V71.09 No Mental Disorder/Diagnosis on Axis II.
Axis III: No General Medical Conditions Reported.
Axis IV: Psychosocial and Environmental Problems:
            Problems related to the home environment (e.g., noncompliant with parental authority, routines, and chores such as cleaning her room; blames others for her mistakes; deliberately annoys other children; cannot play quietly; loses temper).
            Problems related to the school environment (e.g., bossy with classmates and playmates, shunned and often isolated by classmates and playmates).
Axis V: Global Assessment of Functioning: 60 (Intake)

Objectives:
Short Term

1. Reduce tension in the family and Sally through communication about the origin, development, and operation of the Oppositional Defiant Disorder.
2. Reduce tension in the parents by discussing how Sally's oppositional behaviors or attitude toward her parents and classmates/playmates are constructed by the Oppositional Defiant Disorder.

Note: Medium or long-term goals would be established later in the treatment-phase.

Assessments: Instrument choices made by the counselor or clinician in consultation with the parents, teachers, and client.

Counselor/Clinician: Counselor needs to readily build rapport and support for short- and long-term treatment.

Location: Home and/or family environment. School and/or teacher's classrooms.

Interventions: A Behavioral and Cognitive-Behavioral Approach (CBT) and Family Counseling/Therapy.

Strategies/Interventions:

1. Parent education and training on the disorder (ODD).
2. Teacher education and training on the disorder (ODD).
3. Individual counseling emphasizing behavioral techniques and CBT in the sessions (e.g., role-playing, identifying negative self-talk, anger-management training strategies).
4. Social-skills training programs (e.g., focusing on family, teachers, classmates/playmates).
5. Self-esteem-building exercises (e.g., reconstruct Sally's evaluation of self).
6. Activity practice in real-life environmental situations (e.g., home, school, peers).
7. Family counseling/therapy to address how the family can learn to accept and work with Sally and her disorder and how the family unit can become more cohesive.

Note: Additional interventions or more probably the refining of interventions would be accomplished as the counseling treatment progressed. It is anticipated that the treatment would be ongoing or long-term in its application (e.g., home, school).

Emphasis: Structured but highly supportive and empathetic. Goal is to foster client responsibility short-and long-term. No emphasis on missed steps. Emphasis and reinforcement is on successive approximations to the desired behavior (e.g., shaping).

Numbers: Individual and family counseling (e.g., including contacts with the school principal, teachers, school counselor, and school psychologist).

Timing: Initially, the sessions would occur twice a week. The frequency would subsequently be reduced to once per week as treatment progressed. Later, there could be sessions once per month or as needed to monitor and adjust interventions or treatment accordingly.

Medication: Parents would be informed of how medication offers the family, the child, and the school possible additional options for treatment. Potential referral to the family physician, pediatrician, or psychiatrist.

Adjunct Services: Participation in school and/or local community sports activities.

Prognosis: Very good for alleviation/management of the major symptoms of the ODD. Monitoring and follow-up are required.

Closing Remarks

Frick (1998) has provided counselors with several important keys to efficacious treatment or intervention with children and adolescents who have CD. First, the counselor needs to understand the basic nature of Conduct Disorders and the multiple causal pathways that can be involved in the development of these disorders. Counselors cannot assume that the family alone caused the CD and that the family in isolation can be the cure. Counselors need to recognize the various ways CD can be expressed, the variations in impairment that can result, and the patterns of behavior that the disorders can take in their expression. This recognition is necessary for counselors to make decisions on how intensively to focus the interventions in any given case. Second, counselors should have a clear, comprehensive, and individualized case conceptualization to guide the design of a focused and integrated approach to treatment. For example, the case conceptualization is a theory developed by the counselor about the most likely factors that are involved in the development, exacerbation, and maintenance of the conduct problems for the individual child or adolescent. The treatment should also specify the comrobid or secondary problems (e.g., peer rejection) that contribute to the maintenance of the child's conduct problems. Third, successful intervention for children and adolescents with CD typically involves multiple professionals and multiple community agencies working in concert to provide a comprehensive and integrated treatment. For example, the home, school, and community need to be stakeholders in the child's future. Where there is strong coordination of intervention over extended periods of time, the various treatment components are much more effective together than if produced singly or in isolation.

Loeber, Burke, Lahey, Winters, & Zera (2000) have completed a 10-year review of the clinical literature and empirical findings on ODD and CD. These researchers were able to conclude the following:

1. Clinical evidence supports a distinction between the symptoms of ODD and many symptoms of CD; however, there clearly remains a controversy about whether aggressive symptoms (e.g., antisocial actions) should be construed to be part of the ODD or the CD.
2. Some degree of progress has been achieved in documenting gender differences (e.g., given comorbid CD and depression, girls might be more at risk for serious outcomes than many boys).
3. Symptoms that are more serious, more atypical for the child's sex, and more atypical for the child's age, appear to be more prognostic of serious dysfunction and indicate a more problematic course.
4. A proportion of children with ODD later develop CD; however, there is not a definite linear relationship.
5. A small proportion of children with CD are prone to later meet criteria for antisocial personality disorder (APD).
6. ODD, CD, and AD/HD (e.g., when AD/HD is present) can hasten the onset and severity of the CD.
7. Although major advances in the study of the developmental course and treatment of ODD and CD have occurred over the last decade, key issues

about their origin, developmental sequence, and most important, possible prevention remains to be answered.

For example, incoming lines of research evidence suggest that ODD, CD, and APD, in some cases, may be hierarchically and developmentally related (Loeber, Burke, Lahey, Winters, & Zera, 2000). Knowing about broad pathways for the development of these disorders, such as genetics and environment, is only the beginning. We need to learn more about the relationship of specific symptomatic and conceptual pathways that are likely contained in the environment. These can provide conditions that are favorable for the onset of psychopathology. Further clinical investigation to better elucidate the clinical and prognostic implications for these disruptive disorders and their comorbid conditions remains to be conducted. Counselors who are clinically alert to discovering more about these disruptive behavior disorders can expect to provide the higher level of service.

FOR MORE INFORMATION

American Counseling Association
5999 Stevenson Ave.
Alexandria, VA 22304
(703)823-9800
http://www.counseling.org

American School Counselor Association
801 N. Fairfax St., Ste. 310
Alexandria, VA 22304
(703)683-2722/(800)306-4722
http://www.schoolcounselor.org

American Psychiatric Association
1000 Wilson Blvd., Suite 1825
Arlington, VA 22209-3901
(888)357-7924
http://www.psych.org
*http://www.aacap.org/publications/factsfam/
conduct.htm*

American Psychological Association
750 1st St., NE
Washington, DC 20004-4242
(202)336-5500
http://www.apa.org

National Institute of Mental Health
NIMH Public Inquiries
6001 Executive Blvd., Rm. 8184, MSC 9663
Bethesda, MD 20892-9663
(301)443-4513
http://www.nimh.hih.gov
*http://www.mentalhealth.org/publications/allpubs/
CA-0010/conduct.htm*

**Oregon Social Learning Center (pioneers/
leaders in the treatment of Conduct Disorder)**
160 E. 4th Ave.
Eugene, OR 97401
(541)485-2711
http://www.oslc.org

Children and Adults with Attention-Deficit Disorders (CHADD)
8181 Professional Place, Ste. 201
Landover, MD 20785
(301)306-7070/1(800)233-4050
http://chadd.org

Council for Exceptional Children
1110 North Glebe Road, Suit 300
Arlington, VA 22201
(888) 232-7733
http://www.ced.sped.org

Learning Disabilities Association of America
4156 Library Rd.
Pittsburgh, PA 15234
(412)341-1515/341-8077
http://www.ldamerica.org

National Center for Learning Disabilities
381 Park Ave. S., Suit 1402
New York, NY 10016
(212)545-7510/(888) 575-7373

Internet Mental Health-Conduct Disorder
http://www.mentalhealth.com/dis/p20-cho2.html

Office of Civil Rights
U.S. Department of Education
400 Maryland Ave. SW
Washington, DC 20202-4135
(202)401-3020
http://www.ed.gov/about/offices/list/ocr

Chapter 6

ANXIETY DISORDERS IN CHILDREN AND ADOLESCENTS

By

J. Scott Hinkle, Ph.D.

DEFINITION, DIAGNOSTIC FEATURES, AND PREVALENCE

In her book *Anxiety Across the Lifespan: A Developmental Perspective,* Cynthia Last (1993) stated that, "Historically, our understanding and classification of child psychopathology has been based on knowledge obtained from adult disorders" (p. 1). Although Anxiety Disorders are the most common mental health condition reported in the child and adolescent population (see Hollander, Simeon, & Gorman, 1999), much of the information in this chapter is extrapolated from the literature regarding adults, although adult models of anxiety cannot completely explain childhood symptoms (Gullone, King, & Ollendick, 2001). Similarly, Last has elaborated that children manifest anxiety differently than adults and that the interventions for child anxiety disorders have been largely adapted from therapeutic work with adults, although estimates of the prevalence of Anxiety Disorders among children has ranged from largely unknown (Biederman, 1990; Casat, 1988) to the most prevalent of the childhood disorders (Bernstein & Borchardt, 1991; Kashani & Orvaschel, 1988). Estimates of the prevalence of Anxiety Disorder among children range from 5% to 18%. Moreover, various developmental differences have been reported in the manifestation of Anxiety Disorders among children of different age groups (Bernstein & Borchardt, 1991; Muris, 2003).

Etiologically speaking, prenatal stressors have been suggested to increase the risk for anxiety disorders in offspring (Hirshfeld-Becker, Biederman, & Faraone, 2004). Likewise, adolescents with a positive parental history for panic disorder or agoraphobia have an approximately 25% chance of experiencing panic attacks (Hayward, Wilson, & Lagle, 2004).

The Anxiety Disorders in the *DSM-IV-TR* include the following: Panic Disorder (With and Without Agoraphobia), Agoraphobia Without History of Panic Disorder, Specific Phobia (Simple Phobia), Social Phobia, Obsessive-Compulsive Disorder (OCD), Post-Traumatic Stress Disorder (PTSD), Acute Stress Disorder,

Generalized Anxiety Disorder (GAD), Anxiety Disorder Due to a General Medical Condition, Substance-Induced Anxiety Disorder, and Anxiety Disorder NOS (Not Otherwise Specified) (APA, 2000a). Children and adolescents who meet the clinical criteria for these disorders might receive any of these diagnoses. Similarly, they also might obtain diagnoses of anxiety-related disorders in other sections of the *DSM-IV-TR* (e.g., Separation Anxiety Disorder).

SEPARATION ANXIETY DISORDER

Children who experience Separation Anxiety Disorder generally worry that their caregivers will not return to them, possibly due to their caregiver being injured or killed. They also might have anxieties about being harmed themselves or kidnapped (Thyer, 1993). Individuals with this disorder often need to know their parents' whereabouts and need to stay in contact with them by telephone or some other means (APA, 2000a). Symptoms associated with Separation Anxiety Disorder include somatic complaints, school refusal, difficulty going to bed and falling asleep, general avoidance behaviors, and concerns about death and dying. This disorder is manifested by anxiety that is aroused upon separation from significant others (e.g., parents) or upon leaving the home and entering foreign territory. The anxiety reaction is excessive and the anticipation of separation might include somatic symptoms. Following the separation, the child might be inconsolable and fear that the parent is not going to return, possibly due to some unknown tragedy (Rapoport & Ismond, 1990). For example, one young boy assessed by the author cried for 2 hours when his mother left him at the office for a psychoeducational evaluation, pre-empting the completion of any testing. Extreme forms of this disorder are found among children who refuse to go to school in order to avoid the trauma of the separation from the caretaker. (School phobia, on the other hand, entails a true fear of the school setting and persists even in the presence of the caretaker.) In extreme cases of Separation Anxiety Disorder, the child or adolescent might demonstrate anger or even hit a person who might be forcing the separation (APA, 2000a).

Diagnosis of Separation Anxiety Disorder

When making a diagnosis of Separation Anxiety Disorder, it is helpful to interview for anxiety-related symptoms in the child or adolescent's family because these clients often have a family member who has this disorder or overanxiousness (i.e., Generalized Anxiety Disorder). This family-history method of diagnosis consists of gathering information from the client or other family members about related symptoms in the family (Last, 1993).

Separation Anxiety Disorder occurs primarily in younger children between the ages of 5 and 8. This age group outnumbers adolescents with this disorder 2 to 1. This is consistent with the typical finding that separation anxiety *normally* occurs in young children in the general population. Strauss (1993) has indicated that children who develop clinically significant separation anxiety might have experienced stressors such as the death of a major attachment figure, prolonged hospitalization of an attachment figure, or physical/psychological absence of a parental figure during a normal developmental phase when young people typically experience anxiety about separation.

More specifically, younger children with Separation Anxiety Disorder are more likely than adolescents with the same diagnosis to report more symptoms, more nightmares with a separation theme, more worry about harm befalling an attachment figure, and excessive distress upon separation. In contrast, adolescents with separation anxiety symptoms are more apt to report physical complaints on school days than will younger children (Francis, Last, & Strauss, 1987).

The *DSM-IV-TR* (APA, 2000a) criteria for Separation Anxiety Disorder (Table 6.1) include any three of the following: recurrent excessive distress when separated from home or a major attachment figure (e.g., parent); worry about losing a parent

---

TABLE 6.1   Diagnostic Criteria for 309.21 Separation Anxiety Disorder

A. Developmentally inappropriate behavior and excessive anxiety concerning separation from home or from those to whom the individual is attached, as evidenced by three (or more) of the following:

   1. recurrent excessive distress when separation from home or major attachment figures occurs or is anticipated
   2. persistent and excessive worry about losing, or about possible harm befalling, major attachment figures
   3. persistent and excessive worry that an untoward event will lead to separation from a major attachment figure (e.g., getting lost or being kidnapped)
   4. persistent reluctance or refusal to go to school or elsewhere because of fear of separation
   5. persistent and excessive fear or reluctance to be alone or without major attachment figures at home or without significant adults in other settings
   6. persistent reluctance or refusal to go to sleep without being near a major attachment figure or to sleep away from home
   7. repeated nightmares involving the theme of separation
   8. repeated complaints of physical symptoms (such as headaches, stomachaches, nausea, or vomiting) when separation from major attachment figures occurs or is anticipated

B. The duration of the disturbance is at least 4 weeks.

C. The onset is before age 18 years.

D. The disturbance causes clinically significant distress or impairment in social, academic (occupational), or other important areas of functioning.

E. The disturbance does not occur exclusively during the course of a Pervasive Developmental Disorder, Schizophrenia, or other Psychotic Disorder and, in adolescents and adults, is not better accounted for by Panic Disorder With Agoraphobia.

Specify if:

   Early Onset: if onset occurs before age 6 years

From *Diagnostic and Statistical Manual of Mental Disorders,* Fourth Edition, Text Revision (p. 125), American Psychiatric Association (APA), Washington, DC: Copyright 2000 by APA. Reprinted by permission.

or harm coming to a parent; an uncontrollable event leading to separation from a parent; reluctance to go to school due to fear of separation; resistance to being left alone; reluctance to sleep alone or away from home; nightmares with separation themes; and/or physical complaints (e.g., headaches, stomachaches, nausea, or vomiting). As with all of the Anxiety Disorders, the diagnosis of Separation Anxiety Disorder also should include clinically significant distress or impairment in social, academic, or other important areas of functioning. In addition, depressive mood is often present and might become more pronounced over time (APA, 2000a).

PANIC DISORDER AND AGORAPHOBIA

Panic Disorder (With and Without Agoraphobia) and Agoraphobia Without History of Panic Disorder have been described in children and adolescents only in the past 10 years and little is known about the clinical course among this population (Black & Robbins, 1990). It has been estimated that .4% of boys and .7% of girls have Panic Disorder (Whitaker et al., 1990). Developmentally, Thyer and his colleagues (1985) reported that 13% of adult clients with Panic Disorder had symptoms before age 10. Similarly, Moreau and Weissman (1992) found that many adults with Panic Disorder had experienced symptoms before age nine. There is evidence that, although rare among prepubertal children, Panic Disorder does occur but may be manifested differently than it is in adults (Black & Robbins, 1990; Weiss & Hawley, 2002). It is important to note that although there could exist a genetic link between childhood and adult Panic Disorder, this has not been verified by systematic research.

Furthermore, prior to 1987 there were limited published cases of panic attack involving children. Various reports have suggested that children and adolescents with Panic Disorder have multiple symptoms including dizziness, tingling, trembling, palpitations, shortness of breath, feelings of smothering or choking, flushing, sweating, feeling cold and clammy, numbing and tingling (paresthesia), and even thoughts of dying or "going crazy." As with adults, many children with Panic Disorder probably first come to professional attention in emergency rooms with symptoms of palpitations, hyperventilation, and dizziness, resulting in the diagnosis of Panic Disorder often being overlooked (Moreau & Weissman, 1992). In addition, adolescents and children with Panic Disorder typically present to their physicians with somatic complaints, also increasing the chances that many cases of Panic Disorder remain undetected (Black & Robbins, 1990). Unfortunately, diagnosis and subsequent treatment often do not occur because of the lack of accurate detection.

Simply put, Panic Disorder and Agoraphobia (or the fear of incapacitation) are associated with fears (see Gullone, 2000). The *DSM-IV-TR* (APA, 2000a) has indicated that Panic Disorder is characterized by *recurrent* panic attacks. Many panic victims experiencing panic over an extended time will begin to avoid situations where, if a panic attack occurred, escape would be difficult. This is referred to as Panic Disorder With Agoraphobia (APA, 2000a). The degree of avoidance ranges from moderate to extreme, often resulting in constricted lifestyles (National Institute of Health [NIH], 1991). Panic Disorder with concomitant agoraphobia is often described as a fear of open spaces, but it appears that clients are actually more afraid of experiencing panic attacks (Weekes, 1978). Agoraphobia Without History of Panic Disorder occurs infrequently, is generally mild, and often does not result in counseling treatment (Mattick, Andrews, Hadzi-Pavlovic, & Christensen, 1990). Panic attacks are associated with unanticipated, abrupt bouts of overwhelming anxiety and feelings of having a heart attack or losing one's mind, and can even occur during sleep. Panic attacks can be spontaneous or can be precipitated by a fearful stimulus (Laraia, Stuart, & Best, 1989). McNally (1990) reported that in contrast to individuals without Panic Disorder, people who panic "respond fearfully to the bodily sensations produced by the challenge agent" (p. 404). Biology most likely plays an important role in the etiology of panic symptoms. For example, the brain may be hypersensitive to respiratory responses. Respiratory distress and hyperventilation may be misperceived, and such inaccuracy might result in panic attacks (see Bengi & Alkin, 1999; Welkowitz, Papp, Martinez, Browne, & Gorman, 1999).

Thyer (1993) indicated that many individuals with Panic Disorder become polyphobic, resulting in additional symptoms associated with Agoraphobia such as the development of many unreasonable fears. Agoraphobic fears are typically associated with the *anticipatory anxiety* of having a panic attack. Instead of being fearful of externally motivated anxiety, a provoking object (e.g., thunderstorms) or situation, the individual's fears are internal and no control over the event is possible. When the avoidance response controls the individual's life, the diagnosis of Panic Disorder With Agoraphobia is appropriate (Thyer, 1987).

Individuals with Panic Disorder often live restricted lives, suffer from low self-esteem, and have poor social functioning (Laraia et al., 1989). Thyer (1987) stated that although no single theory has emerged as the absolute best to explain Panic Disorder, biological theories are very promising. This is because panic sufferers tend to respond to medications, intravenous infusions of sodium lactate produce panic attacks, panic attacks run in families, and many individuals with Panic Disorder also have mitral-valve prolapse and increased risk for cardiovascular disease.

The occurrence of fear is not essential for triggering a full-blown panic attack (McNally, 1990). According to cognitive theory, panic attacks are associated with the way the stimulus, internal or external, is interpreted. Cognitive interventions espouse the notion that thinking mediates behavior and subsequent changes in thinking will change associated behaviors (Laraia et al., 1989). Specifically, in relation to Panic Disorder, cognitive theory posits that the misinterpretation of bodily sensations results in an individual failing to "distinguish between the triggering bodily sensations and the subsequent panic and so perceive the attack as having no cause and coming out of the blue" (Clark & Ehlers, 1993, p. 132). This is generally referred to as *interoceptive conditioning* (Craske & Barlow, 1993). Some people might go on to respond to autonomic events in a catastrophic manner. Clark (1988) has further elaborated that biological variables can increase the number of potential triggers in individuals with requisite cognitive schemas.

Similarly, the *anxiety sensitivity hypothesis* (Reiss & McNally, 1985) suggests that the anxious individual believes that symptoms have harmful consequences (e.g., a rapid heartbeat signifies a forthcoming heart attack). This may lead to heightened expectations about panic and increase the possibility of their occurrence. Moreover, individuals with Panic Disorder maintain a bias for interpreting ambiguous stimuli as threatening (McNally, 1990). When given false feedback regarding heart rate, individuals with Panic Disorder have demonstrated greater increases in self-reported anxiety, blood pressure, and heart rate (Ehlers, Margraf, Roth, Taylor, & Birbaumer, 1988).

Clark (1988) and others have reflected that individuals in fear of having a heart attack, although they have not expired after recurrent panic attacks—which substantiates the odds that this is not going to occur—continue this thinking for two essential reasons. First, sensations that are frightening may cause these people to become hypervigilant and to constantly scan their bodies for signs of danger. Secondly, avoidance behaviors may interfere with the disconfirmation of the self-defeating belief regarding danger. For instance, a person who is "preoccupied with the idea he is suffering from cardiac disease might avoid exercise and rest whenever he notices a palpitation" (Clark & Ehlers, 1993, p. 135). It is important to keep in mind that this data has not been methodically substantiated in children.

Diagnosis of Panic Disorder and Agoraphobia

In addition to the fear of losing control, losing one's mind, or dying, the symptoms for making a diagnosis of panic attack are numerous. They include heart palpitations, feeling shortness of breath, sensing chest pain, choking, nausea, lightheadedness, and derealization. Also included are shaking, sweating, chills or hot flashes, and paresthesia. The diagnosis of Panic Disorder With Agoraphobia also requires panic attacks and the avoidance of associated situations (e.g., being homebound or anxious in crowds where escape may be perceived as difficult). Relatedly, the *DSM-IV-TR* indicates that a diagnosis of Panic Disorder Without Agoraphobia includes recurrent panic attacks and the absence of Agoraphobia (APA, 2000a). The counselor must accurately evaluate the focus of the fear in order to devise an accurate differential diagnosis. The process of differential diagnosis should exclude other Anxiety Disorders, Mood Disorders, Delusional Disorders, as well as Somatoform Disorders. Furthermore, fear of choking in public is often associated with panic attacks (Turner & Beidel, 1989).

The diagnostic process for Panic Disorder (Table 6.2) and Agoraphobia (Table 6.3) Without History of Panic Disorder (Table 6.4) should include at least three modalities: behavioral, physiological, and cognitive (Laraia et al., 1989). Diagnostic information regarding the family also should be included. For example, Brooks, Baltazar, & Munjack (1989) have reported that case studies have associated parental overprotection and dependency traits with agoraphobic symptoms. Likewise, Mannuzza et al. (1990) have indicated that anxiety symptoms must be assessed within the context of the child or adolescent's disturbance. (Table 6.5)

TABLE 6.2   Criteria for a Panic Attack

Note: A Panic Attack is not a codable disorder. Code the specific diagnosis in which the Panic Attack occurs (e.g., 300.21 Panic Disorder With Agoraphobia [p. 441]).

A discrete period of intense fear or discomfort in which four (or more) of the following symptoms developed abruptly and reached a peak within 10 minutes:

1. palpitations, pounding heart, or accelerated heart rate
2. sweating
3. trembling or shaking
4. sensations of shortness of breath or smothering
5. feeling of choking
6. chest pain or discomfort
7. nausea or abdominal distress
8. feeling dizzy, unsteady, lightheaded, or faint
9. derealization (feelings of unreality) or depersonalization (being detached from oneself)
10. fear of losing control or going crazy
11. fear of dying
12. parenthesis (numbness or tingling sensations)
13. chills or hot flashes

From *Diagnostic and Statistical Manual of Mental Disorders,* Fourth Edition, Text Revision (p. 432), American Psychiatric Association (APA), Washington, DC: APA. Copyright 2000 by APA. Reprinted by permission.

TABLE 6.3   Criteria for Agoraphobia

Note: Agoraphobia is not a codable disorder. Code the specific disorder in which the Agoraphobia occurs (e.g., 300.21 Panic Disorder With Agoraphobia [p. 441] or 300.22 Agoraphobia Without History of Panic Disorder [p. 441]).

A. Anxiety about being in places or situations from which escape might be difficult (or embarrassing) or in which help may not be available in the event of having an unexpected or situationally predisposed Panic Attack or panic-like symptoms. Agoraphobic fears typically involve characteristic clusters of situations that include being outside the home alone; being in a crowd or standing in a line; being on a bridge; and traveling in a bus, train, or automobile.

Note: Consider the diagnosis of Specific Phobia if the avoidance is limited to one or only a few specific situations, or Social Phobia if the avoidance is limited to social situations.

B. The situations are avoided (e.g., travel is restricted) or else are endured with marked distress or with anxiety about having a Panic Attack or panic-like symptoms, or require the presence of a companion.

C. The anxiety or phobic avoidance is not better accounted for by another mental disorder, such as Social Phobia (e.g., avoidance limited to social situations because of fear of embarrassment), Specific Phobia (e.g., avoidance limited to a single situation like elevators), Obsessive-Compulsive Disorder (e.g., avoidance of dirt in someone with an obsession about contamination), Posttraumatic Stress Disorder (e.g., avoidance of stimuli associated with a severe stressor), or Separation Anxiety Disorder (e.g., avoidance of leaving home or relatives).

From *Diagnostic and Statistical Manual of Mental Disorders,* Fourth Edition, Text Revision (p. 433), American Psychiatric Association (APA), Washington, DC: APA. Copyright 2000 by APA. Reprinted by permission.

TABLE 6.4 Diagnostic Criteria for 300.01 Panic Disorder Without Agoraphobia

A. Both (1) and (2):

   (1) recurrent unexpected Panic Attacks (see p. 432)
   (2) at least one of the attacks has been followed by 1 month (or more) of one (or more) of the following:

      (a) persistent concern about having additional attacks
      (b) worry about the implications of the attack or its consequences (e.g., losing control, having a heart attack, "going crazy")
      (c) a significant change in behavior related to the attacks

B. Absence of Agoraphobia (see p. 433).

C. The Panic Attacks are not due to the direct physiological effects of a substance (e.g., a drug of abuse, a medication) or a general medical condition (e.g., hyperthyroidism).

D. The Panic Attacks are not better accounted for by another mental disorder, such as Social Phobia (e.g., occurring on exposure to feared social situations), Specific Phobia (e.g., on exposure to a specific phobic situation), Obsessive-Compulsive Disorder (e.g., on exposure to dirt in someone with an obsession about contamination), Post-Traumatic Stress Disorder (e.g., in response to stimuli associated with a severe stressor), or Separation Anxiety Disorder (e.g., in response to being away from home or close to relatives).

From *Diagnostic and Statistical Manual of Mental Disorders,* Fourth Edition, Text Revision (p. 440), American Psychiatric Association (APA), Washington, DC: APA. Copyright 2000 by APA. Reprinted by permission.

TABLE 6.5 Diagnostic Criteria for 300.21 Panic Disorder With Agoraphobia

A. Both (1) and (2):

   (1) recurrent unexpected Panic Attacks (see p. 432)
   (2) at least one of the attacks has been followed by 1 month (or more) of one (or more) of the following:

      (a) persistent concern about having additional attacks
      (b) worry about the implications of the attack or its consequences (e.g., losing control, having a heart attack, "going crazy")
      (c) a significant change in behavior related to the attacks

B. The presence of Agoraphobia (see p. 433).

C. The Panic Attacks are not due to the direct physiological effects of a substance (e.g., a drug of abuse, a medication) or a general medical condition (e.g., hyperthyroidism).

D. The Panic Attacks are not better accounted for by another mental disorder, such as Social Phobia (e.g., occurring on exposure to feared social situations), Specific Phobia (e.g., on exposure to a specific phobic situation), Obsessive-Compulsive Disorder (e.g., on exposure to dirt in someone with an obsession about contamination), Post-Traumatic Stress Disorder (e.g., in response to stimuli associated with a severe stressor), or Separation Anxiety Disorder (e.g., in response to being away from home or close relatives).

From *Diagnostic and Statistical Manual of Mental Disorders,* Fourth Edition, Text Revision (p. 441), American Psychiatric Association (APA), Washington, DC: APA. Copyright 2000 by APA. Reprinted by permission.

This classification of phobias is associated with an external triggering stimuli that results in an anxiety response. Although the anxiety is typically predictable, at times the intensity of the response may be milder than usual (APA, 2000a). Social and school activities are customarily interrupted and fainting behavior may be reported, especially in those children and adolescents fearful of blood and injections. More importantly, the most significant complication of this disorder is severe restriction in lifestyle (APA, 2000a). Developmentally, it appears that many children and adolescents with Specific Phobias, without treatment, will carry these symptoms into adulthood (see Bernstein & Borchardt, 1991). Moreover, a child's history of control over his or her environment is an important aspect in responding to frightening situations (Mineka & Zinbarg, 2006).

Phobias are typically characterized by a fear of what will happen in the situation that envelopes the stimulus rather than the stimulus itself. Phobic difficulties range from 3% to 8% among children. Females tend to outnumber males with Specific Phobia. Phobic fears appear to have a developmental component. Young children mostly are afraid of the dark and loud noises, whereas older children tend to be afraid of academic tests and being compared or scrutinized socially. Many children with phobia symptoms are resistant to attending school and may complain of physical symptoms in order to avoid school. According to Burke and Silverman's (1987) review, school phobia or school refusal affects about 1% of all school-age children. Deterioration in family and social functioning is often apparent in such cases.

Brulle, McIntyre, and Mills' (1985) review estimated the prevalence of school phobia to be as high as 8% of the school population and to occur more often in girls than in boys. In young children, school phobia has been discussed in two forms: acute and chronic. Acute school phobia has been associated with students with 3 or more prior years of trouble-free attendance. Chronic school phobia is related to students who developed the problem at the beginning of their school experience and have not yet recovered.

Diagnosis of Specific Phobia

The diagnosis of Specific Phobia (Table 6.6) highlights unreasonable or excessive fears that are brought on by specific objects or situations or the anticipation of them. This disorder usually results in the avoidance of the feared stimulus (e.g., school, bridges, or the doctor's office). School counselors should note that in children, the anxiety associated with Specific Phobia may be manifested by tantruming, crying, and clinging behavior. The *DSM-IV-TR* distinguishes among the various types of feared objects or situations (i.e., animals, natural environment, blood, injection, injury, and situational) (APA, 2000a). Differential diagnosis should include other Anxiety Disorders (i.e., Obsessive-Compulsive Disorder, Separation Anxiety Disorder, and Social Phobia).

TABLE 6.6   Diagnostic Criteria for 300.29 Specific Phobia

A. Marked and persistent fear that is excessive or unreasonable, cued by the presence or anticipation of a specific object or situation (e.g., flying, heights, animals, receiving an injection, seeing blood).

B. Exposure to the phobic stimulus almost invariably provokes an immediate anxiety response, which may take the form of a situationally predisposed panic attack. *Note:* In children, the anxiety may be expressed by crying, tantrums, freezing, or clinging.

C. The person recognizes that the fear is excessive or unreasonable. *Note:* In children, this feature may be absent.

D. The phobic situation(s) is avoided or else is endured with intense anxiety or distress.

E. The avoidance, anxious anticipation, or distress in the feared situation(s) interferes significantly with the person's normal routine, occupational (or academic) functioning, or social activities or relationships, or there is marked distress about having the phobia.

F. In individuals under age 18 years, the duration is at least 6 months.

G. The anxiety, panic attacks, or phobic avoidance associated with the specific object or situation are not better accounted for by another mental disorder, such as Obsessive-Compulsive Disorder (e.g., fear of dirt in someone with an obsession about contamination), Post-Traumatic Stress Disorder (e.g., avoidance of stimuli associated with a severe stressor), Separation Anxiety Disorder (e.g., avoidance of school), Social Phobia (e.g., avoidance of social situations because of fear of embarrassment), Panic Disorder With Agoraphobia, or Agoraphobia Without History of Panic Disorder.

Specify type:

Animal Type.

Natural Environment Type (e.g., heights, storms, water).

Blood-Injection-Injury Type.

Situational Type (e.g., airplanes, elevators, enclosed places).

Other Type (e.g., fear of choking, vomiting, or contracting an illness; in children, fear of loud sounds or costumed characters).

From *Diagnostic and Statistical Manual of Mental Disorders*, Fourth Edition, Text Revision (p. 449–450), American Psychiatric Association (APA), Washington, DC: APA. Copyright 2000 by APA. Reprinted by permission.

SOCIAL PHOBIA

Social Phobia among children and adolescents is most often manifested by anxiety around strangers. Turner & Beidel (1989) have indicated that Social Phobia occupies an "intermediate position between simple phobia (specific phobia) and other anxiety states" (p. 16). Social Phobia affects approximately 2% of the general population (Robins et al., 1984). Individuals with Social Phobia may avoid social situations because of shyness and fear of blushing, speaking, incapacitation, negative evaluation from others, or even panic attacks (which reflects a level of comorbidity with the latter) (Hope & Heimberg, 1993; Solyom, Ledwidge,

& Solyom, 1986; Turner & Beidel, 1989). The average age of clients seeking treatment for Social Phobia is 30 (see Turner & Beidel, 1989), suggesting that treating children with this disorder might actually be rare. And, due to the intrinsic social properties of this disorder, many of these clients do not seek counseling. When they do, it is often for fear of public speaking (Thyer, 1987).

Diagnosis of Social Phobia

Social Phobia (Table 6.7) did not become an officially recognized diagnosis until 1980 with the advent of the *DSM-III* (APA, 1980; Mannuzza et al., 1990). Mannuzza et al. (1990) have indicated that there is a limited number of community-based studies regarding the prevalence of Social Phobia; however, general population studies have reflected its over-representation among females, with age of onset

TABLE 6.7   Diagnostic Criteria for 300.23 Social Phobia

A. A marked and persistent fear of one or more social or performance situations in which the person is exposed to unfamiliar people or to possible scrutiny by others. The individual fears that he or she will act in a way (or show anxiety symptoms) that will be humiliating or embarrassing. *Note:* In children, there must be evidence of the capacity for age-appropriate social relationships with familiar people and the anxiety must occur in peer settings, not just in interactions with adults.

B. Exposure to the feared social situation almost invariably provokes anxiety, which may take the form of a situationally predisposed panic attack. *Note:* In children, the anxiety may be expressed by crying, tantrums, freezing, or shrinking from social situations with unfamiliar people.

C. The person recognizes that the fear is excessive or unreasonable. *Note:* In children, this feature is absent.

D. The feared social or performance situations are avoided or else are endured with intense anxiety or distress.

E. The avoidance, anxious anticipation, or distress in the feared social or performance situations(s) interferes significantly with the person's normal routine, occupational (academic) functioning, or social activities or relationships, or there is marked distress about having the phobia.

F. In individuals under 18 years, the duration is at least 6 months.

G. The fear or avoidance is not due to the direct physiological effects of a substance (e.g., a drug of abuse, a medication) or a general medical condition and is not better accounted for by another mental disorder (e.g., Panic Disorder With or Without Agoraphobia, Separation Anxiety Disorder, Body Dysmorphic Disorder, a Pervasive Developmental Disorder, or Schizoid Personality Disorder).

H. If a general medical condition or another mental disorder is present, the fear in Criterion A is unrelated to it; e.g., then the fear is not of stuttering, trembling in Parkinson's Disease, or exhibiting abnormal eating behavior in Anorexia Nervosa or Bulimia Nervosa.

Specify if:

Generalized: if the fears include most social situations (also consider the additional diagnosis of Avoidant Personality Disorder).

From *Diagnostic and Statistical Manual of Mental Disorders,* Fourth Edition, Text Revision (p. 456), American Psychiatric Association (APA), Washington, DC: APA. Copyright 2000 by APA. Reprinted by permission.

ranging from approximately mid to late adolescence (see Turner & Beidel, 1989). Some cases have been diagnosed as early as age 8 (Beidel, Turner, & Morris, 2000). Conversely, research surveys have reported that Social Phobia is equally prevalent among males and females (Bourdon et al., 1988; Turner & Beidel, 1989). Regardless, this disorder reflects a serious and incapacitating mental health problem that can affect the emotional as well as social functioning of children and adolescents (Hope & Heimberg, 1993; Turner & Beidel, 1989).

Social Phobia involves an anxiety response related to the fear of being scrutinized by others, resulting in personal embarrassment or humiliation and ultimate avoidance of feared social situations (APA, 2000a). Children and adolescents with Social Phobia fear that others think they are incompetent, inadequate, or suffering from some type of unacceptable malady.

Individuals with Social Phobia are more likely to report blushing and muscle twitching, whereas difficulty breathing, dizziness, fainting, and limb weakness are more common among clients with Agoraphobia (Mannuzza et al., 1990). People with Social Phobia also will report being more comfortable when alone, whereas individuals with Panic Disorder are more comfortable in the presence of others (Liebowitz et al., 1985). Severe cases may present themselves very much like Agoraphobia, making the diagnostic distinction between the two quite difficult at times.

Many individuals with Social Phobia describe "a gradual buildup of anxiety as they approach the phobic situation, rather than a triggered, intense reaction when in the situation" (Mannuzza et al., 1990, p. 50). Differentiating between Social Phobia and Panic Disorder is a simple process. To illustrate, if clients with Social Phobia encounter the feared phenomena when alone, it will not lead to significant distress (Mannuzza et al., 1990). Individuals with Social Phobia are uncomfortable in social situations but continually struggle to deal with the distress. Differential diagnosis should include Agoraphobia Without History of Panic Disorder (APA, 2000a; Turner & Beidel, 1989). Relatedly, in terms of differential diagnosis, the individual with Avoidant Personality Disorder is more accepting of social limitations and has fewer skills for social interactions (Heimberg, Dodge, & Becker, 1987).

OBSESSIVE-COMPULSIVE DISORDER

Although the symptoms appear to be similar across the lifespan in relation to adults, little is known about Obsessive-Compulsive Disorder (OCD) in children and adolescents due to the lack of epidemiological research (Francis & Borden, 1993). It is estimated that approximately 1% of child inpatients are diagnosed with OCD (McCarthy & Foa, 1988). Childhood cases of OCD closely parallel the clinical picture of that for adults (Rapoport & Ismond, 1990); however, there are some differences. For example, major comorbid affective disorders are significantly less frequently observed among children with OCD (Flament et al., 1985). It has been reported that significant differences occur across age groups on a variety of clinical features associated with OCD (Farrell, Barrett, & Piacentini, 2006). Also, it is not known whether gender differences among children with OCD are the same as those among adults (Francis & Borden, 1993), albeit the rates are assumed to be the same as for adolescents and adults (Flament et al., 1988).

It has been reported that approximately 2% to 3% of the United States population suffers from Obsessive-Compulsive Disorder (OCD). The average age of onset is in the early 20s (Karno, Golding, Sorenson, & Burnam, 1988) and is manifested in 80% of cases by age 30. Although OCD generally is activated initially in late adolescence or early adulthood (Emmelkamp, 1982; Francis & Borden, 1993; Rachman, 1985), it is observed in children (Francis & Borden, 1993). Incidence rates for obsessions and compulsions appear to be near equal for males and females, respectively. More research is needed to clearly elucidate factors that might suggest a genetic vulnerability for OCD (Chabane, Delorme, Millet, Mouren, Leboyer, & Pauls, 2005).

The most frequently reported obsessive-compulsive symptoms among children are fear of germs and dirt, worry about ominous events, excessive washing and grooming, repetitive checking (Zetin & Kramer, 1992), and the fear of AIDS (Rapoport, 1989). Children with Obsessive-Compulsive Disorder also have been known to behave secretively in a manner not unlike that of children with Eating Disorders (Clarizio, 1991). Developmentally, children who are compulsive checkers may later become concerned with contamination; likewise, young obsessive counters may eventually have sexual preoccupations later as adults (Wolff & Rapoport, 1988).

Obsessive thoughts are usually recurrent, are ritualistic in nature, and have a set pattern. They are usually recognized as repugnant, senseless, and not fitting the client's ideas of self (Boyarsky, Perone, Lee, & Goodman, 1991; Zetin & Kramer, 1992). For example, one of the author's child clients with OCD described himself as "stupid" for obsessing about a chemical getting out of a locked container, pouring itself into his mouth, and killing him. Obsessive themes can range from the continuous thoughts of a specific melody to self-deprecating themes that result in extreme distress.

Compulsive behaviors can vary, but compulsive washing is common and usually focuses on the need to be free of germs and potential contamination. For example, the author has counseled children who believe that they might get sick and even die from touching doorknobs. Individuals with obsessions about germs might be involved in compulsive cleaning of their bodies and environments and also might report feeling responsible for contaminating others (Thyer, 1987).

Many children and adolescents with OCD perform variations of ritualistic behaviors such as obsessively *counting* objects. For example, a child might count his or her steps while walking or count automobiles that pass while riding in the family car. Compulsive *checking* behavior is manifested by repeatedly checking to see whether water faucets and lights are off or whether doors and windows are locked. Even though they are unrealistic, checking behaviors are typically performed to ward off catastrophe (Thyer, 1987).

Compulsive *balancing* behaviors, although more rare, tend to come in two varieties, kinesthetic or geographic. Kinesthetic balancing involves repeated attempts to equal the pressure of touch made by the body, typically by the hands or rubbing the body on stationary objects. Geographic balance is an attempt to obtain an exact symmetry of objects in terms of their numbers, order, or height. For example, a child may spend an inordinate amount of time arranging equal numbers of items on the left and right sides of a desk.

Diagnosis of Obsessive-Compulsive Disorder

The diagnostic criteria for Obsessive-Compulsive Disorder are in Table 6.8. According to the *DSM-IV-TR* (APA, 2000a), obsessions are an anxiety response that involve excessive intrusive thoughts and impulses that are a product of the individual's own thinking and result in attempts to ignore or suppress them. Obsessions are often related to actual life problems and can be incongruent with the individual's values and beliefs. A compulsion is related to an obsessive thought and consists of behaviors that are unreasonable, repetitive, and anxiety provoking (APA, 2000a). Compulsions are often explained as the need to neutralize a thought or the alleviation of some type of sensory pressure when the behavior is performed (Boyarsky, Perone, Lee, & Goodman, 1991). Compulsions are typically repetitive, stereotypic, and ritualistic behaviors that are performed to prevent some event or situation from occurring (Zetin & Kramer, 1992). As mentioned, classic compulsive behaviors include the compelling need to engage in washing, counting, checking, and balancing, as well as behaving in a slow, methodical manner. A small number of individuals with Obsessive-Compulsive Disorder have only compulsions or only obsessions.

Differential diagnosis should rule out other Anxiety Disorders and Hypochondriasis (as in the case of excessive health information-seeking). OCD and Major Depression have been postulated to share some comorbid biological markers (Zetin & Kramer, 1992). In contrast to Obsessive-Compulsive Disorder, Obsessive-Compulsive Personality Disorder is identified by characterological perfectionism, rigidity, and inflexibility. The most common Personality Disorders found among clients with OCD are actually Avoidant, Dependent, and Histrionic (Mavissakalian, Hamann, & Jones, 1990).

POST-TRAUMATIC STRESS DISORDER

In terms of psychological trauma, a limited number of studies have focused on children and adolescents with Post-Traumatic Stress Disorder (PTSD) (Armsworth & Holaday, 1993; Lyons, 1987; Vostanis, 2004). Unfortunately, children might not report to anyone their traumatic experiences, which contributes to PTSD being underdiagnosed within this developmental age group (Lyons, 1987). However, the association between trauma and its variants and childhood psychopathology has been well established (Vostanis, 2004). For example, there has been at least one report of a child experiencing PTSD vicariously (i.e., secondary traumatization with contagion symptomatology) via association with his father's Vietnam combat stress (Rosenheck & Nathan, 1985).

Intellectual impairment, language and communication difficulties, withdrawal, and negative self-perceptions have been associated with PTSD among young people. Additionally, depression, guilt and shame, and fears and omens have been

TABLE 6.8   Diagnostic Criteria for 300.3 Obsessive-Compulsive Disorder

A.   Either obsessions or compulsions:

Obsessions as defined by 1, 2, 3, and 4:

1. recurrent and persistent thoughts, impulses, or images that are experienced, at some time during the disturbance, as intrusive and inappropriate and that cause marked anxiety or distress
2. the thoughts, impulses, or images are not simply excessive worries about real-life problems
3. the person attempts to ignore or suppress such thoughts, impulses, or images, or to neutralize them with some other thought or action
4. the person recognizes that the obsessive thoughts, impulses, or images are a product of his or her own mind (not imposed from without as in thought insertion)

Compulsions as defined in 1 and 2:

1. repetitive behaviors (e.g., hand waving, ordering, checking) or mental acts (e.g., praying, counting, repeating words silently) that the person feels driven to perform in response to an obsession, or according to rules that must be applied rigidly
2. the behaviors or mental acts are aimed at preventing or reducing distress or preventing some dreaded event or situation; however, these behaviors or mental acts either are not connected in a realistic way with what they are designed to neutralize or prevent or are clearly excessive

B.   At some point during the course of the disorder, the person has recognized that the obsessions or compulsions are excessive or unreasonable. *Note:* This does not apply to children.

C.   The obsessions or compulsions cause marked distress, are time-consuming (take more than 1 hour a day), or significantly interfere with the person's normal routine, occupational (or academic) functioning, or usual social activities or relationships.

D.   If another Axis I disorder is present, the content of the obsessions or compulsions is not restricted to it (e.g., preoccupation with food in the presence of an Eating Disorder; hair pulling in the presence of Trichotillomania; concern with drugs in the presence of a Substance Use Disorder; preoccupation with having a serious illness in the presence of Hypochondriasis; preoccupation with sexual urges or fantasies in the presence of a Paraphilia; or guilty ruminations in the presence of Major Depressive Disorder).

E.   The disturbance is not due to the direct physiological effects of a substance (e.g., a drug of abuse, a medication) or a general medical condition.

Specify if:

With Poor Insight: if, not for most of the time during the current episode, the person does not recognize that the obsessions and compulsions are excessive or unreasonable.

From *Diagnostic and Statistical Manual of Mental Disorders,* Fourth Edition, Text Revision (p. 462–463), American Psychiatric Association (APA), Washington, DC: APA. Copyright 2000 by APA. Reprinted by permission.

found in traumatized children and adolescents, complicating this often comorbid condition. Conduct Disorders, hyperactivity, enuresis and encopresis, sleep disturbance, somatization, and regressive and repetitive play were all symptoms reported in Armsworth and Holaday's (1993) review of traumatized children. However, children seldom experience the dissociative flashbacks associated with adult PTSD (Lyons, 1987). Childhood trauma also is impacted by parental, family, and contextual factors (Vostanis, 2004).

Girls are significantly more likely to develop PTSD than boys; however, there seems to be no difference by gender of the types of trauma experienced. Sexual abuse is the most often cited stressor among hospitalized, traumatized adolescents (Cohen, Mannarino, & Berliner, 2000). PTSD is often manifested among children and adolescents in natural disasters, life-threatening illness, traffic accidents, rape and sexual abuse, violence, homelessness and displacement, as well as hostage, terrorism, and peer suicide situations (e.g., Cancro, 2004; Cook-Cottone; 2004; Fremont, 2004; Heflin & Deblinger, 2003; Melhim, Day, & Shear, 2004; Stallard, Salter, & Velleman, 2004; Stewart, Steiman, & Cauce, 2004; Stuber, Shemesh, & Saxe, 2003; Thompson, 2005; Zink & McCain, 2003). In addition, some individuals with PTSD will experience *survival guilt* as a function of surviving a calamity.

Diagnosis of Post-Traumatic Stress Disorder

The *DSM-IV-TR* diagnostic criteria for PTSD (Table 6.9) include exposure to as well as the re-experience of a traumatic event that threatens death or injury to self or others and results in fear, helplessness, or horror (APA, 2000a). The reexperience of the trauma might involve recurrent and intrusive thoughts, dreams, distress, and in some cases physiological reactivity. In addition, loss of interest in typical activities, feelings of detachment, avoidance of anything related to the trauma, and restricted affect may be observed in children and adolescents with PTSD. Difficulties with sleep, concentration, hypervigilance, anger, startle responses, and interpersonal relationships are typically present. Children and adolescents can report nightmares regarding the traumatic event. Differential diagnoses can include Adjustment Disorder, Phobias, and Mood Disorders (APA, 2000a; McCormack, 1985).

ACUTE STRESS DISORDER

According to the *DSM-IV-TR* (APA, 2000a), approximately one-fourth of the individuals exposed to a traumatic event will meet the diagnosis of Acute Stress Disorder (Table 6.10). This diagnosis, introduced in *DSM-IV* (APA, 1994), is hierarchically a downgrade from PTSD and includes many of PTSD's clinical features. Approximately 25% of children experiencing an acute stress response will develop PTSD (Ziegler, Greenwald, DeGuzman, & Simon, 2005).

Diagnosis of Acute Stress Disorder

Acute Stress Disorder is diagnosed when a client has been exposed to a traumatic event and experiences symptoms similar to those of PTSD but occurring relatively soon after the event (i.e., 2 days to 4 weeks following the trauma). This disorder usually involves intense fear, numbing or detachment, loss of awareness of environmental surroundings, psychomotor restlessness, and a reexperiencing of the traumatic phenomenon (APA, 2000a). If the symptoms do not dissipate within 4 weeks, a diagnosis of PTSD should be considered. Differential diagnoses typically include Adjustment Disorder and Mood Disorder (e.g., Major Depression).

TABLE 6.9   Diagnostic Criteria for 309.81 Post-Traumatic Stress Disorder

A.   The person has been exposed to a traumatic event in which both of the following were present:

   1. the person experienced, witnessed, or was confronted with an event or events that involved actual or threatened death or serious injury, or a threat to the physical integrity of self or others.
   2. the person's response involved intense fear, helplessness, or horror. *Note:* In children, this might be expressed instead by disorganized or agitated behavior.

B.   The traumatic event is persistently reexperienced in one (or more) of the following ways:

   1. recurrent and intrusive distressing recollections of the event, including images, thoughts, or perceptions. *Note:* In children, repetitive play may occur in which themes or aspects of the trauma are expressed.
   2. recurrent distressing dreams of the event. *Note:* In children, there may be frightening dreams without recognizable content.
   3. acting or feeling as if the traumatic event were recurring (includes a sense of reliving the experience, illusions, hallucinations, or dissociative flashback episodes, including those that occur on awakening or when intoxicated). *Note:* In young children, trauma-specific reenactment may occur.
   4. intense psychological distress at exposure to internal or external cues that symbolize or resemble an aspect of the traumatic event.
   5. physiological reactivity on exposure to internal or external cues that symbolize or resemble an aspect of the traumatic event.

C.   Persistent avoidance of stimuli associated with the trauma and numbing of general responsiveness (not present before the trauma), as indicated by three (or more) of the following:

   1. efforts to avoid thoughts, feelings, or conversations associated with the trauma
   2. efforts to avoid activities, places, or people that arouse recollections of the trauma
   3. inability to recall an important aspect of the trauma
   4. markedly diminished interest or participation in significant activities
   5. feeling of detachment or estrangement from others
   6. restricted range of affect (e.g., unable to have loving feelings)
   7. sense of a foreshortened future (e.g., does not expect to have a career, marriage, children, or normal lifespan)

D.   Persistent symptoms of increased arousal (not present before the trauma), as indicated by two (or more) of the following:

   1. difficulty falling or staying asleep
   2. irritability or outbursts of anger
   3. difficulty concentrating
   4. hypervigilance
   5. exaggerated startle response

E.   Duration of the disturbance (symptoms in Criteria B, C, and D) is more than 1 month.

F.   The disturbance causes clinically significant distress or impairment in social, occupational, or other important areas of functioning.

Specify if:

   Acute: if duration of symptoms is less than 3 months
   Chronic: if duration of symptoms is 3 months or more

Specify if:

   With delayed onset: if onset of symptoms is at least 6 months after the stressor

From *Diagnostic and Statistical Manual of Mental Disorders,* Fourth Edition, Text Revision (p. 467–468), American Psychiatric Association (APA), Washington, DC: APA. Copyright 2000, APA. Reprinted by permission.

TABLE 6.10   Diagnostic Criteria for 308.3 Acute Stress Disorder

A. The person has been exposed to a traumatic event in which both of the following were present:

1. the person experienced, witnessed, or was confronted with an event or events that involved actual or threatened death or serious injury, or a threat to the physical integrity of self or others
2. the person's response involved intense fear, helplessness, or horror

B. Either while experiencing or after experiencing the distressing event, the individual has three (or more) of the following:

1. a subjective sense of numbing, detachment, or absence of emotional responsiveness
2. a reduction in awareness of his or her surroundings (e.g., "being in a daze")
3. derealization
4. depersonalization
5. dissociative amnesia (i.e., inability to recall an important aspect of the trauma)

C. The traumatic event is persistently reexperienced in at least one of the following ways: recurrent images, thoughts, dreams, illusions, flashback episodes, or a sense of reliving the experience; or distress on exposure to reminders of the traumatic event.

D. Marked avoidance of stimuli that arouse recollections of the trauma (e.g., thoughts, feelings, conversations, activities, places, people).

E. Marked symptoms of anxiety or increased arousal (e.g., difficulty sleeping, irritability, poor concentration, hypervigilance, exaggerated startle response, motor restlessness).

F. The disturbance causes clinically significant distress or impairment in social, occupational, or other important areas of functioning or impairs the individual's ability to pursue some necessary task, such as obtaining necessary assistance or mobilizing personal resources by telling family members about the traumatic experience.

G. The disturbance lasts for a minimum of 2 days and a maximum of 4 weeks and occurs within 4 weeks of the traumatic event.

H. The disturbance is not due to the direct physiological effects of a substance (e.g., a drug of abuse, a medication) or a general medical condition, is not better accounted for by Brief Psychotic Disorder, and is not merely an exacerbation of a pre-existing Axis I or Axis II disorder.

From *Diagnostic and Statistical Manual of Mental Disorders*, Fourth Edition, Text Revision (p. 471–472), American Psychiatric Association (APA), Washington, DC: Copyright 2000 by APA. Reprinted by permission.

GENERALIZED ANXIETY DISORDER

Generalized Anxiety Disorder (GAD) is a frequently occurring phenomenon among children and adolescents (Strauss, 1988). However, there is insufficient data on this disorder in children and adolescents (Masi, Millepiedi, Mucci, Poli, Bertini, & Milantoni, 2004). The diagnosis of Generalized Anxiety Disorder (GAD) first appeared in the nomenclature in *DSM-III* in 1980 (APA). Many individuals with this disorder report feeling anxious most of their lives to the point that it has taken on a "free-floating" quality. It is important to note that this disorder has been associated with abuse among children (Thyer, 1991). GAD includes an attitude of apprehension that keeps the person in a state of continual vigilance (Rapoport & Ismond, 1990). Unlike most adult anxieties, children often have overlapping subtypes and other partial mental disorder syndromes in addition to an Anxiety Disorder diagnosis (Rapoport & Ismond, 1990). Accordingly, differential diagnoses should be carefully considered.

Diagnosis of Generalized Anxiety Disorder

Breier, Charney, and Heninger (1985) have suggested that GAD may not be a discrete entity, but simply a prodromal, partial, or residual symptom characteristic of other disorders. GAD has been found in children in the form of *overanxiousness,* where anxiety is intense but generally diffuse and unfocused (Casat, 1988; Strauss, 1988). In effect, overanxiousness is symptomatically identical to adult GAD. Children and adolescents with overanxiousness typically report multiple somatic complaints and continually feel tense. There is some question about overanxiousness' place on a developmental continuum, in that some of the symptoms associated with this problem are related to normal developmental phenomena (Strauss, 1988).

A diagnosis of GAD (Table 6.11) entails uncontrollable, excessive anxiety or worry with various amounts of restlessness, fatigue, irritability, muscle tension, sleep disturbance, and problems with concentration (APA, 2000a). For example, children might be anxious about impending disasters and personal performance. As usual, school and social functioning are impaired with this diagnosis. Considerations for differential diagnosis include all other Anxiety Disorders, Adjustment Disorder, and Mood Disorder (e.g., Major Depression and Dysthymia). As with Panic Disorder

---

TABLE 6.11　Diagnostic Criteria for 300.02 Generalized Anxiety Disorder

A. Excessive anxiety and worry (apprehensive expectation), occurring more days than not for at least 6 months, about a number of events or activities (such as work or school performance).

B. The person finds it difficult to control the worry.

C. The anxiety and worry are associated with three (or more) of the following six symptoms (with at least some symptoms present for more days than not for the past 6 months). *Note:* Only one item is required in children.

　1. restlessness or feeling keyed up or on edge
　2. being easily fatigued
　3. difficulty concentrating or mind going blank
　4. irritability
　5. muscle tension
　6. sleep disturbance (difficulty falling or staying asleep or restless, unsatisfying sleep)

D. The focus of the anxiety and worry is not confined to features of an Axis I disorder, e.g., the anxiety or worry is not about having a panic attack (as in Panic Disorder), being embarrassed in public (as in Social Phobia), being contaminated (as in Obsessive-Compulsive Disorder), gaining weight (as in Anorexia Nervosa), having multiple physical complaints (as in Somatization Disorder), or having a serious illness (as in Hypochondriasis), and the anxiety or worry do not occur exclusively during Post-Traumatic Stress Disorder.

E. The anxiety, worry, or physical symptoms cause clinically significant distress or impairment in social, occupational, or other important areas of functioning.

F. The disturbance is not due to the direct physiological effects of a substance (e.g., a drug of abuse, a medication) or a general medical condition (e.g., hyperthyroidism) and does not occur exclusively during a Mood Disorder, a Psychotic Disorder, or a Pervasive Developmental Disorder.

From *Diagnostic and Statistical Manual of Mental Disorders,* Fourth Edition, Text Revision (p. 476), American Psychiatric Association (APA), Washington, DC: APA. Copyright 2000 by APA. Reprinted by permission.

With Agoraphobia, Major Depression is often encountered with GAD and may be referred to as "anxious depression" (which would be coded as Mood Disorder NOS using the *DSM-IV-TR*) (APA, 2000a).

ANXIETY DISORDER DUE TO A GENERAL MEDICAL CONDITION AND SUBSTANCE-INDUCED ANXIETY DISORDER

To increase the accuracy of differential diagnosis, Anxiety Disorder Due to a General Medical Condition and Substance-Induced Anxiety Disorder are included in the *DSM-IV-TR*. These disorders are etiologically associated with a physical condition or substance intoxication and withdrawal, respectively (APA, 2000a). Interventions will be associated with either medical practice or substance abuse/dependence counseling.

Diagnosis of Anxiety Disorder Due to a General Medical Condition and Substance-Induced Anxiety Disorder

A diagnosis of Anxiety Disorder Due to a General Medical Condition (Table 6.12) is made when clinically significant anxiety is perceived to be the direct result of the physiological effects of a disease process. This diagnosis requires the history, physical examination, or laboratory findings associated with a medical condition. Symptoms

TABLE 6.12   Diagnostic Criteria for 293.84 Anxiety Disorder Due to . . . [Indicate the General Medical Condition]

A. Prominent anxiety, Panic Attacks, or obsessions or compulsions predominate in the clinical picture.

B. There is evidence from the history, physical examination, or laboratory findings that the disturbance is the direct physiological consequence of a general medical condition.

C. The disturbance is not better accounted for by another mental disorder (e.g., Adjustment Disorder With Anxiety in which the stressor is a serious general medical condition).

D. The disturbance does not occur exclusively during the course of delirium.

E. The disturbance causes clinically significant distress or impairment in social, occupational, or other important areas of functioning.

Specify if:

  With Generalized Anxiety: if excessive anxiety or worry about a number of events or activities predominates in the clinical presentation.
  With Panic Attacks: if Panic Attacks . . . predominate in the clinical presentation.
  With Obsessive-Compulsive Symptoms: if obsessions or compulsions predominate in the clinical presentation.

  Coding note: Include the name of the general medical condition on Axis I, e.g., 293.84 Anxiety Disorder Due to Pheochromocytoma, With Generalized Anxiety; also code the general medical condition on Axis III . . .

From *Diagnostic and Statistical Manual of Mental Disorders,* Fourth Edition, Text Revision (p. 479), American Psychiatric Association (APA), Washington, DC: APA. Copyright 2000 by APA. Reprinted by permission.

must be etiologically related to the general medical condition and generally result in Generalized Anxiety, panic attacks, or Obsessive-Compulsive behavior. When making this diagnosis, the medical condition also should be noted on Axis III of the *DSM-IV-TR* multiaxial assessment. Medical problems that might cause anxiety symptoms include cardiovascular, respiratory, and neurological conditions (APA, 2000a).

A diagnosis of Substance-Induced Anxiety Disorder is appropriate when anxiety symptoms are due to the "direct physiological effects of a substance (i.e., a drug of abuse, a medication, or toxin exposure)" (APA, 2000a, p. 479). In the case of anxiety manifestations in the presence of a substance, the full criteria for GAD, Panic Disorder, Phobia, or OCD need not be met. This diagnosis is used when, in addition to the presence of the substance, anxiety symptoms are "sufficiently severe to warrant independent clinical attention" (APA, 2000a, p. 480). The diagnosis should reflect whether the anxiety symptoms are occurring during intoxication or withdrawal. It is important to note that the diagnosis of any Anxiety Disorder in the *DSM-IV-TR* on descriptive data and the categorization of symptoms, etiology, or causal factors is not necessary for the diagnostic process.

CAUSAL FACTORS AND PREVENTION

Anxious symptoms can be etiologically associated with a variety of phenomena including persistent worry, unreasonable fears, fear of separation, social avoidance, family stress, social difficulties, school problems, trauma, and illness (see Last, 1993; Thyer, 1987, 1991; Wells, McQuellon, & Hinkle, 1995). Yet very little is known about the etiology of most Anxiety Disorders, and the cause of Panic Disorder remains particularly controversial. The two major schools of thought are biological mediation, as noted previously, and cognitive-behavioral theory. This has resulted in some degree of polarization in the diagnostic studies of Anxiety Disorders (Mattick et al., 1990). Biological theories (e.g., Klein, 1981) suggest that a genetically transmitted neurochemical abnormality is responsible for Anxiety Disorders. However, cognitive and behavioral theories suggest that biological factors are unnecessary for the explanation of panic (Clark, 1988; Thyer, 1987). It might be that environmental factors and the response to them are determined by a genetically transmitted proneness to Anxiety Disorders (McNally, 1990).

Primary prevention is difficult with many mental disorders including Anxiety Disorders. School counselors and psychologists, parents, and other influential adults can help children and their families effectively cope with anxiety by modeling and applying early interventions. Secondary and tertiary prevention should be applied to keep symptoms from increasing and reducing levels of decompensation over time.

METHODS FOR ASSESSMENT

Few children, especially those under the age of 15, are likely to be self-referred for an Anxiety Disorder. In fact, they are generally referred by a parent, school, or professional community member. Therefore, the clinician must simultaneously evaluate the referral source as well as the child or adolescent. Moreover, the data from each source is rarely consistent. There can even be disagreement between sources when

TABLE 6.13   Diagnostic Criteria for Substance-Induced Anxiety Disorder

A.   Prominent anxiety, panic attacks, or obsessions or compulsions predominate in the clinical picture.

B.   There is evidence from the history, physical examination, or laboratory findings of either 1 or 2:

1. the symptoms in Criterion A developed during, or within 1 month of, Substance Intoxication or Withdrawal.
2. medication use is etiologically related to the disturbance.

C.   The disturbance is not better accounted for by an Anxiety Disorder that is not substance induced. Evidence that the symptoms are better accounted for by an Anxiety Disorder that is not substance induced might include the following: the symptoms precede the onset of the substance use (or medication use); the symptoms persist for a substantial period of time (e.g., about a month) after the cessation of acute withdrawal or severe intoxication or are substantially in excess of what would be expected given the type or amount of the substance used or the duration of use; or there is other evidence suggesting the existence of an independent non–substance-induced Anxiety Disorder (e.g., a history of recurrent non–substance-related episodes).

D.   The disturbance does not occur exclusively during the course of delirium.

E.   The disturbance causes clinically significant distress or impairment in social, occupational, or other important areas of functioning.

Note: This diagnosis should be made instead of a diagnosis of Substance Intoxication or Substance Withdrawal only when the anxiety symptoms are in excess of those usually associated with the intoxication or withdrawal syndrome and when the anxiety symptoms are sufficiently severe to warrant independent clinical attention.

Code [Specific Substance]-Induced Anxiety Disorder

(291.89 Alcohol; 292.89 Amphetamine (or Amphetamine-Like Substance); 292.89 Caffeine; 292.89 Cannabis; 292.89 Cocaine; 292.89 Hallucinogen; 292.89 Inhalant; 292.89 Phencyclidine (or Phencyclidine-Like Substance); 292.89 Sedative, Hypnotic, or Anxiolytic; 292.89 Other [or unknown] Substance)

Specify if:

With Generalized Anxiety: if excessive anxiety or worry about a number of events or activities predominates in the clinical presentation.
With Panic Attacks: if panic attacks (see p. 432) predominate in the clinical presentation
With Obsessive-Compulsive Symptoms: if obsessions or compulsions predominate in the clinical presentation
With Phobic Symptoms: if phobic symptoms predominated in the clinical presentation

Specify if:

With Onset During Intoxication: if the criteria are met for intoxication with the substance and the symptoms develop during the intoxication syndrome
With Onset During Withdrawal: if criteria are met for withdrawal from the substance and the symptoms develop during, or shortly after, a withdrawal syndrome

From *Diagnostic and Statistical Manual of Mental Disorders,* Fourth Edition, Text Revision (p. 483), American Psychiatric Association (APA), Washington, DC: Copyright 2000 by APA. Reprinted by permission.

the same diagnostic procedure is used. The clinician must be aware of potential referral bias, particularly in times of familial, social, and educational turmoil. Furthermore, the child's ability to communicate with the clinician might be limited by age, language development, and conceptual ability (Rapoport & Ismond, 1990).

Psychological testing is often more effective with children than adults in assisting with establishing an accurate anxiety diagnosis. This is because of the strong connection between psychological functioning and symptomology. Traditional instruments for assessing childhood anxiety as well as more recent assessment procedures have been found to have reliable utility as self-report indexes for childhood anxiety in clinical as well as research settings (see Muris, Merckelbach, Gadet, Moulaert, & Tierney, 1999 and Last, 1993, for more assessment information). A reliable teacher rating scale, such as Conners' Teacher Rating Scale (Conners, 1969), is always a reasonable source of collateral diagnostic information.

It is important to note that there is mixed support for the validity of the Anxiety Disorder classification of mental disorder among children and adolescents due to a limited number of adequate developmental measures for these disorders, insufficient construct validity, and a lack of knowledge regarding developmental contributions to symptom constellations (Chorpita & Lilienfeld, 1999). Therefore, multiple diagnoses should be used in the assessment process when appropriate. Additionally, the examiner serves as another observer of the child or adolescent's behavior, particularly when the examinee demonstrates poor self-report. This is especially important when assessing Anxiety Disorders among children and adolescents where critical information can be gleaned by using semistructured interviews (Rapoport & Ismond, 1990).

Applying SUDS (Subjective Units of Discomfort Scales) is often helpful in assessing the levels of improvement in anxiety symptoms across time. For example, a child with fear of strangers might be asked to rate anxiety associated with encountering strangers on a 1–10 scale. Ratings can be tracked over time in order to establish treatment efficacy rates. It is apparent that this type of intervention is contingent upon the child's or adolescent's level of trust in the clinician (see Thyer, 1987).

COMORBIDITY

Unfortunately, children with anxiety symptoms often meet the clinical criteria for other disorders. Such diagnostic overlap (comorbidity) makes the boundary between Anxiety Disorders and other mental disorders difficult to determine among children and adolescents, and also may exacerbate the confusion between threshold and subthreshold symptoms (Labellarte, Ginsburg, Walkup, & Riddle, 1999; Zohar, 1999). For example, there is considerable symptom overlap between Selective Mutism and anxiety symptoms, suggesting that Selective Mutism might actually be a variant of the anxiety spectrum. Moreover, when Selective Mutism is treated as a category of Anxiety Disorder, the treatment tends to be more effective (Anstendig, 1999).

Although Anxiety Disorders and Depressive Mood are often combined in the literature, some research supports the notion that these are two distinct clinical conditions (Kashani, Suarez, Jones, & Reid, 1999), even among children and adolescents. Twenty to 65% of anxious individuals become depressed at some point (see APA, 2000a; Bernstein & Borchardt, 1991; Dubovsky, 1990; Masi, Millepiedi, & Mucci, 2004). Dubovsky's (1990) review indicated that physical disorders also can obscure this comorbid condition. Hence, comorbidity obviously is an important issue in treating children and adolescents with the various Anxiety Disorders.

Furthermore, individuals who are both anxious and depressed are more likely to have comorbid Personality Disorders (i.e., Avoidant, Schizotypal, Schizoid) than those with only anxiety states (Brooks et al., 1989).

More specifically, Separation Anxiety Disorder can present itself with other Anxiety Disorders as well as Dysthymic Disorder or Major Depressive Disorder and might be an associated feature of Pervasive Developmental Disorder (APA, 2000a). Diagnostically, approximately 60% of children with Separation Anxiety Disorder meet the criteria for overanxiousness (GAD), whereas 30% to 50% of children with Anxiety Disorders also have Depressive Mood and about 30% have ADHD (Kutcher, Reiter, Gardner, & Klein, 1992).

The comorbidity of Personality Disorders with Panic Disorder as well as other Anxiety Disorders is relatively sketchy (Brooks et al., 1989). However, Brooks et al. (1989) reported in their review that the prevalence rate of Dependent and Avoidant Personality Disorders among patients with Panic Disorder ranged from 40% to 65%, with Avoidant Personality Disorder having higher rates. This raises the question of whether such personality traits are separate and distinct or an artifact of the Anxiety Disorder itself (Brooks et al., 1989). Moreover, individuals with Panic Disorder and a co-occurring Personality Disorder have been found to have poorer responses to medication treatments and higher relapse rates (Reich, 1988). It is important to note that such clinical comorbidity most likely would be found among older adolescents and not among young children.

Children with panic and non-panic anxiety symptoms have been found to have comorbid major depression (Diler, Birmaher, & Brent, 2004). Panic Disorder shares a concordance rate of about 70% with Major Depressive Disorder, Bipolar Disorder, and Dissociative Disorder as well as other Anxiety Disorders (e.g., Post-Traumatic Stress Disorder and Obsessive-Compulsive Disorder) (NIH, 1991). People with Panic Disorder might be significantly depressed because of self-imposed social restrictions and avoidant functioning (Brooks et al., 1989). Clinicians making the diagnosis of Panic Disorder With or Without Agoraphobia should be sensitive to the strong possibility of physical conditions associated with panic and agoraphobic symptoms (e.g., hyperventilation syndrome, hypoglycemia, Anxiety Disorder Due to a General Medical Condition, Substance-Induced Anxiety Disorder, and Somatoform Disorder (APA, 2000a; Thyer, 1987). Furthermore, Panic Disorder has a high comorbidity rate with Specific Phobia and should always be considered as an additional diagnosis. In school phobia, a child also may develop multiple Specific Phobias.

It is important to understand the significant relationship among Mood Disorders, Personality Disorders, and other comorbid Anxiety Disorders (e.g., Generalized Anxiety Disorder) when making a diagnosis of Social Phobia and devising a treatment plan (Brooks et al., 1989; Turner & Beidel, 1989). Social Phobia is more extensive and disabling than previously thought, and also may be associated with suicide attempts (Aimes, Gelder, & Shaw, 1983; Brooks et al., 1989; Turner & Beidel, 1989). Social Phobia also has been linked to Alcohol Dependence and Substance-Related Disorders among adults, alerting clinicians to be aware of such comorbidity in older adolescents (Liebowitz et al., 1985). In fact, older adolescents (and adults, for that matter) with any Anxiety Disorder might be prone to comorbid alcohol-use disorders (Kushner, Sher, & Erickson, 1999).

Heimberg et al. (1987) highlighted the important relationship between Social Phobia and Personality Disorders when developing treatment plans. Co-occurring Personality Disorders generally predict less improvement and a focus on social-skills training rather than solitary cognitive-behavioral treatments (Turner, 1987). Nearly one-half of children with Generalized Anxiety Disorder or overanxiousness meet the diagnostic criteria for Separation Anxiety Disorder (see Strauss, 1988).

Clients with OCD may present with comorbid disorders that might make the prognosis more unfavorable. Comorbid mental health conditions with OCD include depressive mood and movement disorders, as well as other Anxiety Disorders (e.g., Specific Phobia) (Zohar, 1999). OCD also coexists with abuse of alcohol (Karno et al., 1988; Keane & Wolfe, 1990; Zetin & Kramer, 1992) and has been hypothesized to be associated with the preoccupations of food, weight, and body image associated with Anorexia Nervosa (Fahy, 1991). About 20% of adolescents (and adults) with OCD have other comorbid disorders (e.g., Tourette's, Panic Disorder, Obsessive-Compulsive Personality Disorder) (Clarizio, 1991).

Clients who meet the diagnostic criteria for PTSD often meet the criteria for other diagnoses. Comorbid disorders among boys suffering from PTSD include Eating Disorders, Somatization Disorder, and other Anxiety Disorders. Major Depressive Disorder also may coexist with PTSD. Furthermore, boys and girls with PTSD are likely to report dissociative symptoms (Lipschitz, Winegar, Hartnick, Foote, & Southwick, 1999) as well as problems with sleep, conduct, and attention problems (Caffo & Belaise, 2003).

Scott and Stradling (1992) have indicated that a "pure case of Post-Traumatic Stress Disorder is somewhat of a rarity" (p. 110). For example, Depressive Mood among rape trauma is almost immediate (Steketee & Foa, 1987). Restricted social life, family problems, somatic complaints, and sleep disturbance have been found among trauma victims. Such comorbidity rates are extremely important information for the clinician when making a PTSD diagnosis and devising a treatment plan.

IMPLICATIONS FOR TREATMENT

When treating children and adolescents with Anxiety Disorders, it is always important to gather knowledge of the familial, contextual, social, and biological factors associated with the anxiety symptoms. Additionally, the clinician should take into account the forces that maintain the problem and inhibit the child's or adolescent's development when establishing the treatment plan. Of course, the clinician should always consider the natural outcome of the symptoms without treatment intervention (Rapoport & Ismond, 1990). Early treatment for Anxiety Disorders is critical before complications, chronicity, and social incapacitation occur (Biederman, 1990). Typically, the path to effective treatment is the integration of therapies rather than polarization (Cohen, Mannarino, & Berliner, 2000).

The efficacy of treatments other than cognitive, behavioral, and pharmacological (i.e., psychodynamic therapies) has not been demonstrated (NIH, 1991). Even some treatment components in isolation have no long-term therapeutic efficacy (e.g., relaxation training [Thyer, 1987]). Although well-controlled studies regarding interventions with Anxiety Disorders among children are limited, there is increasing recognition among clinicians that such research is drastically needed (Thyer, 1991). Even with available models for differential diagnosis, weaknesses in assessment and research design have contributed to the lack of effectiveness of prescribing treatment interventions (Burke & Silverman, 1987).

Evidence Based Treatments

During the past decade there has been a growing debate regarding "evidence based" or "empirically supported treatments" (ESTs). This discussion has reflected an ethical imperative to practice ESTs that are based on empirical evidence, even though the conclusions gained from ESTs is quite modest (Follette & Beitz, 2003). It has been argued that such interventions are often rigid, medically-oriented, and tend to advocate cognitive-behavioral therapies (Messer, 2004). ESTs generally represent randomized controlled trials of various types of psychological interventions including those with children and adolescents (e.g., Liberman, Van Horn, & Ippen, 2005).

When considering treatments for childhood and adolescent anxiety disorders, it is important to carefully consider the data presented by ESTs. In some research reports well-controlled studies were efficacious, but little was reported about their effectiveness in uncontrolled, real-world settings. It has been argued that as technical, inflexible adherence to a specified treatment protocol goes up, the therapeutic alliance goes down (Herschell, McNeil, & McNeil, 2004; Sexton & Whiston, 1994). Moreover, representation from minority groups in outcome research has been very low to absent (Bernal, & Scharron-Del-Rio, 2001; Clay, Mordhorst, & Lehn, 2002). There is clearly a need to clearly understanding of the transportability of ESTs, particularly when designing treatments for child and adolescent anxiety disorders (Herschell et al., 2004).

To elaborate, it is important for practitioners working with children and adolescents with anxiety disorders to have an understanding of the benefits *and* weaknesses of ESTs. Some major weaknesses include the all-too-often exclusive reliance on *DSM-IV-TR* diagnoses, applying a medical model to counseling and psychotherapy, and a focus on treatment that occurs immediately after the onset of symptoms, as with PTSD (Honos-Webb, 2005; Messer, 2004). However, individuals with PTSD are likely to seek treatment in a variety of time frames following the initial trauma. Thus, the practitioner needs to ask, *"How well can the treatment be applied with temporal variations? Which aspects of an EST would be practical with this case?"*

Given the weaknesses associated with ESTs, namely supporting internal validity at the risk of reducing external validity, treatment information obtained from ESTs can be useful. But, they are an insufficient guides due to their limited ability to direct clinical decision-making (Herbert, 2003). Clearly, the EST debate has brought into the clinical communities' consciousness the need to be accountable for treatments (Edwards, Dattilio, & Bromley, 2004). Optimally, EST reports combined with single-case studies, local clinical data, and practitioner experience can lead to treatments for child and adolescent anxiety disorders that are efficacious as well as effective. Following is a review of a sample of treatments that have been used for anxiety disorders in young people.

Treatment for Separation Anxiety Disorder

The critical treatment for Separation Anxiety Disorder is to develop a plan for leaving the child in as secure a manner as possible and actually having the caretaker separate from the child as soon as possible. The longer the caretaker indulges the child's fear, the more the symptoms are likely to increase. It is imperative that a treatment strategy be designed that assists the caretaker or parent and child to separate in as positive a manner as possible. Consoling the child after the physical separation from the parent also is important.

Family counseling is a very effective treatment strategy in many Separation Anxiety cases. For example, older children can be asked to assume a hierarchical position and assist the younger, fearful sibling with appropriate separation-coping mechanisms. The clinician can coach the older brother or sister on how to effectively assist the younger, anxious sibling with anxiety symptoms.

Treatment for Panic Disorder and Agoraphobia

A limited number of controlled studies implement cognitive and behavioral treatments for children and adolescents with Panic Disorder. According to a few controlled studies, Cognitive-Behavioral therapy is an efficacious treatment of Anxiety Disorders among the pediatric population (Labellarte et al., 1999; Landon & Barlow, 2004; Roy-Byrne, Craske, & Stein, 2004; Weiss & Hawley, 2002). In terms of developmental treatment, research evaluations regarding children and adolescents have been sparse. Black and Robbins (1990) reported developmental case studies that reflected symptoms of respiratory distress such as hyperventilation, tremors, feeling flushed and hot, intense fear, dizziness, faintness, confusion, palpitations, fear of psychosis, academic difficulty, and comorbid Depressive Mood. As noted previously, Depressive Mood has been found to share symptoms in children with comorbid Anxiety Disorders (Bernstein & Borchardt, 1991). In such cases, increasing a sense of security and anti-depressant counseling are imperative components of treatment. The severity of the aforementioned symptoms, gender, and level of parental anxiety are associated with poor initial response to treatment.

Although early treatment is important, many older adolescents wait several years before seeking therapeutic intervention, largely because of pathological avoidance and concomitant substance abuse used to self-treat. Although substance abuse might seem to the adolescent be an effective way to self-medicate, it only exacerbates the anxious condition. Ultimately, individuals with a combined Panic Disorder and Substance-Related Disorder experience a severe clinical state (Cox et al., 1990). This makes it important to differentiate whether panic is a primary or secondary disorder. It is typically best to treat a secondary Substance-Related Disorder first.

It is critical to note that comorbid alcohol abuse among adolescents with anxiety symptoms increases the risk of suicide attempts (Cox et al., 1990). Moreover, young people not presenting with suicidal ideation, but with a family history of such behavior, should be closely monitored for self-injurious behavior (Schatzberg & Ballenger, 1991). Behavioral interventions for panic typically include *in vivo* (i.e., real life) exposure or desensitization, relaxation, stimulus mapping, and daily logs or diaries of symptoms. Although *in vivo* situations are difficult to control, they are generally superior to imagined situations (Laraia et al., 1989). Essentially, *in vivo* exposure is the supportive exposure to the actual feared stimulus or environment. For example, a child who is afraid of swimming pools would have counseling sessions near or at a pool. Hinkle and Lineberry (1999) have reported that interventions might require the counselor to treat the client in the actual anxiety-provoking context. Likewise, Thyer (1987) has indicated that "therapeutic exposure is a psychosocial intervention that cannot be conducted exclusively from the confines of the human service professional's office. You must go into the real-world context where your client lives, make frequent home visits, and in general abandon the traditions of consulting room practice" (p. 84).

Exposure therapy can be carried out in the client's imagination, *in vivo*, or a combination of both. Therapeutic exposure, followed by persuasion not to escape, are critical components of this treatment. They are typically provided on an outpatient basis and are particularly helpful when a significant other (e.g., parent) is involved for support and encouragement. For example, a parent can be instructed in guiding relaxation training for a child. Exposure therapy includes deliberate contact with the stimulus while the client is urged to extend the discomfort and then become comfortable via imaginative exercises and relaxation. It is important to note that in general, anxious clients with severe comorbid levels of depression are often not good candidates for exposure therapies (Thyer, 1987). In such cases, anti-depressant medication may need to be considered before exposure is begun. Relatedly, effective interventions for Panic Disorder may result in a decrease in comorbid depressive complaints.

Unfortunately, a small percentage of clients who receive this type of treatment do not have a favorable response (Francis & Borden, 1993). Typically, the younger the age at the onset of anxiety symptoms, the more positive the response to treatment (Foa, Grayson, Steketee, & Doppelt, 1983). This is possibly due to the extraneous depression that can be found as the age of the client increases.

Respiratory control training also has been shown to offer some promise (Thyer, 1987), as has interoceptive behavioral conditioning (where the conditioned stimulus is an internal body cue). For example, an innovative treatment by Orwin (1973) has clients engage in aerobic exercise that paradoxically interferes with having a panic attack. In addition, aggressive psychoeducation and demystification of Panic Disorder are often needed (NIH, 1991). Maintenance counseling following the remission of anxiety symptoms also is crucial for long-term, successful intervention with children and adolescents.

The treatment of choice is a function of the desires of the client and the skills and networking resources of the clinician (Mattick et al., 1990). If there is no response in 6 to 8 weeks, the treatment plan should be reassessed. Combinations of therapy are generally needed in more progressive anxiety cases. Combinations of pharmacotherapy and behavioral treatments have been found to be particularly beneficial (Lydiard, Roy-Byrne, & Ballenger, 1988).

Since the 1950s, medications have brought about dramatic changes in the care of people with Anxiety Disorders. The advent of newer medications every year makes the prescription of treatment, both biological and psychological, more efficacious (Rapoport & Ismond, 1990). There are few carefully conducted studies (i.e., without major methodological problems) demonstrating the effectiveness of psychotropic medication for children and adolescents experiencing Anxiety Disorders (Brown & Sammons, 2002; Francis & Borden, 1993; Kutcher, Reiter, Gardner, & Klein, 1992; Moreau & Weissman, 1992; Wolff & Rapoport, 1988). At times the child might respond to counseling only after the symptoms have been pharmacologically controlled (Black & Robbins, 1990). As among adults, benzodiazipines (BZDs) are a psychotropic agent used with young people; however, the efficacy of BZDs is not well established in the younger population. Kutcher et al. (1992) indicated that "as a whole, the literature on high-potency BZDs is too inadequate to offer any clear-cut guidelines for the use of these medications in anxiety disorders of children and adolescents" (p. 47). Although BZDs have been shown to be effective, dependency and relapse when the medication is discontinued become a problem (Lydiard et al., 1988; Mattick et al., 1990).

Clark and Ehlers' (1993) review of the research regarding Panic Disorder has indicated that cognitive interventions among adults have a follow-up success rate of 82%, whereas clients treated pharmacologically (e.g., with imipramine, a tricyclic antidepressant with an anti-panic agent), are more likely to relapse. Unfortunately, relapse rates for tricyclic antidepressants as well as BZDs are estimated as high as 25% and 15%, respectively (NIH, 1991).

The use of antidepressants in childhood Anxiety Disorders is largely uncharted; however, preliminary studies have suggested that they are beneficial (Kutcher et al., 1992). Because suicide attempts have often been reported with some Anxiety Disorders (e.g., Panic Disorder) and adolescents can be erratic and impulsive, it is crucial that psychotropic medications be used judiciously and be closely monitored. Accurate clinical information and diagnosis should always precede pharmacologic treatment (Kutcher et al., 1992). Many clients (10–23%) cannot tolerate anti-panic medications, resulting in higher attrition rates in counseling (Thyer, 1987). Moreover, adolescents with coexisting Personality Disorders or Substance-Related Disorders have an increased risk of abusing habit-forming BZDs (Schatzberg & Ballenger, 1991).

Treatment for Specific Phobias

Specific Phobias are generally treated with a combination of behavioral and cognitive interventions. Counseling approaches typically focus on the aforementioned systematic desensitization, *in vivo* exposure, and relaxation therapy. Medications have been generally ineffective in the direct treatment of Specific Phobias (Lydiard et al., 1988). Clinicians have found play therapy, reality therapy, rational-emotive therapy, relaxation exercises, and various behavioral approaches (Bernstein & Borchardt, 1991) to be the treatments of choice. Systematic desensitization, modeling procedures, social-skills training, and operant conditioning have been found to be beneficial among children and adolescents with phobias (see Ollendick & Francis, 1988; Thyer, 1991). To illustrate, a child with school phobia could be desensitized away from the school setting by the counselor using cognitive therapies, play therapy, and relaxation. Following this, supportive *in vivo* exposure could be attempted.

Treatment for Social Phobia

Combining behavioral treatments such as exposure therapy and cognitive therapies such as rational self-talk is the most frequently reported treatment for Social Phobia (Butler, Cullington, Munby, Amies, & Gelder, 1984; Hope & Heimber, 1993). Hope and Heimberg's review strongly suggests that cognitive behavioral group therapy (CBGT) is one of the more efficacious treatment approaches for Social Phobia. They indicate that CBGT attempts to modify cognitive schemas so that they will be closer to those of nonanxious individuals. This type of treatment requires a great deal of courage on the clients' part because they must confront themselves as well as others within the group-counseling format. In this treatment, barriers to healthy thinking are challenged. For example, an adolescent client might become angry at other group members in an attempt to keep them at a distance (Hope & Heimberg, 1993). This approach to treatment is generally more successful with experienced clinicians working in pairs.

Often adolescents with Social Phobias might have been prescribed psychotropic medication *prior* to treatment. It is important to quickly establish rapport and trust and attempt to obtain some level of phobic relief. Thus, the client attributes progress to the talking-therapy or intervention (Thyer, 1987) and eventually might be able to withdraw from medication treatment.

Treatment for Obsessive-Compulsive Disorder

Obsessive thoughts and compulsive behaviors have historically been considered to be extremely resistant to the treatment process. However, behavioral treatments and advances in psychopharmacotherapy have consistently and effectively challenged this notion. Obsessive-Compulsive Disorder among children and adolescents is manifested earlier in boys than in girls, and there are likely gender differences in symptom manifestation. Complete remission rates among this group are estimated to be within the 10% to 15% range. In addition, treatment outcomes might be less significant if the client truly believes in the obsessions (Thyer, 1987). Cognitive therapy and behavior management, shaping, and modeling have been suggested to be effective treatment strategies (Geffken, Pincus, & Zelikovsky, 1999; Piacentini & Langley, 2004).

Many clients with OCD seek treatment only after the symptoms have become debilitating and have resulted in loss of self-esteem and friendships (Zetin & Kramer, 1992). Although the combination of two behavioral interventions can be time-consuming, exposure plus response prevention is often the intervention of choice for OCD. However, some children and adolescents with OCD will not agree or follow through with the demanding and potentially anxiety-provoking homework required of this approach (Zetin & Kramer, 1992). Psychoeducational and supportive counseling, cognitive restructuring, and relaxation training also have been efficacious in treating OCD among children and adolescents. In addition, encouraging active parental involvement can be beneficial (Friedlander & Desrocher, 2006).

Relaxation training enables the client to decrease anxiety and tension and better prepares the client to cope with other anti–Obsessive-Compulsive interventions. Cognitive distortions and their consequences can likewise be reappraised (Boyarsky et al., 1991). Psychoeducational information about the disorder is an extremely important intervention. Support groups as well as educational family meetings can be helpful in reducing overall Obsessive-Compulsive symptoms.

Unlike the literature for adults, there is a modicum of studies focusing on behavioral interventions for OCD among children (Wolff & Rapoport, 1988). However, Wolff and Rapoport's (1988) review revealed that positive reinforcement, differential reinforcement of other behaviors, thought stopping, cognitive restructuring, systematic desensitization, and relaxation have been found to be therapeutically productive (Biederman, 1990; Clarizio, 1991).

Although behavioral treatments might have a longer lasting impact on Obsessive-Compulsive symptoms, psychotropic medications such as antidepressants (e.g., clomipramine, fluvoxamine, fluoxetine) are often prescribed. Although Obsessive-Compulsive symptoms return for about 70% of clients administered clomipramine when the medication is discontinued (Ananth, 1986), clomipramine's efficacy for Obsessive-Compulsive treatment is more definitive than any other medication (Zetin & Kramer, 1992). Fluoxetine appears to work best when Obsessive-Compulsive Disorder coexists with higher levels of depression (Turner, Beidel, Stanley, & Jacob, 1988).

Treatment for Post-Traumatic Stress Disorder

Unfortunately, progress in the treatment of child and adolescent-related trauma lags far behind that accomplished with adults (Dalgleish, Meiser-Stedman, & Smith (2005). Treatments for PTSD have included cognitive-behavioral therapy, stress-inoculation training, muscle relaxation, controlled breathing, modeling, role-playing, guided self-dialogue, group counseling, and EMDR (Caffo & Belaise, 2003; Calhoun & Resick, 1993; Feeny, Foa, Treadwell, & March, 2004; Cohen, Deblinger, Mannarino, & Steer, 2004; Steketee & Foa, 1987; Wilson, Becker, & Tinker, 1995). It is vital that depression and suicide assessments take place (for instance, one out of five rape victims will attempt suicide). As noted previously, comorbid depression is not uncommon and the various levels of depressive mood must be considered in the treatment plan. Additionally, particular attention should be paid to the nature of traumatic memories and how re-experiencing symptoms maintains cognitive dysfunctions (Meiser-Stedman, 2002).

Younger children might follow a protracted course of PTSD despite early intervention and careful clinical monitoring (Vila, Porche, & Mouren-Simeoni, 1999). Various counseling approaches are utilized with PTSD. Cognitive-behavioral interventions are clearly the most popular. Intrusive imagery and thoughts are the hallmark of PTSD, making it amenable to the cognitive-behavioral approach. The cognitive-behavioral modality targets negative thoughts associated with the traumatic event.

Scott and Stradling (1992) have emphasized treatments including *containment, desensitization, cognitive restructuring,* and *writing assignments.* With containment, the goal is not to eradicate the intrusive imagery but to contain it by watching a "mental video" concerning the trauma. When intrusive thoughts persevere, desensitization is usually needed. This is accomplished by having the client listen for 10 to 15 minutes to a self-made audiotape of the traumatic event. Cognitive restructuring focuses on the accurate perception of the trauma and *balancing out* negative memories with positive ones. Clients also are asked to write about the trauma each day. This is both a containment and desensitization exercise. Avoidant behavior also is addressed in Scott and Stradling's interventions for PTSD.

From a counseling perspective, it is crucial to discuss all aspects of the traumatic event, on some level, with the child. This avoids the potential iatrogenic effect of instilling the perception in the child that the memories regarding the trauma are too uncomfortable for the child to bear (Lyons, 1987) or for the clinician to hear. Art and play therapy and other techniques such as storytelling, puppetry, and working with caretakers also are advantageous in intervening on behalf of traumatized children (Armsworth & Holaday, 1993; Lyons, 1987), although they have not been extensively researched (Kutcher et al., 1992) in child trauma cases. Family and school-directed treatment approaches as well as social support and relationship-focused also might prove efficacious (Bokszczanin, 2003; King, Heyne, & Tonge, 2003; Kruczek & Salsman, 2006; Liberman, Van Horn, Ippen, 2005; Stuber & Shemesh, 2006).

Treatment for Acute Stress Disorder

Treatment of Acute Stress Disorder most often entails similar interventions used for PTSD. However, acute stress often requires crisis counseling. Psychological support in the initial stages of responding to trauma is imperative if the client is to not decompensate. The clinician needs to provide support by making initial contact and focusing on practical matters and the "normal" reactions to trauma and disaster (Scott & Stradling, 1992).

Treatment for Generalized Anxiety Disorder

The majority of clients with Generalized Anxiety Disorder have seen their physicians prior to initiating treatment, which might result in the prescription of medication. Adolescents with a history of drug and alcohol abuse are generally not good candidates for successful medication therapy. Treatments typically include progressive muscle relaxation, systematic desensitization, biofeedback, home-based token economies, cognitive-behavioral interventions, meditation, visual imagery, positive self-statements, problem-solving, or some combination of these (Brown, O'Leary, & Barlow, 1993; Strauss, 1988; Thyer, 1987). Physical exercise such as walking and running also may be therapeutic (Hinkle, 1988). There are few reports regarding the treatment of adolescents with GAD (overanxiousness). However, behavior therapy, relaxation training, and cognitive interventions including positive self-statements (Strauss, 1988; Thyer, 1987) might be helpful.

Treatment for Anxiety Disorder Due to a General Medical Condition and Substance-Induced Anxiety Disorder

Treatment for Anxiety Due to General Medical Condition should include the various strategies used for anxiety symptoms listed previously, in addition to treatment for the medical condition. Treatment for substance-induced anxiety symptoms also generally follows the aforementioned approaches in addition to treatment for the substance, medication, or toxin use. It is important to note that drug therapies might not be applicable when drug abuse or dependence is a part of the clinical picture. In addition, psychoeducation, self-help groups (e.g., AA), and family approaches to treatment should be considered.

BEST PRACTICE GUIDELINES

Counselors need to be knowledgeable of the "practice guidelines" for anxiety disorders in the professional literature. Counselors should consult the practice guidelines for the treatment of anxiety disorders contained *Journal of the American Academy of Child and Adolescent Psychiatry* (October, 1998b, Volume 37); *Journal of the American Academy of Child and Adolescent Psychiatry* (October, 1998c, Volume 37); *Journal of the American Academy of Child and Adolescent Psychiatry* (February, 2007, Volume 46); and *Practice Guidelines for the Treatment of Psychiatric Disorders: Compendium 2006* (American Psychiatric Association, 2006). Clinical and/or practice guidelines are recommendations that are based on limited empirical evidence and/or clinical consensus. The counselor should always consider practice guidelines, but there may be exceptions to their application. Practice guidelines are increasingly being used and/or required by school systems, mental health centers, and managed-care organizations.

SCHOOL AND FAMILY PERSPECTIVES

The importance of including the family in the treatment of the child is evident (Hinkle & Wells, 1995; Rapoport & Ismond, 1990). Casat's (1988) review reported that children with parents suffering a depressive as well as Anxiety Disorder have a greater risk for Depressive Mood or Separation Anxiety Disorder, strongly reflecting a familial influence. Obsessive-Compulsive and Agoraphobic symptoms have been lowered when expressed family anger and stress have been reduced (Chambliss, Bryan, Aiken, Steketee, & Hooley, 2001). Separation Anxiety Disorder also is found more frequently among children of mothers with Panic Disorder (APA, 2000a). Furthermore, Separation Anxiety Disorder can be confused with the high value that some cultures place on strong interdependence among family members (APA, 2000a). Primary caregivers and school personnel should always be included when treating children and adolescents with Anxiety Disorders (Francis & Borden, 1993). Studies have indicated that parents, particularly mothers, can contribute to their child's anxiety symptoms by expecting anxious and avoidant behaviors

(Cobham, Dadds, & Spence, 1999). Therefore, family counseling is often a reasonable and effective part of treatment for children and adolescents with anxiety symptoms in general, and specifically with OCD.

It is imperative that parents and teachers be educated about the various effects of trauma and how to identify them in children. In general, anxious children will attempt to obtain accommodations from parents as well as minimization of the consequences associated with their anxiety. Children, however, typically fail in receiving such from parents and will subsequently feel even more helpless. Therefore, parent training should be included in the antianxiety treatment plan (Kutcher et al., 1992; Lyons, 1987).

Strong arguments have been posited, particularly by family counselors, that psychiatric diagnoses need to focus on more than the individual client. Family counselors indicate that a diagnosis that includes the whole family is more useful in terms of treatment planning and predictive outcome (see Carlson, Hinkle, & Sperry, 1993; Hinkle, 1994a; Rapoport & Ismond, 1990). However, a reliable, systemic diagnostic format has not yet been formulated. Considering *DSM-IV-TR* V-Codes and Axes III and IV diagnoses can enhance the development of a systemic-type diagnosis and indicate that the primary target of treatment for a child or adolescent's anxiety problem includes the family (Rapoport & Ismond, 1990). When parents are involved in the treatment of their child, reductions in anxiety symptoms are often evident (Mendlowitz et al., 1999). For example, home-based token economies have been found to be beneficial (Strauss, 1988; Thyer, 1991). Brief school-based interventions also can produce durable reductions in anxiety symptoms (see Dadds et al., 1999; Hinkle & Wells, 1995). Furthermore, clinicians should deal with school phobia immediately and involve the child's teacher and family in the treatment planning. Although, family counseling is a viable treatment approach for Anxiety Disorders among children and adolescents, it should be attempted by counselors with experience in this therapeutic modality. Family assessment, an accurate assessment understanding of systemic dynamics, treatment sequencing, and barriers to success need to be adequately addressed. Likewise, involving the uninformed school professional is potentially problematic.

MULTICULTURAL CONSIDERATIONS

Professionals working with children with Anxiety Disorders need to be aware of multicultural considerations (Snyder, 1996). When assessing and treating children and adolescents for Anxiety Disorders, it is important to keep in mind the various social structures of class, culture, race, gender, and sexual identity (Neville & Mobley, 2001; Pope-Davis, 2002). It also is important to be aware of clinician variables related to bias and social perceptions (Abreu, 2001; Constantine, Kindaichi, Arorash, Donnelly, & Jung, 2002). Culture-bound values that are used to judge *normality* and *abnormality* are important to keep in mind while working with all people, and especially young children. If having a DSM disorder is not enough, existing in an unfamiliar place between the expectations of home, school, and mainstream society can create more stress and anxiety (Snyder, 1996).

Fears of magic and spirits are present in many cultures and should be considered for a diagnosis of Specific Phobia only if the fears are in excess of the context of the culture. Social Phobia's clinical presentation and degree of impairment may differ across cultures, depending on the various social demands of the respective culture. Moreover, the diagnosis of OCD should be assigned only if the obsessions or ritualistic behaviors exceed the respective cultural norms. In addition, religious and cultural beliefs can influence the themes of obsessions and compulsion (APA, 2000a). Although a few reports have suggested no race effects for some PTSDs, Ruch & Chandler (1983) found people of color to experience greater amounts of psychological trauma. In summary, when assessing children for Anxiety Disorders, it is critical that all cross-cultural information be considered (Hinkle, 1994b) and that potential cultural mistrust and bias be taken into account (Whaley, 2001). Recognizing the importance of exploring multicultural diversity and its consequences related to behavioral change is always necessary (Sellers & Hall, 1998).

CASE ILLUSTRATION

Judy is a 12-year-old, only child who attends sixth grade at a public middle school. Her father is a computer analyst and her mother works at home. Judy is anxious much of the time and often worries about her parents not returning from dinner outings, shopping, or business meetings. Her parents reported that Judy is active and has "always been a nervous child," and that she certainly did not appreciate being left alone when she was an infant. When asked whether she seemed to behave out of the ordinary or overreact upon being separated from her parents, her mother repeated that Judy did not particularly like being left when she was younger, but she did not seem to have any extreme reactions. Recently Judy revealed to her mother that she would like to have a new mattress on her bed. Because it was several years old, her mother agreed and purchased a new mattress. Within days, Judy asked whether she could get another new mattress. Her mother was concerned about this and found Judy to report that she was concerned that the new mattress, as well as the old mattress, might contain germs. She elaborated that she worried that if she became ill from the germs on the mattress, she might die.

In addition, Judy had recently begun to wash her hands frequently, to the point that her hands became dry, cracked, and bleeding in places. Upon further interview, Judy reported that she has "bad dreams" and at times awakens in fear. Judy's parents had no reason to believe that she had abused drugs, and also believed that physical or sexual abuse was not an issue. During the interview, Judy had a difficult time sitting still and appeared to have some difficulty maintaining a line of conversation. She was administered the Digit Span subtest of the Wechsler and obtained a scaled score of 12.

Sample Treatment Plan

It is important to consider all diagnoses that might be applied to Judy's case. First, her nightmares and concern for contracting germs from her mattress suggest possible sexual abuse. The counselor would need to carefully consider this and handle it in a delicate manner. If this were ruled out, Attention-Deficit/Hyperactivity Disorder and Separation Anxiety Disorder would need to be considered for differential diagnosis. Her above-average score on the Digit Span subtest as well as her calm behavior in the waiting room (behavioral observation) suggested that AD/HD was not a valid consideration. However, she did appear to be quite anxious about being in the clinician's office. Although she has experienced some Separation Anxiety, it does not appear to be an issue at this time and might have been "normal" developmental behavior in the past. When considering the diagnostic information for Generalized Anxiety Disorder, it was felt that she met the clinical criteria. Additionally, her hand-washing behavior and concern for germs reflect Obsessive-Compulsive Disorder. It would be important to thoroughly assess Judy for other Anxiety Disorders (e.g., phobias) and any other comorbid conditions (e.g., Depressive Mood).

Diagnosis:

Axis I: 300.02 Generalized Anxiety Disorder
              300.3 Obsessive-Compulsive Disorder (R/O Separation Anxiety, Depressive Mood, phobia, nightmares)
Axis II: V71.09 No diagnosis on Axis II
Axis III: None
Axis IV: Environmental stress
Axis V: Global Assessment of Functioning: 59 (at intake)

In this comorbid case of two Anxiety Disorders, namely GAD and OCD, the first line of treatment included family counseling. This was accomplished in an effort to produce a supportive environment at home and to educate Judy's parents about her psychodiagnoses. Next, Judy was administered a paper-and-pencil assessment (incomplete sentences blank and self-esteem questionnaire) that revealed that she at times thought she was "going crazy" and believed that everyone could tell that she was afraid of becoming sick and dying. This information was quite helpful in further developing Judy's treatment plan. Her parents consented to contact with Judy's school counselor and corroborative clinical information was obtained. Cognitive-behavioral therapies, including stress inoculation and rational thinking, were instituted. Effectively dealing with the fear of germs was accomplished in a few trials by encouraging Judy to shake hands with the counselor and touch the office doorknobs (*in vivo* exposure). Challenging irrational thoughts regarding bacteria and germs as well as a focus on the naturalness of colds and their unlikely chances of killing Judy was successfully completed. Rather than washing her hands, Judy was provided with an antibacterial lotion that eventually cleared up her skin irritations. Finally, after eight counseling sessions, Judy began to discuss her self-esteem issues. Her parents were helpful in family counseling by increasing Judy's level of positive self-perceptions. Judy was monitored for 1 year and remained 80–90% symptom free. If she did not continue to make improvements, she would have been considered for a medication evaluation.

CLOSING REMARKS

Anxiety Disorders among children and adolescents are common and deserve immediate assessment and treatment. Unfortunately, due to the fears and worries involved, many children will not seek treatment and might even be quite fearful of initiating human services. Because many of the Anxiety Disorders are progressive in nature, children and adolescents need care that reflects an accurate diagnosis and an assessment of family and school functioning. Medication might be a part of the treatment plan in some cases. Comorbid disorders, physical illness, and cross-cultural information also should be considered when assessing and treating children with anxiety symptoms.

FOR MORE INFORMATION

Anxiety Disorders Education Program
http://www.nimh.nih.gov/anxiety/whatis/objectiv.htm
Anxiety Disorders Association of America
http://www.adaa.org
Anxiety Disorders in Children and Adolescents
http://www.adaa.org/4_info/4i_child/4i_01.htm

Anxiety.com
http://anxieties.com/home.htm
Anxiety Network International
http://www.anxietynetwork.com

CHAPTER 7

MOOD DISORDERS IN CHILDREN AND ADOLESCENTS

By

Lynn F. Field, *Ph.D., LPC, NCC*
Licensed Professional Counselor
Private Practice, Fairfax, Virginia

Linda Seligman, *Ph.D., LPC*
Licensed Psychologist and Counselor
The Center for Counseling and Consultation, Fairfax, Virginia 22031

and

Professor Emeritus
Graduate School of Education
George Mason University, Fairfax, Virginia 22030

Annette C. Albrecht, *Ph.D., LPC, NCC**
Professor
College of Education
Tarleton State University, Stephenville, Texas, 76402

Childhood and adolescence are marked by many changes physically, cognitively, and emotionally. Most of us recall our own childhood and teen years, particularly the emotions that accompanied those formative times. Not only were our bodies going through numerous changes, but things around us seemed to shift as well. How we felt about what went on around us changed regularly, never allowing us to decide for too long how we really felt about things. Some days we were happy and engaged with the world, whereas other days we felt blue and out of place. Many adults who reflect on their youth and its problems often remark: "I cannot imagine going back to those years; especially with all those feelings!"

---

*Dr. Annette Albrecht revised Chapter 7, Mood Disorders in Children and Adolescents for the second edition.

These were our formative years, which helped to prepare us for adulthood. However, we often could not express the pressures and inner confusion to our parents or caregivers. The different moods that we often experienced on a daily basis, and how these moods changed the way we thought about ourselves and others, cannot, in all cases, be attributed to a developmental stage. Traversing the lifespan from childhood through adolescence can be exciting and challenging and is usually accompanied by highs and lows in mood. The question is, "When do the normal ups and downs typical of these stages of life cross over into a diagnosable Mood Disorder?"

To treat young people with Mood Disorders effectively, clinicians should have a good understanding not only of the diagnostic hallmarks of Mood Disorders, but also of the features that characterize these disorders in young people. In this chapter, clinical information necessary for diagnosing children and adolescents with Mood Disorders is presented, as well as information from research to help clinicians achieve a better understanding of youth experiencing these disorders. The chapter details factors contributing to the onset of Mood Disorders and elements related to prevention. The important assessment tools, along with procedures for use with children and adolescents with Major Depressive Disorder, Dysthymic Disorder, Bipolar Disorder, or Cyclothymic Disorder are reviewed. Comorbid disorders are discussed to enable clinicians to take a holistic view of their clients and to facilitate making a differential diagnosis (e.g., the ability to differentiate a Mood Disorder from another mental disorder). Additionally, the chapter details approaches to counseling children with Mood Disorders, including information on treatment in school and family contexts. A case illustration is provided to enhance and deepen the reader's understanding of important aspects of working with clients in this age group.

DEFINITION AND PREVALENCE

Diagnostic criteria established in the *Diagnostic and Statistical Manual of Mental Disorders* (*DSM-IV-TR*) (American Psychiatric Association [APA], 2000a) for Major Depressive Disorder, Dysthymic Disorder, Bipolar Disorder, and Cyclothymic Disorder are primarily geared to an adult population. Clinicians increasingly appreciate the need to accurately diagnose Mood Disorders in children or adolescents. A number of factors have contributed to this growing awareness, including the following: 1) an increased interest on the part of parents, school personnel (Abrams, Theberge, & Karan, 2005), and mental health professionals in providing the necessary assistance to these children and adolescents; 2) the need to be in compliance with laws and the implications for practice when a disorder is diagnosed (Erk, 1999); 3) improvement in assessment procedures, which has enabled clinicians to coordinate data on making a diagnosis; and perhaps most important, 4) acceptance by professionals and society that developmental psychopathology can emerge in young people (Costello, Foley, & Angold, 2006).

Major Depressive Disorder

The *DSM-IV-TR* (APA, 2000a) criteria for a Major Depressive Episode are noted in Table 7.1. The primary hallmark of this Mood Disorder is a depressed mood that is present most of the time, nearly every day, for at least 2 weeks. This often is evidenced as irritability in young people, although this is not a required symptom. For a diagnosis of Major Depressive Disorder, a child or adolescent must have a depressed mood as described above and four other symptoms. Other criteria of Major Depressive Disorder include diminished interest or pleasure in activities, feelings of guilt

TABLE 7.1   Criteria for Major Depressive Episode

A. Five (or more) of the following symptoms have been present during the same 2-week period and represent a change from previous functioning; at least one of the symptoms is either (1) depressed mood or (2) loss of interest or pleasure. **Note:** Do not include symptoms that are clearly due to a general medical condition or mood-incongruent delusions or hallucinations.

1. depressed mood most of the day, nearly every day, as indicated by either subjective report (e.g., feels sad or empty) or observation made by others (e.g., appears tearful). **Note:** In children and adolescents, can be irritable mood
2. markedly diminished interest or pleasure in all, or almost all, activities most of the day, nearly every day (as indicated by either subjective account or observation made by others)
3. significant weight loss when not dieting or weight gain (e.g., a change of more than 5% of body weight in a month), or decrease or increase in appetite nearly every day. **Note:** In children, consider failure to make expected weight gains
4. insomnia or hypersomnia nearly every day
5. psychomotor agitation or retardation nearly every day (observable by others; not merely subjective feelings of restlessness or being slowed down)
6. fatigue or loss of energy nearly every day
7. feelings of worthlessness or excessive, inappropriate guilt (which may be delusional) nearly every day (not merely self-reproach or guilt about being sick)
8. diminished ability to think or concentrate, or indecisiveness, nearly every day (either by subjective account or observed by others)
9. recurrent thoughts of death (not just fear of dying), recurrent suicidal ideation without a specific plan, or a suicide attempt or a specific plan for committing suicide

B. The symptoms do not meet criteria for a Mixed Episode.
C. The symptoms cause clinically significant distress or impairment in social, occupational, or other important areas of functioning.
D. The symptoms are not due to the direct physiological effects of a substance (e.g., a drug of abuse, a medication) or a general medical condition (e.g., hypothyroidism).
E. The symptoms are not better accounted for by Bereavement, (after the recent loss of a loved one); the symptoms persist for longer than 2 months or are characterized by marked functional impairment, morbid preoccupation with worthlessness, suicidal ideation, psychotic symptoms, or psychomotor retardation.

Reprinted with permission from the *Diagnostic and Statistical Manual of Mental Disorders*, Fourth Edition, text revision. Copyright 2000, American Psychiatric Association.

or worthlessness, a reduced ability to concentrate and think clearly, and recurrent thoughts of death or suicide. Major Depressive Disorder often is also accompanied by vegetative symptoms, including changes in weight or appetite, insomnia or hypersomnia, and psychomotor agitation or retardation. People with Major Depressive Disorder often experience a loss of energy and general fatigue.

Onset of Major Depressive Disorder in childhood or adolescence is strongly associated with an increased likelihood of that disorder becoming chronic or recurrent, and of the disorder persisting into adulthood (Brent, Kolko, Birmaher, Baugher, & Bridge, 1999; Phillips, Corcoran, & Grossman, 2003). The prevalence rate of all depressive disorders is about 2% of children and 5% to 8% of adolescents (Son & Kirchner, 2000). Major Depressive Disorder in children occurs in about the same percentage of boys and girls, whereas in adolescents the rate of occurrence in females is double what it is in males, paralleling the level of depression found in the adult population (Birmaher et al., 1996a; Mellin & Beamish, 2002).

Major Depressive Disorder is by far the most prevalent form of Mood Disorder in adolescents, with puberty signaling a substantial rise in the prevalence of this disorder. However, this does not diminish the seriousness of the disorder or the impact it has on youths and their families. The average duration of a depressive episode lasts approximately 9 months (Dopheide, 2006; Wagner, Robb, Findling, Jin, Gutierrez, & Heydorn, 2004), with duration ranging from 2 weeks to over 10 years (Lewinsohn, Rohde, & Seeley, 1998).

Dysthymic Disorder

In children and adolescents, Dysthymic Disorder is evidenced by depressed or irritable mood for at least 1 year. Symptoms (see Table 7.2) include poor appetite or overeating, insomnia or hypersomnia, low energy or fatigue, feelings of hopelessness, and low self-esteem (APA, 1994). Additionally, there may be evidence of difficulties in concentrating or in making decisions. The depression associated with Dysthymic Disorder is generally milder than that associated with Major Depressive Disorder. However, the enduring nature of a Dysthymic Disorder can still lead to considerable impairment in functioning and development.

The prevalence of Dysthymic Disorder is considered to be about 1% to 2% in children and 2% to 8% in adolescents (Birmaher et al., 1996a; Bostic, Rubin, Prince, & Schlozman, 2005). Among adolescents with unipolar depression (depression without a history of mania or hypomania), about 80% experience Major Depressive Disorder alone or in conjunction with a nondepressive disorder, 10% experience Dysthymic Disorder without a Major Depressive Disorder, and the remaining 10% experience double depression, the combination of Major Depressive Disorder and a more enduring and milder underlying Dysthymic Disorder. This suggests that as many as half of all adolescents who meet the criteria for Dysthymic Disorder will also be found to have a Major Depressive Disorder, although only 7% of those with Major Depressive Disorder will have a coexisting diagnosis of Dysthymic Disorder.

Dysthymic Disorder typically has "an early and insidious onset as well as a chronic course" (APA, 1994, p. 347). When Dysthymic Disorder develops in children, young people have a particularly high risk for the development of a subsequent Mood Disorder (Cicchetti & Toth, 1998; Son & Kirchner, 2000). This pattern should be borne in mind when planning treatment for young people diagnosed with Dysthymic Disorders.

TABLE 7.2   Diagnostic Criteria for 300.4 Dysthymic Disorder

A. Depressed mood most of the day, for more days than not, as indicated either by subjective account or observation by others, for at least 2 years. Note: In children and adolescents, mood can be irritable and duration must be at least 1 year.

B. Presence, while depressed, of two (or more) of the following:

   1. poor appetite or overeating
   2. insomnia or hypersomnia
   3. low energy or fatigue
   4. low self-esteem
   5. poor concentration or difficulty making decisions
   6. feelings of hopelessness

C. During the 2-year period (1 year for children or adolescents) of the disturbance, the person has never been without the symptoms in Criteria A and B for more than 2 months at a time.

D. No Major Depressive Episode has been present during the first 2 years of the disturbance (1 year for children and adolescents); i.e., the disturbance is not better accounted for by chronic Major Depressive Disorder, or Major Depressive Disorder, in Partial Remission. **Note:** There may have been a previous Major Depressive Episode provided there was a full remission (no significant signs or symptoms for 2 months) before development of the Dysthymic Disorder. In addition, after the initial 2 years (1 year in children or adolescents) of Dysthymic Disorder, there may be superimposed episodes of Major Depressive Disorder, in which case both diagnoses may be given when the criteria are met for a Major Depressive Episode.

E. There has never been a Manic Episode, a Mixed Episode, or a Hypomanic Episode, and criteria have never been met for Cyclothymic Disorder.

F. The disturbance does not occur exclusively during the course of a chronic Psychotic Disorder, such as Schizophrenia or Delusional Disorder.

G. The symptoms are not due to the direct physiological effects of a substance (e.g., a drug of abuse, a medication) or a general medical condition (e.g. hypothyroidism).

H. The symptoms cause clinical significant distress or impairment in social, occupational, or other important areas of functioning.

Specify if:

Early Onset: if onset is before age 21 years
Late Onset: if onset is age 21 years or older

Specify (for most recent 2 years of Dysthymic Disorder):

With Atypical Features

Reprinted with permission. from the *Diagnostic and Statistical Manual of Mental Disorders,* Fourth Edition, text revision. Copyright 2000, American Psychiatric Association.

Bipolar Disorder

Bipolar Disorder involves episodes of dysfunctional mood and might include Major Depressive Episodes, Manic Episodes, Hypomanic Episodes, and Mixed Episodes. At least one manic or Hypomanic Episode is required for the diagnosis of Bipolar Disorder. The features of a Major Depressive Episode were described in Table 7.1. Manic Episodes, summarized in Table 7.3, are characterized by at least one week of "abnormally and persistently elevated, expansive, or irritable mood" (APA, 1994, p. 332) with symptoms of grandiosity, reduced need for sleep, greater talkativeness, racing thoughts, and increased distractibility and activity. Additionally, excessive pleasure-seeking may be evident, with a high risk of negative consequences. Hypomania is similar to mania in its array of symptoms and mood; however, episodes have a minimum duration of 4 days and are not severe enough to cause impairment in the individual's functioning. Finally, Mixed Episodes are distinguished by a period of at least 1 week when the person manifests symptoms of both a Major Depressive Episode and a Manic Episode.

Bipolar I Disorder is characterized by one or more Manic Episodes or Mixed Episodes including mania. Additionally, people with this disorder usually also experience Major Depressive Episodes and sometimes Hypomanic Episodes. However, the presence of Major Depressive or Hypomanic Episodes is not necessary to meet the diagnostic criteria. Bipolar II Disorder is characterized by one or more Major

---

TABLE 7.3 Criteria for Manic Episode

A. A distinct period of abnormally and persistently elevated, expansive, or irritable mood, lasting at least 1 week (or any duration if hospitalization is necessary).

B. During the period of mood disturbance, three (or more) of the following symptoms have persisted (four if the mood is only irritable) and have been present to a significant degree:

   1. inflated self-esteem or grandiosity
   2. decreased need for sleep (e.g., feels rested after only 3 hours of sleep)
   3. more talkative than usual or pressure to keep talking
   4. flight of ideas or subjective experience that thoughts are racing
   5. distractibility (i.e., attention too easily drawn to unimportant or irrelevant external stimuli)
   6. increase in goal-directed activity (either socially, at work or school, or sexually) or psychomotor agitation
   7. excessive involvement in pleasurable activities that have a high potential for painful consequences (e.g., engaging in unrestrained buying sprees, sexual indiscretions, or foolish business investments)

C. The symptoms do not meet criteria for a Mixed Episode.

D. The mood disturbance is sufficiently severe to cause marked impairment in occupational functioning or in usual social activities or relationships with others, or to necessitate hospitalization to prevent harm to self or others, or there are psychotic features.

E. The symptoms are not due to indirect physiological effects of a substance (e.g., a drug of abuse, a medication, or other treatment) or a general medical condition (e.g., hyperthyroidism). **Note:** Manic-like episodes that are clearly caused by somatic antidepressant treatment (e.g., medication, electroconvulsive therapy, light therapy) should not count toward a diagnosis of Bipolar I Disorder.

Depressive Episodes and at least one Hypomanic Episode. By definition, people with Bipolar II Disorders have never had a Manic Episode.

Although onset of a true Bipolar Disorder before the age of 12 is uncommon, symptoms can be present in early childhood (El-Mallakh, 1997), and 20% to 40% of children and adolescents diagnosed with Major Depressive Disorder will ultimately be diagnosed as having a Bipolar Disorder (Birmaher, Brent, & Benson, 1998). According to McClellan and Werry (1997), the incidence of Bipolar Disorder appears to increase with the onset of puberty. Findings indicate that approximately 20% of all people diagnosed with Bipolar Disorders had their first episodes during adolescence, with the age of onset usually in the late teens or early twenties (Adler, DelBello, Mills, Schmithorst, Holland, & Strakowski, 2005). Bipolar Disorders appear to be diagnosed about equally in boys and girls (Birmaher et al., 2006). Lewinsohn, Klein, and Seeley (as cited in Practice parameters for the assessment and treatment of children and adolescents with depressive disorders, 1998) indicated that Bipolar II Disorders seem to be more prevalent than Bipolar I Disorders in adolescents.

Cyclothymic Disorder

Cyclothymic Disorder is a milder but more chronic disorder than Bipolar I and II Disorders. Cyclothymic Disorder includes numerous periods of hypomanic symptoms and depressive symptoms that do not meet the criteria for Major Depressive or Manic Episodes (Nicholson & Clayfield, 2004). Cyclothymic Disorder, by definition, lasts for at least 1 year in children and adolescents. Adolescence is a common age of onset for this disorder. Some adolescents with Cyclothymic Disorder subsequently develop Bipolar I or II Disorders (Emslie, Kennard, & Kowatch, 1994). Cyclothymic Disorder is not included separately for discussion, but is considered a Bipolar Disorder.

Mood Disorder Specifiers

There are a number of specifiers available to clarify a Mood Disorder diagnosis in children and adolescents. These specifiers include the following: catatonic, melancholic, atypical, with and without interepisode recovery, seasonal pattern, and rapid-cycling. A postpartum onset specifier also is included in the *DSM-IV-TR* (2000a) but would be used infrequently with this population.

Catatonic features can be specified for the most recent Episode in Major Depressive Disorder and Bipolar Disorder. This specifier is assigned when the clinical picture is highlighted by motor immobility or excessive activity. Additionally, extreme negativism, mutism, peculiarities of voluntary movement, echolalia, or echopraxia (*DSM-IV-TR*, 2000, p. 418) may be noted.

Melancholic features can be specified for the most recent Episode in Major Depressive Disorder and for the most recent major Depressive Episode in Bipolar Disorder. A Major Depressive Episode with melancholic features is characterized by loss of pleasure in most activities or loss of reactivity to something enjoyable.

Additionally, a distinctly depressed mood, depression that is regularly worse in the morning, waking early in the morning, psychomotor retardation or agitation, considerable weight loss, or inappropriate guilt often is noted in melancholic features.

The atypical specifier can be assigned to the current Episode in Major Depressive Disorder or Bipolar Disorder as well as to Dysthymic Disorder. Atypical features are assigned when mood reactivity is present along with two of the following: increased appetite or weight gain, hypersomnia, leaden paralysis, and rejection sensitivity.

The longitudinal course specifiers, with or without full interepisode recovery, can be used to help characterize the course of recurrent Major Depressive Disorder or Bipolar Disorder. These specifiers describe the period of time between the most recent episodes of the Mood Disorder.

The seasonal pattern specifier can be used to describe the pattern of Major Depressive Episodes in recurrent Major Depression or Bipolar Disorder. The fundamental characteristic noted is the onset and remission of Major Depression at particular times of the year, usually winter.

Rapid-cycling can be applied to Bipolar Disorder when there are at least four episodes of mood disturbance during a 12-month period. These episodes can occur in any combination or order.

DIAGNOSTIC FEATURES

Children and adolescents with Mood Disorders often present with symptoms particular to this age group, making an accurate diagnosis difficult for the clinician who is unfamiliar with the presentation of Mood Disorders in young people (Bostic et al., 2005). The following common patterns complicate the diagnosis of Mood Disorders in young people:

1. Symptoms of separation anxiety, phobias, somatic complaints, and behavioral problems often accompany depressive disorders in children and adolescents (Birmaher et al., 1996b; Dopheide, 2006).
2. Depressed children tend to make external and unstable attributions about positive events, displaying an external locus of control and having difficulty finding an inner sense of self (Southam-Gerow, Henin, Chu, Marrs, & Kendall, 1997).
3. Children who are depressed tend to overgeneralize predictions of negative outcomes, catastrophize the consequences of negative events, incorrectly take personal responsibility for negative outcomes, and selectively attend to negative features of an event (Southam-Gerow et al., 1997).
4. Depressed youth have been shown to display problem-solving deficits (Southam-Gerow et al., 1997).

Although there might be similarities among adults, children, and adolescents who present symptoms of Mood Disorders, detecting the subtle differences is critical. Recognizing and diagnosing depression may have the ultimate consequence of saving a life. Suicide associated with Mood Disorders is a leading cause of death in young people (Cash, 2003; Cheung, Emslie, & Mayes, 2005; Emslie & Mayes, 1999).

The likelihood of suicidal ideation was found to be higher in young people with Mood Disorders than in those without this diagnosis, and suicide attempts are much more likely among youth with these disorders (Kovacs, Goldston, & Gatsonis, 1993; Murphy, 2005).

Major Depressive Disorder

The clinical presentation of Major Depressive Disorder, as well as of the other Mood Disorders, varies in children and adolescents across the different developmental stages. Young children generally display more anxiety symptoms, somatic complaints, auditory hallucinations, temper tantrums, and behavioral problems. In middle and late childhood, youth with depression begin to report the cognitive components of dysphoric mood, including distorted thinking, negative attributions, and hopelessness in addition to low self-esteem and guilt. Finally, depressed adolescents typically manifest more sleep and appetite disturbances, delusions, suicidal ideation and attempts, and impairment of functioning than younger children; however, they generally display fewer neurovegetative symptoms and more irritability than adults (Birmaher et al., 1998; Dopheide, 2006, Son & Kirchner, 2000).

Emslie et al. (1994) provided an extensive description of the various features of Major Depressive Disorder specific to children and adolescents. For this age group, dysphoric mood is characterized by sadness, loneliness, unhappiness, hopelessness, mood swings, hypersensitivity, negative attitudes, and displeasure. Children tend to be emotionally labile and overreactive. Some days they might seem to have a pervasive depression, whereas on other days they vacillate between normal moods and periods of depression. Additionally, irritability often is a prominent symptom, generally resulting from sad feelings. Self-deprecatory ideation is another feature often found in this population. Children and adolescents describe feelings of being worthless, dumb, stupid, ugly, or guilty. They might express the belief that they are being persecuted or punished, sometimes reflecting a projection of their own feelings of low self-esteem onto others. Death wishes along with suicidal thoughts and attempts might also be prominent. Aggressive behavior or agitation is common and might be evident in fighting, lack of respect for authority, and argumentativeness or difficulty in getting along with others. Insomnia, difficulty awakening in the morning, and hypersomnolence accompanied by daytime naps are other common features of depression in youth. School refusal or a change in performance might be a problem related to trouble concentrating, loss of interest in school activities, reduced effort in assignments, incomplete work, or even total refusal to complete homework. Additionally, decreased group participation, withdrawal from friends, and a loss of social interest are often characteristics of depressed youth. In adolescents, changes in social interest might manifest as a preference for a less-desirable peer group.

Finally, somatic symptoms often accompany depression in children and teens (Son & Kirchner, 2000). These might take the form of nonspecific headaches, stomachaches, or other physical symptoms that do not seem to have a physical cause. Mental and physical fatigue may be prominent, resulting in less physical activity than is usual for this age group. Additionally, there may be noticeable changes in appetite or sleep patterns (Dopheide, 2006; Evans, Van Velsor, & Schumacher, 2002).

Clearly, recognizing the symptoms of Major Depressive Disorder that are specific to children and adolescents is essential. The classic symptoms of depression, sadness, and hopelessness may be masked in young people. Instead of verbalizing their feelings, which is often difficult for a young population, children might send the message that they are in pain by having temper tantrums, appearing irritable and frustrated, and acting out (Son & Kirchner, 2000). Adolescents are more likely than depressed adults to express feelings of worthlessness and guilt and are less likely to express thoughts of death and suicide or to exhibit weight and appetite changes (Lewinsohn et al., 1998). Strong clinical skills are needed to distinguish depression from normal fluctuation in adolescents' moods (Cash, 2003).

Just as the symptoms of Major Depressive Disorder have a characteristic pattern in young people, so does the usual course of that disorder. The duration of episodes of Major Depressive Disorder was not found to be influenced by gender or comorbidity; instead, an earlier age of onset was associated with longer depressive episodes (McCauley & Myers, 1992). According to Emslie and Mayes (1999), Major Depressive Disorder in children and adolescents tends to be episodic, with either full or partial recovery between episodes. Following an initial Major Depressive Episode in childhood, young people have a higher rate of relapse than people who have an initial episode in adulthood (Reinherz, Paradis, Giaconia, Stashwick, & Fitzmaurice, 2003). Episodes of depressed mood often continue into adulthood.

Dysthymic Disorder

The minimum duration for fulfilling the *DSM-IV-TR* (2000) diagnostic criteria for Dysthymic Disorder is 1 year in children and adolescents as opposed to 2 years in the adult population. Even 1 year of depression is a long time in the life of a young person; consequently, this disorder is likely to appear chronic, with children and adolescents having no prolonged well states for at least a year of their lives. They might have some good days mixed with the bad days, but basically they have no good weeks. As with Major Depressive Disorder, youth diagnosed with Dysthymic Disorder may exhibit an irritable mood (Birmaher et al., 1996a; Nobile, Cataldo, Marino, & Molteni, 2003).

The implications of having Dysthymic Disorder as a child or a teen are significant. Compared to Major Depressive Disorder, Dysthymic Disorder has a much more prolonged course, with the average length of an episode being 3 to 4 years (Cicchetti & Toth, 1998; Nobile et al., 2003; Son & Kirchner, 2000). Young people with long-lasting depression, either Dysthymic Disorder or chronic Major Depressive Disorder, were found to become depressed at a younger age, to experience a more insidious onset of their symptoms, to receive more pharmacological treatment, and to have a slower rate of recovery than those with acute depression (Ferro, Carlson, Grayson, & Klein, 1994). Additionally, early onset of Dysthymic Disorder is associated with an increased risk for diagnosis of subsequent Major Depressive Disorder, Bipolar Disorder, and Substance Use Disorders (Birmaher et al., 1996a).

When evaluating depressive symptoms, clinicians should consider the possibility of a Major Depressive Disorder superimposed on a Dysthymic Disorder, so-called double depression (Dunner, 2005). This combination is particularly severe and is treatment resistant.

Bipolar Disorder

Like adults with Bipolar Disorders, youth may present with Manic, Hypomanic, Depressive, or Mixed Episodes. Geller and Luby (1997) indicated that children with prepubertal-onset Bipolar Disorder are less likely to present with acute onset and reasonably good interepisode functioning than are adolescents and adults with Bipolar Disorders. Instead, they are likely to experience either prolonged episodes of troubling moods or rapid cycling, characterized by multiple brief episodes of dysfunctional mood (Bardick & Bernes, 2005).

According to Emslie et al. (1994), mania in children and adolescents is characterized by an elevated or expansive mood, which might include inappropriate giddiness and silliness, continuous singing, being happier than a situation warrants and, in adolescents, being unrealistically optimistic. Some young people might claim to have super powers. Teens might exhibit dangerous risk-taking behaviors (Bowden, Ketter, Sachs, & Thase, 2005), unusual even for adolescents who commonly have feelings of immortality and invulnerability that are typical of this developmental stage. Distractibility and a short attention span are often apparent. Children and adolescents may be more talkative than usual and may also appear hyperactive, completing multiple projects at one time. Symptoms of hypersexuality may be evidenced by promiscuity (Cash, 2003) frequent and inappropriate masturbation, or a preoccupation with crude sexual comments and jokes (Berenson, 1998).

Irritability (Biederman, Mick, Faraone, & Wozniak, 2004), belligerence, and mixed manic-depressive features are more common than euphoria in children and adolescents with Bipolar Disorders. They also are more likely to have brief rather than persistent episodes of psychomotor agitation and mental excitement (McClellan & Werry, 1997).

While a Bipolar Disorder is often difficult to diagnose in adults, the diagnosis of this disorder in children and adolescents can be an even greater challenge (Faedda, Baldessarini, Glovinsky, & Austin, 2004). It is difficult to differentiate the normal exuberance and excitement of young people from a manic episode. Distinguishing the symptoms of Bipolar Disorders from those associated with other mental disorders can also be challenging (Bardick & Bernes, 2005). Geller and Luby (1997) cautioned clinicians to carefully assess the child for a history of sexual abuse to distinguish sexual acting out related to abuse from manic hypersexuality. In addition, specific language disorders need to be differentiated from the flight of ideas associated with mania. McClellan and Werry (1997) suggested considering a diagnosis of Bipolar Disorder for any youth who presents with marked deterioration in functioning associated with either Mood or Psychotic Disorders.

Hyperactivity associated with mania needs to be distinguished from the symptoms of Attention-Deficit/Hyperactivity Disorder (ADHD). Differentiating ADHD,

Predominantly Hyperactive-Impulsive Type or Combined Type, from Bipolar Disorder can be difficult, even for well-trained clinicians (Adler et al., 2005; Biederman et al., 2004). A good place to begin might be by differentiating the nature of the specific cognitive and ideational impairment often present in people who manifest symptoms of Mania from that of people with ADHD (Botteron & Geller, 1995).

Clearly, similarity between the diagnostic features specific to children and adolescents with Mood Disorders and the characteristics of several other mental disorders complicates the process of diagnosis. Because adolescents with Mood Disorders have a higher risk of suicidality as compared to adolescents with other diagnoses (Barbe, Bridge, Birmaher, Kolko, & Brent, 2004; Geller & Luby, 1997), being thoroughly familiar with the presentation of Mood Disorders in young people is critical.

CAUSAL FACTORS

Many factors contribute to the development of Mood Disorders in children and adolescents. To point the finger at any one specific cause detracts from understanding the complexity of factors that promote these disorders in youth. As is true with the adult population, environmental and biological factors are implicated. What might be more pronounced in a younger population is the impact of both peers and stressful life events on the onset and course of Mood Disorders. Additionally, the presence of negative thinking appears to play a significant role in whether a child or adolescent becomes depressed. Even cigarette smoking in adolescence was found to be a significant risk factor for the development of Major Depressive Disorder (Johnson, Rhee, Chase, & Breslau, 2004; Lewinsohn, Rohde, & Seeley, 1995). Identifying factors that contribute to Major Depressive Disorder, Bipolar Disorder, and Dysthymia in a young population can facilitate better treatment and might even play a role in prevention.

Family Environment

The environment children and teens find themselves in is critical in determining whether they become depressed, and that environment significantly influences the course of the disorder. Family conflict has been found to be a stress factor that triggers depression in children and adolescents who are susceptible to it (Birmaher et al., 1996a; Cuffe, McKeown, Addy, & Garrison, 2005). Additionally, a more stressful family environment has been associated with longer episodes of depression in youth (McCauley et al., 1993).

It seems logical that a child or adolescent who is exposed to problems or stressors in the family is more likely to develop a Mood Disorder. However, clinicians should be familiar with what specific factors have the most impact. The family dynamics of depressed youth were found to be characterized by conflict, maltreatment, rejection, problems with communication, and little expression of positive emotion or support (Birmaher et al., 1998). Depressed children and adolescents in environments with these characteristics perceived their families as significantly less cohesive, supportive, and democratic and more conflictual than nondepressed youth (Garber, Robinson, & Valentiner, 1997; Reinherz et al., 2003).

Child abuse carries a significant number of risks to the physical, cognitive, and emotional development and well-being of youth; depression is clearly a potential consequence (Libby, Orton, Stover, & Riggs, 2005). Brown, Cohen, Johnson, and Smailes (1999) indicated that adolescents and even young adults who had been abused as children were more likely to become depressed and/or suicidal compared to youth without a history of abuse. There was a greater incidence of Dysthymic Disorder and Major Depressive Disorder in those with a history of abuse or neglect, occurring about 4 to 5 times more often in those who had been abused. Specifically, sexual abuse appeared to carry a great risk of subsequent depression (Watts & Markham, 2005).

Although both parents are important in influencing the adjustment of their children, treatment by the mother was found to be a particularly prominent factor in the development of a mental disorder. Pike and Plomin (1996) reviewed studies to determine what environmental influences, rather than genetic components, influenced child and adolescent psychopathology. They concluded that adolescents who are the focus of more negative maternal treatment and attention than their siblings had an increased likelihood of experiencing depression, even independent of genetic effects. Geller, Todd, Luby, and Botteron (1996) found significant differences among depressed youth and non depressed youth, with the depressed youth reporting more problems in mother–child interpersonal functioning and communication and lower global ratings of warmth. However, several measures of father–child relationships, indicating significantly greater impairment in that relationship, were associated with depression in young people. Finally, Sanford et al. (1995) found that low involvement with the father and a poor response to the mother's discipline predicted persistence of depression in adolescents.

Peer Relationships

If the family environment can have such a significant impact on the occurrence of Mood Disorders in children and adolescents, what about peer relationships? Studies with adults indicate that there is a significant relationship between depression and poor interpersonal relationships (e.g., Boyce et al., 1998; Stefos, Bauwens, Staner, Pardoen, & Mendlewicz, 1996). It might, however, be difficult to ascertain whether poor social relationships are precipitants of depression or whether depression leads to the lack of adequate social support.

Puig-Antich et al. (1985b) conducted a thorough study evaluating the quality of social relationships in depressed children. They determined that most aspects of psychosocial relationships were impaired during periods of depression, including those with peers. In support of this finding, Goodyear, Wright, and Altham (1989) found that friendship difficulties before the onset of depression or anxiety did not impact the diagnosis. However, after the onset of the disorder, depressed but not anxious children were at risk for poor friendships. Peterson et al. (1993)

reported that peer support during adolescence plays an important role in protecting against stress-related disorders, but this might not be the case during childhood. Interactions with peers are critical during adolescent development; deficits in peer interactions have been found to place this age group at risk for developing depression (Rice & Leffert, 1997; Spence, Sheffield, & Donovan, 2003). Unfortunately, a vicious circle may be relevant here. Just as young people need positive peer interactions to help them ward off depression, those experiencing depression typically have a more difficult time forming beneficial relationships with peers (Wagner et al., 2004). Goodyer, Herbert, Tamplin, Secher, and Pearson (1997) found that 23% of the 8- to 16-year-olds in their study who were depressed also experienced poor interpersonal relationships, and none of these children had recovered from depression at follow-up. Finally, Geller et al. (1996) noted specific impairment in children with Major Depressive Disorder in three areas of peer relatedness: 1) decreased ability to maintain a special or best friend; 2) decreased overall ability to make and maintain positive peer relations; and 3) increased frequency of teasing by peers.

Parental Depression and Genetic Contributions

The emotional and physical health of parents cannot help but have an impact on their children. In fact, children of depressed parents are three times more likely to have an episode of Major Depressive Disorder at some point in their lives than are children without this history (Practice parameters for the assessment and treatment of children and adolescents with depressive disorders, 1998). Hammen, Burge, Burney, and Adrian (1990) suggested that the lifetime risk for children of depressed parents to develop a Mood Disorder was at least 15% and perhaps as high as 45%. Genetics are clearly a factor in Mood Disorders in children and adolescents (Beardslee, Gladstone, Wright, & Cooper, 2003; Ryan, 2003). According to the *DSM-IV-TR* (2000), Major Depressive Disorder is 1.5 to 3 times more common in first-degree relatives of people who have also been diagnosed with that disorder than in the general population. Puig-Antich et al. (1989) determined that, when compared with Major Depressive Disorder that began later in life, the diagnosis of Major Depressive Disorder before the age of 20 was associated with a particularly increased rate of depression in first-degree relatives; and first- and second-degree relatives of depressed children were found to have higher rates of depression, alcoholism, and other diagnoses. Dysthymic Disorder also is more common among first-degree biological relatives of individuals with Major Depressive Disorder; and first-degree biological relatives of individuals with Bipolar Disorders have elevated rates of Bipolar Disorder and Major Depressive Disorder when compared to the general population (APA, 1994).

Williamson et al. (1995) evaluated 76 adolescents with Major Depressive Disorder and their first- and second-degree relatives to determine whether depression aggregates in the families of depressed youth. Additionally, they addressed whether the presence of clinical features and/or comorbid syndromes in the depressed teens altered the risk of psychopathology in their relatives. Their findings supported the existence of adolescent-onset depression and suggested that familial aggregation of depression is prevalent across the lifespan.

Teasing apart the relative contributions of environment and heredity to the development of a Mood Disorder is difficult. Support, however, for a genetic component of depression has been provided by twin studies showing concordance rates for depression to be higher in monozygotic twins than in dizygotic twins (e.g., McGuffin & Katz, 1989; Watts & Markham, 2005). An interesting study of twins aged 8 to 16 by Thapar and McGuffin (1996) found developmental differences in the etiology of depression in children and adolescents. Monozygotic twin correlations for depressive symptom scores appeared to be greater in early adolescence than in childhood, whereas dizygotic twin correlations appeared to drop markedly from childhood to adolescence. In summary, they found that familial transmission of depressive symptoms in children might best be explained by environment alone, whereas in adolescents, depression appears to be highly heritable whether parent-rated or self-rated.

Shiner and Marmorstein (1998) discovered that a greater number of adolescents who had at some time been depressed had depressed mothers when compared to those adolescents who had never been depressed. Of those adolescents who at some time had been depressed, 47% had mothers who had been depressed. Of those adolescents who had never been depressed, only 18% had mothers who had been depressed.

Neurochemistry

The major hypotheses about the neurobiological aspects of depression in children and adolescents have been extrapolated from studies with adults. The monamine system has been the focus of attention when addressing depressive disorders. This system includes the neurotransmitters dopamine, serotonin, and norepinephrine. For each of these neurotransmitters, many corresponding receptor sites exist. In individuals with depression, it is thought that levels of these neurotransmitters might be low (Watts & Markham, 2005) whereas in individuals with mania, levels may be high (Stark, Vaughn, Doxey, & Luss, 1999).

With the emergence of the newer antidepressant medications, studies examining the action of these drugs have further enhanced our understanding of the neurochemical mechanisms of depression. Similar to most other mental disorders, there are few systematic studies of response to pharmacological treatment in children and adolescents with Mood Disorders (Kaplan & Hussain, 1995; Wagner, 2004). Biologically, there appear to be more similarities than differences among the Mood Disorders in youth and adults, but the developmental differences and differences in brain maturation most likely affect the expression of these underlying biological aspects of depression (Emslie, Walkup, Pliszka, & Ernst, 1999).

Finally, there are also indications that hormonal and neuroendocrine systems are involved in depression (Kutcher, Kusumakar, LeBlanc, Santor, Lagace, & Morehouse, R., 2004; Stark et al., 1999). Hormone changes, particularly estrogen in girls, might be linked to depression. Additionally, irregularities in the hypothalmic-thyroid system may contribute to depression in youth as well.

Life Events

Stress is a factor in everyone's life, regardless of age, and no one can really expect to avoid it. However, certain situations are particularly difficult and stressful and are more likely to have an adverse impact on children and teens, particularly if they are vulnerable to a Mood Disorder. Stressful life events such as divorce, bereavement, and exposure to suicide, alone or together with other risk factors, were found to have a modest but significant positive relationship to the incidence of depression in children and adolescents (Birmaher et al., 1996a; Williamson, Birmaher, Dahl, & Ryan, 2005).

The consequences of a major loss or life change in one's youth might have a long-lasting impact. Evidence was found to support the notion that adverse experiences during childhood and adolescence raise the risk for depression or anxiety in adulthood (Practice parameters for the assessment and treatment of children and adolescents with depressive disorders, 1998). Clinicians should also keep in mind that what might not seem stressful for an adult might be extremely stressful for a child or teen and that loss for a child or adolescent can be real or imagined.

Although children certainly are affected by negative life occurrences, adolescents, too, seem to be considerably affected by such events. More than twice as many depressed adolescents reported having experienced a severe life event during the year prior to the onset of a Mood Disorder than those in a control group of adolescents who had not been diagnosed with a Mood Disorder (Williamson et al., 1998). The types of events that were considered severe to an adolescent included problems in a romantic relationship, a close friend moving away, experiencing pregnancy (Mellin & Beamish, 2002) or abortion, a fight with a friend or a parent, and not doing well in school. Poor physical health might also serve as a risk factor for the onset of Major Depressive Disorder (Lewinsohn, Gotlib, & Seeley, 1995).

When stressful life events are combined with family factors, the child or adolescent might be at an even greater risk for depression (Hammen, Brennan, & Shih, 2004). For example, Shiner and Marmorstein (1998) found that a disproportionate number of adolescents who had been depressed at one time came from families that had experienced divorce. Additionally, when divorce was compounded by depression in the mother, the impact was overwhelming. Forty-three percent of depressed adolescents with depressed mothers experienced their parents' divorce. This was for depression experienced at any point during development. The parental divorce rate was 38% for depressed adolescents whose mother had never been depressed. The control group had a parental divorce rate of only 22%.

Clearly, determining precipitating events when assessing a child or adolescent with a Mood Disorder is important. Pinpointing the specific and immediate stressors that might have played a role in bringing about a Major Depressive Episode or a Manic Episode can help to focus and facilitate the treatment process. Clinicians should also consider any stressors that can be considered chronic, such as a chaotic family environment, a lengthy illness in a family member, chronic abuse, or poverty in the family. Although the onset of depression in adolescents was usually found to be preceded by acute stressful life events, ongoing stressors also were found to contribute to the onset of depression in at least some adolescents (Watts & Markham, 2005; Williamson et al., 1998).

Cognitive Factors

The cognitive symptoms of depression, such as distorted thinking and indecisiveness, are very real, leaving children and adolescents thinking about themselves, other people, and their lives in negative and distorted ways (Evans et al., 2002; Watts & Markham, 2005). Self-esteem may be impaired and the future might seem hopeless.

Gladstone and Kaslow (1995) found evidence supporting the idea that maladaptive attributional patterns in young people are significantly associated with depressive symptoms. Higher levels of depressive symptoms were associated with internal-stable-global attributions for negative outcomes and external-unstable-specific attributions for positive outcomes. What this means is that youth with depressive symptoms tend to explain the negative events that occur in their lives by blaming themselves, seeing these negative events as stable over time, and then generalizing or assuming that other aspects of their lives will become disappointing. Additionally, positive events are seen as being caused by something or someone other than themselves and are perceived as unstable over time and specific to the event, rather than reflective of the way life is going (Evans et al., 2002). For example, if a teen receives a low grade on a math quiz, she might see herself as stupid, certain to fail the next exam, and even certain to fail math or other subjects. Should she get an *A* on an English paper, she might see the assignment as having been too easy, perceive her grade as a fluke, and be certain she will not continue to receive high grades. Youth who have negative attributional styles for interpreting and coping with stressful and negative life events frequently become hopeless and dysphoric and are at higher risk for development of a Major Depressive Disorder (Practice parameters for the assessment and treatment of children and adolescents with depressive disorders, 1998).

Lewinsohn et al. (1995) discovered that negative cognitions also function as a risk factor for Major Depressive Disorder in adolescents. For example, an adolescent who has the tendency to think negatively may interpret an award to another student as a personal rejection of himself and, consequently, become depressed over his perceived failure.

Adolescent girls are at particular risk for depression (Cash, 2003) due to the use of affect-focused coping strategies such as ruminating over their troubles (Rice & Leffert, 1997). This has the potential for intensifying the teens' existing dysphoric mood while at the same time increasing the likelihood of them avoiding direct or more approach- or problem-solving–focused coping strategies.

Self-esteem and self-worth are clearly influenced by a Mood Disorder. Vostanis, Feehan, and Grattan (1998) assessed a group of children and adolescents over a 2-year period to evaluate factors contributing to outcome in treatment. Self-esteem was determined to be the most significant predictor of long-term outcome. The presence of depression at a 2-year follow-up was best predicted by a poor self-esteem rating before and even after nine bi-weekly sessions of cognitive-behavioral treatment.

Specific personality characteristics often contribute to low self-esteem, which in turn may contribute to the likelihood of developing a Major Depressive Disorder. Children or adolescents who judge their own impulses, thoughts, and affects (particularly those that are aggressive or angry in content) in an unrealistic or overly harsh manner are more likely to develop low self-esteem or shame, prominent factors in

Mood Disorders (Practice parameters for the assessment and treatment of children and adolescents with depressive disorders, 1998).

Garber et al. (1997) found that perceived self-worth in adolescents played a factor in the relationship between depression and parenting style. The adolescents' perceptions of themselves partially mediated the negative relationship between maternal acceptance and depression and the positive relationship between maternal overcontrol/intrusiveness and depression.

Causal Factors Specific to Mania

Several factors were found to precipitate or be associated with a Manic Episode in youth diagnosed with Bipolar Disorders (Bowden et al., 2005). Wehr et al. (1982) suggested that sleep deprivation can bring on or aggravate a Manic Episode. Post (as cited in El-Mallakh, 1997) noted that severe psychosocial stressors play a particularly important role in the onset of an initial Manic Episode. Finally, Major Depressive Disorder in adolescents is associated with an increased risk for the onset of Bipolar Disorder (Bostic et al., 2005; Rao et al., 1995).

The following example reflects a typical profile of an adolescent with a Mood Disorder. A 16-year-old girl with low self-esteem feels worthless and pessimistic. She blames herself for what goes wrong and sees things that go right as outside of her control. She receives little support from her family or is in the midst of a family crisis. Her mother has a history of depression. This teen's physical health might be not be good, she might be doing poorly in school, and she might have recently suffered a breakup with a boyfriend. Her combination of risk factors—familial, cognitive, and interpersonal—puts her at high risk for developing a Mood Disorder.

PREVENTION

Identifying the elements that contribute to the onset of Mood Disorders in children and adolescents provides information that can aid in prevention as well as in diagnosis. The goal of preventing the onset, recurrence, or relapse of any of these disorders is important to keep in mind for anyone working with this age group. Identifying groups at risk for depression so that preventive measures can be implemented is an essential step in primary prevention. Educating families, schools, and children and adolescents in age-appropriate ways about risk factors and symptoms of Mood Disorders can contribute to both primary and secondary prevention. Additionally, helping children and teens to develop positive coping skills, good self-esteem, and external resources can provide this group with advantages that will carry them through situations that might otherwise precipitate a Mood Disorder.

As mentioned earlier, the presence of a Dysthymic Disorder is associated with a higher risk for a child or teen to develop another Mood Disorder. The early stages of the Dysthymic Disorder can provide the clinician a window of opportunity for early identification and intervention. If children with Dysthymic Disorders are promptly identified and treated successfully, the first episode of Major Depressive

Disorder as well as subsequent bouts of affective illness may be delayed or even prevented (Kovacs, Akisal, Gatsonis, & Parrone, 1994).

Cognitive behavioral therapy (CBT), discussed later in this chapter, may be an important factor in prevention of relapse and recurrence of Mood Disorders. Birmaher, Ryan, Williamson, Brent, and Kaufman (1996b) found that CBT together with relaxation and group problem-solving therapy could prevent recurrences of depression for as long as 24 months after treatment. Preliminary evidence by Kroll, Harrington, Jayson, Fraser, and Glowers (1996) suggests that monthly CBT sessions occurring after depressive symptoms have remitted can prevent relapse in depressed adolescents.

ASSESSMENT

Thorough and ongoing assessment of adolescents who present symptoms of Mood Disorders is critical to the establishment of an accurate diagnosis and an appropriate treatment plan. The diagnosis of Major Depressive Disorder, Bipolar Disorder, or Dysthymic Disorder is made when the required *DSM-IV-TR* (2000) symptoms are present and all other disorders have been ruled out. Treatment strategies vary depending on the diagnosis. Assessing the range of symptoms such as mania or hypomania, the severity of the Depressed Mood, and whether psychotic features are present is important in determining treatment strategies.

In order to obtain a thorough assessment, the clinician should consider multiple sources of information if possible, including parents, teachers, and peers as well as the young person with mood symptoms (Youngstrom & Duax, 2005). According to Lewinsohn et al. (1995), use of multiple sources of information is important for a number of reasons. Not only is it important for formulating a history, but it is also important in the assessment of comorbid substance use and lethality (Dulmus & Wodarski, 1996). Very young children might be unable to provide certain types of information in reliable and valid ways, and they might deny or minimize undesirable symptoms. Additionally, children, adolescents, and adults all have different perspectives and different thresholds for what is considered problematic behavior. Finally, any one person may have limited knowledge of the full range of situations in which symptoms and associated behaviors occur.

Including informants other than the child or adolescent has advantages (Murphy, 2004) as well as disadvantages (Clarizio, 1994). Disadvantages include an inability of those other than the youth to rate the unobservable and inner aspects of depression such as suicidal ideation; confusion that may arise from multiple impressions of the assessed symptoms; individual differences among those rating the observed behavior; a limited ability to identify and assess stressful events related to the youth's behavior; and the risk of eliciting the youth's mistrust and disapproval in reaction to the clinician's request to talk with significant people in the young person's life. Advantages include drawing on the observer's experience with the youth over time and in different settings; the opportunity to gather data on infrequent behaviors; the low cost and efficiency in gathering important information; and the opportunity to obtain information that the young person might be unable or unwilling to disclose.

Rarely can a diagnosis of a Mood Disorder be made with the input of the parent alone (Emslie et al., 1994); therefore, self-reports by the child or adolescent are critical. Often parents are not aware of symptoms the youth is experiencing, particularly suicidal ideation (Crocker & Hakim-Larson, 1997). Children and adolescents are typically a very reliable source of information for symptoms such as depressed mood, decreased interest, and sleep and appetite changes (Emslie & Mayes, 1999), but parents might be better able to provide information on the course of the illness over time and its behavioral manifestations (Emslie et al., 1994).

Many assessment tools are available for use with young people who might be experiencing affective symptoms. Clinical rating scales are useful in screening for symptoms, assessing the symptom severity, and monitoring improvement, but they might not be sensitive enough to actually determine a diagnosis (Birmaher et al., 1998; Birmaher et al., 1996b; Hodges, 1994; Jones-Hiscock, 2004). An example of a tool to assess Mood Disorders in young people is the Children's Depression Inventory (CDI), which is a version of the Beck Depression Inventory (BDI) specifically for use with children. According to Reynolds (1994), the CDI is considered a good measure of symptom severity and is simple to administer; however, it might not be a good diagnostic measure. That is, the clinical validity of a depression severity measure cutoff score has not been established. Other useful inventories include the Reynolds Child Depression Scale (Murphy, 2004), a self-report measure of depressive symptomatology for use with children 8 to 13 years old, and the Reynolds Adolescent Depression Scale, for use with teens 12 to 18 years old. The BDI is also an alternative for use with adolescents who might not readily volunteer that they are severely depressed or suicidal, but will often respond truthfully when asked directly about their symptoms or given an inventory to measure depressive symptoms.

Hodges (1994) presented a comprehensive review of diagnostic clinical measures, which may provide the clinician with a wealth of information:

1. *Child Assessment Schedule (CAS):* A useful tool for evaluating children and young adolescents who range from healthy to disturbed. The assessment addresses 11 topic areas, including school, friends, activities and hobbies, family, fears, worries and anxieties, self-image, mood, physical complaints, expression of anger, and reality testing.
2. *Interview Schedule for Children (ISC):* This interview inquires about depression-related symptoms, the duration of these symptoms, and the presence of hallucinations and delusions. It is a semistructured interview intended for use by those qualified to make a clinical diagnosis and was designed to rate the severity of current symptoms.
3. *Schedule for Affective Disorders and Schizophrenia in School-Age Children (K-SADS):* The K-SADS is the most widely used interview for the study of depression and is meant to be used only by highly trained professionals. Two versions of this interview are available. The K-SADS-E assesses whether symptoms are currently present and whether they were present in the past, whereas the K-SADS-P is used to determine the symptom severity at its worst during the current episode or in the past 12 months.

Other available measures include the Diagnostic Interview for Children and Adolescents (DICA), the Diagnostic Interview Schedule for Children (DISC), and the Children's Depression Rating Scale—Revised (CDRS). Many of these instruments as well as other clinical measures are discussed in the *Handbook of Psychiatric Measures* (American Psychiatric Association, 2000).

Assessment tools may also be helpful in obtaining information from parents and teachers of young people with symptoms of Mood Disorders. Assessments for use with parents include the Personality Inventory for Children (PIC) (Wirt, Lacher, Klinedinst, & Seat, 1977), the Child Behavior Checklist (CBCL) (Achenbach & Edelbrook, 1982; Aschenbrand, Angelosante, & Kendall, 2005), and the Pediatric Symptom Checklist (Son & Kirchner, 2000). Assessments to be used with teachers include the Behavior Evaluation Scale-2 (BES-2) (McCarney & Leigh, 1990), the Behavior Disorders Identification Scale (BDIS) (Wright, 1988), the Teacher Affect Rating Scale (TARS) (Petti, undated), and the Teacher Report Form and the Direct Observation Form of the CBCL (Achenbach & Edelbrook, 1982).

In addition to assessment with standardized questionnaires and interviews, other more informal methods can also yield a wealth of information. For example, a lifetime mood chart and a mood diary might be helpful in documenting the longitudinal course of the illness (Birmaher et al., 1998; Practice parameters for the assessment and treatment of children and adolescents with depressive disorders, 1998). Many children and adolescents enjoy writing in a journal, which can provide the clinician with a means of obtaining information that would otherwise be lost.

For a complete assessment, clinicians should evaluate many factors in addition to those that are required for a *DSM* diagnosis. A detailed family history of mental disorders, psychosocial stressors, family functioning, school environment, and the youth's coping abilities are important variables and provide the clinician with information on contributing factors. The impact of the young person's symptoms on the family and the family's understanding of the disorder and their attempts to manage it are also vital pieces of information for the clinician (Emslie & Mayes, 1999). Because physical health is a contributing factor in Mood Disorders, determining whether there is a medical issue such as thyroid disease, infectious mononucleosis, or even the effects of substance use (Emslie et al., 1994) is important. Finally, assessment of past and current suicidal ideation or attempts needs to be a routine component of all intake procedures and ongoing assessment with young people, particularly with adolescents.

Of particular concern when assessing symptoms of Bipolar Disorder in youth is being able to properly assess the manic aspects of this disorder. As previously discussed, distinguishing mania in prepubertal children from disruptive behavior disorders such as ADHD and Conduct Disorder can be difficult (Botteron & Geller, 1995). Clinicians assessing a person with a possible Bipolar Disorder should investigate the nature and timing of mood symptoms, especially evidence of hypomanic behavior with pressured speech activity, grandiosity, and hypersexuality (Berenson, 1998). They also should be aware that certain psychiatric and nonpsychiatric medications, including antidepressants, anabolic steroids, corticosteroids, isoniazid, caffeine, and over-the-counter stimulants, might aggravate or precipitate mania (Botteron & Geller, 1995). Steele and Fisman (1997) suggested that clinicians consider a possible diagnosis of juvenile-onset Bipolar Disorder when they are presented with an atypical psychosis in an adolescent or with a volatile behavior disorder accompanied by a marked mood component.

Clinical assessments can provide practitioners with a wealth of information, but these assessments should be combined with a variety of other methods for evaluating this population. Not only should a comprehensive intake assessment be conducted with the child or adolescent, parents, teacher, and peers, but clinicians should continually re-evaluate severity and nature of symptoms over time. This not only will provide a good understanding of young clients and their difficulties, but will aid in treatment planning and in any necessary revisions to that plan.

COMORBID DISORDERS

In general, the presence of depression in children and adolescents was found to significantly increase the likelihood of another mental disorder also being present. Conduct Disorder, Oppositional Defiant Disorder, and Anxiety Disorders are particularly common comorbid disorders (Bardick & Bernes, 2005), and ADHD is also more common in young people diagnosed with Mood Disorders than in those without those diagnoses (Angold & Costello, 1993). In fact, comorbidity of depressive disorders and Conduct Disorder appears to be the rule rather than the exception; both disorders frequently coexist with each other as well as with other behavioral and emotional problems (Reinecke, 1995). The combination of those two disorders is associated with a questionable short-term treatment outcome (Birmaher, et al., 1996a). Anxiety Disorders often precede the emergence of depression (Williamson et al., 2005). Further, the presence of both anxiety and depression in children is likely to increase the likelihood of developing these same disorders in adulthood (Mason, Kosterman, Hawkins, Herronkohl, Lengua, & McCauley, 2004).

Clearly, disorders that are comorbid with a diagnosis of Major Depressive Disorder, Bipolar Disorder, or Dysthymic Disorder are important to identify and will affect treatment. Research has indicated that 40% to 70% of depressed children and adolescents have comorbid psychiatric disorders and at least 20% to 50% have two or more comorbid diagnoses (Birmaher et al., 1996a). Additionally, Marton et al. (1989) reported that a few preliminary studies suggest that more than 60% of depressed adolescents may have comorbid Personality Disorders, with Borderline Personality Disorder accounting for 30% of all comorbid Personality Disorders.

For young people diagnosed with Bipolar Disorder, the incidence of comorbidity is especially high (Biederman et al., 2004). A preliminary study by Geller et al. (1995) suggested that ADHD might be an "age-specific manifestation" (p. 266) of Bipolar Disorder. Additionally, the incidence of substance-use problems is elevated in adolescents who have been diagnosed with Bipolar Disorder (Kafantaris, 1995). Other comorbid disorders commonly found in youth with Bipolar Disorders include Panic Disorder and Bulimia Nervosa (Bowden & Rhodes, 1996; Ramacciotti et al., 2005).

An association exists between suicide and depression (Barbe et al., 2004). For example, Lewinsohn et al. (1995, 1998) found significant consequences to comorbidity including an increase in suicide, a negative impact on academic performance, increased mental health treatment utilization, impaired role functioning, and increased conflict with parents. The co-occurrence of Major Depressive Disorder and a Substance Use Disorder appeared to be the most destructive combination. Although comorbid Anxiety Disorders were not nearly as damaging, those disorders had a high likelihood of persisting after the resolution of the depression (McCauley et al., 1993) and predicted a poorer response to treatment (Birmaher et al., 1996a).

Comorbid depression and alcohol or substance abuse might be particularly problematic (Libby et al., 2005), for some adolescents who use a variety of substances to self-medicate. Depression and alcohol abuse both increase considerably during adolescence (Johnston, O'Malley, & Bachman, 1993; Lewinsohn, Rohde, Seeley, & Hops, 1991), and there are many studies which indicate that comorbidity might be quite common. Stowell and Estroff (1992) indicated that of the substance abusing adolescents they evaluated, 50% had a Mood Disorder, primarily Major Depressive Disorder and Dysthymic Disorder. Deykin, Buka, and Zeena (1992) studied 223 adolescents in a treatment facility and found 25% to meet the criteria for a Major Depression. Riggs, Baker, Mikulichk, Young, and Crowley (1995) evaluated 99 delinquent boys aged 13 to 19 and determined that depressed delinquents tended to have more substance dependence diagnoses, to have behavior problems at an earlier age, to have increased anxiety and attentional problems, and to have more trauma effects than nondepressed delinquents. Finally, a comprehensive study by King et al. (1996) explored the predictors of comorbid alcohol and/or substance abuse and depression in 103 adolescents They found that the depressed substance-abusing adolescents experienced longer and often more persistent episodes of depression than depressed adolescents who were not substance abusers. Depressed adolescents who abused drugs or alcohol reported more overall behavioral impairment (e.g., school performance) and were more likely to have Conduct Disorders than those who were not substance abusers.

Clearly, assessing for comorbidity in youth is critical and will impact treatment in a number of ways, including a need to intervene and address the multiplicity of problems presented. In addition, because depression was found to have a tendency to follow rather than precede the onset of a comorbid disorder (Lewinsohn et al., 1998), identifying and treating other mental disorders in young people can prevent, delay, or reduce the impact of depressive symptoms. Clinicians should also keep in mind that youth with comorbid disorders are at an increased risk for further episodes of depression, show a poorer response to pharmacotherapy, and manifest a greater number of social-skills and problem-solving deficits (Reinecke, 1995).

The child or adolescent with both a Mood Disorder and a comorbid disorder will generally manifest more impairment than a young person with only a Mood Disorder. Clinicians need to be sensitive to this fact and be aware of the added risks for suicide, particularly when drugs and alcohol are present (Wu, Hoven, Liu, Cohen, Fuller, & Shaffer, 2004). Additionally, Disruptive Behavior Disorders, when present along with depression, will impact many areas of the youth's life, including family functioning and academic performance.

This chapter has discussed many aspects of the diagnosis of depression in children and adolescents. Remember that diagnosis and assessment provide the backbone on which to build a treatment plan. Additionally, clinicians should consider appropriate treatment goals, effective treatment approaches and strategies, and other factors that affect the counseling process.

Treatment of Mood Disorders in children and adolescents needs to be multifaceted (Abrams et al., 2005; Emslie et al., 1997; Emslie & Mayes, 1999; Son & Kirchner, 2000), with intervention often occurring not only with the client but also with others, including the family, the school, and those in the youth's social environment. Treatment usually should include individual therapy for the youth as well as family therapy and psychoeducation. A referral for medication might also be necessary.

Overall, when treating children and adolescents with Mood Disorders and their families, it is helpful to keep in mind factors that are related to the likelihood of their receiving treatment as well as those related to their response to treatment. For example, factors that might increase the likelihood of treatment utilization include greater severity of depression (Hannan, Rapee & Hudson, 2000), the presence of a comorbid disorder (Evans et al., 2002), previous history of depression, suicide attempts, academic problems, not residing in an intact family, and being female (Lewinsohn et al., 1998; Watts & Markham, 2005).

Goals of Treatment

When working with this population, a primary goal of treatment is to shorten the episode of the Mood Disorder and decrease its negative consequences (Emslie et al., 1994; Gallagher, 2005). Preventing future episodes of depression and mania in children and adolescents is, of course, also a major concern (Beardslee et al., 2003).

Clinicians should facilitate their clients' spending as much of the day as possible functioning normally, perhaps even in spite of how they feel. Emslie and Mayes (1999) found that allowing children and adolescents to ruminate continuously on their bad feelings not only does little to improve the situation, but actually can worsen the depression. To reduce rumination and promote more positive functioning, it is important to identify the maladaptive thinking and then work in therapy to find more positive and adaptive ways of thinking.

Improving self-control skills is usually an objective in treatment of young people with Mood Disorders (Gallagher, 2005; Southam-Gerow et al., 1997). Self-control skills can be improved by teaching the child techniques of self-monitoring, self-reinforcement, and self-evaluation, which may include helping the child to set less perfectionistic standards for performance, analyze depressogenic beliefs, and monitor mood. Additionally, techniques such as anxiety reduction, increasing pleasant activities, social-skills training, improving communication, teaching negotiation and problem-solving skills, and future planning are helpful (Phillips et al., 2003).

Treatment Modalities

Diagnosis and assessment are important precursors to determining the best type of treatment. The personal characteristics and preferences of the young client will also influence the nature of the treatment plan. Cognitive-Behavioral Therapy (CBT) is the most extensively studied form of psychological treatment for depression in children and adolescents (Dopheide, 2006). Young people who experience depression tend to ruminate and to be preoccupied with negative and self-destructive thoughts of guilt, hopelessness, low self-esteem, and resentment toward others. In addition, they tend to either withdraw from their usual activities or gravitate toward impulsive and rebellious activities. CBT addresses both of these patterns (Maag & Swearer, 2005). It emphasizes the identification and modification of dysfunctional automatic thoughts, assumptions, and beliefs and encourages people to identify and schedule activities that are likely to be empowering and enjoyable. Brent et al. (1997) adapted CBT for use with adolescents by emphasizing the use of concrete examples, educating clients about psychotherapy, actively exploring autonomy and trust, focusing on cognitive distortions and affective shifts that occur in the session, and promoting development of problem-solving, affect-regulation, and social skills. In working with children and adolescents, the clinician plays an active role in the treatment, collaborating with the youth to problem solve, teaching the child or adolescent to monitor and keep records of thoughts and behaviors, and combining behavioral and cognitive strategies (Auger, 2005; Harrington et al., 1998).

Children with mild or moderately severe Mood Disorders respond particularly well to CBT in comparison to children who have more severe depressive disorders (Harrington, Whittaker, & Shoebridge, 1998; Paradise & Kirby, 2005). Additionally, CBT is likely to be effective in alleviating dysphoria (a state of sadness or unhappiness) and depression among adolescents, particularly when treatment includes active, problem-focused interventions (Reinecke, Ryan, & Dubois, 1998). A study by Brent et al. (1997) found that in treatment of adolescents with Major Depressive Disorder, CBT was more effective than systemic behavioral family therapy or nondirective supportive therapy with respect to effect on clinical recovery, rate of symptomatic improvement, and parent-rated treatment credibility.

Other forms of therapy such as psychodynamic therapy, interpersonal therapy (Mufson, Gallagher, Pollack Dorta, & Young, 2004), and family therapy (Crethar, Snow, & Carlson, 2004) were also found to be effective (Practice parameters for the assessment and treatment of children and adolescents with depressive disorders, 1998). Research suggests that these approaches might not have a significant difference when applied to children and adolescents with Mood Disorders (Geller et al., 1996).

Interpersonal psychotherapy, a form of brief psychodynamic psychotherapy, is a promising but relatively untested treatment for depression in children, with its promise stemming both from evidence that it is an effective treatment for adults experiencing depression and its underlying rationale (Harrington et al., 1998; Mellin & Beamish, 2002). Interpersonal therapy is based on the premise that depression is closely linked to a history of problematic interpersonal relationships. It is brief and time limited, concentrates on focal interpersonal concerns and patterns, and has the goals of identifying and treating depressive symptoms and their associated problems.

Emslie et al. (1994) suggested using cognitive therapy to treat children and adolescents in a similar manner to that used with adults, but with some of the following changes or additions: 1) assessing the developmental level of the child or teen and adapting techniques as appropriate; 2) including a family assessment and routinely scheduling family sessions; and 3) placing a greater emphasis on the therapeutic alliance. In fact, Krupnick (1996) reported that the National Institute of Mental Health (NIMH) Treatment of Depression Collaborative Research Program indicated that the therapeutic alliance appears to be even more important than the intervention strategy in determining the outcomes of treatment for depression in adults.

As part of working with the families, educating both client and family about the aspects, consequences, and treatment of depression might facilitate successful treatment and alleviate self-blame (Demaso, Marcus, Kinnamon, & Gonzalez-Heydrich, 2006). Clinicians should be prepared for the possibility that family members, including the client, might not have the same perceptions of how the family is functioning, an issue that might need to be addressed as part of the treatment. Educating parents (Fristad, Goldberg-Arnold, & Gavazzi, 2003) as well as teachers (Auger, 2005) about how the client's developmental level affects the manifestation of and recovery from Mood Disorders also can be helpful. Birmaher et al. (1998) posited that, in addition to seeking to alleviate symptoms, clinicians should help both clients and families to consolidate skills learned during the acute phase of treatment, cope with the psychosocial consequences of the mental disorder, effectively address environmental stressors, understand inner conflicts that might trigger relapse, and teach recognition of early signs of relapse.

Medication is another form of treatment to consider when treating children and adolescents with Mood Disorders (Nilsson, Joliat, Miner, Brown, & Heiligenstein, 2004). Although it should never be the sole treatment, medication can play an important role in a multifaceted treatment plan (Bostic et al., 2005). Factors to consider in determining whether to refer a child or adolescent with a Mood Disorder for medication include the number, severity, and frequency of episodes of dysfunctional mood; whether psychosis is present; the response to psychotherapy; attitudes of client and family members toward medication; and presence of stressors (Dopheide, 2006).

A newer class of antidepressant medication, the Selective Serotonin Reuptake Inhibitors (SSRIs), inhibit the reuptake of serotonin in the brain. Open-trial evidence has indicated that fluoxetine (Prozac), sertraline (Zoloft), and paroxetine (Paxil) were all effective for over 75% of youth with depression, whereas fluvoxamine (Luvox) was effective in 66%, nefazadone (Serzone) was beneficial in 70%, and trazadone (Desryl) appeared to be effective in 50% of depressed youth (Bostic, Wilens, Spencer, & Biederman, 1999; Dopheide, 2006). Tricyclic antidepressants (TCAs) involve the noradrenergic and serotonergic systems, an action that appears to be due to the blocking effects of drugs on the reuptake of these brain neurotransmitters (Bernstein & Perwien, 1995). Although there are mixed reviews on the effectiveness of TCAs in youth, a number of open studies with depressed children and adolescents treated with TCAs have indicated a response rate of up to 75% (Puig-Antich & Westen, 1983). However, more recent studies have not supported the effectiveness of TCAs in the treatment of depression in children or adolescents (Bostic et al., 2005).

Antidepressant medication is often indicated for children and adolescents with non-rapid-cycling bipolar depression, psychotic depression, depression with severe symptoms that prevent effective psychotherapy, and depression that fails to respond to an adequate trial of psychotherapy (Birmaher et al., 1998; Bostic et al., 2005). When treating Major Depressive Disorder, the Selective Serotonin Reuptake Inhibitors (SSRIs) are generally the initial antidepressant of choice (Birmaher et al., 1998), with studies finding 20 mg per day of fluoxetine (Prozac) to be safe and effective in children and adolescents (Emslie et al., 1997). Additional studies have suggested the effectiveness of fluoxetine with dosages ranging from 10 mg to 40 mg per day (Dopheide, 2006).

Although the efficacy of lithium in treating Bipolar Disorder in adults has been established, few studies are available on which to base medication treatment in youth with Bipolar Disorder (Danielyan & Kowatch, 2005; Kafantaris et al., 2004). When treating Bipolar Disorders with medication, lithium has remained the first choice for children and adolescents (Botteron & Geller, 1995). Some studies have documented the effectiveness of using lithium in treatment of mania in young people (Kafantaris, 1995) while other studies have supported the use of lithium in treating acute depression in adolescents with Bipolar Disorder (Patel et al., 2006). Of course, when comorbid conditions exist, the clinician might need to consider other medications (Biederman et al., 2004).

The literature has given some support to the therapeutic potential of electro-convulsive shock therapy (ECT) in youth whose depression is characterized by marked cognitive impairment, psychomotor abnormality, psychotic features, and poor response to psychotherapy (Strober et al., 1998). Although this might seem extreme, and ECT is often not the approach of choice, this method might have a place in the treatment of Mood Disorders that have not responded to psychotherapy or medication (Rabheru, 2001). Future research might support this form of treatment for particularly severe and pervasive episodes of Mood Disorders (Gomez, 2004).

Finally, when working with a child or adolescent client, clinicians should individualize treatment based on factors such as motivation, severity of symptoms, level of impairment, danger to self or others, resources, and assessment of stressors in each case. Multiple sessions per week may be indicated during the acute phase of treatment (Practice parameters for the assessment and treatment of children and adolescents with depressive disorders, 1998). Supportive and other interventions to address individual, family, school, and social precipitants and consequences of depression are essential components of psychotherapy whether or not medication is used.

ADDITIONAL FACTORS TO CONSIDER WHEN TREATING BIPOLAR DISORDER

Due to the nature of Bipolar Disorder and its potential lifelong impact, clinicians providing treatment for this disorder should consider some additional factors. Psychopharmacological intervention is generally considered necessary to effectively treat early-onset Bipolar Disorder, although the literature regarding medication in children and adolescents is limited and based primarily on adult studies (Danielyan & Kowatch, 2005; McClellan & Werry, 1997). Although comorbidity with Personality

Disorders was found to decrease the youth's responsiveness to lithium (Botteron & Geller, 1995), it still is the medication most frequently prescribed for Bipolar Disorders.

Treatment for Bipolar Disorder in children and adolescents should combine psychotherapy, pharmacotherapy, and adjunctive psychosocial therapies, with treatment being flexible and adapted to the phase of the disorder (Kowatch & DelBello, 2006; Wagner, 2004). Primary focus should be on alleviating acute symptoms, preventing relapse, reducing long-term incidence of the disorder, and promoting long-term growth and development (McClellan & Werry, 1997). Additionally, because this disorder can be lifelong, it might require ongoing assessment, psychotherapy, psychosocial interventions, and medication management.

When developing a treatment plan for a child or adolescent with a Bipolar Disorder, there are many important aspects to consider (New treatment guidelines, 2005). To begin with, education for clients and their parents as to the nature, course, and treatment for this disorder is critical. Therapy for youth with this disorder will include elements similar to those used with Major Depressive Disorder. Especially critical is attention to relapse prevention and medication compliance. Use of intensive forms of psychotherapy may be contraindicated in some clients due to their inability to tolerate the affect generated; therefore, more supportive individual, group, or family therapy might be a better choice (McClellan & Werry, 1997). For people with delusional thinking and psychomotor retardation, interpersonal therapy and CBT might not be sufficient and might need to be modified and combined with medication and other approaches to treatment (Kafantaris, 1995).

Children and adolescents who become psychotic during a manic episode might need to be hospitalized (Kafantaris et al., 2004). Many require intensive day-treatment programs; in some cases, long-term residential treatment might be needed. In-patient treatment has a major impact not only on clients, but on their families as well. Young people who are chronically impaired may have complicated clinical and social needs and, according to McClellan and Werry (1997), may need an integrated continuum of services including case management, intensive community and family support, in-home services, out-of-home care, and specialized educational-vocational services.

Education is an important element in treating Bipolar Disorder in children and adolescents and can facilitate relapse prevention (Bardick & Bernes, 2005). The client and family need to become familiar with the types of episodes associated with the onset of this illness, to be aware of the impact of noncompliance with medication, to be able to recognize emergent symptoms, and to be acquainted with factors such as sleep deprivation and substance abuse that can promote a relapse (McClellan & Werry, 1997).

Suicide

Suicide is a special concern for clinicians working with children and adolescents diagnosed with Major Depressive Disorder, Bipolar Disorder, or Dysthymic Disorder (Fleischmann, Berolote, Belfar, & Beautrais, 2005). According to Kovacs et al. (1993), people with a history of Mood Disorders are five times as likely to make a suicide attempt during their lives as are people with a history of other diagnoses. Shaffer et al. (1996) found that 61% of children and adolescents who committed suicide met the criteria for a Mood Disorder, and of that 61%, 52% met the criteria for Major Depressive Disorder, 22% for Dysthymic Disorder, 10% for Adjustment Disorder with Depressed Mood, 4% for Bipolar Disorder, and 12% for Depression, Not Otherwise Specified.

Roberts, Roberts, and Chen (1998) explored the risk of suicidal plans and ideation, depression, and factors such as low self-esteem, loneliness, and pessimism among adolescents with a lifetime history of attempted suicide. Those with a lifetime history of suicide attempts were more likely to think about death, wish to be dead, think about suicide, and plan suicide. In examining the role of depression in relation to suicidal thinking and attempts, the authors determined that depression clearly played a significant role, and in combination with a history of previous attempts, the risk of recent ideation was extremely high. Additionally, it was determined that those who exhibited more suicidal ideation were more likely to be lonely, fatalistic, and pessimistic and to have lower self-esteem and higher levels of stress.

Boergers, Spirito, and Donaldson (1998) explored the psychological functioning and self-reported reasons for suicide attempts in 120 adolescents. They determined that more than half of the adolescents indicated that their attempts to die were to escape or to obtain relief. Those who indicated that the suicide attempts were in order to die were significantly more depressed, hopeless, angry, and perfectionistic. Depression was found to be the most reliable predictor of the motivation to die. Additionally, Bridge, Barbe, Birmaher, Kolko, & Brent (2005) examined suicidal thoughts and behaviors of adolescents during their treatment period involving a clinical trial of antidepressant medication. Their findings were consistent with the theme throughout the literature that suicidality is a common finding when involved with treatment of adolescents who are depressed. A key finding of this study emphasized the use of adolescent self-report as a key part of assessment.

Clearly, adolescents with Mood Disorders are at an increased risk of exhibiting suicidal thoughts and behaviors (Cash, 2003; Murphy, 2005). Assessing risk potential and taking steps to ensure the client's safety is a top priority. Safekeeping contracts between the client and the clinician are a useful first step. Hospitalization should be considered if necessary, as well as notifying parents of their child's risk for suicide and helping them find ways to safeguard the child.

Additionally, Gould et al. (2005) investigated whether suicidal screening increases suidicial ideation among adolescents. They completed a study where an experimental group and a control group participated in a questionnaire. The instrument used with the experimental group contained questions related to suicide while the control group's instrument omitted these items. The experimental group reported no significant suicidial thoughts as a result of the treatment. These findings suggested that suicide screening appears to be safe for use with youth.

Treatment Response and Relapse

Even with successful intervention, the relapse rate for depression in youth is considerable at 40% to 60% (Practice parameters for the assessment and treatment of children and adolescents with depressive disorders, 1998). Given that, continuation of therapy is generally recommended for these clients for at least 6 to 12 months following symptom remission (Birmaher et al., 1998; Practice parameters for the assessment and treatment of children and adolescents with depressive disorders, 1998).

Rao et al. (1995) discussed the implications of an adolescent experiencing an episode of unipolar depression. Their studies indicate that Major Depressive Disorder in adolescence is associated with a continued risk of recurrence and persistence of depressive episodes into adulthood. They caution practitioners that youth coming from lower socioeconomic backgrounds might be at a particularly increased risk for recurrence of depression. However, they also offer the hope that those who do not experience any further episodes during the transition to adulthood can expect to function well as adults.

Even with successful resolution of Major Depressive Episodes, formerly depressed adolescents might continue to experience some related symptoms. Lewinsohn et al. (1998) indicated that these young people might experience an excessive amount of dependency on others, the tendency to internalize problems, and an overly pessimistic outlook. Additionally, their attributions may continue to lean toward being negative, stable, and internal as they relate to failure; and they might experience a greater number of perceived life stressors.

Donaldson, Spirito, and Esposito-Smythers (2005) compared the efficacy of two approaches for treating adolescents who have attempted suicide. A skills-based approach with a cognitive-behavioral focus was compared to a nondirective, affirmative approach. There were no significant differences between the two treatment modalities. However, as a result of receiving either type of treatment, the participants reported significant improvement in overall functioning.

TREATMENT OUTCOME RESEARCH

Until recently, there were very few controlled studies testing the efficacy of treatment issues related to Mood Disorders in childhood and adolescence. Evidence-based practices, often referred to as outcome research, are fast becoming the norm in treatment strategies when working with medical and mental health issues. Evidence-based translates to the use of scientific methods when making a determination of the usefulness of a treatment approach (McClellan & Werry, 2003) whether it involves the use of medications such as antidepressants, types of therapy approaches, or use of both of these strategies. These studies typically involve the use of a group, or groups receiving the treatment interventions and a group who receives either a placebo or no treatment. Although much progress has been made in this area, there are many issues that complicate this type of study in children and adolescents with Mood Disorders (McClellan, 2005).

In 2004, interest was sparked in the use of antidepressant medication with youth in the treatment of Mood Disorders when the United States Food and Drug Administration (FDA) intervened and issued a "black box warning" on these medications (Department of Health and Human Services, 2005). This warning came about after indications of youth suicide ideation were suggested to have been related to use of antidepressant medication. The FDA analyzed 24 different studies with a total of more than 4,400 participants (Ferren, 2006). The findings indicated an elevated risk for suicidal thoughts or behaviors during the first few months of treatment on antidepressants. It is important to note that there were no completed suicides by adolescents in these studies. This warning states that there may be an increase in suicidal thoughts and behaviors in children with Major Depressive Disorder.

At the time of issuing the black box warning, the FDA did not mandate discontinuation of use of antidepressants with children and adolescents, but strongly encouraged physicians, mental health professionals, and parents to carefully assess youth in their care who take these prescription medications. Furthermore, based on the analysis of 24 studies of nine different medications, the FDA issued a statement supporting the use of fluoxetine in treatment of child and adolescent Mood Disorders in spite of the previously issued black box warning (Raz, 2006). Therefore, controlled studies have been completed with more underway to determine efficacy of the use of these medications due to the controversial nature of treatment implications.

As the result of the conflicting FDA statements, Bostic et al. (2005) noted that there has been a recent emergence of outcome-based research related to antidepressants and children. These studies examine the effects of treatment of youth with antidepressant medication, psychotherapy, or a combination of approaches. Following is a brief introduction to some evidence-based literature that has been published about youth with Mood Disorders.

A major study designed to measure the effectiveness of use of antidepressants in children was sponsored by the National Institute of Mental Health (NIMH). The Treatment of Adolescents with Depression Study (TADS) is fast becoming a benchmark in the area of effectiveness of treatment options with child and adolescent Mood Disorders. Participants in the study (N = 439) were 12 to 17 years old with a primary diagnosis of Major Depressive Disorder. They were divided into four treatment groups: 1) fluoxetine only, 2) CBT only, 3) fluoxetine along with CBT, or 4) a placebo group. Over a 12-week period, the participants were assessed using the Children's Depression Rating Scale—Revised. A statistically significant finding of the research was that in 71% of the youth participating in the study, use of fluoxetine along with cognitive behavioral therapy showed improvement in their depressive symptomology (March et al., 2004). A similar finding was noted related to suicidal thoughts. However, for a small group of participants, the use of fluoxetine increased suicidal behaviors (NIMH, 2005).

In addition to fluoxetine, citalopram is another SSRI that was studied to determine its effectiveness in treatment of children and adolescents with Mood Disorders. Wagner et al. (2004) conducted an 8 week double-blind study that compared groups of children (ages 7–11) and adolescents (ages 12–17) receiving this medication to like groups who received a placebo. All participants (N = 178) met the criteria for Major Depressive Disorder. Using the Children's Depression Rating Scale—Revised, those treated with citalopram demonstrated statistically significant improvement in their depressive symptoms. Additionally, limited side effects were experienced by participants.

Asarnow et al. (2005) also conducted a controlled study comparing two intervention techniques for the treatment of Mood Disorders in adolescents (ages 13 to 21). Specifically, 211 participants were randomly assigned to an enhanced intervention group and the remaining 207 participants were in the normal treatment group. The enhanced intervention group received a combination of psychopharmacological treatments as well as psychotherapeutic treatments. Using the Center for Epidemiological Studies—Depression Scale (CES-D), after 6 months, the enhanced intervention group reported significantly fewer depressive symptoms than the normal treatment group.

While other researchers have focused on the treatment of unipolar depression, a few authors have conducted outcome-based inquiries related to adolescents with Bipolar Disorders. For example, according to Kafantaris et al. (2004), they conducted the first evidence-based study focusing on the effectiveness of using lithium to treat acute mania in adolescents (ages 12 to 18). The researchers randomly assigned participants (N = 40) to one of two groups in this double-blind study. Both groups of bipolar adolescents were stabilized on lithium. After 2 weeks, the lithium was discontinued from one group and replaced with a placebo. The findings of this study did not support the efficacy of lithium as a monotherapy in treating youth with Bipolar Disorder. Rather, Kafantaris et al. suggested that lithium might be more effective when used as part of a combination therapy with another drug.

In addition to investigating the efficacy of lithium, Delbello, Schwiers, Rosenberg, and Strakowski (2002) conducted a double-blind, randomized, placebo-controlled study of quetiapine as adjunctive treatment for adolescent mania. The participants in this study were 30 adolescents (ages 12 to 18) with Bipolar Disorder. These youth were randomly assigned to either a combination therapy group which consisted of a mood stabilizer (i.e., divalproex) and an antipsychotic (i.e., quetiapine), or to the control group which consisted of divalproex and a placebo. The Young Mania Rating Scale (YMRS) was used to measure participants throughout the study. The results suggested that the combination therapy was more effective than the monotherapy approach (i.e., divalproex only).

In a follow-up study, Delbello et al. (2006) researched the effectiveness of using a mood stabilizer (i.e., divalproex) or an atypical antipsychotic (i.e., quetiapine) in the treatment of acute mania in adolescents (ages 12 to 18) with Bipolar Disorder. In this study, adolescents with Bipolar Disorder were randomly assigned to either use divalproex (N = 25) or quetiapine (N = 25) for 28 days. The YMRS was used to measure participants throughout the study. The results revealed that both quetiapine and divalproex were effective in the treatment of acute manic symptoms. However, participants using quetiapine demonstrated a more rapid reduction in manic symptoms.

In lieu of psychopharmacological approaches for treating Mood Disorders, a few researchers have conducted outcome-based research related to the efficacy of psychotherapeutic applications. For example, Diamond, Reis, Diamond, Siqueland, and Issacs (2002) attempted to determine the effectiveness of attachment-based family therapy (ABFT) on adolescents (ages 13 to 17) with major Depressive Disorder by comparing a group (N = 16) who received ABFT treatment compared with a wait list control group (N = 16) who received minimal support. The findings of the study supported the effectiveness of the approach with 81% of the treatment group no longer qualifying for a Major Depressive Disorder diagnosis, as compared to 47% of the control group participants.

The school setting is an additional area where evidence-based treatment approaches for adolescents with depression is minimal. Kowalenko et al. (2005)

compared a treatment group (N = 76) and a wait list control group (N = 50) of high school students with an elevated score on the Children's Depression Inventory (CDI). The treatment consisted of cognitive behavioral therapy and interpersonal skills development. After 10 weeks, the participants were re-measured using the CDI. The results of the study indicated that participation in the treatment lowered depressive symptoms and increased coping skills.

Another study evaluating the efficacy of an identified therapy approach compared to standard treatment offered by a school-based health provider was conducted by Mufson, Pollack Dorta, Wickramaratne, Nomura, Olfson, and Weissman (2004). A sample of mostly female participants (ages 12 to 18) with diagnosable Mood Disorders was randomly divided into either a treatment group (N = 34) who received interpersonal psychotherapy for 16 weeks or a wait list control group (N = 29) who received the usual care provided by the staff of the school clinic. Based on post-test results from the Hamilton Depression Rating Scale, the Children's Global Assessment Scale, the Social Adjustment Scale—Self-Report, and the Clinical Global Impression Scale, findings supported the supposition that interpersonal psychotherapy was a more effective intervention for youth with Mood Disorders.

The last few years have indeed produced an increased number of evidence-based studies in the literature related to the area of child and adolescent mental health. However, much more outcome-based research needs to be conducted. Some areas to be addressed include commonly utilized approaches which are not validated, evidence approaches in nonacademic clinical settings, and strategies that can be used by both community-based and school-based mental health professionals (McClellan, 2005).

SCHOOL AND FAMILY PERSPECTIVES

The presence of a Mood Disorder almost always has a clear impact on a child or adolescent. The steps a clinician takes in treatment with these youth are critical to their functioning at school and with their families. The following sections discuss the impact Major Depressive Disorder, Dysthymic Disorder, and Bipolar Disorder can have on school and family.

School

Even a mild depression affects children and adolescents in most areas of their lives, including school. Young people with Mood Disorders commonly experience low self-perceived academic and social competence (Evans et al., 2002; Harrington et al., 1998). That self-image, perhaps compounded by psychomotor retardation, fatigue, and problems in concentration, can make completion of school work and even regular school attendance a challenge. Many children who display school refusal behaviors have depressive disorders (Angold & Costello, 1993; Kearney & Bates, 2005).

The social and academic consequences of Mood Disorders for children and adolescents can be significant. As a result of the decreased interest and energy that often accompany depression (Abrams et al., 2005), they might drop out of their usual activities at school and avoid contact with friends. This can further compound their depression (Emslie et al., 1994), suggesting once again the importance of encouraging daily attendance.

As has been discussed earlier in this chapter, depression in young people might not be readily apparent. Not only are the diagnostic features particular to this population often misleading, but other conditions or behaviors can mask the Mood Disorder. Although children with comorbid disorders are generally aware of their depressive symptoms, their teachers are usually more aware of their conduct problems (Angold & Costello, 1993). The behavior problems of young people diagnosed with Bipolar Disorder are particularly likely to overshadow their mood symptoms; they frequently harass their teachers, criticize their teaching abilities, and fail subjects intentionally, believing that the courses are being taught incorrectly (Geller & Luby, 1997).

Certain subpopulations within the school environment may be at particular risk for depression. The prevalence of Mood Disorders in learning disabled youth was found to be higher than in those who are not learning disabled (Emslie et al., 1994; Maag & Reid, 2006). Additionally, children who are homosexual or bisexual are particularly at risk for depression (Galliher, Rostosky & Hughes, 2004; Kitts, 2005; Rice & Leffert, 1997).

Teachers (Auger, 2004) and school counselors (Evans et al., 2002) should be well-versed in and sensitive to the symptoms and needs of children and adolescents with Mood Disorders. The school setting is important in the treatment process, which might even include adapting the setting or shortening the school day to reduce the client's stress (Emslie & Mayes, 1999). Consultation with the school can be particularly helpful for students with recurrent disorders; teachers and counselors can be trained to spot the early warning signs of depression or mania.

School counselors can play a vital role in dealing with children and adolescents with Mood Disorders (Abrams et al., 2005). The counselors might need to act as the child's advocate at school or at home, ensuring that parents and teachers are understanding and contributing to the child's need for help. School counselors need to be familiar with their school's policies and procedures regarding crisis management, and might even need to develop such policies and procedures if none exist in order to help a child in crisis. School counselors can also play an important part in the initial identification and assessment of the Mood Disorder, in coordination of referrals, and in treatment and in follow-up.

Family

Aspects of family life that contribute to depression in children and adolescents have already been discussed. However, it is also important to mention that a depressed youth will have an impact on the family (Demaso et al., 2006). Kircaldy and Siefen (1998) found that adolescents with a greater level of assessed depression were likely to display lower family involvement, achievement motivation, and family cohesiveness than those with lower depression scores. Additionally, research suggests that the higher the depressive state in children and adolescents, the lower the level of cohesiveness experienced within the family and the more intense the degree of intra-family conflict. Needless to say, everyone in a family will be affected by a young person's depression, leaving the clinician to carefully consider who will be included in treatment and what referrals need to be made.

Educating family members about Mood Disorders can help alleviate some of the negative feelings they might be having about the diagnosis and treatment of a Mood Disorder in a family member (Beardslee et al., 2003). Informing them about what is known as well as what is not known is essential and may reduce the tendency for them to blame themselves or others or to view the mood symptoms as a character flaw or a sign of laziness. Particularly important is letting them know that Mood Disorders have biological aspects and might be present in other family members.

According to McCauley et al. (1993), the family environment does appear to be a significant predictor of long-term success in achieving recovery and preventing relapse following a depressive episode. Their study indicated that increased levels of stress in the family environment were associated with poorer psychosocial competence over a 3-year period. Conversely, it is reasonable to conclude that those in families with less stress will generally express greater psychosocial competence. Having parents and other family members become well informed and including them in treatment planning can facilitate their openness to making needed changes in the environment to help their children (Son & Kirchner, 2000).

MULTICULTURAL CONSIDERATIONS

Emotions have biological and cultural aspects, and how emotions are expressed and labeled is influenced by culture as well. According to Matsumoto (1994), Western society encourages emotions that separate the self from social relations and promote independence, such as pride and superiority; non-Western cultures view the self and society as interdependent and validate emotions such as friendly feelings, respect, indebtedness, and guilt (Iwasaki, 2005).

The impact of ethnic and cultural factors is mediated by the developmental process (Bosacki & Moore, 2004). The cognitive level of development of adolescents or children is a critical consideration when attempting to understand their thinking in general, as well as their ethnic-racial awareness, identity, attitudes, and behavior (Wehrly, 1995). For adolescents in particular, a stable ethnic identity may provide an anchor at a time when they are exposed to the considerable stressors that often influence their level of psychological functioning.

The current research addressing the role of multicultural factors in childhood and adolescent Mood Disorders is extremely limited (Choi, 2002; Hallfors, Brodish, Khatapoush, Sanchez, Cho, & Steckler, 2006). This is unfortunate, considering the current and continuing shift in the demographic make-up in Western society, reflecting a trend toward greater cultural diversity (U.S. Census Bureau, 2001).

As a general rule, it is important to consider children's and adolescents' ethnic and cultural context when assessing for the presence of a Mood Disorder (Wright, Aneshensel, Botticello, & Sepúlveda, 2005). The *DSM-IV-TR* (2000a) suggests that a narrative summary be written for all clients, which includes 1) the cultural identity of the individual; 2) a cultural explanation of the illness; 3) cultural factors related to the psychosocial environment and functioning of the individual; 4) cultural elements of the therapeutic alliance; and 5) the overall cultural assessment relevant to diagnosis and treatment. Additionally, Murphy (2004) noted the importance of culture when considering the use of psychopharmacological treatment options.

Social class and race-ethnicity have been noted as correlates of adolescent depressive symptoms (Kuperminc, Blatt, Shahar, Henrich, & Leadbeater, 2004). Siegel, Anehensel, Taub, Cantewell, and Driscoll (1998) cautioned that there is a tendency to confound race with social class and possibly with family structure. Lower social class has been associated with higher emotional distress among adolescents (Kaplan, Hong, & Weinhold, 1984); this link is partly due to the greater number of undesirable life events that economically disadvantaged youth experience (Garrison, Schluchter, Shoenback, & Kaplan, 1989; Gore, Aseltine, & Colton, 1992). These are important considerations, given that African American adolescents are four times more likely and Hispanics three times more likely to be living below the poverty line than white adolescents (Jessor, 1993); and single-parent families, half of which are generally below the poverty line, are twice as common among African Americans as they are among whites (Garfinkel & McLanahan, 1986).

Siegel et al. (1998) compared African American, Asian American, Latino, and non-Hispanic white adolescents and found Latino adolescents to be the most depressed. Additionally, they determined that higher levels of depression were associated with particularly early or late puberty for Latino teens. Finally, there were significant social-class effects on depression, indicating that as income diminished, the average level of depression increased.

Although each child and adolescent deserves special consideration when being assessed for a Mood Disorder, some additional considerations should be kept in mind when culture-ethnicity is a factor. Youngstrom et al. (2005), reported success in using some assessment tools with culturally diverse groups of adolescents. However, the efficacy of Western assessment tools for non-Western individuals can be a concern (Nguyen & Peterson, 1993). For example, in Chinese cultures, emotional disturbances tend to be expressed as somatic symptoms (Cheung, Lau, & Waldmann, 1981; Kleinman, 1977; Kleinman, 2004; Marsella, Kinzie, & Gorson, 1973), an important consideration in the overall assessment process. Finally, whereas mental illness often carries a stigma in Western culture, in non-Western cultures the social stigma is likely to be much greater (Chen, Roberts, & Aday, 1998), further complicating children's and teens' access to treatment. These same differences related to social stigma are also found when working with adolescents in other multicultural populations (Fornos, Mika, Bayles, Serrano, Jimenez, & Villarreal, 2005).

BEST PRACTICE GUIDELINES

Based on the recent emergence of the outcome-based practice literature, much emphasis has been placed on how practitioners can best use this information when working with children and adolescents. It has become relatively common in the medical and mental health fields for practice guidelines to be published. According to the American Psychiatric Association (APA, 2004), practice guidelines do not guarantee treatment results or provide an exact treatment plan for clients. Rather, the guidelines provide a structure and some general suggestions based on recommendations from practitioners with extensive experience in the subject area. Often academic researchers will proffer strategies in the form of practice guidelines based on findings from their research studies. Some of the available best practice guidelines and recommendations in the area of child and adolescent Mood Disorders will be reviewed below.

When assessing Major Depressive Disorder, treatment of children and adolescents can present differently than treatment in adults. The APA (2004) purported that it is imperative to note the difference in childhood presentation, possibly in the form of behavior disruption or somatic complaints. A suicide evaluation is also a necessity when working with youth with Mood Disorders. Those assessing suicidality in children and adolescents are well-advised to review the "Summary of Practice Parameters for the Assessment and Treatment of Children and Adolescents with Suicidal Behavior" (American Academy of Child and Adolescent Psychiatry, 2001). These guidelines issued explicit suggestions regarding suicide assessment, risk, and information on certain types of interventions.

Given the relationship between Major Depressive Disorder and electroconvulsive therapy (ECT), practice parameters have been developed pertaining to the use of ECT with adolescents. Specifically, Ghaziuddin et al. (2004) provided a comprehensive set of recommendations related to ECT for adolescents. The guidelines pointed out that an adolescent must meet specific diagnostic criteria as well as display severe symptoms that are life threatening prior to qualifying for ECT.

In the area of Bipolar Disorder with children, the APA (2004) indicated that psychopharmacological approaches should be considered as viable treatment alternatives. They further offered comment on stabilization and discontinuation of medications when treating children and youth with Bipolar Disorder. In addition to the APA, Kowatch et al. (2005) provided clinicians with guidelines for working with youth who are diagnosed with Bipolar Disorder. They precisely addressed issues related to diagnosis, comorbidity, and treatment.

Like the APA, the Food and Drug Administration (n.d.) has also issued a medication guide with recommendations for youth taking antidepressant medications. This document includes warning signs related to suicide. Furthermore, the American Psychiatric Association and the American Academy of Child and Adolescent Psychiatry (n.d.) have jointly prepared a comprehensive document outlining the use of medication in treating childhood and adolescent depression. Like the FDA guidelines, this document provides extensive coverage of suicide-related risk factors.

Practitioners should also consult *Practice Guidelines for the Treatment of Psychiatric Disorders: Compendium 2006* (American Psychiatric Association, 2006). This compendium contains the latest guidelines for Major Depressive Disorder, second edition; Bipolar Disorder, second edition; and Suicidal Behaviors.

The various practice guidelines provide a starting point for working with children and adolescents with various types of Mood Disorders. However, it is imperative that counselors and/or clinicians consider the individual needs and treatment goals of each client when reviewing these guidelines. Moreover, as more outcome-based research is reported in the literature, practice parameters will continue to evolve to reflect the new knowledge. Professionals must be diligent in keeping current with advances in psychopharmacological and psychotherapeutic treatments when working with youth.

SAMPLE TREATMENT PLAN

The following is an example of the diagnosis and treatment plan of an adolescent experiencing symptoms of dysfunctional mood. This is organized according to the 12 steps of the DO A CLIENT MAP, developed by Seligman (1998). Each of the 12 steps begins with one of the letters in DO A CLIENT MAP, which facilitates recall of that format.

Client

The client is a 16-year-old African American girl, Recee, who is living with her mother and 10-year-old brother. Her parents separated approximately 18 months ago and will soon be divorced. Since her parents' separation, Recee has been experiencing moderate depression almost every day. She has felt hopeless and discouraged, blaming herself for the end of her parents' marriage. Her school grades declined from As and Bs to Bs and Cs because Recee reportedly had difficulty concentrating and felt tired most of the time.

About 3 months ago, Recee began dating a young man who was 4 years older than she. She made efforts to see him every day and became almost consumed with thoughts about her boyfriend. Three weeks ago, he ended their relationship, telling Recee that he had met someone to whom he was more attracted. Since that time, Recee's depression has worsened considerably. Her enjoyment of her friends and activities has diminished greatly, she has lost nearly 10 pounds, and she has been sleeping 12 to 14 hours a day. Her schoolwork has declined further. Recee reports that she is just like her mother, "depressed and unlovable," and will never be able to have a good relationship. She hints that life is not worth living without her boyfriend.

Prior to her parents' separation, Recee was a lively and popular girl who did well in school and played on the school basketball team. Although her mood has changed considerably, Recee reports no problems with drugs or alcohol, or with her conduct.

Diagnosis:

Axis I: 296.23 Major Depressive Disorder, Single Episode, Severe Without Psychotic Features, Early Onset 300.4 Dysthymic Disorder, Early Onset, Moderate

Axis II: V71.09 No Mental Disorder on Axis II

Axis III: No General Medical Conditions Reported

Axis IV: Psychosocial and Environmental Problems:
            Problems with primary support group (parents' separation, mother's depression)
            Problems related to the social environment (break-up with boyfriend)
            Educational problems (decline in grades)

Axis V: Global Assessment of Functioning: 50 (Current)

Objectives:

Short Term:

1. Reduce level of depression at least 5 points as measured by the Beck Depression Inventory.
2. Maintain regular school attendance.
3. Ensure client's safety.
4. Reestablish contact with at least one friend and participation in at least one activity.
5. Reduce level of self-blame as measured by a self-report scale.

(Medium and perhaps long-term objectives would be established later in treatment.)

Assessments: Beck Depression Inventory Life History Questionnaire.

Clinician: Either male or female, able to build rapport readily.

Location: Outpatient community mental health center, although the possibility of a day-treatment program will be considered if client does not respond to treatment rapidly and if she seems to present a danger to herself.

Interventions: Theoretical approach: Cognitive-Behavioral Therapy.

Strategies:

1. Stress inoculation training
2. Identification and modification of dysfunctional thoughts
3. Activity scheduling
4. Education on the impact of divorce on families
5. Self-talk and thought-stopping to reduce ruminating
6. Journal writing
7. Development of problem-solving and social skills
8. Safe-keeping contract
9. Affirmations

(Additional interventions would probably be added to the treatment plan as counseling progressed.)

Emphasis: Supportive but structured, promoting client responsibility.

Numbers: Individual and family counseling as well as contact with school counselor. Perhaps later involvement in group counseling.

Timing: Initially, client would be seen twice a week, reducing frequency to once a week when she was no longer in danger. Approximately 20 sessions of counseling would be anticipated.

Medication: Referral would be made to a psychiatrist for evaluation of Recee's need for medication.

Adjunct services: Tutoring, resumption of involvement in school basketball team, bibliotherapy.

Prognosis: Very good for alleviation of Major Depressive Disorder; good for alleviation of Dysthymic Disorder. Extended follow-up would be needed.

CLOSING REMARKS

Mood disorders in children and adolescents have a major impact on their lives. The potential for disruption of healthy social, emotional, and cognitive growth is great and the impact on the child or adolescent, family, school performance, and peer relationships can be profound and long lasting.

Understanding the diagnoses of Major Depressive Disorder, Bipolar Disorder, and Dysthymic Disorder is only a first step. The clinician needs to be aware of the diagnostic features of Mood Disorders in young people as well as the most common comorbid disorders that can further complicate treatment. Thorough assessment, which includes gathering information from multiple sources and using assessment tools, is an important precursor to diagnosis and treatment planning. Additionally, familiarity with the range of causal factors not only adds important information to facilitate treatment, but also can provide an understanding of critical factors in prevention.

Individual Cognitive-Behavioral Therapy is perhaps the most widely used approach to treatment. However, other forms of treatment, including Interpersonal Psychotherapy and family and group counseling, hold promise as well. The importance of a good therapeutic alliance with a child or an adolescent is critical. Also important is considering involvement of the family and even the school and peer group in the treatment process.

A child's or adolescent's experience with depression can have a lifelong impact. Major Depressive Disorder, Bipolar Disorder, and Dysthymic Disorder are often chronic and need to be identified early to maximize the likelihood of successful treatment. Risks associated with these disorders, such as their strong association with suicidal ideation and family dysfunction, make it imperative that clinicians be extremely knowledgeable about the assessment, diagnosis, and treatment of Mood Disorders in children and adolescents.

FOR MORE INFORMATION

American Academy of Child & Adolescent Psychiatry

3615 Wisconsin Ave., NW
Washington, DC 20016-3007
(202)966-7300
http://www.aacap.org

American Psychological Association

750 First Street, N.E.
Washington, DC 20002
(202)336-5500
http://www.apa.org

Depression and Bipolar Support Alliance (DBSA)

730 N. Franklin St., Ste. 501
Chicago, IL 60610-7224
1(800)826-3632
http://www.dbsalliance.org

Federation of Families for Children's Mental Health

9605 Medical Center Drive, Suite 280,
Rockville, MD 20850
(240) 403-1901
http://www.ffcmh.org

International Foundation for Research and Education on Depression (iFred)

7040 Bembe Beach Road, Suite 100
Annapolis, MD 21403
(410) 268-0044
http://www.ifred.org

National Alliance for the Mentally Ill (NAMI)

200 N. Glebe Rd., Ste. 1015
Arlington, VA 22203-3754
1(800)950-6264
(703) 524-9094
http://www.nami.org

National Institute of Mental Health (NIMH)

Public Information and Communications Branch
6001 Executive Boulevard, Room 8184, MSC 9663
Bethesda, MD 20892-9663
(866)615-6464
(301)443-4513
http://www.nimh.nih.gov

Substance Abuse and Mental Health Services Administration's (SAMHSA) National Mental Health Information Center

P.O. Box 42557
Washington, DC 20015
(800)789-2647
http://www.mentalhealth.samhsa.gov

Chapter 8

SUBSTANCE-RELATED DISORDERS

By

Nick J. Piazza, *Ph.D.*
The University of Toledo

INTRODUCTION

Counseling students who first encounter alcohol- or other drug-using clients during their internship often come to the startling realization that they are woefully ill prepared for the task. Students and interns frequently complain they lack the knowledge base or skill set to deal with substance-abusing clients or their families. This lack of training is not acceptable in light of the fact that Substance-Related Disorders are among the most common mental health problems in the United States, and upwards of 50% of counseling interns report working in substance abuse treatment facilities (Salyers, Ritchie, Luellen, & Roseman, 2005).

I recall evaluating my client caseload after my first year as a therapist in a rural mental health center. I was surprised to discover that substance-abusing clients or their family members comprised nearly 60% of my caseload. This alarming realization became a tremendous motivator for learning all I could about Substance-Related Disorders. While I learned that working with this population was often challenging and frustrating, I also learned that I enjoyed it very much. Consequently, I hope this chapter will provide students with an overview of a much neglected problem and, perhaps, inspire some students to make this their life's work.

DEFINITION AND PREVALENCE

It is important to recognize that using substances to alter consciousness is apparently integral to human nature. People have used alcohol and other psychoactive substances for millennia to relieve suffering, alleviate boredom or fatigue, improve concentration, or alter consciousness. Using alcohol and other substances is not just limited to humans. Interestingly, wild and domesticated animals will use psychoactive plants or fermented fruits or berries to relieve pain or induce intoxication (e.g., catnip). This suggests that many organisms may possess an innate biological need or drive to use psychoactive substances to intentionally modify consciousness or induce euphoria (Seigel, 1986).

Early in human history, the relatively limited and/or seasonal availability of alcohol and other psychoactive substances mitigated the destructive potential of substance use. In more recent times, however, the number, availability, and potency of drugs have greatly increased. As a result, there has been a concomitant increase in concern over substance abuse and dependence. This is especially true with respect to substance use by young people. Helzer, Burnam, and McEvoy (1991) noted that approximately 40% of people with a Substance Use Disorder developed their first symptoms between the ages of 15 and 19.

Data collected by Piazza and Ivoska (2006) indicate that substance use, including nicotine, by young people is still alarmingly high. Table 8.1 provides a summary of the prevalence of substance use for various psychoactive substances. These data are consistent with national results obtained in the University of Michigan's annual *Monitoring the Future Survey* (Johnston, O'Malley, Bachman, 2005) of eighth, tenth, and twelfth graders.

Substance use by young people can have serious consequences even when the level of use falls short of abuse or dependence. Substance use can interfere with performing age-appropriate developmental tasks, inhibit ability to cope, impair cognitive functioning, and disrupt social and familial relationships.

Substance-Related Disorders include diagnoses related to the use of alcohol or other drugs, the side effects of medication, or exposure to a chemical toxin. Generally, it is considered *substance use* if the person intentionally uses alcohol or other drugs for the purpose of becoming intoxicated. It is considered *toxin exposure* if the use is unintentional or part of an intentional poisoning (e.g., taking an overdose during a suicide attempt).

The *Diagnostic and Statistical Manual of Mental Disorders* (Fourth Edition, Text Revision) (*DSM-IV-TR;* American Psychiatric Association [APA], 2000a) divides Substance-Related Disorders into two groups. The first group contains the *Substance Use Disorders*. These disorders are defined by either abuse of or dependence on alcohol or other drugs. The second group consists of *Substance-Induced Disorders*. This includes intoxication and withdrawal from alcohol or other drugs,

TABLE 8.1   Annual and 30-Day Prevalence Rates for Various Drugs for 8th, 10th, and 12th Graders

Substance	Annual Prevalence Rate			30-Day Prevalence Rate		
	8th	10th	12th	8th	10th	12th
Alcohol	32.9	56.5	70.2	19.8	36.6	51.4
Marijuana	11.0	26.7	37.3	6.4	16.5	23.7
Cigarettes	—	—	—	7.3	14.4	20.6
Cocaine	1.6	3.4	6.7	—	—	—

Piazza, N. J., & Ivoska, W. (2006). *ADAS Student Survey for Toledo, Lucas County, and Northwest Ohio.* Toledo, OH: Alcohol and Drug Addiction Services Board.

but can also include any cognitive, psychotic, mood, anxiety, sexual, sleep, or other disorder induced by use of or exposure to a substance.

The *DSM-IV-TR* lists 124 numbered Substance-Related Disorders. This is a considerable increase from the second edition of the *Diagnostic and Statistical Manual of Mental Disorders* (*DSM-II;* APA, 1968), which listed only 28 alcohol- or other drug-related disorders. The *DSM-IV-TR* divides disorders into 11 classes of substances (see Table 8.2). However, most substances fall into one of three broad categories.

1. *Central Nervous System Stimulants:* Amphetamines, caffeine, cocaine, and tobacco products containing nicotine.
2. *Central Nervous System Depressants:* Alcohol; opiate analgesics; sedatives, hypnotics, and anxiolytics (i.e., anti-anxiety medications or tranquilizers)
3. *Perception-distorting drugs:* Cannabis (marijuana or hashish), hallucinogens, inhalants, and phencyclidine (PCP).

Clinicians are frequently distressed to discover that, while searching for information on Substance-Related Disorders, many available resources contain little information that is practice oriented. To help clinicians meet their needs better, this chapter begins with a review of the diagnostic features for substance dependence, abuse, intoxication, and withdrawal. The chapter proceeds with causal factors and prevention, followed by methods or procedures for assessment, and comorbidity. Finally, the chapter will conclude with school and family considerations, multicultural considerations, treatment implications and practice guidelines, a case illustration, and closing remarks.

TABLE 8.2   Substance Use and Substance Induced Disorders by Substance

Substance	Substance Use Disorder		Substance Induced Disorder	
	Dependence	Abuse	Intoxication	Withdrawal
1. Alcohol	303.90	305.00	303.00	291.81
2. Amphetamines	304.40	305.70	292.89	292.0
3. Caffeine	—	—	305.90	—
4. Cannabis	304.30	305.20	292.89	—
5. Cocaine	304.20	305.60	292.89	292.0
6. Hallucinogens	304.50	305.30	292.89	—
7. Inhalants	304.60	305.90	292.89	—
8. Nicotine	305.1	—	—	292.0
9. Opioids	304.00	305.50	292.89	292.0
10. Phencyclidine	304.60	305.90	292.89	—
11. Sedatives, Hypnotics, or Anxiolytics	304.10	305.40	292.89	292.0

Reprinted with permission from the *Diagnostic and Statistical Manual of Mental Disorders*, Fourth Edition, Text Revision. Copyright 2000 American Psychiatric Association. The number given is the diagnostic code for each disorder. Missing codes indicate there is no diagnosis.

DIAGNOSTIC FEATURES

The *DSM-IV-TR* uses Substance Dependence, Substance Abuse, Substance Intoxication, and Substance Withdrawal as generic terms intended to be descriptive of their respective conditions regardless of substance used. My intention is to discuss these four diagnostic categories in general and leave it to the reader to consult the *DSM-IV-TR* for criteria specific to a particular substance.

SUBSTANCE DEPENDENCE

The *DSM-IV-TR* diagnostic criteria for Substance Dependence are contained in Table 8.3. The *DSM-IV-TR* defines Substance Dependence as "a cluster of cognitive, behavioral, and physiological symptoms indicating that the individual continues use of the substance despite significant substance-related problems" (APA, 2000a, p. 192). The *DSM-IV-TR* goes on to state that substance dependence arises from "a pattern of repeated self-administration that usually results in tolerance, withdrawal, and compulsive drug-taking behavior" (APA, 2000a, p. 192). Ten of the 11 substance classes are believed to produce dependence. The one putative exception is caffeine.

Core Characteristics of Substance Dependence

Morrison (1995) noted that there are four core characteristics to a diagnosis of Substance Dependence. The first core characteristic is that the *substance use must be maladaptive*. This means that the individual's substance use causes or aggravates life problems. It can also mean that substance use is distressing not only for the individual user, but also for family members, employers, or others.

Morrison's second core characteristic emphasized *a pattern to the substance use*. Typically this has come to mean that an individual's substance use or the consequences of that use tend to follow a predictable course or pattern. Examples of a pattern of maladaptive use are the individual who consistently becomes intoxicated once substance use is initiated or someone who repeatedly misses work or school because of substance use.

The third core characteristic requires that *the effects of substance use are clinically important or significant*. Morrison believes that the consequences of a person's pattern of substance use become clinically significant when they come to the attention of some third party such as a family member, an employer, or a professional.

Finally, *the substance use must cause the user distress or impairment*. Generally, this means that personal functioning has been harmed in some important life area such as family, job, school, social relationships, or legal status.

Tolerance, Withdrawal, and Compulsive Use

Tolerance   The *DSM-IV-TR* provides two definitions of tolerance. Tolerance is first defined as the need for greatly increased amounts of a substance in order to achieve a desired effect (e.g., intoxication, euphoria, etc.). Tolerance is also defined as a

TABLE 8.3   Criteria for Substance Dependence

A maladaptive pattern of substance use, leading to clinically significant impairment or distress, as manifested by three (or more) of the following, occurring at any time in the same 12-month period:

(1) tolerance, as defined by either of the following:

  (a) a need for markedly increased amounts of the substance to achieve intoxication or desired effect
  (b) markedly diminished effect with continued use of the same amount of the substance

(2) Withdrawal, as manifested by either of the following:

  (a) the characteristic withdrawal syndrome for the substance (refer to Criteria A and B of the criteria sets for Withdrawal from the specific substances)
  (b) the same (or a closely related) substance is taken to relieve or avoid withdrawal symptoms

(3) the substance is often taken in larger amounts or over a longer period than was intended
(4) there is a persistent desire or unsuccessful efforts to cut down or control substance use
(5) a great deal of time is spent in activities necessary to obtain the substance (e.g., visiting multiple doctors or driving long distances), use the substance (e.g., chain-smoking), or recover from its effects
(6) important social, occupational, or recreational activities are given up or reduced because of substance use
(7) the substance use is continued despite knowledge of having a persistent or recurrent physical or psychological problem that is likely to have been caused or exacerbated by the substance (e.g., current cocaine use despite recognition of cocaine-induced depression, or continued drinking despite recognition that an ulcer was made worse by alcohol consumption)

Specify if:

  With Physiological Dependence: evidence of tolerance or withdrawal (i.e., either Item 1 or 2 is present)
  Without Physiological Dependence: no evidence of tolerance or withdrawal (i.e., neither Item 1 nor 2 is present)

Course specifiers:

  Early Full Remission
  Early Partial Remission
  Sustained Full Remission
  Sustained Partial Remission
  On Agonist Therapy
  In a Controlled Environment

greatly diminished response to a substance's effects after regular or repeated use of a fixed amount of that substance.

Tolerance is produced through a number of physiological mechanisms that can occur individually or in combination. The primary mechanism by which tolerance occurs is enhanced metabolism of the substance in the liver or "metabolic tolerance" (Julien, 2005, p. 34). The liver produces enzymes that are instrumental in the metabolism of the substances found in the blood supply. Exposure to a variety of substances can induce the liver to manufacture more enzymes. This results in more efficient metabolism with a concomitant decrease in the duration and intensity of the effect of the substance.

A second type of tolerance is "cellular-adaptive tolerance" (Julien, 2005, p. 34). Cellular-adaptive tolerance occurs when neurons in the brain adapt to the presence of a drug by reducing receptor number for or sensitivity to the substance. Julien states that "such reduction in numbers or sensitivity is termed *down regulation* [original emphasis], and higher levels of drug are necessary to maintain the same biological effect" (p. 34).

Neural accommodation is a third mechanism for producing tolerance. Neural accommodation occurs when the brain tries to compensate for or counteract the effects of a substance. Consequently, the brain may increase stimulation to counter the effects of a depressant drug or may decrease activity to correct for the effects of a stimulant drug. In either case, the brain becomes less sensitive to the effects of a substance over time.

The degree to which tolerance develops can vary significantly across substances. People who use excessive amounts of substances like nicotine, alcohol, or opiate analgesics can grow to tolerate doses that would be lethal for nonusers or initiates. Other substances may produce very little tolerance (e.g., cannabis, phencyclidine) or no tolerance (e.g., LSD).

Often the best way to determine the degree to which tolerance has developed is through determining blood concentration. For example, it is not unusual for novice or occasional drinkers to achieve blood alcohol concentrations of .08 (the legal limit of intoxication in most states). Blood alcohol concentrations of .2 or higher, however, are usually found only in regular or heavy drinkers with a high degree of tolerance.

Tolerance can be a difficult criterion to apply to adolescents and is only "modestly associated" with adolescent substance dependence (National Institute on Alcohol Abuse and Alcoholism [NIAAA], 2004/2005b). For example, many adolescent drinkers may report a "marked increase" in tolerance to the effects of alcohol, even though their consumption has gone from one drink to three. Tolerance, as a consequence, appears to be a high prevalence criterion with only limited clinical utility. Diagnosticians applying the criterion of tolerance would be advised to consider the client's developmental period, frequency and duration of use, and drug of choice.

Withdrawal   Withdrawal refers to the physical syndrome that results when a dependency-producing substance is abruptly discontinued or significantly reduced after a prolonged period of regular or heavy use. Withdrawal syndromes typically occur in individuals who have developed a physical dependency on a substance, are substance specific, and begin to appear as the blood concentration starts to drop. The withdrawal syndrome can usually be relieved or avoided by either ingesting more of the substance or by substituting a similarly acting substance (e.g., administering methadone to a heroin addict or giving lorazepam [Ativan®] to someone who is alcohol dependent).

As with tolerance, the presence and intensity of withdrawal symptoms can vary considerably across substances. The withdrawal syndromes for alcohol, sedatives, hypnotics, and opiate analgesics can be quite dramatic and even life threatening. Withdrawal from stimulants such as amphetamines or cocaine is less dramatic, while there may be no overt signs of withdrawal from cannabis or the hallucinogens.

Like tolerance, withdrawal can be another criterion that is difficult to apply to adolescents. NIAAA authors (2004/2005b) have noted that withdrawal tends to occur only after years of heavy use, has a low prevalence, and is of limited utility when applied to teens. Adolescents frequently lack the histories of prolonged and regular use necessary to create the degree of physical dependence required to produce symptoms of withdrawal.

Compulsive Substance Use   The *DSM-IV-TR* correctly notes that "neither tolerance nor withdrawal [is] necessary or sufficient for a diagnosis of Substance Dependence" (APA, 2000a, p. 194). Many individuals may in fact develop tolerance or experience withdrawal symptoms, but never go on to develop Substance Dependence. Chronic pain patients may develop tolerance and physical dependence on opiate analgesics, for example, but are able to give up their drug use once their condition has improved. Substance use must become compulsive in order for it to be considered Substance Dependence.

Compulsive use, sometimes called psychological dependence, generally refers to the inability to moderate or refrain from using a substance in spite of the problems that the substance use is causing or aggravating. Compulsive use is often evident in the client's preference for the drugged state over a normal state, by craving, or by drug seeking.

Criteria 3 through 5 in Table 8.3 describe the *DSM-IV-TR* symptoms that constitute compulsive use. In contrast to tolerance and withdrawal, compulsive use *is* a necessary and sufficient condition for a diagnosis of Substance Dependence. *DSM-IV-TR* conventions allow the diagnostician to specify whether the Substance Dependence occurs with or without physiological dependence.

Course Specifiers

The *DSM-IV-TR* allows for the use of six course specifiers to describe the individual's remission status. These six course specifiers can only be used after none of the criteria for Substance Dependence or Substance Abuse have been met for at least a 1-month period. Four of the specifiers are called "Remission specifiers" (p. 195) and the other two are used to identify individuals who are on drug-replacement therapy or who have restricted access to alcohol or other drugs.

Remission specifiers are used to identify individuals who no longer meet criteria for Substance Abuse or Dependence because they have either significantly curtailed their substance use or they are abstinent. *Early Full Remission* is specified if the individual has not met any diagnostic criteria for either Substance Dependence or Abuse for a period of not less than 1 month or more than 12 months. *Sustained Full Remission* would be used for individuals who have been symptom-free for 12 or more months. *Early Partial Remission* would be used to specify an individual who has met one or more, but not all, the criteria for a diagnosis of Substance Dependence or Abuse for a period of not less than 1 month or more than 12 months. *Sustained Partial Remission* specifies individuals who have not met the full criteria for a diagnosis of Substance Dependence or Abuse for a period of 12 or more months.

The diagnostician would specify *On Agonist Therapy* for those individuals participating in some form of drug replacement therapy. Examples of drug replacement therapies include methadone maintenance programs for narcotics users or nicotine patches or gum for persons trying to stop using tobacco products.

The specifier *In a Controlled Environment* would be used to describe individuals who no longer meet criteria for a diagnosis of Substance Dependence or Abuse because they are in an environment where access to alcohol or other drugs is restricted. Examples of such environments include jails, therapeutic communities, or locked residential facilities. It is probably best to use this specifier when there is some question as to whether the individual is voluntarily abstinent or not.

SUBSTANCE ABUSE

Morrison (1995) refers to Substance Abuse as a "residual category" (p. 62). A diagnosis of Substance Abuse is made for those individuals "whose substance use produces problems but does not fulfill the more rigorous criteria for Substance Dependence" (p. 62). Caffeine and nicotine are the only substances exempt from this diagnosis. The full diagnostic criteria for Substance Abuse can be found in Table 8.4.

Individuals who experience significant tolerance or physiological dependence, by definition, would not qualify for a diagnosis of Substance Abuse. Rather, they would meet criteria for Substance Dependence and should be diagnosed accordingly. Morrison suggests reserving the diagnosis of Substance Abuse for those individuals experiencing social or legal problems resulting from their substance use, while Substance Dependence implies physiological changes or loss of control over substance use.

TABLE 8.4   Criteria for Substance Abuse

A. A maladaptive pattern of substance use leading to clinically significant impairment or distress, as manifested by one (or more) of the following, occurring within a 12-month period:

   (1) recurrent substance use resulting in a failure to fulfill major role obligations at work, school, or home (e.g., repeated absences or poor work performance related to substance use; substance-related absences, suspensions, or expulsions from school; neglect of children or household)
   (2) recurrent substance use in situations in which it is physically hazardous (e.g., driving an automobile or operating a machine when impaired by substance use)
   (3) recurrent substance-related legal problems (e.g., arrests for Substance-Related Disorderly conduct)
   (4) continued substance use despite having persistent or recurrent social or interpersonal problems caused or exacerbated by the effects of the substance (e.g., arguments with spouse about consequences of intoxication, physical fights)

B. The symptoms have never met the criteria for Substance Dependence for this class of substance.

TABLE 8.5   Criteria for Substance Intoxication

A.   The development of a reversible substance-specific syndrome due to recent ingestion of (or exposure to) a substance. *Note:* Different substances may produce similar or identical syndromes.

B.   Clinically significant maladaptive behavioral or psychological changes that are due to the effect of the substance on the central nervous system (e.g., belligerence, mood lability, cognitive impairment, impaired judgment, impaired social or occupational functioning) and develop during or shortly after use of the substance.

C.   The symptoms are not due to a general medical condition and are not better accounted for by another mental disorder.

Reprinted with permission from the *Diagnostic and Statistical Manual of Mental Disorders,* Fourth Edition, Text Revision. Copyright 2000 American Psychiatric Association.

SUBSTANCE INTOXICATION

Substance Intoxication refers to the substance-specific maladaptive psychological or behavioral effects experienced by an individual who has recently ingested or been exposed to a substance (see Table 8.5 for full diagnostic criteria). Intoxication results in a typically reversible condition that is the result of neither a general medical condition nor a different mental disorder. Intoxication can be voluntary or accidental. It can also occur in individuals who do not meet criteria for a diagnosis of Substance Abuse or Substance Dependence. The *DSM-IV-TR* identifies nicotine as the only substance class that does not produce intoxication.

SUBSTANCE WITHDRAWAL

Substance withdrawal has already been discussed above (see Table 8.6 for diagnostic criteria). The *DSM-IV-TR* notes that Substance Withdrawal becomes significant enough to diagnose when it begins to interfere with "social, occupational, or other important areas of functioning" (p. 202). Withdrawal is usually associated with

TABLE 8.6   Criteria for Substance Withdrawal

A.   The development of a substance-specific syndrome due to the cessation of (or reduction in) substance use that has been heavy and prolonged.

B.   The substance-specific syndrome causes clinically significant distress or impairment in social, occupational, or other important areas of functioning.

C.   The symptoms are not due to a general medical condition and are not better accounted for by another mental disorder.

Reprinted with permission from the *Diagnostic and Statistical Manual of Mental Disorders,* Fourth Edition, Text Revision. Copyright 2000 American Psychiatric Association.

Substance Dependence, but it is important to note that this may not always be the case. Those substances recognized as clearly producing a withdrawal syndrome include alcohol; amphetamines; cocaine; nicotine; opioids; and sedatives, hypnotics, or anxiolytics.

DSM-IV-TR DIAGNOSTIC LIMITATIONS

Martin and Winters (1998a) argue that in general, applying *DSM-IV-TR* Substance Use Disorder criteria to adolescents has shown some validity. There are, however, a number of limitations to this practice. First, Martin and Winters note that *DSM-IV-TR* criteria do not include symptoms that are typical of adolescent problem users. Second, there is a heavy emphasis on medical problems associated with substance use that often only occur after years of heavy drinking (e.g., cirrhosis of the liver). Third, some symptoms are overemphasized. For example, one would expect a significant increase in tolerance to develop in the months after an adolescent begins drinking alcohol on a regular basis. Fourth, *DSM-IV-TR* criteria were developed for adults, and have not been established as applicable to adolescents (American Academy of Child and Adolescent Psychiatry [AACAP], 1997). Brown (cited in NIAAA 2004/2005b) argued that the numerous developmental differences between adult and adolescent substance users "indicate the need to adapt criteria to make them relevant to and properly scaled for an adolescent's stage of maturation" (p. 164).

Finally, it is apparent that substance use and Substance Use Disorders represent a "continuum of severity distinguished more by the number than the type of symptoms" (NIAAA, 2004/2005b, p. 166). The *DSM-IV-TR*, unfortunately, tries to take a continuous variable like Substance Use Disorders and force it into the dichotomous categories of Substance Abuse and Substance Dependence. Martin and Winters (1998a) point out that there is no conceptual or empirical basis to support making a distinction between abuse and dependence. Some researchers have also argued that artificially creating categorically distinct disorders has led to the appearance of so-called "diagnostic orphans" (Pollock & Martin, 1999) and "diagnostic impostors" (Martin, cited in NIAAA, 2004/2005b).

DIAGNOSTIC ORPHANS AND DIAGNOSTIC IMPOSTORS

The term diagnostic orphans refers to those individuals who have "fallen through the cracks" (Pollock & Martin, 1999) between the diagnostic criteria for Substance Abuse and those for Substance Dependence. The medical model of illness followed by the *DSM-IV-TR* requires that Substance Abuse and Substance Dependence be separate categories with mutually exclusive diagnostic criteria. Consequently, it is possible for some adolescents to meet *some* of the criteria for Dependence and *some* of the criteria for Abuse, without meeting the full criteria for either.

Studies have shown that anywhere from 9.9 percent to 13.5 percent of high school students were diagnostic orphans (Lewinsohn, Rohde, & Seeley, 1996; Harrison, Fulkerson, & Beebe, 1998). Martin and Winters (1998b) reported that diagnostic orphans had levels of substance use that were similar to individuals with a diagnosed Substance Use Disorder and which were higher than levels reported by regular users without a DSM diagnosis. Pollock and Martin (1999) found that 31 percent of a sample of adolescent drinkers were diagnostic orphans.

The limitations inherent in the *DSM-IV-TR* are such that significant numbers of individuals may not meet criteria for a Substance Use Disorder, but could nonetheless benefit from treatment. They may also represent a high-risk group for later development of a full-blown Substance Use Disorder and, therefore, could benefit from early intervention and prevention. Perhaps future editions of the DSM will abandon a categorical perspective on Substance Use Disorders in favor of a more realistic dimensional approach such as Marlatt's (1996) "harm reduction" model.

Diagnostic impostors result from the algorithm-based approach of the *DSM-IV-TR*. For example, a diagnosis of Substance Abuse Disorder can be assigned if an adolescent user meets only one out of four criteria. "Some adolescents who engage in relatively low levels of . . . use meet criteria for an abuse diagnosis only because of arguments with their parents" about alcohol or other drug use (NIAAA, 2004/2005b, p. 166).

"Diagnostic impostors and orphans limit the ability of the *DSM-IV* diagnostic system to provide appropriate categories for research studies and to guide the allocation of scarce health care resources" (NIAAA, 2004/2005b, p. 166). One solution for minimizing the number of diagnostic impostors and orphans would be to use "V-codes." V-codes are used to identify problems or concerns that would benefit from treatment, but which do not meet criteria for disorder. Unfortunately, many of the recommended substance-related V-codes are not listed in the *DSM-IV-TR*.

V65.49 Substance Use Variation   is employed to identify adolescents who use occasionally in the context of experimentation. A key feature of this diagnosis is that use occurs in a social or peer context. "If the substance use is associated with a social/emotional problem in the child, or if it occurs while the child is alone, it is less likely to represent experimentation" (Wolraich, Felice, & Drotar, 1996, p. 137). Another key feature is that use is typically limited to alcohol, nicotine, and marijuana.

V71.09 Substance Use Problem   would be diagnosed in those situations where 1) the individual has used an illegal substance more than once, 2) has used a legal substance in an illicit or unauthorized manner more than once, or 3) the substance use occurs while the individual is alone or in the context of behavioral/emotional difficulties (Wolraich et al., 1996). The key feature for this diagnosis is that use has progressed beyond experimentation to problematic use. Use has also become more frequent; however, it still does not meet criteria for a "repeated pattern of alcohol or other drug use" (Wolraich et al., 1996, p. 139).

While V-codes can be useful in expanding the pool of individuals who may qualify or be eligible for treatment, it is important to recognize that many third-party payers will not reimburse for a V-code diagnosis. Most mental health benefits extend only to the treatment of disorder. V-codes are not considered disorders and, therefore, may not qualify for insurance, Medicaid, or Medicare reimbursement.

CAUSAL FACTORS AND PREVENTION

The etiology of Substance Dependence and Substance Abuse is multifactorial, and based on the interaction between biological, environmental, and personality factors. The presence of these factors increases the *risk* that a young person will initiate and continue using substances. Consequently, these factors can be thought of as risk rather than causal factors. At present, there are no known causal factors for Substance Abuse or Substance Dependence. It is believed, rather, that it is the unique interplay of these risk factors within each individual that ultimately leads someone to use, abuse, or become dependent on alcohol or other drugs.

BIOLOGICAL RISK FACTORS

Researchers have long-noted the family transmissibility of Substance Use Disorders—especially alcoholism. Initial investigation confirmed the familial nature of alcoholism, but failed to reveal whether etiology was attributable to genetics or a shared family environment. Studies of twins and adopted away offspring have since shown that the basis of alcoholism and other Substance Use Disorders is at least "partly genetic" (Department of Health and Human Services [DHHS], 1993, p. 61). Twin studies of alcoholism have revealed greater concordance rates (i.e., the extent to which a trait is found in both members of a twin pair) between identical twins than between fraternal twins (DHHS, 1997). Adoption studies have also shown higher rates of alcoholism among the biological offspring of alcoholic parents even when the children are adopted away and raised by non-relatives (DHHS, 1997).

Genetics and Neurotransmission

Biological vulnerability to developing a Substance Use Disorder is based in genetics. Certain inherited genetic codes affect the way different neurotransmitters work in the brain (Anglin, 1997). Specifically, dopamine, serotonin, gamma aminobutyric acid, glutamate, and norepinephrine are all thought to play a role in mediating the effects of several classes of substances. These inherited individual differences are believed to regulate an individual's sensitivity to the effects of certain substances and place them at increased risk of compulsive substance use.

Eisner and McClellan (1999) noted that certain personality risk factors may be mediated by variations in specific neuronal or neurotransmitter systems in the brain that are largely heritable. Dopamine-using neurons in the midbrain may be responsible for regulating novelty seeking. Individuals with a propensity for seeking out new or stimulating experiences may derive greater satisfaction from substance use. Serotonin-using neurons in the dorsal raphe are believed to govern harm avoidance. Serotonin dysregulation in this part of the brain may allow individuals to seek out or participate in higher risk activities. Finally, norepinephrine- and/or dopamine-using neurons in the reward centers of the brain (e.g., locus coeruleus, ventral tegmental area, nucleus accumbens, and the pre-frontal area) may cause the effects of certain substances to be more rewarding or pleasurable.

Genetic Markers

The human genome project has made it possible to identify genetic markers for different disorders that are located in different areas of a person's DNA (Collins & Fink, 1995). In the future, it may be possible to locate these marker genes to determine an individual's susceptibility to various complex disorders such as Substance Use Disorder. Early research has shown that groups of genes distributed across a number of chromosomes may influence dopamine transmission when substances are abused (Blum et al., 1990), while other groups of genes may serve to regulate drug metabolism (DHHS, 1997).

ENVIRONMENTAL RISK FACTORS

Social Factors

Social Bonding Theory   (also called *social control theory*) emphasizes the degree of affiliation with traditional institutions such as family and school. Ellickson and Hays (1992) noted that adolescents are much more likely to use substances when "attachment to family and school and belief in conventional norms are weak" (p. 377). Piazza and Ivoska (1998, 2000, 2002, & 2004) found that school suspensions, expulsions, and gang involvement increased with substance use, while involvement in school athletics, extracurricular activities, and church sponsored activities decreased.

Social Learning Theories   emphasize the impact of associating with people who use substances, model substance-using behavior, and reinforce continuing substance use. Marshall, Molina, and Pelham (2003) noted that "deviant peer group affiliation is a central component of most, if not all, adolescent substance use theories" (p. 294). Marshall et al. go on to claim that membership in a deviant peer group is "the strongest and most consistent correlate of adolescent substance use" (p. 294).

Social learning theories are especially helpful in explaining the effect that peers have on adolescent substance use. Peer substance use and approval are consistently identified as risk factors for later use (DHHS, 1997; Chassin & DeLucia, 1996; Ellickson & Hays, 1992). Ellickson and Hays believe that "exposure to people who use drugs and who make drugs available to young adolescents appears to play the dominant role in early drug use" (p. 383). Parents appear to exert an initial moderating influence by actively monitoring their children's substance use and through providing positive role models. As adolescents develop, however, "parental influences continue to be important, but there is a progressive increase in the influence of peers" (NIAAA, 2004/2005a, p. 122).

Family Factors

The most extensive study of family factors comes from the field of alcoholism. "A positive family history for alcoholism is one of the most consistent and powerful predictors" of a person's risk for developing alcohol dependence (DHHS, 1997, p. 34). The DHHS reports that:

> . . . the odds of alcohol dependence were 45 percent greater among individuals with a problem-drinking second- or third-degree relative only, 86 percent greater among individuals with a problem-drinking first-degree relative only, and 167 percent greater among individuals with at least one problem drinking first-degree relative and at least one problem-drinking second- or third-degree relative. (p. 35)

In spite of this increased risk, most individuals raised in alcoholic homes never develop an alcohol-related problem or disorder. This suggests that while there are familial factors that increase an individual's vulnerability, there may also be family factors that increase an individual's resistance to developing a problem.

Family Modeling Theories emphasize the role of family factors on substance use. Family risk factors that increase offspring vulnerability include parents who use alcohol or other drugs to excess, parents who show high levels of antisocial behavior, and families where siblings use substances (Chassin & DeLucia, 1996). Other family factors that may contribute to adolescent substance use include low levels of support or closeness, little monitoring of children's behavior, inconsistent discipline, and high levels of conflict (Barnes, Farrell, & Cairns, 1986).

Individuals who grow up in alcoholic homes, but do not develop an alcohol-related problem are called "resilient offspring" (DHHS, 1997, p. 35). A number of factors appear to contribute to this resilience in spite of the presence of an alcoholic family member. First, "high levels of parental support, close monitoring of adolescent activity by parents, and positive adolescent-parent communication" (DHHS, 1997, p. 35) all appear to modify the effects of parental alcohol abuse. Second, perceived positive external social support may also protect individuals from the effects of parental abuse (Ohannessian & Hesselbrock, 1993). Finally, Harburg et al. (1990) reported that resilient offspring may develop an aversion to drinking after witnessing the negative consequences associated with a father's abusive drinking. Harburg et al. found that 63 percent of children of alcoholic fathers drank very little or not at all compared to 48 percent of children from nonalcoholic homes.

Cultural and Community Factors

In addition to peer and family influences, cultural and community factors play a role as well. An important community factor is access or availability of a substance. Chassin and DeLucia (1996) noted that "greater alcohol availability is associated with higher rates of drinking. In contrast, greater regulation of alcohol availability is associated with older ages of initiation, decreased consumption, and fewer alcohol-related problems" (p. 177). Piazza and Ivoska (2002) determined that social regulation and parental monitoring play an important role in limiting availability. They found that adolescents reported stores and friends were the two most common sources for alcohol and other drugs. This implies that community-level interventions like limiting the number of retail outlets, better police enforcement of age requirements, and closer supervision by parents would have a positive effect on adolescent substance use. Finally, the AACAP (1997d) cites community or neighborhood characteristics such as "low socioeconomic status, high population density, physical deterioration of the neighborhood, and high crime" (p. 142S) as contributing to greater substance use during adolescence.

Cultural factors may also affect the drug of choice selected by people of different sexes. Frone, Cooper, and Russell (1994) found that stressful life events caused an increase in alcohol consumption in men, but not women. Stress, however, was associated with an increase in women's consumption of tranquilizers, amphetamines, and painkillers. This study suggests that while both men and women may turn to pharmacological means to relieve stress, culturally acceptable drugs may vary with gender.

PERSONALITY RISK FACTORS

Rose (1998) noted that behavioral or personality risk factors for substance use are identifiable "as early as kindergarten and elementary school" (p. 132). Risk factors seem to vary with the sexes, with some risk factors associated with males, others with females, and still others with both sexes.

Males

A number of studies identified novelty-seeking and low harm avoidance as risk factors (Cloninger, Sigvardsson, Bhoman, 1988; Mâsse & Tremblay, 1997). Several forms of conduct problems are also predictive of substance use, including aggression (Pulkkinen & Pitkänen, 1994), impulsivity and restlessness (Knop, Teasdale, Schulsinger, & Goodwin, 1985), hyperactivity (Mâsse & Tremblay, 1997), sensation-seeking (Brook, Cohen, Whiteman, & Gordon, 1992), and low self-regulation (Rose, 1998).

Females

It has only been recently that studies of risk factors have started to include women. Much of the early research was conducted on samples that included men only. As a result, there is far less data regarding risk factors for adolescent women. One risk factor identified as more salient for women is negative emotionality or affect. Myers, Aarons, Tomlinson, and Stein (2003) described individuals who were high in negative affectivity as tending to feel "distressed, nervous, upset, and tense, even in the absence of overt stressors" (p. 277–278). Myers et al. write that "affect-regulation models suggest that negative affective states may increase the risk for substance use because of negative reinforcement" (i.e., anxiety relief), "self-medication," or "social facilitation" (p. 277).

Several researchers argue, however, that studies linking negative emotionality and substance use are contradictory (Myers et al., 2003) or equivocal at best (Chassin & DeLucia, 1996). Rose (1998) noted that "anxiety correlated positively with later [alcohol and other drug] abuse for females but negatively for males" (p. 133), while Myers et al. (2003) cite the example of how "social anxiety has been found to both protect against and facilitate using substances during adolescence" (p. 278).

Males and Females

School performance is an important risk factor for both sexes. Low expectations for academic success, not valuing academic success, and poor school performance have all been associated with increased risk for alcohol and other drug use (Knop et al., 1985; Pulkkinen & Pitkänen, 1994). Piazza and Ivoska (1998) found an inverse relationship between grade point, the number of substances used, and the frequency of substance use.

Another risk factor is a high tolerance for deviant behavior (Chassin & DeLucia, 1996). Adolescents choosing to use alcohol or other drugs must seek out like-minded individuals who will facilitate, encourage, and support their decision. The relationship between associating with deviant peer groups and substance use appears to be reciprocal. Chassin and DeLucia note that "adolescents who drink are more likely to select friends who drink, and those friends in turn influence adolescents' drinking" (p. 178).

Finally, a history of psychiatric disorder increases the risk of developing a Substance Use Disorder. Caton, Gralnick, Bender, and Simon (1980) found that almost 51 percent of individuals in a long-term adolescent psychiatric facility also had a Substance Use Disorder. Piazza (1996) reported that nearly 41 percent of patients in an acute adolescent psychiatric hospital were also positive for a Substance Use Disorder. Finally, Drake and Wallach (1989) claim that psychiatric patients with a co-existing Substance Use Disorder are more difficult to treat.

PREVENTION

Individual Approaches to Prevention

Young people at risk of developing a Substance Use Disorder "may decrease that risk by remaining abstinent throughout adolescence" (Rose, 1998, p. 135) or by delaying the initiation of substance use (Grant & Dawson, 1997). The NIAAA (2004/2005b) stated that "individual-level interventions seek to change knowledge, attitudes, and skills so that youth are better able to resist influences that support drinking [or other drug use]" (p. 163).

Early attempts at prevention, unfortunately, met with little success. Kaminer (1994) noted that initial prevention efforts relied on educational programs and media campaigns. Educational programs used fear-arousal models to discourage young people from experimenting with alcohol, tobacco products, and marijuana. Kaminer reported that "the assumption that increased knowledge will decrease drug use was found to be invalid," and that educational programs "may serve to increase adolescents' curiosity, which may initiate substance use" (p. 418).

Media campaigns achieved mixed results. Media coverage was largely responsible for the decrease in alcohol-related traffic injuries, however, the media also "indirectly provokes the adolescent to seek out cigarettes and alcohol by portraying the products as harmless and 'cool' to use" (p. 419).

Kaminer felt that effective prevention programs typically incorporated four components. The first component was positive peer and adult role modeling. Second, effective programs incorporated positive support and reinforcement for not using alcohol or other drugs. Third, group norms were established that discouraged alcohol or other drug use. Finally, successful programs raised awareness of social pressures to use substances, helped manage negative emotionality, and taught assertiveness and drug-resistance skills.

Family Approaches to Prevention

Family approaches to prevention arose in response to the growing evidence supporting the familial transmissibility of Substance-Use Disorders. NIAAA (2004/2005b) stated that family-level interventions should "encourage parents to be aware of the risks from underage [use], communicate with children, clarify expectations, set rules and consequences about . . . use, and monitor children's activities" (p. 163). In addition to the above activities, families can also "create an environment that reduces alcohol availability and increases the costs associated with use" (p. 163).

Initial results suggest that parental participation in prevention programming "could be effective in reducing adolescent substance use. . . . Furthermore, parental participation seemingly influenced young people's selection of non–drug-using friends" (DHHS, 1997, p. 304). This early research on family approaches to prevention provides strong "support for the importance of involving parents in drug abuse prevention programs" (DHHS, 1997).

Programs for Minorities and Women

Most prevention programs were tested on white, male users; however, minorities, women, and other special populations are generally recognized as having specialized prevention needs. Unfortunately, there is little research that demonstrates "whether minority populations would benefit from interventions specifically designed for them" (DHHS, 1997). Most research, thus far, has focused on defining the differences between white males and African Americans, Hispanic Americans, Native

Americans, women, and persons with disabilities. It is hoped that analysis of these differences will ultimately lead to the development of prevention strategies to meet the special needs of minority persons who may be at risk of developing Substance-Related Disorders.

Environmental Approaches to Prevention

Environmental approaches focus on ways to minimize substance-related problems across an entire population, rather than focus only on "high risk" users. This approach recognizes that most users are moderate users and, therefore, experience only a low level of risk. The aggregate of this low level of risk, however, can be much greater that the risk experienced by a small group of heavy users. For example, most alcohol-related deaths and disabilities are attributable to moderate drinkers and not to alcohol addicts (DHHS, 1997). A number of prevention efforts have been developed that reflect an environmental approach to prevention.

The most apparent prevention effort was to raise the minimum legal drinking age from 18 to 21 years. Raising the minimum legal drinking age "was associated with a significant decline in alcohol use and a 15-percent decline in traffic fatalities. . . . Moreover, compensatory use of marijuana did not increase when the legal drinking age made alcohol less available" (DHHS, 1997, p. 312). Examples of other approaches include 1) using liquor licensing laws to limit the number and density of retail outlets where alcohol can be obtained, 2) better enforcement of existing laws regulating or restricting the sale or use of alcohol or other drugs, 3) increase enforcement of laws against driving under the influence (DUI), 4) training servers to detect and refuse to serve individuals who are underage or legally intoxicated, 5) deterring adults from purchasing or providing alcohol to minors, and 6) extending liability for damages to individuals who provide alcohol or other drugs to users.

School-Based Approaches to Prevention

Recently, prevention efforts have focused on how schools and families can work together to reduce adolescent substance use. These combined approaches focus on both individual-level and environmental-level interventions. "School curricula operate at the individual level by trying to provide students with the knowledge, skills, and motivation to resist pressures" to use alcohol or other drugs (NIAAA, 2004/2005b, p. 163). At the environmental level, schools enact policies and rules that discourage substance use and encourage student participation in school and extracurricular activities.

The most comprehensive federally-funded school-based prevention program was Project Northland, which was tested in 22 counties in Minnesota (NIAAA, 2004/2005b). Results from Project Northland showed that such comprehensive programs were able to reduce initiation of alcohol use among non-drinkers at the start of the study, but produced no effect on those who were already drinking. It would appear, then, that prevention efforts are relatively effective at supporting adolescents' resistance to substance use. It would also appear, however, that prevention activities are relatively ineffective at reversing substance use once it has begun.

METHODS OR PROCEDURES OF ASSESSMENT

Early identification, diagnosis, and treatment are dependent on appropriate screening and assessment. Screening instruments are used to determine which individuals might have a particular disorder and should be assessed further. Assessments are used to determine the number, frequency, and severity of symptoms, as well as diagnosis. A good assessment will ultimately serve as the basis for treatment planning.

Screening Instruments

Screening instruments are a necessary first step in identifying who may or may not have a Substance Use Disorder. Adger and Werner (1994) stated that the goal of screening is to determine whether a problem exists and the "need for an in depth assessment" (p. 124). Adger and Werner recommended that all patients be screened, and warned that failure by a clinician to detect a latent Substance Use Disorder could lead to charges of inappropriate treatment or professional negligence.

Salaspuro (1994) noted that a screening instrument should have good *sensitivity* (i.e., a good true positive rate) and good *specificity* (i.e., a good true negative rate). In fact, specificity is probably more important than sensitivity. Most professionals use screening instruments to determine who does *not* need an assessment in order to conserve expensive time and resources. Only those individuals who cannot be ruled out by the screen undergo a more time- and labor-intensive assessment.

Professionals need to be aware that there are several types of screens and that not all screens are equally valid for all purposes. It is important to know the different types of screens and the purposes to which they are best suited. Screening instruments fall into one of three types: 1) biological screens, 2) logically derived psychosocial screens, and 3) empirically derived psychosocial screens.

Biological Screening Instruments   Biological screening instruments are best used to identify individuals who have recently used or who may be under the influence of a substance. Biological screening is usually done by analyzing blood or urine, but can also involve hair, sweat, sputum, or breath. Biological screens typically look for high concentrations of the substance (e.g., breath and blood analysis) or for high concentrations of metabolic by-products (e.g., urinalysis).

Biological screens are of limited clinical value. While they may tell us who has used or is under the influence of a substance, they do not tell us if the user is dependent, abusing, or just experimenting with a substance. The three best uses for biological screens are to determine if an individual is 1) in danger from overdose or exposure to a toxin, 2) too impaired by substance use or toxin exposure to operate a motor vehicle or engage in hazardous activities, or 3) in compliance with treatment or probation/parole requirements to remain abstinent. The AACAP suggests that biological screens may also "provide a check of adolescent truthfulness" (1997d, p. 143S).

There are also a number of other limitations to using biological screens. Short periods of abstinence can lead to false negatives on some screens like urinalysis. Conversely, some procedures like hair analysis will yield positive results weeks or months after use has stopped. Laboratory procedures can be invasive and embarrassing, and can be quite expensive. Consequently, they may not be cost-efficient for universal screening. In fact, studies (Horrigan, Piazza, & Weinstein, 1996; Horrigan & Piazza, 1999) have shown that self-reports combined with psychosocial screening were just as effective and more cost-efficient than urinalysis.

Logically Derived Screens   Logically derived screens, sometimes referred to as *face valid* screens, are developed through a process called *logical keying*. Logically derived items are selected because they obviously measure the construct in question. In this case, logically derived instruments contain items that question respondents about their alcohol and/or other drug use. Logically derived screens include such instruments as the Michigan Alcoholism Screening Test (MAST; Selzer, 1971), the CAGE (Nilssen & Cone, 1994, p. 136), the T-ACE (Sokol, Martier, & Ager, 1989), the TWEAK (Russell, 1994), and the Alcohol Use Disorders Identification Test (AUDIT; Babor & Grant, 1989).

The principal advantages of using logically derived screens are they are typically brief, easy to score and interpret, often can be administered from memory as part of an interview, have good construct validity, and provide direct data regarding an individual's substance use. Limitations on using logically derived instruments include the fact that they are often specific to alcohol, but not other drugs (e.g., MAST, CAGE); may be standardized on one sex and not the other (e.g., TWEAK); and may not have representative norm groups.

The principal disadvantage to using a logically derived screen, however, is that these instruments are highly vulnerable to denial and deception. In fact, it could be said that logically derived screens are really only good at catching people who want to be caught. An individual who is motivated to avoid detection can usually do so with little difficulty. This is a significant limitation, because the clinician should expect evasion and deception due to the "covert, deviant nature of substance use, as well as the component of denial" (AACAP, 1997d, p. 143S).

Empirically Derived Screens   Empirically derived screens are developed using a procedure called *criterion keying*. Items on an empirically derived instrument are selected for their predictive validity and not their content. Predictive validity means that the instrument is able to discriminate between members of a criterion group (e.g., individuals with a Substance Use Disorder) and members of a control group (e.g., people without any known Substance Use Disorder) without asking questions that are obviously related to alcohol or other drug problems. Because the items are less obvious, they are less vulnerable to denial, deception, or defensiveness.

Examples of empirically derived screens include the revised MacAndrew (MAC-R) scale on both the *Minnesota Multiphasic Personality Inventory-2* (MMPI-2) and the *Minnesota Multiphasic Personality Inventory-Adolescent* (MMPI-A) which help identify psychiatric patients who may also have a Substance Use Disorder. The *Client Substance Index-Short* (CSI-S; Thomas, 1990) was developed specifically to screen individuals in the juvenile justice system. The *Drug Use Screening Inventory-Revised* (DUSI-R; Tarter, Laird, Bukstein, & Kaminer, 1992) screens for substance-related problems and 10 other problem areas as well. In addition, the DUSI-R includes a lie scale to assess the validity of results. Finally, the adolescent version of the *Substance Abuse Subtle Screening Inventory* (SASSI; Miller, 1985) combines both a logically derived screen with an empirically derived screen. The SASSI also has two defensiveness scales to help identify individuals who may be denying or minimizing a Substance Use Disorder.

Empirically derived screens tend to be much longer and more complicated to administer, score, and interpret than logically derived screens. Empirically derived screens can also cost more (typically $2–3 per administration), but are still cost effective. The major advantages to using empirically derived screens, however, are their greater accuracy and their resistance to denial and deception.

Assessment Instruments

The goal of assessment is to "determine whether a problem of using one or more psychoactive substances exists and whether the problem fits the diagnostic criteria for substance abuse or dependence" (AACAP, 1997d, p. 143S). Structured diagnostic interviews are probably the most frequently used methods to assess Substance Use Disorders in adolescents. Martin and Winters (1998a) identified two advantages to using structured diagnostic interviews. First, they can "more precisely and reliably elicit the information needed to make a diagnosis" (p. 101). Second, they use "standardized symptom definitions and question formats, which help minimize variability in responses" (p. 101). The main disadvantage is that they often require specialized training to administer and interpret the results of the interview.

Martin and Winters (1998a) stated that the following criteria should be considered when selecting a diagnostic interview:

- The interview should have demonstrated validity and reliability.
- Historical assessment should cover both lifetime and recent substance use.
- The instrument should review both when problems first occurred, and when and if they remitted.
- The interview should enable the examiner to determine if a symptom is clinically significant enough to contribute to a diagnosis.
- Questions on the instrument should cover a variety of substances, drug using behaviors, treatment experiences, family history, and possible consequences of use.
- The examiner needs to consider ease and length of administration, as well as training requirements.

Examples of commonly used diagnostic interviews for young people include the *Diagnostic Interview Schedule for Children* (DISC-C; Shaffer, Fischer, & Dulcan, 1996), the *Structured Clinical Interview for the DSM* (SCID; Spitzer, Williams, & Gibbon, 1987), and the *Teen Addiction Severity Index* (T-ASI).

The DISC-C shows a high level of agreement with independent diagnoses made by other clinicians, however, it does not relate as directly to DSM diagnostic criteria as other interviews (Martin & Winters, 1998a). The SCID is directly tied to DSM diagnostic criteria and questions are asked in a decision-tree format. Specific follow-up questions are asked whenever an individual endorses an item on the SCID. The T-ASI is a brief assessment inventory and uses a combination of objective data as well as patient self-reports (Winters, 1999). The T-ASI can be used to tailor treatment recommendations based on the severity of the patient's Substance Use Disorder.

COMORBIDITY OR CO-OCCURRING CONDITIONS

Adolescents with Substance Use Disorders consistently have high rates of co-morbid or co-occurring psychopathology. Rohde, Lewinsohn, and Seeley (1996) reported that more than 80% of adolescents diagnosed with a Substance Use Disorder were also positive for some other form of psychopathology. Clark and Bukstein (1998) reported that common co-morbid psychopathology included disruptive behavior disorders (e.g., Attention-Deficit/Hyperactivity Disorder, Oppositional Defiant Disorder, and Conduct Disorder) and negative affect disorders (e.g., mood- and anxiety-related disorders). The presence of co-morbid conditions can have significant implications for client safety and welfare. Piazza and Ivoska (1998) found that substance users were twice as likely as non-users to report suicidal ideation, three times as likely to report suicide attempts, and nearly four times as likely to report being the victim of violence.

Brems (2000) noted that it is important to separate Substance-Related Disorders from independent psychiatric disorders in order to achieve a reliable and valid diagnosis of comorbidity. An accurate diagnosis is "best achieved by delaying testing and assessment for a time period sufficient to allow for substance-related and -induced symptoms to subside" (p. 59). This will afford the opportunity to assess the relationship between Substance-Related Disorders and other psychiatric disorder.

There are two possible relationships between co-existing disorders (Brems, 2000). First, one disorder may cause the other. Second, the two disorders may exist independently and simultaneously. The AACAP (1997d) stated that the chronology of symptom onset was important to assessing the relationship between two disorders. If symptoms of a mental or emotional disorder were present before the initiation of substance use or are present during periods of abstinence, then the clinician should consider the possibility of comorbidity. Symptoms that are present only during intoxication or withdrawal are most likely attributable to a Substance-Induced Disorder.

Related to the issue of comorbidity is the use of substances to self-medicate a pre-existing mental or emotional disorder (Brems, 2000). For example, individuals with Attention-Deficit/Hyperactivity Disorder (ADHD) or depression may use central nervous system stimulants to relieve or control their symptoms. Other individuals may use marijuana to relieve anxiety or drink alcohol to relieve stress. Generally, one would expect the substance use to resolve itself once the underlying condition was properly treated. If the substance use persists, then comorbidity should be considered.

EMPIRICALLY SUPPORTED TREATMENT

Substance dependence is probably best viewed as a chronic, relapsing condition. Treatment of a Substance Use Disorder is at least "as successful as treatment of other chronic diseases, such as diabetes, hypertension, and asthma" (Leshner, 1999, p. 1316). In addition to reducing substance use by 40 to 60%, treatment significantly reduces criminal activity and the risk of contracting infectious diseases such as HIV and hepatitis (Leshner, p. 1316).

THE PROCESS OF CHANGE

Not everyone, however, is equally ready to benefit from treatment. Prochaska, DiClemente, and Norcross (1992) claimed that modifying addictive behavior involved progressing through five stages. The first stage is *precontemplation*. Individuals during this stage have no intention of changing their behavior and may even lack insight into or deny a substance use problem.

Contemplation is the stage where individuals reach the point where they recognize their behavior is problematic, but feel no press to change anytime in the foreseeable future. Individuals in the contemplation stage are characterized by insight into their substance use problem, but no commitment to change. "Contemplators appear to struggle with their positive evaluations of the addictive behavior and the amount of effort, energy, and loss it will cost to overcome the problem" (Prochaska et al., 1992, p. 1103).

During the *preparation* stage, individuals state their imminent intent to change their behavior or have unsuccessfully attempted to change their behavior in the past year, but have yet to take effective action. Many individuals, in fact, may need to make several attempts before effecting lasting change. This stage can be particularly frustrating for counselors. Clients state that they want to change, but they appear to be ambivalent about or uncommitted to change. In reality, they are working up to change and should be encouraged in the process.

The *action* stage is where individuals actually change their behavior and their environments to overcome their substance use problems. Clients are ready at this point to make the considerable commitment of time, energy, and personal resources to making long-term and sustainable changes in their lives. Counselors need to be careful during this stage not to confuse progress with change. Progress occurs when clients start to say the right things. Change occurs when clients actually begin to act to modify their circumstances. Progress may be a necessary precursor to change, but behavioral change is the ultimate criterion for success.

The goal of the *maintenance* stage is to consolidate and sustain the gains made during treatment and to prevent relapse. Maintenance is not a passive stage. For many individuals, resisting relapse and sustaining important changes may require a lifetime of effort and support. Prochaska et al. believe that individuals should be symptom- and relapse-free for a period of 6 months before considering them to be in the maintenance stage.

Although the model is presented as linear with one stage leading to another, Conners, Donovan, and DiClemente (2001) point out that, in practice, people commonly cycle back to an earlier stage from a more advanced one. "It is not uncommon for several such reversions to occur before a durable behavioral change pattern has been established" (p. 203). Cycling is considered normative for individuals with substance-related disorders (Brownell, Marlett, Lichtenstein, & Wilson, 1986).

PRINCIPLES OF EFFECTIVE TREATMENT

When confronted with treating clients who present with a Substance Use Disorder, it is important to consider what elements constitute effective treatment. The National Institute on Drug Abuse (NIDA) enumerated what they call 13 principles of effective treatment that are supported in the scientific literature (NIDA, 1999). These principles are summarized below:

1. No single treatment works for all individuals. Treatment must be individualized to meet the specific needs of each client.
2. Treatment needs to be readily available. Motivation for treatment may be fleeting and opportunities to recruit clients into treatment may be lost if treatment is not accessible when the client is ready.
3. Effective treatment addresses any client medical, psychosocial, vocational, or legal problems, and not just the client's substance use.
4. An individual's treatment plan is continually monitored and modified to meet the client's changing needs.
5. Staying in treatment for an adequate time is important and early termination should be avoided.
6. Individual and/or group counseling is a critical component of effective treatment.
7. Medication is an important adjunct to treatment for many patients, especially when combined with psychotherapy.
8. Individuals with Substance Use Disorders and other mental disorders should be treated in an integrated setting where both disorders can be addressed.
9. Medical detoxification, while important, is not treatment and does little to change substance use. Detoxification, however, may be a necessary precursor to treatment.
10. Involuntary treatment can still be effective. Enticements from family, employers, the criminal justice system, etc., can induce motivation and facilitate the treatment process.
11. Individuals should be monitored continuously for substance use during treatment. Compliance testing can help ensure client resistance to relapse.

12. Individuals should be regularly assessed for infectious diseases such as HIV/AIDS, hepatitis, and tuberculosis. Clients should be counseled on modifying or changing behavior to reduce the risk of infection.
13. Recovery from Substance Dependence is a life-long process and frequently requires multiple episodes of treatment. Participation in self-help groups can facilitate relapse prevention.

TREATMENT PLANNING

There are three main goals to treatment planning (AACAP, 1997d). The first is to select specific and appropriate treatment modalities. The second consists of selecting an appropriate treatment setting. Third is determining the duration and intensity of treatment.

Modality

There are many treatment modalities or approaches that can be used to develop a comprehensive treatment plan. The components of a comprehensive treatment plan can be divided into core services and adjunct services (National Institute on Drug Abuse [NIDA], 1999). Core services are those treatments that would be considered for incorporation into almost any treatment plan and include assessment, diagnosis, and treatment planning; detoxification; individual, group, or family therapy; pharmacotherapy; or referral to a self-help group. Adjunct services are not necessarily essential to treatment, but would be selected as needed for individual clients. Adjunct services can include mental health counseling, medical services, education, legal services, credit counseling, child care, housing, etc.

Level of Care

In addition to type of treatment services, another consideration would be level of care. It is preferable to treat individuals in the least restrictive setting. Inpatient or residential treatment is probably the most restrictive level of care. It is typically reserved for those individuals who require detoxification, suffer from medical complications, need to be removed from access to substances, or do not have access to services readily available in their communities. Less restrictive treatment environments include group homes, day treatment programs, intensive outpatient programs, and traditional office approaches such as individual, group, or family therapy.

Brems (2000) recommends evaluating individuals along six dimensions for referral to a particular level of care. More restrictive levels of care should be considered if the individual 1) is currently intoxicated or likely to experience withdrawal complications; 2) suffers from a medical condition that needs to be treated concurrently; 3) is experiencing a psychiatric condition that complicates treatment [especially if the individual is dangerous to self or others]; 4) is resistant or unreceptive to treatment; 5) has failed to stay substance-free in less restrictive treatment environments; and 6) is experiencing family, living, legal, vocational, or other problems that may interfere with or impede recovery.

Duration

Duration of treatment depends on the level of care and the severity of the disorder. "Treatment should be intensive and of sufficient duration to achieve [lasting] changes in the patient's attitude and behavior regarding substance use and related behaviors" (AACAP, 1997d, p. 145S). Duration should depend on factors such as level of motivation, family involvement, quality of social supports, presence of co-morbid conditions, self-help group attendance, just to name a few.

Polysubstance Abuse

Another consideration would be the number of substances used by the individual. Piazza and Ivoska (2000; 2002) found that polysubstance use was related to a higher frequency of use, using more of a substance, greater binge drinking, and more school and life problems. Polysubstance users were also 10 times more likely to describe themselves as having a substance-related problem than respondents who reported using only alcohol. This suggests that polysubstance users as a group may have more severe forms of Substance-Use Disorders than individuals who use just one or two substances. Consequently, polysubstance users may need more treatment services, of greater intensity, and for a longer duration.

The Planning Process

A final consideration would be the steps involved in actually putting together a treatment plan. Applegate (1980) described eight steps to constructing a good treatment plan. The first step is ensuring that the plan is *simple* so that it is easily understood. Next, the plan should emphasize *small* changes to ensure success and protect the client from a failure experience. The plan should include a focus on what the client is going to *start* doing differently, and not just on what behaviors the client needs to stop. The treatment plan should be *noncontingent*. In other words, successful completion of the plan should be dependent on the client's actions and not on what others do. The plan should be *specific* as to what is expected of the client and the consequences of the client's behavior. Plans should be *repetitive* so that clients have the opportunity to repeatedly practice new behavior. Treatment plans should encourage *immediate* action and avoid delaying behavior change. Finally, clients should take ownership of the plan and make a *commitment* to following through on its success.

In addition to the steps enumerated by Applegate, counselors should avoid using vague terms such as "improved self-esteem" or "increased self-worth." Counselors should operationalize the terms used in treatment plans so that goals and outcomes are measurable and objective. Achieving measurable and objective goals are tangible evidence of the client's success and, therefore, are more meaningful and rewarding to the client.

OUTCOME RESEARCH

Dealing effectively with adolescent substance use and abuse requires that we provide both effective prevention and intervention services. Any discussion of outcomes must address not only the effectiveness of our treatments, but must also address how well we prevent the initiation of adolescent substance use.

Prevention

Prevention has been implemented primarily through the use of school-based policies and curricula. The effects of policy-based versus curriculum-based approaches will be considered separately.

School-Based Policy Approaches   Evans-Whipp et al. (2004) noted that "the overarching goal of US [sic] federal drug policy is . . . manifested at the school level by policies that are exclusively abstinence-based and reflect zero tolerance for substance use" (p. 232). These authors contrast the U.S. approach with harm reduction orientations employed in other countries where abstinence is only one component of prevention. Evans-Whipp et al. noted that there is "currently little empirical evidence regarding the effectiveness of either . . . the abstinence only or harm minimization orientations" (p. 232). They do caution, however, that the U.S. zero tolerance policy approach may have unintended negative consequences. They argued that suspending or expelling students is not likely to prevent their further drug use, and may actually have the opposite effect by "adding lack of involvement in school and school failure to the list of risk factors experienced by these students" (p. 232).

Piazza and Ivoska (1998; 2000; 2002) found that a policy of school monitoring plays an important role in preventing adolescent substance use. We found that students reported very little substance use while attending school-sponsored activities. Students reported that they were most likely to use alcohol or other drugs either before or after rather than while attending school activities. Apparently, a policy of faculty monitoring adolescents' behavior acts as a barrier to their substance use.

School-Based Curricular Approaches   Ringwalt et al. (2002) stated that "school-based curricula constitute the nation's primary means of preventing youth substance use" (p. 257). School-based approaches are popular because they offer easy access to current and potential substance users. Typically, school-based programs have adopted one or more of the following approaches. The first is life skills training. This approach emphasizes the acquisition of important life skills that facilitate social interaction, help resolve interpersonal conflict, and encourage assertiveness. The results of research on the effectiveness of life skills training programs, unfortunately, have been mixed (DHHS, 1997).

Resistance education focuses on helping young people identify situations in which they may be pressured to use substances and learn ways to resist this pressure. Project DARE (Drug Abuse Resistance Education) is probably the best-known resistance education program. Recently, and unfortunately, two well-controlled studies of the DARE program have shown that it has had relatively little effect on eventual substance use (DHHS, 1997).

One approach that does show promise is normative education. This approach is based on the discovery that young people consistently believe that substance use is more common among their peers than it actually is. They are also more likely to believe in the positive effects of substance use. Hansen and Graham (1991) showed that substance use among students who completed a normative education program was significantly lower than students who participated in programs that were more traditional.

There were two findings, however, that seem to stand out across the literature. First, peer-led programs appear to be more effective than teacher-led programs (Botvin, Baker, Filazzola, & Botvin, 1990). Second, parental participation in school-based programs was "effective in reducing adolescent substance use" and "influenced young people's selection of non-drug-using friends" (DHHS, 1997, p. 305).

TREATMENT AND INTERVENTION

While the need for effective substance use treatment programs is widely accepted, Brannigan, Schackman, Falco, and Millman (2004) pointed out that "research on the effectiveness of treatment for adolescents is still a new field" and there are "relatively few scientifically rigorous studies published to date" (p. 904). Brannigan et al. rated 144 so-called exemplary programs along nine key components and found that 40 percent fulfilled fewer than half of the components while only 3 percent fulfilled four-fifths of the components.

Muck et al. (2001) observed that efforts to treat adolescent substance use disorders were "based on adult models that did not seem to consider the unique needs of adolescents" (p. 145). They also noted an "increased emphasis on developing and evaluating theoretically based and empirically supported substance abuse intervention models designed specifically for adolescents" (p. 145).

Muck et al. reviewed existing adolescent substance use treatment programs and found they could be categorized into four main modalities: "12 step, behavioral or cognitive behavioral, family based, and therapeutic communities" (p. 146).

12-Step Approaches

The classic model and basis for all other 12-step programs is Alcoholics Anonymous and its derivatives such as Narcotics Anonymous and Cocaine Anonymous. Programs based on a 12-step approach tend to view substance use disorders as "diseases" that require lifetime management where abstinence is the only treatment goal that offers complete recovery.

Typically, 12-step programs operate as self-help groups that meet informally on a regular basis. There are examples, however, of professional treatment services that are based on the 12-step philosophy. Professional treatment programs that incorporate a 12-step approach are often said to be based on the "Minnesota Model," and the best example of such programs is the Hazelton Center for Youth and Families. This program is located in Plymouth, MN, and serves clients aged 14 to 25.

Muck et al. report that "studies examining the effectiveness of 12-step programs typically focus on comparisons between program completers and noncompleters rather than comparisons to other treatment models" (p. 147). Generally, completers tend to have significantly higher abstinence rates than noncompleters at 6-month follow-up, however, abstinence rates tend to decline over time until there is "no significant difference between completers and noncompleters by 2 years posttreatment" (p. 148).

Behavioral and Cognitive-Behavioral Approaches

Behavioral approaches tend to focus on the external or environmental cues associated with adolescent substance use, while cognitive-behavioral approaches emphasize the attitudes, values, thoughts, and beliefs underlying adolescent substance use. Both approaches view substance use as a behavior that is subject to the laws and principles of learning and behavior modification. Treatment interventions focus on learning coping skills that will preclude or help the client resist substance use. Examples of coping skills include:

> . . . drug and alcohol refusal skills, resisting peer pressure to use drugs and alcohol, communication skills (nonverbal communication, assertiveness training, and negotiation and conflict resolution skills), problem-solving skills, anger management, relaxation training, social network development, and leisure time management. (Muck et al., 2001, p. 149)

Studies of effectiveness typically compare behaviorally-based or cognitive-behaviorally-based programs to other treatment approaches. Muck et al. (2001) reviewed comparisons with supportive therapies, insight-oriented therapies, and psychoeducational approaches. They found that behavioral and cognitive-behavioral approaches were superior to these other approaches in such areas as treatment completion rates, abstinence rates, school and/or work attendance, and satisfaction ratings. Statistically significant improvement was found primarily for short-term follow-up (e.g., less than 6 months), however, long-term follow-up failed to reveal any differences on measures like alcohol use; drug use; psychiatric problems; problems with peers, family, or school; and legal problems" (p. 150).

Family-Based Approaches

Henggeler et al. (2002) noted that there were several promising family-based approaches. These included functional family therapy, multidimensional family therapy, conjoint family therapy, and multisystemic therapy. Muck et al. (2001) noted that most family-based approaches drew their techniques from structural, strategic, functional, or behavioral family approaches, often combining one or more models.

Family-based approaches view the family system, and not just the substance using adolescent, as the client. The family system is comprised of a variety of subsystems (e.g., parents and children) each with a variety of roles and role relationships. The focus of treatment is on these subsystems and how they interrelate, communicate, and function (or not function) relative to one another.

Muck et al. (2001) report that a number of studies have compared the effectiveness of family-based approaches to family drug education, adolescent group therapy, parent effectiveness training, 12-step programs, and individual outpatient therapy. Their review revealed that the literature supports the effectiveness of family therapy. Muck et al. claim that family therapy results in a decrease in substance use and the seriousness of the use, improved school performance, improved overall family functioning, greater satisfaction with family communication, and fewer arrests. Unfortunately, most of the research cited by Muck et al. has follow-up data for 6- and 12-months only. Whether treatment benefits are sustained beyond this time is not yet known, as studies with longer follow-up periods were not noted.

Therapeutic Communities The basic model of the therapeutic community (TC) is a residential program reserved for the most severely problematic adolescent substance users. Typically, residents stay within the TC for up to a year or longer. The TC environment is highly structured and restrictive, and residents progress through treatment by earning privileges that allow them to advance to less restrictive levels of care. TCs are viewed as most appropriate for those individuals whose development has been so severely impaired that they are more in need of *habilitation* rather than *rehabilitation*.

Muck et al. report that 6-month follow-up data arising from a study of six different TCs revealed significant reductions in substance use and abuse, and that more than two-thirds of adolescents "reported that their alcohol use was either greatly reduced or at an abstinent level" (p. 155). There were two limitations to the data reviewed by Muck et al. First, follow-up data were limited to 6 months and there were no post-treatment data for longer periods. Second, completion rates for TCs were relatively low—about 45%. This is probably due to the length of the treatment as well as its rigor.

Brannigan et al. (2004) probably best summarized the state of research into substance abuse treatment outcomes. They noted that "no 1 particular treatment modality is associated with superior outcome" (p. 907). There seems to be a general consensus that outcome research is important and necessary. The current lack of outcome research has been attributed to the fact that "adolescent drug treatment research is a relatively new field" (Brannigan et al., p. 908). In addition, "given the high cost of conducting rigorous outcome evaluations, few of even the best programs in the country can be expected to undertake such studies on their own" (p. 908). Fortunately, the federal government has stepped in and is funding extensive research into adolescent treatment outcomes. The Center for Substance Abuse Treatment (CSAT) has established the Adolescent Treatment Model (ATM) program. The goals of the ATM program are to identify "existing potentially exemplary models of adolescent treatment" (Dennis et al., 2003, p. 19), standardize treatments, and then evaluate treatment effectiveness across multiple sites. CSAT then intends to make these evidence-based models of treatment available through publication of manuals, conferences, and workshops (Dennis et al., 2003, p. 20).

FAMILY PERSPECTIVES FOR COUNSELORS

The surest way to predict who may develop a problem with alcohol or other drugs is to identify those adolescents raised in a family with a substance-abusing parent. Windle (1996) noted that Substance Use Disorders disrupt "parent–adolescent relations and adversely affect adolescent development and adjustment in several ways" (p. 181). There appear to be at least five prominent family factors that mediate development of a Substance Use Disorder.

Family Factors

First, is the strength of positive emotional ties with parents and among other family members. Jacob and Johnson (1997) suggested that the "extent to which a child models the behavior of his or her parent(s) . . . is moderated by the warmth and degree of reinforcement shown by the parent(s)" (p. 205). Windle (1996) claimed that higher levels of warmth and nurturance correlated with "lower levels of alcohol and substance use and higher levels of general mental health and well-being among adolescents" (p. 182). In addition, Windle noted that high levels of marital conflict and domestic violence are associated with high levels of substance use.

Observing family rituals would appear to be a second important factor. Rituals such as taking meals as a family and celebrating special events like birthdays, anniversaries, and holidays provide adolescents with "more stability, predictability, and perceived support" (Windle, 1996, p. 183).

The third factor emphasizes consistent rules based on open parent–child communication. Windle (1996) argued that "inconsistency in parenting may undermine a child's sense of order, control and stability in the family environment, reducing both feelings of self-esteem and perceptions of self-competency" (p. 181). Parents should establish clear rules, consistently enforce reasonable consequences for violating the rules, and provide adolescents with some say in how rules are established and modified.

A factor related to consistency is providing adequate parental monitoring. "Higher levels of parental monitoring are associated with lower levels of adolescent alcohol and other drug use as well as other forms of delinquent behavior" (Windle, 1996, p. 181). Adequate parental monitoring decreases the risk of adolescent substance use by encouraging healthy choices, avoiding substance using peers, and preventing risky behavior.

Finally, parental attitudes toward substance use are important. Windle (1996) reports that families with higher levels of parental tolerance of substance abuse have children who start drinking at an earlier age and escalate to higher levels of use.

Enabling versus Empowering

An important family perspective to consider is the difference between enabling versus empowering an individual with a substance-use problem. Often family members will minimize and deny a Substance Use Disorder to the same extent as the user. In these cases, family members become "co-conspirators" in concealing an individual's alcohol- or other drug-related problems (e.g., informing the school or an employer that a family member is ill rather than hung-over). Such behavior protects users from the negative consequences of their behavior and "enables" them to continue using as if nothing were wrong. Family members often engage in enabling behavior out of the mistaken belief that they are helping or supporting their loved one.

Empowering family members means supporting them as they face and overcome their problems. Empowerment often begins with what is known as an "intervention" where family members help break through denial and encourage the user into treatment (Johnson, 1973). One important job for the counselor is helping family members distinguish between what is empowering the user and what is enabling the drinking or drug use.

MULTICULTURAL CONSIDERATIONS

Group membership can be a useful indicator for social behavior such as alcohol or other drug use. Group membership helps to establish the social structures, rules, role expectations, norms, and sanctions that regulate an individual's substance use. Proper assessment, diagnosis, and treatment of a substance-related disorder require that the clinician consider important group memberships.

One important group membership is age cohort. Social changes in the second half of the 20th century have been "characterized by increasingly earlier ages for the onset of alcohol [and other drug] use" (DHHS, 2000, p. 40). The literature would seem to support that within a given culture, people develop a pattern of use during their youth and early adulthood, and "the pattern is largely set for a person's lifetime" (p. 40).

Gender represents a second important group membership. In the past, there were considerable gender differences on substance use, initiation of use, amounts used, and problem prevalence. This "gender gap" appears to be closing, and there is increasing similarity between the consumption patterns of men and women. For example, "males born before World War II were 2.4 times as likely as females to use alcohol," while males born during the Vietnam era are "only 1.2 times as likely as females to use alcohol" (DHHS, 2000, p. 40). Men born before World War II were also nearly 5 times more likely to develop alcohol dependence than were females. Men born during the Vietnam era are only 1.4 times more likely than women to develop alcohol dependence (DHHS, 2000, p. 41).

Race and ethnicity represent a highly significant group membership. While it is obvious that there is considerable variability between racial and ethnic groups relative to substance use, it is also important to recognize that there is considerable within group variability as well. It would be a serious mistake to assume that all individuals within a racial or ethnic group are like all others. For example, there is a tendency to think of Hispanics as a fairly homogeneous group; however, this term can be used to identify individuals from Cuba, Puerto Rico, Mexico, and the countries of Central and South America.

There are a number of risk factors common to the acculturation process that can contribute to substance use. First, is the stress of trying to integrate into a more dominant culture. This may occur at the same time as one's original culture is being devalued or lost. Second, income, standard of living, and opportunity may all be limited for members of different groups. For example, the median income for African American families was only 60% of the median income of white families, while unemployment was twice that of the general population (Smith-Stevens & Smith, 1998, p. 227). Other factors include under-education, poor housing, prejudice, discrimination, and cultural and linguistic barriers to treatment and prevention services (pp. 230–231).

Smith-Stevens & Smith (1998) argued that clinicians need to evaluate and be aware of their own worldview. They noted that:

> The challenge is to develop an awareness of how one perceived the culturally different client. In developing this awareness, counselors need to gain an understanding of the history and background of their clients to address the clients' issues within the context in which they are presented. By doing so they will not only serve their clients needs more fully, they will also empower them within the process. (p. 235)

CASE ILLUSTRATION

Jerry was a 17-year-old, white, male referred for a substance abuse evaluation by his mother who was concerned that he may have an "alcohol or drug problem." Jerry reported that he drank between 2 and 4 nights per week, and consumed approximately 12 cans of beer (or its equivalent in spirits) per drinking episode. Jerry admitted that even he was concerned about his drinking, as friends had told him that he "becomes a different person" when drinking.

Jerry claimed that he quit drinking about 3 weeks ago after an episode where he became verbally abusive with his mother and then ran from the house. Jerry reported that he was picked up, but not arrested, by the police at his mother's request. He also stated that he has no recollection of the events of that evening.

Jerry described his biological father as an alcoholic, and reported that his father died when Jerry was about 6 years old. Jerry claimed that his father died when he became intoxicated and "overdosed on pills." Jerry did not know if his father's death was accidental or a suicide.

Jerry stated that he had no history of prior treatment for a mental, emotional, or substance use disorder. Jerry claimed he started drinking when he was about 14. He denied any problems until about 3 months ago. He reported that he became concerned about his drinking at that time and quit for about 30 days.

A mental status evaluation revealed that Jerry was oriented for time, place, and person. Memory was intact for recent, remote, and immediate recall. The only exception was his inability to recall events around his last drinking episode 3 weeks prior. Mood and affect were unremarkable. Jerry denied any suicidal ideation or intent, and he denied hallucinations or delusions. Jerry's drinking was evaluated along three parameters: compulsive use, psychological dependence, and physical dependence.

Compulsive use was defined as often drinking more or over a longer period than was intended. Jerry admitted that this might be a problem. He stated that he felt unable to predict how much he might drink or whether or not he would drink to intoxication on any given night.

Jerry denied any other symptoms of compulsive use. He did not believe he spent an inordinate amount of time in alcohol-related activities. He had not given up or reduced important activities to engage in drinking. Finally, he claimed that his grades had not suffered as a result of his drinking. He did admit he was afraid he might jeopardize his eligibility to play high school sports if his drinking were discovered, because his school had a zero use policy. Jerry claimed to be a good athlete with a chance to win an athletic scholarship for college, so he was motivated to maintain his eligibility for athletics.

A developing physical dependence was evident in Jerry's marked tolerance for alcohol and the presence of an alcohol-induced blackout. He did deny, however, any symptoms of alcohol withdrawal.

Sample Treatment Plan

Jerry may very well be an example of the previously described diagnostic orphan. Jerry's drinking does not clearly meet criteria for a diagnosis of Alcohol Abuse. There is no evidence of recurrent failure to fulfill major role obligations. Jerry did not report engaging in hazardous alcohol-related activities (e.g., driving while intoxicated). There was no history of recurrent alcohol-related legal problems, and there was no evidence of continued use in spite of significant interpersonal problems. In fact, Jerry stopped drinking in response to the altercation he experienced with his mother. While Jerry certainly exhibited behavior that would meet the criteria, there was no *pattern* of *recurrent* behavior that would satisfy any one criterion.

It is also not clear that Jerry's behavior would meet the full criteria for a diagnosis of Alcohol Dependence. There is evidence of tolerance and drinking more than intended, however, other symptoms were denied. The only questionable symptom relates to Jerry's desire and efforts to control his alcohol use. Jerry's desire to moderate his drinking is relatively recent and he has made only one unsuccessful attempt to quit drinking. This most likely does not meet the criteria of "persistent desire" or repeated "unsuccessful efforts" to cut down or control alcohol use (APA, 2000a, p. 197).

Clearly, Jerry has a problem with alcohol. Unless one is prepared to stretch the evidence, however, Jerry's drinking does not meet full criteria for either 305.00 Alcohol Abuse or 303.90 Alcohol Dependence at this time. Three points need to be made, however, concerning Jerry's alcohol use. First, Jerry could very well be denying or minimizing his symptoms. Further investigation or a more honest self-appraisal on Jerry's part may reveal additional evidence to permit a diagnosis. Second, without some form of intervention, Jerry's drinking will no doubt get progressively worse until it does meet full criteria for either Alcohol Abuse or Alcohol

Dependence. Third, any treatment plan developed for Jerry is going to have to take into consideration that he is a minor and it is illegal for him to drink. Consequently, the treatment plan should emphasize abstinence regardless of problem severity.

Diagnosis

Axis I: V71.09 Substance Use Problem.
           Rule out: 303.90 Alcohol Dependence and 305.00 Alcohol Abuse.
Axis II: V71.09 No Mental Disorder/Diagnosis on Axis II
Axis III: No General Medical Conditions Reported
Axis IV: Psychosocial and Environmental Problems: None
Axis V: Global Assessment of Functioning:
           Current: 80
           Past year: 90

Long-Term Goal

Clarify the legal, health, and educational risks inherent in Jerry's current alcohol use.

Objectives

1. Complete a program of alcohol education emphasizing the legal consequences of underage drinking, health risks associated with heavy alcohol consumption, and how these could adversely affect future educational opportunities.
2. Relate father's history of alcohol dependence to Jerry's current drinking behavior.
3. Explore extended family history of Substance Use Disorder to determine level of genetic risk.
4. Refer Jerry for a physical examination to determine if there are any adverse physical effects related to Jerry's drinking.
5. Have Jerry attend an open Alcoholics Anonymous (AA) meeting and discuss the impact of the meeting with the therapist.

Long-Term Goal

Acquire necessary skills to avoid using alcohol while still a minor.

Objectives

6. Sign an abstinence contract wherein Jerry agrees to remain abstinent for a specified period.
7. Identify ways that remaining abstinent can have a positive impact on Jerry's life.
8. Seek out friends and activities that encourage abstinence.
9. Review negative consequences of maintaining drinking-related friendships and activities.
10. Identify positive impact abstinence will have on relationship with mother.

11. Identify situational and social stress factors that may undermine Jerry's commitment to abstinence.
12. Encourage Jerry to consider remaining abstinent until age 21, after the contract expires.

Prognosis: Prognosis for short-term abstinence is very good. Prognosis for abstinence until Jerry reaches the age of majority is guarded.

BEST PRACTICE GUIDELINES

An important resource for practitioners or clinicians, is access to treatment guidelines that reflect the best practices and evidence-based approaches available. The best place to begin searching for best practice guidelines is the National Guideline Clearinghouse (NGC), which can be located at *http://www.guidelines.gov*. The NGC is a program of the Agency for Healthcare Research and Quality (AHRQ) of the U.S. Department of Health and Human Services (DHHS). The NGC is a comprehensive database of evidence-based clinical practice guidelines across a variety of conditions.

The practice guideline most applicable to substance abuse treatment and adolescence is published by the American Academy of Child and Adolescent Psychiatry (AACAP, 1997d). The AACP Practice Parameters for Substance Use Disorders can be downloaded from *http://www.aacap.org/galleries/PracticeParameters/ substanceUseDisorder.pdf.*

The American Psychiatric Association (APA) practice guideline applies to clients in general and not just adolescents. The APA's Practice Guideline for the Treatment of Patients with Substance Use Disorders: Alcohol, Cocaine, Opioids can be located on the Internet at *http://www.psych.org/psych_pract/treatg/pg/pg_substance.cfm.*

The American Society of Addiction Medicine (ASAM) has published practice guidelines for the management of alcohol withdrawal (Mayo-Smith et al., 1997). This and other practice guidelines are available on the ASAM website at *http://www .asam.org/publ/pg.htm.*

Professionals should also consult *Practice Guidelines for the Treatment of Psychiatric Disorders: Compendium 2006* (American Psychiatric Association, 2006). The latest edition of practice guidelines for Substance Use Disorders and Suicidal Behaviors are contained in this compendium.

CLOSING REMARKS

Counseling individuals with Substance-Related Disorders can be challenging, yet rewarding, work. For many years, people were discouraged from entering this field of practice in the belief that clients with Substance-Related Disorders were untreatable and did not get better. We have since learned that Substance-Related Disorders are no less responsive to treatment than other chronic, relapsing disorders like depression or anxiety. The keys to effectively treating this class of disorder are to 1) become proficient in the knowledge base unique to the Substance-Related Disorders, 2) make a good diagnosis, and 3) tailor treatment to meet the needs of the individual.

FOR MORE INFORMATION

Alcoholics Anonymous (AA), Al-anon, and Alateen
Address and telephone numbers for local chapters available in the yellow pages.
http://www.alcoholics-anonymous.org
http://www.al-anon.alateen.org

Treatment of Adolescents with Substance Use Disorders
12-Step–Based Programs
http://www.athealth.com/Practitioner/ceduc/health_tip32g.html

American Counseling Association
5999 Stevenson Avenue
Alexandria, VA 22304
(703)823-9800
http://www.counseling.org

American Psychiatric Association
1400 K Street, N.W.
Washington, D.C. 20005
1(888)357-7924
http://www.psych.org
Practice Guideline for the Treatment of Patients with Substance Use Disorder: Alcohol, Cocaine, Opioids (available at *http://www.psych.org/clin_res/pg_substance.cfm*)

American Psychological Association
750 First Street, NE
Washington, D.C. 20002-4242
(202)336-5500
http://www.apa.org

American Society of Addiction Medicine (ASAM)
4601 North Park Ave, Arcade Suite 101
Chevy Chase, MD 20815
(301)656-3920
http://www.asam.org

Center for Substance Abuse Prevention (CSAP)
5600 Fishers Lane, Rockville, II
Rockville, MD 20857
(301)443-0365
http://www.samhsa.gov/csap

Join Together
441 Stuart Street
Boston, MA 02116
(617)437-1500
http://www.jointogether.org

Mothers Against Drunk Driving (MADD)
P.O. Box 541688
Dallas, TX 75354-1688
1(800)GET-MADD
http://www.madd.org

National Clearinghouse for Alcohol and Drug Information (NCADI).
11426 Rockville Pike, Suite 200
Rockville, MD
1(800)487-4890
http://www.health.org

National Council on Alcoholism and Drug Dependence (NCADD)
12 West 21 Street
New York, NY 10010
(212)206-6770
http://www.ncadd.org

National Institute on Alcohol Abuse and Alcoholism (NIAAA)
6000 Executive Boulevard—Willco Building
Bethesda, MD 20892-7003
http://www.niaaa.nih.gov

National Institute on Drug Abuse (NIDA)
6001 Executive Blvd
Bethesda, MD 20892-9561
(301)443-1124
http://www.nida.nih.gov/NIDAHome1.html

National Institutes of Health (NIH)
Bethesda, MD 20892
http://www.nih.gov

SMART Recovery—Self Management and Recovery Training
Mercantile Road, Suite 11
Beachwood, OH 44122
(216)292-0220
http://www.smartrecovery.org

Substance Abuse and Mental Health Services Administration (SAMHSA)
Room 12, 105 Parklawn Building
5600 Fishers Lane
Rockville, MD 20857
http://www.samhsa.gov

Chapter 9

ADOLESCENTS AND EATING DISORDERS

By

Gina Scarano-Osika, *Ph.D.*
Kathleen Maloney, *M.A.*

Eating disorders or what can more accurately be described as eating-disordered behaviors have received increasing attention in recent years. These deficits in eating behavior are highly enmeshed with a preoccupation with body weight; these deficits simultaneously coexist with distorted concepts of body image. Points or questions, for example, that most often occur to counseling practitioners or clinicians who work with clients with eating disorders are twofold. First, why the individual affected cannot develop a reliable picture of body image or weight, and second, why the individual cannot develop an accurate forecast of the consequences of poor or inadequate nutrition. Answers down the road may come from the research emanating from the study of human genetics (e.g. the Human Genome Project); hopefully, from this research will come a better understanding of how the anatomy of the brain and the interaction of neurochemicals in the brain can affect the individual's cognitive processes (e.g., as they relate to eating-disordered behavior and body image). This information has the potential to supply answers to questions that have perplexed practitioners in this field for years. Mizes (1995) and Kauffman (2005) believed that a genetic predisposition to eating disorders exists and that this view is being increasingly recognized by researchers; moreover, environmental triggers (e.g., in the social-cultural environment) are where early dysfunctional eating patterns are likely to be developed and maintained. For now, however, eating-disordered behavior is an area for the counseling practitioner or clinician that is still evolving. We have relatively little understanding of the actual causes or effective treatments, especially when the onset of these disorders is in the childhood years (Lask & Bryant-Waugh, 1993). What is important is that eating-disordered behavior and preoccupation with weight gain are becoming more and more common, among younger and younger children. Indeed, in some of these cases, eating disorders have the potential for a fatal consequence. What follows in this chapter are pertinent topics to help you gain a better understanding of eating disorders and to enhance your knowledge regarding appropriate treatment methods. Other areas of discussion include diagnosis and prevalence, the diagnostic features contained in the *DSM-IV-TR*, an outline of comorbid conditions, methods of assessment, causal factors, implications for practice and treatment, school and public perspectives, and a case illustration.

DIAGNOSIS AND PREVALENCE

Eating disorders are characterized by deviant eating behaviors designed to alter body composition. The most commonly recognized eating disorders are anorexia nervosa and bulimia nervosa. Anorexia nervosa is defined as a condition in which the patient insists on maintaining a low body weight, at least 15% below what is expected given an individual's age and height. Bulimia nervosa is characterized by episodes of excessive overeating (binges), followed by self-induced vomiting, excessive use of laxatives, or other purgative behaviors. Pathological thoughts and emotions concerning the control of body weight and shape are an essential feature in both of these related disorders. Bulimia nervosa and anorexia nervosa are psychiatric disorders characterized by a preoccupation with weight, food intake, and body image. The *DSM-IV-TR* (American Psychiatric Association, 2000a) identifies both anorexia nervosa and bulimia nervosa in a category titled "Eating Disorders."

Diagnostic Features

Bulimia Nervosa   Three main clinical features characterize bulimia nervosa. The keystone behavior of bulimia nervosa is binge eating. Bingeing is defined as the consumption of large amounts of food that most people would not eat under similar circumstances. This excessive amount of eating is accompanied by a feeling of loss of control. The individual attempts to compensate for these episodes with purgative behaviors, which is the second feature of bulimia nervosa. These include techniques such as self-induced vomiting, laxative abuse, diuretic abuse, stimulant abuse, rigorous dieting or fasting, or vigorous exercise. The third criteria required for the diagnosis of bulimia nervosa is a self-evaluation that is unduly influenced by body shape and weight. Weight regulation and evaluation of one's body are important factors in determining self-esteem in bulimic individuals. To qualify for the diagnosis of bulimia nervosa, binge eating and purging behaviors must be present an average of at least twice weekly for 3 months. The *DSM-IV-TR* diagnostic criteria for bulimia nervosa are listed in Table 9.1. As you can see, the *DSM-IV-TR* further subtypes bulimia nervosa into purging and non-purging types. The purging subtype distinguishes those who engage in self-induced vomiting or the misuse of laxatives or diuretics, while the non-purging subtype refers to those individuals who use alternative compensatory behaviors such as excessive fasting or exercise. Approximately two-thirds of individuals diagnosed with bulimia nervosa are of the purging type, while the remaining one-third is subtype non-purging (Hsu, 1990).

TABLE 9.1   *DSM-IV-TR* Diagnostic Criteria for Bulimia Nervosa

A.   Recurrent episodes of binge eating. An episode of binge eating is characterized by both of the following:

     (1)   eating in a discrete period of time (e.g., within any 2 hour period, an amount of food that is definitely larger than most people would eat in a similar period of time in similar circumstances; and,

     (2)   a sense of lack of control over eating during the episode (e.g., a feeling that one cannot stop eating or control what or how much one is eating).

B.   Recurrent inappropriate compensatory behavior in order to prevent weight gain, such as: self-induced vomiting; misuse of laxatives, diuretics or other medications; fasting; or excessive exercise.

C.   The binge eating and inappropriate compensatory behaviors both occur, on average, at least twice a week for 3 months.

D.   Self-evaluation is unduly influenced by body shape and weight.

E.   The disturbance does not occur exclusively during episodes of Anorexia Nervosa

Specify type:

     Purging type: The person regularly engages in self-induced vomiting or the misuse of laxatives or diuretics.
     Non-purging type: The person uses other inappropriate compensatory behaviors, such as fasting or excessive exercise, but does not regularly engage in self-induced vomiting or the misuse of laxatives or diuretics.

Reprinted with permission from the *Diagnostic and Statistical Manual of Mental Disorders,* Fourth Edition, Text Revision. Copyright 2000 American Psychiatric Association.

Anorexia Nervosa   The *DSM-IV-TR* diagnostic criteria for anorexia nervosa are listed in Table 9.2 and, as you can see, three main features define it. The first criteria is the presence of a body weight that is 15% below what is expected with no known medical conditions accountable for weight loss. The second feature is an intense fear of gaining weight. The third criterion is a marked disturbance in body image, or the misperception of the shape or size of one's body. Additionally, in postmenarcheal females, an absence of three consecutive menstrual cycles is required for the diagnosis. The *DSM-IV-TR* distinguishes that in children and adolescents, a failure to meet expected normal weight gains may substitute for the criteria of weight loss. The *DSM-IV-TR* further subtypes anorexia nervosa into binge-eating/purging and restricting types. The restricting type refers to individuals who limit food intake, while the binge-eating/purging type refers to individuals who rely on purgative behaviors. The binge-eating/purging subtype of anorexia is distinct from bulimia nervosa in that the anorexic binges on relatively small amounts of food and purges on a more consistent basis. Also, for anorexics there is a weight criterion (e.g., anorexics must be 15% below normal weight, whereas bulimics can be of normal weight or overweight). Research examining prevalence rates of these subtypes indicates that half of the individuals diagnosed with anorexia nervosa engage in binge eating and purging. In perhaps 10% of these cases, the end result of this self-starvation is death.

Eating Disorder Not Otherwise Specified   The *DSM-IV-TR* also recognizes a third category of eating disturbances, which are described as those "Not Otherwise Specified." This category is relatively new and is slowly gaining recognition in the

TABLE 9.2   *DSM-IV-TR* Diagnostic Criteria for Anorexia Nervosa

A.   Refusal to maintain body weight at or above a minimally normal weight for age and height (e.g., weight loss leading to maintenance of body weight less than 85% of that expected; or failure to make expected weight gain during period of growth, leading to body weight less than 85% of that

B.   Intense fear of gaining weight or becoming fat, even though underweight.

C.   Disturbance in the way in which one's body weight or shape is experienced, undue influence of body weight or shape on self-evaluation, or denial of the seriousness of the current low body weight.

D.   In postmenarcheal females, amenorrhea, i.e., the absence of at least three consecutive menstrual cycles. (A woman is considered to have amenorrhea if her periods occur only following hormone, e.g., estrogen administration.)

Specify type:

Restricting Type: during the current episode of Anorexia Nervosa, the person has not regularly engaged in binge-eating or purging behavior (i.e., self-induced vomiting or the misuse of laxatives, diuretics, or enemas)

Binge-Eating/Purging Type: during the current episode of Anorexia Nervosa, the person has regularly engaged in binge-eating or purging behavior (i.e., self-induced vomiting or the misuse of laxatives, diuretics, or enemas)

Reprinted with permission from the *Diagnostic and Statistical Manual of Mental Disorders,* Fourth Edition, Text Revision. Copyright 2000 American Psychiatric Association.

research and practice of psychology (Rodin, Silberstein, & Striegel-Moore, 1985; Scarano-Kalodner-Martin, 1994). Researchers have coined the term *subclinical* or *nonspecific* eating disorders to describe a few of the disorders that fall into this category (Scarano & Kalodner-Martin, 1994). According to the *DSM-IV-TR*, this category includes those eating disordered behaviors which are not sufficient (in duration or frequency) to meet the criteria for bulimia or anorexia. Examples include Binge Eating Disorder (BED), which describes a person who engages in uncontrollable bouts of overeating but does not engage in the compensatory behaviors such as vomiting, laxative use, diuretics, or dieting to control weight. Chronic dieters are another group of subclinical eating disorders and are described as those who chronically restrict calories or fat in order to lose weight. Purgers are those who self-induce vomiting after eating only a small amount of food, without engaging in binge eating. Subclinical bulimics are those who engage in binge eating and compensatory behaviors, but less than two times per week.

POPULATION AND PREVALENCE

Eating disorders occur primarily in females, and adolescence is a major risk period for the development of these disorders. Age of onset for eating disorders is typically 16 to 19 years of age (Garfinkel, Lin, Goering, & Spegg, 1995). Research examining the prevalence of anorexia nervosa reports that 1% of adolescents and young women meet full criteria for the disorder. The prevalence of bulimia nervosa in adolescent girls is estimated to be 1% to 3% (Fairburn & Beglin, 1990). Limited data are available concerning the prevalence of eating disorders in males, although estimates of its occurrence are stated to be approximately 20:1 to 15:1 of that in females (Gettelman & Thompson, 1993). Epidemiological studies report that 5% of adolescent girls meet *DSM-IV-TR* criteria for eating disorders, and an additional 18–46% of this population demonstrate non-specific or sub-clinical levels of these disorders (Lifshitz & Moses, 1988; Mellin, Irwin, & Scully, 1992). More specifically, research indicates that approximately 40 to 60% of adolescent girls in the United States diet to lose weight, using a variety of dangerous weight loss methods (Mintz & Betz, 1988). Moreover, epidemiological studies report that about 13% of adolescents induce vomiting, or inappropriately use diet pills, laxatives, or diuretics. Lifshitz and Moses (1988) reported that in an investigation surveying 798 teenage girls, 39% of the sample were dieting to lose weight, 27% reported uncontrollable eating binges, 8% had impulses to vomit after meals, and 3% stated that they engaged in vomiting behavior to control their body weight. Current research shows that the prevalence of eating disturbances in adolescence has increased dramatically over the last 50 years. While the incidence rate for eating disorders in adult women has, for the most part, remained constant, in recent years there has been a significant increase in females 15–24 years old with eating disordered behavior (Killen, Taylor, Telch, Saylor, Maron, & Robinson, 1987; Patton, 1988). Certainly, a claim can be made that when specific and subclinical levels of eating pathology are taken into account, there exists an epidemic of eating disorders among young adult women (Kalodner & Scarano, 1992; Mintz & Betz, 1988). These prevalence rates are alarming, especially when we consider that eating disordered behavior places females at higher risk for other physical ailments and co-occurring psychopathology.

EATING DISORDERS IN MALES

Information about eating disorders in males has been long awaited by many. Do the symptoms manifest themselves differently? Are men influenced by thinness standards or do they feel pressure to look masculine, muscular, and strong? These are all questions which have been the focus of very recent research studies (see McCreary, Saucier, & Courtenay, 2005; Morrison, Morrison, & Hopkins, 2003; Olivardia, Pope, Borowiecki, & Cochrane, 2004; Ridgeway & Tylka, 2005; Smolak, Murnen, & Thompson, 2005). Although eating disorders are much more common in females, there is growing evidence that males also suffer from these disorders. Research suggests that about 10% of eating-disordered individuals coming to the attention of mental health professionals are male (American Psychiatric Association, 2000a; Wolf, 1991; Fairburn & Beglin, 1990).

While statistically there is a large difference between male and females presenting with eating disorders, there is some consensus that eating disorders in males are clinically similar to eating disorders in females (Margo, 1987; Schneider & Agras, 1987). Similar to females, the age of onset for boys appears to be puberty and influences from the media, peer comparisons, and parents appear to be contributing factors (Smolak, Murnen & Thompson, 2005). Further, Ricciardelli and McCabe (2004) found that among boys (as is with girls), disordered eating behaviors were associated with Body Mass Index, a fear of obesity, negative affect, self-esteem, and perfectionism. Older studies have documented the presence of both Anorexia and Bulimia among samples of males (Anderson & Mickalide, 1983; Andersen & Holman, 1997; Schneider & Agras, 1987). Like girls, boys appear to feel added pressures from their participation in sports, especially sports which demand a specific weight class or body image (i.e., wrestling, swimmers, runners; Ricciardelli and McCabe, 2004). For both males and females, body dissatisfaction appears to spawn from unhealthy media images and stringent societal standards for body shape. There are several risk factors identified, which have been shown to increase vulnerability to eating disorders among males. Males who have been previously obese seem more likely to develop eating disorders. Additionally, males in occupations which encourage a weight class or a lean body image are particularly vulnerable to eating disorders. Consistent with this, males have been shown to demonstrate higher levels and more frequently use excessive and obsessive exercise and body building prior to and during their eating disorder.

Research has also been presented which suggests that a disproportionate amount of males with anorexia may have persisting or preexisting problems in testosterone production (Anderson & Mickalide, 1983). These findings are consistent with research, which indicates homosexual males are over-represented in many samples of eating disordered men. While the proportion of male homosexuals in the general population cross-culturally is estimated to be 3–5% (Whitman, 1983), samples of eating-disordered men are commonly twice as high or greater (Fichter & Daser, 1987). Several authors have also noted that homosexual conflict preceded the onset of an eating disorder in up to 50% of male patients (Scott, 1986; Dally, 1969). Homosexual males may be at an increased risk for developing an eating disorder because of cultural pressures within the homosexual community to be thin (Schneider & Agras, 1987). Herzog, Keller, Strober, & Yeh (1992) found that homosexual men weighed significantly less than heterosexual men, were more likely to be underweight and to desire an underweight ideal weight. Compared to the heterosexuals, homosexual men were less satisfied with their body build and scored significantly higher on the "Drive for Thinness" scale of the Eating Disorders Inventory (EDI), which is consistent with clinical reports which suggest eating disorders are associated with individuals who have issues relating to gender identity and also a high prevalence among homosexual males (Herzog, Norman, Gordon, & Pepose, 1984).

In general, these disorders are very similar in males and females. However, while the signs and symptoms of eating disorders between these two populations are similar, it is not clear regarding the best treatment for eating problems in males at this time. Both because men are less likely to seek treatment for eating disorders (which have the social stigma of being a "female problem") and because of the low base rate of males with eating disorders, treatment research is scarce. However, it is essential to recognize that the problem does occur and to recognize the importance of providing psychological and health services to males battling eating disorders.

Growth, Hormonal Disturbance, and Infertility

For the majority who develop eating disorders, onset occurs during the period of adolescent growth and maturation. As such, eating disorders carry profound hazards for interrupting somatic and physiological development (Lifshitz & Moses, 1988), especially in females. Semistarvation in prepubescent girls might delay menarche and minimize stature and breast development (Russell, 1985). Dieting and weight loss affect body hormones, resulting in irregular or absent menstruation, even when body fat is adequate. At least 17% of body weight needs to be fatty tissue in order to begin menstruating during puberty, and at least 22% must be fat to maintain regular menstrual cycles (Rintala & Mustajoki, 1992). Although the connection between eating-disordered behavior and infertility is not as well documented, it is worthy of mentioning. Women with either a history of anorexia or who were actively anorexic at the time of conception were more likely to have birthing complications or give birth to babies of low birth weight (American Psychiatric Association, 2000a). Of 29 "infertile" chronic dieters, 26 gained a sufficient amount of weight to approach their healthy weight, and 19 of these 26 immediately became pregnant without the use of infertility procedures (Bates, Bates, & Whitworth, 1982). Three would not accept the idea that dieting could be responsible for their infertility problems (Bates et al., 1982). This connection, however, remains in need of further research; nonetheless, for females, growth, hormonal disturbance, and infertility can portend consequences across the lifespan.

Obesity

Many with Binge Eating Disorder (BED) will understandably be overweight since they are not engaging in compensatory behaviors after binge eating. Although this is not always the case, BED occurs in 50% of the obese (Fairburn, 1995). Dieting has been a trigger to binge eating and can subsequently result in obesity. This is especially true for those fad diets or diets which unrealistically restrict the type or amount of food eaten. In the case of severe food restriction, a state of physiological and psychological deprivation results which sets the stage for binge eating. Also, chronic dieting and calorie restriction results in a lowered metabolic rate, which makes weight gain effortless. That is why "yo-yo dieting" (repeatedly going on and off diets) is counterproductive. Yet the obese are likely to be more desperate to lose weight and utilize these futile methods of weight loss.

Medical Complications and Fatalities

Self-induced vomiting abuse of laxatives, diuretics, and enemas may produce fluid and electrolyte imbalances, leading to serious medical complications and death. Other general medical conditions associated with malnutrition and purgative behaviors in eating disorders include the development of impaired renal function, cardiovascular problems, dental problems, and osteoporosis. For those who binge eat, tearing and stretching of the stomach wall can lead to severe abdominal pain and internal bleeding. Labored breathing can also result from an over-stretched and full stomach pressing on the diaphragm. For those patients whose weight is dangerously low, mortality rates are drastically increased. While most individuals with Bulimia Nervosa are within the normal weight range, those diagnosed with Anorexia Nervosa are often grossly underweight. In general, the incidence of death increases 12-fold in women aged 15–24 with eating disorders, with the mortality rate reaching 10–15% for anorexics (American Psychiatric Association, 2000a; Sullivan, 1995). Further, 66% of anorexics in treatment had a prognosis rated, at best, as poor, with 5% of these cases ending in fatalities (American Psychiatric Association, 2000a). Repeat vomiting also causes damage to the teeth, swelling of the salivary glands, inflammation or infections of the throat, and bleeding or tearing of the esophagus. Russell's sign are the abrasions or scarring on the hands of those who self-induce vomiting via their fingers. Chronic laxative abuse can result in permanent damage to the intestines.

Psychiatric Disorders

In addition to physiological conditions, other psychiatric conditions can co-exist with eating disordered behavior (American Psychiatric Association, 2000a). For example, there is an uncanny similarity between the diagnostic criteria for eating disordered behavior and depression. As you review the diagnostic criteria for Bulimia and Anorexia, you will note that the criteria for a depressive episode include low self-esteem and an increase or decrease in appetite. In fact, depression is one of the most common comorbid disorders (APA, 2000a) and may even predate the eating disorder. In this scenario, the client develops either a loss of appetite or an increase in appetite, which leads to a respective weight loss or gain. Since most females have a propensity to be weight conscious, this weight loss or gain may put in motion other characteristics of eating-disordered behavior. For example, a female who gains weight because of a depressive disorder may feel overly guilty about the weight gain and then turn to unhealthy practices to lose the weight. Or the female who is depressed and experiences a loss of appetite may find that this weight loss boosts her self-esteem and temporarily "cures" her depression, thus becoming more addicted to weight loss practices. Again, be aware that this association is based more on clinical observation, rather than on research data.

Other comorbid conditions would be the class of anxiety disorders. For example, Obsessive Compulsive Disorder (OCD) is characterized by persistent and rigidly held beliefs that may or may not result in repetitive behaviors to reduce feelings of fear and anxiety. This trend can be seen in eating-disordered women who hold rigid and perfectionistic beliefs about eating and weight, which make them feel anxious and fearful of gaining weight. In turn, these feelings of anxiety are temporarily soothed by engaging in ritualistic and repetitive behaviors (e.g., purging) to lose weight and reduce the fear of gaining weight. Also, the fear of gaining weight can be conceptualized as similar to Body Dysmorphic Disorder.

In adult women, a case can be made that personality disorders are a common co-occuring condition with eating-related difficulties, with such diagnosis co-occurring in 42 to 75% of eating-disordered females (American Psychiatric Association, 2000a). Common examples include Obsessive Compulsive Personality Disorder, Borderline Personality Disorder, and Dependent Personality Disorder. One study directly observed a higher incidence of codependency among college-aged eating-disordered females which points to this possibility (Meyer & Russell, 1998). These researchers found that college-aged females were beginning to develop a lack of internal awareness and social insecurity that hypothetically predisposed them to internalizing strict standards of thinness from the media or unsupportive significant others. It is important to remember that it is rarely ever appropriate to diagnose a young woman with personality pathology, but these researchers highlight the importance of considering pathological personality traits, rather than a full-blown personality disorder, when establishing diagnosis and treatment plans with adolescent eating-disordered women.

Because one of the diagnostic criteria for Borderline Personality pathology is self-mutative behavior, which in addition to drug abuse and superficial cutting can include self-induced vomiting, self-starvation, addictive exercise, and abuse of laxatives or diuretics to lose weight, the comorbidity of Borderline Personality traits and eating disorders is common. This is best documented by the increased incidence of drug and substance abuse among women with eating disorders. Substance abuse has been found to exist in as many as 30% to 37% of patients with Bulimia and 12% to 18% of women with Anorexia (American Psychiatric Association, 2000a). With some eating-disordered clients, inquiry into the psychogenic reasons for their behavior reveals that the behavior is not only a way to lose weight by extreme denial of nutrition, but also a way to abuse oneself and cause self-harm. Again, this hypothesis is not empirically based, so obviously, much research is needed in this area; however, counseling practitioners or clinicians should be cognizant of these possible co-occurring conditions.

METHODS AND PROCEDURES OF ASSESSMENT

Although there is a proliferation of assessment measures established for evaluating eating disorders, their assessment remains a complex area of clinical activity due to the presentation of a mix of disturbances in a range of domains. Moreover, assessment of eating disorders in adolescents poses particular difficulty. For example, assessment measures in this area are primarily developed for use with adult populations, and psychometric properties are often not available for younger populations. Following is a review of the more commonly used eating-disorder-assessment measures. Please note that very few self-report instruments provide normative data for adolescent or child populations, and even fewer have been designed specifically for use with either of these populations.

Clinical Interviews

The Eating Disorder Examination (EDE)   The structured clinical interview is among the most widely used means of assessing eating disorders. While there are a number of clinical interviews available that vary widely in their structure, the most widely recognized is the Eating Disorders Examination (Fairburn and Cooper, 1993). This structured clinical interview is designed to assess for the specific psychopathology of eating disorders. The EDE provides the practitioner with a complete clinical picture of the patient's behaviors and attitudes regarding eating through a detailed analysis of caloric intake, food preoccupation, skipping meals, food avoidance, and relationship to self-imposed dietary rules. The EDE provides a comprehensive evaluation of the diagnostic criteria of all eating disorders, and provides a depth and breadth of assessment that is unmatched by other assessment measures. This instrument is especially useful in determining the difference between overeating and binge eating episodes.

The Structured Clinical Interview for *DSM-IV* Disorders (SCID)   The eating disorders section of the Structured Clinical Interview for *DSM-IV* disorders is another measure providing a comprehensive assessment for evaluating the symptoms of Anorexia and Bulimia Nervosa (Segal, Hersen, & VanHasselt, 1994). While clinical interviews provide a comprehensive assessment of eating disorders, disadvantages include length of administration, training required to administer interview, and the intrusive quality of investigator-based interviews (Fairburn & Beglin, 1994). Confessing behaviors such as binge eating and self-induced vomiting can be embarrassing for individuals and may create response biases. For these reasons supplementary methods of assessment are often desirable.

Self-Report Questionnaires

Eating Disorders Inventory 2 (EDI-2)   A number of self-report questionnaires have been developed to assess the specific psychopathology of eating disorders. One of the more widely used measures is the Eating Disorders inventory (EDI-2; Garner, 1991). The EDI-2 has well-established reliability and validity and provides a broad-based assessment of both psychological and behavioral features common to Anorexia Nervosa and Bulimia Nervosa. Although this measure does not provide specific information required to assign a diagnosis, it does provide the clinician with important information regarding treatment planning and tracking patient improvement and outcome. Normative data for the Eating Disorders Inventory has been collected with adolescent populations, in which the psychometric characteristics are reported to be similar to those obtained with adults (Shore & Porter, 1990).

Eating Attitudes Test (EAT)   Another self-report questionnaire, the Eating Attitudes Test (EAT; Garner & Garfinkel, 1979) is a 40-item questionnaire that assesses a variety of attitudes and behaviors associated with Anorexia Nervosa and Bulimia Nervosa. The EAT is one of the most widely used self-report measures in assessing eating patterns. The Child Eating Attitudes Test (Maloney, McGuire, & Daniels,

1988) is a 25-item version of the EAT that is applicable to school-aged children for assessing symptoms associated with eating disorders.

Body Satisfaction Scale   The Body Satisfaction Scale (BSS; Slade, Dewey, Newton, & Brodie, 1990) is a simple paper-and-pencil test designed to measure satisfaction/dissatisfaction with 16 body parts. The BSS takes only 2 to 3 minutes to complete and provides three summative scales (general, head parts, and body parts dissatisfaction). The psychometric properties of the scales are excellent.

Kids' Eating Disorder Survey   The Kids' Eating Disorder Survey (KEDS; Childress, Jarrell, & Brewerton, 1993) is a 14-item self-report questionnaire on eating disorders pathology. The KEDS identifies predictors of weight dissatisfaction and purging behavior in children. The survey is comprised of questions derived from the Eating Symptoms Inventory and eight child-figure drawings. The KEDS is an excellent tool to administer to children in the screening for and prevention of eating disorders, demonstrating high levels of internal consistency and reliability.

Three additional measures assessing behaviors associated with eating disorders are available. The Three Factor Eating Questionnaire (TFEQ; Stunkard & Messick, 1985) is a 51-item, self-report measure that assesses levels of dietary restraint across the three subscales of cognitive restraint, disinhibition of eating, and perceived hunger. The TFEQ provides a useful assessment measure for the clinician to monitor behaviors of dietary restraint. The revised Restraint Scale also provides a psychometrically sound measure of dietary restraint (Herman, Polivy, Pliner, & Threlkeld, 1978). The Body Shape Questionnaire (BSQ; Cooper, Taylor, Cooper, & Fairburn, 1987) provides a specific measure of attitudes regarding body shape and weight, which are central features of both Anorexia Nervosa and Bulimia Nervosa.

Self-Monitoring

Self-monitoring provides for a valuable and unique method of assessment in eating disorders. This form of assessment is typically conducted by having patients record their eating behaviors and attitudes on weekly monitoring sheets. However, others, including parents and peers, can extend monitoring to include observations. In addition, self-monitoring can provide information regarding the context in which these behaviors occur and what circumstances preceded the episode, providing clues to the clinician of both the subjective and objective context. Although this technique does contain potential obstacles concerning consistency and accuracy, an explanation regarding the purpose and significance of the process can help to alleviate potential problems.

CAUSAL FACTORS AND TREATMENT OUTCOMES: EMPIRICAL STUDIES

Theories addressing the development of eating disorders are relatively new, with most contributing their works in the last third of the 20th century. For example, Bruch (1969) was one of the first to state that eating-disordered women might have a deficit in self-awareness. Other early postulates pointed to the role of dysfunctional family interaction in maintaining eating-disordered symptoms (Bruch, 1973; Selvini-Palazzoli, 1974). Crisp (1980) was one of the first to pinpoint the adolescent period as a modal point of body dissatisfaction and eating disorders. Not surprisingly, many aspects of some classical theories have remained supported by recent research. What follows is a summary of the traits and factors that have repeatedly been deemed as causal factors in the development of eating disorders and weight concerns.

Family Relationships

Researchers have postulated that families of eating-disordered women are wrought with relationship and communication difficulties (Friedlander & Siegel, 1990; Heesacker & Neimeyer, 1990; Sharpe, Killen, Bryson, Shisslak, Estes, Gray, Crago, & Taylor, 1998; Smolack & Levine, 1993). In fact, family dysfunction was deemed the strongest correlate of disturbed eating behavior among adolescent females (Sharpe, et al., 1998). More specifically, despite having similar levels of body shape distortion, insecurely attached adolescent females reported significantly higher weight concerns, lower self-esteem, and a greater sense of rejection from others as compared to securely attached females (Sharpe et al., 1998). Researchers have also pointed to disturbed family relationships as being a variable that predicts poor treatment outcome and higher relapse rates (Hsu, 1991; Strober, Freeman, & Morrell, 1997). As you will see, myriad family dynamics are common to eating-disordered women (Humphrey, 1989; Kog & Vandereycken, 1989; Scalf-McIver & Thompson, 1989).

Eating-disordered behaviors have been associated with poor self–other differentiation, insecure attachment, social incompetence, and overresponsibility (Friedlander & Siegel, 1990; Heesacker & Neimeyer, 1990; Smolack & Levine, 1993). Families of bulimic females are characterized by hostile enmeshment (inability to distinguish between self and others), nonnurturance, emotional unresponsiveness, conflictual dependence on parents, and excessive guilt, mistrust, and resentment (Humphrey, 1989; Scalf-McIver & Thompson, 1989; Smolack & Levine, 1993). Among adolescent females, Humphrey (1986) reported that Bulimics not only felt negatively about their bodies, but also felt negatively about themselves and their relationships with their parents. More specifically, they felt deprived of nurturance and empathy and felt abused and neglected by both parents. Families of eating-disordered females were also described as discussing disagreements less openly, having poor communication skills, being unresponsive to their children, and having deficits in conflict-resolution skills (Kog & Vandereycken, 1989; Maharaj, Rodin, Olmsted, & Daneman, 1998). Further, the overall family environments were perceived to be conflictual and inadequate in support and structure (Kog & Vandereycken, 1989; Maharaj, et al., 1998). These researchers suggest that separation individuation problems (difficulty being an adult person with distinct needs, wants, and desires) emerge as a result of pervasive disturbances in family dynamics and suppressed affective expression (Armstrong & Roth, 1989; Friedlander & Siegel, 1990; Heesacker & Neimeyer, 1990; Strober & Humphrey, 1987). These family characteristics consequently reduce the child's ability to cope with adult relationships.

Codependency is a term that initially emerged from the addictions literature to describe people whose lives have become unmanageable as a result of being involved with someone who is chemically dependent (Beattie, 1988). Recently, the term has expanded beyond the addictions literature to include any person who has worry or concern for others at the expense of their own needs, thoughts, and feelings (Meyer & Russell, 1998). Consequently, codependent people are obsessed with managing the behaviors of others and can be equated with women who adopt the traditionally female sex-role stereotype. Spann and Fischer (1990) described codependency as an "extreme focus outside of oneself, a lack of open expression of feelings, and an attempt to derive a sense of purpose through relationships." Similar to other researchers (Cowan, Bommersbach, & Curtis, 1995; Cowan & Warren, 1994), Wright and Wright (1990) sought to empirically support this theoretical concept and found that women deemed to be codependent experienced less emotional expression, higher control needs, greater feelings of responsibility, and a higher tendency to evaluate personal self-worth on the basis of their partners' opinions. Fischer and Crawford (1992) reported higher codependency scores among women whose fathers were perceived as demonstrating a parental style characterized by high control and low support.

Only one study has questioned a dependent relationship style as being a factor in the development of eating disorders (Meyer & Russell, 1998). Among college eating-disordered women, results of two multivariate analyses indicated that codependency was associated with greater amounts of eating-disorder symptomology and less psychological separation from parents. Further, results of a regression analysis indicated that separation from parents predicted a lack of interoceptive awareness (see Bruch, 1969) and social insecurity. Similar claims have been made by others (Streigel-Moore, 1993), who state that young women are particularly vulnerable to the opinions of others. They state that "girls who feel insecure about their identity, or how they are valued by others, may focus on physical appearance because such a focus provides a concrete way to construct identity." The vicious cycle of low self-esteem begins as young girls become aware that the beauty ideal is unattainable because their physical maturation takes them further and further away from that goal. These authors then claim that body disturbances and eating disorders might evolve as a result of females being more reliant on acceptance from others (e.g., peers, parents, society, the media) rather than on an internal sense of self-satisfaction. Further, they suggest that adolescent females might be more prone to idealize or internalize the values and standards of their peers or the media when they lack a supportive family environment (Sharpe et al., 1998). In summary, adolescents may develop a codependent interpersonal style; they learn, for example, that a lack of warmth and emotional insecurity are typical of both familial and nonfamilial relationships. Poor communication skills, conflict avoidance, nonnurturance, and emotional neglect seem to make it difficult for eating-disordered women to develop a secure sense of self, thus making them more likely to internalize or idealize societal or peer values, especially in regard to thinness. Thinness, unfortunately, might be mistaken for developing a sense of self and seemingly a correct way to regain lost or damaged self-esteem.

Sociocultural Factors and Body Image Disturbance

Although the incidence of eating disorders is increasing diversity in ethnic and socioeconomic groups, these disturbances are presently more prevalent in Western, industrialized countries of white ethnicity and in middle- and upper-class females. Research has shown that an overall correlation exists between the cultural expectations of thinness and the prevalence of eating disorders across populations (Striegel-Moore, McAvay, & Rodin, 1986). The relationship between social class and pressures to attain a thin body ideal suggests that sociocultural influences play an important role in mediating concerns about shape and weight. It is suggested that the increase of prevalence in the younger population and in specific social classes is representative of the impact of popular-culture images, which play a significant role in determining the disorder in these populations (Garfinkel & Garner, 1982; Fallon & Rozin, 1985).

The influence of the popular culture schema in characterizing women's idealized bodies as thin and slender has put considerable pressure on females to conform to this physical standard (Striegel-Moore, Silberstein, & Rodin, 1986). The vulnerability of younger individuals to these cultural pressures is suggested to be largely responsible for the high rates of dieting in young women and the increasing incidence rates of eating disorders in adolescent females. Eating-disordered behavior has recently been correlated within societies that have a stringent standard for thinness (Lucas, Beard, O'Fallon, & Kolind, 1991). For example, Lucas, et al. (1991) performed a population-based incidence study of Anorexia over the 50-year span from 1935 to 1984. They found that the base rate of Anorexia increased from 7 per 100,000 in 1950–1954 to 26 per 100,000 in 1980–1984, a time that parallels when the media began portraying models as thinner. Similarly, the incidence of eating disorders is higher among samples of dancers, models, and athletes, where the expectation to be thin is more pronounced (Garner & Garfinkel, 1980). Furnham and Manning (1997) found that of 147 males and females between the ages of 16 and 19, a majority indicated that social pressures and the media were factors that they believed to be most important in causing eating-disordered behavior. Levine, Smolack, Moodey, Shuman, & Hessen (1994) found two factors were correlates of dieting behavior among middle-school females: 1) exposure to the dieting habits of their adolescent peers or mothers; and 2) perceived parental pressure to be slender. It seems as though young females who feel insecurely attached and emotionally neglected by the family are more susceptible to the media's standards for thinness and are expected to maintain those unrealistic standards by their nonnurturing parents, which in turn contributes to a perception that they are overweight (i.e., body image distortion).

Body image distortion is a perceptual distortion in which one inaccurately perceives him- or herself as larger than he or she actually is. Body image distortion understandably has been documented to result in low body esteem and eating disturbances (Eisele, Hertsgaard, & Light, 1986; Fabian & Thompson, 1989). Eisele and colleagues (1986) found that although 81% of adolescent females in their sample were within normal weight, 78% preferred to weigh less. Similar results have been found among other researchers (Halmi, Goldberg, & Cunningham, 1977; Leon, Fulkerson, Perry, & Cudeck, 1993). Further, in a well-controlled 2-year longitudinal study, Attie and Brooks-Gunn (1989) demonstrated that eating problems were more likely to develop among women who felt negatively about their bodies. Among 939 adolescent girls, eating-disordered symptoms were most likely among those who had significant weight concerns or were dissatisfied with body shape over a 3-year period (Killen, Taylor, Hayward, Wilson, Haydel, Hammer, Simmons, Robinson, Litt, Varady, & Kraemer, 1994). These results are consistent with researchers who have noted that the incidence of eating disorders has reached epidemic proportions, during a time in which the media portrays models that appear "waif-like" and gaunt. Others have pointed to the adolescent time period in which many females begin to feel dissatisfied with their body images as they begin to become shapely and loose their "boyish" figures.

Onset of Puberty

Puberty is a time when a variety of maturational and physiological changes occur for adolescent females. Scientific evidence supports a rapid accumulation of body fat for females during puberty, and that this event is, in fact, a "triggering event" that elicits first attempts at weight-loss diets. Although some researchers have refuted these results (Fabian & Thompson, 1989; Leon, et al., 1993), results of a well-controlled 2-year longitudinal study support this claim (Attie & Brooks-Gunn, 1989). Among 193 normal-weight, white, middle-school females, eating problems were most common for those females who had the highest body-fat index (Attie & Brooks-Gunn, 1989). Similarly, Levine, Smolack, Moodey, Shuman, and Hessen (1994) found that girls who had recently begun menstruating used more weight-management techniques than those who had not begun to menstruate. The most worrisome aspect of these results is that body dissatisfaction contributed to eating-disordered behavior among *normal-weight* females. During puberty, when normal increases in weight are present, the desire to lose weight or maintain a certain level of thinness is exacerbated. Increased levels of dissatisfaction in body image, fear of becoming fat, and a desire to lose weight might predispose adolescents toward the development of unhealthy weight-regulation practices.

In summary, it appears that females who recently accumulated body fat (as part of the natural maturational process) are at a higher risk of adhering to the unrealistic standards of thinness if they are not provided with support, a model of healthy eating attitudes, a positive view of both healthy mind and body, and reminders of the consequences of attempting to adhere to unrealistic standards of thinness. The psychodynamic theory of eating disorders takes this statement a step further and suggests that parental nonnurturance contributes to eating-disordered behavior in that the child or adolescent is likely inhibited from developing positive coping skills such as internal awareness and assertiveness.

Stress, Trauma, and Coping

Bruch (1969) was one of the first theorists to postulate that a poor awareness of needs and difficulty becoming aware of one's feelings (e.g., interoceptive awareness) during stressful times can be associated with eating-disordered behavior. *Alexithymia* is a similar term developed by Sifneos (1972) to describe difficulties in finding words to express feelings and a subsequent reliance on external factors rather than one's own internal thoughts and feelings. For example, among 937 adolescent females in the 7th through 10th grades, the strongest predictors of risk for eating-disordered behavior were body dissatisfaction, negative emotionality, a high degree of stress, and a lack of interoceptive awareness (Leon et al., 1993). A family history of depression, poor interoceptive awareness, and feelings of ineffectiveness significantly contributed to a predictive model of eating disorders (Lyon, Chatoor, Atkins, Silber, Mosimann, & Gray, 1997). These results are concerning given the high degree of stress associated with the period of adolescence. Also, tension and affect regulation describe one's capacity to relieve, modulate, and organize negative emotional states (Goodsitt, 1983).

A firm body of research states that eating disorders are more likely to emerge during adolescence due to the tremendous stress (e.g., increased achievement pressures, dating, and social conflict) that is typical of normal development (Attie & Brooks-Gunn, 1989; Fabian & Thompson, 1989; Fryer, Waller, & Stenfert-Kroese, 1997; Furnham & Manning, 1997; Levine, Smolack, Moodey, Shuman, & Hessen, 1994; Margo, 1985). For example, Margo (1985) found that 60% of eating-disordered women identified a major life event within the year prior to the onset of their eating disturbance. These events were classified as a real or threatened separation from a significant individual, a major life change, increased academic pressure, or interpersonal conflict. Others have indicated that emotion-focused coping (which results only in the control of negative affect), rather than solution-oriented skills, was directly associated with eating disturbances and lower self-esteem among adolescent females (Fryer et al., 1997). Levine and Smolack (1992) proposed a cumulative stressor model of eating disturbances that emphasizes three aspects of early adolescence: 1) weight gain associated with puberty; 2) the onset of dating; and 3) the intensification of academic demands. Among 382 middle-school females, for example, those who had begun menstruating and dating within the same year tended to engage in significantly more weight-management behavior than girls who had undergone only one of these changes. Coupled with their poor coping skills and inability to be aware of needs or feelings, it seems as though the stressors associated with normal development enhance the development of eating disturbances among adolescent females. These results are consistent with the psychoanalytic hypothesis of eating disorders, which suggests that eating-disordered women turn to food, rather than people or their own internal resources, to find nurturance and soothing during a stressful period. Among adult women, Smolack and Levine (1993) have noted that binge eating might be a method of self-soothing because seeking support from significant others cannot be relied on as a method to nurture their negative emotions.

Childhood sexual abuse has recently gained attention as a correlate of eating disturbances and body-image distortion (Bryant-Waugh & Lask, 1995; Connors & Morse, 1993; Everill & Waller, 1995; Wonderlich, Brewerton, Jocic, Dansky, & Abbott, 1997), but the inconsistent results have led to the conclusion that the relationship here is complex. The prevalence of sexual abuse among the general psychiatric population has been reported to be approximately 30%, which is not significantly different than the prevalence of sexual abuse among eating-disordered women (Connors & Morse, 1993; Steiger & Zanko, 1990). As a result of a meta-analysis of research conducted between 1987 and 1994, Wonderlich and colleagues (1997) stated that although childhood sexual abuse is not directly associated with greater eating-disorder severity, family variables, interpersonal skills, and the emotional reaction following a sexual trauma might mediate or influence this relationship. Child sexual abuse is neither necessary nor sufficient for the development of eating-disordered behavior; however, family systems that tolerate the perpetration of sexual abuse might have higher levels of addictive disorders, physical abuse, emotional neglect, or other psychiatric disorders (Connors & Morse, 1993).

Treatment Outcome Studies

One outcome study documents the effectiveness of a multimodal and intensive inpatient treatment program for adolescent Anorexia Nervosa at UCLA's Neuropsychiatric Institute (Strober, Freeman, & Morrell, 1997). Patients in this sample were 12 to 17 years of age at intake. During inpatient admissions, each patient received 14 hours of individual, group, or family therapy per week, dietary counseling, and high-intensity nursing management, and mealtimes were controlled to gradually increase the client's calorie intake to gain no less than 2 pounds per week. Patients were discharged when they gained 20 to 25% of their expected weight. After discharge, assessments were taken of these clients every 6 months, during which time all participated in some form of outpatient or partial-hospitalization program. Follow-up assessments were taken for 10 to 15 years after discharge from the hospital. Partial recovery was obtained by 86% of the sample. The mean time it took to partially recover was 57 months, whereas full recovery took 79 months. Factors that predicted poor outcomes or a chronic eating disorder included a compulsive drive to exercise and poor social skills. Another study assessed the outcome of an inpatient treatment program at Massachusetts General Hospital for eating-disordered adult women and found that the recovery rate for Bulimic women was 56%, whereas only 10% of anorexics reached full recovery. This study pointed to low body weight as a significant risk factor in the chronicity of eating disorders and suggests aggressive treatment with such women to prevent further weight loss or death (Herzog, Sacks, Keller, Lavori, VonRanson, & Gray, 1993).

What follows is a review of outcome studies completed on adult eating-disordered women to provide some information regarding those interventions, which have been empirically supported. Be aware that it is uncertain whether these interventions would be effective with adolescent females.

Many research studies have pointed to the success of Cognitive-Behavioral interventions in the treatment of Bulimia among adult women (Fairburn, Marcus, & Wilson, 1993; Whittal, Agras, & Gould, 1999). These writers claim that research over the past 15 years points to the combination of antidepressant medications and Cognitive-Behavioral treatment as being more effective than medication treatment alone, nondirective therapy, and psychodynamic therapy in treating adult women with Bulimia. Only one other type of treatment (i.e., interpersonal therapy) was as effective as Cognitive-Behavioral Therapy, but that was based on only one study (Fairburn, Jones, Peveler, Carr, Solomon, O'Connor, Burton, & Hope, 1991).

The components of Cognitive-Behavioral Therapy include exposure to feared foods, response prevention, normalization of food intake, cognitive restructuring, and relapse prevention (Fairburn et al., 1993; Whittal, et al., 1999). Exposure is a Cognitive-Behavioral intervention in which the client is exposed to feared foods in an attempt to confront the irrational thoughts and feelings associated with the food. For example, a client is instructed to imagine, look at, or ingest a feared food (e.g., french fries), after which the clinician asks what their beliefs are about the food and themselves. Response prevention is a behavioral intervention in which the client is actually prevented, via environmental control, from engaging in unhealthy eating practices after the forbidden food is ingested. Cognitive restructuring is a cognitive method to refute irrational beliefs about food and weight. This type of intervention also relies heavily on nutritional education to refute the strongly held beliefs that certain dangerous behaviors are productive at weight loss. Constantly reminding the client of the consequences and ineffectiveness of his or her current practices and of the benefits of a healthy and balanced diet is the goal here. Relapse prevention is a paradoxical way to discuss the prediction that relapse is inevitable and that it is unrealistic to expect that mistakes will not be made. This allows the client to be in a "win-win" situation in terms of her recovery: It is a positive thing if she doesn't relapse, but it is also positive if she does relapse because a great deal of useful information regarding triggers can be gained from it.

There is some overlap between eating disorders and those who also abuse psychoactive substances, but this relationship is uncertain at the current time (Fairburn, 1995; Wilson, 1993). Treatment implications for this nonempirical association are called The Myth of the Addiction Model because the addiction model of eating-disorders treatment is not supported by the facts (American Psychiatric Association, 2000a; Fairburn, 1993; Vandereycken, 1990). It is, unfortunately, the treatment of choice by some patients with eating-related disturbances, and a national organization called "Overeaters Anonymous" (OA) adheres to this treatment model. Please note that the OA model of eating-disorder treatment flies in the face of psychologically based treatment protocols in four major ways. The addictions model claims that: 1) There is no cure for eating disorders, which are described as a chronic illness; 2) immediate abstinence is paramount, and anything but that is less tolerated; 3) avoidance of "toxic" foods is a major strategy to healing; and 4) black-and-white thinking is encouraged regarding being abstinent or not and being out of or in control, and foods are or are not toxic. If a client enters treatment already involved in OA, it is the clinician's responsibility to educate him or her about how the treatment philosophies are different and a matter of personal choice.

As demonstrated, the effective treatment of eating disorders among adolescent females is not as well documented as it is among adults. Consequently, effective treatment relies heavily upon research regarding the psychological correlates of eating disorders and research regarding those interventions that is deemed as effective in treating adult eating-disordered women. For example, family dysfunction has been well documented as a correlate of eating pathology that is consistent with the effectiveness of Interpersonal Therapy (IPT) in the treatment of eating disorders (Fairburn, et al., 1991). However, no such study exists to document the effectiveness of IPT among adolescent eating-disordered females.

Similarly, Cognitive-Behavioral Therapy (CBT) is well known as an effective eating-disorder treatment among adult women (Whittal, et al., 1999), but no studies to date document CBT's effectiveness among adolescent eating-disordered women. Please keep this in mind when reading the following section.

IMPLICATIONS FOR PRACTICE/TREATMENT

What follows is an outline and description of the crucial elements of the successful treatment of eating-related disturbances. We must make a number of notes before we begin. Most clients, especially after realizing that their goal is to eliminate dangerous weight-control methods, are likely to be concerned about changes in their weight (American Psychiatric Association, 2000a; Fairburn, 1993). Research documents that changes in weight during treatment are likely to be minimal, and any significant weight gain is likely to be temporary and a result of rehydration, especially for those who use laxatives and diuretics (American Psychiatric Association, 2000a; Fairburn, 1993). Although weight loss cannot be guaranteed, it is sometimes an outcome, especially in those with Binge Eating Disorder. Adjunctive services, Cognitive-Behavioral, and Interpersonal Therapy are discussed as effective intervention strategies.

The Treatment Team

As can be seen by the preceding sections, the treatment of eating disorders among adolescent women is likely to be complex and multidimensional. The clinician who is reluctant to involve other skilled or licensed service providers or who is afraid to confront persistent resistance to therapeutic suggestions can easily make grave or dangerous error. Consequently, the practitioner must not only be privy to what is in the best interest of the client, but also be apprised of how to protect himself or herself when possible treatment failure becomes more evident. The key word is "teamwork." See Table 9.3 for an outline of the various team members involved in treating eating disorders.

TABLE 9.3   The Treatment Team

1. Nutritionist
2. Psychiatrist
3. Physician
4. Inpatient or Partial-Hospitalization Programs
5. Counseling Practitioner
6. Consultant to Counseling Practitioner

Nutritionist

Education by a nutritionist is essential to highlight the role that physiology and a lack of balanced nutrition can play in both weight loss and binge eating. A nutritionist will serve as another person to refute those rigidly held beliefs that dieting needs to involve starvation or food avoidance. For example, a great deal of research has pointed to the role of glucose and stable blood sugars in preventing binge eating and weight loss. Diets lacking in protein can result in excessively low or high blood-sugar levels, which makes one more prone to overeating or weight gain. Also, a nutritionist can be helpful in determining one's basal metabolic rate and the number of calories needed in order to maintain the efficiency of various metabolic functions.

The nutritionist should repeatedly remind the client that eating an insufficient number of calories depletes lean muscle mass, which further lowers metabolic rate, making weight gain more likely. Further, the roles of fats in making one feel satiated, feel psychologically satisfied, and actually consume fewer calories needs to be addressed to challenge the clients beliefs about low- or nonfat diets.

Together, the nutritionist and therapist can reduce the client's fear of avoided foods by gradually introducing more and more foods of a wider and wider variety. The therapist and the nutritionist, ideally, should work together to be sure that the client is getting enough nutritionally, but is not overwhelmed with trying to eat too much, too soon into the treatment. A good rule of thumb is that a weight gain of .5 to 1 lb. per week is adequate (American Psychiatric Association, 2000a). Sometimes a feared-food hierarchy is helpful here. The goal here is for the client to agree to gradually work her way up the hierarchy so that she is slowly confronting her fear of various foods and expanding the variety of her diet. This can be tricky, however and progress will for the most part ultimately be decided upon by the client. For example, clients with a very restrictive diet might not be able to progress up the hierarchy in a rapid manner and might be very slow in adding more calories and variety to their diets. This again highlights the importance of having other medical professionals involved in the treatment to continually assess for the arrival of medical illnesses.

Psychiatrist

Psychotropic medications (e.g., neuroleptics, imipramine, desipramine, and fluoxetine) have been well documented as being effective in remitting eating-disordered symptoms as well as the disorders that might co-exist, such as depression and anxiety (American Psychiatric Association, 2000a; Goldstein, Wilson, Thompson, Potvin, Rampey, & the Fluoxetine Bulimia Nervosa Collaborative Research Group, 1995; Walsh, Hadigan, Devlin, Gladis, & Roose, 1991). Consequently, assisting a client in seeking the services of a qualified psychiatrist is likely to be a critical component of the treatment plan. However, when making a referral to a psychiatrist, try to choose a professional that you feel you can communicate with openly and who will be a "team player." A psychiatrist who is willing to exchange ideas and respects the judgment of all members of this team is an invaluable asset to a treatment team. Note that some research points to the possibility that the positive effects of such medications are very short-lived (Walsh et al., 1991), so using medications in conjunction with psychological therapies is the best combination.

Physician

Some researchers have pointed to the role of biological factors in the cause and cure of eating disorders (Bryant-Waugh & Lask, 1995; Russell, 1985). For example, endocrine disorders affecting the pituitary and hypothalamus might result from eating-disordered behavior, which might cause reproductive difficulties. Also, a variety of hormones (e.g., cholecystokinin or CCK) regulate eating and satiety and have been found to be elevated in Anorexic women and below normal in Bulimic women. Further, binge eating, purging, diet pill use, and diuretic use are dangerous addictive behaviors that carry the potential to be fatal. Deaths have occurred from eating-disordered behavior as a result of renal failure, electrolyte imbalances (ketosis), dehydration, and cardiac arrest (Herzog, Keller, & Lavori, 1988; Hsu, 1988; Steinhausen, Rauss-Mason, & Seidel, 1991). Among people with cases of juvenile-onset Anorexia whose illness was active at the time of death, mortality rates can reach as high as 14%, including suicides (Casper & Jabine, 1996). Mortality rates among eating-disordered women have been found to be 12 times the expected incidence of death from all other causes in women 15 to 24 years of age (Sullivan, 1995). Furthermore, many of these deaths are sudden. Other consequences of eating-disordered behavior include pubertal delays, slowed growth, persisting menstrual irregularities, infertility, and osteoporosis (Russell, 1992; Bryant-Waugh & Lask, 1995). Consequently, a medical doctor or psychiatrist is an essential member of the treatment team because he or she would be able to identify a medical problem and treat it before the condition became fatal.

A medical professional is also able to set a predetermined criterion (e.g., further weight loss, ketosis, or insufficient weight gain) to determine when specialized psychiatric inpatient treatment is needed. This criterion usually works best when it is agreed upon with the client and parents at the beginning of treatment. Again, communicating this criterion to other members of the treatment team is essential to ensure quality treatment and reduce fatalities.

The medical professional is the only professional who can involuntarily hospitalize the client when an acute medical illness or condition emerges, which is critical for those clients or parents who refuse to set a criterion for needed inpatient care. Without this professional on the team, the client and counseling practitioner might not even realize that a potentially fatal medical condition exists. The nonmedical members of the team (e.g., the counseling practitioner) will then have no grounds to say that the client is in imminent danger. In other words, if medical consultation is ignored, the ability to hospitalize the unwilling eating-disordered client is limited because eating disorders are considered imminently dangerous only when there is an acute medical condition resulting from the eating disorder.

Specialized Inpatient Treatment or Partial-Hospitalization Programs

A number of elite hospitals in the United States specialize in the treatment of eating disorders (see the "For More Information" section). Although eating-disorder treatment is not usually an advertised focus of many conventional psychiatric hospitals, with some searching, one is likely to find a hospital relatively close to home that has a subspecialty in eating disorders. Obviously, it is best to try to choose a hospital that has experience treating such disorders. As the clinician, your task is to find a suitable program for the client. Phone calls to local hospitals with a good reputation are a fine place to start.

Specialized inpatient treatment is recommended to be in the treatment plan of many clients diagnosed with Anorexia Nervosa. This might sound drastic, but someday this little rule of thumb might save a life and your professional reputation. When I present this item on the treatment plan, I use words such as "as a precaution" or "if you don't respond to treatment as I expect, we may want to consider. . . ." Although research suggests that a majority of people with eating-related difficulties can be treated successfully on an outpatient basis (Fairburn, 1993), it is recommended to be in the treatment plan from the start as a way to have a plan of treatment in case outpatient treatment begins to fail. As you can see, discussing inpatient treatment sets the stage for discussing the client's expectations of outpatient therapy. This is helpful for avoiding the client or the client's parents expecting "too much, too soon" out of the outpatient therapy process. If a client prefers to choose inpatient treatment from the start, this is not necessarily a bad choice. Hospitals that specialize in eating-disorder treatment typically provide intensive psychotherapy (2–3 hours per day), group sessions, and family meetings. They also have greater control over the patient's use of laxatives or diuretics, can monitor the amount of food eaten during meals, and can restrict or supervise the use of the bathroom. Some cons of inpatient treatment include the fact that the eating-disordered behavior is not occurring within a naturalistic setting, which limits the information that can be gathered regarding stressors that trigger such behavior (Fairburn, 1993). A number of conditions do indicate that inpatient treatment would be the best and most effective mode of treatment (American Psychiatric Association, 2000a; Fairburn, 1993). These include the following: 1) when a client is too depressed to utilize outpatient treatment; 2) when a client is actively suicidal; 3) when there exists a medical ailment caused by the eating disorder; 4) when a client is in the early stages of pregnancy; and 5) when a patient has not responded to outpatient treatment and continues to lose weight. According to Fairburn (1993), these situations occur in about 5% of cases.

Consultant

With only a minority of eating-disordered females achieving a good prognosis after treatment (American Psychiatric Association, 2000a), it behooves each counseling practitioner to seek frequent consultation or supervision from a well qualified colleague. Because these illnesses are difficult to ameliorate, these clients often evoke strong feelings of inadequacy, frustration, or demoralization within the counseling practitioner. Also, loosening of therapeutic boundaries and sexualized counter-transference reactions are not out of the realm of possibility, which increase the likelihood of engaging in unethical behavior with your client. Frequent collaboration can strengthen your stance when the patient challenges your limits and can help the counseling practitioner regain a sense of power and authority in the therapeutic relationship.

OUTPATIENT MENTAL HEALTH TREATMENT

The effectiveness of Cognitive-Behavioral group interventions (group therapy) to address Bulimic behavior and chronic dieting is well established among adult women (McNamara, 1989; Weiss, Katzman, & Wolchik, 1985), so a case could be made that providing the preceding Cognitive-Behavioral interventions in a group format can be cost-effective. Keep in mind, however, that the effectiveness of Cognitive-Behavioral group therapy among adolescents has been documented as effective only when it is administered during inpatient hospitalizations (Strober et al., 1997). When in a group setting, eating-disordered females might start to "compete" as to who is the thinnest and unhealthiest, which would be very difficult to manage on an outpatient basis (American Psychiatric Association, 2000a).

Psychosocial History and Diagnostic Impressions

A good place to start with any client is with a thorough and complete psychosocial history. Standard and customary procedures of a diagnostic exam include assessments of parental alcohol or drug use, client alcohol or drug use, domestic violence, educational history, medical history, sexual/physical abuse, and the history of the client's parents' marriage. Further, with a client presenting with eating-related concerns, it is important to spend some extra time asking specifically about current dieting and eating habits. Reviewing a "typical day" with the client is an effective way to gauge calories consumed. Most important, asking specific questions about the frequency of various behaviors such as vomiting, diet-pill and laxative use, and hours of exercise per day will be the most productive line of questioning to generate a diagnosis. Further, keeping track of these frequencies over the course of subsequent sessions will also help the clinician evaluate the effectiveness of treatment. If a client feels uncomfortable with these questions, gently explain that these are important questions to answer because of the potential for medical complications and the need to evaluate her risk for treatment failure. If someone is simply unsure of these frequencies, assign them homework to keep track of their behaviors and assure them that accuracy will help you to monitor whether treatment is helpful. As you can see, honesty is a process issue that is likely to emerge in the treatment of eating-disordered women. Address it; don't ignore it. You also must assess for concomitant disorders such as depression and anxiety.

Be careful to obtain information about the client's definition of a "binge." The client might perceive herself as binge eating, but in actuality, she might simply be "overeating." Remember that binge eating involves a feeling of loss of control when an extraordinary amount of food is eaten. Binge eating involves the rapid consumption of large amounts of food, which results in feelings such as an altered state of consciousness, guilt, and a loss of control (Fairburn, 1995). Typically, binge eating is done in private. As a reference point, according to Mitchell, Pyle, & Eckert (1981), the average binge ranges in length from 15 minutes to 8 hours and involves the consumption of between 1,200 to 11,500 calories (an average of 3,415 calories). The most typical binge involves the consumption of only between 1,000 and 2,000 calories (Fairburn, 1995). A variety of the assessment procedures described previously can be helpful here.

Meeting individually with the client during the first session is a good opportunity to ask her opinion regarding her family and the information gathered during the history taking. Asking her opinion about her illness and how serious she thinks it is is a productive way to gather information about her level of defensiveness and whether she uses any denial, which can significantly diminish her prognosis. Assessing the client's insight and judgment is the initial goal here.

Treatment Planning

After all relevant diagnoses are established, the clinician, client, and family review and agree upon the treatment plan. A sample treatment plan follows in the next section. Each of the "team" members and their respective responsibilities are outlined. The treatment plan should also include reminders to have appropriate releases of information signed. Also, the actual goals of the mental health treatment, as discussed by the client and her family, are outlined here. Typically, goals of the mental health treatment include at least one statement that the eating-disordered behavior(s) will be reduced in frequency as treatment progresses. Other goals will be specific to the stressors outlined by the client, the client's parents, and the clinician (e.g., assertiveness, empathy, listening, or positive communication). After an agreement is made, the "team" is chosen based upon whom the clinician and client have had positive experiences with. After this session, the clinician contacts all relevant personnel (in both writing and via phone) to invite them to participate. It is also best if regular team meetings are held so that everyone can review progress and share clinical opinions. The most important part of this phase of treatment, however, is the actual signing of the treatment plan by the clinician, the parent(s), and the client. This is your safety net on a journey that has the potential to be both rewarding and exasperating.

The "meat" of the mental health therapy can then begin, which can feel overwhelming because of the many things that need to be addressed. Conceptualizing therapy as running on two tracks may be helpful here. The first track consists of Cognitive-Behavioral Interventions to address food- and weight-related concerns. The second track consists of Interpersonal Therapy to address those stressors, situations, persons, feelings, places, or events, that trigger eating-disordered behavior.

Cognitive-Behavioral Therapy

Consistent with the Cognitive-Behavioral approach, goals of individual therapy are outlined in Table 9.4 and include to 1) identify those situations, feelings, people, or events that trigger eating-disordered behavior (self-monitoring); 2) cognitively restructure the client's irrational beliefs about body image, food, weight gain, and nutrition; 3) establish a schedule of regular eating and use alternative behaviors to substitute for unhealthy eating behaviors; 4) encourage the client to improve the variety of foods she eats by incorporating more forbidden foods into her meal plan (exposure), while assisting the client's family in supervising the client after meals to prevent unhealthy habits from occurring (response prevention); 5) use constructive problem-solving when negative emotions arise; and 6) prevent relapses.

Many engage in unhealthy eating habits after breaking a dietary rule, gaining weight, or ignoring insatiable hunger. Many eating-disordered women are able to diet because of staunch beliefs about weight loss, dieting, and the consequences of eating forbidden foods. Early in the treatment process, clients are recommended to explore those cognitive triggers. Techniques such as self-monitoring or keeping a journal of eating behaviors and the antecedents and consequential thoughts and feelings is most effective here. Information gathered should include the time of the eating behavior, the quantity and type of food eaten or the behavior that was engaged in, the place that the behavior occurred, and the thoughts and feelings before and after the behavior was engaged in. For example, by using self-monitoring, it might become known that the person vomited after eating a few cookies because she irrationally believed that the cookies would result in a 5-lb weight gain. Or, the client might have been starving herself in the hopes of loosing 4 lbs in 1 week after she gained some weight during her spring break. Self-monitoring is the cornerstone of Cognitive-Behavioral interventions because it highlights the cognitive triggers and irrational thoughts and feelings that precede eating-disordered behavior. Only with this information can a clinician begin to refute these beliefs about dieting and weight loss.

Body-image dissatisfaction is likely to be a trigger for some eating-disordered women (e.g., "I purged because I felt fat"). Consistent with the Cognitive-Behavioral approach, the goal here as a clinician is to challenge the feeling of "feeling fat" and beliefs that go along with it. This will involve discussing the definition of "fat,"

TABLE 9.4   Goals of Cognitive-Behavioral Therapy (Track 1)

1. Identify triggers of eating-disordered behavior via self-monitoring.
2. Restructure irrational beliefs about weight and attraction via BMI and family involvement.
3. Establish a regular schedule of eating.
4. Discuss the physiological consequences of maintaining unhealthy eating habits.
5. Expose the client to a variety of foods while avoiding unhealthy eating habits.
6. Support realistic beliefs about physiological changes during recovery.
7. Use alternative behaviors to manage stress and improve coping skills.
8. Seek the support of other family members to supervise eating behavior.
9. Prevent relapse and establish realistic expectations for treatment.

talking about beliefs about people perceived as "fat," and focusing on positive, non–weight-related aspects of their appearance. Also, you must underscore for the client the fact that weight gain is developmentally appropriate during adolescence. Encouraging clients to accept that the body is developing and changing in order to prepare for motherhood is helpful. Discussing the Body Mass Index—BMI; (weight [lbs] × 703/height [in])/height [in]—will challenge the belief that the number on the scale is "too big." The BMI is a standardized index increasingly used in research to determine who is significantly over- and underweight (American Psychiatric Association, 2000a). Women with a BMI of less than 18.5 would be considered underweight; those with a BMI of higher than 25 would be considered overweight. For example, a woman standing 62 inches tall can weigh as much as 135 pounds before actually being considered overweight. This same woman would be considered underweight if she weighed 95 pounds; so a healthy weight range for her is between 100 and 135 pounds. Consequently, one can say that falling outside the recommended range (i.e., either too thin or overweight) can place someone at risk for developing a life-threatening disease later in life. Discussing this with the client will enable her to become aware of a healthy range of weights that are realistic, rather than a target weight that would be dangerous to achieve.

Family and significant others can help the client refute irrational beliefs about attraction and their own body images. At these times, inviting such persons to therapy sessions or assigning the client homework to discuss these issues is most helpful. Irrational beliefs about what significant others believe is attractive can be reconstructed by actually having her discuss with her parents and male peers those body traits that they feel make someone attractive. In the healthiest of relationships, the client is told that the waif-like and excessively thin females portrayed in the media are actually unattractive. Family and significant others can also tell the client about those aspects of the client's body, shape, and non–weight-related traits that are valued and seen as attractive (e.g., eye color, hands, arms). Discussing family and parental pressure to be thin, as well as her parents' own eating and body attitudes, is likely to be helpful here.

Encouraging the client to reject the media's portrayal of thin women as being most attractive can be supported by using interventions taken from Feminist Theory. Feminist Theory is a contemporary theory about the psychology of females, which encourages females to reject traditional female sex-typed behavior when choosing to bear children, have a career, or establish significant relationships. From a feminist-therapy perspective, one could say that the same anti–sex-role approach would hold true when choosing a body image to adhere to and adopting models of thinness. Adopting approaches from the feminist perspective can highlight the dilemma of eating-disordered females who feel caught between traditional models of thinness and more contemporary theories that such adherence is unhealthy.

Facts about nutrition and physiology are needed here in order for the clinician to refute stringent beliefs. For example, research supports the idea that strict dieting (a diet in which 1,200 or fewer calories are consumed) lowers metabolic rate, or the number of calories needed to gain a pound of fat. More specifically, for a person whose metabolism is running at full efficiency, a pound of fat is gained after 3,500 extra calories are consumed. Taking into account calories needed to maintain basal functioning, the average female would need to consume 5,300 calories to gain 1 pound. However, when strict dieting results in a metabolic slowdown, a pound can be gained after eating as few as 2,500 calories. Vomiting is not an effective weight-loss method because research indicates that up to 50% of the food is absorbed, regardless of repeated and immediate vomiting after a meal or binge (Fairburn, 1993). In fact, vomiting might actually enhance the probability of overeating because the client irrationally believes that she can eat more and just purge it later. Also, vomiting is easier if the stomach is full, so more calories are absorbed. Laxatives and diuretics attack the food within the bowels and intestines, well after the food is absorbed into the bloodstream and passes through the stomach. The only weight loss occurring when laxatives and diuretics are consumed is water weight, which is not only dangerous to lose but is temporary and easily returns after the abuse ends. Clients using laxatives and diuretics are most likely to gain weight at the beginning of treatment. Reminding them that they were only losing water, not fat, will help keep them motivated for treatment.

Although the nutritionist will play a role in expanding the client's diet to include forbidden foods and to establish a schedule of regular eating, the counseling practitioner also can be helpful here because the client is likely to hold rigid beliefs about food, nutrition, and weight loss. Initially, a forbidden-food hierarchy is likely to be helpful. This is a list of forbidden foods ranging from the least forbidden to the most forbidden. Clients would be encouraged to slowly begin incorporating forbidden foods into their diets, beginning with the least forbidden foods. During this time, irrational beliefs about fats and calories are likely to be uncovered and need to be refuted. The clinician can outline the constructive role of fats (i.e., fats make one feel satiated and psychologically satisfied so that less calories are consumed in the long run) to help the client avoid the fad of nonfat diets. Accurate information about how weight is gained (e.g., by eating at least 5,000 calories per day) can be discussed to refute the idea that one fatty serving will lead to a substantial weight gain. Remind the client that "easy and quick fixes" are the problem here and not the cure. Encourage her to choose a lifestyle free of starvation, deprivation, and hunger rather than another diet. Convey facts that metabolism is increased by moderate exercise and eating every 3 to 4 hours, which are habits that make weight maintenance easier. You can also outline the physical hazards and potential death from dangerous eating habits here (e.g., ketosis, tooth decay, cardiac arrest, dehydration). As she eats previously restricted foods, the client is normalizing the quantity of her food intake and reprogramming her body on how to metabolize that food again. The cramping and bloating that result are not a sign that vomiting is necessary or that weight gain is imminent. Help the client understand that cramping and bloating are to be expected as she improves her eating habits. Initial weight gain is normal because her fluids are normalizing as she becomes less dehydrated, and this is temporary. Feeling excessively full does not mean she overate; rather, it means that her stomach is becoming healthier as it relearns how to metabolize healthy amounts of food. At this stage, it is very important that the client *not* rely on her internal feelings of hunger or satiation when deciding whether to eat. These physiological cues, especially in the beginning of treatment, are not reliable indicators. That is why the client must adhere to a schedule of regular eating. Reprogramming these cues to be more accurate is the goal of treatment.

Highlighting the importance of parents increasing their supervision of the client during and after meals is greatly needed to reduce the occurrence of vomiting, reduce the use of diuretics and laxatives, and ensure that an adequate number of calories is being consumed. This is especially important as the variety and quantity of the client's diet increase because the urge to eliminate food is likely to increase as she eats forbidden foods. Encouraging the client to discuss (in sessions) and journal (between sessions) her thoughts and feelings after eating forbidden foods is a very fruitful way to do some cognitive therapy. For example, the rationality of her stating "I think I am an unhealthy person when I eat french fries" or "I feel so guilty after I eat french fries" can be scrutinized. Remind her that one fatty portion does not make one fat or unhealthy. In fact, fat is a very important nutrient because it provides us with a satisfied feeling and is a protective sheath surrounding a number of our internal organs. It is excessive fat intake that is unhealthy. Parents and family can also assist the client in grocery shopping and being sure that a balance of safe and forbidden foods is available within the home. Replacing unhealthy behaviors with alternative coping skills is also useful here. Constructing a list of alternative activities such as going to the movies, taking a bath, visiting a friend, shopping, or playing music can be helpful during a time of crisis. Parents can be helpful here as well by reminding the client or suggesting such activities at a time they know is difficult for the client (e.g., after meals or at a food-oriented social gathering).

The clinician should continually highlight realistic expectations about progress and the process of treatment as the client moves through treatment. The client needs to realize that her unhealthy eating behaviors are not going to disappear, but rather gradually will diminish in frequency and urgency. She needs to realize that her unhealthy habits are also likely to continue to increase during times of stress, despite long periods of abstinence. A lapse is a setback, whereas a relapse is when one returns to square one (Fairburn, 1993). When relapses occur, identifying the unhealthy behavior as soon as possible is important. Then you should immediately reinstitute the program. Lastly, you should try to identify and problem-solve around the source of emotional stress.

Other goals of these individual sessions include encouraging the client to listen and speak about her feelings. This is likely to be difficult for some because as outlined above, a lack of interoceptive awareness is one of the suspected factors causing eating disorders. Journaling (writing down one's thoughts and feelings in a private place within a special notebook) is a very effective way to assist these clients in becoming more aware of their feelings and to manage stress. This technique has been documented as effective in improving eating-disordered symptoms among adolescents (Guernina, 1998). It is a very productive way to develop an understanding of those negative feelings, besides feeling fat, that trigger unhealthy eating behaviors. Examples include boredom, tension, anger, and loneliness. Fairburn (1993) outlines six components of effective problem-solving: 1) Identify the negative emotion as early as possible; 2) specify the problem accurately; 3) consider many solutions; 4) think about the implications of each solution; 5) choose the best solution or combination of solutions; and 6) act on the solution.

Family Therapy and Interpersonal Skill Building

Family therapy is likely to be productive if it focuses on the needs of the client as gleaned from individual sessions. Helping parents gain some degree of understanding about those family factors that are maintaining the illness needs to be directly discussed. Consequently, individual sessions work nicely along with family sessions (e.g., with one or more family members present). Completing solely individual or family therapy throughout the entire treatment is a mistake because it will narrow the information available to the clinician. When listening to the client and her family, a number of treatment issues or triggers might emerge: physical or sexual abuse, verbal abuse, excessive criticism, high expectations, fear or nonsupport for independent behaviors, denial or avoidance of negative affect, destructive anger-management skills, poor empathy skills, poor listening skills, and a lack of communications/connectedness. When these issues become a topic of discussion between the client and clinician, it is then the responsibility of the clinician to encourage the client to discuss her thoughts and feelings with a family member present. The goal of this discussion would then be twofold: first, to problem-solve around the specific issue at hand so that the client's needs are met (e.g., content goal), and second, to teach the family members and client to communicate, listen, and problem-solve more productively (e.g., process goal).

Because other triggers might include peer relations, during sessions with the client it is also a good idea to assess the quality of the client's interpersonal relationships, as well as the family functioning. It is possible that an adolescent eating-disordered female is in a currently abusive heterosexual relationship or is being mistreated by her same-sex peers. Also, try to get an idea of the mental health of the client's peer group to assess for any group norms accepting self-destructive behavior such as purging, self-abuse, superficial cutting, and drug use. Also, when discussing the client's peer group, try to get an idea of their beliefs about thinness and weight loss. Instead of taking a dependent or caretaking role in interpersonal relationships, the client should be taught to choose significant others who are a source of strength. Encourage the client to be realistic with herself in maintaining both physical and mental health. In short, therapy will hopefully teach the adolescent client how to seek out supportive others when she is feeling stressed about the many challenges that she faces every day (e.g., dating, achievement pressure, social acceptance). Choosing productive coping skills will enhance the clients feeling of control over her life, relationships, and other stressful situations. Helping clients to become aware of the stress, to accurately identify the stress, to communicate with others about the stress, to organize their resources, to perceive themselves as having control over the stress, and to take care of themselves physically and mentally are productive interventions. Boosting their stress-management skills can help them use other resources (e.g., a friend, a good book, a day trip, a shopping spree, a good movie, a warm bath), rather than food, to manage stress. The goals of Interpersonal Therapy are outlined in Table 9.5.

TABLE 9.5 Goals of Family Therapy and Interpersonal Skill Building (Track 2)

1. Explore issues such as physical or sexual abuse, perfectionism, and verbal abuse.
2. Explore the family's support of independent and age-appropriate behaviors.
3. Explore the use of denial or avoidance of negative affect.
4. Explore the use of destructive anger-management techniques.
5. Explore the health of both same- and opposite-sex peer relationships.
6. Teach the client how to choose healthy peers and set limits in relationships.
7. Teach the client how to identify and manage stress productively.
8. Teach significant others how to listen and communicate with empathy and understanding.

BEST PRACTICE GUIDELINES

The disordered eating patterns identified in this chapter present a serious medical risk. Practice guidelines provide recommendations to help practitioners make treatment decisions that are supported by the best available evidence, including current research and expert consensus. The third edition (latest revision) of practice guidelines for "eating disorders" are contained in *Practice Guidelines for the Treatment of Psychiatric Disorders: Compendium 2006* (American Psychiatric Association, 2006). Professionals should review and utilize these guidelines to improve treatment decision making for clients with disordered eating behavior.

PRIMARY PREVENTION: SCHOOL AND PUBLIC PERSPECTIVES

Weight concerns have been documented in samples of younger and younger women. Girls as young as 9 years old are restricting their food intakes unnecessarily and do not seem to have sufficient knowledge about how to diet safely. This has resulted in many young girls having unhealthy diets that are insufficient in quantity and quality of food (Dixey, 1998). Further, restrictive dieting is well documented as a factor that predicts future eating-disordered behavior, which places these young girls at severe risk for future medical pathology and psychopathology (Killen, Taylor, Telch, Saylor, Maron, & Robinson, 1986). Some blame the health movement for this pattern and state that messages that encourage adults to be thin, fit, and lean are difficult for children to ignore. Further, children often don't have a parent who can put their dieting needs aside to focus on their child, assist the child in assimilating the information, and outline why this eating style is not healthy for the child. Young girls are already "hungry" for an adult female figure and can very easily assimilate the media's portrayal of ultra-thin women, especially if their mothers are preoccupied with their own thinness.

The National Eating Disorders Screening Program (NEDSP) is a new service that provides the public with accurate information regarding eating disorders, free screenings, and referrals to appropriate treatment sources. Clinicians pay a small fee and are provided with advertising, screening, and informational materials to serve the public. This is one way to enhance public knowledge of eating disorders; refute beliefs about dieting, weight, and body image; and assist clients in finding quality services for their disorders. This is very important because eating disorders are secretive in nature, and women affected by them feel very ashamed of their behavior and are not sure where to turn. Attending a program such as this is also a way to ensure that the knowledge the client receives is accurate and of quality. The NEDSP also had a new component in 2002 that specifically addressed adolescents with eating disorders. A note of caution: Some research suggests that imparting knowledge to young women about eating disorders actually can do more harm than good (Carter, Stewart, Dunn, & Fairburn, 1997; Dixey, 1998; Killen, Taylor, Hammer, Litt, Wilson, Rich, Hayward, Simmons, Kraemer, & Varady, 1993). More specifically, these authors note that disseminating such information to females without any eating-related disturbance can actually predispose them to developing eating-disordered behavior. Conversely, when such information is disseminated to females with some degree of eating-related disturbance, their symptoms can be alleviated. This highlights the importance of screening large groups of females before such information is distributed.

Many researchers (Carter et al., 1997; Dixey, 1998; Killen et al., 1993) outline how educators should present nutritional information to young women. They highlight the importance of addressing societal pressures to be thin, promoting a positive body image by emphasizing health rather than thinness, outlining the harmful effects of unhealthy weight regulation, accepting weight gain as a normal developmental process, and strengthening coping skills to resist the diverse sociocultural influences regarding thinness. Because the positive effects of such programs is very short-lived, these researchers point to the possibility that such interventions might do more harm than good. They also point to the wisdom of targeting "at-risk" females and providing only them with prevention efforts. More specifically, educational seminars would be helpful if provided only to those who score above a certain threshold on one of the assessment measures outlined in the previous section. At the very least, more research regarding the effectiveness of prevention programs and ways to identify at-risk youth is needed.

MULTICULTURAL CONSIDERATIONS

Some speculate that eating disorders are more common among specific cultures and genders; however, these conclusions might be be an artifact of poorly defined concepts and very few studies. Only a fair amount of research explores the incidence of eating disorders among various ethnic and multicultural groups. When reading this section, please keep in mind that the conclusions are tentative, and that many of the statements are theoretical rather than empirically based.

The one cultural specification that is well founded is that eating disorders are more common among the female population (*DSM-IV-TR*). According to many studies, 90% of eating-disordered persons are female (*DSM-IV-TR*). However, this could be a residual effect of the disorders manifesting themselves differently in the male population and not being well defined. For example, according to the *DSM-IV-TR*, Bulimia and Anorexia are characterized by an intense desire to be thinner, which might not be a trait to which eating-disordered men adhere. In fact, some speculate that eating-disordered men actually desire to gain lean muscle mass and utilize unhealthy means to do so (e.g., using steroids, creatine, or excessive weightlifting). Obviously, much more research is needed in this area.

Bulimia is noted to occur with roughly similar frequencies among highly industrialized countries such as the United States, Canada, Europe, Australia, Japan, New Zealand, and South Africa (*DSM-IV-TR*). Within these countries, the ideal female body type is at the thinnest 5% of the normal weight distribution (i.e., an ideal female weighs 13 to 19% below normal weight), which excludes 95% of American women (Berg, 1997). But again, unfortunately, few studies have actually examined the prevalence of Bulimia and the ideal body images of Third-World countries. Further, because the media's influence is not substantial in many Third-World countries, exploring the incidence and prevalence of eating disorders within these cultures will help us determine the influence of the media in the etiology of eating disorders. No studies to date have explored this specific question.

For now, many have written about eating disorders in the United States and have started a revolution against ultra-thin images being portrayed in the media. In *Afraid to Eat,* Frances Berg (1997) writes ". . . worldwide, there is a backlash against fashion's severe excesses in portraying malnutrition as glamorous, although the industry's resistance to change is nearly as strong" (p. 258). Berg then cites a striking example of this resistance in which the Omega watch company pulled its ads from *Vogue* magazine in protest of their use of extremely thin models, for fear that the ads would encourage eating disorders among women. When Omega reversed its position and reinstated the ads, *Vogue* arrogantly lauded the decision as a triumph. Another example is cited by Berg (1997, p. 27) when he quotes *Newsweek* as it describes the "look" of the late 1990s: "it is a slimmer, more dissipated vision . . . reedy, hollow curves and sinewy lines, . . . small, frail looking . . . austere at times . . . human coat hangers . . . clothes just fall off them . . . it's proof that men and their appetites do not rule the earth," he writes. Diet promotion, nonexistent in 1973, now compromises about 5% of TV advertisements in the U.S. (Berg, 1997). If this trend is not challenged, it is scary to think of what could happen to our culture.

A number of organizations have attempted to address this problem head on. The Boston-based consumer group BAM (Boycott Anorexic Marketing) forced the cancellation of Diet Sprite ads that depicted a bony, apathetic girl sipping a diet drink and boasting of her nickname, "Skeleton." Berg himself has designated a Healthy Weight Day in the third week in January, in which he gives awards to television networks, shows, and magazines that portray the message that beauty and health come in all sizes. The National Education Association has declared itself ready to combat size prejudice in the schools because they claim that schools are a site of ongoing prejudice, unnoticed discrimination, and almost constant harassment for large students. As Berg (1997) writes (p. 257), "changing culture is a huge task . . . it won't be easy, nor will it happen overnight." Berg (1997) proposes that such cultural change is possible only with the help of families, schools, and communities working together and reiterates that there are sure signs that people are ready for a change.

CASE ILLUSTRATION

Jane presented herself for treatment at the age of 13 after being referred by her school counselor for Bulimic behavior. Upon intake, she was self-inducing vomiting two to three times per day after eating only 800 calories per day. She denied use of laxatives, diuretics, or diet pills. She weighed 110 pounds and stood 65 inches tall at intake. Her menstrual cycle was regular and sufficient and no binge eating was reported. Upon intake, she completed the EAT, the BSS, and the Beck Depression Inventory (BDI). Indicative of eating-disordered behavior, she scored above clinical cutoff scores on all measures. She also complained of chronic depression, sleep difficulties, suicidal ideations, and concentration difficulties. No suicide attempts were noted in her history. Her psychosocial history was also positive for academic difficulties, frequent school suspensions for fighting, and divorced parents.

Jane was seen individually during the first session, at which time she reported a history of being physically abused by her father in the recent past. She discussed her parents' divorce and the pressure she was feeling to remain in contact with her father, who remains explosive and an active alcoholic. A report was taken by Child Protective Services and Jane and her mother were educated about the CPS investigative process (e.g., it's only a preliminary investigation and a caseworker will come to your house and ask questions). Jane also disclosed being physically and verbally abused by her older brothers as recently as the day before the session. As a result of this session, more specific goals for the mental health treatment were outlined and included: 1) Reduce her vomiting frequency; 2) improve the degree to which her mother supervises her after meals; 3) reconstruct irrational beliefs regarding weight loss, nutrition, and body image; 4) reduce depressive symptoms and suicidal thoughts; 5) improve her assertiveness skills with abusive persons in her family; 6) improve her mother's ability to protect Jane from abusive persons; 7) improve Jane's mother's ability to listen to Jane and support her negative feelings, especially those feelings involving family members; and 8) decrease physical fights at school via anger-management training. The treatment plan and diagnostic impressions below were verbally presented to Jane and her hearing-impaired mother at the first intake session. Jane was asked to begin keeping a food journal and to bring it to the second session. A session with her brothers was also scheduled.

Diagnostic Impressions

Axis I: 307.50 Eating Disorder, NOS
             300.40 Dysthymic Disorder
             315.90 R/O Learning Disorder, NOS
Axis II: 301.90 Borderline Personality Traits
Axis III: R/O Medical Complication secondary to Bulimic behavior
Axis IV: Psychosocial and Environmental Problems:
             V61.21 Physical Abuse of Child
             V61.20 Parent–Child Relational Problem
Axis V: Global Assessment of Functioning: 60—Current

Sample Treatment Plan

1. Jane will be seen at this agency for a combination of individual and family therapy. Cognitive-Behavioral, behavioral, stress-management, object relational, and family process interventions will be utilized in order to meet the following goals:

    (a) reduce her vomiting frequency
    (b) improve the degree to which her mother supervises her after meals
    (c) reconstruct irrational beliefs regarding weight loss, nutrition, and body image
    (d) reduce depressive symptoms and suicidal thoughts
    (e) improve her assertiveness skills with abusive persons in her family
    (f) improve her mother's ability to protect Jane from abusive persons
    (g) improve Jane's mother's ability to listen to Jane and support her negative feelings, especially those feelings involving family members
    (h) decrease physical fights at school via anger-management training.

2. Jane will be referred to see a nutritionist to receive nutritional counseling and education. A release of information will be signed.
3. Jane will be followed by her primary care physician so that her physiological health can be monitored and medical complications that arise can be treated. Releases will be signed.
4. Jane will be seen by a psychiatrist to assess her need for psychotropic medications.
5. Jane will be screened to assess the possibility that she has a learning disability. If results are positive, a release will be signed and a letter will be written to her school psychologist requesting that Jane be further evaluated by the Committee on Special Education.
6. Jane will be educated about emergency mental health procedures. In the case of suicidal ideations, Jane will be instructed to call the emergency beeper service of this writer. If this is unsuccessful, Jane will be instructed to contact the local emergency room to request an Emergency Mental Health Assessment to evaluate her need for inpatient mental health treatment. Jane and her mother agree that these procedures will take place in the event that Jane is thinking of suicide and has a method in mind.
7. The need for specialized inpatient treatment specific to an eating disorder may be needed if Jane does not make sufficient progress after 10 to 12 sessions. Appropriate releases of information will be signed to make such a referral.

Mother	Jane	Clinician

Before the second appointment, all referral sources were contacted and the need for their services was explained via both phone consultations and writing. At the second session, Jane had appointments to be seen by her physician, a nutritionist, and a psychiatrist. She was subsequently medicated on an antidepressant and her medical tests remained normal throughout subsequent sessions.

At the second session, Jane reviewed her food journal and the cognitive triggers that made her feel fat and feel the need to vomit. She had a number of irrational beliefs about fatty foods, believing that she could gain an excessive amount of weight after eating a small portion of fatty food. The constructive role of fats was outlined and she was educated about the physiological process of weight loss (e.g., basal metabolism). Other cognitive triggers included her beliefs that vomiting is a successful weight-loss technique. These were refuted, again, with more accurate information. Jane again referred to her brothers' verbal abuse of her and was very saddened that they repeatedly call her "fat mama." She prepared herself for the next session, in which she was to discuss this abuse and set limits with her brothers.

At the third session, Jane was seen with her mother and brothers, and the alleged verbal abuse was discussed. Jane very appropriately told her brothers how their abusive statements made her feel and requested that they stop making these statements. Jane's mother also supported Jane during this session and placed the boys on a behavior-management program to discipline them when they verbally abused Jane. The boys openly discussed the verbal abuse they experienced from their father, who also called the boys "fat slobs" throughout much of their lives. The boys discussed how they felt with their own weight and admitted that they themselves feel fat. Because both boys were verbally abused by their father, they were recommended for their own mental health treatment. Subsequent sessions were spent with Jane and her mother. Interventions addressed supervising Jane after meals to enhance response (vomiting) prevention, refuting irrational beliefs about Jane feeling fat, following through with the behavior-management program, and improving Jane's communication skills.

Four sessions later, Jane's neglect by her mother became evident. Jane's vomiting frequency was unchanged and her mother was not sufficiently supervising her after meals. Jane also reported that her mother was not implementing the behavioral-management plan on her brothers and they remained verbally abusive to her. Shortly thereafter, Jane was hospitalized for 6 weeks at a hospital with a specialized eating-disorder program. Outpatient treatment continued upon discharge but was fraught with difficulties (e.g., poor attendance, a lack of parental supervision, and discontinuing medications). Ironically, the low point of treatment occurred after Jane was discharged from the hospital. At this time, her attendance to therapy was poor. When this was discussed directly with her and her mother, financial issues emerged as the primary reason for her poor attendance. Consequently, her fee was significantly reduced and her attendance did improve, but only temporarily. At this point in the treatment, the psychologist at Jane's school was contacted to seek her assistance in providing Jane with some portions of the existing treatment plan. Jane received in-school counseling along with visits to my office, which was a very effective strategy. School professionals were also contacted regarding Jane's scores on a learning-disabilities screening measure. Jane completed this instrument during a previous session and results indicated that she might have a learning disability in reading. These results were provided to the school.

The mode of treatment was then changed to see whether Jane's attendance and progress would improve. She became a member of an anger-management group for adolescents. When Jane was discharged from treatment 8 months later, she cited this group as being one of the most effective intervention strategies. This group consisted of eight other males and females referred by Social Service agencies, schools, or juvenile court for assistance in learning more effective strategies for managing their anger.

From my perspective, two topics seemed to really help Jane recover. One topic included the group's discussion regarding their feelings about being abused or neglected by their parents or guardians. Expression of negative feelings, empathy, and problem-solving skills were the hallmark of these group sessions. The other topic that seemed to affect Jane in a powerful way was when she disclosed her eating disorder and received feedback from other group members regarding her purging and body image. This feedback helped her reconstruct her irrational beliefs about her body, weight, and appearance. Jane was unable to receive this feedback from her significant family relationships, but as soon as she received it from people that she cared about in group, a substantial improvement was seen. After Jane's disclosure, the group wanted Jane to be weighed at each session because they were worried about further weight loss. Not only was this helpful for Jane to see that others were concerned, but other non–weight-conscious females jokingly weighed themselves and Jane could see just how thin she really was. Another perk was that pizza or some other snack food was a regular part of the group, which served as a built-in exposure and prevention technique for Jane. When she did not partake in the enjoyment, she was usually asked why. Jane was eventually able to reduce her vomiting frequency to once every 2 months, but this did not happen until 12 months after intake. Upon discharge from treatment, her scores on the EAT, BSS, and BDI were all in the normal range.

As you can see, in some cases, the treatment of eating disorders can be long term. Progress can seem like a series of peaks and valleys rather than a line sloped upright. During the valleys, it behooves each clinician to go back to the diagnosis on all three axes and be a bit creative in addressing barriers to treatment. In Jane's case, creating an artificial family within her therapy group allowed her to receive feedback to refute her irrational beliefs about her body image, food, and weight-related issues. The Cognitive-Behavioral components of the needed treatment were provided to her within a group context rather than from her family of origin.

CLOSING REMARKS

The prevalence of eating disorders among adolescent females is on the rise and still carries with it the potential for death. The point that needs to be stressed here is that much more research is needed to investigate appropriate assessment and treatment methods for eating-disordered women. Given the prevalence and dangerousness of eating-disordered behaviors, the paucity of current research leaves the clinician in a very difficult situation. Questions remain about the effectiveness of group therapy with adolescent eating-disordered women and the interventions that would constitute an effective group. In fact, some have stated that some preventative interventions might have done more harm than good. Also, although the effectiveness of intervention for eating-disordered adult women has been documented, only a handful of outcome studies on adolescent females exist. Further, there is a need to establish the reliability and validity of more assessment techniques. What we do know is that eating disorders are increasing at alarming rates, despite the possibility that many people are secretive and too ashamed to admit to such behavior. Also, we know that these difficulties carry a potential for death from many physiological ailments as well as from suicide. Further, the role of family pathology and teamwork is a hall-mark of the treatment of eating disorders. Other correlates of eating disorders include body dissatisfaction secondary to the normal weight gains associated with adolescence and adhering to societal standards of thinness. But again, some aspects of treatment (e.g., addressing pathological social skills and moving around defensiveness) are left to speculation and rely on a fine sense of clinical judgment.

FOR MORE INFORMATION

Professional Associations

National Association to Advance Fat Acceptance (NAAFA)
(916)558–6880
www.naafa.org

National Association of Anorexia Nervosa and Associated Disorders (ANAD)
(847)831–3438
www.anad.org

National Eating Disorders Association (NEDA)
(800)931–2237
www.edap.org

The American Anorexia and Bulimia Association (AABA)
www.aabainc.org
(212)734–1114

Academy for Eating Disorders (AED)
(847)498–4274
www.aedweb.org

International Association of Eating Disorders Professionals (IAEDP)
(800)800–8126
www.iaedp.com

Anorexia Nervosa & Related Eating Disorders (ANRED)
(847)831–3438
www.anred.com

Eating Disorders Resources on the Web
www.edreferral.com
www.healthtouch.com
www.edrecovery.com

Eating Disorders Support on the Web
www.ednewsletter.com
www.something-fishy.com
www.dcregistry.com/users/eatingaddictions/index
www.angelfire.com

ADDITIONAL INFORMATION

National Eating Disorders Screening Program (NEDSP)
(781)239-0071
www.mental health screening.org/events/nedsp /index.aspx

Gurze Books: Specializing in eating disorders publications
www.bulimia.com
www.gurze.com

ADDITIONAL READING FOR CLIENTS

Being Fat is Not a Sin by Shelley Bovey
Body Traps by Judith Rodin
Fat Is a Feminist Issue by Susie Orbach
Making Peace with Food by Susan Kano
The Body Myth by Naomi Wolf
The Hungry Self by Kim Chernin

PART THREE
EFFECTIVE TREATMENT PLANNING

Chapter 10
Treatment Planning Guidelines For Children and Adolescents

Chapter 11
Case Studies In Treatment Planning

Chapter 10

TREATMENT PLANNING GUIDELINES FOR CHILDREN AND ADOLESCENTS

By

Gary G. Gintner
Louisiana State University

INTRODUCTION

Treatment planning is a core clinical activity that describes the proposed course of treatment. In this era of managed care and greater utilization review, reimbursement is often made contingent on documentation that the proposed services are deemed necessary and have a reasonable chance of success (Domino, Salkever, Zarin, & Pincus, 1998; Lawless, Ginter, & Kelly, 1999). As a result, treatment planning has emerged as a more critical component in the overall treatment process (Cormier & Cormier, 1998). Although the specific aspects of a treatment plan vary depending on institutional and agency requirements, typical components include a problem list, measurable goals, and interventions designed to meet those goals (Berman, 1997; Beutler & Clarkin, 1990; Lyman & Campbell, 1996; Seligman, 1990). The intervention component addresses issues such as level of care (e.g., inpatient versus outpatient), modality of therapy (e.g., individual, group, or family), and the specific interventions that will be used (e.g., social-skills training, cognitive restructuring). Although the components of a treatment plan appear rather straightforward, each part requires the clinician to make important clinical decisions that ultimately influence treatment success or failure (Cormier & Cormier, 1998; Gaw & Beutler, 1995; Fonagy, Target, Cottrell, Phillips, & Kurtz, 2002).

These treatment planning decisions, however, can be particularly challenging when the identified client is a child or an adolescent. First, it might be difficult to clearly specify a problem list. Because children and adolescents are usually not self-referred (Fonagy et al., 2002; Wu et al., 1999), they might not see themselves as having a problem or might attribute the problem to others (Kazdin & Weisz, 1998). For those who do admit to having a problem, cognitive and emotional developmental factors can make it difficult to clearly describe the problem and the conditions under which it occurs. This is compounded by the fact that child and adolescent problems are frequently nested in family, peer, and school settings

(Borduin, 1999; Fonagy et al., 2002). As a result of these types of issues, collateral informants such as teachers and parents must be included in the assessment process (Fonagy et al., 2002; Lambert, Salzer, & Bickman, 1998). Thus, treatment planning frequently requires the integration of information from various informants across multiple contexts in order to identify the client's problem.

Goal-setting is also frequently challenging for many of the same reasons. Clients referred by a third party might not be interested in change or might state goals in terms of changing others (DiClemente, 1991). Because problems often vary by the particular context (Kazdin, 1993), teachers and parents may have different ideas about appropriate treatment goals (Fonagy et al., 2002). Furthermore, children might have difficulty stating goals because they cannot abstract how things in their lives could be different. A critical issue in treatment planning, then, is to ensure that goal-setting is developmentally sensitive and addresses relevant contexts (e.g., home, school, and neighborhood).

Designing the intervention itself also presents a special set of challenges. First, because of the emotional, physical, and cognitive changes inherent in a child's maturation, interventions need to be developmentally appropriate. Unfortunately, many treatments for children are simply downward extensions of treatments that have been validated on adult populations (Eyberg, Schuhmann, & Rey, 1998; Kaslow & Thompson, 1998). There is mounting evidence that a number of standard treatments that are offered to children and adolescents (e.g., cognitive therapy, parent training) have age-limiting windows of effectiveness (Dishion & Patterson, 1992; Durlak, Fuhrman, & Lampman, 1991; Fonagy et al., 2002). Thus, treatment planning requires familiarity with age-specific interventions that are developmentally anchored (Holmbeck, Greenley, & Franks, 2003; Weisz & Hawley, 2002).

A second factor that complicates intervention selection is the fact that the family and school frequently need to be involved in the treatment (Borduin, 1999; Kazdin, 1997; Fonagy et al., 2002; Kazdin & Weisz, 1998). However, families might resist participation (Kazdin & Wassell, 1998; Szapocznik, Kurtines, Santisteban, & Rio, 1990), and school personnel might be reluctant or too busy to become involved (Fonagy et al., 2002). A key issue in treatment planning is engaging significant third parties, even when they do not see themselves as part of the problem.

Finally, intervention selection is also influenced by client characteristics such as personality factors, expectations about treatment, and demographic features (e.g., socioeconomic status [SES], race, and ethnicity). In fact, these factors are among the most robust predictors of treatment outcome (Beutler & Clarkin, 1990; Cormier & Cormier, 1998). For example, expectations about treatment and the client's readiness to change have been shown to predict premature dropout (Kazdin & Wassell, 1999; Smith, Subich, & Kalodner, 1995) and clinical outcome (Prochaska, DiClemente, & Norcross, 1992). Importantly, matching treatment recommendations to these types of client characteristics has been shown to enhance persistence in treatment and long-term outcome (Cormier & Cormier, 1998; Fonagy et al., 2002; Prochaska et al., 1992; Smith et al., 1995). Simply put, the treatment plan must address, "What works for this client with this set of characteristics?"

The purpose of this chapter is to provide a guide for thinking through the numerous clinical decisions involved in constructing a treatment plan. Table 10.1

TABLE 10.1   Treatment Planning Flowchart

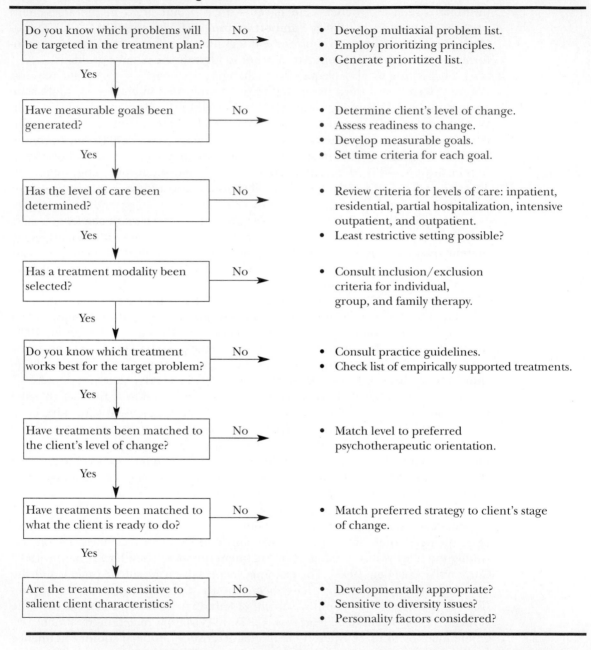

Do you know which problems will be targeted in the treatment plan?	No →	• Develop multiaxial problem list. • Employ prioritizing principles. • Generate prioritized list.
↓ Yes		
Have measurable goals been generated?	No →	• Determine client's level of change. • Assess readiness to change. • Develop measurable goals. • Set time criteria for each goal.
↓ Yes		
Has the level of care been determined?	No →	• Review criteria for levels of care: inpatient, residential, partial hospitalization, intensive outpatient, and outpatient. • Least restrictive setting possible?
↓ Yes		
Has a treatment modality been selected?	No →	• Consult inclusion/exclusion criteria for individual, group, and family therapy.
↓ Yes		
Do you know which treatment works best for the target problem?	No →	• Consult practice guidelines. • Check list of empirically supported treatments.
↓ Yes		
Have treatments been matched to the client's level of change?	No →	• Match level to preferred psychotherapeutic orientation.
↓ Yes		
Have treatments been matched to what the client is ready to do?	No →	• Match preferred strategy to client's stage of change.
↓ Yes		
Are the treatments sensitive to salient client characteristics?	No →	• Developmentally appropriate? • Sensitive to diversity issues? • Personality factors considered?

provides an overview of the key clinical questions that will be addressed. The chapter breaks down the treatment-planning process into three major steps: 1) turning problems into goals; 2) deciding on the structure and type of treatment; and 3) tailoring aspects of treatment to client characteristics. Throughout the chapter, the term "children" refers to both children and adolescents unless otherwise specified.

Although the discussion focuses on designing effective treatments, pragmatic issues such as treatment planning in a managed-care environment are also addressed. At the end, a completed treatment plan on a sample case is presented.

TURNING PROBLEMS INTO GOALS

After the clinician has collected the assessment information, the next issue is translating complex clinical information into a meaningful treatment plan. As an initial step in this process, this section discusses how to 1) generate a comprehensive problem list from the assessment data; 2) prioritize the list in terms of more immediate and long-term targets; and 3) convert these problems into goal statements. A basic principle in this process is that the more specific and focused both the problems and the goals are, the better the long-term outcome (Cormier & Cormier, 1998; Kazdin, 1993; Meichenbaum & Turk, 1987; Woody, Detweiler-Bedell, Teachman, & O'Hearn, 2003). In this regard, it is not surprising that many managed-care entities require that treatment plans include a set of specific problems and measurable goals as a prerequisite for authorizing reimbursement (Domino et al., 1998; Lawless et al., 1999).

Developing a Comprehensive Problem List

Traditional methods of problem identification have tended to simply rely on a diagnosis such as depression or Attention-Deficit/Hyperactivity Disorder (AD/HD). However, this global approach does not clarify the particular symptoms, contextual factors, and developmental issues that need to be addressed in the treatment plan. As an alternative way of formulating the problem, *The Diagnostic and Statistical Manual of Mental Disorders* (Fourth Edition, Text Revision; *DSM-IV-TR;* American Psychiatric Association [APA], 2000a) uses a multiaxial system that can be adapted to generate a more detailed problem list (Gintner, 1995; Kennedy, 1992; Nathenson & Johnson, 1992). Each axis refers to a particular domain of the client's problem; together they provide a comprehensive way of systematically considering relevant areas of functioning. This list will be referred to as the *multiaxial problem list* (Gintner, 1995). A case vignette is presented next to illustrate how to develop the problem list.

CASE EXAMPLE

Becky is a 16-year-old Caucasian female in her sophomore year of high school. About 2 weeks prior to seeking treatment, she told her mother that she had to do something about her weight problem. She reports that she feels "fat" despite the fact that she is only slightly overweight. Her efforts to lose weight have included trying to fast at least 2 days a week and exercising $1\frac{1}{2}$ hours per day. However, at night when her parents are asleep, it is not unusual for her to eat large amounts of potato chips and cookies, which she has hidden in her room. Another pattern is that she stops at several fast-food restaurants after school. She describes life as a constant battle between her efforts to curb her eating and episodes of binge eating. Although this pattern of eating has been evident for the past 4 months, it became worse about a month ago after her boyfriend broke up with her. She believes her weight problem contributed to the breakup. She finds herself so preoccupied by food and ways of controlling her eating that her social life has been significantly curtailed. Personally, she describes herself as shy and reports that she never feels "good enough." She does well in school and her academics have not suffered up to this point.

The Multiaxial Problem List   The case example meets diagnostic criteria for Bulimia Nervosa, Non-Purging Type (APA, 2000a). The first step in translating diagnostic information into a multiaxial problem list is to query which Axis I symptoms of the psychiatric disorder(s) need to be addressed. In terms of the case example, these include fasting, excessive exercise, binge eating, and weight preoccupation. Axis I considerations also include developmental issues (e.g., V-codes such as Phase of Life Problem). Developmental issues such as identity formation and peer acceptance probably explain why the problem has appeared at this time of her life.

Axis II is used primarily to code personality disorders as well as clinically significant traits and defenses (APA, 2000a). Because personality disorders usually do not emerge full blown until mid- to late adolescence, clinicians need to be cautious in using these codes with a youthful population (APA, 2000a). Instead, it might be more practical to consider whether the treatment plan needs to target maladaptive traits and ineffectual coping or defensive styles. For example, Gaw and Beutler (1995) suggest that the way an individual deals with threat or anxiety can be conceptualized as a point on a continuum from acting out against others (externalizer) to withdrawing and criticizing oneself (internalizer). Internalizers tend to direct anxiety to things within the person's control in the form of worry, self-blame, and obsessive-compulsive behaviors. Externalizers deal with anxiety by acting out (e.g., drug use, running away), rationalizing, and blaming others. In the case example, Becky appears to be shy and shows internalizing tendencies. As a result, self-evaluations are likely to be excessively self-critical. These stylistic traits also limit the potential moderating effect of outside feedback from others on her self-concept. The focus on food and weight might be part of a defensive pattern of redirecting anxiety from identity issues to more personally controlled activities such as weight control. Thus, the problem list might include shyness and excessive internalizing or self-blame.

Axis III reminds the clinician to consider whether any medically related action needs to be taken. This includes the need for a medical evaluation or a psychiatric consultation. In terms of the former, medical conditions can cause or exacerbate psychiatric symptoms and vice versa (APA, 2000a). For example, the presence of hypothyroidism can cause depressive-like symptoms and weight gain in children. Conversely, psychiatric conditions such as depression can interfere with a child's compliance to medical conditions such as Type I diabetes. In either case, it would be important to include a medical evaluation as an initial priority on the problem list. Another consideration is whether psychotropic medication is indicated. In the case example, a medical evaluation is typically recommended for an eating disorder to rule out medical complications or underlying medical conditions. However, psychotropic medications are generally not recommended with the nonpurging type of Bulimia in the absence of other complicating factors such as Major Depression (Roth & Fonagy, 2005).

Axis IV considerations examine the role of more contextual factors in the form of psychosocial and environmental problems. For those who are disadvantaged in some way or who are of lower SES, environmental stressors such as poverty, discrimination, and crime victimization are particularly important to consider in the overall treatment plan (Sue & Sue, 1990). In terms of contextual issues, stressors should be considered from each of three major life spheres: family, school, and peers (Borduin & Henggeler, 1990). For example, for children with severe forms of Conduct Disorder, the problem typically manifests itself with family conflict, peer problems, and academic difficulties (Gintner, 2000; Moffitt, 1993). Each of these contextual problems contributes to the overall development and maintenance of the disorder. In the case of Becky, an important stressor to note is the breakup with her boyfriend.

Whereas Axis IV checks for environmental pressures on the individual, Axis V looks at the person side of the equation in terms of psychological, social, and academic or occupational functioning. With regard to the problem list, do any of these areas need to be targeted? In Becky's case, her psychiatric symptoms are moderately severe, but her academic and family functioning seem intact. However, her shyness and weight preoccupation have curtailed social functioning, making the breakup particularly stressful. Thus, the fact that she has few friends would be placed on her problem list.

Keeping developmental limitations in mind, the clinician should develop the problem list collaboratively with the client (Lyman & Campbell, 1996). The next step in the treatment planning process is to prioritize these problems in terms of the order in which they will be addressed.

Principles of Prioritizing   Four general questions can guide decisions about prioritizing the set of identified problems. First, would any of the problems be considered life-threatening or high-risk? Life-threatening behaviors or situations include suicidal and homicidal ideation and gestures as well as serious neglect and physical abuse. High-risk problems have the potential for serious physical or psychological harm (Woody et al., 2003). Examples include sexual abuse, self-mutilation, substance dependence, high-risk sexual activity, and running away. These types of problems would be given top priority and targeted first.

The next prioritizing question would ascertain what the client wants to change the most. Research shows that treatment outcome and commitment to change are a function of the extent to which clients perceive treatment as addressing their model of the problem (Beutler & Clarkin, 1990; Kazdin & Wassell, 1999; Meichenbaum & Turk, 1987; Prochaska et al., 1992). The following are examples of leads for identifying what the client perceives as the most important problem area:

- "Which of the problems on the list would you like to change the most?"
- "If you could pick one problem on the list to change, what would it be?"
- "If your child was doing much better at home and at school, which problem would be the most important to work on first?"

In the case example, there are no life-threatening or high-risk behaviors or situations. Moving to the second prioritizing consideration, Becky's model of the problem is that she is overweight and has trouble controlling her food intake. She believes that if this area improved, she would feel much better about herself. Initial priorities that were agreed upon included addressing late-night snacking and frequenting fast-food restaurants. Another immediate priority was ruling out any kind of medical condition that could be contributing to her "weight problem."

A third prioritizing principle is to identify the problem that cues the occurrence of other problems. For example, an adolescent's anger-management problems at school might be fueled by earlier disagreements with family members at home. By dealing with family issues, subsequent work on anger management will be less demanding. Similarly, in the case of Becky, night binge eating and frequenting fast-food restaurants are good initial target problems because they encourage weight-neutralizing efforts such as fasting and exercise.

For those who have multiple problems or feel discouraged, a fourth principle is to select the problem that is the easiest to resolve or is a subcomponent of a more complex problem. The success in overcoming the easier or proximal problem will not only increase the individual's confidence, but will also result in greater effort being put forth toward subsequent problems (Bandura, 1982). In Becky's case, her shyness might make it difficult for her to make friends. This type of problem can be broken down into prerequisite steps such as initiating and maintaining conversations with others.

In the case of Becky, the prioritized list is as follows:

A. What needs to be addressed initially?
    1. Rule out medical complication
    2. Binge eating at night
    3. Frequenting fast-food restaurants

B. What needs to be addressed next or are prerequisites for more long-term issues?
    4. Excessive exercise
    5. Fasting
    6. Breakup with boyfriend

C. What are subsequent or more long-term issues?
    7. Few friends
    8. Not feeling "good enough" (related to internalizing and self-image issues)

After the clinician generates the problem list, the next step is to turn each of these problems into a goal statement.

Goal-Setting

Like selecting a destination on a map, goal-setting provides direction to the therapeutic endeavor. In this sense, the goal is the destination, whereas the rest of the treatment plan is the set of directions to get there. The more specific the destination, the easier it will be to develop clear directions (Woody et al., 2003). Not surprisingly, many consider goal setting to be the most critical step in the treatment-planning process (Cormier & Cormier, 1998; Kazdin, 1993; Kennedy, 1992; Lyman & Campbell, 1996). In this section, three major issues in goal-setting are discussed: 1) determining the scope of the treatment goals; 2) ensuring that goals are sensitive to the client's readiness to change; and 3) developing goals collaboratively that are specific and measurable.

Scope of Change   The introduction of goal-setting into the treatment process shifts the discussion from "problem talk" to "change talk." As the clinician reviews the problem list, it is important to determine the scope or the nature of change that will be required. Beutler and Clarkin (1990) have made distinctions between more narrow-band change that focuses on symptom removal versus broad-band change that targets repetitive maladaptive patterns or dysfunctional family systems. Similarly, Lyddon (1990) makes distinctions between first-order change, which is directed at specific symptoms or stressors, and second-order change, which attempts to alter personality structure or the family system itself. Prochaska and Norcross (2003) have further differentiated these concepts by outlining five levels of change: 1) symptom/situational problems; 2) maladaptive cognitions; 3) current interpersonal conflict; 4) family/systems conflict; and 5) intrapsychic conflict. As one goes from the symptom/situational level to "deeper" levels, the cause of the problem usually goes back further in time and manifests itself more pervasively in the person's day-to-day functioning (Prochaska & Norcross, 2003). Thus, the upper levels of the model are akin to the concepts of symptom removal (Beutler & Clarkin, 1990) and first-order change (Lyddon, 1990), whereas lower levels are akin to pattern/system change or second-order change. A key concept in treatment planning is to match goal statements with the level of change reflected in the client's model of the problem. When there is a discrepancy between where the problem appears to lie (e.g., intrapsychic conflict) and how the client describes the problem (e.g., symptom/situational), the consensus in the literature is to start where the client is ready to work (Berman, 1997; Beutler & Clarkin, 1990; Prochaska & Norcross, 2003). If in doubt, it is generally better to write goals at the symptom/situational level rather than at "deeper" and potentially more threatening levels of change (Beutler & Clarkin, 1990; Prochaska & Norcross, 2003). In the case of Becky, she describes her problem at a symptom/situational level of change (e.g., excessive weight, binge eating, and the breakup). As treatment progresses, it should be possible to shift to the intrapsychic level to deal with her internalizing style and issues with self-blame and identity.

Stage of Change   Goal-setting assumes that the client is willing to do something about the problem. Research on therapy clients and self-changers, however, has shown that there are various stages of readiness to change (Prochaska & Norcross, 2003). In their review of this literature, Prochaska et al. (1992) describe five stages of change: 1) precontemplation; 2) contemplation; 3) preparation; 4) action; and 5) maintenance. Each stage has a characteristic set of issues and client attitudes. Clients coming into treatment in the precontemplation stage will report no intention to change in the foreseeable future. Clinically, they would be considered resistant or unaware of the problem. They frequently enter treatment at the request of a third party (e.g., school, probation) or to change someone else (e.g., their child). They also might admit to a problem (e.g., alcohol abuse), but be unwilling to change at this time. Research shows that individuals in this stage of change have the highest likelihood of dropping out of treatment or relapsing as soon as external contingencies are removed (DiClemente, 1991; Prochaska & Norcross, 2003; Smith et al., 1995). In this regard, low motivation to change is common among children who visit community clinics (Weisz & Hawley, 1998). Their parents frequently initiate treatment only after the strong urgings or mandates of third parties such as the police, school, or child protection (Weisz & Hawley, 1998). Thus, children, adolescents, and their parents frequently enter treatment at the precontemplation stage. To move forward in the stages of change, precontemplators must admit that they have a problem. In terms of goal-setting, a key issue is for the client to be able to recognize maladaptive aspects of the problem and to realize that change is in their best interest. For example, stating at least three negative consequences of drinking and three benefits of abstaining might be initial goals for an adolescent problem drinker who is in precontemplation.

In the contemplation stage, individuals admit that they have a problem and report wanting to change in the foreseeable future (Prochaska et al., 1992). They are frequently self-referred and show the greatest distress at initial presentation, in comparison to those at other stages of change. However, they are not yet ready to take action because they are unsure of or ambivalent about what to do (DiClemente, 1991). Important goals for individuals in this stage of change include identifying potential solutions to the problem as well as clarifying ambivalence about change. For example, an 11-year-old male reported that he wanted to quit getting into fights, but did not know how to control his temper. Another aspect of the problem was that fighting was a way he maintained his reputation among his peers. Thus, although he was upset about the problem, he was also ambivalent about changing. In this case, the initial goal was stated in terms of identifying at least three ways that he could control his temper without "losing face."

In the preparation stage, individuals intend to take action in the immediate future or have begun to take some small steps to curb the problem. The key issue in this stage is to develop an action plan to change the problem itself, based on what was learned in the contemplation stage. For example, having identified ways to control his temper during the contemplation phase, the 11-year-old described previously is now ready to set goals to reduce fighting.

In the action stage, the client is actually attempting to change the identified problem. A common difficulty is trying to change too many things at one time. As a result, it is often useful to focus on one goal at a time, especially for those with multiple problems. It is also important to reevaluate whether goals that were set earlier require modification. For example, a particular goal might need to be broken down into more manageable sub-goals.

The maintenance stage frequently receives very little attention in the literature, despite the fact that it is the longest period over which change must be sustained. Goal-setting at this stage of change aims at streamlining the plan into essential components that the client can easily maintain. For example, if family conflict was a central focus during the action stage, a maintenance goal might be to have weekly family meetings at a prescribed time. In the case of Becky, her maintenance goals might include eating three meals a day, exercising three times a week with a friend, and doing something for herself each day.

In actuality, these stages do not consistently unfold in this linear fashion (Prochaska & Norcross, 2003). Rather, it is not uncommon for clients to reach a particular stage and then to either discontinue treatment or take a step back. By setting goals that are sensitive to the client's readiness to change, backsliding problems or even dropout can be prevented (Prochaska et al., 1992; Smith et al., 1995).

Generating Specific Goals Collaboratively   This section offers suggestions for developing specific goals that maximize the client's input. The attribution literature suggests that the more the client participates in and is given a choice about a particular endeavor, the greater the commitment to it and the more likely the client will be to make an internal attribution about the change (Meichenbaum & Turk, 1987). Change that is internally attributed (e.g., "I'm doing it because I choose to") is more stable over time than change that is attributed to some outside force (e.g., "I'm only doing it because they are making me do it"). When clients learn to turn problems into goals, they are also acquiring an important skill for solving future problems. A central aspect of this skill is to be able to state goals that 1) specify the desired outcome; 2) set a criteria that will indicate when the outcome has been achieved; and 3) estimate a time frame for reaching the outcome (Cormier & Cormier, 1998; Kennedy, 1992). I offer suggestions for eliciting each of these goal components from the client.

In terms of specifying the desired outcome, clients can be asked questions such as the following:

- "If you had better . . . e.g., self-esteem, control of your temper, give me some examples of things you would be doing that you are not doing now."
- "If you got over this, what would others notice that is different about you?"
- "If you woke up tomorrow and the problem was solved, what would be different about you?"

Some examples of leads that could be used with younger children and their parents include the following:

- To children, "If I had a magic wand and could make things all better, what would be different? What would you be like? What would your friends (or parents) see that would be different about you?"
- To parents, "Let's suppose that our sessions are finished and that you are very happy about what has changed. What would be different? How would your child be different? What would we notice about you?"
- To parents, "If you and your daughter were getting along better, what would we notice?"

There are several common problems that can occur in response to these questions. First, respondents might simply say that they do not know what they would be doing. A useful counter is to ask about times when the problem is better and to inquire about what is different about those times. Another counter is to ask whether they know anyone who handles the problem better and to have them describe what they do. A second common problem is that the client responds with a vague response such as, "I'd feel better." If this occurs, it is helpful to ask, "If you were feeling better, what would people notice about you?" A third problem is when the response indicates that another person would need to change. When this occurs, it is important to point out that although changing others might not be possible, there might be things that the client could do to improve the situation. This can be followed up by asking the following:

> I wonder what we can do to make it better for you? Are there ever times when things are better with. . . ? What's different about those times? What do you do differently? I wonder if you did that more, if it would help?

Note that these questions help to minimize blame and highlight how personal change might be in the client's best interest.

When the desired outcome has been clarified, it is important to determine criteria that will indicate when the goal has been reached. Criteria can be set in terms of four possible dimensions: 1) frequency; 2) duration; 3) intensity; and 4) amount. Frequency focuses on how many times the desired outcome would need to occur. Goals that lend themselves to frequency criteria include problems in which the client wants to decrease or increase a behavior (e.g., fighting, arguing, initiating conversations, or arriving home on time). In the case of Becky, a goal statement that used a frequency criterion was as follows: "Reduce eating at fast-food restaurants from eight times a week to two times or less." The following are examples of leads that can help to specify frequency criteria:

- "How often would you like to be able to do that?"
- "You said that you usually do it . . . times per week. How many times a week would you be satisfied with?"
- To parent, "If your child was doing better, how many times would . . . occur?"

Duration criteria delineate how much time will be spent engaging in a particular behavior. Examples include time spent doing activities such as studying, completing chores, socializing with peers, and engaging in pleasant events. In the case of Becky, her excessive exercise was transformed into the following goal: "Reduce exercise time per day from one and a half hours to 40 minutes." Leads that can generate duration criteria include the following:

- "How much time would you be willing to spend . . . (e.g., studying)?"
- "If you were doing better, how much time would you be spending each day on . . . ?"
- "On a typical day, how much time would you like to spend on . . . ?"

Intensity criteria can be used when the goal is changing the qualitative nature of responses such as anger, sadness, self-deprecation, grief, or self-confidence. You can use a Likert scale to calibrate the desired intensity of response. For example, a depressed adolescent might have a goal of improving his or her daily mood rating from an average of "2" on a 7-point scale to "5" or more (with higher numbers reflecting a more positive mood). Some examples of leads to obtain intensity ratings for the goal are the following:

- "When you come to school now, you said that your nervousness is "7"—real anxious. If things got better, what number would it be?"
- "Pretend that this picture of a thermometer measures how mad you get. What number is it when you fight with your mom now? If things were better, where would you be on the thermometer?"

If more behavioral criteria are required in the particular clinical setting, the clinician can follow up these intensity questions by simply asking, "If the anger rating did drop to 3 or less, what would you be doing that you are not doing now?"

A goal can also be calibrated in terms of the amount of something. Examples would include the amount of money, ounces of alcohol, number of calories, and pounds of weight. This type of criterion is probably used the least with children and adolescents because it can be cumbersome to use. For example, in the case of Becky, it would be difficult to "weigh" the food she consumes or translate it into calories. Instead, we would measure food intake by the number of servings or the number of times she stops at a fast-food establishment (i.e., frequency). However, one possible goal would be to target the amount of money she could save by not buying food.

Finally, each goal should have a statement about the expected time needed to accomplish the goal. Setting a target date motivates the client to get started and to sustain his or her efforts to the completion date. Many managed-care companies also require time estimates for treatment goals. Useful leads to elicit time estimates include the following:

- "How long do you think it will take to . . . ?"
- To parents, "What would be a realistic estimate of how long it would take to . . . ?"

If the client is unable to give an estimate, it is helpful to say, "So it's kind of hard to say. What do you think about 5 weeks? Does that sound reasonable?" It might be difficult or impossible to obtain this type of information from younger children or clients who are hospitalized. Nevertheless, it is often useful to share timelines with clients to the best of their abilities to understand.

Many authors have recommended tiering goals into those that are long-term and those that are short-term (Berman, 1997; Cormier & Cormier, 1998; Kennedy, 1992; Woody et al., 2003). Although this approach helps to delineate ultimate outcomes and the subgoals to achieve them, there are also contraindications to consider. First, this approach might be difficult to use with clients who are in the precontemplation stage. Discussing any goal that suggests major change on the client's part might make treatment appear less relevant (Kazdin & Wassell, 1998) and potentially more threatening (DiClemente, 1991). An alternative approach would be to tier goals in terms of the client's stage of change (Berman, 1997; Prochaska et al., 1992). For example, with precontemplators, goal-setting can be discussed in terms of identifying the pros and cons of the problem behavior and alternative responses. As the client progresses along the stages of change, the goal-setting process can be revisited and new stage-sensitive goals can be created (Woody et al., 2003).

A second problem is that setting long-term goals might not be sensitive to developmental and cultural differences (Baruth & Manning, 1999; Cormier & Cormier, 1998; Sue & Sue, 1990). Young children are not cognitively able to understand abstract long-range goals. Abstract or long-range goals might also be inconsistent with the worldviews of clients from particular ethnic or racial backgrounds (Baruth & Manning, 1999; Paniagua, 1998; Sue & Sue, 1990). For example, many Asian American clients prefer pragmatic goals and seek a solution in a timely fashion (Baruth & Manning, 1999). Thus, decisions about constructing long- and short-range goals need to be considered on a case-by-case basis.

In summary, the multiaxial problem list translates diagnostic information into a set of specific problems. Goal-setting leads help change these problems into specific and measurable goals. Clinically, these goals need to be sensitive to the client's age, ethnic and racial background, scope or level of change, and stage of readiness to change. Individualizing goals in this way also meets the requirements of many utilization-review entities such as managed care. The next step in the treatment-planning process is to develop the therapeutic plan to meet these treatment goals.

DECISIONS ABOUT THE STRUCTURE AND TYPE OF TREATMENT

In this section, I suggest a number of decision rules for selecting 1) the level of care; 2) the therapeutic modality; and 3) the indicated intervention for particular problems and disorders. More global issues such as the level of care are discussed first, followed by progressively more specific considerations about the type of treatment offered.

Level of Care

Children come to treatment with varying needs for structure, supervision, contact, and medical backup. Matching the appropriate level of care to these variables determines the kind of setting in which the treatment will occur. In the current mental health environment, there is a continuum of care that spans from the most restrictive setting (inpatient hospitalization) to those that are less restrictive (e.g., partial hospitalization, intensive outpatient). A basic principle is to select the least restrictive setting that can successfully meet the client's needs (Beutler & Clarkin, 1990; Kennedy, 1992; Lyman & Campbell, 1996). Ideally, this setting will be close to the client's home to maximize family involvement and treatment generalization (Fonagy et al., 2002; Lyman & Campbell, 1996). Using a setting that is more restrictive than is required or that precludes family involvement has been associated with poorer outcome (Lyman & Campbell, 1996; Waggoner, 1992).

Table 10.2 describes admission criteria for various levels of care. Although there is no single standard used nationally, managed-care entities (e.g., Health

TABLE 10.2   Admission Criteria by Level of Care

Inpatient Hospitalization. Must have numbers 1 through 3:

1. Documented *DSM-IV-TR* diagnosis.
2. Requires a 24-hour medically supervised program as indicated by a, b, or c:
   a. Imminent danger to self or others.
   b. Severe self-care impairment or inability to perform activities of daily living.
   c. A significant medical-related complication or condition requires close medical management (e.g., previous psychotropic adverse reaction, uncontrolled diabetes).
3. A lower level of care has either failed or is insufficient to stabilize the client.

Residential Treatment. Must have numbers 1 through 3:

1. Documented *DSM-IV-TR* diagnosis.
2. Requires a 24-hour structured program as indicated by a, b, or c:
   a. Risk of danger to self, others, or property.
   b. Significant impairments in activities of daily living or social, familial, or academic functioning. Social or familial resources are inadequate to ameliorate these deficits.
   c. A medical condition requires regular monitoring or care (e.g., diabetic regime).
3. A lower level of care has failed or is insufficient to lead to improvement.

Partial Hospitalization. Must have numbers 1 through 3:

1. Documented *DSM-IV-TR* diagnosis.
2. Requires a structured daily program as indicated by a, b, or c:
   a. Risk of danger to self, others, or property but does not require 24-hour supervision.
   b. A structured program is needed to maintain activities of daily living or social, familial, or academic functioning.
   c. Periodic medical monitoring or care is required.
3. A lower level of care has failed or is insufficient to lead to improvement.

Intensive Outpatient. Must have numbers 1 through 3:

1. Documented *DSM-IV-TR* diagnosis.
2. Multiple weekly contacts are necessary as indicated by a, b, or c:
   a. Some risk of danger to self, others, or property.
   b. Regular contacts are needed to maintain social, familial, or academic functioning.
   c. Periodic medical monitoring is required throughout the week.
3. A lower level of care has failed or is insufficient to lead to improvement.

Outpatient. Must have numbers 1 through 3:

1. Documented *DSM-IV-TR* diagnosis.
2. Outpatient contacts are necessary as indicated by a, b, or c:
   a. Some risk of danger to self, others, or property.
   b. Clinically significant distress or impairment in social, familial, or academic functioning.
   c. Weekly medical monitoring is required.
3. A lower level of intervention (e.g., support group) is unlikely to lead to improvement.

Note: Criteria are adapted from Mattson (1992) and Health Associates of America (1997).

Associates of America [HAA], 1997) and quality-assurance standards published by professional groups (e.g., Mattson, 1992) typically employ three major criteria for determining the appropriate level of care. First, a *DSM-IV-TR* diagnosis must be clearly documented in terms of symptom presentation. Second, the level of care is determined by judging the severity of symptoms and/or degree of impairment present. Third, justification must be provided that a lower level of care would not be adequate. In this section, each level of care is examined relative to the specific indications for admission.

Inpatient Psychiatric hospitalization affords a secure setting in which 24-hour medical supervision and a therapeutic milieu are provided. Treatment usually includes individual and group therapy as well as periodic family sessions. The primary goal is to stabilize the client and ameliorate the condition that necessitated hospitalization (Kennedy, 1992; Lyman & Campbell, 1996). The length of stay generally ranges from days to weeks (Lyman & Campbell, 1996).

In terms of admission criteria, the diagnostic picture usually is characterized by a severe psychiatric disorder such as a marked Mood Disorder (American Academy of Child and Adolescent Psychiatry [AACAP], 1997b), early-onset Schizophrenia (Fonagy et al., 2002; McClellan & Werry, 1994), or severe Conduct Disorder (AACAP, 1997c). In adolescents, other common disorders are Anorexia (Fonagy et al., 2002), Substance-Related Disorders (AACAP, 1997d), and Bipolar Disorder (AACAP, 1997b). It is important to note that most cases that present at this level of care are characterized by comorbidity (Lyman & Campbell, 1996).

A second major indication for inpatient treatment is that the psychiatric disorder has the potential for incurring significant harm without immediate hospitalization. Although suicidal or homicidal intent are well-recognized examples of this, potential harm could also occur if a medical condition is not closely monitored and managed (Waggoner, 1992). Examples include monitoring withdrawal, stabilizing a serious medical condition (e.g., weight loss in Anorexia), and treating a medical concern that requires an inpatient setting (e.g., overdose complications, the initiation of psychotropic medication in a child who has a significant medical disorder). Lastly, harm can result due to the child's inability to function and self-manage his or her behavior. This can be so severe that activities of daily living (ADLs) such as bathing, grooming, dressing, and feeding are significantly impaired. As a way of gauging the degree of impairment evident at this level of care, Global Assessment of Functioning (GAF; APA, 2000a) scores for inpatient hospitalization are usually about 30 or less (HAA, 1997).

There are a number of inappropriate uses of hospitalization. For example, a child who has suicidal ideation but has no plan and has reliable family support could probably be managed at a lower level of care. A major contraindication for hospitalization is mere custodial care. For example, it would be inappropriate to hospitalize a child in lieu of placement availability at a boarding school or residential center (Hersov, 1994). In terms of justifying this level of care, documentation needs to indicate that a lower level of care has either failed or is unlikely to stabilize a serious condition.

Two major reviews of inpatient treatment outcome for children have been reported. Blotcky, Dimperio, and Gossett (1984) reviewed published articles between

1936 and 1982 and concluded that although findings were positive, these data needed to be interpreted cautiously due to the lack of well controlled studies. In a subsequent review, Pfeifer and Strzelecki (1990) also reported that inpatient treatment yielded positive outcome, especially when a specialized treatment program is offered and aftercare is provided. Interestingly, the relationship between length of inpatient treatment and outcome was mixed, with about half of the studies showing no relationship. Like the previous review, however, many of the reported studies were poorly controlled in terms of research design. Although the quality of many of the studies is problematic, the available data suggest that program specialization and aftercare are important ingredients of a good outcome.

Residential Care   Residential treatment settings provide a structured 24-hour program for those who do not require the close medical supervision that inpatient care affords. Services include counseling, medical monitoring, schooling, special education services, and recreational therapy. Ideally, a family therapy component is also present if home placement is expected. Lengths of stay typically range from weeks to months (Wilson & Phillips, 1992; Lyman & Campbell, 1996).

Diagnostically, many of the disorders that are common in an inpatient setting are also present at this level of care, but they are less acute and potentially less harmful. Disruptive behavior disorders and Posttraumatic Stress Disorder (PTSD) are also prevalent (Lyman & Campbell, 1996). GAF scores at admission are generally less than 50 (HAA, 1997). Common problems in the history of these youths include chronic truancy, school failure, running away, and impulse-control problems that result in destruction of property or danger to self or others (Wilson & Phillips, 1992). Because the family is frequently quite dysfunctional, parents are unable to provide a stable home environment. As a result of these types of problems, out-of-home placement is necessary in order to provide the stability and intensity of services that is required.

Partial Hospitalization   Partial hospitalization provides a structured day program in which services are delivered in a therapeutic milieu. Services offered usually include individual, group, and family therapy; medical monitoring; schooling; and recreational therapy. Participants attend the program at least 3 days per week for approximately 5 to 7 hours a day (Waggoner, 1992). Common disorders at this level of care include Mood Disorders, disorders with psychotic features, Anorexia, Substance-Use Disorders, PTSD, and Disruptive Behavior Disorders. Although danger to self or others and psychosocial impairments are significant, there is no longer the necessity for a 24-hour program. GAF scores are typically 50 or less (HAA, 1997). The major indication for partial hospitalization is that a structured support system is needed to maintain functioning in the community (Wilson & Phillips, 1992).

Although positive findings for partial hospitalization have been reported, outcome studies in this area often suffer from weak research designs that do not include a control group or long-term followup (Sayegh & Grizenko, 1991). To address these problems, Grizenko, Sayegh, & Papineau (1994) compared a group of severely behavior-disordered children in partial hospitalization with a control group. Evaluation included a 6-month followup. Results showed that partial-hospitalization subjects showed significantly more improvement in symptomotology and self-esteem in comparison to the control group.

Intensive Outpatient   Intensive outpatient participants generally meet 3 to 5 days a week for at least 2 to 4 hours each day. Like partial hospitalization, intensive outpatient treatment provides a structured therapeutic milieu and medical monitoring as well as individual, group, and family therapy. GAF scores for these patients at admission are generally 50 or less. Participants at this level of care are more likely to have a sustained period of much better functioning in the past year compared to those at more restrictive levels of care (Lyman & Campbell, 1996). The range of *DSM-IV-TR* disorders can be quite broad, but the primary indication for this level of care is that regular weekly contacts are needed to sustain functioning and minimize the threat to self or others.

Outpatient   At the outpatient level of care, distress or impairment in functioning is clinically significant, but not to the degree evident in more restrictive settings. Treatment usually entails weekly or even biweekly individual, group, or family therapy. Most managed-care plans require a documented *DSM-IV-TR* disorder as a prerequisite for reimbursement (HAA, 1997). In this regard, V-codes such as Bereavement and Parent–Child Problems are typically excluded. GAF scores for outpatients usually range from about 70 to about 30. Well-designed outcome studies of outpatient treatment for children have generally shown positive results that are comparable to findings with adults (Fonagy et al., 2002).

  In summary, the various levels of care provide a continuum of service settings depending on the intensity and type of care required. When the conditions necessitating a particular level of care are ameliorated, treatment is stepped down to a less-intensive level. In this way, the client is always afforded the least-restrictive therapeutic environment possible. Familiarity with clinical indicators for each level of care ensures optimal matching of clinical needs to the appropriate setting.

Therapeutic Modality

The next treatment-planning decision is to select the modality of treatment that will be offered within the particular clinical setting. Earlier reviews suggested that treatment modality did not have a significant impact on treatment outcome (Smith, Glass, & Miller, 1980). However, more recent studies suggest that modality is important depending on the type of disorder (Kazdin, 1997; Pinsof & Wynne, 1995), the age of the client (Weisz & Hawley, 1998; Weisz, Weiss, Alicke, & Klotz, 1987; Weisz, Weiss, Han, Granger, & Morton, 1995), and other client characteristics such as delinquency (Dishion, McCord, & Poulin, 1999), introversion (Weisz et al., 1995), and impulsivity (Gaw & Beutler, 1995; Yalom, 1995). Indications and contraindications for each treatment modality are examined in this section.

Individual Therapy   Of the three treatment modalities, individually oriented approaches offer the greatest flexibility in tailoring treatment to the client's special needs and characteristics (Weisz & Hawley, 1998). Table 10.3 lists some of these special

TABLE 10.3   Selecting a Treatment Modality: Individual, Group, and Family Therapy

Indications for Individual Therapy:

1.   Is the client in crisis?
2.   Is the problem based on an intrapsychic conflict?
3.   Is the problem very specific or intimate?
4.   Is the client unlikely to participate in group therapy?
5.   Does the client meet group therapy exclusion criteria?

Indications for Group Therapy:

1.   Is the problem interpersonal in nature?
2.   Will feedback, modeling, or support from others be therapeutic?
3.   Does the client need to learn a specific skill?
4.   Does the client have the capacity to be accepted by other group members?

Indications for Family Therapy:

1.   Is the problem related to family rules, relationships, or interaction patterns?
2.   Do intergenerational patterns contribute to the problem?
3.   Does the problem reflect a trauma or developmental issue that affects the whole family?
4.   Because of the identified client's age, is family involvement needed to address the problem?
5.   Does the family show the capacity to participate in treatment?

situations. A basic principle is that individual therapy is indicated when the problem requires more time or specialized attention than can be afforded in the other therapeutic modalities. Examples include stabilizing a suicidal adolescent, working through trust issues due to early abandonment, and discussing intimate problems such as sexual orientation or sexual abuse.

A second principle for selecting individual therapy is that the client is unlikely to attend or actively participate in group or family therapy. For example, very shy or socially anxious clients frequently are reluctant to participate in a group (Seligman, 1990). Similarly, the adolescent who is asserting independence might refuse to participate in family sessions. As these types of issues are dealt with individually, there is a greater likelihood that the client will be open to group or family therapy later, if this is indicated.

Finally, individual therapy is indicated when the client is not suitable for either group therapy or the groups that are available (Yalom, 1995). First, there might be no developmentally appropriate group available with children of comparable ages. Second, group therapy might be contraindicated because the client's presence in the group has a high potential for adversely affecting the other participants' therapy. For example, a hostile and resistant antisocial child can undermine the group experience for those who do show the potential to improve (Dishion et al., 1999; Kazdin, 1997; Yalom, 1995). Third, the individual might not be able to accept feedback from others (e.g., strong narcissistic traits) or provide constructive feedback (e.g., socially detached, floridly psychotic). There is mounting evidence that the inappropriate placement of youth in groups can actually worsen the condition that prompted referral (Dishion et al., 1999; Kazdin, 1997).

Group Therapy   The most common modality of treatment offered to children and adolescents in published outcome studies is group therapy (Weisz & Hawley, 1998). A number of empirically supported treatments have been delivered in a group format. These include treatments for depression (Clarke, Debar, & Lewinsohn, 2003; Kaslow & Thompson, 1998), anger management (Feindler, Marriott, & Iwata, 1984; Lochman, Barry, & Pardini, 2003), conduct problems (Lochman, Burch, Curry, & Lampron, 1984), and Posttraumatic Stress Disorder (AACAP, 1998b). Group therapy can also be an excellent vehicle for teaching social and coping skills because training can take advantage of peer modeling and varied rehearsal situations.

A primary indication for group therapy is that the identified problem is interpersonal in nature (Yalom, 1995). Examples include social inhibition, impulse-control problems, social-skill deficits, chronic interpersonal conflicts, and the need for social support (e.g., no friends, coping with the death of a loved one).

Cormier & Cormier (1998) have outlined criteria for placing individuals in heterogeneous versus homogenous groups depending on the type of problem. Homogenous groups, in which participants share a common problem, are indicated for clients who have specific impulse-control problems (e.g., anger management), display similar symptoms (e.g., depression), are coping with a stressful live event (e.g., dealing with parental divorce), or need training in a specific skill (e.g., social problem-solving skills). Developmentally, because of their specific needs, elementary and middle-school-aged children tend to profit more from homogenous groups (Thompson & Rudolph, 2000). Heterogeneous groups, in which members have different interpersonal problems, are more appropriate for older adolescents, whose interpersonal problems occur across a range of contexts. In composing this type of group, it is important to evaluate how members will be able to relate to and accept each other. Those who are considered by other members to be deviant or too dissimilar are likely to have a poor outcome (Yalom, 1995).

Longitudinal studies suggest that group therapy might be contraindicated for young adolescents with delinquency problems (e.g., see Dishion et al., 1999, for a review). A number of studies have shown that peer influence is a significant contributor to the onset and maintenance of antisocial behavior (Gintner, 2000; Moffitt, 1993). Young adolescents, in comparison to older adolescents or younger children, appear to be particularly prone to this type of deviant peer influence (Dishion et al., 1999; Moffitt, 1993). Several studies have shown that a form of "deviancy training" (Dishion et al., 1999) might occur in groups in which delinquent youth are congregated. Family therapy, as well as interventions designed to limit deviant peer affiliation, show the most promise with this population (Borduin, 1999; Henggeler & Lee, 2003).

Family Therapy   Because of the powerful role of the family in a child's life, family therapy is frequently a primary or adjunctive treatment (Kazdin & Weisz, 1998; Pinsof & Wynne, 1995). Table 10.3 lists a number of common problems that would be indications for family therapy. Typically, the younger the child, the greater the probability of family or parental involvement in the treatment. In fact, a common quality-assurance standard in the care of children and adolescents is the involvement of the family in the treatment process (Waggoner, 1992).

Clinical research supports this strong emphasis on family involvement for a number of different problems. In the treatment of adolescent substance abusers, family therapy has been shown to increase treatment initiation, reduce dropout, and enhance long-term success (AACAP, 1997d; Pinsof & Wynne, 1995). Family therapy appears to be superior to an individual therapy approach for mild-to-moderate Conduct Disorder (Brestan & Eyberg, 1998). Family or parental involvement has also been shown to be a key intervention in multicomponent programs for severe Conduct Disorder (Borduin, 1999; Gintner, 2000), AD/HD (Anastopoulos & Farley, 2003; Pinsof & Wynne, 1995; Pelham, Wheeler, & Chronis, 1998), and eating disorders (Fonagy et al., 2002). Typically, these treatments involve weekly meetings with the family or the parents.

Of the three modalities, family therapy is probably the most underutilized. A major problem is that family members are difficult to engage in treatment. For example, Szapocznik et al. (1990) reported that of 650 families invited to treatment by experienced family therapists, only 145 completed the intake procedure. Of those families that do participate in therapy, about 40% to 60% will drop out of treatment prematurely (Szapocznik et al., 1990).

Two major approaches can be used to deal with this engagement problem. First, actual and perceived barriers for entering or remaining in treatment can be addressed. Kazdin & Wassell (1999) identified a number of factors that inhibit treatment participation and therapeutic change. These include practical problems (e.g., transportation), a perception that treatment is not consistent with the parent's view of the problem, a perception that the treatment is overly demanding, and a poor therapeutic alliance. To the extent that the treatment plan can be sensitive to these issues, engagement and therapeutic change can be enhanced.

A second approach to improving family participation is to consider the engagement problem as an example of the family's dysfunctional interaction pattern and to attempt to intervene as such (Szapocznik et al., 1990). For example, if the father does not want to be involved, the therapist might work with the mother to enhance the marital relationship and thereby encourage his involvement. A study that compared the standard manner in which families are invited to attend therapy versus a systems-oriented engagement approach found that dropout was significantly lower for the systems approach (7%) relative to the comparison condition (57%; Szapocznik et al., 1990). Findings like these suggest that there are some promising approaches for dealing with the engagement problem.

Practice Guidelines

There has been increasing pressure from managed care, Health Maintenance Organizations (HMOs), and other utilization-review organizations to show that mental health services are indeed necessary and effective (Domino et al., 1998; Lawless et al., 1999). As a result, professional groups such as the American Academy of Child and Adolescent Psychiatry (AACAP) and the American Psychological Association have sought to develop practice guidelines before these outside agencies attempt to impose their own standards. Basically, these guidelines are designed to help the clinician select and implement the most appropriate treatment for a particular disorder. From a treatment-planning perspective, these guidelines help to delineate the type of treatment that will be delivered within the particular modality.

There have been several approaches for identifying effective treatments, each with its own particular strengths and weaknesses. Although an in-depth discussion of these approaches is beyond the scope of this chapter, a brief overview is presented that includes salient reference material for the interested reader.

Meta-Analyses   A meta-analysis (Smith, Glass, & Miller, 1980) is a way of pooling findings across studies so that the magnitude of the overall treatment effect, referred to as the *effect size* (ES), can be calculated. ES can be considered small (.20), medium (.50), or large (.80 or larger; Cohen, 1988). There have been four meta-analyses of the child and adolescent outcome literature, encompassing over 300 studies of children from 2 to 18 years of age (Weisz & Hawley, 1998). Across these meta-analytic studies, the findings have consistently shown the ES for treated children to range from .71 (Casey & Berman, 1985) to .88 (Kazdin, Bass, Ayers, & Rogers, 1990). In terms of the latter ES, this would mean that the average treated child did better than 81% of the control-group children. Additionally, findings indicate that treatments are equally effective for overcontrolled problems (e.g., anxiety disorders) and undercontrolled problems (e.g., Conduct Disorder, AD/HD; Weisz et al., 1995). In terms of treatment approaches, behavioral treatments have yielded larger effect sizes than nonbehavioral approaches (Weisz & Hawley, 1998). A weakness of these meta-analytic studies is that most of the studies (about 75%) test Behavioral or Cognitive-Behavioral Interventions (Weisz & Hawley, 1998). As a result, nonbehavioral approaches are sorely underrepresented. Thus, although meta-analytic findings have shown that counseling is effective for a broad range of childhood problems, results should be interpreted cautiously with this limitation in mind.

AACAP Practice Parameters   Professional groups have also used task-force reports to suggest best practices. In the area of child and adolescent treatment, AACAP has been quite active in delineating practice parameters. In terms of their procedures, a task force of experts reviews available research findings on a particular disorder or problem and develops a set of recommendations. When insufficient data is available, the committee develops a consensus opinion. AACAP has published a number of practice standards for the treatment of child and adolescent disorders, including Depressive Disorders (1998a), Posttraumatic Stress Disorder (AACAP, 1998b), Anxiety Disorders (Bernstein & Shaw, 1997), AD/HD (AACAP, 1997a), Bipolar Disorder (AACAP, 1997b), Conduct Disorder (AACAP, 1997c), Substance-Use Disorders (AACAP, 1997d), and Schizophrenia (McClellan & Werry, 1994). The major strength of these guidelines is that they are comprehensive in the range of clinical decisions that are addressed. Guidelines are provided for conducting an assessment, selecting a level of care, choosing a treatment modality, and selecting effective psychotherapy approaches and medications. The major shortcoming, however, is that there are no clear criteria for determining the strength of the findings. Rather, it is left to the opinion of the group to judge the quality of the evidence. Nevertheless, these guidelines provide a rich source of assessment and treatment recommendations.

American Psychological Association Task Force A third effort to identify effective treatments was undertaken by the Task Force on Promotion and Dissemination of Psychological Procedures (1995), Division 12 (Clinical Psychology), of the American Psychological Association. This group was asked to identify empirically supported treatments for the purpose of educating clinicians, students, and third-party providers. The task force developed a set of strict research criteria for classifying treatments as well-established, probably efficacious, or experimental. Unfortunately, most of the treatments that were examined focused on adult psychiatric disorders. A subsequent group was asked specifically to examine treatments for child and adolescent disorders (Lonigan, Elbert, & Johnson, 1998). Their findings were published in a special issue of the *Journal of Clinical Child Psychology* (*1998*, Volume 27, #2). The issue contains reviews for disorders such as AD/HD (Pelham et al., 1998), Depression (Kaslow & Thompson, 1998), Conduct and Oppositional problems (Brestan & Eyberg, 1998), and Anxiety Disorders (Ollendick & King, 1998). A recent meta-analysis of child and adolescent psychotherapy outcome found that evidence-based treatments outperformed usual care interventions (Weisz, Hensen-Doss, & Hawley, 2006).

A weakness of the American Psychological Association list of empirically supported treatments is that the treatment studies cited 1) generally exclude children with comorbid disorders; 2) use manualized treatments that are highly structured; and 3) tend to test only Behavioral and Cognitive approaches (Westen & Morrison, 2001). As a result, a major criticism of this approach is that findings might not generalize to "real-world" therapy in which client populations and treatments are more varied (Westen & Morrison, 2001).

Although these various efforts to identify "best practices" can be useful, the counseling practitioner or clinician needs to consider whether this client with this set of characteristics is likely to profit. Unfortunately, most treatment-outcome studies that attempt to identify empirically supported treatments rarely test how findings are moderated by client factors such as age, gender, race, personality style, and readiness to change (Gaw & Beutler, 1995; Prochaska et al., 1992; Weisz & Hawley, 1998). As a way of addressing this problem, the next section examines how these individual difference factors can be addressed in the overall treatment plan.

TAILORING INTERVENTIONS TO CLIENT CHARACTERISTICS

Sensitivity to client characteristics has been shown to improve client satisfaction, reduce dropout, and enhance treatment outcome (Duncan & Miller, 2000; Gaw & Beutler, 1995; Prochaska et al., 1992). Factors that have been studied include the client's level and stage of change, developmental factors, demographic factors (e.g., race, ethnicity, and socioeconomic status), and personality characteristics such as impulsivity and coping style. Each of these variables is discussed in terms of tailoring various aspects of the treatment plan.

Matching Treatments to the Level of Change

Levels of change were discussed earlier with regard to determining the scope of change in the goal-setting process. In this section, levels of change are considered relative to selecting treatment approaches. Prochaska & Norcross (2003) suggest that certain theories of psychotherapy are more relevant at particular levels of change. Behavioral interventions would be indicated when the primary focus is changing symptoms (e.g., school avoidance, anxiety, fighting). Cognitive therapies would be most appropriate for problems involving maladaptive cognitions. Interpersonal therapy (Weissman et al., 2000) has been shown to be particularly effective for current interpersonal problems (e.g., role disputes, role transitions). Strategic and structural family therapies would be indicated for family systems problems. Psychodynamic and existential approaches would be most relevant for intrapsychic problems. By matching treatment approaches to the indicated level of change, the proposed intervention "makes sense" in terms of the client's model of the problem. As treatment progresses, other levels of change can be addressed, as needed, to the extent that the client is receptive to broadening the scope of change.

Matching Interventions to the Stage of Change

A key treatment-planning issue is determining what the client is ready to do. In this regard, the stages-of-change model provides a motivational map of the client's involvement in the therapeutic process. These stages suggest *when* particular interventions are likely to be successful in relation to the degree of motivation. Each stage has specific tasks that must be addressed in order for the client to move on to the next stage (DiClemente, 1991; Gintner & Choate. 2003; Prochaska & Norcross, 2003). Table 10.4 outlines how the clinician can match interventions to address the particular tasks of each stage of change.

Precontemplation   In the precontemplation stage, clients do not see themselves changing in the foreseeable future. The major tasks at this stage are to help the client to 1) "see" the problem and its maladaptive consequences; 2) realize that change is possible and in the client's best interest; and 3) increase commitment to the therapeutic endeavor. Interventions discussed in this section are based upon the principles of motivational interviewing developed by Miller and Rollnic (1991), as well as by extensive research on ways of increasing commitment to change (Gintner & Choate, 2003; Meichenbaum & Turk, 1987).

Table 10.4 lists helpful strategies for addressing these tasks. First, paraphrasing a classic psychodynamic dictum, it is important to deal with defensiveness before tackling the conflict itself. As a result, it is important to understand the client's reasons for avoiding change. For example, the clinician might say, "I bet there's a good reason why you do not want to be here. I'd like to understand that." This type of response validates the client's experience and helps to elucidate his or her model of the problem. This discussion can set the stage for reframing treatment as a way of dealing with personal concerns. To quote an old cowboy saying, "It's easier to ride a horse in the direction that it is going" (Hoyt, 2000, p. 208).

TABLE 10.4   Tasks and Relevant Strategies by Stage of Change

| | Stage of Change | | | | |
	Precontemplation	Contemplation	Preparation	Action	Maintenance
Tasks	Own the problem	Identify causes of the problem	Develop a specific plan	Be systematic	Streamline the plan
	Realize that change is possible	Resolve ambivalence	Learn prerequisite skills	Grade progress realistically	Prevent relapse
	Become committed to therapy	Reevaluate the meaning of change	Make commitment to act	Know how to recover from a slip	Incorporate change into lifestyle
			Prepare environment	Check support systems	
Strategies	Get their model of the problem	Consciousness-raising	Use leads to get specifics	Change one thing at a time	Provide a model of maintenance
	Be empathetic Provide choices	Bibliotherapy	Consult best practice guidelines	Arrange for proximal success	Plan for high-risk situations
	Have client give you the answers	Experiential activities	Teach prerequisite skills	Address unsupportive environment	Develop a plan for slips
	Do "balanced" pros and cons	Pros/cons of change for self and others	Encourage public commitment	Plan how to recover from a slip	Incorporate change into a positive lifestyle
	Expose to coping models		Engage support system	Fine-tune the plan regularly	

Another helpful strategy in dealing with resistance is to respond empathetically. Empathic responses promote the development of the relationship and will enhance the clinician's social influence with the client (Meichenbaum & Turk, 1987; Miller & Rollnick, 1991). A former student of the author shared a personal experience that exemplifies this principle. After the first group meeting for adolescent substance abusers, his more seasoned cotherapist commented that he had been "pretty easy" on the group members because he had primarily made reflective comments. The former student responded, "I believe in opening an account before making a withdrawal."

A number of techniques have been found to increase commitment and motivation to change. The basic social psychological principle is that commitment is enhanced when the individual attributes behavior change to internal factors versus outside pressure (Meichenbaum & Turk, 1987; Miller & Rollnick, 1991). Clinicians can facilitate this set by providing children and parents with choices about different aspects of treatment. To the extent that they perceive participation to be due to their own volition, they will be more committed to the endeavor. In the same way, using leads that elicit their participation enhances the perception of personal involvement in the process. For example, instead of pointing out negative consequences of drug-using behavior, the clinician could ask the client questions about how the drug use is affecting personal, social, and scholastic spheres. Another principle is that if individuals make a small commitment now, they are more likely to make a bigger one later. For example, parents who question the value of being involved in their child's treatment might be asked, "Would you be willing to come to three sessions, after which we can re-evaluate the need for you to participate?" By the third session, there is a greater likelihood of the parent continuing because time and effort has been invested willingly in the therapeutic endeavor (Meichenbaum & Turk, 1987; Prochaska & Norcross, 2003).

As a therapeutic alliance is established, the client is more ready to examine the problem. A useful technique is to discuss the pros and cons of the problem in a "balanced" manner (Janis & Mann, 1977). This means that the counseling practitioner or clinician needs to appear neutral or fair to each side of the equation. This approach has been shown to increase the likelihood that the client will make a more responsible decision (Meichenbaum & Turk, 1987).

Finally, in terms of social influence, individuals are more likely to be persuaded by a coping model (e.g., someone like themselves) than a "master model" (e.g., a person who is seen as an expert; see Prochaska & Norcross, 2003). This principle is especially salient for those who do not believe that they have the power to change the problem. For example, an adolescent client might be asked to talk to someone who was initially resistant to attending an adolescent drug-treatment program, but who subsequently participated and profited from treatment.

Tactics to avoid with precontemplators include giving them strongly loaded educational materials and aggressively confronting them with the problem (DiClemente, 1991; Miller & Rollnick, 1991). These clients are not at a place where they can "hear" these types of messages. The strategies discussed in this section, hopefully, will help clients recognize that change is possible and in their own best interests.

Contemplation   In the contemplation stage, individuals admit that they have a problem, but are not yet ready to act. Table 10.4 lists the major tasks for this stage, which include 1) identifying the factors that contribute to the problem; and 2) considering what change will mean personally and for those around the client.

Consciousness-raising strategies are particularly indicated at this stage of change. The type of consciousness-raising, however, depends on "what" level of change the treatment is addressing. At the symptom/situational level, it might entail pinpointing the antecedents, the responses, and the consequences to the problem. Having the client self-monitor these factors might be a particularly useful exercise. At the maladaptive cognition level, irrational beliefs, negative automatic thoughts, and other forms of distorted thinking could be delineated. If the problem is due to current interpersonal conflicts, issues such as role transitions (e.g., child leaving home), loss, and conflict-resolution skills would be explored (Weissman et al., 2000). At the family-systems level, techniques such as sculpting would be used to help family members see how close they feel to one another. Consciousness-raising at the intrapersonal level would focus on working through defenses, buried feelings, and unconscious conflicts.

In the contemplation stage, clients are more open to reading books and participating in experiential activities such as watching a relevant movie. For example, a family who had lost a child in a tragic accident was helped greatly by watching the movie *Ordinary People,* which portrays a family's reaction to the sudden loss of a family member. Books can also be excellent adjunctive vehicles for helping clients understand the problem. For example, elementary-age children who are coping with a loss might be asked to read *When Dinosaurs Die* (Brown & Brown, 1996).

Discussing the pros and cons of change helps clients identify potential investments in the problem as well as the benefits of change. It is particularly helpful to frame this exercise in terms of the pros and cons for the client as well as significant others. This has the advantage of clarifying potential stumbling blocks and the positive ramifications of change for all parties involved.

As the causes of the problem are identified, potential solutions become more evident. By the end of contemplation, the client frequently feels more empowered and confident that a resolution is possible. Motivationally, the client is ready to prepare for action.

Preparation   Typical problems encountered at this stage include a premature jump into action without thinking through the specifics of the plan and the potential responses of significant others. Table 10.4 lists common tasks that must be addressed at this stage and relevant interventions.

A number of strategies can facilitate progress through the preparation stage. First, it is useful to use leads that prompt the client to generate specific aspects of the action plan. For example, clients can be asked to clarify "what they would be doing" and "when they would be doing it." Another avenue for generating aspects of the plan is to consider the practice guidelines for the particular problem. In this regard, it is important to frame the recommendation in a way that is consistent with the client's model of the problem. As the plan is elaborated, it might be clear that the client might need to acquire prerequisite skills. For example, a shy and depressed 11-year-old who wants to make friends might need to first practice basic skills such as initiating a conversation and maintaining eye contact.

At this stage, it is important to encourage activities that will enhance the client's motivation to undertake action. For example, commitment to act can be enhanced by letting others know about the intended change (Meichenbaum & Turk, 1987). For example, a student who had previously been quite disruptive might inform his teacher that he is going to try to earn stars on the board instead of Xs. It is also important to prepare significant others so that they can support efforts to change. For example, a parent who needs to take more personal time off from work might inform her family of her intentions.

Action   At this stage, the plan that was outlined during the preparation stage now begins to be carried out. (Prochaska & Norcross, 2003). Common problems include changing too many things at one time and becoming dissatisfied with the rate of change. Related to the latter, a lapse in the plan can occur that leads to giving up altogether. As the action phase unfolds, it also might be necessary to modify the original plan to address unanticipated problems or issues.

As a way of addressing these problems, Table 10.4 lists the major tasks and strategies of this stage. In terms of tasks, it is important that the client carry out the plan in a systematic fashion. It is usually best to target one behavior or area at a time. This approach can also help to deal with impatience about the rate of change because this more focused approach makes success experiences more likely and proximal.

As the individual begins to change, those in the environment might respond in ways that sabotage these efforts. This is particularly problematic when there are family-systems problems. If this occurs, it might be necessary to modify the treatment plan to include significant others.

As in most learning, it is not unusual to take three steps forward and one step back. As a result, it is useful to have a plan for dealing with a lapse. Research shows that how you think and act following the slip predicts whether it is a temporary setback or a full-blown relapse (Marlatt & Gordon, 1985; Witkeiwitz & Marlatt, 2004). All-or-nothing thinking such as "My slip means I can't do it" portends a negative emotional reaction and a greater likelihood of giving up. On the other hand, if the client is prepared to think more realistically and has a plan about what to do, these types of slips are more likely to be only temporary setbacks (see Marlatt & Gordon, 1985). Thus, treatment planning for this stage of change should include ways to handle a breakdown in the plan.

Finally, if additional problems emerge or the plan is not working, modifications in the plan can be made as needed. The attribution bias under these conditions is to blame the client. Instead, collaboratively working with the client might suggest important issues that were overlooked. A good rule of thumb is to revisit the treatment plan periodically to assess whether changes are necessary.

Maintenance   As the problem resolves, the client enters the maintenance stage. Key tasks at this stage are streamlining the action plan, preventing relapse, and incorporating change into the overall lifestyle pattern. Table 10.4 lists relevant interventions for these tasks.

First, providing a cognitive model for maintenance can help clients understand the differences between action plans and maintenance plans. For example, parents who had successfully carried out a behavioral-management plan with their son were told the following:

> Do you remember what it was like when you first came to see me? You felt like your child was running the household. You worked real hard, however, at implementing a consistent and positive behavior-management plan. It made a big difference. That was like making a down payment on a new house. But to keep that house, you have to make your monthly payments. In the same way, there are family routines that can help to sustain the changes that you have made.

This metaphor sets the stage for creating a maintenance plan.

The maintenance plan has three major components. First, a decision has to be made about which maintenance activities need to be woven into the daily lifestyle. For example, in the preceding case, the parents decided to have weekly family meetings and to simplify the behavior-management plan. A second component is to anticipate high-risk situations that could trigger a lapse in the plan (Marlatt & Gordon, 1985; Witkeiwitz & Marlatt, 2004). These are typically situations that might have triggered a lapse in the past. The client can also be asked about what sorts of events could make it difficult to stay on the plan. Coping plans for these situations can be devised and even rehearsed. Third, as was done in the action stage, procedures for coping with a lapse in the plan need to be considered. The client can use a "maintenance notebook" to outline each of these steps and then refer to the notebook as needed.

Developmental Considerations

Another important client characteristic to consider in treatment planning is the client's age, which is the most commonly used index of a child's developmental level (Eyberg et al., 1998). There is a paucity of data on the effectiveness of specific treatments at different ages (Eyberg et al., 1998; Lonigan et al., 1998). As a result, there has been a call in the literature to design interventions that are sensitive to the child's physiological, cognitive, and emotional developmental level (Lonigan et al., 1998). With this in mind, this section examines age-related considerations in treatment design and delivery.

Developmentally, younger children are more dependent and more influenced by their caretakers compared to older children and adolescents. As a result, parental or family involvement is especially indicted to ensure that parent–child relationships are positive and discipline is effective. In this regard, several studies have shown that parent training is more effective in the treatment of younger children in comparison to adolescents (Dishion & Patterson, 1992; Pelham et al., 1998; Ruma, Burke, & Thompson, 1996).

Another consideration in treating younger children is that their level of cognitive and emotional development limits their ability to clearly understand or explain inner turmoil (Eyberg et al., 1998). Instead, problems tend to be expressed in behavioral terms. Not surprisingly, effective treatments for this age group typically entail action-oriented interventions such as play activities to instill social skills (see Webster-Stratton & Hammond, 1997). For older children and adolescents, however, more cognitively oriented treatments become appropriate. In a meta-analysis that examined the relationship between a child's age and the effectiveness of cognitively based treatments, Durlak et al. (1991) found that older children (i.e., 11 years old and above) appeared to profit more from cognitively oriented therapy than younger children.

In early and later adolescence, peers become particularly influential as youth begin to individuate from their families (Dishion et al., 1999). In fact, peer affiliation has been shown to either protect against or promote behavior problems, depending on whether the peers are more prosocial or more deviant (Dishion et al., 1999; Moffitt,

1993). For example, arranging strong prosocial peer contacts can moderate an adolescent's antisocial behavior (Gintner, 2000; Weisz & Hawley, 2002). As a result, treatment plans with this age group need to be particularly sensitive to whether peer affiliation needs to be addressed.

Family problems during adolescence reflect attempts to delineate personal identity and autonomy. Parents no longer have the extent of environmental control evident in younger children. As a result, conflicts over rules and family values are common. These developmental considerations suggest that the role of family therapy is different for adolescents in comparison to younger children (Weisz & Hawley, 2002). There is some evidence that more interactional forms of family therapy (versus a parental-skill training format) might be more indicated to deal with these types of problems (Alexander & Parsons, 1982; Gintner, 2000).

Multicultural Issues

Cultural, ethnic, racial, and SES group differences are receiving more attention as critical factors to address in designing effective treatment plans (Baruth & Manning, 1999; Cauce et al., 2002; Cormier & Cormier, 1998; Paniagua, 1998). Three important factors to consider are the level of acculturation (Paniagua, 1998), the client's worldview (Sue & Sue, 1990), and the social context in which the problem is embedded (Baruth & Manning, 1999). The level of acculturation reflects the extent to which the new culture is integrated with or replaces the old cultural beliefs, language, values, and lifestyle (Paniagua, 1998). For example, Hispanics who speak primarily Spanish and whose friends are also primarily Spanish speaking probably have a low level of acculturation (Paniagua, 1998). As a result, the treatment plan needs to be especially sensitive to the client's traditional Hispanic culture (Baruth & Manning, 1999). It might also suggest the inclusion of indigenous practices such as the use of folk tales to help children understand important life lessons (Paniagua, 1998).

Worldview can be defined as the way the individual perceives his or her relationship to the world (Sue & Sue, 1990). It includes the views of human nature, relationships, time orientation, and the extent of self-expression. For example, in many Asian cultures, managing emotions is seen as a sign of maturity, and family honor is held in high esteem. Consequently, an Asian American adolescent might perceive uncovering work in psychotherapy as taboo, especially if it means speaking badly of his or her family (Baruth & Manning, 1999). Instead, a more effective approach would be to focus on the present and solve the problem at hand (Paniagua, 1998). The principle of understanding the client's model of the problem as an initial task in psychotherapy ensures that each client's particular worldview will be honored.

Contextual contributors to the problem are especially salient to consider for various multicultural groups due to the history of disadvantage, prejudice, disenfranchisement, and poverty (Cauce et al., 2002; Sue & Sue, 1990). Axis IV aspects of the problem list are especially salient in this regard. These contextual factors include family, school, community, work, and peer areas. Interestingly, treatments that have addressed various life domains such as multisystemic therapy have been shown to be especially effective for clients of color (Henggeler, Melton, & Smith, 1992).

SES is another important determinant of an individual's values and lifestyle. In fact, Baruth and Manning (1999) suggest that:

> Social class differences may be more pronounced than cultural differences. For example, as social class differences separate members of the European cultures, a lower-class African American may share more cultural commonalities with a lower-class European American than with middle- or upper-class African Americans. (p. 10)

SES differences have been shown to affect the likelihood of seeking treatment, being accepted into treatment, and continuing in treatment (Gaw & Beutler, 1995). Beutler and Clarkin (1990) warn, "Lower socioeconomic class patients may have expectations of the therapy relationship and the treatment process which are so discrepant with those of the treating clinician that they rapidly become discouraged and lose their motivation (p. 62)." In this regard, there is some evidence that lower SES clients prefer active and time-limited treatments to those that are long-term or nondirective (Beutler & Clarkin, 1990). This suggests that brief therapy approaches which address the upper levels of change (e.g., symptom/situational) might be more appropriate for lower SES clients and their families.

Personality Factors

Personality factors have been shown to influence treatment outcome (Gaw & Beutler, 1995). For example, of the characteristics studied, impulsivity and coping style are particularly relevant to consider in designing treatment plans for children. Impulsivity refers to an individual's tendency to be readily pulled by and act on internal or external stimuli. More structured treatments, such as Cognitive-Behavioral approaches, appear better suited to these types of individuals (Gaw & Beutler, 1995). On the other hand, those who are low on impulsivity might profit more from a less structured or non-directive approach.

Earlier internalization and externalization were given as examples of coping styles that could be noted on the multiaxial problem list. Gaw & Beutler (1995) suggest that the treatment plan can be optimally designed to accommodate each style. Because externalizers tend to deal with anxiety by avoidance, acting out, or projecting blame, they tend to be less aware of their own emotions and as a result, tend to do poorly in insight-oriented types of therapy. More structured behavioral approaches provide a better fit for this style. In contrast, internalizers tend to be over-controlled, self-critical, and introspective. As a result, they are more likely to respond to insight-oriented approaches.

In summary, a well-constructed treatment plan attempts to design the treatment to fit these client factors. The challenge is to consider not only the child, but also other relevant parties that will be involved. As a way of illustrating the application of the treatment-planning principles discussed in this chapter, the next section describes a case example of a treatment plan.

Case Background

Ken is a 12-year-old Caucasian fifth grader who was brought to treatment by his mother at the school's urging. The precipitating event was an incident in which he taunted a visually impaired female student at school.

For the past 6 years, he has had numerous academic and behavioral problems. At school, the behavioral problems include swearing at teachers and, on two occasions, actually hitting and kicking them. These types of problems have resulted in five suspensions in the past 2 years. He also has a great deal of conflict with his classmates. When he does not get his way, he either tries to bully them or pick a fight. On one occasion, he hit a classmate so hard in the ear that it required surgery to restore the victim's hearing.

Academically, he barely makes passing grades. He was held back the past year for failing grades. About a month ago, he was placed in an alternative program for behavior-disordered students after his most recent suspension. Although he seems to have average mathematical ability, he has a great deal of difficulty with any task that requires reading. On two occasions, the school system attempted to test him for reading problems, but he became so disruptive that the testing could not be continued. Despite these problems, he has unusually good artistic ability, especially in the area of drawing.

At home, there are constant arguments about house rules. The mother is the primary disciplinarian and the father plays a more passive role. This pattern is compounded by the fact that the father's construction work requires him to be out of town for extended periods of time. The main discipline technique is taking away privileges and grounding. When confronted with his misbehavior, Ken typically fabricates a story that places the blame on someone else.

In the neighborhood, he has no friends. He has a reputation as the "mean meany" because he seems to enjoy intimidating the other children, especially those who are younger. He has been arrested for theft and vandalism in the neighborhood on four separate occasions that date back to the age of 8.

Ken is an only child. Both parents dropped out of high school in the eleventh grade and were married shortly after. They have been married for 13 years, but have had several separations in that time. Each time, his father left for a few months. The family is considered low SES. Financial problems are a frequent source of family arguments.

Ken has had various forms of mental health treatment in the past. In the first grade, he saw a play therapist for about five sessions. On two other occasions, the family was referred for treatment, but only the mother and son attended. Each time, they discontinued after a couple of sessions. Ken was hospitalized about a year ago after threatening the life of a neighborhood child. He was discharged after a month and referred to outpatient therapy. However, he did not continue after the first session because, "The counselor was in my face."

In the interview, Ken presents in a confident and swaggering manner. He reports that the real problem is that everyone is on his back. He appears to be proud of his bullying and his acting out. On the other hand, it is clear that much of his disruptive behavior is a way that he gains attention from others, especially adults.

Case Conceptualization

This section discusses the various treatment-planning decisions relative to this case. Diagnostically, Ken meets criteria for Conduct Disorder, Childhood Onset. As is common for those with this diagnosis, the clinical picture is also dominated by Oppositional Defiant symptoms (APA, 2000a). Key symptoms that need to be targeted in the treatment plan include bullying, fighting, aggressive behavior toward school staff, and opposition to rules at home and in the school. There are also partner relational problems and parenting-skill problems that appear to exacerbate the conduct problems. From a systems perspective, Ken is overinvolved with his mother, which stabilizes emotional distance between the parents. Interpersonally, Ken appears to have significant skill deficits in social skills and social problem-solving (e.g., considering alternative solutions to interpersonal conflict). His externalizing style minimizes personal culpability and helps him maintain his positive image of himself. However, he also seems to be a lonely and very frustrated child who uses his misbehavior as a way of getting attention from others in the only way that he knows how. One unanswered question is whether he has a reading disorder that might be contributing to his academic difficulties.

In terms of decisions about the most appropriate treatment, he clearly meets criteria for outpatient treatment. There is no imminent danger to himself or others, and the structure of the alternative school helps him to function throughout the day. The optimal modalities would be family therapy to address the systems and parenting problems and individual treatment to ameliorate Ken's social-skill deficits. The latter could also provide a corrective interpersonal experience. Group therapy would be contraindicated because of his potential adverse effects on others and his need for more intensive and individualized treatment. Best-practice standards suggest that a multisystemic approach, which targets family, school, peer, and personal domains, would be an effective treatment approach (Brestan & Eyberg, 1998; Henggeler et al., 1992; Gintner, 2000). This approach has been shown to be particularly effective with chronic violent delinquents, many of whom are from low SES families.

Finally, client characteristics need to be considered. In terms of levels of change, the mother and father see the problem as Ken's bothersome symptoms, despite the family system's contribution. Ken sees the problem as the behavior of others who are always on his back. Each family member sees the problem as requiring someone else to change. Consequently, they appear to be at the precontemplation stage and, as a result, need to be sold on the idea that change is in their best interest. Initial treatment goals need to emphasize the development of a collaborative relationship in which action on their part is not seen as a sign of "fault" for the problem. Ken's externalizing style suggests that he might have difficulty with an insight-oriented approach. Instead, the individual therapy component would be structured, focusing on building social and conflict-resolution skills. These efforts can be extended to developing more positive relationships with peers and adults.

The family component would emphasize increasing positive interactions between family members and decreasing family arguments. By helping the parents become more consistent and positive in their parenting, a subtle systems intervention is also made. The increased communication that these efforts would entail will reduce the couple's emotional distance. It also will enable them to respond to discipline problems with a "united front." Increasing communication between the parents and school could further enhance home discipline and consistency across settings.

With this case conceptualization in mind, we can outline a detailed treatment plan. Although this sample treatment plan might appear more detailed than most, remember that this is a multiple-problem case in which participants are precontemplative as to change. As a result, the treatment plan exemplifies how to address a variety of problems systematically and how to tailor the treatment plan to the participants' stage of change. The extent to which part or all of this plan would be required depends on the particular clinical setting. For example, managed-care agencies might require a plan for only the next five to eight sessions. As such, the treatment plan provides an overall model that spans from the initiation of treatment to problem resolution. Comments have been added in italics as explanatory points, but would not appear in the actual treatment plan. Throughout the therapeutic process, these plans can be modified or readjusted to meet the client's changing needs.

Sample Treatment Plan for Ken

Problem List:
1. Conflict with teachers
2. Bullying and conflict with peers
3. Social skill deficits
4. Externalizing style
5. Family conflict over rules
6. No friends
7. Reading and academic problems

Prioritized List:

What needs to be addressed initially?

1. Family conflict over rules
2. Conflicts with teachers
3. Rule out reading disorder

What needs to be addressed next? What are prerequisites to long-term goals?

4. Social skill deficits
5. Bullying and conflict with peers

What problems require more long-term work?

6. No friends
7. Externalizing

Treatment Goals and Plan   More immediate goals (within the next 4 weeks):

1. Be able to state at least three benefits of reduced conflict over family rules.
   (Precontemplation: Arrange activities in which family members provide the rationale for the benefits of treatment.)

   Plan:
   a. Arrange weekly outpatient family therapy session initially focusing on current and past instances when family members got along *(instill hope that change is possible).*
   b. Elicit a verbal commitment to attend therapy with the goal of more positive interactions.

2. Identify at least three differences between times when family members are cooperating and times when there is an argument. *(Contemplation: identify solutions.)*

   Plan:
   a. Assign a family homework project of monitoring positive and negative interactions.
   b. Have family members share their monitoring information in session *(starting with positive instances to set a positive tone).*

3. Complete a reading assessment administered by pupil appraisal.
   (Rule out a reading problem as a potential contributing factor to school problems.)

   Plan:
   a. Arrange a referral for testing.
   b. Discuss the testing with Ken, pointing out its potential benefits for him.

Short-term goals (within the next 10 weeks):

4. Decrease arguments over family rules from three times a day to one time or less a day.
   (Preparation to Action: Have family generate specifics to increase commitment. Emphasize positive interactions first to create a warmer family atmosphere and then target discipline.)

Plan:

  a. In session, have family members write out family rules. Then, develop a system that recognizes and rewards cooperation and compliance and withholds privileges for noncompliance.

  b. Role-play and provide feedback in following parenting skills: 1) attending to positive behaviors; 2) delivering positive reinforcement; and 3) withholding privileges.

  c. Arrange family pleasant event time each week.

  d. Arrange a regular time each week that the parents discuss parenting efforts *(united front)*.

5. Decrease classroom misbehavior from five times a day to one time or less a day.
   (Precontemplation to Action: Clarifying the specific changes related to school behavior.)

   Plan:

   a. Arrange a parent-teacher conference in which each participant describes what would be different at school if Ken were doing better *(solution talk)*. Identify times when this has occurred already *(Precontemplation to Contemplation)*.

   b. Develop a school-home report in which Ken is responsible for getting his teacher to sign a card rating his conduct that day. The report is then taken home to the parents, who either administer a reward or withhold a privilege, depending on his behavior. Ken's access to his favorite activity (video games) is made contingent on getting the report to school and back *(Action)*.

   c. Arrange activities with the male art teacher, contingent on behavior that day.

6. Increase positive interactions with peers from one time a day to three or more times a day.
   (Precontemplation to Action: Help him see the benefits of prosocial interactions first. Next, work on developing the social skills that will facilitate positive social interactions.)

   Plan:

   a. As acute family and school problems subside, family-oriented treatment will be faded to biweekly meetings. Individually oriented weekly sessions will be initiated to deal with peer-related problems. The initial intervention will be writing the pros and cons of changing how Ken responds to others versus staying the same *(Precontemplation)*.

   b. A list of situations will be developed that indicate when he is getting along with others versus times when there is a conflict *(Contemplation—consciousness raising)*.

   c. The first target will be promoting positive interactions with others (e.g., starting a conversation, making requests, and sharing). Each skill will be modeled, role-played, and followed by a homework assignment *(Preparation to Action)*.

7. Decrease verbal and behavioral aggressive responses toward peers from daily to two times or less per week.
   (Preparation to Action: Once he can deal with peers in low-conflict situations, the focus will shift to handling interpersonal disputes.)

   Plan:
   a. Social problem-solving skills training (Kazdin, 1997) will be initiated to help Ken learn to generate alternatives to conflict situations, weigh alternatives, and select an optimum solution.
   b. Role-plays will be used to ensure that Ken knows how to carry out the solution in an actual situation.

Long-term goals (within the next 4 months):

8. Time spent with peers in play or cooperative activities will increase from 1 hour per week to 5 or more hours per week
   (Action to Maintenance: As socializing and conflict-resolution skills are mastered, activities are scheduled that will facilitate building positive peer relationships).

   Plan:
   a. Ken will attend swimming classes at the local recreation center each weekend.
   b. He will identify at least one school classmate that he can eat lunch with each day.
   c. Each week, he will invite one peer to his home for play activities.

Case Outcome

Ken had the reputation of being the "worst kid in the school." At the outset of treatment, both his parents and the teachers held little hope for him being able to continue in the public school system. However, 4 months after treatment was initiated, the clinical picture looked considerably different. Ken's numerous conflicts with teachers and classmates now occurred on only a biweekly basis. The parents reported that although he still could be difficult to manage at times, at least they knew what to do and felt that things were improving. On a personal basis, Ken seemed happier and less irritable. His improved social and conflict-resolution skills helped him deal with frustration in a more constructive manner. Academically, the testing did confirm the presence of a significant reading disorder. He was able to receive special educational services that had a positive outcome on his school success. The attention he was now receiving focused on his accomplishments and his improvement. His friendlier style invited like behavior from others. As treatment goals were attained, the weekly sessions were faded to monthly for 5 months. During the following school year, he was mainstreamed back into the regular classroom.

CLOSING REMARKS

The treatment-planning model discussed in this chapter emphasizes how to make clinical decisions so that the eventual plan meets each client's special set of needs. The model also highlights how the treatment-planning process itself has many therapeutic aspects. The collaborative nature of the process helps to involve and empower clients and their families. Interestingly, this client-focused approach also meets the requirements of managed-care entities that demand individualized treatment plans and evidence that clients are participating in the treatment process. Practice guidelines help to pinpoint treatments with the best evidence of success. The art in treatment planning is weaving each of these pieces together to provide the most favorable fit for the client.

Chapter 11

CASE STUDIES IN TREATMENT PLANNING

By

Gary G. Gintner
Louisiana State University

INTRODUCTION

Child and adolescent treatment planning can be complicated by issues such as differential diagnosis, problems in multiple life areas, and client or family resistance. Unfortunately, these types of problems tend to be the rule rather than the exception (Eyberg, Schuhmann, & Rey, 1998; Fonagy, Target, Cottrell, Phillips, & Kurtz, 2002). The purpose of this chapter is to illustrate by case examples how the clinician can address issues such as these in the treatment-planning process.

The treatment-planning guide outlined in Chapter 10 is used in each of the cases that will be presented. Briefly, this approach integrates a number of empirically derived principles for: 1) developing goals from a problem list; 2) determining a level of care (e.g., outpatient, partial hospitalization, inpatient); 3) selecting a modality (individual, group, or family); 4) choosing an evidenced-based intervention; and 5) tailoring interventions to client factors such as developmental level, cultural background, and coping style. A key organizing principle is to match interventions to the client's stage of readiness to change (Prochaska & Norcross, 2003). Five stages of change have been identified: precontemplation, contemplation, preparation, action, and maintenance. Research has shown that different interventions are likely to be more effective at different stages of change (Prochaska & Norcross, 2003). For example, motivational interventions are more indicated for precontemplators and contemplators, whereas action-oriented strategies are more appropriate for those in the preparation and action stages. A basic assumption is that client involvement and treatment outcome will be enhanced when treatment goals and intervention plans are written to correspond with a client's stage of change.

With these caveats in mind, I present six case examples, each with a different type of challenging issue. The first case describes a child who witnessed his father being murdered. The case depicts how bereavement can be complicated by the traumatic nature of the loss. The second case describes how to make a treatment plan gender-sensitive to the special issues of girls with Conduct Disorder. The third case portrays a child with Attention-Deficit/Hyperactivity Disorder. The fourth case illustrates a treatment plan for a depressed adolescent with acute suicidal ideation. The fifth case describes a child with school refusal problems. The last case deals with an adolescent who uses numerous substances and also has depressive symptoms that might be substance-induced or part of a primary mental disorder. This case also illustrates a treatment plan for a structured substance-abuse program. For each case, background information is presented first, followed by sections on diagnostic issues, case conceptualization, and formal treatment planning.

CASE ILLUSTRATION

Traumatic Loss

The experience of losing a loved one by violent means such as homicide, suicide, or a vehicular accident is more common than we would like to believe (Gintner, 2001). By some estimates, one in three Americans will have a loved one die by some type of violent means (Norris, 1992). Several studies have indicated that inner city youth are particularly vulnerable to experiencing violent losses due to the fact that they live in high-crime neighborhoods (Berman, Kurtines, Silverman, & Serafani, 1996; Gintner, 2001; Horowitz, Weine, & Jekel, 1995). For example, Berman et al. (1996) found that 42% of their urban youth sample had witnessed someone being murdered. Of those who experience a violent loss, 30% or more will go on to develop Posttraumatic Stress Disorder (PTSD; Berman et al., 1996; Horowitz et al., 1995). Other common psychiatric complications include Major Depressive Disorder and substance use problems (American Academy of Child and Adolescent Psychiatry [AACAP], 1998a). Untreateated, many of these youths will experience psychiatric or behavioral problems for years (AACAP, 1998a; Gintner, 2001).

The following case describes the treatment of a child who developed PTSD after witnessing his father's murder. The treatment plan illustrates how PTSD symptoms as well as bereavement issues were treated using available best-practice guidelines (AACAP, 1998a).

Case Background

Anthony is a 9-year-old African American who was referred for counseling by school personnel 5 weeks after the death of his father. Anthony witnessed his father being attacked by two men who broke into their house as part of a burglary. A struggle ensued, in which his father was shot three times. After the intruders left, Anthony tried unsuccessfully to revive his father. He then ran to a neighbor's house to get help. When Anthony learned that his father was pronounced dead at the scene by the emergency-response team, he started to cry and scream out, "He's not dead! He's not dead!" For nearly 2 hours he sat on a neighbor's steps repeating these words to himself despite the attempts of his grandmother and family friends to console him.

After the event, he moved in with his grandmother, who lives about 2 miles away. In the subsequent weeks he kept to himself and played alone in his room. On several occasions, the grandmother witnessed Anthony play-acting the event in his room with a toy gun. About every other night he awakened in a panic after having a vivid dream about the event. He was also afraid that the two gunmen would try to find and kill him as well. On two occasions he suddenly developed panic symptoms when his grandmother happened to drive near his old house. In fact, he refused to go near the house and even avoided two friends who used to be neighbors. He also refused to visit the gravesite despite his grandmother's attempts to take him with her.

A marked change in his behavior was also evident at school. He had been a "B" student, but now he began making poor grades. The teachers commented that he appeared to be in a daze. On one occasion he told a teacher, "What's the point? It doesn't matter anyway." Socially, he became more withdrawn. When he did interact with others, he was irritable. On three occasions in a 1-week period, he got into fights with classmates over minor disagreements. Once considered easygoing, his fellow students now described him as having an "attitude."

Anthony has not seen his mother since he was 2. The grandmother described her as a "lost child" who was a chronic drug user. The mother moved to another city and has only sporadically maintained contact with Anthony and the rest of her family. The father had always been Anthony's primary caretaker, although the grandmother also helped out. By both the child's and grandmother's accounts, Anthony and his father had a close and very positive relationship.

In session, Anthony appeared anxious and edgy. He wished that he could stop thinking about his father's death. He was unable to get the image of his father's body out of his head and wondered whether this was a sign that he was "going crazy." His grandmother was very worried about him and tried her best to cheer him up. She wanted some practical suggestions on helping her grandson. The grandmother's primary way of coping with the loss of her son was through prayer. She also had received a great deal of support from her fellow church members.

Diagnostic Issues

The diagnostic workup included interviews with both the child and the grandmother. Anthony was also taken to a pediatrician to rule out the presence of any medical problems.

The concept of diagnostic hierarchies as described in the *Diagnostic and Statistical Manual of Mental Disorders* (4th ed., text revision; *DSM-IV-TR;* APA, 2000a) is a useful heuristic for thinking through diagnostic possibilities. First, medical disorders, medications, and substance use need to be ruled out as potential causes of the observed symptoms. In this case, the medical checkup showed no indications of any type of medical or substance-related problem. Next, major psychiatric disorders such as Schizophrenia, Bipolar Disorder, or Major Depressive Disorder should be considered as potential contributing factors. Although Anthony feels like he is "going crazy," his symptoms are not indicative of a break with reality. The intrusive image of his father's death is a good example of a re-experiencing symptom that is often associated with trauma (APA, 2000a). Although Anthony has some mood symptoms, they do not meet criteria for any Mood Disorder. In fact, sadness and grief are noticeably absent in the clinical picture, suggesting that normal bereavement might be blocked in some way.

Instead of grief, the clinical picture is dominated by symptoms of anxiety and hyperarousal. These symptoms suggest that an Anxiety Disorder needs to be considered. Although panic symptoms are present, they are cued or situationally tied to reminders of the traumatic loss. This rules out Panic Disorder as a possible diagnostic consideration. Because the symptoms appear to be a response to a traumatic, stressful event, PTSD should be considered (APA, 2000a). The diagnostic criteria require that the stressful event be responded to with intense fear, helplessness, or horror. In addition, there need to be symptoms of re-experiencing, avoidance or numbing, and hyperarousal. Anthony's reaction following the death of his father clearly showed helplessness and horror over what transpired. His re-experiencing symptoms include the nightmares, intrusive thoughts and images of the event, repetitive re-enactment in play, and panic symptoms when confronted with reminders. Behavioral avoidance is manifested in his reluctance to visit his old house, his neighborhood friends, and the gravesite. Numbing symptoms are suggested by his general social withdrawal, his "don't care" attitude, and the appearance of being in a daze. His fear that the intruders will return contributes to an overall sense of hyperarousal, irritability, and being on edge. Importantly, all these symptoms are not typical of his premorbid functioning. Because symptoms have persisted for 5 weeks, the appropriate subtype of PTSD would be Acute (symptoms persisting less than 3 months).

DSM-IV-TR Diagnosis:

Axis I: 308.81 Posttraumatic Stress Disorder, Acute
Axis II: V71.09 No diagnosis
Axis III: None
Axis IV: Homicide of father, change in living arrangements, academic problems
Axis V: GAF = 50 (Current)

Case Conceptualization

Violent loss is considered one of the most difficult types of traumas to overcome (APA, 2000a; Gintner, 2001). Part of the problem is that traumatic aspects of the loss interfere with the survivor's efforts to grieve the loss. For example, anxiety-arousing recollections of the death might prompt the use of avoidant coping strategies, but these efforts can also interfere with bereavement work. As a result, treatment is usually directed at resolving the traumatic aspects first, followed by bereavement work per se (Gintner, 2001). This focus is also consistent with Anthony's and the grandmother's model of the current problem.

Practice guidelines recommend that the trauma-specific work should first attempt to stabilize functioning before confronting the trauma directly (AACAP, 1998b; Gintner, 2001). In Anthony's case, this would entail limiting stressors, providing social and school support, and teaching him how to better control symptoms of re-experiencing, hyperarousal, and avoidance. Trauma work per se would then focus on graded exposure to aspects of the trauma so that the event can be mastered and reintegrated in a revised view of himself and the world around him. Avenues for this exposure work include retelling of the trauma, journaling, activity-based forms of reexperiencing (e.g., drawing the event), and progressive *in vivo* exposure to avoided reminders (e.g., visiting the grave and neighborhood friends). Strategies learned to control anxiety during the stabilization phase can be adapted to modulate excessive emotional reactions during these various exposure activities. Throughout this process, family members, such as the grandmother, need to be involved to evaluate the child's, as well as the family's, response to the trauma. In addition, family members can provide very useful support for therapeutic activities (AACAP, 1998b). With appropriate release information, relevant school personnel such as the school counselor can also be enlisted as treatment aides.

As PTSD symptoms subside, the focus of treatment can shift to bereavement issues. The literature suggests that dealing with the death of a loved one requires loss-oriented coping as well as restoration-oriented work (Gintner, 2001). The former emphasizes efforts to deal with the emotional aspects of the loss, whereas the latter entails making life adjustments, re-establishing social networks, and modifying life goals. In the case of Anthony, restoration work would include making friends in his new neighborhood, adjusting to his new living arrangements, and finding new meaning in school and sports activities. Like the trauma work, it will be important to deal with not only Anthony but the grandmother, who has also been significantly affected by the loss.

Treatment-Planning Issues

Consistent with the guidelines outlined in Chapter 10, a problem list can help to specify what needs to be addressed in the treatment plan. Anthony's PTSD diagnosis can be broken down into relevant treatment targets such as intrusive thoughts of his father's death, irritability, panic symptoms, and avoidance of reminders. Further, the treatment plan needs to address the disruption in academic and interpersonal functioning so that additional adverse consequences can be prevented. Lastly, bereavement issues need to be dealt with as these more immediate concerns subside.

Treatment would be initiated at an outpatient level of care because there is no imminent danger or high-risk behavior present. Both individual and family modalities would be indicated. The individual sessions would initially focus on resolving PTSD symptoms and later on doing bereavement work. Conjoint sessions with the grandmother and Anthony would be scheduled at the beginning and at periodic points throughout the therapy process. Practice guidelines recommend that the treatment plan include stress-management techniques, exposure and retelling activities, and involvement of significant others including relevant school personnel (AACAP, 1998b).

These general treatment considerations, however, have to be tailored to client characteristics. Fortunately, both Anthony and the grandmother see a need for counseling and therefore appear to be in the contemplation stage of change. Indicated interventions at this stage are designed to enhance understanding of the problem and build confidence that change is indeed possible

(Prochaska & Norcross, 2003). As these issues are successfully dealt with, more action-oriented techniques can be introduced (Prochaska & Norcross, 2003). Because many African American women and their families are quite involved in their local churches (Paniagua, 1998), church involvement can be incorporated into the treatment plan as a vehicle for various therapeutic activities.

The following is the treatment plan that was developed with the preceding considerations in mind:

Problem List:

1. Marked anxiety associated with thoughts and images of the father's death
2. Avoidance of reminders
3. Declining grades
4. Social withdrawal
5. Inhibited bereavement

Treatment Goals and Plan: Immediate Goals (within the next 2 weeks):

1. Reduce daily anxiety rating from an average of 8 on a 10-point scale to 6 or less.

   Plan:
   a. In conjoint session with Anthony and his grandmother, provide education about PTSD, ways of reducing distress, and recommended interventions.
   b. Develop a daily planned schedule of activities that limits rumination time. The schedule will also include availability of adult supervision to enhance a sense of safety.
   c. Teach Anthony how to use thought-stopping to deal with intrusive thoughts.
   d. After completing appropriate release information, Anthony's teacher and the school counselor will be contacted to discuss ways of decreasing school stress and improving overall school functioning.

Short-Term Goals (within the next 5 weeks)

2. Anthony will increase his in-therapy talk about the circumstances of his father's death from 5 minutes each session to 15 or more minutes.

   Plan:
   a. As his functioning stabilizes, therapy will help him reintegrate the trauma through retelling and exploration of thoughts and feelings associated with the circumstances of the death. Relaxation exercises will be used before and after the retelling component to modulate anxiety.
   b. Cognitively based techniques geared at the appropriate developmental level will be used to attenuate beliefs about personal vulnerability, self-blame, and helplessness.
   c. A list of behavioral and cognitive coping techniques will be developed that Anthony can use whenever he does not feel safe.

    d. A conjoint session with the grandmother will be scheduled to discuss how the trauma has impacted "the family."

3. Anthony will be able to visit his father's grave and his old neighborhood friends at least two times.

Plan:

    a. As Anthony masters trauma-related reminders in sessions, the focus will shift to *in vivo* exposure to avoided places and people. A gradual exposure hierarchy will include talking with his old neighborhood friends at school, playing with them at a nearby playground, and visiting them at their houses.

    b. A similar hierarchy will be arranged for visiting the father's gravesite. The grandmother will accompany him and be instructed in how to help him cope with his anxiety.

Long-Term Goal (within 12 weeks)

4. Anthony will be able to express at least three feelings related to the loss of his father.

Plan:

    a. As he gains control over traumatic aspects of the death, the focus will shift to bereavement-related issues in order to process the loss. First, in a family session with the grandmother, the loss will be discussed in terms of implications for each of them. This will be followed by individual sessions with Anthony to further process bereavement issues.

    b. Anthony will be asked to spend 5 minutes a day writing about any thoughts or feelings related to his father. These notes will be discussed at each session.

5. Anthony will be able to state at least three things that he likes about his new living arrangements (restoration-oriented adjustment).

Plan:

    a. The grandmother and Anthony will develop a list of privileges and home responsibilities.

    b. Membership at a local recreation center will be arranged for Anthony.

    c At least one church-affiliated youth group will be identified for Anthony to join.

    d. Regular playtimes will be scheduled with peers in the new neighborhood.

Case Outcome

The combination of conjoint family sessions and individual sessions was very useful in helping both Anthony and his grandmother deal with the traumatic and bereavement aspects of the loss. During the initial weeks of treatment, stabilization measures helped Anthony to develop a sense of predictability, support, and greater control over his symptoms. Interestingly, just these steps resulted in a marked improvement in his sleep and irritability. The cognitive work helped him understand that he was blaming himself, to some extent, because he did not do more to stop the intruders. Visible relief was evident when he recognized that he was not capable of "saving" his father. By the fourth week, he was willing to talk with his old friends, who he had been avoiding. The biggest turn in therapy occurred when he visited the grave on the sixth week. Although he was anxious and ambivalent about going, afterwards he admitted that he did better than he had expected. This was a particularly empowering experience for him because he was able to pay respects at his father's grave. Afterwards, grief issues became a more prominent focus of the therapy for both Anthony and the grandmother. The minister at the grandmother's church was a particularly strong source of support for her, and this appeared to help her be more available emotionally for Anthony. The restoration activities helped Anthony start to feel more at home with his new life situation. By the twelfth week of treatment, Anthony's anxiety had dissipated considerably and he was doing much better academically and socially.

A GIRL WITH CONDUCT DISORDER

Most of the research on Conduct Disorder (CD) has focused on males, despite the fact that conduct problems are the second most common reason girls are referred for psychiatric services (Loeber & Stouthamer-Loeber, 1998). One problem with this research literature, however, is that findings that are characteristic of boys might not be as applicable to girls with CD. For example, in comparison to boys, girls with CD are more likely to be diagnosed in adolescence, have less overtly aggressive behaviors, and engage in more covert antisocial acts, such as running away and relational aggression (APA, 2000a; Loeber & Stouthamer-Loeber, 1998). Relational aggression is characterized by behaviors such as spreading rumors, excluding peers, and disrupting social bonds (Loeber & Stouthamer-Loeber, 1998).

There are also gender differences in risk factors. Girls are more adversely affected by factors such as poor family relationships, sexual and physical abuse, and early physical maturation (Weisz & Hawley, 2002). Whereas deviant peer affiliation has been shown to be an important risk factor for the adolescent-onset type of CD in both sexes (Gintner, 2000; Moffitt, 1993), girls might be particularly susceptible because of their greater sensitivity to peer relationships and social status (Loeber & Stouthamer-Loeber, 1998). There is some evidence that these gender differences in symptomotology and risk factors might impede early identification and timely referral of girls (Loeber & Stouthamer-Loeber, 1998). Failure to recognize CD and intervene can result in a number of adverse consequences such as teen pregnancy, suicide, violent death, academic failure, and substance abuse (APA, 2000a; Loeber & Stouthamer-Loeber, 1998). The following case exemplifies how a girl with CD might initially present and how the clinician can design the treatment plan to address these gender differences.

Case Background

Jill is a 13-year-old Caucasian female who appears 3 years older than her stated age. Her parents referred her for counseling after an incident in which she sneaked out of the house in the middle of the night with a 16-year-old male friend. The police picked her up about 12 hours later in front of a popular teen hangout. This was the second time that she had run away in the past year. In the past 2 years she already had been picked up for shoplifting, running away, and destroying school property. The parents describe her as "totally out of control."

According to the parents' report, prior to the past 2 years, Jill was a model child and her school reports were always good. Her problems started shortly after the family moved from out of state to their current residence. Jill began spending time with two girls who lived a few blocks down from her. In the beginning, it seemed that Jill had found some good friends her own age. But within a month or so, the police contacted Jill's parents about shoplifting charges, in which the three girls had been caught on videotape stealing clothing from a local mall. In the months that followed, it seemed that not a week went by that someone in the neighborhood was not making some kind of complaint about Jill and her two friends. Jill's parents responded by restricting her privileges for each transgression. In response, Jill, who had been an easygoing child, became more "willful" and obstinate. Loud shouting matches with her father became a standard part of everyday life. The situation worsened after her parents became aware of her involvement with older boys who were suspected of being in a gang.

Her behavior problems were also evident at school. She was suspended for 2 days for skipping school. Her grades had dropped from As and Bs to Cs and Ds. Her most serious offense was vandalizing the assistant principal's car with her two neighborhood friends. The principal informed Jill and her parents that another incident could lead to expulsion or transfer to an alternative school.

In terms of family background, Jill's older sister, with whom she had a close relationship, left for college about a year ago. Unlike Jill, the older sister is described as outgoing, popular, and socially active. The father is the major disciplinarian in the family, whereas the mother tends to provide the social and emotional support. The mother states that talking to Jill is like "walking on eggs." However, they are still able to do things together such as shopping and visiting relatives. The mother often feels like a referee, mediating arguments between Jill and her father.

In the initial family session, Jill was sullen and clearly unhappy with her home situation. Most of the interchanges involved the father making critical comments and Jill responding in a flip, sarcastic tone. Periodically, the mother would plead with both of them to try to get along "so that we can be a family again."

Diagnostic Issues

Jill's primary symptoms include numerous conduct problems and oppositional behavior. These are more than developmental aspects of adolescence because they result in clinically significant impairment in functioning. Her CD symptoms include running away, shoplifting, skipping school, and destroying school property. Because her symptoms first appeared after the age of 10, she would meet criteria for the Adolescent/Onset type of CD (APA, 2000a). She would also warrant the specifier of Moderate because the number of CD symptoms are more than is required but the harm to others is not marked (APA, 2000a). Although she also has ODD symptoms, this disorder is not coded separately in the presence of CD (APA, 2000a).

The *DSM-IV-TR* Diagnosis:

Axis I: 312.82 Conduct Disorder, Adolescent Onset Type, Moderate
Axis II: V71.09 No Diagnosis
Axis III: None
Axis IV: Legal problems, failing at school, parent-child conflict
Axis V: GAF = 48 (Current)

Case Conceptualization

The initiation of Jill's behavior problems appears to coincide with her association with neighborhood friends and older males. Jill manifests two critical risk factors that have been shown to increase a girl's susceptibility to deviant peer influence: proximity to deviant peers and her early physical maturation (Weisz & Hawley, 2002). The latter has been associated with increased association with older males who introduce girls to substance use, sexual activity, and other antisocial behaviors (Loeber & Stouthamer-Loeber, 1998; Weisz & Hawley, 2002).

In terms of family dynamics, Jill and her parents are locked into reciprocal interaction patterns that alienate Jill from her family attachments and inadvertently strengthen her deviant peer friendships. Jill's behavior and sarcastic style might be manifestations of her attempts to be more independent. However, these behaviors invite critical comments and controlling behaviors that only heighten Jill's attempts for more independence. The father is overinvolved in the discipline, whereas the mother tends to be underinvolved. During the initial family session, it appeared as if the mother was reluctant to confront the daughter for fear of alienating her. Therapeutically, it will be important to try to empower the mother to exert a more positive influential role with the daughter, and to moderate the father's involvement. A key component in this process is rekindling a positive family atmosphere that will facilitate parental influence and cooperative interactions. Positive family attachments have been shown to be inversely associated with serious conduct problems and deviant peer affiliation (Loeber & Stouthamer-Loeber, 1998).

Treatment Planning Issues

Jill's problem list would include violation of house rules, family arguments, undesirable peer associations, skipping school, and academic problems. Violation of house rules would be of the highest priority because it is associated with high-risk behaviors (e.g., running away, association with older males).

Treatment would be initiated at the outpatient level of care because there is no imminent danger to self or others, the parents are willing to participate in the treatment process, and there is no history of prior treatment. Best-practice recommendations suggest that a multisystemic approach (Borduin, Mann, Cone, Henggeler, Fucci, Blaske, & Williams, 1995) that targets the family, school, and peer systems would be particularly indicated in this type of case (AACAP, 1997c; Brestan & Eyeberg, 1998). Family therapy would be the primary modality in this type of approach. Developmentally, the parenting approach needs to become more authoritative, blending limit-setting with warmth and autonomy granting (Weisz & Hawley, 2002). As a result, a key family issue will be to involve Jill in the negotiation of house rules. This authoritative approach can then be applied to resolving school- and peer-related problems. Because Jill tends to externalize her problems in the form of acting-out behaviors, a more behavioral approach is indicated as opposed to an insight-oriented strategy (see Chapter 10).

A challenging issue at the outset is crafting interventions in line with the family's stage of change. Although the parents recognize the problem (contemplation stage), Jill is precontemplative about change, seeing the problem in all the authority figures around her. A key task will be motivating Jill to see that change is in her own best interest. Goal 1 of the following treatment plan describes how this motivational issue was addressed.

Problem List:

1. Family arguments
2. Violation of house rules
3. Association with undesirable peers
4. Skipping school
5. Poor academic performance

Treatment Goals and Plan: Immediate Goal (within the next 2 weeks):

1. Jill will be able to state at least two benefits of attending counseling sessions.

   Plan:
   a. Have family members discuss the "good and not so good" things about attending counseling sessions.
   b. Have each member identify personally relevant benefits of an improved family atmosphere.

Short-Term Goals (within the next 8 weeks):

2. Increase positive exchanges between Jill and her parents from one time per week to at least twice a day.

   Plan:
   a. Discuss and model ways of attending to positive behaviors as they occur.
   b. Have each family member practice the attending skill in session.
   c. Have each family member self-monitor positive exchanges that occur in the home. They will then share these observations at the outset of the following session.

3. Increase family's pleasant events from one time per month to at least once a week.

   Plan:
   a. Have the family develop a list of mutually acceptable pleasant family events.
   b. Schedule a regular time each week for at least one family activity.

4. Decrease violations of house rules from daily to three times or less per week.

   Plan:
   a. Jill and her parents will develop a list of house rules (e.g., curfews, acceptable peers, substance use, school attendance), responsibilities (e.g., chores, notifying parents of whereabouts), and privileges (e.g., allowance, attendance at social activities and special events). Jointly, they will negotiate a system of rewards and punishments.
   b. Arrange a time each week for the family to discuss any issues related to house rules.

5. Decrease associations with undesirable peers from daily to one time or less per week.

   Plan:
   a. Discuss short-term and long-term consequences of different types of peer associations.
   b. Increase parental monitoring of peer contacts.
   c. Develop house rules regarding peer associations.
   d. Increase parental support of prosocial peer activities (e.g., driving to events, providing financial support).

6. Decrease the number of days that Jill earns a detention at school from one time per week to one time or less per month.

   Plan:
   a. Schedule parent-teacher conference to develop a home-school report form for Jill's school behavior (e.g., completion of assignments, attendance, class behavior).
   b. Arrange a system in which the form is taken home each day to be reviewed by the parents, who award privileges or restrictions depending on Jill's behavior.

7. Increase study time from a 1/2 hour a day to 1 hour or more per day.

   Plan:
   a. Have Jill and her mother develop a study schedule for the week.
   b. Arrange consequences for daily compliance.
   c. Have parents monitor academic progress on a daily home-school report form.

Long-Term Goal (within 12 weeks):

8. Increase time in prosocial recreational activities from 1 hour a week to 5 or more hours a week.

Plan:

a. Review a list of community- and school-related activities, organizations, and clubs with Jill and her parents. Have Jill select at least three that she will investigate.
b. Contract with Jill to attend at least one meeting for each of the selected groups.
c. Have Jill commit to attending at least one of the groups on a weekly basis.

Case Outcome

Jill's initial resistance subsided when she realized that the focus of the session was not going to be on recriminations but on how to make things better. The encouragement of an authoritative discipline style further involved Jill as a true contributor in the negotiation of house rules. The work with the father helped him become less reactive and more positive. As a result, daily arguments began to subside. During each of the first 6 weeks of treatment, Jill got into trouble in much the same way as she did before treatment started. However, each incident was framed as an opportunity to try out new things and to apply the new family rules. Because of Jill's involvement in developing these rules and the way in which the parents now responded, her reactions were less volatile. She spent less and less time with her former two friends, who were often in trouble at school. The upward spiral of increased privileges at home and at school helped Jill appreciate the benefits of these changes in comparison to the way things used to be. Developmentally, she and her family had turned a corner. After 12 sessions, the identified treatment goals were accomplished. Two follow-up sessions spaced at 6-month intervals were scheduled to ensure maintenance of treatment changes.

AD/HD AND PARENTAL RESISTANCE TO STIMULANT MEDICATIONS

AD/HD is one of the most common childhood disorders referred for outpatient treatment (AACAP, 1997a; Fonagy et al., 2002). Overall, stimulant medications (e.g., Ritalin, Adderal) have been shown to be more effective than psychosocial treatments for reducing core AD/HD symptoms such as inattention, hyperactivity, and impulsivity (AACAP, 1997a; Fonagy et al., 2002). However, such medications have a number of limitations. First, although the children's behaviors improve on stimulant medications, the children still function in the clinical range, and one in five children will have significant side-effects (AACAP, 1997a). Second, stimulant medications do not alleviate common concurrent problems such as social skill deficits and comorbid disorders (e.g, anxiety disorder, substance use disorder, learning disorder; Root & Resnick, 2003). Finally, many parents are uncomfortable with the idea of only using medication (Root & Resnick, 2003). As a result, psychosocial treatments are considered a first-line treatment when: 1) the ADHD symptoms are not severe; 2) there are comorbid conditions that need to be treated (e.g., social skill deficit); and 3) the parents prefer counseling over medication (Root & Resnick, 2003). With these points in mind, this case illustrates the common problems of a child with AD/HD and the treatment considerations that need to be addressed when parents oppose the use of medications.

Case Background

Maurice is a 7-year-old African-American first grader who was referred as part of his Individual Educational Plan (IEP) recommendations. He was evaluated for special education services because of his chronic behavioral problems and academic concerns. This evaluation, which included intellectual, academic, and psychological testing, indicated that while he is in the average range of intellectual functioning, his reading ability is over two standard deviations below that expected of a child his age. On the other hand, he also demonstrated above-average arithmetic ability. These scores were consistent with the failing grades that he was receiving in reading and the As he had consistently made in arithmetic. From a behavior standpoint, classroom observations, as well as teacher and parent reports using standardized assessment questionnaires, indicated that Maurice was an overactive child who had difficulty maintaining attention on school and home tasks.

A complete physical examination by the family's pediatrician ruled out any physical or neurological problems. The pediatrician recommended that the parents consider placing Maurice on a stimulant (Ritalin) to improve his attention and hyperactivity problems. However, the parents were uncomfortable about the medication option and preferred trying psychosocial interventions first.

During the initial counseling assessment, his parents provided a detailed history of Maurice's behavioral problems. His overactivity became evident by the age of 3. His mother said she could not leave him for more than a couple of minutes "without him getting into something." For example, on one occasion he accidentally pulled down the television and almost seriously injured himself. Furthermore, by the age of 4 he was having difficulty playing with other children because "he could be very rough in his play." Maurice had difficulty at preschool because he was so rambunctious that he frequently disrupted play activity. Similar problems began to emerge when he started kindergarten, especially during recess, play activities, and other unstructured times. His mother added, however, that the teacher was particularly good at structuring the daily program, which seemed to moderate much of Maurice's behavioral problems. His first-grade teacher, however, was described as being less organized and "doing a lot of yelling" when Maurice was off task or being disruptive in the classroom.

His parents admitted that he was difficult to manage at home but also added that he had "plenty of good days." Maurice does better whenever one of his parents is monitoring him. His mother admitted, however, that she becomes worn-out having to constantly correct him. His father added that he spanks Maurice if the reprimands are ineffective. Despite these problems, it was clear that Maurice had a good relationship with both of his parents.

Economically, Maurice's parents would be considered to be middle class. His father runs his own carpeting business and his mother works as a teacher. Maurice has a 14-year-old brother who is considered to be academically gifted.

After the IEP meeting, his parents realized that Maurice may not perform at the level of his older brother.

During the initial session, Maurice was quite fidgety. Within minutes of being in session, his mother was correcting him about touching and picking up things in the office. Maurice usually responded to the first reprimand; however, it was not unusual for his mother to have to remind him two or three times. Despite his activity level, Maurice seemed friendly and willing to participate. His parents wanted concrete suggestions for managing him at home and improving his school performance. In addition, they also were concerned that he had few friends and was rarely invited to play with other neighborhood children.

Diagnostic Issues

The diagnostic work-up included interviews with Maurice's parents and Maurice, as well as a phone consultation with his first-grade teacher. In addition, school records (e.g., grades, conduct reports) evaluation reports (e.g., IEP, testing results, behavioral rating scales) and medical records were reviewed. Information from these sources suggested that Maurice manifested the core symptoms of AD/HD, such as numerous symptoms of inattention (e.g., failing to listen, being highly distractible, failing to follow instructions), hyperactivity (e.g., being fidgety, having difficulty playing quietly, leaving his seat in the classroom) and impulsivity (e.g., often interrupting other or intruding on others). These symptoms clearly had persisted for at least 6 months and were clinically significant as evidenced by his problems at home and school. Diagnostic criteria for AD/HD (APA, 2000a) also require that these symptoms are present in two or more settings, which in Maurice's case would include the school and home as well as with his peers. The extensive diagnostic information ruled out other potential causes for his behavioral problems (e.g., depression, an anxiety disorder, Oppositional Defiant Disorder, trauma). Because Maurice has numerous symptoms of inattention and hyperactivity/impulsivity, he would be coded as the Combined Type (APA, 2000a).

Comorbidity is common in those with AD/HD, and about one in four children will meet the criteria for a learning disorder (AACAP, 1997a). Maurice meets the criteria for a reading disorder due to his low reading score on a standardized test of achievement and his failing grades in reading (APA, 2000). However, because the referral was to deal with the behavioral problems per se, AD/HD will be listed first on Axis I, followed by the reading disorder.

DSM-IV-TR Diagnosis:

Axis I: 314.01 Attention-Deficit/Hyperactivity Disorder, Combined Type
            315.1 Reading Disorder
Axis II: V71.09 No diagnosis
Axis III: None
Axis IV: Academic problems, discord with peers, discipline problems in the home
Axis V: GAF = 55 (Current)

Case Conceptualization

Maurice demonstrates how AD/HD problems can play out in each of the major life domains. In the school environment, his symptoms interfere with self-directed study, classroom behavior, and play activities with peers. In fact, studies show that hyperactive symptoms, in particular, are associated with peer rejection that can, in turn, contribute to lower self-esteem (AACAP, 1997a; Root & Resnick, 2003). Similarly, conduct problems also can undermine a positive working relationship with the teacher. This is exacerbated by the fact that most teachers do not receive training in classroom management techniques for at-risk children. Likewise, the home atmosphere can be tense because typical parenting techniques may not be adequate to deal with the particular demands of an AD/HD child. Although both of his parents and his first-grade teacher want Maurice to be successful, they may not have the skills to manage his behavior. Fortunately, in this case the teacher was willing to become involved in the overall treatment plan. The kindergarten teacher's earlier success with Maurice suggests that improved child management skills can make a dramatic difference in his behavior.

Developmentally, first grade is a time that sets the tone for the school experience both academically and socially. Maurice appears clearly discouraged and feels like a troublemaker much of the time. The school's IEP plan will help him with his reading problems. A key therapeutic issue, however, will be to teach him social skills that compensate for his AD/HD symptoms.

Finally, resistance to medication is common among parents, especially those of color (Panaigua, 1998). Part of building a collaborative working alliance is to ensure that treatment goals and methods are in line with our clients' wishes as well as their racial and ethnic background. Otherwise, the research shows that drop out and non-compliance are likely (Gintner, 2000; Miller & Rollnick, 1991).

Treatment Planning Issues

Maurice's problem list would include difficulty staying on task at school, having conduct problems in the classroom (staying in seat, excessively talking, interrupting), needing constant redirection at home, difficulty playing with peers, and reading problems. Of these, the parents wanted to first work on improving his school behavior. Maurice, too, wanted to get into less trouble at school. Although reading problems are on his problem list, his school had designed a specialized program for Maurice that included instructions to the parents on how to help him with his reading assignments.

Because Maurice's AD/HD symptoms are in the mild-to-moderate range, psychosocial treatments alone can be effective (Root & Resnick, 2003). Practice guidelines recommend behavioral parent training and behavioral consultation with the teacher as the best empirically supported treatments (AACAP, 1997a; Root & Resnick, 2003). Parent training entails teaching parents skills to: 1) immediately attend to and reward on-task behavior; 2) provide concrete specific instruction in making a request or redirecting the child; and 3) respond to non-compliance or misbehavior with immediate consequences such as loss of privileges or a time-out from preferred activities (e.g., TV, playing with a toy). In addition, environmental management components can be added, such as a sign in the kitchen indicating the day's activities and chores. Teacher consultation regarding classroom management techniques includes similar training components, but it emphasizes their application not only to misbehavior but also to learning. Like the Conduct Disorder case described previously, including a home-school daily report ensures consistency in both settings.

Social skills training has mixed results as far as a primary treatment for AD/HD (AACAP, 1997a). However, in this case, it appears to be an important additional concern that standard treatments do not directly address. The skills training would help Maurice learn how to initiate and sustain reciprocal play activities with peers.

These treatments, however, must be tailored to client characteristics such as stage of change, developmental issues, and race factors. Because both the parents and Maurice recognize the problem and are interested in making changes soon, they appear to be in the preparation stage of change, and therefore, would be ready to consider undertaking the required behavioral assignments. Developmentally, Maurice is probably not ready to use cognitive self-control skills such as self-instructional training or problem-solving (AACAP, 1997a). However, simple self-talk reminders about staying on task may be useful to include in his treatment.

In terms of the frequency and modality of treatment, parenting skills training will be delivered through weekly sessions with the parents. There also will be a meeting with Maurice's teacher individually as well as a parent–teacher meeting to design the home–school report. Individual sessions with Maurice will focus on social skills training and the use of self-talk reminders. With these points in mind, the following treatment plan illustrates how these issues can be systematically addressed.

Problem List:

1. Conduct problems in the classroom (staying in seat, excessive talking)
2. Staying on task at school
3. Needing constant redirection at home
4. Difficulty playing with peers

Treatment Goals and Plan: Immediate Goals (within the next 3 weeks):

1. Implement the use of a home-school report that will be completed at least 4 out of 5 days a week.

   Plan:
   a. Meet with the parents and provide educational and reading material about AD/HD and effective types of parenting practices and school interventions.
   b. Arrange a meeting with the teacher to solicit her involvement and provide learning materials about using behavioral strategies in the classroom.

    c. Arrange a parent-teacher meeting in which the home-school report is developed with particular consequences for compliance and non-compliance. The parents will explain the plan to Maurice and set up reminders for him to take the card back and forth to school.

    d. Initiate a weekly telephone consultation with Maurice's teacher with regard to classroom management issues.

Short-Term Goals (within the next 8 weeks)

2. Increase on-task behavior at school from 40% of the time to at least 60% or more of the time.

   Plan:

   a. During weekly phone consults, help Maurice's teacher implement environmental management strategies to increase his on-task behavior (e.g., sitting Maurice at the front of the class).

   b. Provide suggestions to Maurice's teacher for presenting and sequencing planned classroom assignments.

   c. Help Maurice's teacher to develop a point-reward system for on-task and appropriate behavior.

   d. Provide educational materials on attending to and reinforcing appropriate and on-task behavior and on ignoring or punishing misbehavior (e.g., losing points, time-out).

3. Increase Maurice's on-task and appropriate behaviors at home from 3 times a day to at least 6 or more times a day.

   Plan:

   a. In sessions with Maurice's parents, develop a time schedule of activities for Maurice (e.g., getting dressed for school, doing homework between 4 and 5 o'clock).

   b. Provide educational material, modeling, and practice in using immediate positive reinforcement for on-task behaviors.

   c. Teach Maurice's parents how to implement a point system for rewards that are tied to privileges (access to TV, video games).

   d. Teach Maurice's parents skills in giving directives (e.g., tone of voice, one reminder, etc.).

Long-Term Goal (within 15 weeks)

4. Increase Maurice's play time with peers from 2 hours a week to 8 hours a week.

   Plan:

   a. In individual sessions, provide educational materials, modeling (video of child), and practice in reciprocal play activities.

   b. Ask Maurice's parents to monitor play behavior throughout the week. Teach them how to use prompts for the appropriate behaviors.

   c. Teach Maurice self-talk reminders to wait his turn and handle frustration during play activities.

   d. Arrange a weekly play schedule with neighborhood and school peers.

Case Outcome

A fortunate aspect of this case is the teacher's willingness to participate. The home–school report and the classroom management plan helped Maurice increase his on-task behavior and decrease his talking and out-of-seat behaviors. His behavior was still problematic at times, however, the teacher felt that at least she knew what to do and was confident that things could improve further. Because of Maurice's mother's background in education, the point system that was instituted was familiar to her and she took the lead in implementing the system. Maurice's father was pleased that he was doing better at school and in the home, and his father did not feel compelled to use paddling throughout the duration of treatment. Although the older brother was not directly involved in treatment, Maurice's parents reported that his behavior had improved, too, due to the clearer expectations of household rules. Maurice was visibly a happier child and was able to make several friends, one of which visited the house regularly.

Monthly follow-up sessions with Maurice and his parents were scheduled a year later to ensure that these gains persisted. Had his behavior gotten worse even with the behavior management plan, the possibility of adding medication would have been discussed with the parents.

ADOLESCENT DEPRESSION AND SUICIDALITY

Roughly one in four adolescents will have a bout of significant depression (AACAP, 1998a). Gender differences emerge after puberty, with girls showing about twice the prevalence as boys (AACAP, 1998a). Despite the high incidence of depression in adolescence, epidemiological evidence indicates that depressed youth are significantly under-referred for treatment (AACAP, 1998a). Untreated, depression can become a chronic disorder over the individual's lifetime and can lead to adverse outcomes such as suicide and substance abuse (Weisz & Hawley, 2002). The case that follows illustrates an example of Major Depressive Disorder that is complicated by the presence of suicidal ideation.

Case Background

Amy is a 13-year-old Caucasian seventh grader who was initially seen at an outpatient mental health center on emergency. Earlier that day a teacher had found a suicide note in a schoolbook. After talking with the school counselor, Amy admitted that she had written the note and agreed to go with her mother to be evaluated.

For the past month, Amy has had thoughts about killing herself nearly every day. Her most common ideation is to just step in front of a car. There have been no prior attempts or gestures. She explained that she is just tired of all the teasing and harassment she receives from a group of girls in her class. The harassment has included making derogatory comments (e.g., "trailer-park trash"), spreading rumors, and playing pranks on her.

Amy also reported a number of depressive symptoms. She feels like a "loser" and cries several times a day. Her thinking is dominated by thoughts of her own inadequacy and hopelessness about the future. She does not believe that anyone could ever really like her. She also feels like a burden to her mother and her two older sisters, who she believes worry about her. She currently finds little in her life that is pleasurable. It usually takes her an hour to fall asleep because she ruminates about something she did that day. These symptoms have been present for the past 8 weeks and coincide with the onset of the teasing at school.

The family has lived in a small trailer for the past several years. Amy's older sisters are 18 and 19 years old, and no longer live in the home. The mother is 37 years old but looks much older than her stated age. She cleans houses and works about 12 hours a day to try to make ends meet. She divorced her husband about 4 years ago after a chronic history of verbal and physical abuse. It is not clear whether any of the children were also abused. The mother also reported a significant history of depressive episodes throughout her life, although she stated that she has felt much better since the divorce. The children have had very little contact with the father since the dissolution of the marriage.

Amy has few pleasant events in her day-to-day life. She has numerous household chores to complete because of her mother's long work hours. Although they get along, they do not spend much time in any quality activities together. There are no girls her age who live in her trailer park, so she spends most of her time by herself or socializing with adult neighbors. She does have one friend at school, who is also occasionally teased.

Despite the social problems at school, she makes adequate grades and is liked by her teachers. One area in which Amy does excel in is gym class. She is athletically talented, but financial problems have made it difficult for her to participate in any of the school's sports teams.

She has had one previous episode of significant depression that occurred during the marital separation, but her symptoms cleared within a year or so. There has been no previous treatment.

Diagnostic Issues

Amy's symptoms would meet criteria for a Major Depressive Episode (APA, 2000a). Her symptoms include depressed mood, loss of pleasure in activities, sleep disturbance, feelings of worthlessness, and suicidal ideation. There is no evidence that these symptoms are due to any substance use or medical condition. The severity of her episode is in the Moderate range because of the daily rumination about suicide. She would be coded as the Recurrent subtype because there has been a previous episode. Between these episodes she has had a period of sustained remission of symptoms that will be important to note as a course specifier in the diagnosis. She does not meet criteria for any other mood specifier (e.g., melancholic, atypical, chronic).

DSM-IV-TR **Diagnosis:**

Axis I: 296.32 Major Depressive Disorder, Recurrent, Moderate, With Full Interepisode Recovery
Axis II: V71.09 No diagnosis
Axis III: None
Axis IV: Harassment from peers, family financial problems
Axis V: GAF = 50 (Current)

Case Conceptualization

Amy's suicidal thoughts reflect the depths of her hopelessness. Her coping style, stressful peer environment, and living arrangements are all important contributors to her current depressive episode. She tends to cope with stress by avoidance and by turning her attention inward and criticizing herself (Gaw & Beutler, 1995). Her style of thinking exemplifies the classic triad of negative cognitions about the self, the world, and the future so frequently associated with depression (Beck, 1987a). Family financial problems and her living arrangements limit opportunities for success experiences and alternative peer interactions. Her history of depression suggests that her current depression is not simply due to school peers, but to a tendency to amplify the adverse impact of negative life events by the way she interprets them. A critical component of treatment will be to teach Amy a more adaptive and realistic way of thinking about herself and her life experiences.

Behaviorally, her avoidance limits anxiety in the short run but does nothing about changing the source of the stress or creating positive experiences. Assertiveness skills would help her to deal with situations in which others try to intimidate her or violate her rights. She also needs skills to initiate new positive peer relationships. Her self-esteem and positive expectation about the future could be enhanced by arranging success experiences and positive events.

Her home life plays a role in her depression. Her relationship with her mother is not very close or warm. The time they do have together tends to be highly task-oriented. The departure of her sisters has systematically eliminated her few warm relationships. With only one remaining child in the home, both Amy and her mother are adjusting to role transitions in the family. A key task will be to build a better bond between them.

Treatment Planning Issues

Amy's problem list would include suicidal ideation, depressed mood, her self-deprecating thinking style, harassing classmates, few positive peer relationships, and improving the mother-daughter relationship. The initial focus would be reducing her suicidal risk. Typically, interventions such as a no-harm contract as well as increased social support and monitoring are effective ways of stabilizing the situation. When the risk of suicide has subsided, the next targets for treatment would be her negative thinking and dealings with harassing peers. Amy is interested in changing both of these areas. As key contributors to the depression are ameliorated, the focus will shift to bolstering the quality of her life through improved relationships and pleasant events.

The level of care would be outpatient because Amy is not an imminent threat to herself. She has no prior history of attempts and her plan is not well-thought out. Medication for her depression would not be indicated because her depression is in the Mild to Moderate range and there are no significant vegetative symptoms (AACAP, 1998a). The recommended first-line treatment for her depression would be Cognitive-Behavioral or Interpersonal Therapy (AACAP, 1998a; Kaslow & Thompson, 1998). Because of her negative thinking style, a Cognitive-Behavioral approach would be a good match for her particular coping style (Prochaska & Norcross, 2003). Treatment would include cognitive restructuring as well as skills training in areas such as assertion, social problem-solving, and initiating a peer relationship (Kaslow & Thompson, 1998). It would also be desirable to add a family component to the treatment to improve her relationship with her mother and quality of life at home.

Amy is at the contemplation stage of change. She sees that there is a problem but is not ready to act because she has very low self-efficacy about her ability to deal with either the harassing peers or her negative attitude toward herself. An early focus of treatment will be to increase her self-efficacy so that she will be more motivated to try things out. Arranging small success experiences has been shown to be one of the most powerful ways of enhancing self-efficacy (Bandura, 1982). For example, teaching her ways of cutting down her contact with harassing peers can show her that there are things she can do that will improve the way she feels at the end of the day. As her confidence increases, she will be more open to more direct ways of dealing with those who bother her.

When the more acute aspects of her depression lift, efforts will be directed at building areas that will improve Amy's quality of life. These include establishing good peer relationships, increasing involvement in mastery activities (e.g., sports), increasing regular pleasant events, and improving her relationship with her mother.

With these comments in mind, the following treatment plan illustrates how these various issues can be systematically addressed.

Problem List:

1. Suicidal ideation
2. Depressed mood
3. Negative thinking
4. Harassing classmates
5. Few positive relationships

Immediate Goals (within the next week):

1. Reduce suicidal thoughts from five or more times a day to one time or less a day.

   Plan:
   a. Client will be seen two times in the next week in outpatient therapy. She will be asked to sign a no-harm contract for the next 7 days.
   b. A daily activity schedule will be constructed that maximizes time with those who can be supportive. Each day she will also make a mood rating on a 10-point scale and indicate at least two events that contributed to it.
   c. A coping menu will be developed with the client that lists at least 10 things she can do when she gets a suicidal thought.
   d. A portion of one session will include a conjoint session with the mother, enlisting her involvement in support and monitoring activities.

Short-Term Goals (within the next 6 weeks):

2. The client's daily mood rating will increase from an average of 2 on a 10-point scale (with 10 being very good mood) to 5 or more.

Plan:

  a. A new no-harm contract will be signed for the next 4 weeks.
  b. The daily mood monitoring will be used to identify activities that affect her mood, especially when she is at school. A schedule will be constructed that systematically increases mood-enhancing activities and limits exposure to events that depress mood.
  c. Education will be provided on how thinking affects mood and various types of distorted thinking.
  d. Five ways to change distorted thinking will be discussed and practiced in sessions.
  e. Client will practice realistic thinking exercises at least 10 minutes a day.
  f. Coping self-talk scripts for before, during, and after a stressful encounter will be developed and practiced.

3. Client will be able to make an assertive statement to a classmate at least 75% of the time when it is indicated.

Plan:

  a. Education will be provided on the differences between aggressive, assertive, and passive responses.
  b. Assertive responses will be modeled and practiced using monitoring situations.
  c. Social problem-solving will be discussed relative to deciding when to say something to harassing peers and when to use an alternative strategy.

Long-Term Goal (within 10 weeks):

4. Time spent in positive social interactions will increase from 2 hours a week to 1 hour or more a day.

Plan:

  a. Several family sessions will be scheduled to improve positive interactions between mother and daughter. At least one pleasant activity will be scheduled for a regular time each week.
  b. The client and her mother will identify one school sports activity that the client can join.
  c. The client will select at least two peers with whom she would like to socialize. The mother and daughter will problem-solve ways to arrange meeting times.
  d. A weekly home schedule will be developed that allows for regular pleasant events and socializing time.

Case Outcome

After the first session, Amy had more optimism about her life possibly improving than she had had in a long time. She later reported that the structure and attention helped her feel that she was not alone and that there were others in her corner. Her daily mood monitoring showed her that her mood did vary and was associated with the quality of her life activities. The cognitive work that initially helped her the most was creating self-talk scripts for encountering her non-supportive classmates. This experience sold her on the idea that changing the way she thinks could make a difference. This was further amplified by pointing out to her that many successful athletes use their thinking to "psych out" their opponents. Her daily cognitive homework assignment helped her to monitor and re-evaluate her automatic thoughts about herself. By the fifth week of treatment, her mood ratings were consistently 5 or greater. She had the most difficulty with acting assertively. Unexpectedly, she became markedly anxious at the prospect of "saying something." The treatment plan was altered to more gradually introduce assertive behaviors.

The largest jump in her mood occurred when she learned that she would be able to join the school's volleyball team. Her mother was able to work out a plan with a neighbor to solve a transportation problem. Although some expense was involved, the mother was able to work out an arrangement with the coach. Her talent was apparent immediately and she became a key member of the team. This also helped her make more friends and improved her reputation around the school. At follow-up 6 months later, she was still doing well and was considering joining the school's basketball team.

School Refusal

School refusal is characterized by difficulty attending school due to some kind of emotional distress such as anxiety and somatic symptoms (e.g., stomach aches; Heyne & King, 2004). Prevalence rates range from about 1 to 5 percent of school-age children (Heyne, King, Tongue & Cooper, 2001). Rates tend to peak when a child starts school or transitions to another school. Other common triggering events include illness, family problems (e.g., marital separation), problems with peers (e.g., bullying), and academic difficulties (e.g., test anxiety, academic failure). Typically, children complain about somatic symptoms or significant anxiety in anticipation of going to school in the morning. This may escalate into tantrums if the parent attempts to force the child to go. A chronic pattern of school refusal may then evolve over days to weeks which can have significant effects in the child's school, family and peer functioning. Treatments can be challenging to implement because they require the cooperation of the child, the parent and school personnel.

Case Background

José is an 11-year-old Hispanic male who lives with his mother and two older sisters. The family recently moved to Houston from Austin following the parents' divorce. He attended classes the first three weeks of school but became ill with a stomach virus during the fourth week. After he appeared to recover during the ensuing weekend, the nausea and stomachaches returned each morning of the following week. The mother kept José home thinking he was still suffering from a lingering aspect of the illness. However, the following weekend he appeared fine again until Monday morning, when the symptoms returned. A follow-up visit to the pediatrician confirmed that the symptoms were most likely due to anxiety and not a physical illness. At this point the mother attempted to force José to go to school. The more she nagged about going, the more anxious José became, until he began to vomit. At this point the mother contacted the principal at the school who put her in touch with the school counselor. After a lengthy phone conversation, the school counselor referred her to a local mental health counselor who specialized in child and adolescent problems.

José has had a long history of anxiety-related symptoms. His mother describes him as an anxious child who has to be constantly reassured. He has a history of bedwetting that continued until he was 8 years old. It is not unusual for him to have trouble sleeping because he feels on edge and ruminates about something that happened during the day. He has always been able to make friends, but often worries about "saying something stupid" or being unliked. Academically, he has made As and Bs in the past but last year he almost flunked the fifth grade because of a number of illnesses that coincided with his parents' separation. He seemed to be doing better during the past summer but then began expressing worry a few days before classes were scheduled to begin at the new school.

Two school incidents appeared to trigger his recent bout of school refusal. Two boys began teasing José in gym class during the third week of classes. Then his teacher made a number of critical remarks about his acting "whiny" in class when the teacher would ask him to hurry up and finish an assignment. Apparently, his racing thoughts were interfering with his ability to stay on task. These thoughts usually entailed concerns about what the teacher and other students might be thinking about him.

In terms of the family history, the parents divorced about 6 months ago. The mother decided to move to Houston because she has extended family there and knew about a job opportunity as a restaurant manager. She describes her relationship with José as close but admitted that he needs "a lot of growing up." The two older sisters have graduated from high school but still live in the home. One is working and the other is attending a local university.

José and his mother attended the initial counseling session. The mother did most of the talking, while her son fidgeted and seemed preoccupied. While José was reluctant to agree that he was ready to return to school, he also admitted that he wished the situation was better because he "felt bad" about upsetting his mother.

Diagnostic Issues

The first diagnostic distinction that needs to be made is to determine whether the school refusal is due to emotional distress or is simply truancy. Children who are truant lack the anxiety about going to school and often have other antisocial behaviors like stealing, conduct problems, or substance use. José clearly has marked emotional distress and lacks any significant conduct problems. This type of school refusal can be associated with a range of disorders like Separation Anxiety Disorder

(SAD), Generalized Anxiety Disorders (GAD), Panic Disorder With Agoraphobia, Social and Specific Phobias, Posttraumatic Stress Disorder (PTSD) and depression (APA, 2000a). The symptom profile is not consistent with SAD because José does not have excessive worry about being separated from his mother or being away from home. Depression can often present with somatic symptoms in children but José has no other significant mood symptoms. While he does have phobic-like behaviors, the cause appears to be his excessive worry and apprehension that give rise to physical symptoms. These symptoms appear to be part of along-standing pattern of worry and anxiety characteristic of GAD. José is not so much phobic of the school but rather the potential adverse events he believes could befall him there. His worry also appears to contribute to his distractibility and poor academic performance. Because his somatic symptoms are part of GAD, they would not be coded on Axis III. His Axis V score would reflect serious impairment in his school functioning due to the school refusal.

DSM-IV-TR **Diagnosis:**

Axis I: 300.02 Generalized Anxiety Disorder
Axis II: V71.09 No diagnosis
Axis III: None
Axis IV: School non-attendance, academic problems, and peer problems
Axis V: GAF = 50 (Current)

Case Conceptualization

José's worry and apprehension predispose him to chronic anxiety. Avoidance behaviors are strengthened through the process of negative reinforcement because they immediately reduce an aversive state. They also interfere with approach behaviors that have the potential to help José habituate or get use to anxiety provoking situations. The divorce and move are difficult for any child, but are particularly challenging for someone with GAD. His thinking appears to magnify danger and self-doubt and interferes with his ability to stand up for himself with other children.

Family factors are also important to consider. His father was disengaged from the family even before the divorce. This may be why José seems very close to his mother. His place in the family as the youngest child with older siblings is probably another contributing factor. As a result he is very dependent on caretakers and has difficulty with being separate and autonomous. All these factors conspire to contribute to his appearance of immaturity.

Treatment Planning Issues

School refusal problems require a comprehensive assessment that includes the child, parents, and relevant school personnel. The primary goal of treatment is return to school as soon as possible. The prioritized problem list includes missing school, excessive worry and anxiety, peer conflicts, and academic problems. Treatment will be implemented at an outpatient level of care and include both individual counseling for José, meetings with the mother and school personnel and family sessions with José and his mother (Bernstein & Shaw, 1997; Heyne & King, 2004).

Interventions with José will include relaxation training to control physiological arousal as well as cognitive therapy to counter negative thinking. Social skills training in assertion and social problem-solving will help him deal with his difficulties with peers. The therapeutic approach needs to be positive with the underlying aim to encourage autonomy and self-reliance.

Parent interventions will emphasize how the mother can support José's return to school. She can be instructed in child management techniques that reward approach and "courageous" behaviors and ignore avoidance and somatic behaviors. It will be important to acknowledge the mother's distress and life changes and help her generate better ways to deal with her new life circumstances. This may help her develop more of a life for herself that, from a system's perspective, will help to support José's efforts at greater self-reliance.

The school component will involve José's gradual reintroduction to school which has been termed *in vivo desensitization* (Heyne & King, 2004). Prior to implementation, a meeting with the parent and school personnel is needed to clearly lay out a step by step plan for school attendance. The procedure entails having the child gradually increase class attendance each day over a 1-week period. It is critical that the first day entail positive welcoming by school faculty and a selection of a low-stress class. If the child becomes anxious, procedures should be in place to ensure that he stays in the school for the scheduled time for that day. The parent is instructed in how to manage the morning separation routine and how to reward successful attendance.

In terms of stages of change, José seems to be in the early phase of contemplation because he recognizes some down side to the school refusal. Prior to implementing *in vivo desensitization*, it will be important to do a motivational intervention that will help him buy into the school attendance plan.

With these clinical points in mind, the following treatment plan was implemented:

Problem List:

1. School non-attendance
2. Excessive worry and anxiety
3. Problem with peers
4. Academic problems

Immediate Goals (within the next two weeks):

1. Jose will state at least three advantages of attending school.

    Plan:
    a. In conjoint session with the mother discuss the "good and not so good" things about staying home.
    b. Identify at least three benefits of school participation (e.g., friends, pleasant events, peace at home).
    c. Provide a model for coping with uncomfortable symptoms: ways to decrease physiological arousal (relaxation), negative thinking (coping thoughts) and behavioral avoidance (gradual exposure, school and family support).

    d. Train both parties in breathing relaxation, a brief relaxation exercise in which breathing is balanced through a system of five counts in and five counts out. The exercise will be practiced in session and then at home daily. Breathing relaxation is to be implemented whenever he begins to feel anxiety.

2. The client will attend school four out of five days a week for the designated time.

Plan:

    a. Arrange a meeting with the parent and school personnel to structure the in vivo desensitization plan. The plan will include rewards at home and at school for attendance. A graduated reward system will be used that is arranged so that reward values increase each consecutive day that he attends school. In the event of an unexpected absence, the reward value returns to the level of the first day, and increases with each day of attendance.

    b. José who will have opportunities to provide input into the reward schedule to insure compliance and commitment.

    c. School and home compliance to the plan will be monitored by counselor phone contacts during the week.

Short-Term Goals (within the next 6 weeks):

3. José will attend school for the entire day at least 90% of the time.

Plan:

    a. Continue implementation of the *in vivo* exposure but extend duration to include the whole school day.

    b. Include rewards for completion of homework.

    c. In conjoint sessions with Jose and his mother, troubleshoot any potential barriers to implementation. Encourage the mother to engage in pleasant events to help her take care of herself.

4. José's distractibility during class time will decrease from every hour to two times or less per day.

Plan:

    a. Meet with teachers to arrange a classroom plan for task completion. Discuss the importance of positive attention and encouraging comments for on-task behavior.

    b. Have José use the breathing exercise whenever he begins to feel anxiety in the classroom.

    c. Implement home-school report to provide a mechanism for teachers to provide feedback to the mother for school performance.

5. Client will be able to make an assertive statement to a classmate at least 75% of the time when it is indicated.

Plan:

    a. Education will be provided on the differences between aggressive, assertive, and passive responses.

    b. Assertive responses will be modeled and practiced using peer conflict situations.

    c. Social problem-solving will be discussed to help José decide whether to speak up or use an alternative strategy.

Long-Term Goal (within 10 weeks):

6. Negative thoughts will decrease from ten or more times a day to two times or less per day.

    Plan:

    a. Provide psychoeducation about the relationship between thinking, anxiety arousal and behavior.

    b. Review a five-step process for changing negative thinking: 1) identify the triggering situation; 2) note the feeling; 3) identify the thought associated with the feeling; 4) ask yourself what's true about the thought and what's untrue about the thought; and 5) make a decision to either change the thought (mostly untrue) or develop an action plan to deal with the situation if the thought is justified.

    c. Arrange daily practice using a worksheet that outlines the five steps.

Case Outcome

Initially José was opposed to the school plan. However, his resistance softened after he contemplated the positives and negatives of staying home. He admitted that deep down he wanted to be like his fellow students but did not know how to control his overwhelming sense of anxiety. The model that was presented during the first session helped him see that there was a manageable way of controlling his discomfort. Breathing relaxation provided a simple intervention that could provide some immediate relief. As far as the school plan, the first two days went well. On the third day, when he needed to attend three classes, he became ill during the second period. Per the school plan, he was instructed to go to the nurse's office. The symptoms worsened over a 30-minute period and then began to subside. This was an important turning point in the treatment because it showed the value of not giving in to avoidance behavior as the only way to reduce symptoms. A similar episode was handled successfully at the end of the week when he needed to attend gym. The following Monday he complained of nausea, but his mother was able to implement the behavior plan and encourage him to get on the school bus. He was able to attend school for the entire week. The graded reward system placed a higher response cost on slipping back to avoidance as a way of controlling anxiety. His regular school attendance helped with forming new relationships that served as a buffer for his tendency to internalize his doubts about himself. On one occasion he was able to express his discontent to the two students who had teased him. Their apologetic response suggested that their earlier comments may have been misinterpreted or magnified by José's negative thinking style.

    Work on his negative thinking moved more slowly, however. One important stuck point was the frequent lapses he would have after a period of several good days. Another critical point in the treatment was being able to see these situations as "slips" rather than signs that he would never get better. The mother's successful behavior management gave her a sense that she could be freed up to pursue more activities for herself. She felt more comfortable going out and pursuing a social life for herself. By the third month of treatment, plans were made to fade treatment to every other week for four sessions.

POLYSUBSTANCE DEPENDENCE

Substance-use problems in adolescence can be particularly difficult to diagnose. First, hallmark symptoms of dependence such as withdrawal and psychological and physical problems associated with usage are much less common in adolescents (Chung, Martin, Armstrong, & Labouvie, 2002). Instead, adolescents are more likely to show symptoms such as tolerance and using the substance longer than intended (Chung et al., 2002). Second, the pattern of substance use is also different in adolescents. Because adolescents have a more difficult time purchasing and obtaining substances, they are more likely to use whatever mind-altering drugs are available. As a result, they are more prone to show a pattern of polysubstance use (AACAP, 1997d; APA, 2000a). Last, the presence of a comorbid psychiatric disorder is common and must be distinguished from symptoms that are the result of the substance use (AACAP, 1997d).

Treatment has its own special set of challenges. Treatment outcome is generally poorer for adolescent substance users in comparison to adults (AACAP, 1997c). Part of the problem is that serious substance use might interfere with the development of an adolescent's coping repertoire (e.g., dealing with loss and loneliness). Furthermore, adolescents are more susceptible to the adverse influence of family and peer factors (AACAP, 1997d). Consequently, successful treatment programs not only must deal with ameliorating substance-use issues per se, but also must target coping deficits, family problems, and peer affiliation. These issues can be further complicated by the presence of a comorbid psychiatric disorder that also requires treatment. The case that follows illustrates how the clinician can design the treatment plan to deal with these types of issues.

Case Background

Todd is a 16-year-old Caucasian male who was initially evaluated in the emergency room after he collapsed at a party an hour earlier. He was running a body temperature of 104 degrees. Fortunately, the friend who brought him told the doctor that he had been taking Ecstasy (a stimulant with hallucinogenic properties), which can elevate body temperature to life-threatening levels. When his medical condition was stabilized, the after-hour emergency team from the local mental health center was notified and asked to evaluate him. His mother also participated in the evaluation.

Todd has been using various drugs for about 3 years. In the past year he has regularly used Ecstasy, Xanax, marijuana, and alcohol. On weekends he attends raves, which are all-night dance parties where drugs such as Ecstasy and Xanax are frequently available. Toward the end of the evening, he unwinds by having a few beers, or more commonly by taking Xanax. His Ecstasy use has escalated from one time a week to taking several pills each day of the weekend. Apparently, this is what it now takes to "get rolling." On weekdays it is not unusual for him to smoke marijuana before going to school. He likes to do this because "It takes the edge off school." Although he usually smokes only about one joint, it is not unusual for him to smoke another and subsequently skip school. At these times, he typically hangs out at an abandoned building until school is over. He supports his drug habit by selling small quantities of the drugs that he purchases at the raves to other classmates.

Although his mother was aware of his drug use, she did not realize the extent or the severity. She works as a nurse on the 11 P.M. to 7 A.M. shift at a local hospital during the week and works overtime on weekends. She explains that as a single parent, she has to work these long hours just to cover her monthly expenses. Her dilemma is that her long work hours compromise her ability to supervise Todd. She is also concerned that Todd might not be providing the right kind of supervision for his 13-year-old brother, who is often left in Todd's care.

Despite his drug use, Todd is unusually dutiful about taking care of responsibilities around the house. After school each day, he helps his mother with various chores around the house (e.g., laundry, yard work, cleaning). When he sneaks out at night, he instructs his brother to keep the doors locked and to stay in the house.

Todd's parents divorced about 4 years ago. The father moved to another city and has had only limited contact with the boys. However, about 2 years ago Todd went to live with his father for a couple of months after he was caught at school with marijuana in his locker. Although Todd initially seemed to be doing better in the new environment, he was expelled from school for selling some "pills" to his classmates. Apparently, he was using this money to buy marijuana. He then moved back with his mother.

In addition to his substance use, Todd also has a history of depressive symptoms such as depressed mood, sleep disturbance, and fatigue. These symptoms started about 2 years ago. One thing that he likes about Ecstasy is that it counters his fatigue symptoms and makes him feel more energetic and outgoing. He likes Xanax because it helps him unwind so that he can sleep.

He makes only marginally passing grades at school. He rarely turns in his homework assignments, and preparation for tests is limited to his study-hall period. Although he is not considered to have a behavior problem, his teachers are concerned about him because his friends are known drug users. Todd tends to stay to himself, and his involvement with teachers and other students is minimal.

Previous treatment involvement is limited. About 8 months ago, his mother took him to a local outpatient clinic after he was sent home from school for suspected drug use. However, they discontinued going after three meetings. The mother did not feel that the counseling sessions were very helpful because Todd would become upset and argumentative after each session.

Diagnostic Issues

Todd's substance use is certainly clinically significant and more than drug experimentation. However, he does not meet dependence criteria for any single substance. His Ecstasy use shows evidence of tolerance because he needs to use more of the substance to achieve the desired effect. His chronic use of marijauna, although fairly stable, does result in episodes in which he uses the substance longer than intended. His use of Xanax, Extacy, and marijuana interferes with other social, school, and recreational activities. Although he has had a physical problem (i.e., emergency-room visit) as a result of substance use, this can be counted only if there is prior knowledge of the likelihood of the physical problem occurring (APA, 2000a). Although no single substance has the necessary number of dependence symptoms, together they do meet the criteria of three or more symptoms present in the same 12-month period. A Polysubstance Dependence diagnosis would, therefore, best fit the symptom picture. The specifier With Physiological Dependence would be added because he has tolerance (APA, 2000a).

Todd also has a number of low-grade depressive symptoms that have persisted for a couple of years. The diagnostic conundrum is whether these symptoms are substance-induced or indicative of another psychiatric disorder such as Dysthymic Disorder. Fortunately, the *DSM-IV-TR* (APA, 2000a) provides a number of important guidelines to help differentiate substance-induced conditions from those that are attributable to an independent psychiatric disorder. First, if the symptoms began before the onset of the substance use, the presence of an independent psychiatric disorder is more probable. In this case, however, depressive symptoms were not present prior to the onset of substance use. A second consideration is whether the symptoms are typical or atypical of the suspected primary psychiatric disorder. Todd's depressive symptoms are consistent with the presentation of Dysthymic Disorder with an early onset. The only caveat is that low self-esteem is not present, which is common in the presentation of adolescent depression. Last, if symptoms persist for longer than 4 weeks after the last intoxication or withdrawal period, this is evidence that the symptoms are probably not substance-induced but the result of a primary psychiatric disorder. Unfortunately, there has been no period of time in the last 3 years in which this has occurred. As a result, there is not clear evidence of an independent primary psychiatric disorder. In the absence of a substance-free period of time, a basic rule of thumb is to re-evaluate Todd after 4 weeks of cessation to ascertain the status of these depressive symptoms before coding a diagnosis of Dysthymic Disorder (APA, 2000a).

DSM-IV-TR Diagnosis:

Axis I: 304.80 Polysubstance Dependence, With Physiological Dependence
Axis II: V71.09 No diagnosis
Axis III: None
Axis IV: Selling drugs, academic problems
Axis V: GAF = 60 (Current)

Case Conceptualization

Todd lives a double life. On the one hand, he shoulders a fair amount of home responsibilities while his mother works. From a family-systems perspective, there is a blurred generational boundary between him and his mother, in which he plays a parent-like role in the family. On the other hand, his substance use occupies the other half of his life. From a developmental perspective, the drug use provides an avenue to act independent and adult-like (e.g., using adult substances and staying out late). However, the substances now have become a focal point around which the rest of his life revolves.

The drugs have also become part of his coping repertoire. He uses them to deal with the strains of his home life as well as the typical stresses of the teen years. However, the drug use has also stunted his personal development in areas such as identity, intimacy, and vocational interests. Life without drugs will require Todd to develop not only a new lifestyle and social network, but also a very different way of approaching his everyday anxieties and uncertainties.

Treatment Planning Issues

Todd's problem list would include substance use, dealing to support his access to drugs, violation of house rules (staying out, skipping school), his externalizing coping style, and depressive symptoms. In terms of prioritizing this list, substance use would be targeted first for several reasons. First, it is associated with high-risk behaviors with potentially harmful consequences. Second, resolving substance use would break the chain of events that led to other problems such as dealing, skipping school, and staying out all night. Finally, from a pragmatic standpoint, efforts to change other problem behaviors will be extremely difficult to resolve as long as Todd is actively using drugs. As substance-related problems resolve, it will be important to address factors that can create high-risk situations for usage such as family conflicts, contact with substance-using peers, and coping with negative emotional states.

A key component to getting Todd's substance use under control is providing more daily structure and supervision. He does not meet inpatient admission criteria because he is not an imminent danger to self or others and there is no evidence that he needs to be medically supervised for withdrawal complications. Residential treatment would provide a structured 24-hour program, but this level of care might be too restrictive for this particular case. After all, there is a stable home base, and more community-based treatment would allow for direct treatment of family and peer factors. An intensive outpatient (IOP) level of care would strike a more optimal balance between needs for structure and maintenance in the community. Typically, IOP programs require participants to meet from 3 to 5 days a week for about 3 hours per meeting. These programs are usually scheduled after school and include a combination of group therapy, family therapy, drug education, and 12-step work. These components are consistent with recommended practice guidelines (AACAP, 1997d). Group therapy often includes skills training in areas such as anger management, substance refusal, problem-solving, communication, and relapse prevention. There is also attention to developing alternative peer relationships and leisure activities.

An important issue at the outset will be motivating Todd to give up his drug use. Although he appears to be in the precontemplation stage, the medical emergency might provide a window of opportunity in which Todd is more open to reconsidering his substance use. In this regard, motivational interviewing (MI; Miller & Rollnick, 1991) has been shown to be particularly effective in motivating resistant substance users. This approach consists of five basic strategies: listening empathetically, rolling with resistance, avoiding argumentation, creating discrepancies, and increasing self-efficacy. MI is particularly developmentally sensitive for adolescents because it minimizes the use of pressure or confrontation from adults. Instead, counselors use leads that encourage collaboration and client participation as a way of increasing intrinsic motivation for change.

The following is a treatment plan for an IOP setting. The usual length of stay is 3 to 5 weeks, depending on the type of case presented. This particular program requires participants to attend three meetings per week from 6:00 to 9:00 P.M. One of the meeting days is devoted entirely to meeting with the family. During the other 2 days, clients participate in group therapy as well as educational sessions on substance abuse. In addition, participants are required to attend two 12-step meetings a week outside of the time at the IOP facility.

Problem List:

1. Substance use
2. Dealing drugs
3. Violation of house rules
4. Peers and social activities associated with substance use
5. Externalizing coping style
6. Depressive symptoms

Immediate Goals (within the next week):

1. Be able to state at least three reasons why drug use is a problem.

   Plan: The client will:
   a. Attend group-therapy sessions 2 days a week with adolescents with similar substance-use problems as part of an IOP program. The focus of these sessions will be on discussing the adverse consequences of substance use and the benefits of cessation.
   b. Attend a 2-hour family-group-therapy session in which family members share their experiences, concerns, and feelings about the client's substance use.
   c. Attend at least two 12-step meetings for adolescent substance users.
   d. Sign a substance no-use contract for the duration of program participation.

Short-Term Goals (within the next 4 weeks):

2. Decrease substance use from daily to one time or less in the next 4 weeks.

   Plan:
   a. Continue 3-day-a-week attendance at the IOP program. The group therapy will focus on identifying triggers for usage (times, places, and emotional states) and developing a plan to cope with these situations.
   b. In the family sessions, the client and his mother will develop specific consequences for substance-related activities, staying out late, skipping school, and associating with known drug users.
   c. The mother will increase supervision by one of the following three methods: exploring ways to change her work schedule, enlisting the support of

her sister to monitor after-school activities if she is working, or asking school personnel to call her immediately if her son is not at school.

3. Increase positive interactions between the client and his mother from three times a week to one or more times per day.

   Plan:
   a. Each family member will monitor the occurrence of appreciated or valued activities by another family member.
   b. Schedule at least one pleasant family activity per week.
   c. Schedule a regular time each week for family to discuss house issues.

4. The client will engage in at least one positive leisure activity per day.

   a. Conduct an assessment of potential pleasant activities.
   b. Have client create a pleasant events menu of activities.
   c. Have the client write a weekly schedule of activities.

5. Increase time spent with nonusing peers from 1 hour per week to at least 5 hours a week.

   a. From the pleasant events menu, have the client select at least two activities he can perform with a peer.
   b. Have client select at least two nonusing peers for planned activity.
   c. In family session, arrange home support for participation in prosocial activities (e.g., arranging a ride).

6. Be able to state at least three things to do when there is an urge to use a substance.

   a. Client will write a list of high-risk situations that could trigger a lapse in cessation.
   b. At least two coping plans for each situation will be developed.
   c. Each coping plan will be role-played in sessions.

Long-Term Goal (by the 5th week)—Discharge Planning

7. The client will initiate weekly outpatient group therapy.

   a. Once IOP goals have been met, client will be referred to the outpatient unit for group therapy.
   b. Recommend periodic family therapy and weekly attendance at 12-step group to augment group work.
   c. Conduct case followup 6 months after IOP program discharge.

Case Outcome

The emergency-room visit not only scared Todd, but also helped him see more clearly the impact of his behavior on both his mother and his brother. He reluctantly agreed to participate in the IOP program. Between the program's schedule, school, and the increased home monitoring, Todd's daily lifestyle no longer made it easy to use drugs. When his substance use stopped, so did his need to sell drugs and deal with the consequences of using (e.g., taking Xanax to come down). The group and family therapy helped him deal more directly with issues that he was avoiding. After 2 weeks of being substance free, his mood markedly improved and his sleep problems dissipated. Apparently these symptoms were highly substance-induced. The program's focus of acquiring coping skills to deal with high-risk situations helped him learn how to deal with stress in ways other than simply externalizing through drug use.

He did have an occurrence of using during the third week of IOP, in which he sneaked out on the weekend. However, this only provided the mother an opportunity to implement "home rules" with the benefit of program support. Now the costs of using began to outweigh any temporary benefits. As more leisure activities and nonusing peers were included in his regular weekly routine, Todd began to see that life could be enjoyable without drugs. About 3 months later, Todd had another incident in which he came home drunk. However, he was able to recover and use the experience as another example of situations he still needed to learn to master. At the 6-month follow-up point, Todd and his family were still attending the outpatient program regularly. Although his attendance at 12-step meetings became more sporadic, he was able to maintain an abstinent lifestyle.

CLOSING REMARKS

These cases highlight how treatment planning needs to be sensitive to a range of individual differences. Although the diagnosis provides some general suggestions for what clients might need, treatment planning has to be far more finely tuned. This is why popular "cookbooks" on treatment planning for particular problems (e.g., anger, oppositional behavior) are inadequate on their own. Rather, an effective treatment plan tailors the interventions to a range of factors and attempts to involve the client in the process. From this perspective, the process of treatment planning itself is therapeutic.

REFERENCES

Abrams, K., Theberge, S. K., & Karan, O. C. (2005). Children and adolescents who are depressed: An ecological approach. *Professional School Counseling, 8,* 284–292.

Abreu, J. M. (2001). Theory and research on stereotypes and perceptual bias: A didactic resource for multicultural counseling trainers. *Counseling Psychologist, 29,* 487–512.

Achenbach, T. M. (1991a). *Manual for the Child Behavior Checklist and 1991 Profile.* Burlington, VT: University of Vermont, Department of Psychiatry.

Achenbach, T. M. (1991b). *Manual for the Youth Self-Report and 1991 Profile.* Burlington: University of Vermont, Department of Psychiatry.

Achenbach, T., & Edelbrock, C. (1982). *Manual for the Child Behavior Checklist and Child Behavior Profile.* Burlington: Department of Psychiatry, University of Vermont.

Achenbach, T. M., & Edelbrock, C. (1983). *Manual for the Child Behavior Checklist and Revised Child Behavior Profile.* Burlington, VT: University of Vermont, Department of Psychiatry.

Adger, H., & Werner, A. J. (1994). The pediatrician. *Alcohol Health & Research World, 18,* 121–126.

Adler, C. M., DelBello, M. P., Mills, N.P., Schmithorst, V., Holland, S., & Strakowski, S. M. (2005). Comorbid ADHD is associated with altered patterns of neuronal activation in adolescents with bipolar disorder performing a simple attention task. *Bipolar Disorders, 7,* 577–588.

Aimes, P. L., Gelder, M. G., & Shaw, P. M. (1983). Social phobia. A comparative clinical study. *British Journal of Psychiatry, 142,* 174–179.

Ainsworth, M. D. S. (1979). Infant–mother attachment. *American Psychologist, 34,* 932–937.

Ainsworth, M. D. S., Blehar, M. C., Waters, E., & Walls, S. (1978). Patterns of attachment: A psychological study of the strange situation. Hillsdale, NJ: Lawrence Erlbaum.

Alberto, P., & Troutman, A. (1995). *Applied behavior analysis for teachers* (4th ed.). Upper Saddle River, NJ: Merrill Prentice Hall.

Alexander, J. F., Holtzworth-Munroe, A., & Jameson, P. B. (1994). The process and outcome of marital and family therapy research: Review and evaluation. In A. E. Bergin & S. L. Garfield (Eds.), *Handbook of Psychotherapy and Behavior Change* (pp. 595–630). New York: John Wiley & Sons.

Alexander, J. P., & Parsons, B. V. (1982). *Functional family therapy.* Pacific Grove, CA: Brooks/Cole.

Alsobrook, J. P., & Pauls, D. L. (1997). The genetics of Tourette Syndrome. *Neurological Clinics, 15,* 381–393.

Ambrosini, P. J. (2000). Historical development and present status of the schedule for Affective Disorders and Schizophrenia for school-age children. *Journal of the American Academy of Child and Adolescent Psychiatry, 39,* 49–58.

American Academy of Child and Adolescent Psychiatry (1997c). Practice parameters for the assessment and treatment of children and adolescents with Conduct Disorder. *Journal of the American Academy of Child and Adolescent Psychiatry, 36*(10, Suppl.), 122S–139S.

American Academy of Child and Adolescent Psychiatry (1998c). Practice parameters for the assessment and treatment of children and adolescents with obsessive-compulsive disorder. *Journal of the American Academy of Child and Adolescent Psychiatry, 27,* 27–46.

American Academy of Child and Adolescent Psychiatry (2002). Practice parameters for the use of stimulant medications in the treatment of children, adolescents, and adults *Journal of the American Academy of Child and Adolescent Psychiatry, 41,* 26S–49S.

American Academy of Child and Adolescent Psychiatry (2007). Practice parameters for the assessment and treatment of children and adolescents with anxiety disorders. *Journal of the American Academy of Child and Adolescent Psychiatry, 46,* 267–284.

American Academy of Child and Adolescent Psychiatry (2007). Practice parameters for the assessment and treatment of children and adolescents with oppositional defiant disorder. *Journal of the American Academy of Child and Adolescent Psychiatry, 46,* 126–142.

American Academy of Child and Adolescent Psychiatry. (1997a). Practice parameters for the assessment and treatment of children, adolescents and adults with Attention-Deficit/Hyperactivity Disorder. *Journal of the American Academy of Child Adolescent Psychiatry, 36*(10, Suppl.), 85S–121S.

American Academy of Child and Adolescent Psychiatry. (1997b). Practice parameters for the assessment and treatment of children and adolescents with Bipolar Disorder. *Journal of the American Academy of Child and Adolescent Psychiatry, 36*(10, Suppl.), 157S–176S.

American Academy of Child and Adolescent Psychiatry. (1997d). Practice parameters for the assessment and treatment of children and adolescents with Substance-Use Disorders. *Journal of the American Academy of Child and Adolescent Psychiatry, 36*(10, Suppl.), 140S–156S.

American Academy of Child and Adolescent Psychiatry. (1998a). Practice parameters for the assessment and treatment of children and adolescents with Depressive Disorders. *Journal of the American Academy of Child and Adolescent Psychiatry, 37*(10, Suppl.), 63S–83S.

American Academy of Child and Adolescent Psychiatry. (1998b). Practice parameters for the assessment and treatment of children and adolescents with Posttraumatic Stress Disorder. *Journal of the American Academy of Child and Adolescent Psychiatry, 37*(10, Suppl.), 4S–26S.

American Academy of Child and Adolescent Psychiatry. (2001). Summary of practice parameters for the assessment and treatment of children and adolescents with suicidal behavior. *Journal of the American Academy of Child & Adolescent Psychiatry, 44,* 495–499.

American Academy of Pediatrics (2000). Clinical practice guideline: Diagnosis and evaluation of the child with attention-deficit/hyperactivity disorder. *Pediatrics, 105.* 1158–1170.

American Academy of Pediatrics (2001). Clinical practice guideline: Treatment of the school-aged child with attention-deficit/hyperactivity disorder. *Pediatrics, 108,* 1033–1044.

American Guidance Service. (1987). *Woodcock reading mastery test—revised.* Circle Pines, MN: Author.

American Guidance Service. (1988). *KeyMath—revised: A diagnostic inventory of essential mathematics.* Circle Pines, MN: Author.

American Psychiatric Association & American Academy of Child and Adolescent Psychiatry. (n.d.). The use of medication in treating childhood and adolescent depression: Information for physicians. Retrieved, April 15, 2006, from http://www.parentsmedguide.org/physicians-medguid.pdf

American Psychiatric Association (2000b). Practice guidelines for the treatment of patients with eating disorders (revision). *The American Journal of Psychiatry. 157,* 1–39.

American Psychiatric Association (2006). *Practice guidelines for the treatment of psychiatric disorders: Compendium 2006.* Washington, DC: Author.

American Psychiatric Association. (1968). *Diagnostic and statistical manual of Mental Disorders* (2nd ed.). Washington, DC: Author.

American Psychiatric Association. (1980). *Diagnostic and statistical manual of Mental Disorders* (3rd ed.). Washington, DC: Author.

American Psychiatric Association. (1987). *Diagnostic and statistical manual of Mental Disorders.* (3rd ed., text revision). Washington, DC: Author.

American Psychiatric Association. (1994). *Diagnostic and statistical manual of Mental Disorders* (4th ed.). Washington, DC: Author.

American Psychiatric Association. (2000). *Handbook of psychiatric measures.* Washington, DC: Author.

American Psychiatric Association. (2000a). *Diagnostic and statistical manual of Mental Disorders* (4th ed., text revision). Washington, DC: Author.

American Psychological Association (1998). Empirically supported treatments. *Journal of Clinical Child Psychology, 27,* 138–226.

Americans with Disabilities Act of 1990, 42 U.S.C., Section 121010 *et seq.*

Ames, L. B., Gillespie C., Haines, J., & Ilg, F. L. (1979). *The Gesell Institute's child from one to six: Evaluating the behavior of the preschool child.* New York: Harper & Row.

Ananth, J. (1986). Clomipramine: An antiobsessive drug. *Canadian Journal of Psychiatry, 31,* 253–258.

Anastopoulous, A. D., & Barkley, R. A. (1991). Biological factors in Attention-Deficit Disorder. *CH. A. A. D. ER, 5,* 1.

Anastopoulous, A. D., & Farley, E. F. (2003). A cognitive-behavioral training program for parents of children with Attention-Deficit/Hyperactivity Disorder. In A. E. Kazdin & J. R. Weisz (Eds.), *Evidence-based psychotherapies for children and adolescents* (pp. 187–203). New York: Guilford Press.

Anastopoulous, A. D., Smith, J. M., & Wien, E. E. (1998). Counseling and training parents. In R. A. Barkley (Ed.), *Attention-Deficit/Hyperactivity Disorder: A handbook for diagnosis and treatment* (pp. 373–393). New York: Guilford Press.

Andersen, A. E., & Mickalide, A. D. (1983). Anorexia Nervosa in the male: An undiagnosed disorder. *Psycho-somatics, 24,* 1067–1075.

Andersen, A. E., and Holman, J. E. (1997). Males with eating disorders: Challenges for treatment and research. *Psychopharmacology Bulletin, 33,* 391–397.

Andreasen, N. C., & Hoenk, P. R. (1982). The predictive value of Adjustment Disorders: A follow-up. *American Journal of Psychiatry, 139,* 584–590.

Andreasen, N. C., & Wasek, P. (1980). Adjustment Disorders in adolescents and adults. *Archives of General Psychiatry, 37,* 1166–1170.

Anglin, T. M. (1997). Adolescent substance abuse. In *Current Pediatric Diagnosis* (13th ed.). Retrieved from *STAT! Ref Medical Information CD-ROM,* 1998. Jackson Hole, WY: Teton Data Systems.

Angold, A., & Costello, E. J. (1993). Depressive comorbidity in children and adolescents: Empirical, theoretical, and methodological issues. *American Journal of Psychiatry, 150,* 1779–1791.

Anstendig, K. D. (1999). Is selective mutism an Anxiety Disorder? Rethinking its *DSM-IV* classification. *Journal of Anxiety Disorders, 13,* 417–434.

Applegate, G. (1980). If only my spouse would change: Marriage counseling with a young couple. In N. Glasser (Ed.), *What are you doing? How people are helped through reality therapy* (pp. 34–47). New York: Harper & Row.

Araoz, D. L., & Carrese, M. A. (1997). Adjustment Disorders and brief treatment. In S. R. Sauber (Ed.), *Managed mental health care: Major diagnosis and treatment approaches* (pp. 216–243). Bristol, PA: Brunner/Mazel.

Armsden, G. C., & Greenberg, M. T. (1987). The inventory of parent and peer attachment: Individual differences and their relationship to psychological well-being in adolescence. *Journal of Youth and Adolescence, 16,* 427–453.

Armstrong, J. G., & Roth, D. M. (1989). Attachment and separation difficulties in Eating Disorders: A preliminary investigation. *International Journal of Eating Disorders, 8,* 141–155.

Armsworth, M. W., & Holaday, M. (1993). The effects of psychological trauma on children and adolescents. *Journal of Counseling and Development, 72,* 49–56.

Arngold, A., & Costello, E. J. (2000). The child and adolescent psychiatric assessment. *Journal of the American Academy of Child and Adolescent Psychiatry, 39,* 39–48.

Arnold, E. L. (1996). Sex differences in AD/HD: Conference summary. *Journal of Abnormal Child Psychology, 24,* 555–569.

Arrendondo, P. (1998). Integrating multicultural counseling competencies and universal helping conditions in culture-specific contexts. *The Counseling Psychologist, 26,* 592–601.

Arrendondo, P. (1999). Multicultural counseling competencies as tools to address oppression and racism. *Journal of Counseling and Development, 77,* 102–108.

Arrendondo, P., & Arciniega, G. M. (2001). Strategies and techniques for counselor training based on the multicultural counseling competencies. *Journal of Multicultural Counseling, 29,* 263–269.

Arrendondo, P., Toporek, R., Brown, S. P., Jones, J., Locke, D. C., Sanchez, J., & Stadler, H. (1996). Operationalizing of the multicultural counseling competencies. *Journal of Multicultural Counseling and Development, 24,* 42–78.

Asarnow, J. R., Jaycox, L. H., Duan, N., LaBorde, A .P., Rea, M. M., Murray, P., et al. (2005). Effectiveness of a quality improvement intervention for adolescent depression in primary care clinics: A randomized controlled trial. *JAMA: The Journal of the American Medical Association, 293*, 311–319.

Aschenbrand, S. G., Angelosante, A. G., & Kendall, P. C. (2005). Discriminate validity and clinical utility of the CBCL with anxiety-disordered youth. *Journal of Clinical Child and Adolescent Psychology, 34*, 735–746.

Attie, I. & Brooks-Gunn, J. (1987). Weight-related concerns in women: A response to or a cause of stress? In R. C. Barnett, L. Biener, & G. K. Baruch (Eds.), *Gender and stress* (pp. 218–254). New York: Free Press.

Attie, I., & Brooks-Gunn, J. (1989). Development of eating problems in adolescent girls: A longitudinal study. *Developmental Psychology, 25*(1), 70–79.

Auger, R. W. (2004). The accuracy of teacher reports in the identification of middle school students with depressive symptomatology. *Psychology in Schools, 41*, 379–389.

Auger, R. W. (2005). School-based interventions for students with depressive disorders. *Professional School Counseling, 8*, 344–352.

Babinski, L. M., Hartsough, C. S., & Lambert, N. M. (1999). Childhood conduct problems, hyperactivity-impulsivity, and inattention as predictors of adult criminal activity. *Journal of Child Psychology and Psychiatry, 40*, 347–355.

Babor, T. F., & Grant, M. (1989). From clinical research to secondary prevention: International collaboration in the development of the Alcohol Use Disorders Identification Test (AUDIT). *Alcohol Health & Research World, 13*, 371–374.

Baby Center. (1997–2000). *Cognitive development: Age 2 and ages 6–8.* Retrieved November 21, 2000, from http://www.parentcenter.com:80/general/parenting/development/13233.html.

Bacon, S. F., Collins, M. J., & Plake, E. V. (2002). Does the Global Assessment of Functioning assess functioning? *Journal of Mental Health Counseling, 24*, 202–212.

Baider, L., Cooper, C. L., & De-Nour, A. K. (Eds.). (1996). *Cancer and the family.* Chichester, England: John Wiley & Sons.

Ballis, G. U. (1997). General principles of neuropsychiatric diagnosis. In W. H. Reid, G. U. Ballis, & B. J. Sutton (Eds.), *The treatment of Psychiatric Disorders: Revised for the DSM-IV* (pp. 3–13). Levittown, PA: Brunner/ Mazel.

Bandura, A. (1977). *Social learning theory.* Upper Saddle River, NJ: Merrill Prentice Hall.

Bandura, A. (1982). Self-efficacy mechanisms in human agency. *American Psychologist, 37*, 122–147.

Bandura, A. (1986). *Social foundations of thought and action: A social-cognitive theory.* Upper Saddle River, NJ: Merrill Prentice Hall.

Bandura, A. (1995). Exercise of personal and collective self-efficacy in changing societies. In A. Bandura (Ed.), *Self-efficacy in changing societies* (pp. 1–45). New York: Cambridge University Press.

Bandura, A., & Walters, R. H. (1963). *Social learning and personality development.* New York: Holt, Rinehart and Winston.

Barbe, R. P., Bridge, J., Birmaher, B., Kolko, D., & Brent, D. A. (2004). Suicidality and its relationship to treatment outcome in depressed adolescents. *Suicide & Life-Threatening Behavior, 34*, 44–55.

Bardick, A. D., & Bernes, K. B. (2005). A closer examination of bipolar disorder in school-age children. *Professional School Counseling, 9*, 72–77.

Barker, P. (2004). *Basic child psychiatry* (7th ed.). Malden, MA: Blackwell Publishing.

Barkley, R. A. (1981). *Hyperactive children: A handbook for diagnosis and treatment.* New York: Guilford Press.

Barkley, R. A. (1985). The social interactions of hyperactive children: Developmental changes, drug effects, and situational variation. In R. McMahon & R. Peters (Eds.), *Childhood Disorders: Behavioral developmental approaches* (pp. 218–243). New York: Brunner/Mazel.

Barkley, R. A. (1995). *Taking charge of AD/HD: The complete authoritarian guide for parents.* New York: Guilford Press.

Barkley, R. A. (1996). Attention-Deficit/Hyperactivity Disorder. In E. J. Mash & R. A. Barkley (Eds.), *Child psychopathology* (pp. 63–112). New York: Guilford Press.

Barkley, R. A. (1997a). *AD/HD and the nature of self-control.* New York: Guilford Press.

Barkley, R. A. (1997b). *Defiant children: A clinician's manual for assessment and parent training* (2nd ed.). New York: Guilford Press.

Barkley, R. A. (1998). *Attention-Deficit Hyperactivity Disorder: A handbook for diagnosis and treatment* (2nd. ed.). New York: Guilford Press.

Barkley, R. A. (2000a). Commentary on the multimodal treatment study of children with AD/HD. *Journal of Abnormal Psychology, 28*, 595–599.

Barkley, R. A. (2000b). Commentary: Issues in training parents to manage children with behavior problems. *Journal of the American Academy of Child and Adolescent Psychiatry, 39*, 1004–1007.

Barkley, R. A. (2005). *Attention deficit hyperactivity disorder: A handbook for diagnosis and treatment* (3rd ed.). New York: Guilford Press.

Barkley, R. A., & Cunningham, C. E. (1979). The effects of methylphenidate on the mother–child interactions of hyperactive children. *Archives of General Psychiatry, 36*, 201–208.

Barkley, R. A., DuPaul, G. J., & McMurray, M. B. (1990). A comprehensive evaluation of Attention-Deficit Disorder with and without hyperactivity. *Journal of Consulting and Clinical Psychology, 58*, 775–789.

Barkley, R. A., & Edelbrock, C. S. (1987). Assessing situational variation in children's behavior problems: The home and school questionnaires. In R. J. Prinz (Ed.), *Advances in behavioral assessment of children and families* (pp. 157–176). Greenwich, CT: JAI Press.

Barkley, R. A., Guevremont, D. C., Anastopoulous, A. D., & Fletcher, K. E. (1992). A comparison of three family therapy programs for treating family conflicts in adolescents with Attention-Deficit/Hyperactivity Disorder. *Journal of Consulting and Clinical Psychology, 60*, 450–462.

Barnes, G. M., Farrell, M. P., & Cairns, A. (1986). Parental socialization factors and adolescent drinking behaviors. *Journal of Marriage and the Family, 48*, 27–36.

Barnow, S., Linden, M., Lucht, M., & Freyberger, H. J. (2002). The importance of psychosocial factors, gender, and severity of depression in distinguishing between adjustment and depressive disorders. *Journal of Affective Disorders, 72*, 71–78.

Barrett, R. J. (1997). Cultural formulation of psychiatric diagnosis; Death on a horse's back: Adjustment Disorder with panic attacks. *Culture, Medicine and Psychiatry, 21*, 481–496.

Bartholomew, K., Henderson, A., & Dutton, D. (2001). Insecure attachment and abusive intimate relationships. In C. Clulow (Ed.), *Adult attachment and couple psychotherapy: The "secure base" in practice and research* (pp. 43–61). Philadelphia: Taylor & Francis.

Baruth, L. G., & Manning, M. L. (1999). *Multicultural counseling and psychotherapy: A lifespan perspective* (2nd ed.). Upper Saddle River, NJ: Prentice Hall.

Bates, G. W., Bates, S. R., & Whitworth, N. S. (1982). Reproductive failure in women who practice weight control. *Fertility and Sterility, 37*, 373–378.

Baumgaertel, A., Wolraich, M. L., & Dietrich, M. (1995). Comparison of diagnostic criteria for Attention-Deficit Disorders in a German elementary school sample. *Journal of the American Academy of Child and Adolescent Psychiatry, 34*, 629–638.

Baving, L., Laucht, M., & Schmidt, M. H. (1999). Atypical frontal brain activation in AD/HD: Preschool and elementary school boys and girls. *Journal of the American Academy of Child and Adolescent Psychiatry, 38*, 1363–1371.

Beardslee, W. R. (2000). Prevention of Mental Disorders and the study of developmental psychopathology: A natural alliance. In J. L. Rapoport (Ed.), *Childhood-onset of adult psychopathology: Clinical and research advances* (pp. 333–355). Washington, DC: American Psychiatric Press.

Beardslee, W. R., Gladstone, T. R. G., Wright, E. J., & Cooper, A. B. (2003). Family-based approach to the prevention of depressive symptoms in children at risk: Evidence of parental and child change. *Pediatrics, 112*, 119–131.

Beattie, H. J. (1988). Eating Disorders and the mother–daughter relationship. *International Journal of Eating Disorders, 7*, 453–460.

Beck, A. T. (1987a). Cognitive models of depression. *Journal of Cognitive Psychotherapy, 1*, 5–37.

Beck, A. T. (1987b). *Beck depression inventory*. San Antonio, TX: Psychological Corporation.

Beck, A. T. (1987c). *Beck hopelessness scale*. San Antonio, TX: Psychological Corporation.

Beck, A. T. (1990). *Anxiety inventory*. San Antonio, TX: Psychological Corporation.

Beidel, D. C., Turner, S. M., Morris, T. L. (2000). Behavioral treatment of childhood social phobia. *Journal of Consulting and Clinical Psychology, 68*, 1072–1080.

Beiser, M., Jenkins, J. H., Kinzie, J. D., & Spiegel, D. (1996). Adjustment and Stress Disorders. In J. E. Mezzich & A. Kleinman (Eds.), *Culture and psychiatric diagnosis: A DSM-IV perspective* (pp. 215–239). Washington, DC: American Psychiatric Press.

Bell, C. C. (2001). Diagnostic and statistical manual of Mental Disorders, fourth edition, text revision: *DSM-IV-TR/* quick reference to the diagnostic criteria from *DSM-IV-TR. The Journal of the American Medical Association, 285*, 811–812.

Bell, R. Q., & Harper, L. V. (1977). *Child effects on adults*. New York: John Wiley & Sons.

Bengi, B., & Alkin, T. (1999). Panic Disorder subtypes: Differential response to CO_2 challenge. *American Journal of Psychiatry, 156*, 739–744.

Berenson, C. K. (1998). Frequently missed diagnoses in adolescent psychiatry. *The Psychiatric Clinics of North America, 21*, 917–926.

Berg, F. M. (1997). *Afraid to eat: Children and teens in weight crisis*. Hettinger, ND: Healthy Weight Journal.

Berk, L. E., & Potts, M. K. (1991). Development and functional significance of private speech among Attention-Deficit/Hyperactivity Disorder and normal boys. *Journal of Abnormal Child Psychology, 19*, 357–377.

Berman, P. S. (1997). *Case conceptualization and treatment planning: Exercises for integrating theory with clinical practice*. Thousand Oaks, GA: Sage Publications.

Berman, S. L., Kurtines, W. M., Silverman, W. K., & Serafini, L. T. (1996). The impact of exposure to crime and violence on urban youth. *American Journal of Orthopsychiatry, 66*, 329–336.

Bernal, G., & Scharron-del-Rio, M. R. (2001). Are empirically supported treatments valid for ethnic minorities? Towards an alternative approach for treatment research. *Cultural Diversity and Ethnic Minority Psychology, 7*, 328–342.

Bernstein, G. A., & Borchardt, C. M. (1991). Anxiety Disorders of childhood and adolescence: A critical review. *Journal of the American Academy of Child and Adolescent Psychiatry, 30*, 519–532.

Bernstein, G. A., & Perwien, A. R. (1995). Anxiety Disorders. Children and adolescents. *Psychiatric Clinics of North America, 4*, 305–322.

Bernstein, G. A., & Shaw, K. (1997). Practice parameters for the assessment and treatment of children and adolescents with Anxiety Disorders. *Journal of the American Academy of Child and Adolescent Psychiatry, 36*(10, Suppl.), 69S–84S.

Bettelheim, B. (1967). *The empty fortress: Infantile autism and the birth of the self*. New York: Free Press.

Beutler, L. E., & Clarkin, J. F. (1990). *Systematic treatment selection*. New York: Brunner/Mazel Publishers.

Biederman, J. (1990). The diagnosis and treatment of adolescent Anxiety Disorders. *Journal of Clinical Psychiatry, 51*, 20–26.

Biederman, J., Faraone, S. V., Keenan, K., Knee, D., & Tsuang, M. T. (1990). Family-genetic and psychosocial risk factors in *DSM-III* Attention Deficit Disorder. *Journal of the American Academy of Child and Adolescent Psychiatry, 145*, 526–533.

Biederman, J., Faraone, S. V., & Lapey, K. (1992, October). Comorbidity of diagnosis in Attention-Deficit/ Hyperactivity Disorder. *Child and Adolescent Psychiatric Clinics of North America, 1*, 335–360.

Biederman, J., Faraone, S. V., Mick, E., Williamson, S., Wilens, T. E., Spencer, T. J., Weber, W., Jetton, J., Kraus, I., Pert, J., & Zallen, B. (1999). Clinical correlates of AD/HD in females: Findings from a large group of girls ascertained from pediatric and psychiatric referral sources. *Journal of the American Academy of Child and Adolescent Psychiatry, 38*, 966–975.

Biederman, J., Faraone, S. V., Milberger, S., Jetton, J. G., Chen, L., Mick, E., Greene, R. W., & Russell, R. L. (1996). Is childhood Oppositional Defiant Disorder a precursor to adolescent Conduct Disorder? Findings from a four-year follow-up study of children with AD/HD. *Journal of the American Academy of Child and Adolescent Psychiatry, 35*, 1193–1204.

Biederman, J., Mick, E., Faraone, S. V., Braaten, E., Doyle, A., Spencer, T., Wilens, T. E., Frazier, E., & Johnson, M. A. (2002). Influence of gender on Attention-Deficit/ Hyperactivity Disorder in children referred to a psychiatric clinic. *American Journal of Psychiatry, 159*, 36–42.

Biederman, J., Mick, E., Faraone, S .V., & Wozniak, J. (2004). Pediatric bipolar disorder or disruptive behavior disorder? *Primary Psychiatry, 11*, 36–41.

Biederman, J., Newcorn, J., & Sprich, S. (1991). Comorbidity of Attention-Deficit/Hyperactivity Disorder with conduct, depressive, anxiety, and other disorders. *American Journal of Psychiatry, 148*, 564–577.

Bierman, K. L., & Greenberg, M. T. (1996). Social skills training in the FAST Track program. In R. D. Peters & R. J. McMahon (Eds.), *Preventing childhood disorders, substance abuse, and delinquency* (pp. 65–89). Thousand Oaks, CA: Sage.

Binet, A., & Simon, Th. (1916). *The development of intelligence in children (The Binet-Simon Scale)* (E. S. Kite, Trans.). Baltimore: Williams & Wilkins. (Original work published 1905.)

Bird, H. R. (1996). Epidemiology of childhood disorders in a cross-cultural context. *Journal of Child Psychology and Psychiatry, 37*, 35–49.

Bird, H. R., Gould, M., Staghezza, B. (1993). Patterns of diagnostic comorbidity in a community sample of children aged 9 through 16 years. *Journal of the American Academy of Child and Adolescent Psychiatry, 32,* 361–368.

Bird, H. R., Gould, M., Yager, T., Staghezza, B., & Canino, G. (1989). Risk factors for maladjustment in Puerto Rican children. *Journal of the American Academy of Child and Adolescent Psychiatry, 28,* 847–850.

Birmaher, B., Axelson, D., Strober, M., Gill, M. K., Valeri, S., Chiappetta, L., et al. (2006). Clinical course of children and adolescents with bipolar spectrum disorders. *Archives of General Psychiatry, 63,* 175–183.

Birmaher, B., Brent, B., & Benson, R. S. (1998). Summary of the practice parameters for the assessment and treatment of children and adolescents with Depressive Disorders. *Journal of the American Academy of Child and Adolescent Psychiatry, 37,* 1234–1238.

Birmaher, B., Ryan, N. D., Williamson, D. E., Brent, D. A., & Kaufman, J. (1996b). Childhood and adolescent depression: A review of the past 10 years. Part II. *Journal of the American Academy of Child and Adolescent Psychiatry, 35,* 1575–1583.

Birmaher, B., Ryan, N. D., Williamson, D. E., Brent, D. A., Kaufman, J., Dahl, R. E., Perel, J., & Nelson, B. (1996a). Childhood and adolescent depression: A review of the past 10 years. Part I. *Journal of the American Academy of Child and Adolescent Psychiatry, 35,* 1427–1439.

Black, B., & Robbins, D. R. (1990). Panic Disorder in children and adolescents. *Journal of the American Academy of Child and Adolescent Psychiatry, 29,* 36–44.

Blotcky, B. J., Dimperio, T. J., & Gossett, J. T. (1984). Follow-up of children treated in psychiatric hospitals: A review of studies. *American Journal of Psychiatry, 141,* 1499–1507.

Blum, K., Noble, E. P., Sheridan, P. J., Montgomery, A., Ritchie, T., Jagedeeswaran, P., Nogami, H., Briggs, A. H., & Cohen, J. B. (1990). Allelic association of human dopamine D2 receptor gene in alcoholism. *Journal of the American Medical Association, 263,* 2055–2060.

Boergers, J., Spirito, A., & Donaldson, D. (1998). Reasons for adolescent suicide attempts: Associations with psychological functioning. *Journal of the American Academy of Child and Adolescent Psychiatry, 37,* 1287–1293.

Bokszczanin, A. (2003). The role of coping strategies and social support in adolescent's well-being after a flood. *Polish Psychological Bulletin, 34,* 67–72.

Bonafina, M. A., Newcorn, J. H., McKay, K. E., Koda, V. H., & Halperin, J. M. (2000). AD/HD and reading disabilities: A cluster analytic approach for distinguishing subgroups. *Journal of Learning Disabilities, 33,* 297–307.

Borduin, C. M. (1999). Multisystemic treatment of criminality and violence in adolescents. *Journal of the American Academy of Child and Adolescent Psychiatry, 38,* 242–248.

Borduin, C. M., & Henggeler, S. W. (1990). A multisystemic approach to the treatment of serious delinquent behavior. In R. J. McMahon & R. DeV. Peters (Eds.), *Behavior Disorders of adolescence* (pp. 63–80). New York: Plenum Press.

Borduin, C. M., Mann, B. J., Cone, L. T., Henggeler, S. W., Fucci, B. R., Blaske, D. M., & Williams, R. A. (1995). Multisystemic treatment of serious juvenile offenders: Long-term prevention of criminality and violence. *Journal of Consulting and Clinical Psychology, 63,* 569–578.

Bosacki, S. L., & Moore, C. (2004). Preschoolers' understanding of simple and complex emotions: Links with gender and language, *Sex Roles, 50,* 659–675.

Bostic, J. Q., Rubin, D. H., Prince, J., & Schlozman, S. (2005). Treatment of depression in children and adolescents. *Journal of Psychiatric Practice, 11,* 141–154.

Bostic, J. Q., Wilens, T. E., Spencer, T., & Biederman, J. (1999). Antidepressant treatment of juvenile depression. *International Journal of Psychiatry in Clinical Practice, 3,* 171–179.

Botteron, K. N., & Geller, B. (1995). Pharmacologic treatment of childhood and adolescent mania. *Child and Adolescent Psychiatric Clinics of North America, 4,* 283–304.

Botvin, G. J., Baker, E., Filazzola, A. D., & Botvin, E. (1990). A cognitive-behavioral approach to substance abuse prevention: One-year follow-up. *Addictive Behavior, 15,* 47–63.

Bourdon, K. H., Boyd, J. H., Rae, D. S., Burns, B. J., Thompson, J. W., & Locke, B. Z. (1988). Gender differences in phobia: Results of the ECA Community Survey. *Journal of Anxiety Disorders, 2,* 227–241.

Bowden, C. L., & Rhodes, L. J. (1996). Mania in children and adolescents: Recognition and treatment. *Psychiatric Annals, 26,* S430–S434.

Bowden, C. L., Ketter, T. A., Sachs, G. S., & Thase, M. E. (2005). Focus on bipolar disorder treatment. *Journal of Clinical Psychiatry, 66,* 1598–1609.

Bowlby, J. (1973). *Attachment and loss: Vol. II. Separation: Anxiety and anger.* New York: Basic Books.

Bowlby, J. (1980). *Attachment and loss: Vol. III. Loss: Sadness and depression.* New York: Basic.

Boyarsky, B. K., Perone, L. A., Lee, N. C., & Goodman, W. K. (1991). Current treatment approaches to Obsessive-Compulsive Disorder. *Archives of Psychiatric Nursing, V,* 299–306.

Boyce, P., Harris, M., Silove, D., Morgan, A., Wilhelm, K., & Hadzi-Pavlovic, D. (1998). Psychosocial factors associated with depression: A study of socially disadvantaged women with young children. *The Journal of Nervous & Mental Disease, 186,* 3–11.

Boyle, M. H., & Offord, D. R. (1991). Psychiatric Disorder and substance use in adolescence. *Canada Journal of Psychiatry, 36,* 699–705.

Bracken, B. A. (1992). *The multidimensional self-concept scale.* Austin, TX: Pro-Ed.

Brandenburg, N. A., Friedman, R. M., & Silver, S. E. (1990). The epidemiology of childhood Psychiatric Disorders: Prevalence findings from recent studies. *Journal of the American Academy of Child and Adolescent Psychiatry, 29,* 76–83.

Brannigan, R., Schackman, B. R., Falco, M., & Millman, R. B. (2004). The quality of highly regarded adolescent substance abuse treatment programs. *Archives of Pediatric and Adolescent Medicine, 158,* 904–909.

Breen, M. J. (1989). Cognitive and behavioral differences in AD/HD boys and girls. *Journal of Child Psychology and Psychiatry, 30,* 711–716.

Breier, A., Charney, D. S., & Heninger, G. R. (1985). The diagnostic validity of Anxiety Disorders and their relationship to depressive illness. *American Journal of Psychiatry, 142,* 787–797.

Brems, C. (2000). *Dealing with challenges in psychotherapy and counseling.* Belmont, CA: Brooks/Cole.

Brent, D. A., Holder, D., Kolko, D., Birmaher, B., Braugher, M., Roth, C., Iyengar, S., & Johnson, B. A. (1997). A clinical psychotherapy trial for adolescent depression comparing cognitive, family, and supportive therapy. *Archives of General Psychiatry, 54,* 877–885.

Brent, D. A., Kolko, D. J., Birmaher, B., Baugher, M., & Bridge, J. (1999). A clinical trial for adolescent depression: Predictors of additional treatment in the acute and follow-up phases of the trial. *Journal of the American Academy of Child and Adolescent Psychiatry, 38,* 263–270.

Brestan, E. V., & Eyberg, S. M. (1998). Effective psychosocial treatments of Conduct-Disordered children and adolescents: 29 years, 82 studies, and 5,272 kids. *Journal of Clinical Child Psychology, 27*(2), 180–189.

Bretherton, I. (1995). Attachment theory and developmental psychopathology. In D. Cicchetti & S. Toth (Eds.), *Emotion and representation in developmental psychopathology.* Rochester, NY: University of Rochester Press.

Bridge, J. A., Barbe, R. P., Birmaher, B., Kolko, T. J., & Brent, D. A. (2005). Emergent suicidality in a clinical psychotherapy trial for adolescent depression. *American Journal of Psychiatry, 162,* 2173–2175.

Bronfenbrenner, U. (1979). *The ecology of human development: Experiments by nature and design.* Cambridge, MA: Harvard University Press.

Brook, J. S., Cohen, P., Whiteman, M., & Gordon, A. S. (1992). Psychosocial risk factors in the transition from moderate to heavy use or abuse of drugs. In M. Glantz & R. Pickens (Eds.), *Vulnerability to drug abuse* (pp. 359–388). Washington, DC: American Psychological Association.

Brook, J. S., Whiteman, M., Finch, S. J., & Cohen, P. (1996). Young adult drug use and delinquency: Childhood antecedents and adolescent mediators. *Journal of the American Academy of Child and Adolescent Psychiatry, 35,* 1584–1592.

Brooks, D. K., Jr. (1984). *A life-skills taxonomy: Defining elements of effective functioning through the use of the Delphi technique.* Unpublished doctoral dissertation, The University of Georgia, Athens, GA.

Brooks, R. B., Baltazar, P. L., & Munjack, D. J. (1989). Co-occurence of Personality Disorders with Panic Disorder, Social Phobia, and Generalized Anxiety Disorder: A review of the literature. *Journal of Anxiety Disorders, 3,* 259–285.

Brown, J., Cohen, P., Johnson, J., & Smailes, E. (1999). Childhood abuse and neglect: Specificity of effects on adolescents and young adult depression and suicidality. *Journal of the American Academy of Child and Adolescent Psychiatry, 38,* 1490–1496.

Brown, L. K., & Brown, M. (1996). *When dinosaurs die.* Boston: Little, Brown, and Company.

Brown, R. T., & Ivers, C. E. (1999). Gilles de la Tourette syndrome. In S. Goldstein & C. R. Reynolds (Eds.), *Handbook of Neurodevelopmental and Genetic Disorders in children* (pp. 185–215). New York: Guilford Press.

Brown, R. T., & Sammons, M. T. (2002). Pediatric psychopharmacology: A review of new developments and recent research. *Professional Psychology: Research and Practice, 33,* 135–147.

Brown, T. A., O'Leary, T. A., & Barlow, D. H. (1993). Generalized Anxiety Disorder. In D. H. Barlow (Ed.), *Clinical handbook of Psychological Disorders* (2nd. ed., pp. 137–188). New York: Guilford.

Brown, T. E. (1994). The many faces of ADD: Comorbidity. *Attention! The Magazine of Children and Adults with Attention-Deficit Disorders, 2,* 29–36.

Brown, T. E. (1995). *Brown Attention-Deficit Disorder scales.* San Antonio, TX: Psychological Corporation.

Brownell, K. D., Marlett, G. A., Lichtenstein, E., & Wilson, G. T. (1986). Understanding and preventing relapse. *American Psychologist, 41,* 765–782.

Bruch, H. (1969). Hunger and instinct. *Journal of Nervous and Mental Diseases, 149,* 91–114.

Bruch, H. (1973). *Eating Disorders.* New York: Basic Books.

Brulle, A. R., McIntyre, T. C., & Mills, J. S. (1985). School phobia: Its educational implications. *Elementary School Guidance and Counseling, 20,* 19–28.

Bryant-Waugh, R., & Lask, B. (1995). Annotation: Eating Disorders in children. *Journal of Child Psychology and Psychiatry, 36*(2), 191–202.

Bukstein O. G. (2004). *Practice parameter for the assessment and treatment of children and adolescents with substance use disorders.* Washington, DC: American Academy of Child and Adolescent Psychiatry.

Burke, A. E., & Silverman, W. K. (1987). The prescriptive treatment of school refusal. *Clinical Psychology Review, 7,* 353–362.

Butler, G., Cullington, A., Munby, M., Amies, P., & Gelder, M. (1984). Exposure and anxiety management in the treatment of social phobia. *Journal of Consulting and Clinical Psychology, 52,* 642–650.

Buydens-Branchey, L., Branchey, M. H., & Noumair, D. (1989). Age of alcoholism onset I: Relationship to psychopathology. *Archives of General Psychiatry, 46,* 225–230.

Caffo, E., & Balaise, C. (2003). Psychological aspects of traumatic injury in children and adolescents. *Child and Adolescent Psychiatric Clinics of North America, 12,* 493–535.

Calhoun, K. S., & Resick, P. A. (1993). Post-traumatic Stress Disorder. In D. H. Barlow (Ed.), *Clinical handbook of Psychological Disorders* (2nd. ed., pp. 48–98). New York: Guilford.

Cancro, R. (2004). Mental health impact of September 11. *Molecular Psychiatry, 9,* 1055–1056.

Cantwell, D. P., & Baker, L. (1989). Stability and natural history of *DSM-III* childhood diagnoses. *Journal of the American Academy of Child and Adolescent Psychiatry, 28,* 691–700.

Cantwell, D. P., & Baker, L. (1992). Association between Attention-Deficit/Hyperactivity Disorder and learning disabilities. In S. E. Shaywitz & B. A. Shaywitz (Eds.), *Attention-Deficit Disorder comes of age: Toward the twenty-first century* (pp. 145–164). Austin, TX: Pro-Ed.

Cantwell, D. P., & Satterfield, J. H. (1992). The prevalence of academic underachievement in hyperactive children. *Journal of Pediatric Psychology, 3,* 168–171.

Capaldi, D. M. (1992). The co-occurrence of conduct problems and depressive symptoms in early adolescent boys: II. A 2-year follow-up at grade 8. *Development and Psychopathology, 4,* 125–144.

Carey, G., & DiLalla, D. L. (1994). Personality and psychopathology: Genetic perspectives. *Journal of Abnormal Psychology, 103,* 32–43.

Carey, W. B., & McDevitt, S. C. (Eds.). (1989). *Clinical and educational applications of temperament research.* Amsterdam: Swets & Zeitlinger.

Carlson, J., Hinkle, J. S., & Sperry, L. (1993). Using diagnosis and *DSM-III-R* and *IV* in marriage and family counseling and therapy: Increasing treatment outcomes without losing heart and soul. *The Family Journal: Counseling and Therapy for Couples and Families, 1,* 308–312.

Carter, J. C., Stewart, D. A., Dunn, V. J., & Fairburn, C. G. (1997). Primary prevention of Eating Disorders: Might it do more harm than good? *International Journal of Eating Disorders, 22,* 167–172.

Carter, J. D., & Swanson, H. L. (1995). The relationship between intelligence and vigilence in children at risk. *Journal of Abnormal Psychology, 23,* 201–220.

Casat, C. D. (1988). Childhood Anxiety Disorders: A review of the possible relationship to Adult Panic Disorder and Agoraphobia. *Journal of Anxiety Disorders, 2,* 51–60.

Casey, B. J., Castellanos, X. F., Giedd, J. N., Marsh, W. L., Hamburger, S. D., Schubert, A. B., Vauss, Y. C., Vaituzis, A. C., Dickstein, D. P., Sarafatti, S. E., & Rapoport, J. L. (1997). Implication of right frontostriatal circuitry in response inhibition and Attention-Deficit/Hyperactivity Disorder. *Journal of the American Academy of Child and Adolescent Psychiatry, 36,* 374–383.

Casey, B. J., Giedd, J., Vauss, Y., Vaituzis, C. K., & Rapoport, J. L. (1992). Selective attention and the anterior cingulate: A developmental neuroanatomical study. *Social Neuroscience Abstracts, 18,* 332.

Casey, R. J., & Berman, J. S. (1985). The outcome of psychotherapy with children. *Psychological Bulletin, 98,* 388–400.

Cash, R. E. (2003). When depression brings teens down. *Education Digest, 69,* 35–42.

Casper, R. C., & Jabine, L. N. (1996). An eight-year follow-up: Outcome from adolescent compared to adult onset Anorexia Nervosa. *Journal of Youth and Adolescence, 25,* 499–518.

Caspi, A., Henry, B., McGee, R. O., Moffitt, T., & Silva, P. A. (1995). Temperamental origins of child and adolescent behavior problems: From age three to age fifteen. *Child Development, 66,* 55–68.

Caspi, A., & Moffitt, T. (1995). The continuity of maladaptive behavior: From description to understanding in the study of antisocial behavior. In D. Cicchetti & D. J. Cohen (Eds.), *Developmental psychopathology: Risk, disorder, and adaptation* (pp. 472–511). New York: John Wiley & Sons.

Castellanos, X. F., Giedd, J. N., Eckburg, P., Marsh, W. L., Vaituzis, A. C., Kaysen, D., Hamburger, S. D., & Rapoport, J. L. (1994). Quantitative morphology of the caudate nucleus in Attention-Deficit/Hyperactivity Disorder. *American Journal of Psychiatry, 151,* 1791–1796.

Castellanos, X. F., Giedd, J. N., Marsh, W. L., Hamburger, S. D., Vaituzis, A. C., Dickstein, D. P., Sarfatti, S. E., Vauss, Y. C., Snell, J. W., Pajapakse, J. C., & Rapoport, J. L. (1996). Quantitative magnetic brain imaging in Attention-Deficit/Hyperactivity Disorder. *Archives of General Psychiatry, 53,* 607–616.

Caton, C. L., Gralnick, A., Bender, S., & Simon, R. (1980). Young chronic patients and substance abuse. *Hospital & Community Psychiatry, 40,* 1037–1040.

Cauce, A. M., Dommenech-Rodriguez, M., Paradise, M., Cochran, B. N., Shea, J. M., Srebnik, D., & Baydar, N. (2002). Cultural and contextual influences in mental health help seeking: A focus on ethnic minority youth. *Journal of Consulting and Clinical Psychology, 70,* 44–55.

Chabane, N., Delorme, R., Millet, B., Mouren, M., Leboyer, M., & Pauls, D. (2005). Early-onset obsessive-compulsive disorder: A subgroup with a specific clinical and familial pattern? *Journal of Child Psychology and Psychiatry, 46,* 881–887.

Chamberlain, P., & Reid, J. B. (1987). Parent observation and report of child symptoms. *Behavioral Assessment, 9,* 97–109.

Chambliss, D. L., Bryan, A. D., Aiken, L. S., Steketee, G., & Hooley, J. M. (2001). Predicting expressed emotion: A study with families of obsessive-compulsive and agoraphobic outpatients. *Journal of Family Psychology, 15,* 225–240.

Chassin, L., & DeLucia, C. (1996). Drinking during adolescence. *Alcohol Health & Research World, 20*(3), 175–180.

Chen, I. G., Roberts, R. E., & Aday, L. (1998). Ethnicity and adolescent depression: The case of Chinese Americans. *The Journal of Nervous and Mental Diseases, 186,* 623–630.

Chess, S., & Thomas, A. (1977). Temperament individuality from childhood to adolescence. *Journal of the American Academy of Child and Adolescent Psychiatry, 16,* 218–226.

Cheung, A. H., Emslie, G. J., & Mayes, T. L. (2005). Review of the efficacy and safety of antidepressants in youth depression. *Child Psychology and Psychiatry, 46,* 735–754.

Cheung, F. M., Lau, B. W. K., & Waldmann, E. (1981). Somatization among Chinese depressives in general practice. *International Journal of Psychiatry and Medicine, 10,* 361–374.

Chilcoat, H. D., & Breslau, N. (1999). Pathways from AD/HD to early drug use. *Journal of the American Academy of Child and Adolescent Psychiatry, 38,* 1347–1354.

Childress, A. C., Jarrell, M. P., & Brewerton, T. D. (1993). The Kids' Eating Disorders Survey (KEDS): Internal consistency, component analysis, and reliability. *Eating Disorders: The Journal of Treatment and Prevention, 1,* 123–133.

Choi, H. (2002). Understanding adolescent depression in ethnocultural context. *Advances in Nursing Science, 25,* 71–85.

Chorpita, B. F., & Lilienfeld, S. O. (1999). Clinical assessment of anxiety sensitivity in children and adolescents: Where do we go from here? *Psychological Assessment, 11,* 212–224.

Chung, T., Martin, C. S., Armstrong, T. D., & Labouvie, E. (2002). Prevalence of *DSM-IV* alcohol diagnoses and symptoms in adolescent community and clinical samples. *Journal of the American Academy of Child and Adolescent Psychiatry, 41,* 546–554.

Cicchetti, D., Ackerman, B. P., & Izard, C. E. (1995). Emotions and emotional regulation in developmental psychopathology. *Development and Psychopathology, 7,* 1–10.

Cicchetti, D., & Cannon, T. D. (1999). Neurodevelopmental processes in ontogenesis and epigenesis of psychopathology. *Development and Psychopathology, 11,* 375–393.

Cicchetti, D,, & Cohen, D. J. (1995). *Developmental psychopathology* (Vols. 1 and 2). New York: John Wiley & Sons.

Cicchetti, D., & Sroufe, L. A. (2000). Editorial: The past as prologue to the future: The times, they've been a-changin'. *Development and Psychopathology, 12,* 255–264.

Cicchetti, D., & Toth, S. L. (1998). The development of depression in children and adolescents. *American Psychologist, 53,* 221–241.

Cicchetti, D., & Tucker, D. (1994). Development and self-regulatory structures of the mind. *Development and Psychopathology, 6,* 533–549.

Clarizio, H. F. (1991). Obsessive-Compulsive Disorder: The secretive syndrome. *Psychology in the Schools, 28,* 106–115.

Clarizio, H. F. (1994). Assessment of depression in children and adolescents by parents, teachers, and peers. In W. M. Reynolds & H. E. Johnston (Eds.), *Handbook of depression in children and adolescents* (pp. 235–248). New York: Plenum Press.

Clark, A. J. (1991). The identification and modification of defense mechanisms in counseling. *Journal of Counseling & Development, 69,* 231–236.

Clark, A. J. (2002). *Early recollections: Theory and practice in counseling and psychotherapy.* New York: Brunner-Routledge.

Clark, D. B., & Bukstein, O. G. (1998). Psychopathology in adolescent alcohol abuse and dependence. *Alcohol Health & Research World, 22*(2), 117–121, 126.

Clark, D. M. (1988). A cognitive model of panic. In S. Rachman & J. Maser (Eds.), *Panic: Psychological perspectives.* Hillsdale, NJ: Earlbaum.

Clark, D. M., & Ehlers, A. (1993). An overview of the cognitive theory and treatment of Panic Disorder. *Applied and Preventive Psychology, 2,* 131–139.

Clarke, G. N., L. L. Debar, & Lewinsohn, P. M. (2003). Cognitive-behavioral group treatment for adolescent depression. In A. E. Kazdin & John R. Weisz. (Eds.), *Evidence-based psychotherapies for children and adolescents* (pp. 120–134). New York: Guilford Press.

Clay, D. L., Mordhorst, H. J., & Lehn, L. (2002). Empirically supported treatments in pediatric psychology: Where is the diversity? *Journal of Pediatric Psychology, 27,* 325–337.

Cloninger, C. R., Sigvardsson, S., & Bhoman, M. (1988). Childhood personality predicts alcohol abuse in young adults. *Alcoholism: Clinical and Experimental Research, 12,* 494–505.

Cobham, V. E., Dadds, M. R., & Spence, S. H. (1999). Anxious children and their parents: What do they expect? *Journal of Clinical Child Psychiatry, 28,* 220–231.

Coddington, R. D. (1981a). *Life Event Scale—Adolescents.* St. Clairsville, OH: Stress Research Company.

Coddington, R. D. (1981b). *Life Event Scale—Children.* St. Clairsville, OH: Stress Research Company.

Cohen, J. (1988). *Statistical power analyses for the behavioral sciences* (2nd ed.). Hillsdale, NJ: Erlbaum.

Cohen, J. A., Deblinger, E., Mannarino, A. P., & Steer, R. A. (2004). A multisite randomized controlled trial for children with sexual abuse-related PTSD symptoms. *Journal of the American Academy of Child & Adolescent Psychiatry, 43,* 393–402.

Cohen, J. A., Mannarino, A. P., & Berliner, L. (2000). Trauma-focused cognitive behavioral therapy for children & adolescents: An empirical update. *Journal of Interpersonal Violence, 15,* 1202–1223.

Cole, P. M., Zahrn-Waxler, C., & Smith, D. (1994). Expressive control during disappointment: Variations related to preschoolers' behavior problems. *Developmental Psychology, 30,* 835–846.

Coleman, P. K., & Karraker, K. H. (1998). Self-efficacy and parenting quality: Findings and future applications. *Developmental Review, 18,* 47–85.

Collins, F. S., & Fink, L. (1995). The human genome project. *Alcohol, Health, & Research World, 19,* 190–195.

Colvin, G., Greenberg. S., & Sherman, R. (1993). The forgotten variable: Improving academic skills for students with serious emotional disturbance. *Effective School Practices, 12,* 20–25.

Compas, B. E., & Bond, L. A. (Eds.). (1989). *Primary prevention and promotion in the schools.* Newbury Park, CA: Sage Publications.

Conduct Problems Prevention Research Group. (1992). A developmental and clinical model for the prevention of Conduct Disorder. The FAST Track program. *Development and Psychopathology, 4,* 509–527.

Conners, C. K. (1969). A teacher rating scale for use in drug studies with children. *American Journal of Psychiatry, 126,* 884–888.

Conners, C. K. (1990). *Conners rating scales manual.* North Tonawanda, NY: Multi-Health Systems.

Connors, G. J., Donovan, D. M., & DiClemente, C. C. (2001). *Substance abuse treatment and the stages of change.* New York: Guilford Press.

Connors, M. E., & Morse, W. (1993). Sexual abuse and Eating Disorders: A review. *International Journal of Eating Disorders, 13*(1), 1–11.

Constantine, M. G. (2001). Theoretical orientation, empathy, and multicultural counseling competence in school counselor trainees. *Professional School Counseling, 4,* 342–348.

Constantine, M. G., Kindaichi, M., Arorash, T. J., Donnelly, P. C., & Jung, K. K. (2002). Clients' perceptions of multicultural counseling competence: Current status and future directions. *The Counseling Psychologist, 30,* 407–416.

Cook, E. H. (2000). Genetics of Psychiatric Disorders: Where have we been and where are we going? *American Journal of Psychiatry, 157,* 1039–1040.

Cook-Cottone, C. (2004). Childhood post-traumatic stress disorder: Diagnosis, treatment, and school reintegration. *School Psychology Review, 33,* 127–139.

Cooper, P. J., & Goodyer, I. (1997). Prevalence and significance of weight and shape concerns in girls aged 11–16. *British Journal of Psychiatry, 171,* 542–544.

Cooper, P. J., Taylor, M., Cooper, Z., & Fairburn, C. G. (1987). The development and validation of the Body Shape Questionnaire. *International Journal of Eating Disorders, 6,* 485–494.

Cooper, Z., & Fairburn, C. G. (1987). The Eating Disorder examination: A semi-structured interview for the assessment of the specific psychopathology of Eating Disorders. *International Journal of Eating Disorders, 6,* 1–8.

Cooper, Z., & Fairburn, C. G. (1993). Demographic and clinical correlates of selective information processing in patients with Bulimia Nervosa. *International Journal of Eating Disorders, 13,* 109–116.

Copeland, A. D. (1974). *Textbook of adolescent psychopathology and treatment.* Springfield, IL: Thomas.

Copeland, A. P. (1979). Types of private speech produced by hyperactive and nonhyperactive boys. *Journal of Abnormal Child Psychology, 7,* 169–177.

Copeland, E. D., & Love, V. L. (1991). *Attention please! A comprehensive guide for successfully parenting children with Attention-Deficit Disorders and Hyperactivity.* Atlanta, GA: Southeastern Psychological Institute Press.

Corey, G. (2001). *Theory and practice of counseling and psychotherapy.* Pacific Grove, CA: Brooks/Cole.

Corey, G. (2005). *Theory and practice of counseling and psychotherapy* (7th ed.). Pacific Grove, CA: Brooks/Cole.

Cormier, S., & Cormier, B. (1998). *Interviewing strategies for helpers.* Pacific Grove, CA: Brooks/Cole.

Corsini, R. J. (Ed.). (2002). *The dictionary of psychology.* New York: Brunner-Routledge.

Costello, A. J., Edelbrock, C. S., Dulcan, M. S., Kales, R., & Klavic, R. S. (1984). *Report on the NIMH diagnostic interview schedule for children (DISC).* Bethesda, MD: National Institute of Mental Health.

Costello, E. J., Foley, D. L., & Angold, A. (2006). 10-year research update review: The epidemiology of child and adolescent psychiatric disorders: II. Developmental epidemiology. *Journal of the American Academy of Child & Adolescent Psychiatry, 45,* 8–25.

Cottone, R. R. (1992). *Theories and paradigms of counseling and psychotherapy.* Boston: Allyn & Bacon.

Cotugno, A. L. (1995). Personality attributes of Attention-Deficit Hyperactivity Disorder (AD/HD) using the Rorschach inkblot test. *Journal of Clinical Psychology, 51,* 554–561.

Cowan, G., & Warren, L. W. (1994). Codependency and gender-stereotyped traits. *Sex Roles, 30,* 631–645.

Cowan, G., Bommersbach, M., & Curtis, S. R. (1995). Codependency, loss of self, and power. *Psychology of Women Quarterly, 19,* 221–236.

Cox, B. J., Norton, G. R., Swinson, R. P., & Endler, N. S. (1990). Substance abuse and panic-related anxiety: A critical review. *Behaviour Research and Therapy, 28,* 385–393.

Craske, M. G., & Barlow, D. H. (1993). Panic Disorder and Agoraphobia. In D. H. Barlow (Ed.), *Clinical handbook of Psychological Disorders: A step-by-step treatment manual* (2nd. ed., pp. 1–47). New York: Guilford.

Crawford, C., & Krebs, D. L. (Eds.). (1998). *Handbook of evolutionary psychology: Ideas, issues, and applications.* Mahwah, NJ: Lawrence Erlbaum.

Creasey, G. L. (2006). *Research methods in lifespan development.* Boston: Pearson.

Crethar, H. C., Snow, K., & Carlson, J. (2004). It's all in the family: Family counseling for depressed children. *The Family Journal: Counseling and Therapy for Couples and Families, 12,* 222–229.

Crick, N. R., & Dodge, K. A. (1994). A review and reformulation of social information-processing mechanisms in children's social adjustment. *Psychological Bulletin, 115,* 73–101.

Crisp, A. (1980). *Anorexia Nervosa: Let me be.* London: Academic Press.

Crocker, A. D., & Hakim-Larson, J. (1997). Predictors of pre-adolescent depression and suicidal ideation. *Canadian Journal of Behavioural Science, 29,* 76–82.

Cuffe, S. P., McKeown, R. E., Addy, C. L., & Garrison, C. Z. (2005). Family and psychosocial risk factors in a longitudinal epidemiological study of adolescents. *Journal of the American Academy of Child & Adolescent Psychiatry, 44,* 121–129.

Dadds, M. R., Holland, D. E., Laurens, K. R., Mullins, M., Barrett, P. M., & Spence, S. H. (1999). Early intervention and prevention of Anxiety Disorders in children: Results at 2-year follow-up. *Journal of Clinical and Consulting Psychology, 67,* 145–150.

Dalgleish, T., Meiser-Stedman, R., & Smith, P. (2005). Cognitive aspects of post-traumatic stress reactions and their treatment in children and adolescents: An empirical review and some recommendations. *Behavioural and Cognitive Psychotherapy, 33,* 459–486.

Dally, P. (1969). *Anorexia Nervosa.* London: Heinemann Medical Books.

D'Andrea, M., & Daniels, J. (1995). Promoting multiculturalism and organizational change in the counseling profession: A case study. In J. G. Ponterotto, J. M. Casas, L. A. Suzuki, & C. M. Alexander (Eds.), *Handbook of Multicultural Counseling* (pp. 17–33). Thousand Oaks, CA: Sage.

Danforth, J. S., Barkley, R. A., & Stokes, T. F. (1991). Observations of parent-child interactions with hyperactive children: Research and clinical implications. *Clinical Psychology Review, 11,* 703–727.

Danielyan, A., & Kowatch, R. A. (2005). Management options for bipolar disorder in children and adolescents. *Pediatric Drugs, 7,* 277–294.

Darden, C. A., Gazda, G. M., & Ginter, E. J. (1996). Life-skills and mental health counseling. *Journal of Mental Health Counseling, 18,* 134–141.

Das, A. K. (1995). Rethinking multicultural counseling: Implications for counselor education. *Journal of Counseling & Development, 74,* 45–52.

DeBellis, M., Burke, L., Trickett, P., & Putnam, F. (1996). Antinuclear antibodies and thyroid function in sexually abused girls. *Journal of Traumatic Stress, 9,* 369–378.

Delbello, M. P., Kowatch, R. A., Adler, C. M., Stanford, K. E., Welge, J. A., Barzman, D. H., et al. (2006). A double-blind randomized pilot study comparing quetiapine and divalproex for adolescent mania. *Journal of the American Academy of Child & Adolescent Psychiatry, 45,* 305–313.

Delbello, M. P., Schwiers, M. L., Rosenberg, H. L., & Strakowski, S. M. (2002). A double-blind, randomized, placebo-controlled study of quetiapine as adjunctive treatment for adolescent mania. *Journal of the American Academy of Child & Adolescent Psychiatry, 41,* 1216–1223.

Demaso, D. R., Marcus, N. E., Kinnamon, C., & Gonzalez-Heydrich, J. (2006). Depression experience journal: A computer-based intervention for facilities facing childhood depression. *Journal of the American Academy of Child & Adolescent Psychiatry, 45,* 158–165.

Demetriou, A., Doise, W., & van Lieshout, C. F. M. (1998). *Life-span developmental psychology.* New York: John Wiley & Sons.

Denckla, M. (1991, February). *Brain behavior insights through imaging.* Paper presented at the Learning Disabilities Association National Conference, Chicago, IL.

Denckla, M. B., & Rudel, R. G. (1978). Anomalies of motor development in hyperactive boys. *Annals of Neurology, 3,* 231–233.

Dennis, M. L., Dawud-Noursi, S., Muck, R. D., & McDermeit, M. (2003). The need for developing and evaluating adolescent treatment models. In S. J. Stevens & A. R. Morral (Eds.), *Adolescent substance abuse treatment in the United States: Exemplary models from a national evaluation study* (pp. 3–34). New York: The Haworth Press.

Department of Health and Human Services. (1993). *Eighth special report to the U.S. Congress on alcohol and health.* Washington, DC: Author.

Department of Health and Human Services. (1997). *Ninth special report to the U.S. Congress on alcohol and health.* Washington, DC: Author.

Department of Health and Human Services. (2000). *Tenth special report to the U.S. Congress on alcohol and health.* Washington, DC: Author.

Department of Health and Human Services. (2005). Antidepressant use in children, adolescents, and adults. Retrieved March 27, 2006, from http://www.fda.gov/cder/drug/antidepressants.

Desland, M. (1995). Hypnosis in the treatment of Adjustment Disorder. *Australian Journal of Clinical and Experimental Hypnosis, 23,* 58–69.

Despland, J. N., Monod, L., & Ferrero, F. (1995). Clinical relevance of Adjustment Disorder in *DSM-III-R* and *DSM-IV. Comprehensive Psychiatry, 36,* 454–460.

Deykin, E. Y., Buka, S. L., & Zeena, T. H. (1992). Depressive illness among chemically dependent adolescents. *American Journal of Psychiatry, 149,* 1341–1347.

Diamond, G. S., Reis, B. F., Diamond, G. M., Siqueland, L., & Issacs, L. (2002). Attachment-based family therapy for depressed adolescents: A treatment development study. *Journal of the American Academy of Child & Adolescent Psychiatry, 41,* 1190–1196.

DiClemente, C. C. (1991). Motivational interviewing and the stages of change. In W. R. Miller & S. Rollnick (Eds.), *Motivational interviewing: Preparing people to change addictive behavior* (pp. 191–202). New York: Guilford Press.

Diler, R. S., Birmaher, B., & Brent, D. A. (2004). Phenomenology of panic disorder in youth. *Depression and Anxiety, 20,* 39–43.

Dishion, T. J., Andrews, D. W., & Crosby, L. (1995). Antisocial boys and their friends in early adolescence: Relationship characteristics, quality, and interactional process. *Child Development, 66,* 139–151.

Dishion, T. J., French, D. C., & Patterson, G. R. (1995). The development and ecology of antisocial behavior. In D. Cicchetti & D. J. Cohen (Eds.), *Developmental Psychopathology: Risk, disorder, and adaptation* (pp. 421–471). New York: John Wiley & Sons.

Dishion, T. J., McCord, J., & Poulin, F. (1999). When interventions harm. *American Psychologist, 54,* 755–764.

Dishion, T. J., & Patterson, G. R. (1992). Age effects in parent training outcome. *Behavior Therapy, 23,* 719–729.

Dixey, R. (1998). Healthy eating in schools, overweight "Eating Disorders": Are they connected? *Educational Review, 50*(1), 29–34.

Dodge, K. A., & Crick, N. R. (1990). Social information-processing bases of aggressive behavior in children. *Personality and Social Psychology Bulletin, 16,* 8–22.

Dodge, K. A., Lochman, J. E., Harnish, J. D., Bates, J. E., Pettit, G. S. (1997). Reactive and proactive aggression in school children and psychiatrically impaired chronically assultive youth. *Journal of Abnormal Child Psychology, 106,* 37–51.

Domino, M. E., Salkever, D. S., Zarin, D. A., & Pincus, H. A. (1998). The impact of managed care on psychiatry. *Administration and Policy in Mental Health, 26,* 149–157.

Donaldson, D., Spirito, A., & Esposito-Smythers, C. (2005). Treatment of adolescents following a suicide attempt: Results of a pilot trial. *Journal of the American Academy of Child and Adolescent Psychiatry, 44*, 113–120.

Dopheide, J. A. (2006). Recognizing and treating depression in children and adolescents. *American Journal of Health-System Pharmacy, 63*, 233–243.

Douglas, V. I. (1983). Attention and cognitive problems. In M. Rutter (Ed.), *Developmental neuropsychiatry* (pp. 280–329). New York: Guilford Press.

Dowdy, C. A., Patton, J. R., Smith, T. E. C., & Polloway, E. A. (1998). *Attention-Deficit/Hyperactivity Disorder in the classroom: A practical guide for teachers.* Austin, TX: Pro-Ed.

Drake, R. E., & Wallach, M. A. (1989). Substance abuse among the chronically mentally ill. *Hospital & Community Psychiatry, 40*, 1041–1046.

Dubovsky, S. L. (1990). Generalized Anxiety Disorder: New concepts and psychopharmacologic therapies. *Journal of Clinical Psychiatry, 51*, 3–10.

Ducharme, J. M., Atkinson, L., & Poulton, L. (2000). Success-based, noncoercive treatment of oppositional behavior in children from violent homes. *Journal of the American Academy of Child and Adolescent Psychiatry, 39*, 995–1004.

Dulmus, C. N., & Wodarski, J. S. (1996). Assessment and effective treatments of childhood psychopathology: Responsibilities and implications for practice. *Journal of Child and Adolescent Group Therapy, 6*, 75–99.

Duncan, B. L., & Miller, S. D. (2000). *The heroic client: Doing client-directed, outcome-informed therapy.* San Francisco: Jossey-Bass.

Dunn, J., & McGuire, S. (1992). Sibling and peer relationships in childhood. *Journal of Child Psychology and Psychiatry, 33*, 67–105.

Dunner, D. L. (2005). Dysthymia and double depression. *International Review of Psychiatry, 17*, 3–8.

DuPaul, G. J., & Stoner, G. (1994). *AD/HD in the schools: Assessment and intervention strategies.* New York: Guilford Press.

Durlak, J. A. (1997). Primary prevention programs in schools. In T. H. Ollendick & R. J. Prinz (Eds.), *Advances in clinical child psychology* (Vol. 19). New York: Plenum.

Durlak, J. A., Fuhrman, T., & Lampman, C. (1991). Effectiveness of cognitive-behavior therapy for maladapting children: A meta-analysis. *Psychological Bulletin, 110*, 204–214.

Durlak, J. A., & Wells, A. M. (1997). Primary prevention mental health programs for children and adolescents: A meta-analytic review. *American Journal of Community Psychology, 25*, 115–152.

Dykeman, C., & Appleton, V. E. (1999). Family therapy. In D. Capuzzi & D. R. Gross (Eds.), *Counseling and Psychotherapy* (2nd ed., pp. 319–343). Upper Saddle River, NJ: Merrill Prentice Hall.

Dykman, R. A., & Ackerman, P. T. (1991). Attention-Deficit Disorder and specific reading disability: Separate but often overlapping disorders. *Journal of Learning Disabilities, 24*, 96–103.

Edwards, D. J. A., Dattilio, F. M., & Bromley, D. B. (2004). Developing evidence-based practice: The role of case-based research. *Professional Psychology: Research and Practice, 35*, 589–597.

Ehlers, A., Margraf, J., Roth, W. Y., Taylor, C. B., & Birbaumer, N. (1988). Anxiety produced by false heart rate feedback in patients with Panic Disorder. *Behaviour Research and Therapy, 26*, 1–11.

Eisele, J., Hertsgaard, D., & Light, H. K. (1986). Factors related to Eating Disorders in young girls. *Adolescence, 21*, 283–290.

Eisner, A., & McClellan, J. (1999). Drugs of abuse. In J. S. Werry & M. G. Aman (Eds.), *Practitioner's guide to psychoactive drugs for children and adolescents* (2nd ed.). New York: Plenum Medical Book Company.

Ellickson, P. L., & Hays, R. D. (1992). On becoming involved with drugs: Modeling adolescent drug use over time. *Health Psychology, 11*, 377–385.

Elliott, D. S., Huizinga, D., & Ageton, S. S. (1985). *Explaining delinquency and drug use.* Beverly Hills, CA: Sage.

El-Mallakh, R. S. (1997). New insights into the course and prognosis of bipolar illness. *Psychiatric Annals, 27*, 478–481.

Emde, R. N., & Spicer, P. (2000). Experience in the midst of variation: New horizons for development and psychopathology. *Development and Psychopathology, 12*, 313–331.

Eme, R. F., & Kavanaugh, L. (1995). Sex differences in Conduct Disorder. *Journal of Clinical Child Psychology, 24*, 406–426.

Emery, R. E., Fincham, R. D., & Cummings, E. M. (1992). Parenting in context: Systemic thinking about parental conflict and its influence on children. *Journal of Consulting and Clinical Psychology, 60*, 909–912.

Emmelkamp, P. M. G. (1982). *Phobic and ObsessiveCompulsive Disorders: Theory, research, and practice.* New York: Plenum.

Emslie, G. J., Kennard, B. D., & Kowatch, R. A. (1994). Affective Disorders in children: Diagnosis and management. *Journal of Child Neurology, 10*, S42–S49.

Emslie, G. J., & Mayes, T. L. (1999). Depression in children and adolescents: A guide to diagnosis and treatment. *CNS Drugs, 11*, 181–189.

Emslie, G. J., Rush, A. J., Weinberg, W. A., Kowatch, R. A., Hughes, C. W., Carmody, T., & Rintelmann, J. (1997). A double-blind, randomized, placebo-controlled trial of fluoxetine in children and adolescents with depression. *Archives of General Psychiatry, 54*, 1031–1037.

Emslie, G. J., Walkup, J. T., Pliszka, S. R., & Ernst, M. (1999). Nortricyclic antidepressants: Current trends in children and adolescents. *Journal of the American Academy of Child & Adolescent Psychiatry, 38*, 517–528.

Enzer, N. B., & Cunningham, S. D. (1991). Adjustment and Reactive Disorders. In J. M. Wiener (Ed.), *Textbook of child and adolescent psychiatry* (pp. 468–476). Washington, DC: American Psychiatric Press.

Epstein, J. N., Conners, C. K., Erhardt, D., March, J. S., & Swanson, J. M. (1997). Asymmetrical hemispheric control of visual-spatial attention in adults with Attention-Deficit/Hyperactivity Disorder. *Neuropsychology, 11*, 467–473.

Epstein, M. A., Shaywitz, S. E., Shaywitz, B. A., & Woolston, J. L. (1991). The boundaries of Attention-Deficit Disorder. *Journal of Learning Disabilities, 24*, 78–86.

Erikson, E. H. (1963). *Childhood and society* (2nd ed., Revised). New York: W. W. Norton.

Erikson, E. H. (1968). *Identity: Youth and crisis.* New York: W. W. Norton.

Erk, R. R. (1995a). A diagnosis of Attention-Deficit Disorder: What does it mean for the school counselor? *The School Counselor, 42*, 292–299.

Erk, R. R. (1995b). The conundrum of Attention-Deficit Disorder. *Journal of Mental Health Counseling, 17*, 131–145.

Erk, R. R. (1995c). The evolution of Attention-Deficit Disorders terminology. *Elementary School Guidance and Counseling, 29*, 243–248.

Erk, R. R. (1997). Multidimensional treatment of Attention-Deficit Disorder: A family-oriented approach. *Journal of Mental Health Counseling, 19*, 3–22.

Erk, R. R. (1999). Attention-Deficit/Hyperactivity Disorders: Counselors, laws, and implications for practice. *Professional School Counseling, 2*, 318–326.

Erk, R. R. (2000). Five frameworks for increasing understanding and effective treatment of Attention-Deficit/ Hyperactivity Disorder: Predominantly Inattentive Type. *Journal of Counseling and Development, 78*, 389–399.

Evans, J. R., Van Velsor, P., & Schumacher, J. E. (2002). Addressing adolescent depression: A role for school counselors. *Professional School Counseling, 5*, 211–219.

Evans-Whipp, T., Beyers, J. M., Lloyd, S, LaFazia, A. N., Toumbourou, J. W. Arthur, M. W., & Catalano, R. F. (2004). A review of school drug policies and their impact on youth substance use. *Health Promotion International, 19*(2), 227–234.

Everill, J. T., & Waller, G. (1995). Reported sexual abuse and eating psychopathology: A review of the evidence for a causal link. *International Journal of Eating Disorders, 18*(1), 1–11.

Eyberg, S. M. (1992). Parent and teacher behavior inventories for the assessment of conduct problem behaviors in children. In L. VanderCreek, S. Knapp, & T. L. Jackson (Eds.), *Innovations in clinical practice: A source book* (pp. 261–270). Sarasota, FL: Professional Resource Exchange.

Eyberg, S. M., Bessmer, J., Newcomb, K., Edwards, D., & Robinson, E. (1994). *Dyadic parent-child interaction coding system II: A manual.* Unpublished manuscript, University of Florida.

Eyberg, S. M., & Robinson, E. A. (1983). Dyadic parent-child interaction coding system: A manual. *Psychological Documents, 13*, 24.

Eyberg, S. M., Schuhmann, E. M., & Rey, J. (1998). Child and adolescent psychotherapy research: Developmental issues. *Journal of Abnormal Child Psychology, 26*, 71–82.

Fabian, L. J., & Thompson, J. K. (1989). Body image disturbance in young females. *International Journal of Eating Disorders, 8*(1), 63–74.

Faedda, G. L., Baldessarini, R. J., Glovinsky, I. P., & Austin, N. P. (2004). Pediatric bipolar disorder: Phenomenology and course of illness. *Bipolar Disorders, 6*, 305–313.

Fahy, T. A. (1991). Obsessive-compulsive symptoms in Eating Disorders. *Behaviour Research and Therapy, 29*, 113–116.

Fairburn, C. G. (1995). *Overcoming binge eating.* New York: Guilford Press.

Fairburn, C. G., & Beglin, S. J. (1990). Studies of the epidemiology of Bulimia Nervosa. *American Journal of Psychiatry, 147*, 401–408.

Fairburn, C. G., & Beglin, S. J. (1994). Assessment of Eating Disorders: Interview or self-report questionnaire? *International Journal of Eating Disorders, 16*(4), 363–370.

Fairburn, C. G., & Cooper, Z. (1993). The Eating Disorder examination (12th ed.). In C. G. Fairburn & G. T. Wilson (Eds.), *Binge eating: Nature, assessment and treatment.* New York: Guilford Press.

Fairburn, C. G., Jones, R., Peveler, R. C., Carr, S. J., Solomon, R. A., O'Connor, M. E., Burton, J., & Hope, R. A. (1991). Three psychological treatments for Bulimia Nervosa: A comparative trial. *Archives of General Psychiatry, 48*, 463–469.

Fairburn, C. G., Marcus, M. D., & Wilson, G. T. (1993). Cognitive-Behavioral therapy for binge eating in Bulimia Nervosa: A comprehensive treatment manual. In C. G. Fairburn & G. T. Wilson (Eds.), *Binge eating: Nature, assessment, and treatment* (pp. 361–404). New York: Guilford Press.

Fallon, A. E., & Rozin, P. (1985). Sex differences in the perception of desirable body shape. *Journal of Abnormal Psychology, 94*, 102–105.

Faraone, S. V., Biederman, L., Lehman, B., Keenan, K., Norman, D., Seidman, L. J., Kolodny, R., Kraus, I., Perrin, J., & Chen, W. (1993). Evidence for the independent familial transmission of Attention-Deficit/Hyperactivity Disorder and learning disabilities: Results from a family genetic study. *American Journal of Psychiatry, 150*, 891–895.

Faraone, S. V., Tsuang, M. T., & Tsuang, D. W. (1999). *Genetics of Mental Disorders: A guide for students, clinicians, and researchers.* New York: Guilford Press.

Farmer, T. W., Farmer, E. M. Z., & Gut, D. (1999). Implications of social development research for school-based interventions for aggressive youth with Emotional and Behavioral Disorders. *Journal of Emotional and Behavioral Disorders, 7*, 130–136.

Farrell, L., Barrett, P., & Piacentini, J. (2006). Obsessive-compulsive disorder across the developmental trajectory: Clinical correlates in children, adolescents and adults. *Behaviour Change, 23*, 103–120.

Fauber, R. L., & Long, N. (1991). Children in context: The role of the family in child psychotherapy. *Journal of Consulting and Clinical Psychology, 59*, 813–820.

Feeny, N. C., Foa, E. B., Treadwell, K. R. H., & March, J. (2004). Post-traumatic stress disorder in youth: A critical review of the cognitive and behavioral treatment outcome literature. *Professional Psychology: Research and Practice, 35*, 466–476.

Feindler, D. L., Marriott, S. A., & Iwata, M. (1984). Group anger control training for junior high school delinquents. *Cognitive Therapy and Research, 8*, 299–311.

Ferren, P. M. (2006). Demystifying the black box warning on antidepressants: A protocol for safe prescribing in your practice. *Contemporary Pediatrics, 23*, 28–36.

Ferro, T., Carlson, G. A., Grayson, P., & Klein, D. N. (1994). Depressive Disorders: Distinctions in children. *Journal of the American Academy of Child and Adolescent Psychiatry, 33*, 664–670.

Fichter, M. M., & Daser, C. (1987). Symptomatology, psychosexual development and gender identity in 42 Anorexic males. *Psychological Medicine, 17*, 409–418.

Finzi, R., Ram, A., Dov, H. E., Shnit, D., & Weizman, A. (2001). Attachment styles and aggression in physically abused and neglected children. *Journal of Youth and Adolescence, 30*, 769–787.

Fiore, T. A., Becker, E. A., & Nero, R. C. (1993). Educational interventions for students with Attention-Deficit Disorder. *Exceptional Children, 60*, 163–173.

Fischer, J. L., & Crawford, D. W. (1992). Codependency and parenting styles. *Journal of Adolescent Research, 7*, 352–363.

Fisher, P., Wicks, J., Shaffer, D., Piacentini, J., & Lapkin, J. (1992). *National institute of mental health diagnostic interview schedule for children user's manual.* New York: New York State Psychiatric Institute, Division of Child and Adolescent Psychiatry.

Flament, M. F., Rapoport, J. L., Berg, C. J., Sceery, W., Kilts, C., Mellstrom, B., & Linnoila, M. (1985). Clomipramine treatment of childhood OCD. *Archives of General Psychiatry, 42*, 977–983.

Flament, M. F., Whitaker, A., Rapoport, J. L., Davies, M., Berg, C. Z., Kalikow, K., Sceery, W., & Shaffer, D. (1988). Obsessive-Compulsive Disorder in adolescence: An epidemiological study. *Journal of the American Academy of Child and Adolescent Psychiatry, 27*, 764–771.

Fleischmann, A., Berolote, J. M., Belfar, M., & Beautrais, A. (2005). Completed suicide and psychiatric diagnoses in young people: A critical examination of evidence. *American Journal of Orthopsychiatry, 75*, 676–683.

Foa, E. B., Grayson, J. B., Steketee, S., & Doppelt, H. (1983). Treatment of obsessive-compulsives: When do we fail? In E. B. Foa

& P. M. G. Emmelkamp (Eds.), *Failures in behavior therapy*. New York: John Wiley & Sons.

Follette, W. C., & Beitz, K. (2003). Adding a more rigorous scientific agenda to the empirically supported treatment movement. *Behavior Modification, 27*, 369–386.

Fonagy, P., Target, M., Cottrell, D., Phillips, J., & Kurtz, Z. (2002). *What works for whom: A critical review of treatments for children and adolescents*. New York: Guilford Press.

Fontes, L. A. (2002). Child discipline and physical abuse in immigrant Latino families: Reducing violence and misunderstandings. *Journal of Counseling & Development, 80*, 31–40.

Food and Drug Administration. (n.d.). Medication guide: About using antidepressants in children and teenagers. Retrieved April 1, 2006, from http://www.fda.gov/medwatch/SAFETY/2005/Feb_PI/AntidepressantMedGuide.pdf.

Forehand, R., & McMahon, R. J. (1981). *Helping the noncompliant child: A clinician's guide to parent training*. New York: Guilford Press.

Forehand, R., Armistead, L., & David, C. (1997). Is adolescent adjustment following parental divorce a function of predivorce adjustment? *Journal of Abnormal Child Psychology, 25*, 157–164.

Forness, S. R. (2005). The pursuit of evidence-based practice in special education for children with emotional and behavioral disorders. *Behavioral Disorders, 30*, 311–331.

Fornos, L. B., Mika, V. S., Bayles, B., Serrano, A. C., Jimenez, R. L., & Villarreal, R. (2005). A qualitative study of Mexican American adolescents and depression. *Journal of School Health, 75*, 162–170.

Fowler, M. (1992). *CH.A.D.D. educators manual: An in-depth look at Attention-Deficit Disorder from an educational perspective*. Plantation, FL: CH.A.D.D.

Francis, G., & Borden, J. (1993). Expression and treatment of Obsessive-Compulsive Disorder in childhood, adolescence, and adulthood. In C. G. Last (Ed.), *Anxiety across the lifespan: A developmental perspective* (pp. 148–166). New York: Springer.

Francis, G., Last, C. G., & Strauss, C. C. (1987). Expression of Separation Anxiety Disorder: The roles of age and gender. *Child Psychiatry and Human Development, 87*, 82–89.

Freemont, W. P. (2004). Childhood reactions to terrorism-induced trauma: A review of the past 10 years. *Journal of the American Academy of Child and Adolescent Psychiatry, 43*, 381.

Freud, A. (1966). *The writings of Anna Freud: Vol. II. The ego and the mechanisms of defense*. (Rev. ed., C. Baines, Trans.) New York: International Universities Press. (Original work published 1937)

Frick, P. J. (1998). *Conduct Disorders and severe antisocial behavior*. New York: Plenum.

Frick, P. J., & Jackson, Y. K. (1993). Family functioning and childhood antisocial behavior: Yet another reinterpretation. *Journal of Clinical Child Psychology, 22*, 410–419.

Frick, P. J., Lahey, B. B., Applegate, B., Kerdyck, L., Ollendick, T., Hynd, G. W., Garfinkel, B., Greenhill, L., Biederman, J., Barkley, R. A., McBurnett, K., Newcorn, J., & Waldman, I. (1994). *DSM-IV* field trials for the Disruptive Behavior Disorders: Symptom utility estimates. *Journal of the American Academy of Child and Adolescent Psychiatry, 33*, 529–539.

Friedlander, L., & Desrocher, M. (2006). Neuroimaging studies of obsessive-compulsive disorder in adults and children. *Clinical Psychology Review, 26*, 32–49.

Friedlander, M. L., & Siegel, S. M. (1990). Separation-individuation difficulties and Cognitive-Behavioral indicators of Eating Disorders among college women. *Journal of Counseling Psychology, 37*, 74–78.

Friedman, R. J., & Doyal, G. T. (1992). *Management of children and adolescents with Attention-Deficit/Hyperactivity Disorder*. Austin, TX: Pro-Ed.

Fristad, M. A., Goldberg-Arnold, J. S., & Gavazzi, S. M. (2003). Multi-family psychoeducation groups in the treatment of children with mood disorders. *Journal of Marital and Family Therapy, 29*, 491–504.

Frone, M. R., Cooper, M. L., & Russell, M. (1994). Stressful life events, gender, and substance use: An application of tobit regression. *Psychology of Addictive Behavior, 8*(2), 59–69.

Fryer, S., Waller, G., & Stenfert-Kroese, B. (1997). Stress, coping, and disturbed eating attitudes in teenage girls. *International Journal of Eating Disorders, 22*, 427–436.

Furnham, A., & Manning, R. (1997). Young people's theories of Anorexia Nervosa and obesity. *Counseling Psychology Quarterly, 10*(4), 389–414.

Furth, H. G., & Wachs, H. (1975). *Thinking goes to school: Piaget's theory in practice*. New York: Oxford University Press.

Gallagher, R. (2005). Evidence-based psychotherapies for depressed adolescents: A review and clinical guidelines. *Primary Psychiatry, 12*, 33–39

Galliher, R. V., Rostosky, S. S., & Hughes, H. K. (2004), School belonging, self-esteem, and depressive symptoms in adolescents: An examination of sex, sexual attraction status, and urbanicity. *Journal of Youth and Adolescence, 33*, 235–245.

Gallucci, F., Bird, H. R., Berardi, C., Gallai, V., Pfanner, P., & Weinberg, A. (1993). Symptoms of Attention-Deficit/Hyperactivity Disorder in an Italian school sample: Findings of a pilot study. *Journal of The American Academy of Child and Adolescent Psychiatry, 32*, 1051–1058.

Garber, J. (1984). Classification of childhood psychopathology: A developmental perspective. *Child Development, 55*, 30–48.

Garber, J., Robinson, N. S., & Valentiner, D. (1997). The relation between parenting and adolescent depression: Self-worth as a mediator. *Journal of Adolescent Research, 12*, 12–33.

Garfinkel, I., & McLanahan, S. (1986). *Single mothers and their children: A new American dilemma*. Washington, D.C.: Urban Institute Press.

Garfinkel, P. E., & Garner, D. M. (1982). *Anorexia Nervosa: A multidimensional perspective*. New York: Brunner/ Mazel.

Garfinkel, P. E., Lin, E., Goering, P., & Spegg, C. (1995). Bulimia Nervosa in a Canadian community sample: Prevalence and comparison of subgroups. *American Journal of Psychiatry, 152*, 1052–1058.

Garner, D. M. (1991). *Eating Disorders inventory-2*. Odessa, FL: Psychological Assessment Resources.

Garner, D. M., & Garfinkel, P. E. (1979). The Eating Attitudes Test: An index of the symptoms of Anorexia Nervosa. *Psychological Medicine, 9*, 273–279.

Garner, D. M., & Garfinkel, P. E., (1980). Sociocultural factors in the development of Anorexia Nervosa. *Psychological Medicine, 10*, 647–656.

Garner, D. M., & Garfinkel, P. E. (1985). *Handbook of psychotherapy in Anorexia and Bulimia*. New York: Guilford Press.

Garrison, C. Z., Schluchter, M., Schoenback, V. J., & Kaplan, B. K. (1989). Epidemiology of depressive symptoms in young adolescents. *Journal of the American Academy of Child Psychology, 28*, 343–351.

Garvey, M. A., Giedd, J., & Swedo, S. E. (1998). PANDAS: The search for environmental triggers of Pediatric Neuropsychiatric Disorders. Lessons from rheumatic fever. *Journal of Neurology, 13*, 413–423.

Gaub, M., & Carlson, C. L. (1997). Gender differences in AD/HD: A meta-analysis and critical review. *Journal of the American Academy of Child and Adolescent Psychiatry, 36,* 1036–1045.

Gaulin, S. J. C., & McBurney, D. H. (2001). *Psychology: An evolutionary approach.* Upper Saddle River, NJ: Prentice Hall.

Gaw, K. F., & Beutler, L. E. (1995). Integrating treatment recommendations. In L. E. Beutler & M. R. Berren (Eds.), *Integrative assessment of adult personality* (pp. 280–314). New York: Guilford Press.

Gazda, G. M., Ginter, E. J., & Horne, A. M. (2001). *Group counseling and group psychotherapy: Theory and application.* Boston: Allyn & Bacon.

Geffken, G. R., Pincus, D. B., & Zelikovsky, N. (1999). Obsessive-Compulsive Disorder in children and adolescents: Review of background, assessment, and treatment. *Journal of Psychological Practice, 5,* 15–31.

Gelfand, D. M., Ficula, T., & Zarbatany, L. (1986). Prevention of Childhood Behavior Disorders. In B. A. Edelstein & L. Michelson (Eds.), *Handbook of Prevention* (pp. 133–152). New York: Plenum.

Geller, B., & Luby, J. (1997). Child and adolescent Bipolar Disorder: A review of the past 10 years. *Journal of the American Academy of Child and Adolescent Psychiatry, 36,* 1168–1176.

Geller, B., Sun, K., Zimerman, B., Luby, J., Frazier, J., & Williams, M. (1995). Complex and rapid-cycling in Bipolar children and adolescents: A preliminary study. *Journal of Affective Disorders, 34,* 259–268.

Geller, B., Todd, R., Luby, J., & Botteron, K. N. (1996). Treatment-resistant depression in children and adolescents. *The Psychiatric Clinics of North America, 19,* 253–267.

Gemelli, R. (1996). *Normal child and adolescent development.* Washington, DC: American Psychiatric Press.

Gesell, A., Halverson, H. M., Thompson, H., Ilg, F. L., Castner, B. M., Ames, L. B., & Amatruda, C. S. (1940). *The first five years of life: A guide to the study of the preschool child.* New York: Harper & Brothers.

Gettelman, T. E., & Thompson J. K. (1993). Actual differences and stereotypical perceptions in body image and eating disturbance: A comparison of male and female heterosexual and homosexual samples. *Sex Roles, 29,* 545–562.

Ghaziuddin, N, Kutcher, S. P., Knapp, P., Bernet, W., Arnold, V., Beitchman, A. V., et al. (2004). Practice parameter for use of electroconvulsive therapy with adolescents. *Journal of the American Academy of Child & Adolescent Psychiatry, 43,* 1521–1539.

Gilligan, C. (1993). *In a different voice: Psychological theory and women's development.* Cambridge, MA: Harvard University Press.

Gilligan, C., & Belenky, M. F. (1994). A naturalistic study of abortion decisions. In B. Puka (Series Ed.), *Moral development: A compendium: Vol. 6. Caring voices and women's moral frames: Gilligan's view* (pp. 39–60). New York: Garland.

Gilvarry, E. (2000). Substance abuse in young people. *Journal of Child Psychology and Psychiatry, 41,* 55–80.

Ginter, E. J. (1989). If you meet Moses/Jesus/Mohammed/Buddha (or associate editors of theory) on the road, kill them! *Journal of Mental Health Counseling, 11,* 335–344.

Ginter, E. J. (1999). David K. Brooks' contribution to the developmentally based life-skills approach. *Journal of Mental Health Counseling, 21,* 191–202.

Ginter, E. J. (2001). Private practice: The professional counselor. In D. C. Locke, J. E. Myers, & E. L. Herr (Eds.), *The handbook of counseling* (pp. 355–372). Thousand Oaks, CA: Sage.

Ginter, E. J. (2002). *Journal of Counseling & Development (JCD)* and counseling's interwoven nature: Achieving a more complete understanding of the present through "historization" (musings of an exiting editor—an editorial postscript). *Journal of Counseling & Development, 80,* 219–222.

Ginter, E. J. (2003). David Kendrick Brooks, Jr. In J. D. West, C. J. Osborn, & D. L. Bubenzer (Eds.), *Leaders and legacies: Contributions to the profession of counseling* (pp. 135–142). New York: Brunner-Routledge.

Ginter, E. J. (2005). Wellness research: An agenda for the future. In J. E. Myers & T. J. Sweeney (Eds.), *Counseling for wellness: Theory, research, and prac*tice (pp. 151–165). Alexandria, VA: American Counseling Association.

Ginter, E. J., & Bonney, W. (1993). Freud, ESP, and interpersonal relationships: Projective identification and the Mobius interaction. *Journal of Mental Health Counseling, 15,* 150–169.

Ginter, E. J., & Glauser, A. (2001). Effective use of the *DSM* from a developmental/wellness perspective. In E. R. Welfel & R. E. Ingersoll (Eds.), *The mental health desk reference* (pp. 69–77). New York: John Wiley & Sons.

Gintner, G. G. (1995). Differential diagnosis in older adults: Dementia, depression, and delirium. *Journal of Counseling and Development, 73,* 346–351.

Gintner, G. G. (2000). Conduct Disorder and chronic violent offending: Issues in diagnosis and treatment selection. In D. S. Sandhu & C. B. Aspy (Eds.), *Violence in American schools: A practical guide for counselors* (pp. 335–351). Alexandria, VA: American Counseling Association.

Gintner, G. G. (2001). Sudden violent loss: Clinical guidelines for screening and treating survivors. In D. S. Sandhu (Ed.), *Faces of violence: Psychological correlates, concepts, and intervention strategies* (pp. 355–376). Huntington, NY: Nova Science.

Gintner, G. G., & Choate, L. H. (2003). Stage-matched motivational interventions for college student binge drinkers. *Journal of College Counseling, 6,* 99–113.

Gjone, H., Stevenson, J., & Sundet, J. M. (1996). Genetic influence on parent-reported attention-related problems in a Norwegian general population twin sample. *Journal of the American Academy of Child and Adolescent Psychiatry, 35,* 588–596.

Gladding, S. T. (2007). *Family therapy: History, theory, and practice* (4th ed.). Upper Saddle River, NJ: Merrill/Prentice Hall.

Gladstone, T. R., & Kaslow, N. J. (1995). Depression and attributions in children and adolescents: A meta-analytic review. *Journal of Abnormal Child Psychology, 23,* 597–606.

Goldberg, S. (2000). *Attachment and development.* New York: Oxford University Press.

Goldenberg, H., & Goldenberg, I. (1994). *Counseling today's families* (2nd ed.). Pacific Grove, CA: Brooks/Cole.

Goldfried, M. R., & Castonguay, L. G. (1992). The future of psychotherapy integration. *Psychotherapy, 29,* 4–10.

Goldstein, D. J., Wilson, M. G., Thompson. V. L., Potvin, J. H., & Rampey, A. H., Jr. (1995). The Fluoxetine Bulimia Nervosa Collaborative Research Group: Long-term fluoxetine treatment of Bulimia Nervosa. *British Journal of Psychiatry, 166,* 660–666.

Goldstein, S. (1999). Attention-Deficit/Hyperactivity Disorder. In S. Goldstein & C. R. Reynolds (Eds.), *Handbook of Neurodevelopmental and Genetic Disorders in children.* (pp. 154–188). New York: Guilford Press.

Goldstein, S., & Goldstein, M. (1998). *Understanding and managing Attention-Deficit/Hyperactivity Disorder in children: A guide for practitioners* (2nd ed.). New York: John Wiley & Sons.

Goldstein, S., & Reynolds, C. R. (Eds.). (1999). *Handbook of Neurodevelopmental and Genetic Disorders in children.* New York: Guilford Press.

Gomez, G. (2004). Electroconvulsive therapy: Present and future. *Issues in Mental Health Nursing, 25*, 473–486.

Goodman, G., & Poillion, M. (1992). ADD: Acronym for any dysfunction or difficulty. *Journal of Special Education, 26*, 37–56.

Goodsitt, A. (1983). Self-regulatory disturbances in Eating Disorders. *International Journal of Eating Disorders, 2*, 51–60.

Goodyear, P., & Hynd, G. W. (1992). Attention-Deficit Disorder with (ADD/H) and without (ADD/WO) hyperactivity: Behavioral and neuropsychological differentiation. *Journal of Child Psychology, 21*, 273–305.

Goodyer, I. M., Wright, C., & Altham, P. M. E. (1989). Recent friendships in anxious and depressed school-age children. *Psychological Medicine, 19*, 165–174.

Goodyer, I., Herbert, J., Tamplin, A., Secher, S., & Pearson, J. (1997). Short-term outcome of major depression: II. Life events, family dysfunction, and friendship difficulties as predictors of Persistent Disorder. *Journal of the American Academy of Child & Adolescent Psychiatry, 36*, 474–480.

Gordon Systems, Inc. (1983). *Gordon diagnostic system*. DeWitt, NY: Author.

Gore, S., Aseltine, R. H., Jr., & Colton, M. E. (1992). Social structure, life stress and depressive symptoms in a high school-aged population. *Journal of Health and Social Behavior, 33*, 97–113.

Gotay, C. C. (1996). Cultural variation in family adjustment to cancer. In L. Baider, C. L. Cooper, & A. K. De-Nour (Eds.), *Cancer and the family* (pp. 31–52). Chichester, England: John Wiley & Sons.

Gottesman, I., & Goldsmith, H. (1994). Developmental psychopathology of antisocial behavior: Inserting genes into it: ontogenesis and epigenesis. In C. A. Nelson (Ed.), *Threats to optimal development: Integrating biological, psychological, and social risk factors* (pp. 69–104). Hillsdale, NJ: Erlbaum.

Gould, M. S., Marrocco, F. A., Kleinman, M., Thomas, J.G., Mostkoff, K., Cote, J., et al. (2005). Evaluating iatrogenic risk of youth suicide screening programs: A randomized controlled trial. *JAMA: Journal of the American Medical Association, 293*, 1635–1643.

Gould, S. J. (1981). *The mismeasure of man*. New York: W. W. Norton.

Grant, B. F., & Dawson, D. A. (1997). Age at onset of alcohol use and its association with *DSM-IV* alcohol abuse and dependence: Results from the National Longitudinal Alcohol Epidemiologic Survey. *Journal of Substance Abuse, 9*, 103–110.

Gray, J. A. (1987). *The psychology of fear and stress* (2nd ed.). New York: Cambridge University Press.

Grayson, P., & Carlson, G. A. (1991). The utility of a *DSM-III-R*-based checklist in screening child psychiatric patients. *Journal of the American Academy of Child and Adolescent Psychiatry, 30*, 669–673.

Gredler, M. E. (2005). *Learning and instruction: Theory into practice* (5th ed.). Upper Saddle River, NJ: Merrill/Prentice Hall.

Green, A., & Keys, S. (2001). Expanding the developmental school counseling paradigm: Meeting the needs of the 21st century student. *Professional School Counseling, 5*, 84–95.

Greenberg, W. M., Rosenfeld, D. N., & Ortega, E. A. (1995). Adjustment Disorder as an admission diagnosis. *American Journal of Psychiatry, 152*, 459–461.

Greene, R. W., & Doyle, A. E. (1999). Toward a transactional conceptualization of Oppositional Defiant Disorder: Implications for assessment and treatment. *Clinical Child and Family Psychology Review, 2*, 129–148.

Gresham, F. M., & Elliott, S. N. (1990). *The social skills rating system—parent and teacher forms*. Circle Pines, MN: American Guidance Press.

Grizenko, N., Sayegh, L., & Papineau, D. (1994). Predicting outcome in a multimodal day treatment program for children with severe behavior problems. *Canadian Journal of Psychiatry, 39*, 557–562.

Grodzinsky, G. M., & Diamond, R. (1992). Frontal lobe functioning in boys with Attention-Deficit/Hyperactivity Disorder. *Developmental Neuropsychology, 8*, 427–445.

Guernina, Z. (1998). Adolescents with Eating Disorders: A pilot study. *Counseling Psychology Quarterly, 11*(1), 117–124.

Guevremont, D. C., & Dumas, M. C. (1994). Peer relationship problems and Disruptive Behavior Disorders. *Journal of Emotional and Behavioral Disorders, 2*, 164–172.

Gullone, E. (2000). The development of normal fear: A century of research. *Clinical Psychology Review, 20*, 429–451.

Gullone, E., King, N. J., & Ollendick, T. H. (2001). Self-reported anxiety in children and adolescents: A three-year follow-up study. *Journal of Genetic Psychology, 162*, 5–15.

Hallfors, D., Brodish, P. H., Khatapoush, S., Sanchez, V., Cho, H., & Steckler, A. (2006). Feasibility of screening adolescents for suicide risk in "real world" high school settings. *American Journal of Public Health, 96*, 282–287.

Halmi, K. A., Goldberg, S. C., & Cunningham, S. (1977). Perceptual distortion of body image in adolescent girls: Distortion of body image in adolescence. *Psychological Medicine, 7*, 253–257.

Hamlett, K. W., Pellegrini, D. S., & Conners, C. K. (1987). An investigation of executive processes in the problem-solving of Attention-Deficit Disorder-Hyperactive children. *Journal of Pediatric Psychology, 12*, 227–240.

Hammen, C., Brennan, P. A., & Shih, J. H. (2004). Family discord and stress predictors of depression and other disorders in adolescent children of depressed and nondepressed women. *Journal of the American Academy of Child and Adolescent Psychiatry, 43*, 994–1002.

Hammen, C., Burge, D., Burney, E., & Adrian, C. (1990). Longitudinal study of diagnoses in children of women with Unipolar and Bipolar Affective Disorder. *Archives of General Psychiatry, 47*, 1112–1117.

Hanna, F. J., Hanna, C. A., & Keys, S. G. (1999). Fifty strategies for counseling defiant, aggressive adolescents: Reaching, accepting, and relating. *Journal of Counseling and Development, 77*, 395–404.

Hannan, A. P., Rapee, R. M., & Hudson, J. L. (2000). The prevention of depression in children: A pilot study. *Behaviour Change, 17*, 78–83.

Hansen, W. B., & Graham, J. (1991). Preventing alcohol, marijuana, and cigarette use among adolescents: Peer pressure resistance training versus establishing conservative norms. *Prevention Medicine, 20*, 414–430.

Harburg, E., DiFrancesico, W., Wevster, D. W., Gleiberman, L., & Schork, A. (1990). Familial transmission of alcohol use. *Journal of Studies on Alcohol, 51*, 245–256.

Harrington, R. (1993). *Depressive Disorder in childhood and adolescence*. New York: John Wiley & Sons.

Harrington, R., Whittaker, J., & Shoebridge, P. (1998). Psychological treatment of depression in children and adolescents. A review of treatment research. *The British Journal of Psychiatry, 173*, 291–298.

Harris, J. R. (1995). Where is the child's environment? A group socialization theory of development. *Psychological Review, 102*, 458–489.

Harrison, P. A., Fulkerson, J. A., & Beebe, T. J. (1998). *DSM-IV* Substance Use Disorder criteria for adolescents: A critical examination based on a statewide school survey. *American Journal of Psychiatry, 155,* 486–492.

Harter, S. (1985). *Self-perception profile for children.* Denver, CO: University of Denver, Department of Psychology.

Harter, S. (1988). *Self-perception profile for adolescents.* Denver, CO: University of Denver, Department of Psychology.

Hartman, A. (1979). *Finding families: An ecological approach to family assessment in adoption.* Beverly Hills, CA: Sage.

Hatfield, T., & Hatfield, S. R. (1992). As if your life depended on it: Promoting cognitive development to promote wellness. *Journal of Counseling & Development, 71,* 164–167.

Havighurst, R. J. (1972). *Developmental tasks and education* (3rd ed.). New York: David McKay.

Hayward, C., Wilson, K. A., & Lagle, K. (2004). Parent-reported predictors of adolescent panic attacks. *Journal of the American Academy of Child and Adolescent Psychiatry, 43,* 613–620.

Health Associates of America. (1997). *Health care management consultants: Review protocols for psychiatric and substance abuse services.* Baton Rouge, LA: Author.

Heaton, R. K., Chelune, G. J., Talley, J. L., Kay, G. G., & Curtiss, G. (1993). *Wisconsin card sort manual—revised.* Odessa, FL: Psychological Assessment Resources, Inc.

Heesacker, R. S., & Neimeyer, G. J. (1990). Assessing object relations and social-cognitive correlates of Eating Disorders. *Journal of Counseling Psychology, 37,* 419–426.

Heflin, A. H., & Deblinger, E. (2003). Treatment of a sexually abused adolescent with post-traumatic stress disorder. In Reinecke, A., Dattilio, F. M., & Freeman, A., *Cognitive therapy with children and adolescents: A casebook for clinical practice* (2nd Ed.) (pp. 214–246). New York: Guilford.

Heimberg, R. G., Dodge, C. S., & Becker, R. E. (1987). Social phobia. In L. Michelson & M. L. Asher (Eds.), *Anxiety and Stress Disorders* (pp. 280–309). New York: Guilford.

Helzer, J. E., Burnam, A., & McEvoy, L. T. (1991). Alcohol abuse and dependence. In L. Robins & D. Reiger (Eds.), *Psychiatric disorders in America: The epidemiologic catchment area study* (pp. 81–115). New York: Macmilian.

Hendrix, N. C., & Morrison, J. P. (2000). *"Fact sheets" for 12 months, 15 months, 18 months, and 2–9 years.* Athens, GA: Authors.

Hengeller, S. W., & Lee, T. (2003). A multsystemic treatment of serious clinical problems. In A. E. Kazdin & J. R. Weisz (Eds.), *Evidence-based psychotherapies for children and adolescents* (pp. 301–322). New York: Guilford Press.

Henggeler, S. W. (1994). A consensus: Conclusions of the APA task force on innovative models of mental health services for children, adolescents, and their families. *Journal of Clinical Child Psychology, 23,* 3–6.

Henggeler, S. W., & Borduin, C. M. (1990). *Family therapy and beyond: A multisystemic approach treating the behavior problems of children and adolescents.* Pacific Grove, CA: Brooks/Cole.

Henggeler, S. W., Clingempeel, W. G., Brondino, M. J., & Pickrel, S. G. (2002). Four-year follow-up of multisystemic therapy with substance-abusing and substance-dependent juvenile offenders. *Journal of the American Academy of Child and Adolescent Psychiatry, 41*(7).

Henggeler, S. W., Melton, G. B., & Smith, L. A. (1992). Family preservation using multisystemic therapy: An effective alternative to incarcerating serious juvenile offenders. *Journal of Consulting and Clinical Psychology, 60,* 953–961.

Henggeler, S. W., Rodick, J. D., Borduin, C. M., Hanson, C. L., Watson, S. M., & Urey, J. R. (1986). Multisystemic treatment of juvenile offenders: Effects on adolescent behavior and family interaction. *Developmental Psychology, 22,* 132–141.

Henggeler, S. W., Schoenwald, S. K., Borduin, C. M., Rowland, M. D., & Cunningham, P. B. (1998). *Multisystemic treatment of antisocial behavior in children and adolescents.* New York: Guilford Press.

Henin, A., Biederman, J., Mick, E., Sachs, G. S., Hirschfield-Becker, D. R., Siegel, R. S., et al. (2005). Psychopathology in the offspring of parents with bipolar disorder: A controlled study. *Biological Psychiatry, 58,* 554–561.

Herbert, J. D. (2003). The science and practice of empirically supported treatments. *Behavior Modification, 27,* 412–430.

Herman, C. P., Polivy, J., Pliner, P., & Threlkeld, J. (1978). Distractibility in dieters and nondieters: An alternative view of "externality." *Journal of Personality and Social Psychology, 5,* 536–548.

Herring, R. D. (1997). *Multicultural counseling in schools: A synergetic approach.* Alexandria, VA: American Counseling Association.

Herschell, A. D., McNeil, C. B., McNeil, D. W. (2004). Clinical child psychology's progress in disseminating empirically supported treatments. *Clinical Psychology, 11,* 267–288.

Hersen, M., & Ammerman, R. T. (Eds.). (1995). *Advanced abnormal psychology.* Hillsdale, NJ: Erlbaum.

Hersov, L. (1994). Inpatient and day-hospital units. In M. Rutter, E. Taylor, & L. Hersov (Eds.), *Child and adolescent psychiatry* (3rd ed., pp. 983–995). Oxford: Blackwell Scientific Publications.

Herzog, D. B., Keller, M., & Lavori, P. (1988). Outcome in Anorexia Nervosa and Bulimia Nervosa: A review of the literature. *Journal of Nervous and Mental Disorders, 176,* 131–143.

Herzog, D. B., Keller, M. B., Strober, M., & Yeh, C. J. (1992). The current status of treatment for Anorexia Nervosa and Bulimia Nervosa. *International Journal of Eating Disorders, 12*(2), 215–220.

Herzog, D. B., Norman, D. K., Gordon, C., & Pepose, M. (1984). Sexual conflict and Eating Disorders in 27 males. *American Journal of Psychiatry, 141*(8), 989–990.

Herzog, D. B., Nussbaum, K. M., & Marmot, A. K. (1996). Comorbidity and outcomes in Eating Disorders. *Psychiatric Clinics of North America, 19,* 681–697.

Herzog, D. B., Sacks, N. R., Keller, M. B., Lavori, P. W., VonRanson, K. B., & Gray, H. M. (1993). Patterns and predictors of recovery in Anorexia Nervosa and Bulimia Nervosa. *Journal of the American Academy of Child and Adolescent Psychiatry, 32*(4), 835–842.

Hetherington, E. M., & Martin, B. (1986). Family factors and psychopathology in children. In H. C. Quay & J. S. Werry (Eds.), *Psychopathological Disorders of childhood* (3rd ed., pp. 332–390). New York: John Wiley & Sons.

Heyne, D., & King, N. J. (2004). Treatment of school refusal. In P. M. Barrett & T. H. Ollendick (Eds.), *Handbook of interventions that work with children and adolescents: Prevention and treatment* (pp. 241–2720). West Sussex, England: John Wiley.

Heyne, D., King, N. L., Tonge, B. J., & Cooper, H. (2001). School refusal: Epidemiology and management. *Pediatric Drugs, 1,* 719–732.

Hinkle, J. S. (1988). Psychological benefits of aerobic running: Implications for mental health counselors. *Journal of Mental Health Counseling, 10,* 245–253.

Hinkle, J. S. (1994a). Ecosystems and mental health counseling: Reaction to Becvar and Becvar. *Journal of Mental Health Counseling, 16,* 33–36.

Hinkle, J. S. (1994b). Practitioners and cross-cultural assessment. *Measurement and Evaluation in Counseling and Development, 27,* 103–115.

Hinkle, J. S., & Lineberry, S. (1999, March). *A case presentation of phobia of the dead human body*. Presentation at the 72nd Annual Convention of the North Carolina Counseling Association (NCCA), Greensboro, NC.

Hinkle, J. S., & Wells, M. E. (1995). *Family counseling in the schools: A practical guide for counselors, teachers, and psychologists*. Greensboro, NC: ERIC.

Hinshaw, S. P. (1987). On the distinction between Attentional Deficits/Hyperactivity and conduct problems/ aggression in child psychopathology. *Psychological Bulletin, 101,* 443–463.

Hinshaw, S. P. (1992). Externalizing behavior problems and academic underachievement in childhood and adolescence: Causal relationships and underlying mechanisms. *Psychological Bulletin, 111,* 127–155.

Hinshaw, S. P., & Anderson, C. A. (1996). Conduct and Oppositional Defiant Disorders. In E. J. Mash and R. A. Barkley (Eds.), *Child psychopathology* (pp. 113–149). New York: Guilford Press.

Hinshaw, S. P., Buhrmeister, D., & Heller, T. (1989). Anger control in response to verbal provocation: Effects of stimulant medication for boys with AD/HD. *Journal of Abnormal Child Psychology, 17,* 393–408.

Hinshaw, S. P., Lahey, B. B., & Hart, E. L. (1993). Issues of taxonomy and comorbidity in the development of Conduct Disorder. *Development and Psychopathology, 5,* 31–49.

Hinshaw, S. P., Owens, E. B., Wells, K. C., Kraemer, H. C., Abikoff, H. B., Arnold, E., et al. (2000). *Journal of Abnormal Child Psychology, 28,* 555–568.

Hinshaw, S. P., Zupan, B. Z., Simmel, C., Nigg, J. T., & Melnick, S. (1997). Peer status in boys with and without AD/HD: Predictions from overt and covert antisocial behavior, social isolation, and authoritative parenting beliefs. *Child Development, 68,* 880–896.

Hirshfeld-Becker, D. R., Biederman, J., & Faraone, S. V. (2004). Pregnancy complications associated with childhood anxiety disorders., *Depression and Anxiety, 19,* 152–162.

Hobbs, N. (1982). *The troubled and troubling child*. San Francisco: Jossey-Bass.

Hodges, K. (1987). Assessing children with a clinical interview: The child assessment schedule. In R. J. Prinz (Ed.), *Advances in behavioral assessment of children and families* (pp. 133–166). Greenwich, CT: JAI.

Hodges, K. (1994). Evaluation of depression in children and adolescents using diagnostic clinical interviews. In W. M. Reynolds & H. E. Johnston (Eds.), *Handbook of depression in children and adolescents* (pp. 183–208). New York: Plenum Press.

Hollander, E., Simeon, D., & Gorman, J. M. (1999). Anxiety Disorders. In R. E. Hales, S. C. Yudofsky, & J. A. Talbott (Eds.), *Textbook of psychiatry* (3rd ed., pp. 567–633). Washington, DC: American Psychiatric Press.

Hollon, S. D., & Beck, A. T. (1994). Cognitive and cognitive-behavioral therapies. In S. L. Garfield & A. E. Bergin (Eds.), *Handbook of psychotherapy and behavior change* (pp. 428–466). New York: John Wiley & Sons.

Holmbeck, G. G., Creeenley. R. N., & Franks, E. A. (2003). Developmental issues and considerations in research practice. In A. E. Kazdin & J. R. Weisz (Eds.), *Evidence-based psychotherapies for children and adolescents* (pp. 21–41). New York: Guilford Press.

Honos-Webb, L. (2005). The meaning vs. the medical model in the empirically supported treatment program: A consideration of the empirical evidence. *Journal of Contemporary Psychotherapy, 35,* 55–65.

Hood, A. B., & Johnson, R. W. (2002). *Assessment in counseling: A guide to the use of psychological assessment procedures* (3rd ed.). Alexandria, VA: American Counseling Association.

Hope, D. A., & Heimberg, R. G. (1993). Social phobia and social anxiety. In D. H. Barlow (Ed.), *Clinical handbook of Psychological Disorders* (2nd ed., pp. 99–136). New York: Guilford.

Horowitz, M. J., Weine, S., & Jekel, J. (1995). PTSD symptoms in urban adolescent girls: Compounded community trauma. *Journal of the Academy of Child and Adolescent Psychiatry, 34,* 1353–1361.

Horrigan, T. J., & Piazza, N. J. (1999). SASSI minimizes the need for toxicology screening of prenatal patients. *Journal of Substance Abuse Counseling, 17,* 243–247.

Horrigan, T. J., Piazza, N. J., & Weinstein, L. (1996). The Substance Abuse Subtle Screening Inventory is more cost-effective and has better selectivity than urine toxicology for the detection of substance abuse in pregnancy. *Journal of Perinatology, 16,* 326–330.

Hosie, T. W., & Erk, R. R. (1993, January). American Counseling Association reading program: Attention-Deficit Disorder. *Guidepost,* 15–18.

Hovens, J. G. F. M., Cantwell, D. P., & Kiriakos, R. (1994). Psychiatric comorbidity in hospitalized adolescent substance abusers. *Journal of the American Academy of Child and Adolescent Psychiatry, 33,* 476–483.

Hoyt, M. F. (2000). *Some stories are better than others: Doing what works in brief therapy and managed care*. Philadelphia: Brunner/Mazel.

Hoza, B., Owens, J. S., Pelham, W. E., Swanson, J. M., Conners, C. K., Hinshaw, S. P., Arnold, L. E., & Kraemer, H. C. (2000). Parent cognitions as predictors of child treatment response in Attention-Deficit/Hyperactivity Disorder. *Journal of Abnormal Child Psychology, 28,* 569–583.

Hsu, L. (1988). The outcome of Anorexia Nervosa: A reappraisal. *Psychological Medicine, 18,* 807–812.

Hsu, L. (1990). *Eating Disorders*. New York: Guilford Press.

Hsu, L. (1991). Outcome studies in patients with Eating Disorders. In S. M. Miren, J. T. Gossett, & M. C. Grob (Eds.), *Psychiatric treatment: Advances in outcome research* (pp. 159–180). Washington, DC: American Psychiatric Press.

Huizinga, D. H., Menard, S., & Elliot, D. S. (1989). Delinquency and drug use: Temporal and developmental patterns. *Justice Quarterly, 6,* 419–455.

Humphrey, L. L. (1986). Structural analysis of parent-child relationships in Eating Disorders. *Journal of Abnormal Psychology, 95*(4), 395–402.

Humphrey, L. L. (1989). Observed family interactions among subtypes of Eating Disorders using structural analysis of social behavior. *Journal of Consulting and Clinical Psychology, 57,* 206–214.

Hynd, G. W., Semrud-Clikeman, M., Lorys, A. R., Novey, E. S., Eliopulos, D., & Lyntinen, H. (1991). Corpus callosum morphology in Attention-Deficit/Hyperactivity Disorder: Morphmetric analysis of MRI. *Journal of Learning Disabilities, 24,* 141–146.

Hynd, G. W., Semrud-Clikeman, M., Nieves, Huettner, & Lahey, B. B., (1991). *Journal of Child Neurology, 6,* 37–43.

Ilg, F. L., & Ames, L. B. (1972). *School readiness: Behavior tests used at the Gesell Institute* (New ed.). New York: Harper & Row.

Individuals with Disabilities Education Act of 1990, 20 U.S.C. Section 1400 *et seq.*

Ingalls, S., & Goldstein, S. (1999). Learning disabilities. In S. Goldstein & C. R. Reynolds (Eds.), *Handbook of Neurodevelopmental and Genetic Disorders in children* (pp. 101–153). New York: Guilford Press.

Ivey, A. E., D'Andrea, M., Ivey, M. B., & Simek-Morgan, L. (2002). *Theories of counseling and psychotherapy: A multicultural perspective* (5th ed.). Boston: Allyn & Bacon.

Ivey, A. E., & Ivey, M. B. (1998). Reframing *DSM-IV*: Positive strategies from developmental counseling and therapy. *Journal of Counseling & Development, 76,* 334–350.

Iwasaki, M. (2005). Mental health and counseling in Japan: A path toward societal transformation. *Journal of Mental Health Counseling, 27,* 129–141.

Jackson, B., & Farrugia, D. (1997). Diagnosis and treatment of adults with Attention-Deficit/Hyperactivity Disorder. *Journal of Counseling and Development, 75,* 312–319.

Jacob, T., & Johnson, S. (1997). Parenting influences on the development of alcohol abuse and dependence. *Alcohol Health & Research World, 21*(3), 204–209.

Jacobs, B. L. (1994). Serotonin, motor activity, and Depression-related Disorders. *American Scientist, 82,* 456–463.

Janis, I. L., & Mann, L. (1977). *Decision making.* New York: Free Press.

Jessor, R. (1993). Successful adolescent development among youth in high-risk settings. *American Psychologist, 48,* 117–126.

Johnson, E. O., Rhee, S. H., Chase, G. A., & Breslau, N. (2004). Comorbidity of depression with levels of smoking: An exploration of the shared familial risk hypothesis. *Nicotine & Tobacco Research, 6,* 1029–1038.

Johnson, L. S. (1997). Developmental strategies for counseling the child whose parent or sibling has cancer. *Journal of Counseling & Development, 75,* 417–427.

Johnson, V. E. (1973). *I'll quit tomorrow.* New York: Harper & Row.

Johnston, C., & Ohan, J. L. (1999). Externalizing disorders. In W. K. Silverman & T. H. Ollendick (Eds.), *Developmental issues in the clinical treatment of children* (pp. 278–294). Boston: Allyn & Bacon.

Johnston, L. D., O'Malley, P. M., & Bachman, J. G. (1993). *National survey results on drug use from monitory the future study, 1975–1992* (NIH Publication 93–3597, Vol. 1, Secondary School Students). Rockville, MD: National Institute on Drug Abuse.

Johnston, L. D., O'Malley, P. M., & Bachman, J. G. (1998). *Drug use by American young people begins to turn downward.* Retrieved May, 19, 1999, from http://www.isr.umich.edu/src/mtf/.

Johnston, L. D., O'Malley, P. M., Bachman, J. G., & Schulenberg, J. E. (2005). *Monitoring the Future national survey results on drug use, 1975–2004. Volume I: Secondary school students* (NIH Publication No. 05-5727). Bethesda, MD: National Institute on Drug Abuse, 680 pp.

Jones, R., Yates, W. R., & Zhou, M. H. (2002). Readmission rates for adjustment disorders: comparison with other mood disorders. *Journal of Affective Disorders, 71,* 199–203.

Jones, R., Yates, W. R., Williams, S., Zhou, M., & Hardman, L. (1999). Outcome for adjustment disorder with depressed mood: Comparison with other mood disorders. *Journal of Affective Disorders, 55,* 55–61.

Jones-Hiscock, C. (2004). Using depression inventories: Not a replacement for clinical judgment. *Canadian Journal of Psychiatry, 49,* 646–647.

Jordan, D. R. (1992). *Attention-Deficit Disorder: AD/HD and ADD syndromes.* Austin, TX: Pro-Ed.

Julien, R. M. (2005). *A Primer of Drug Action* (10th ed.). New York: Worth Publishers.

Kadish, T. E., Glaser, B. A., Calhoun, G. B., & Ginter, E. J. (2001). Identifying the developmental strengths of juvenile offenders: Assessing four life-skills dimensions. *Journal of Addictions & Offender Counseling, 21,* 85–95.

Kafantaris, V. (1995). Treatment of Bipolar Disorder in children and adolescents. *Journal of the American Academy of Child and Adolescent Psychiatry, 34,* 732–741.

Kafantaris, V., Coletti, D. J., Dicker, R., Padula, G., Pleak, R. R., Alvir, J. M. J., et al. (2004). Lithium treatment of acute mania in adolescents: A placebo-controlled discontinuation study. *Journal of the American Academy of Child & Adolescent Psychiatry, 43,* 984–993.

Kagan, J. (1964). *The matching familiar figures test.* Unpublished manuscript. Harvard University, Cambridge, MA.

Kagan, J., Snidman, N., Arcus, D., & Reznick, J. S. (1994). *Galen's prophecy: Temperament in human nature.* New York: Basic Books.

Kalodner, C. R. (1999). Cognitive-behavioral theories. In D. Cappuzzi & D. C. Gross (Eds.), *Counseling and psychotherapy* (pp. 261–286). Upper Saddle River, NJ: Merrill Prentice Hall.

Kalodner, C. R., & Scarano, G. (1992) A continuum of non-clinical Eating Disorders: A review of behavioral and psychological correlates and suggestions for intervention. *Journal of Mental Health Counseling, 14,* 30–41.

Kaminer, Y. (1994). Adolescent substance abuse. In M. Galanter & H. D. Kleber (Eds.), *Textbook of substance abuse treatment* (pp. 415–437). Washington, DC: American Psychiatric Press.

Kamphaus, R. W., & Frick, P. J. (1996a). *Clinical assessment of child and adolescent psychiatry and behavior.* Boston: Allyn & Bacon.

Kamphaus, R. W., & Frick, P. J. (1996b). *The clinical assessment of children's emotion, behavior, and personality.* Boston: Allyn & Bacon.

Kanbayashi, Y., Nakata, Y., Fujii, K., Kita, M., & Wada, K. (1994). ADHD–related behavior among nonreferred children. Parents' ratings of *DSM-III-R* symptoms. *Child Psychiatry and Human Development, 25,* 13–29.

Kann, T. R., & Hanna, F. J. (2000). Disruptive Behavior Disorders in children and adolescents: How do girls differ from boys? *Journal of Counseling and Development, 78,* 267–274.

Kaplan, B. J., Crawford, S. G., Dewey, D. M., & Fisher, G. C. (2000). *Journal of Learning Disabilities, 33,* 425–432.

Kaplan, C. A., & Hussain, S. (1995). Use of drugs in child and adolescent psychiatry. *The British Journal of Psychiatry, 166,* 291–298.

Kaplan, S. L., Hong, G. K., & Weinhold, C. (1984). Epidemiology of depressive symptomatology in adolescents. *Journal of the American Academy of Child Psychology, 23,* 91–98.

Karmiloff, K., & Karmiloff-Smith, A. (1999). *Everything your baby would ask . . . if only he or she could talk.* New York: Golden Books.

Karno, M., Golding, J. M., Sorenson, S. B., & Burnam, M. A. (1988). The epidemiology of Obsessive-Compulsive Disorder in five U.S. communities. *Archives of General Psychiatry, 45,* 1094–1099.

Karp, S. A., & Konstadt, N. (1969). *Childrens' embedded figures test.* Palo Alto, CA: Consulting Psychologists Press.

Kasen, S., Johnson, J., & Cohen, P. (1990). The impact of school emotional climate on student psycho-pathology. *Journal of Abnormal Child Psychology, 18,* 165–177.

Kashani, J. H., & Ovaschel, H. (1988). Anxiety Disorders in mid-adolescents: A community sample. *American Journal of Psychiatry, 145,* 960–964.

Kashani, J. H., Suarez, L., Jones, M. R., & Reid, J. C. (1999). Perceived family characteristic differences between depressed and anxious children and adolescents. *Journal of Affective Disorders, 52,* 269–274.

Kaslow, N. J., Celano, M., & Dreelin, E. D. (1995). A cultural perspective on family theory and therapy. *Cultural Psychiatry, 18,* 621–633.

Kaslow, N. J., & Thompson, M. P. (1998). Applying the criteria for empirically supported treatments to studies of psychosocial interventions for child and adolescent depression. *Journal of Clinical Child Psychology, 27*(2), 146–155.

Katz, M. (1997). *On playing a poor hand well: Insights from the lives of those who have overcome childhood risks and adversities.* New York: W. W. Norton.

Kauffman, J. M. (2005). *Characteristics of emotional and behavioral disorders of children and youth* (8th ed.). Upper Saddle River NJ: Merrill/Prentice Hall.

Kay, J. (2001). Integrated treatment: An overview. In J. Kay (Ed.), *Integrated treatment of Psychiatric Disorders* (pp. 1–29). Washington, DC: American Psychiatric Press.

Kazdin, A. E. (1993). Evaluation in clinical practice: Clinically sensitive and systematic methods of treatment delivery. *Behavior Therapy, 24,* 11–45.

Kazdin, A. E. (1995). *Conduct Disorders in childhood and adolescence* (2nd ed.). Thousand Oaks, CA: Sage.

Kazdin, A. E. (1997). Parent management training: Evidence, outcomes, and issues. *Journal of the American Academy of Child and Adolescent Psychiatry, 36,* 1349–1356.

Kazdin, A. E. (1997). Practitioner review: Psychosocial treatments for Conduct Disorder in children. *Journal of Child Psychology and Psychiatry, 38,* 161–178.

Kazdin, A. E. (2003). Problem-solving skills training and parent management training for conduct disorder. In A. E. Kazdin & J. R. Weisz (Eds.), *Evidence based psychotherapies for children and adolescents* (pp. 241–262). New York: Guilford Press.

Kazdin, A. E., & Crowley, M. (1997). Moderators of treatment outcome in cognitively based treatment of antisocial behavior. *Cognitive Therapy and Research, 21,* 185–207.

Kazdin, A. E., & Mazurick, J. L. (1994). Dropping out of child psychology: Distinguishing early and late dropouts over the course of treatment. *Journal of Consulting and Clinical Psychology, 62,* 1069–1074.

Kazdin, A. E., & Wassell, G. (1998). Treatment completion and therapeutic change among children referred for outpatient therapy. *Professional Psychology: Research and Practice, 29,* 332–340.

Kazdin, A. E., & Wassell, G. (1999). Barriers to treatment participation and therapeutic change among children referred for Conduct Disorder. *Journal of Clinical Child Psychology, 28,* 160–172.

Kazdin, A. E., & Wassell, G. (2000a). Predictors of barriers to treatment and therapeutic change in outpatient therapy for antisocial children and their families. *Mental Health Services Research, 2,* 27–40.

Kazdin, A. E., & Wassell, G. (2000b). Therapeutic changes in children, parents, and families resulting from treatment of children with conduct problems. *Journal of the American Academy of Child and Adolescent Psychiatry, 39,* 414–420.

Kazdin, A. E., & Weisz, J. R. (1998). Identifying and developing empirically supported child and adolescent treatments. *Journal of Consulting and Clinical Psychology, 66,* 19–36.

Kazdin, A. E., Bass, D., Ayers, W. A., & Rogers, A. (1990). The empirical and clinical focus of child and adolescent psychotherapy research. *Journal of Consulting and Clinical Psychology, 58,* 729–740.

Kazdin, A. E., Esveldt-Dawson, K., French, N. H., & Unis, A. S. (1987a). The effects of parent management training and problem-solving skills training combined in the treatment of antisocial behavior child behavior. *Journal of the American Academy of Child and Adolescent Psychiatry, 26,* 416–424.

Kazdin, A. E., Esveldt-Dawson, K., French, N. H., & Unis, A. S. (1987b). Problem-solving skills training and relationship therapy in the treatment of antisocial child behavior. *Journal of Consulting and Clinical Psychology, 55,* 76–85.

Kazdin, A. E., Siegel, T. C., & Bass, D. (1992). Cognitive problem-solving skills training and parent management training in the treatment of antisocial behavior in children. *Journal of Consulting and Clinical Psychology, 60,* 733–747.

Kazdin, A., E., & Whitley, M. K. (2003). Treatment of parental stress to enhance therapeutic change among children referred for aggressive and antisocial behavior. *Journal of Consulting and Clinical Psychology, 71,* 504–515.

Kazdin, A.E., Bass, D., Siegel, T., & Thomas, C. (1989). Cognitive-behavioral treatment and relationship therapy in the treatment of children referred for antisocial behavior. *Journal of Consulting and Clinical Psychology, 21,* 522–535.

Keane, T. M., & Wolfe, J. (1990). Comorbidity in Post-traumatic Stress Disorder: An analysis of community and clinical studies. *Journal of Applied Social Psychology, 20,* 1776–1788.

Kearney, C. A., & Bates, M. (2005). Addressing school refusal behavior: Suggestions for frontline professionals. *Children & Schools, 27,* 207–216.

Kearney, C. A., & Silverman, W. K. (1995). Family environment of youngsters with school refusal behavior: A synopsis with implications for assessment and treatment. *American Journal of Family Therapy, 23,* 59–72.

Kearney, C. A., & Silverman, W. K. (1996). The evolution and reconciliation of taxonomic strategies for school refusal behavior. *Clinical Psychology: Science and Practice, 3,* 339–354.

Keenan, K., Loeber, R., & Green, S. (1999). Conduct Disorder in girls: A review of the literature. *Clinical Child and Family Psychology Review, 2,* 3–19.

Keenan, K., Shaw, D. S., Walsh, B., Delliquardi, E., & Giovannelli, J. (1997). *DSM-III-R* Disorders in preschool children from low-income families. *Journal of the American Academy of Child and Adolescent Psychiatry, 36,* 620–627.

Keenan, K., & Wakschlag, L. S. (2000). More than the terrible twos: The nature and severity of behavior problems in clinic-referred preschool children. *Journal of Abnormal Child Psychology, 28,* 33–46.

Kendall, P. C. (1993). Cognitive-behavioral therapies for youth: Guiding theory, current status, and emerging developments. *Journal of Consulting and Clinical Psychology, 62,* 100–110.

Kendall, P. C., & Braswell, L. (1985). *Cognitive-behavioral therapy for impulsive children.* New York: Guilford Press.

Kendall, P. C., & Dobson, K. S. (1993). On the nature of cognition and its role in psychopathology. In K. S. Dobson & P. C. Kendall (Eds.), *Psychopathology and cognition* (pp. 3–17). San Diego, CA: Academic Press.

Kendall, P. C., & MacDonald, J. P. (1993). Cognition in the psychopathology of youth and implications for treatment. In K. S. Dobson & P. C. Kendall (Eds.), *Psychopathology and cognition* (pp. 387–427). San Diego, CA: Academic Press.

Kennedy, J. A. (1992). *Fundamentals of psychiatric treatment planning.* Washington, DC: American Psychiatric Press, Inc.

Kessler, R. C., Berglund, P., Demler, O., Jin, R., Merikangas, K. R., & Walters, E. E. (2005a). Lifetime prevalence of age-of-onset distributions of *DSM-IV* disorders in the national comorbidity survey replication. *Archives of General Psychiatry, 62,* 593–602.

Kessler, R. C., Chiu, W. T., Demler, O., & Walters, E. E. (2005b). Prevalence, severity, and comorbidity of 12 month *DSM-IV* disorders in the national comorbidity survey replication. *Archives of General Psychiatry, 62,* 617–627.

Kessler, R. C., McGonagle, K. A., Zhao, S., Nelson, C. B., Hughes, M., Eshlman, S., Wittchen, H. U., & Kendler, K. S. (1994). Lifetime and twelve-month prevalence of *DSM-III-R* Psychiatric Disorders in the United States: Results from the national comorbidity study. *Archives of General Psychiatry, 51,* 8–19.

Keys, S. G., & Bemak, F. (1997). School-family community linked services: A school counseling role for changing times. *The School Counselor, 44*, 255–263.

Keys, S. G., Bemak, F., & Lockhart, E. (1998). Transforming school counseling to meet the mental health needs of at-risk youth. *Journal of Counseling and Development, 76*, 381–388.

Killen, J. D., Taylor, C. B., Hammer, L. D., Litt, I., Wilson, D. M., Rich, T., Hayward, C., Simmons, B., Kraemer, H., & Varady, A. (1993). An attempt to modify unhealthful eating attitudes and weight-reduction practices of young adolescent girls. *International Journal of Eating Disorders, 13* (4), 369–384.

Killen, J. D., Taylor, C. B., Hayward, C., Wilson, D. M., Haydel, K. F., Hammer, L. D., Simmons, B., Robinson, T. N., Litt, I., Varady, A., & Kraemer, H. (1994). Pursuit of thinness and onset of Eating Disorder symptoms in a community sample of adolescent girls: A three-year prospective analysis. *International Journal of Eating Disorders, 16* (3), 227–238.

Killen, J. D., Taylor, C. B., Telch, M. J., Saylor, K. E., Maron, D. J., & Robinson, T. N. (1986). Self-induced vomiting and laxative and diuretic use among teenagers: Precursors of the binge-purge syndrome? *Journal of the American Medical Association, 255*, 1447–1449.

Killen, J. D., Taylor, C. B., Telch, M. J., Saylor, K. E., Maron, D. J., & Robinson, T. N. (1987). Depressive symptoms and substance use among adolescent binge eaters and purgers: A defined population study. *American Journal of Public Health, 77*, 1539–1541.

King, C. A., Ghaziuddin, N., McGovern, L., Brand, E., Hill, E., & Naylor, M. (1996). Predictors of comorbid alcohol and substance abuse in depressed adolescents. *Journal of the American Academy of Child and Adolescent Psychiatry, 35*, 743–751.

King, N. J., Heyne, D., & Tonge, B. J. (2003). Sexually abused children suffering from post-traumatic stress disorder: Assessment and treatment strategies. *Cognitive Behaviour Therapy, 32*, 2–12.

Kirkcaldy, B., & Siefen, G. (1998). Depression, anxiety and self-image among children and adolescents. *School Psychology International, 19*, 135–149.

Kiselica, M. S., & Robinson, M. (2001). Bringing advocacy to life: The history, issues, and human dramas of social justice work in counseling. *Journal of Counseling & Development, 79*, 387–397.

Kitts, R. (2005). Gay adolescents and suicide: Understanding the association. *Adolescence, 40*, 621–628.

Klein, D. F. (1981). Anxiety reconceptualized. In D. F. Klein & J. G. Rabkin (Eds.), *Anxiety: New research and changing concepts* (pp. 235–263). New York: Raven.

Klein, R. G. (1994). Anxiety Disorders. In M. Rutter, E. Taylor, & L. Hersov (Eds.), *Child and adolescent psychiatry: Modern approaches* (pp. 351–374). Oxford: Blackwell.

Klein, R. G., Abikoff, H., Klass, E., Ganeles, D., Seese, L. M., & Pollack, S. (1997). Clinical efficacy of methylphenidate in Conduct Disorder with and without Attention-Deficit/Hyperactivity Disorder. *Archives of General Psychiatry, 54*, 1073–1080.

Klein, R. G., & Mannuzza, S. (1991). Long-term outcome of hyperactive children: A review. *Journal of the American Academy of Child and Adolescent Psychiatry, 30*, 383–387.

Kleinman, A. (1977). Depression, somatization and the new cross-cultural psychiatry. *Social Science Medicine, 11*, 3–10.

Kleinman, A. (2004). Culture and depression. *The New England Journal of Medicine, 351*, 951–953.

Knop, J., Teasdale, T. W., Schulsinger, F., & Goodwin, D. W. (1985). A prospective study of young men at high risk for alcoholism: School behavior and achievement. *Journal of Studies on Alcohol, 46*, 273–278.

Kochanska, G. (1995). Children's temperament, mothers' discipline, and security of attachment: Multiple pathways to emerging internalization. *Child Development, 66*, 597–615.

Kog, E., & Vandereycken, W. (1989). Family interaction in Eating Disorder patients and normal controls. *International Journal of Eating Disorders, 8*(1), 11–23.

Kohlberg, L. (1994). Stages and sequences: The cognitive-developmental approach to socialization. In B. Puka (Series Ed.), *Moral development: A compendium: Vol. 1. Defining perspectives in moral development* (pp. 1–134). New York: Garland.

Kohnstamm, G. A., Bates, J. E., & Rothbart, M. K. (Eds.). (1989). *Temperament in childhood*. New York: John Wiley & Sons.

Koss-Chioino, J. D., & Vargas, L. A. (1999). *Working with Latino youth: Culture, development, and context*. San Francisco: Jossey-Bass.

Kovacs, M. (1992). *The Children's Depression Inventory*. North Tonawanda, NY: Multi-Health Systems.

Kovacs, M., Akisal, H. S., Gatsonis, C., & Parrone, P. L. (1994a). Childhood-onset Dysthymic Disorder: Clinical features and prospective naturalistic outcome. *Archives of General Psychiatry, 51*, 365–374.

Kovacs, M., Akisal, H. S., Gatsonis, C., & Parrone, P. L. (1994a). Childhood-onset Dysthymic Disorder: Clinical features and prospective naturalistic outcome. *Archives of General Psychiatry, 51*, 365–374.

Kovacs, M., Gatsonis, C., Pollock, M., & Parrone, P. L. (1994b). A controlled prospective study of *DSM-III* Adjustment Disorder in childhood: Short-term prognosis and long-term predictive validity. *Archives of General Psychiatry, 51*, 535–541.

Kovacs, M., Gatsonis, C., Pollock, M., & Parrone, P. L. (1994b). A controlled prospective study of *DSM-III* Adjustment Disorder in childhood: Short-term prognosis and long-term predictive validity. *Archives of General Psychiatry, 51*, 535–541.

Kovacs, M., Goldston, D., & Gatsonis, C. (1993). Suicidal behaviors and childhood-onset Depressive Disorders: A longitudinal investigation. *Journal of the American Academy of Child and Adolescent Psychiatry, 32*, 8–20.

Kovacs, M., Ho, V., & Pollock, M. H. (1995). Criterion and predictive validity of the diagnosis of Adjustment Disorder: A prospective study of youths with new-onset insulin-dependent diabetes mellitus. *American Journal of Psychiatry, 152*, 523–528.

Kowalenko, N., Rapee, R. M., Simmons, J., Wignall, A., Hoge, R., Whitefield, K., et al. (2005). Short-term effectiveness of a school-based early intervention program for adolescent depression. *Clinical Child Psychology & Psychiatry, 10*, 493–507.

Kowatch, R. A., & DelBello, M. P. (2006). Pediatric bipolar disorder: Emerging diagnostic and treatment issues. *Child and Adolescent Psychiatric Clinics of North America, 15*, 73–108.

Kowatch, R. A., Fristad, M., Birmaher, B., Wagner, K. D., Findling, R. L., Hellander, M., et al. (2005). Treatment guidelines for children and adolescents with bipolar disorder: Child psychiatric workgroup on bipolar disorder. *Journal of the American Academy of Child & Adolescent Psychiatry, 44*, 213–235.

Kranzler, E. M. (1988). Adjustment Disorders. In C. J. Kestenbaum & D. T. Williams (Eds.), *Handbook of clinical assessment of children and adolescents.* (pp. 812–828). New York: New York University.

Kroll, L., Harrington, R., Jayson, D., Fraser, J., & Glowers, S. (1996). Pilot study of continuation cognitive-behavioral therapy for major depression in adolescent psychiatric patients. *Journal of the American Academy of Child and Adolescent Psychiatry, 35,* 1156–1161.

Kruczek, T., & Salsman, J. (2006). Prevention and treatment of post-traumatic stress disorder in the school setting. *Psychology and the Schools, 43,* 461–470.

Krupnick, J. L. (1996). The role of therapeutic alliance in psychotherapy and pharmacotherapy outcome: Findings in the National Institute of Mental Health treatment of depression collaborative research program. *Journal of Consulting and Clinical Psychology, 64,* 532–539.

Kryshanovskaya, L., & Canterbury, R. (2001). Suicidal behavior in patients with adjustment disorders. *Crisis, 22,* 125–131.

Kuperminc, G. P., Blatt, S. J., Shahar, G., Henrich, C., & Leadbeater, B. J. (2004). Cultural equivalence and cultural variance in longitudinal associations of young adolescent self-definition and interpersonal relatedness to psychological and school adjustment. *Journal of Youth and Adolescence, 33,* 13–30.

Kushner, M. G., Sher, K. J., & Erickson, D. J. (1999). Prospective analysis of the relation between *DSM-III* Anxiety Disorders and Alcohol Use Disorders. *American Journal of Psychiatry, 156,* 723–732.

Kutcher, S. P., Reiter, S., Gardner, D. M., & Klein, R. G. (1992). The pharmacotherapy of Anxiety Disorders in children and adolescents. *Psychiatric Clinics in North America, 15,* 41–67.

Kutcher, S., Kusumakar, V., LeBlanc, J., Santor, D., Lagace, D., & Morehouse, R. (2004). The characteristics of asymptomatic female adolescents at high risk for depression: The baseline assessment from a prospective 8-year study. *Journal of Affective Disorders, 79,* 177–185.

Labellarte, M. J., Ginsburg, G. S., Walkup, J. T., & Riddle, M. A. (1999). The treatment of Anxiety Disorders in children and adolescents. *Biological Psychiatry, 46,* 1567–1578.

LaFreniere, P. J. (1999). *Emotional development.* New York: Wadsworth.

Lahey, B. B., Hart, E. L., Pliszka, S., Applegate, B., & McBurnett, K. (1993). Neurophysiological correlates of Conduct Disorder: A rationale and review of current research. *Journal of Clinical Child Psychology, 22,* 141–153.

Lahey, B. B., Hartdagen, S. E., Frick, P. J., McBurnett, K., Connor, R., & Hynd, G. W. (1988). Conduct Disorder: Parsing the confounded relationship between parental divorce and antisocial personality. *Journal of Abnormal Psychology, 97,* 334–337.

Lahey, B. B., & Loeber, R. (1994). Framework for a developmental model of Oppositional Defiant Disorder and Conduct Disorder. In D. K. Routh (Ed.), *Disruptive Behavior Disorders in children* (pp. 139–180). New York: Plenum.

Lahey, B. B., Loeber, R., Frick, P. J., & Grimm, J. (1997). In A. Frances, T. Widiger, H. Pincus, R. Ross, M. B. First, & W. Davis (Eds.), *DSM-IV source book* (pp. 189–209). Washington, DC: American Psychiatric Publishing.

Lahey, B. B., Loeber, R., Quay, H. C., Applegate, B., Shaffer, D., Waldman, I., Hart, E., McBurnett, K., Frick, P. J., Jensen, P. S., Dulcan, M. K., Canino, G., & Bird, H. R. (1998). Validity of *DSM-IV* subtypes of Conduct Disorder based on age of onset. *Journal of the American Academy of Child and Adolescent Psychiatry, 37,* 435–442.

Lahey, B. B., Loeber, R., Quay, H. C., Frick, P. J., & Grimm, S. (1992). Oppositional Defiant and Conduct Disorders: Issues to be resolved for *DSM-IV. Journal of the American Academy of Child and Adolescent Psychiatry, 31,* 539–546.

Lahey, B. B., Schwab-Stone, M., Goodman, S. H., Waldman, I. D., Canino, G., Rathouz, P. J., Miller, T. L., Dennis, K. D., Bird, H., & Jensen, P. S. (2000). Age and gender differences in oppositional behavior and conduct problems: A cross-sectional household study of middle childhood and adolescence. *Journal of Abnormal Psychology, 109,* 488–503.

Lahey, B. B., Waldman, I. D., & McBurnett, K. (1999). The development of antisocial behavior: An integrative causal model. *Journal of Child Psychology and Psychiatry, 40,* 669–682.

Lamb, M. E. (Ed.). (1999). *Parenting and child development in "nontraditional" families.* Mahwah, NJ: Lawrence Erlbaum.

Lambert, W., Salzer, M. S., & Bickman, L. (1998). Clinical outcome, consumer satisfaction, and ad hoc ratings of improvement in children's mental health. *Journal of Consulting and Clinical Psychology, 66,* 270–279.

Landon, T. M., & Barlow, D. H. (2004). Cognitive-behavioral treatment for panic disorder: Current status. *Journal of Psychiatric Practice, 10,* 211–226.

Laraia, M. T., Stuart, G. W., & Best, C. L. (1989). Behavioral treatment of Panic-Related Disorders: A review. *Archives of Psychiatric Nursing, III,* 125–133.

Lask, R., & Bryant-Waugh, R. (Eds.). (1993). *Childhood-onset Anorexia Nervosa and related Eating Disorders.* Hillsdale, NJ: Lawrence Erlbaum Associates.

Last, C. G. (Ed.). (1993). *Anxiety across the lifespan: A developmental perspective.* New York: Springer.

Lavenstein, B. (1995). Neurological comorbidity patterns/ differential diagnosis in adult Attention-Deficit Disorder. In K. G. Nadeau (Ed.), *A comprehensive guide to Attention-Deficit Disorder in adults: Research, diagnosis, and treatment* (pp. 74–92). New York: Brunner/Mazel.

Lawless, L. L., Ginter, E. J., & Kelly, K. R. (1999). Managed care: What mental health counselors need to know. *Journal of Mental Health Counseling, 21,* 50–65.

Learner, J. W. (1989). *Learning disabilities: Theories, diagnosis, and teaching strategies* (5th ed.). Boston: Houghton Mifflin.

Learner, J. W. (1993). *Learning disabilities: Theories, diagnosis, and teaching strategies* (6th ed.). Boston: Houghton Mifflin.

Learner, J. W., Lowenthal, B., & Learner, S. R. (1995). *Attention-Deficit Disorders: Assessment and teaching.* Pacific Grove, CA: Brooks Cole.

Lee, C. C. (2001). Culturally responsive school counselors and programs: Addressing the needs of all students. *Professional School Counseling, 4,* 257–261.

Lee, K. (Ed.). (2000). *Childhood cognitive development: The essential readings.* Malden, MA: Blackwell.

Lemerise, E. A., & Arsenio, W. F. (2000). An integrated model of emotional processes and cognition in social information processing. *Child Development, 71,* 107–118.

Leon, G. R., Fulkerson, J. A., Perry, C. L., & Cudeck, R. (1993). Personality and behavioral vulnerabilities associated with risk status for Eating Disorders in adolescent girls. *Journal of Abnormal Psychology, 102*(3), 438–444.

Leshner, A. I. (1999). Science-based views of drug addiction and its treatment. *Journal of the American Medical Association, 282,* 1314–1316.

Levine, M. P., & Smolack, L. (1992). Toward a developmental psychopathology of Eating Disorders: The example of early adolescence. In J. H. Crowther, S. E. Hobfoll, M. A. P. Stephens, & D. L. Tennenbaum (Eds.), *The etiology of Bulimia: The individual and familial context* (pp. 59–80). Washington, DC: Taylor & Francis.

Levine, M. P., Smolack, L., Moodey, A. F., Shuman, M. D., & Hessen, L. D. (1994). Normative developmental challenges and dieting and eating disturbances in middle school girls. *International Journal of Eating Disorders, 15*(1), 11–20.

Lewinsohn, P. M., Gotlib, I. H., & Seeley, J. R. (1995a). Adolescent psychopathology: IV. Specificity of psychosocial risk factors for depression and substance abuse in older adolescents. *Journal of the American Academy of Child and Adolescent Psychiatry, 34,* 1221–1229.

Lewinsohn, P. M., Rohde, P., & Seeley, J. R. (1995). Adolescent psychopathology: III. The clinical consequences of comorbidity. *Journal of the American Academy of Child and Adolescent Psychiatry, 34,* 510–519.

Lewinsohn, P. M., Rohde, P., & Seeley, J. R. (1995b). Adolescent psychopathology: III. The clinical consequences of comorbidity. *Journal of the American Academy of Child and Adolescent Psychiatry, 34,* 510–519.

Lewinsohn, P. M., Rohde, P., & Seeley, J. R. (1996). Alcohol consumption in high school adolescents: Frequency of use and dimensional structure of associated problems. *Addiction, 91,* 375–390.

Lewinsohn, P. M., Rohde, P., & Seeley, J. R. (1998). Major Depressive Disorder in older adolescents: Prevalence, risk factors, and clinical implications. *Clinical Psychology Review, 18,* 765–794.

Lewinsohn, P. M., Rohde, P., Seeley, J. R., & Hops (1991). Comorbidity of Unipolar Depression: I. Major Depression with Dysthymia. *Journal of Abnormal Psychology, 100,* 205–213.

Lewis, F. M. (1996). The impact of breast cancer on the family: Lessons learned from the children and adolescents. In L. Baider, C. L. Cooper, & A. K. De-Nour (Eds.), *Cancer and the family* (pp. 271–287). Chichester, England: John Wiley & Sons.

Lewis, M. (2000). Toward a developmental psychopathology: Models, definitions, and predictions. In A. Sameroff, M. Lewis, & S. Miller (Eds.), *Handbook of developmental psychopathology* (pp. 15–27). New York: Plenum.

Lewisohn, P. M., Rohde, P., & Seeley, J. R. (1993). Prosocial characteristics of adolescents with a history of suicide attempts. *Journal of the American Academy of Child and Adolescent Psychiatry, 32,* 60–68.

Li, C. Y., Copeland, E. P., & Martin, J. D. (1995). Peer relations of children in Taiwan with characteristics of Attention-Deficit/Hyperactivity Disorder. *School Psychology International, 16,* 379–388.

Libby, A. M., Orton, H. D., Stover, S. K., & Riggs, P. D. (2005). What came first, major depression or substance use disorder? Clinical characteristics and substance use comparing teens in a treatment cohort. *Addictive Behaviors, 30,* 1649–1662.

Liberman, A. F., Van Horn, P., & Ippen, C. G. (2005). Toward evidence-based treatment: Child-parent psychotherapy with preschoolers exposed to marital violence. *Journal of the American Academy of Child and Adolescent Psychiatry, 44,* 1241–1248.

Lickey, M. E., & Gordon, B. (1991). *Medicine and mental illness.* New York: Freeman.

Liebowitz, M. R., Fyer, A. J., Gorman, J. M., Dillon, D., Davies, S., Stein, J. M., Cohen, B. S., & Klein, D. F. (1985). Specificity of lactate infusions on social phobia versus Panic Disorders. *American Journal of Psychiatry, 142,* 947–950.

Lifshitz, F., & Moses, N. (1988). Nutritional dwarfing: Growth, dieting, and fear of obesity. *Journal of the American College of Nutrition, 7,* 367–376.

Lipschitz, D. S., Winegar, R. K., Hartnick, E., Foote, B., & Southwick, S. M. (1999). Post-traumatic Stress Disorder in hospitalized adolescents: Psychiatric comorbidity and clinical correlates. *Journal of the American Academy of Child & Adolescent Psychiatry, 38,* 385–392.

Livingston, R. (1999). Cultural issues in diagnosis and treatment of AD/HD. *Journal of the American Academy of Child and Adolescent Psychiatry, 38,* 1591–1594.

Lochman, J. E., Burch, P. R., Curry, J. F., & Lampron, L. B. (1984). Treatment and generalization effects of Cognitive-Behavioral and goal-setting interventions with aggressive boys. *Journal of Consulting and Clinical Psychology, 52,* 915–916.

Lochman, J. E., & Dodge, K. A. (1994). Social-cognitive processes for severely violent, moderately aggressive, and nonaggressive boys. *Journal of Consulting and Clinical Psychology, 62,* 366–374.

Lochman, J. E., & Wells, K. C. (1996). A social-cognitive intervention with aggressive children: Prevention effects and contextual implementation issues. In R. D. Peters & R. J. McMahon (Eds.), *Preventing childhood disorders, substance abuse, and delinquency* (pp. 111–143). Thousand Oaks, CA: Sage.

Lochman, J. E., Barry, T. D., & Pardini, D. A. (2003). Anger control training for aggressive youth. In A. E. Kazdin & J. R. Weisz (Eds.), *Evidence-based psychotherapies for children and adolescents* (pp. 263–281). New York: Guilford Press.

Lochman, J. E., White, K. J., & Wayland, K. K. (1991). Cognitive-behavioral assessment with aggressive children. In P. C. Kendall (Ed.), *Child and adolescent therapy: Cognitive-behavioral procedures* (pp. 25–65). New York: Guilford Press.

Locke, D. C. (1992). *Increasing multicultural understanding.* Newbury Park, CA: Sage.

Lockhart, E., & Keys, S. (1998). The mental health counseling role of the school counselor. *Professional School Counseling, 1,* 3–6.

Loeber, R. (1982). The stability of antisocial and delinquent child behavior: A review. *Child Development, 53,* 1431–1446.

Loeber, R. (1988). Natural histories of conduct problems, delinquency, and associated substance use: Evidence for developmental progressions. In B. B. Lahey & A. E. Kazdin (Eds.), *Advances in clinical child psychology* (pp. 73–124). New York: Plenum.

Loeber, R., Burke, J. D., Lahey, B. B., Winters, A., & Zera, M. (2000). Oppositional Defiant and Conduct Disorder: A review of the past 10 years, part I. *Journal of the American Academy of Child and Adolescent Psychiatry, 39,* 1468–1484.

Loeber, R., Farrington, D. P., Stouthamer-Loeber, M., & Van Kammen, W. B. (1998). Multiple risk factors for multiproblem boys: Co-occurrence of delinquency, substance use, Attention Deficit, conduct problems, physical aggression, covert behavior, depressed mood, and shy/withdrawn behavior. In R. Jessor (Ed.), *New perspectives on adolescent risk behavior* (pp. 90–149). New York: Cambridge University Press.

Loeber, R., Green, S. M., Lahey, B. B., Christ, M. A. G., & Frick, P. J. (1992). Developmental sequences in the age of onset of disruptive child behaviors. *Journal of Child and Family Studies, 1,* 21–41.

Loeber, R., & Keenan, K. (1994). The interaction between Conduct Disorder and its comorbid conditions: Effects of age and gender. *Clinical Psychology Review, 14,* 497–523.

Loeber, R., & Schmaling, K. B. (1985). Empirical evidence for overt and covert patterns of antisocial conduct problems. *Journal of Abnormal Child Psychology, 13,* 337–352.

Loeber, R., & Stouthamer-Loeber, M. (1998). Development of juvenile aggression and violence: Some common misconceptions and controversies. *American Psychologist, 53,* 242–259.

Loeber, R., Stouthamer-Loeber, M., Van Kammen, W. B., & Farrington, D. P. (1989). Development of a new measure of self-reported antisocial behavior for young children: Prevalence and reliability. In M. W. Klein (Ed.), *Cross-national research and self-reported crime and delinquency* (pp. 203–225). Dordrecht, The Netherlands: Kluwer-Nijhoff.

Lonigan, C. J., Elbert, J. C., & Johnson, S. B. (1998). Empirically supported psychosocial interventions for children: An overview. *Journal of Clinical Child Psychology, 27*(2), 138–145.

Lopez, F. G. (1995). Contemporary attachment theory: An introduction with implications for counseling psychology. *The Counseling Psychologist, 23,* 395–415.

Lou, H. C., Henriksen, L., & Bruhn, P. (1984). Focal cerebral hypoperfusion in children with dysphasia and/or Attention-Deficit Disorder. *Archives of Neurology, 41,* 825–829.

Lucas, A., Beard, C., O'Fallon, W., & Kolind, L. (1991). Fifty-year trends in instance of Anorexia Nervosa in Rochester, Minnesota: A population-based study. *American Journal of Psychiatry, 148,* 917–922.

Lucker, J. R., & Molloy, A. T. (1995). Resources for working with children with Attention-Deficit/Hyperactivity Disorder (AD/HD). *Elementary School Guidance & Counseling, 29,* 260–277.

Lufi, D., & Parish-Plass, J. (1995). Personality assessment of children with Attention-Deficit/Hyperactivity Disorder. *Journal of Clinical Psychology, 51,* 94–99.

Lyddon, W. J. (1990). First- and second-order change: Implications for rationalist and constructivist cognitive therapies. *Journal of Counseling and Development, 69,* 122–127.

Lyddon, W. J. (1995). Attachment theory: A metaperspective for counseling psychology? *The Counseling Psychologist, 23,* 479–483.

Lyddon, W. J., & Sherry, A. (2001). Developmental personality styles: An attachment theory conceptualization of Personality Disorders. *Journal of Counseling & Development, 79,* 405–414.

Lydiard, R. B., Roy-Byrne, P. P., & Ballenger, J. C. (1988). Recent advances in the post psychopharmacological treatment of Anxiety Disorders. *Hospital and Community Psychiatry, 39,* 1157–1165.

Lyman, R. D., & Campbell, N. R. (1996). The clients: Admissions and treatment planning. In M. Lingre (Ed.), *Treating children and adolescents in residential and inpatient settings* (pp. 25–44). Thousand Oaks, CA: Sage Publications, Inc.

Lyon, M., Chatoor, I., Atkins, D., Silber, T., Mosimann, J., & Gray, J. (1997). Testing the hypothesis of the multidimensional model of Anorexia in adolescents. *Adolescence, 32*(125), 101–110.

Lyons, J. A. (1987). Post-traumatic Stress disorder in children and adolescents: A review of the literature. *Journal of Developmental and Behavioral Pediatrics, 8,* 349–356.

Lyons, J. S., Uziel-Miller, N. D., Reyes, F., & Sokol, P. T. (2000). Strengths of children and adolescents in residential settings: Prevalence and associations with psychopathology and discharge placement. *Journal of the American Academy of Child and Adolescent Psychiatry, 39,* 176–181.

Lyons-Ruth, K., Zeanah, C. H., & Benoit, D. (1996). Disorder and risk for disorder during infancy and toddlerhood. In E. J. Mash and R. A. Barkley (Eds.), *Child psychopathology* (pp. 457–491). New York: Guilford Press.

Maag, J. W., & Reid, R. (2006). Depression among student with learning disabilities: Assessing the risk. *Journal of Learning Disabilities, 39,* 3–10.

Maag, J. W., & Swearer, S. M. (2005). Cognitive-behavioral interventions for depression: Review and implications for school personnel. *Behavioral Disorders, 30,* 259–276.

Maccoby, E. E. (1992). The role of parents in the socialization of children: A historic overview. *Developmental Psychology, 28,* 1006–1017.

Magnusson, D. (1988). Aggressiveness, hyperactivity, and autonomic activity/reactivity in the development of social maladjustment. In D. Magnusson (Ed.), *Paths through life* (pp. 153–172). Hillsdale, NJ: Erlbaum.

Maguire, L. (1993). Brief social support interventions with adolescents. In R. A. Wells & V. J. Giannetti (Eds.), *Casebook of brief psychotherapies.* (pp. 91–107). New York: Plenum.

Maharaj, S. I., Rodin, G. M., Olmsted, M. P., & Daneman, D. (1998). Eating disturbances, diabetes, and the family: An empirical study. *Journal of Psychosomatic Research, 44*(3/4), 479–490.

Maloney, M. J., McGuire, J., & Daniels, S. R. (1988). Reliability testing of the children's version of the Eating Attitudes Test. *Journal of the American Academy of Child and Adolescent Psychiatry, 5,* 541–543.

Manassis, K., & Monga, S. (2001). A therapeutic approach to children and adolescents with Anxiety Disorders and associated co-morbid conditions. *Journal of the American Academy of Child and Adolescent Psychiatry, 40,* 115–117.

Mann, B. J., Borduin, C. M., Henggeler, S. W., & Blaske, D. M. (1990). An investigation of systemic conceptualizations of parent-child coalitions and symptom change. *Journal of Consulting and Clinical Psychology, 58,* 336–344.

Mannuzza, S., Fyer, A. J., Liebowitz, M. R., & Klein, D. F. (1990). Delineating the boundaries of social phobia: Its relationship to Panic Disorder and Agoraphobia. *Journal of Anxiety Disorders, 4,* 41–59.

Mannuzza, S., Klein, R. G., Bonagura, N., Malloy, P., Giampino, T. L., & Addalli, K. A. (1991). Hyperactive boys almost grown up: V. Replication of psychiatric status. *Archives of General Psychiatry, 48,* 77–83.

March, J., Silva, S., Petrycki, S., Curry, J., Wells, K., Fairbank, J., et al. (2004). Fluoxetine, cognitive-behavioral therapy, and their combination for adolescents with depression: Treatment for Adolescents with Depression Study (TADS) randomized controlled trial. *JAMA: The Journal of the American Medical Association, 292,* 807–820.

Margo, J. L. (1985). Anorexia Nervosa in adolescents. *British Journal of Medical Psychology, 58,* 193–195.

Margo, J. L. (1987). Anorexia Nervosa in males: A comparison with female patients. *British Journal of Psychiatry, 151,* 80–83.

Mariani, M., & Barkley, R. A. (1997). Neuropsychological and academic functioning in preschool children with Attention-Deficit/Hyperactivity Disorder. *Developmental Neuropsychology, 13,* 111–129.

Marlatt, G. A. (1996). Harm reduction: Come as you are. *Addictive Behaviors, 21,* 779–788.

Marlatt, G. A., & Gordon, J. (1985). *Relapse prevention: Maintenance strategies in the treatment of Addictive Disorders.* New York: Guilford Press.

Marsella, A. J., Kinzie, D., & Gorson, P. (1973). Ethnic variation in the expression of depression. *Journal of Cross-Cultural Psychology, 4,* 435–456.

Marshall, M. P., Molina, B. S. G., & Pelham, W. E. (2003). Childhood ADHD and adolescent substance use: An examination of deviant peer group affiliation as a risk factor. *Psychology of Addictive Behaviors, 17,* 293–302.

Martin, C. S., & Winters, K. C. (1998a). Diagnosis and assessment of Alcohol Use Disorders among adolescents. *Alcohol Health & Research World, 22*(2), 95–101, 104–105.

Martin, C. S., & Winters, K. C. (1998b). Diagnostic orphans: Adolescents with alcohol symptoms but without a *DSM-IV* Alcohol Use Disorder. *Alcohol Health & Research World, 22*(2), 100.

Marton, P., Korenblum, M. P., Kutcher, M., Stein, S., Kennedy, B., & Pakes, J. (1989). Personality dysfunction in depressed adolescents. *Canadian Journal of Psychiatry, 34*, 810–813.

Marttunen, M. J., Hillevi, M. A., Henriksson, M. J., & Lonnqvist, J. K. (1994). Adolescent suicides with Adjustment Disorders or no psychiatric diagnosis. *European Child and Adolescent Psychiatry, 3*, 101–110.

Mash, E. J. (1998). Treatment of child and family disturbance: A behavioral-systems perspective. In E. J. Mash & R. A. Barkley (Eds.), *Treatment of childhood disorders* (pp. 3–54). New York: Guilford Press.

Mash, E. J., & Barkley, R. A. (Eds.). (1996). *Child psychopathology.* New York: Guilford Press.

Mash, E. J., & Dozois, D. J. A. (1996). Child psychopathology: A developmental-systems approach. In E. J. Mash & R. A. Barkley (Eds.), *Child psychopathology* (pp. 3–60). New York: Guilford Press.

Mash, E. J., & Terdal, L. G. (Eds.). (1997). *Assessment of childhood disorders.* New York: Guilford Press.

Mash, E. J., & Wolfe, D. A. (2002). *Abnormal child psychology.* Belmont, CA: Wadsworth.

Mâsse, L. C., & Tremblay, R. E. (1997). Behavior of boys in kindergarten and the onset of substance use during adolescence. *Archives of General Psychiatry, 54*, 62–68.

Masi, G., Millepiedi, S., & Mucci, M. (2004). Generalized anxiety disorder in referred children and adolescents. *Journal of the American Academy of Child and Adolescent Psychiatry, 43*, 752–760.

Masi, G., Millepiedi, S., Poli, P., Bertini, N., Milantoni, L. (2004). *Journal of the American Academy of Children and Adolescent Psychiatry, 43*, 752–760.

Mason, W. A., Kosterman, R., Hawkins, J. D., Herronkohl, T. I., Lengua, L. J., & McCauley, E. (2004). Predicting depression, social phobia, and violence in early adulthood from childhood behavior problems. *Journal of the American Academy of Child & Adolescent Psychiatry, 43*, 307–315.

Masten, A. S., & Coatsworth, J. D. (1998). The development of competence in favorable and unfavorable environments: Lessons from research on successful children. *American Psychologist, 53*, 205–220.

Matsumoto, D. (1994). *People: Psychology from a cultural perspective.* Pacific Grove, CA: Brooks/Cole.

Mattick, R. P., Andrews, G., Hadzi-Pavlovic, D., & Christensen, H. (1990). Treatment of panic and agoraphobia. *Journal of Nervous and Mental Disease, 178*, 567–576.

Mattson, M. R. (1992). *Manual of psychiatric quality assurance: A report of the American Psychiatric Association Committee on Quality Assurance.* Washington, DC: American Psychiatric Association.

Mavissakalian, M., Hamann, M. S., & Jones, B. (1990). Correlates of *DSM-III* Personality Disorders in Obsessive-Compulsive Disorder. *Comprehensive Psychiatry, 31*, 481–489.

Mayer, G. R. (1995). Preventing antisocial behavior in the schools. *Journal of Applied Behavioral Analysis, 28*, 467–478.

Mayo-Smith, M. F., Cushman, Jr., P., Hill, A. J., Jara, G., Kasser, C., Kraus, M., Nauts, D., Saitz, R., Smith, J. W., Sullivan, J., & Thiessen, N. (1997). Pharmacological management of alcohol withdrawal: A meta-analysis and evidence-based practice guideline. *Journal of the American Medical Association, 278.*

McAuliffe, G. J., & Eriksen, K. P. (1999). Toward a constructivist and developmental identity for the counseling profession: The context-phase-stage-style model. *Journal of Counseling & Development, 77*, 267–280.

McBurnett, K. (1992). Psychobiological approaches to personality and their application to child psychopathology. In B. B. Lahey & A. E. Kazdin (Eds.), *Advances in child psychology* (pp. 107–164). New York: Plenum.

McBurnett, K., & Lahey, B. B. (1994). Neuropsychological and neuroendocrine correlates of Conduct Disorder and antisocial behavior in children and adolescents. In D. C. Fowles, P. Sutker, & S. H. Goodman (Eds.), *Progress in experimental personality and psychopathology research* (pp. 199–231). New York: Springer.

McCarney, S., & Leigh, J. (1990). *Behavior evaluation scale.* Austin, TX: Pro-Ed.

McCarthy, P. R., & Foa, E. D. (1988). Obsessive Compulsive Disorder. In M. Hersen & C. G. Last (Eds.), *Child behavior therapy casebook* (pp. 55–70). New York: Plenum.

McCartney, S. B. (1989). *Attention-Deficit Disorders evaluation scales.* Columbia, MO: Hawthorne Educational Services.

McCauley, E., & Myers, K. (1992). Family interactions in mood-disordered youth. *Child and Adolescent Psychiatric Clinics of North America, 1*, 111–127.

McCauley, E., Myers, K., Mitchell, J., Calderon, R., Schloredt, K., & Treder, R. (1993). Depression in young people: Initial presentation and clinical course. *Journal of the American Academy of Child and Adolescent Psychiatry, 32*, 714–722.

McClellan, J. (2005, September). Evidence-based therapies in child and adolescent psychiatry. *Psychiatric Times, 22*(10). Retrieved March 15, 2006, from http://www.psychiatrictimes.com/showArticle.jhtml?articleId=171201534.

McClellan, J. M., & Werry, J. S. (2003). Evidence-based treatments in child and adolescent psychiatry: An inventory. *Journal of the American Academy of Child & Adolescent Psychiatry, 42*, 1388–1400.

McClellan, J., & Werry, J. (1994). Practice parameters for the assessment and treatment of children and adolescents with Schizophrenia. *Journal of the American Academy of Child and Adolescent Psychiatry, 33*, 616–635.

McClellan, J., & Werry, J. (1997). AACAP official action: Practice parameters for the assessment and treatment of children and adolescents with Bipolar Disorder. *Journal of the American Academy of Child and Adolescent Psychiatry, 36*, 138–157.

McCormack, N. A. (1985). Cognitive therapy of Post-traumatic Stress Disorder: A case report. *American Mental Health Counselors Association Journal, 7*, 151–155.

McCreary, D. R., Saucier, D. M., & Courtney, W. H. (2005). The drive for muscularity, and masculinity: Testing the associations among general traits, attitudes, and conflict. *Psychology of Men and Masculinity, 6*, 83–94.

McDermott, P. A. (1996). A nationwide study of developmental and gender prevalence for psychopathology in children and adolescence. *Journal of Abnormal Child Psychology, 24*, 53–66.

McDermott, P. A., Marston, N. C., & Stott, D. H. (1993). *Adjustment scales for children and adolescents.* Philadelphia: Edumetric and Clinical Science.

McDermott, P. A., & Weiss, R. V. (1995). A normative typology of healthy, subclinical, and clinical behavior styles among American children and adolescents. *Psychological Assessment, 7*, 162–170.

McGuffin, P., & Katz, R. (1989). The genetics of depression and Manic-Depressive Disorder. *British Journal of Psychiatry, 155*, 294–304.

McMahon, R. J., & Estes, A. M. (1997). Conduct problems. In E. J. Mash & L. G. Terdal (Eds.), *Assessment of childhood disorders* (3rd ed.). New York: Guilford Press.

McMahon, R. J., & Wells, K. C. (1998). Conduct problems. In E. J. Mash & R. A. Barkley (Eds.), *Treatment of childhood disorders* (pp. 111–207). New York: Guilford Press.

McMahon, R. J., Wells, K. C., & Kotler, J. S. (2006). Conduct problems. In E. J. Mash & R. A. Barkley (Eds.), *Treatment of childhood disorders* (pp. 137–268). New York: Guilford Press.

McNally, R. J. (1990). Psychological approaches to Panic Disorder: A review. *Psychological Bulletin, 108,* 403–419.

McNamara, K. (1989). A structured group program for repeat dieters. *Journal for Specialists in Group Work, 14,* 141–150.

Meents, C. K. (1989). Attention-Deficit Disorder: A review of the literature. *Psychology in the Schools, 26,* 168–178.

Meichenbaum, D., & Turk, D. C. (1987). *Facilitating treatment adherence.* New York: Plenum Press.

Meiser-Stedman, R. (2002). Towards a cognitive-behavioral model of PTSD in children and adolescents. *Clinical Child and Family Psychology Review, 5,* 217–232.

Meiser-Stedman, R., Yule, W., Smith, P., Gluckman, E., & Dalgleish, T. (2005). Acute stress disorder and posttraumatic stress disorder in children and adolescents involved in assaults or motor vehicle accidents. *The American Journal of Psychiatry, 162,* 1381–1382.

Melhem, N. M., Day, N., & Shear, M. K. (2004). Traumatic grief among adolescents exposed to a peer's suicide. *American Journal of Psychiatry, 161,* 1411–1416.

Mellin, E. A., & Beamish, P. M. (2002). Interpersonal theory and adolescents with depression: Clinical update. *Journal of Mental Health Counseling, 24,* 110–125.

Mellin, L. M., Irwin, C. E. Jr., & Scully, S. (1992). Disordered eating characteristics in girls: A survey of middle-class children. *Journal of the American Dietetic Association, 92,* 851–853.

Mendlowitz, S. L., Manassis, K., Bradley, S., Scapillato, D., Miezitis, S., & Shaw, B. F. (1999). Cognitive-behavioral group treatments in childhood Anxiety Disorders: The role of parental involvement. *Journal of the American Academy of Child and Adolescent Psychiatry, 38,* 1223–1229.

Merrill, K. W. (1994). *Assessment of behavioral, social, and emotional problems: Direct and objective methods for use with children and adolescents.* New York: Longman.

Messer, S. B. (2004). Evidence-based practice: Beyond empirically supported treatments. *Professional Psychology: Research and Practice, 35,* 580–588.

Meyer, D. F., & Russell, R. K. (1998). Caretaking, separation from parents, and the development of Eating Disorders. *Journal of Counseling and Development, 76*(2), 166–173.

Middleton, F. A., & Strick, P. L. (1994, October 21). Anatomical evidence for cerebellar and basal ganglia involvement in higher cognitive function. *Science, 266,* 458–461.

Miller, G. (1985). *The substance abuse subtle screening inventory—adolescent.* Bloomington, IN: SASSI Institute.

Miller, G. A. (1956). The magical number seven, plus or minus two: Some limits on our capacity for processing information. *The Psychological Review, 63,* 81–97.

Miller, S. A. (1995). Parents' attributions for the children's behavior. *Child Development, 66,* 1557–1584.

Miller, W. R. & Rollnick, S. (1991). *Motivational interviewing: Preparing people to change addictive behavior.* New York: Guilford Press.

Miller, W. R., & Rollnick, S. (1991). *Motivational interviewing: Preparing people for change.* New York: Guilford Press.

Millon, T., Green, C. J., & Meager, R. B. (1982). *Millon multiaxial personality inventory.* Minneapolis, MN: National Computer Systems.

Mineka, S., & Zinbarg, R. (2006). A contemporary learning theory perspective on the etiology of anxiety disorders. *American Psychologist, 61,* 10–26.

Mintz, L. B., & Betz, N. E. (1988). Prevalence and correlates of eating behaviors among college women. *Journal of Counseling Psychology, 35,* 463–471.

Mitchell, J. E., Pyle, R. L., & Eckert, E. D. (1981). Frequency and duration of binge-eating episodes in patients with Bulimia. *American Journal of Psychiatry, 138,* 835–836.

Mizes, J. S. (1995). Eating Disorders. In M. Hersen & R. T. Ammerman (Eds.), *Advanced abnormal child psychology* (pp. 375–391). Hillsdale, NJ: Lawrence Erlbaum Associates.

Moffitt, T. (1993). Adolescence-limited and life-course-persistent antisocial behavior: A developmental taxonomy. *Psychological Review, 100,* 674–701.

Moffitt, T. E. (1990). Juvenile delinquency and Attention-Deficit Disorder: Boys' developmental trajectories from age 3 to age 15. *Child Development, 61,* 893–910.

Moffitt, T. E. (1993). Adolescence-limited and life-course-persistent antisocial behavior: A developmental taxonomy. *Psychological Review, 100,* 674–701.

Moffitt, T. E., Caspi, A., Dickson, N., Silva, P., & Stanton, W. (1996). Childhood-onset versus adolescent-onset antisocial conduct problems in males: Natural history from ages 3 to 18 years. *Development and Psychopathology, 8,* 399–424.

Moreau, D., & Weissman, M. M. (1992). Panic Disorder in children and adolescents: A review. *American Journal of Psychiatry, 149,* 1306–1314.

Moritsugu, J., & Sue, S. (1983). Minority status as a stressor. In R. D. Felner, L. A. Jason, J. N. Moritsugu, & S. S. Farber (Eds.), *Preventive psychology: Theory, research and practice* (pp. 162–174). Elmsford, NY: Pergamon Press.

Morrison, J. R. (1995). *DSM-IV made easy: The clinician's guide to diagnosis.* New York: The Guilford Press.

Morrison, R. G., Morrison, M. A., & Hopkins, C. (2003). Striving for bodily perfection? An exploration of the drive for masculinity in Canada. *Psychology of Men and Masculinity, 4,* 111–120.

Mucher, J. (1996). MFT and schools: A perfect combination. *Family Therapy News, 27,* 12–25.

Muck, R., Zempolich, K. A., Titus, J. C., Fishman, M., Godley, M. D., & Schwebel, R. (2001). An overview of the effectiveness of adolescent substance abuse treatment models. *Youth & Society, 33,* 143–168.

Mufson, L., Gallagher, T., Pollack Dorta, K., & Young, J. F. (2004). A group adaptation of interpersonal psychotherapy for depressed adolescents. *American Journal of Psychotherapy, 58,* 220–237.

Mufson, L., Pollack Dorta, K., Wickramaratne, P., Nomura, Y., Olfson, M., & Weissman, M. M. (2004). A randomized effectiveness trial of interpersonal psychotherapy for depressed adolescents. *The Archives of General Psychiatry, 61,* 577–584.

Multi-Health Systems. (1992). *Conners' continuous performance test.* North Tonawanda, NY: Author.

Mumma, G. H. (1998). Improving cognitive case formulations and treatment planning in clinical practice and research. *Journal of Cognitive Psychotherapy: An International Quarterly, 12,* 251–274.

Munoz, R. F., Mrazek, P. J., & Haggerty, R. J. (1996). Institute of medicine report on prevention of mental disorders: Summary and commentary. *American Psychologist, 51,* 1116–1122.

Muris, P. (2003). Information processing abnormalities in childhood anxiety. *Behaviour Change, 20,* 129–130.

Muris, P., Merckelbach, H., Gadet, B., Moulaert, V., & Tierney, S. (1999). Sensitivity for treatment effects of the screen for child Anxiety Related Emotional Disorders. *Journal of Psychopathology and Behavioral Assessment, 21,* 323–335.

Muro, J. J., & Kottman, T. (1995). *Guidance and counseling in the elementary and middle schools: A practical approach.* Madison, WI: Brown & Benchmark.

Murphy, K. (2004). Recognizing depression. *The Nurse Practitioner, 29,* 18–29.

Murphy, K. (2005). What can you do to prevent teen suicide? *Nursing, 35,* 43–45.

Murphy, K. R. (1998). Psychological counseling of adults with AD/HD. In R. A. Barkley (Ed.), *Attention-Deficit/Hyperactivity Disorder: A handbook for diagnosis and treatment* (pp. 582–591). New York: Guilford Press.

Myers, J. E. (1992). Wellness, prevention, development: The cornerstone of the profession. *Journal of Counseling & Development, 71,* 136–139.

Myers, M. G., Aarons, G. A., Tomlinson, K., & Stein, M. B. (2003). Social anxiety, negative affectivity, and substance use among high school students. *Psychology of Addictive Behaviors, 17,* 277–283.

Nadeau, K. G. (1991). *Adult AD/HD questionnaire.* Annandale, VA: Chesapeake Psychological Services.

Nadeau, K. G. (1995). Life management skills for the adult with ADD. In K. G. Nadeau (Ed.), *A comprehensive guide to Attention-Deficit Disorder in adults: Research, diagnosis, and treatment* (pp. 191–217). New York: Brunner/Mazel.

Nathenson, P., & Johnson, C. (1992). The psychiatric treatment plan. *Perspectives in Psychiatric Care, 28,* 32–35.

National Institute of Mental Health. (2005). Antidepressant medications for children and adolescents: Information for parents and caregivers. Retrieved February 12, 2006, from http://www.nimh.nih.gov/healthinformation/antidepressant_child.cfm.

National Institute on Alcohol Abuse and Alcoholism. (2004/2005a). Developmental issues in underage drinking research. *Alcohol Health & Research World, 28*(3), 121–123.

National Institute on Alcohol Abuse and Alcoholism. (2004/2005b). Interventions for alcohol use and alcohol use disorders in youth. *Alcohol Health & Research World, 28*(3), 161–174.

National Institute on Drug Abuse. (1999). *Principles of drug addiction treatment: A research-based guide* (NIH Publication No. 99–4180). Washington, DC: Author.

National Institutes of Health. (1991). Treatment of Panic Disorder. *NIH Consensus Statement, 9,* 3–24.

Neale, E. L. (1994). The children's diagnostic drawing series. *Art Therapy: Journal of the American Art Therapy Association, 11,* 119–126.

Neville, H. A., & Mobley, M. (2001). Social identities contexts: An ecological model of multicultural counseling processes. *Counseling Psychologist, 29,* 471–486.

New treatment guidelines available for children and adolescents with bipolar disorder. (2005, March). *Brown University Child & Adolescent Psychopharmacology, 7* (3), 2–4.

Newcombe, N. (1996). *Child development: Change over time* (8th ed.). New York: HarperCollins.

Newcomer, P. L. (2000). *Understanding and teaching emotionally disturbed children and adolescents* (3rd ed.). Austin, TX: Pro-Ed.

Newcorn, J. H., & Strain, J. (1992). Adjustment Disorder in children and adolescents. *Journal of the American Academy of Child and Adolescent Psychiatry, 31,* 318–326.

Nguyen, L., & Peterson, C. (1993). Depressive symptoms among Vietnamese-American college students. *The Journal of Social Psychology, 133,* 65–72.

Nicholson, J., & Clayfield, J. C. (2004). Responding to depression in parents. *Pediatric Nursing, 30,* 136–142.

Nilssen, O., & Cone, H. (1994). Screening patients for alcohol problems in primary care settings. *Alcohol Health & Research World, 18*(2), 136–139.

Nilsson, M., Joliat, M. J., Miner, C. M., Brown, E. B., & Heiligenstein, J. H. (2004). Safety of subchronic treatment with fluoxetine for major depressive disorder in children and adolescents. *Journal of Child and Adolescent Psychopharmacology, 14,* 412–417.

Noam, G. G., Chandler, M., & LaLonde, C. (1995). Clinical-developmental psychology: Constructivism and social cognition in the study of psychological dysfunctions. In D. Cicchetti & D. J. Cohen (Eds.), *Developmental psychopathology: Vol. 1. Theory and methods* (pp. 424–443). New York: John Wiley & Sons.

Nobile, M., Cataldo, G. M., Marino, C., & Molteni, M. (2003). Diagnosis and treatment of dysthymia in children and adolescents. *CNS Drugs, 17,* 927–946.

Norcross, J. C., & Newman, C. R. (1992). Psychotherapy integration: Setting the context. In J. C. Norcross & M. R. Goldfried (Eds.), *Handbook of psychotherapy integration* (pp. 3–45). New York: Basic Books.

Norris, F. H. (1992). Epidemiology of trauma: Frequency and impact of different potentially traumatic events on different demographic groups. *Journal of Consulting and Clinical Psychology, 60*(3), 409–418.

Nottelman, E. D., & Jensen, P. S. (1995). Comorbidity of disorders in children and adolescents: Developmental perspectives. In T. H. Ollendick & R. J. Prinz (Eds.), *Advances in clinical child psychology* (pp. 109–155). New York: Plenum.

O'Brien, B. S., & Frick, P. J. (1996). Reward dominance: Associations with anxiety, conduct problems, and psychopathology in children. *Journal of Abnormal Child Psychology, 24,* 223–335.

O'Brien, J. D. (1992). Children with Attention-Deficit/ Hyperactivity Disorder and their parents. In J. D. O'Brien, D. J. Pilowsky, & O. W. Lewis (Eds.), *Psychotherapies with children and adolescents: Adapting the psychodynamic process* (pp. 109–124).

Ohannessian, C. M., & Hesselbrock, V. M. (1993). The influence of perceived social support on the relationship between family history of alcoholism and drinking behaviors. *Addiction, 88,* 1651–1658.

Olivardia, R., Pope, H. G., Borwiecki, J. J., & Cohane, G. H. (2004). Biceps and body image: The relationship between masculinity and self-esteem and eating disorders symptoms. *Psychology of Men and Masculinity, 5,* 112–120.

Ollendick, T. H. (1978). *The fear survey schedule for children—Revised.* Unpublished manuscript, Indiana State University, Terre Haute, Indiana.

Ollendick, T. H. (1983). Reliability and validity of the revised fear survey schedule for children (FSSC-R). *Behavior Research and Therapy, 21,* 685–692.

Ollendick, T. H., & Francis, G. (1988). Behavioral assessment and treatment of childhood phobias. *Behavior Modification, 12,* 165–204.

Ollendick, T. H., & King, N. J. (1994). Diagnosis, assessment, and treatment of internalizing problems: The role of longitudinal data. *Journal of Consulting and Clinical Psychology, 62,* 918–927.

Ollendick, T. H., & King, N. J. (1998). Empirically supported treatments for children with Phobic and Anxiety Disorders:

Current status. *Journal of Clinical Child Psychology, 27*(2), 156–167.

O'Malley, P. M., Johnston, L. D., & Bachman, J. G. (1999). Epidemiology of substance abuse in adolescence. In P. J. Ott & R. E. Tarter (Eds.), *Sourcebook on substance abuse: Etiology, epidemiology, assessment, and treatment* (pp. 14–31). Boston: Allyn & Bacon.

Orwin, A. (1973). "The running treatment": A preliminary communication on a new use for an old therapy (physical activity in the agoraphobic syndrome). *British Journal of Psychiatry, 122,* 175–179.

Osborne, J. L., & Collison, B. B. (1998). School counselors and external providers: Conflict or complement? *Professional School Counseling, 1,* 7–11.

Osborne, W. L., Brown, S., Niles, S., & Miner, C. U. (1997). *Career development, assessment, and counseling: Applications of Donald E. Super C-DAC Approach.* Alexandria, VA: American Counseling Association.

Overstreet, S., Nelson, C. C., & Holden, E. W. (1999). Adjustment Disorders in children and adolescents. In S. D. Netherton, D. Holmes, & C. E. Walker (Eds.), *Child and Adolescent Psychological Disorders: A comprehensive textbook* (pp. 464–476). New York: Oxford University.

Paisley, P. O., & Hubbard, G. T. (1994). *Developmental school counseling programs: From theory to practice.* Alexandria, VA: American Counseling Association.

Paniagua, F. A. (1998). *Assessing and treating culturally diverse clients: A practical guide.* Thousand Oaks, CA: Sage Publication.

Paradise, L. V., & Kirby, P. C. (2005). The treatment and prevention of depression: Implications for counseling and counselor training. *Journal of Counseling & Development, 83,* 116–119.

Patel, N. C., Delbello, M. P., Bryan, H. S., Adler, C. M., Kowatch, R. A., Stanford, K., et al. (2006). Open-label lithium for the treatment of adolescents with bipolar depression. *Journal of the American Academy of Child & Adolescent Psychiatry, 45,* 289–297.

Paternite, C. E., Loney, J., & Roberts, M. A. (1995). External validity of Oppositional Defiant Disorder and Attention-Deficit Disorder with hyperactivity. *Journal of Abnormal Child Psychology, 23,* 453–469.

Patterson, G. R., DeGarmo, D. S., & Knutson, N. (2000). Hyperactive and antisocial behaviors: Comorbid or two points in the same process. *Development and Psychopathology, 12,* 91–106.

Patterson, G. R., Reid, J. B., & Dishion, T. J. (1992). *Antisocial boys.* Eugene, OR: Castalia Press.

Patton, G. C. (1988). The spectrum of Eating Disorders in adolescence. *Journal of Psychosomatic Research, 32,* 579–584.

Pauls, D. L., Leckman, J. F., & Cohen, D. J. (1993). Familial relationship between Guilles de la Tourette's Syndrome, Attention-Deficit Disorder, learning disabilities, speech disorders, and stuttering. *Journal of the American Academy of Child and Adolescent Psychiatry, 32,* 1044–1050.

Pedersen, P. (1994). *A handbook for developing multicultural awareness* (2nd ed.). Alexandria, VA: American Counseling Association.

Pelham, W. E., Wheeler, T., & Chronis, A. (1998). Empirically supported psychosocial treatments for Attention-Deficit Hyperactivity Disorder. *Journal of Clinical Child Psychology, 27*(2), 190–205.

Pelkonen, M., Marttunen, M., Henriksson, M., & Lonnqvist, J. (2005). Suicidality in adjustment disorder: Clinical characteristics of adolescent outpatients. *European Child & Adolescent Psychiatry, 14,* 174–180.

Peterson, A. C., Compas, B. E., Brooks-Gunn, J., Stemmler, J., Ey, S., & Grant, K. E. (1993). Depression in adolescence. *American Psychology, 48,* 155–168.

Petti, T. (n.d.). *Teacher Affect Rating Scale (TARS).* Indiana University School of Medicine, Indianapolis, IN.

Pfeifer, S. I., & Strzelecki, S. C. (1990). Inpatient treatment of children and adolescents: A review of outcome studies. *American Academy of Child and Adolescent Psychiatry, 29,* 286–293.

Pfiffner, L. J., & Barkley, R. A. (1998). Treatment of AD/HD in school settings. In R. A. Barkley (Ed.), *Attention-Deficit/Hyperactivity Disorder: A handbook for diagnosis and treatment* (pp. 458–490). New York: Guilford Press.

Pfiffner, L. J., & McBurnett, K. (1997). Social skills training with parent generalization: Treatment effects for children with ADD. *Journal of Consulting and Clinical Psychology, 65,* 749–757.

Phillips, J. H., Corcoran, J., & Grossman, C. (2003). Implementing a cognitive-behavioral curriculum for adolescents with depression in the school setting. *Children & Schools, 25,* 147–158.

Piacentini, J., & Langley, A. K. (2004). Cognitive-behavioral therapy for children who have obsessive-compulsive disorder. *Journal of Clinical Psychology, 60,* 1181–1194.

Piaget, J. (2000). Piaget's theory. In K. Lee (Ed.), *Childhood cognitive development: The essential readings* (pp. 33–47). Malden, MA: Blackwell. (Reprinted from *Carmichael's manual of child psychology* [3rd ed.] by P. H. Mussen, Ed., 1970, New York: John Wiley & Sons).

Piazza, N. J. (1996). Dual diagnosis and adolescent psychiatric inpatients. *Substance Use & Misuse, 31,* 215–223.

Piazza, N. J., & Ivoska, W. (1998). ADAS Student Survey for Toledo, Lucas County, and Northwest Ohio. Toledo, OH: Alcohol and Drug Addiction Services Board.

Piazza, N. J., & Ivoska, W. (2000). ADAS Student Survey for Toledo, Lucas County, and Northwest Ohio. Toledo, OH: Alcohol and Drug Addiction Services Board.

Piazza, N. J., & Ivoska, W. (2002). ADAS Student Survey for Toledo, Lucas County, and Northwest Ohio. Toledo, OH: Alcohol and Drug Addiction Services Board.

Piazza, N. J., & Ivoska, W. (2004). *ADAS Student Survey for Toledo, Lucas County, and Northwest Ohio.* Toledo, OH: Alcohol and Drug Addiction Services Board.

Piazza, N. J., & Ivoska, W. (2006). *ADAS Student Survey for Toledo, Lucas County, and Northwest Ohio.* Toledo, OH: Alcohol and Drug Addiction Services Board.

Piazza, N. J., Martin, N., & Dildine, R. J. (manuscript in submission). Screening instruments for alcohol and other drug problems.

Pike, A., & Plomin, R. (1996). Importance of nonshared environmental factors for childhood and adolescent psychopathology. *Journal of the American Academy of Child and Adolescent Psychiatry, 35,* 560–570.

Pinsof, W. M., & Wynne, L. C. (1995). The efficacy of marital and family therapy: An empirical overview, conclusions, and recommendations. *Journal of Marital and Family Therapy, 21,* 585–613.

Pisterman, S., McGrath, P., Firestone, P., & Goodman, J. T. (1989). Outcome of parent-mediated treatment of preschoolers with Attention-Deficit Disorder with Hyperactivity Disorder. *Journal of Consulting and Clinical Psychology, 57,* 636–643.

Plessen, K. J., Bansal, R., Zhu, H., Whiteman, R., Amat, J., Quackenbush, G. A., Martin, L., Durkin, K., Blair, C., Royal, J., Hugdahl, K., & Peterson. B. S. (2006). Hippocampus and amygdala morphology in attention-deficit/hyperactivity disorder. *Archives of General Psychiatry, 63,* 795–807.

Pliszka, S. R., Carlson, C. L., & Swanson, J. M. (1999). *ADHD with Comorbid Disorders: Clinical assessment and management.* New York: Guilford Press.

Pliszka, S. R., & Olvera, R. L. (1999). Anxiety Disorders. In S. Goldstein & C. R. Reynolds (Eds.), *Handbook of Neurodevelopmental and Genetic Disorders in children* (pp. 216–246). New York: Guilford Press.

Plomin, R., & DeFries, J. C. (1998). The genetics of abilities and disabilities. *Scientific American, 278,* 40–48.

Plomin, R., & Dunn, J. (Eds.) (1986). *The study of temperament: Changes, continuities and challenges.* Hillsdale, NJ: Lawrence Erlbaum.

Plomin, R., DeFries, J. C., & McClearn, G. E. (1990). *Behavioral genetics: A primer* (2nd ed.). San Francisco: W. H. Freeman.

Plomin, R., Owen, M. J., & McGuffin, P. (1994). The genetic basis of complex human behaviors. *Science, 264,* 1733–1739.

Polanski, P. J. (1998). Alternative pathways among dropouts: An ecodevelopmental model of educational persistence (Doctoral dissertation, The University of North Carolina at Greensboro, 1998). *Dissertation Abstracts International,* A60/02, p. 384, Aug 1999.

Pollock, N. K., & Martin, C. S. (1999). Diagnostic orphans: Adolescents with alcohol symptoms who do not qualify for *DSM-IV* abuse or dependence diagnoses. *American Journal of Psychiatry, 156,* 897–901.

Pope-Davis, D. B., Toporek, R. L., Ortega-Villabos, L., Ligiero, D. P., Brittan-Powell, C. S., Liu, W. M., Bashshur, M. R., Codrington, J. N., & Liang, C. T. H. (2002). Client perspectives of multicultural competence: A qualitative examination. *The Counseling Psychologist, 30,* 355–393.

Popper, C. W. (1988). Disorders usually first evident in infancy, childhood, or adolescence. In J. A. Talbott, R. E. Hales, & S. C. Yudofsky (Eds.), *Textbook of psychiatry* (pp. 649–735). Washington, DC: American Psychiatric Press.

Popper, C. W., & Steingard, R. J. (1994). Disorders usually first diagnosed in infancy, childhood, or adolescence. In R. E. Hales, S. C. Yudofsky, & J. A. Talbott (Eds.), *The American psychiatric press textbook of psychiatry,* (pp. 729–832). Washington, DC: American Psychiatric Press.

Portzky, G., Audenaert, K., & van Heeringen, K. (2005). Adjustment disorder and the course of the suicidal process in adolescents. *Journal of Affective Disorders, 87,* 265–270.

Powers, S. W., & Roberts, M. W. (1995). Simulation training with parents of oppositional children: Preliminary findings. *Journal of Clinical Child Psychology, 24,* 89–97.

Practice parameters for the assessment and treatment of children and adolescents with Depressive Disorders. *Journal of the American Academy of Child and Adolescent Psychiatry, 37,* 63S–83S.

Prior, M. (1992). Childhood temperament. *Journal of Child Psychology and Psychiatry, 33,* 249–279.

Prochaska, J. O., & Norcross, J. C. (2003). *Systems of psychotherapy: A transtheoretical analysis* (5th ed.). Pacific Grove, CA: Brooks/Cole.

Prochaska, J. O., DiClemente, C. C., & Norcross, J. C. (1992). In search of how people change: Applications to addictive behaviors. *American Psychologist, 47,* 1102–1114.

Prout, H. T. (1999). Counseling and psychotherapy with children and adolescents: An overview. In H. T. Prout & D. T. Brown (Eds.), *Counseling and psychotherapy with children and adolescents: Theory and practice for school and clinical settings* (3rd ed., pp. 1–25). New York: John Wiley & Sons.

Puig-Antich, J., & Chambers, W. (1978). *The schedule for Affective Disorders and Schizophrenia for school-age children.* New York: New York State Psychiatric Association.

Puig-Antich, J., Goetz, D., Davies, M., Kaplan, T., Davies, S., Ostrow, L., Asnis, L., Toomey, J., Iyengar, S., & Ryan, N. (1989). A controlled family history of prepubertal Major Depressive Disorder. *Archives of General Psychiatry, 46,* 406–418.

Puig-Antich, J., Lukens, E., Davies, M., Goetz, D., Brennan-Quattrock, J., & Todak, G. (1985a). Psychosocial functioning in prepubertal Depressive Disorders. I: Interpersonal relationships during the depressive episode. *Archives of General Psychiatry, 42,* 500–507.

Puig-Antich, J., Lukens, E., Davies, M., Goetz, D., Brennan-Quattrock, J., & Todak, G. (1985b). Psychosocial functioning in prepubertal Depressive Disorders. II: Interpersonal relationships after sustained recovery from affective episode. *Archives of General Psychiatry, 42,* 511–517.

Puig-Antich, J., & Weston, B. (1983). The diagnosis and treatment of Major Depressive Disorder in childhood. *Annual Review of Medicine, 34,* 231–245.

Pulkkinen, L., & Pitkänen, T. A. (1994). Prospective study of the precursors to problem drinking in young adulthood. *Journal of Studies on Alcohol, 55,* 578–587.

Quay, H. C. (1986a). Classification. In H. C. Quay & J. S. Werry (Eds.), *Psychopathological Disorders of childhood* (3rd ed., pp. 1–34). New York: John Wiley & Sons.

Quay, H. C. (1986b). Conduct Disorders. In H. C. Quay & J. S. Werry (Eds.), *Psychopathological Disorders of childhood* (3rd ed., pp. 35–72). New York: John Wiley & Sons.

Quay, H. C. (1993). The psychobiology of undersocialized aggressive Conduct Disorder: A theoretical perspective. *Development and Psychopathology, 5,* 165–180.

Quay, H. C., & Peterson, D. R. (1987). *Manual for the revised behavioral problem checklist.* Coral Gables, FL: Author.

Quinn, P. O. (1997). *Attention-Deficit Disorder: Diagnosis and treatment from infancy to adulthood.* New York: Brunner/Mazel.

Rabheru, K. (2001). The use of electroconvulsive therapy in special patient populations. *Canadian Journal of Psychiatry, 46,* 710–719.

Rachman, S. J. (1985). An overview of clinical and research issues in Obsessive-Compulsive Disorders. In M. Mavissakalian, S. M. Turner, & L. Michelson (Eds.), *Obsessive-Compulsive Disorders: Psychological and pharmacological treatment* (pp. 1–47). New York: Plenum.

Rak, C. F., & Patterson, L. E. (1996). Promoting resilience in at-risk children. *Journal of Counseling & Development, 74,* 368–373.

Ramacciotti, C. E., Paoli, R. A., Marcacci, G., Piccinni, A., Burgalassi, A., Dell'Osso, L., et al. (2005). Relationship between bipolar illness and binge-eating disorders. *Psychiatry Research, 135,* 165–170.

Rao, U., Ryan, N. D., Birmaher, B., Dahl, R. E., Williamson, D. E., Kaufman, J., Rao, R., & Nelson, B. (1995). Unipolar Depression in adolescents: Clinical outcome in adulthood. *Journal of the American Academy of Child and Adolescent Psychiatry, 34,* 556–578.

Rapoport, J. (Ed.). (1989). *Obsessive-Compulsive Disorder in children and adolescents.* Washington, DC: American Psychiatric Association.

Rapoport, J. L. (1996, Winter). Questions and answers: An interview with Judith Rapoport, M.D. *Attention! The Magazine of Children and Adults With Attention Deficit Disorder,* 7–10.

Rapoport, J. L. (2000). Introduction. In J. L. Rapoport (Ed.), *Childhood-onset of adult psychopathology: Clinical and research advances* (pp. xiii–xviii). Washington, DC: American Psychiatric Press.

Rapoport, J. L., & Ismond, D. R. (1990). DSM-III-R *training guide for diagnosis of childhood disorders.* New York: Brunner/Mazel.

Raz, A. (2006). Perspectives on the efficacy of antidepressants for child and adolescent depression. *PLoS Medicine, 3,* 35–41.

Reed, L. J., Carter, B. D., & Miller, L. C. (1992). Fear and anxiety in children. In C. E. Walker and M. C. Roberts (Eds.), *Handbook of clinical child psychology* (2nd ed., pp. 237–260). New York: John Wiley & Sons.

Reeves, J. C., Werry, J. S., Elkind, G. S., & Zametkin, A. (1987). Attention-Deficit, Conduct, Oppositional, and Anxiety Disorders in children: II. Clinical characteristics. *Journal of the American Academy of Child and Adolescent Psychiatry, 26,* 144–155.

Reich, J. (1988). *DSM-III* Personality Disorders and the outcome of treated Panic Disorder. *American Journal of Psychiatry, 145,* 1149–1152.

Reich, W., & Welner, Z. (1989). *Diagnostic interview for children and adolescents—Revised.* St. Louis, MO: Washington University, Division of Child Psychiatry.

Reid, R., DuPaul, G. J., & Power, T. J. (1998). Assessing culturally different students for Attention-Deficit/ Hyperactivity Disorder using behavioral rating scales. *Journal of Abnormal Child Psychology, 26,* 187–189.

Reif, S. F. (1993). *How to reach and teach ADD/ADHD children.* West Nyack, NY: Center for Applied Research in Education.

Reinecke, M. A. (1995). Comorbidity of Conduct Disorder and depression among adolescents: Implications for assessment and treatment. *Cognitive and Behavioral Practice, 2,* 299–326.

Reinecke, M. A., Ryan, N. E., & Dubois, D. (1998). Cognitive-Behavioral Therapy of depression and depressive symptoms during adolescence: A review and meta-analysis. *Journal of the American Academy of Child and Adolescent Psychiatry, 37,* 26–34.

Reinherz, H. Z., Paradis, A D., Giaconia, R M., Stashwick, C. K., & Fitzmaurice, G. (2003). Childhood and adolescent predictors of major depression in the transition to adulthood. *The American Journal of Psychiatry, 160,* 2141–2147.

Reiss, D., & Neiderhiser, J. M. (2000). The interplay of genetic influences and social processes in developmental theory: Specific mechanisms are coming into view. *Development and Psychopathology, 12,* 357–374.

Reiss, S., & McNally, R. J. (1985). Expectancy model of fear. In S. Reiss & R. R. Bootzin (Eds.), *Theoretical issues in behavior therapy* (pp. 107–121). San Diego, CA: Academic Press.

Resnick, R. J. (2000). *The hidden disorder: A clinician's guide to Attention-Deficit/Hyperactivity Disorder in adults.* Washington, DC: American Psychological Association.

Reynolds, C. R., & Kamphaus, R. W. (1992). *Behavior assessment system for children (BASC).* Circle Pines, MN: American Guidance Services.

Reynolds, C. R., & Richmond, B. O. (1978). "What I think and feel": A revised measure of children's manifest anxiety. *Journal of Abnormal Child Psychology, 6,* 271–280.

Reynolds, W. M. (1994). Assessment of depression in children and adolescents by self-report questionnaires. In W. M. Reynolds & H. E. Johnston (Eds.), *Handbook of depression in children and adolescents* (pp. 209–234). New York: Plenum Press.

Rhode, G., Jenson, W. R., & Reavis, H. K. (1992). *The tough kid book: Practical classroom management strategies.* Longmont, CO: Sopris West.

Ricciardelli, L. A., & McCabe, M. P. (2004). Biopsychosocial model of disordered eating and the pursuit of masculinity in boys. *Psychological Bulletin, 130,* 179–205.

Riccio, C. A., Hynd, G. W., Cohen, M. J., & Gonzalez, J. J. (1993). Neurological basis of Attention-Deficit/Hyperactivity Disorder. *Exceptional Children, 60,* 118–124.

Rice, K. G., & Leffert, N. (1997). Depression in adolescence: Implications for school counsellors. *Canadian Journal of Counseling, 31,* 18–34.

Ridgeway, R. T., & Tylka, T. L. (2005). College men's perceptions of ideal body composition and shape. *Psychology of Men and Masculinity. 6,* 209–220.

Ridley, M. (1999). *Genome: The autobiography of a species in 23 chapters.* New York: HarperCollins.

Riggs, P. D., Baker, S., Mikulich, S., Young, S., & Crowley, T. (1995). Depression in substance-dependent delinquents. *Journal of the American Academy of Child and Adolescent Psychiatry, 34,* 764–771.

Ringwalt, C. L., Ennett, S., Vincus, A., Thorne, J., Rorbach, L.A., & Simons-Rudolph, A. (2002). The prevalence of effective substance use prevention curricula in U.S. middle schools. *Prevention Science, 3*(4), 257–265.

Rintala, M., & Mustajoki, P. (1992). Could mannequins menstruate? *British Medical Journal, 305,* 1575–1576.

Riverside Publishing Company. (1989). *Woodcock-Johnson psychoeducational battery—Revised.* Chicago: Author.

Roberts, M. A. (1990). A behavioral observation method for differentiating hyperactive and aggressive boys. *Journal of Abnormal Child Psychology, 18,* 131–142.

Roberts, R. E., Roberts, C. R. , & Chen, Y. R. (1998). Suicidal thinking among adolescents with a history of attempted suicide. *Journal of the American Academy of Child and Adolescent Psychiatry, 37,* 1294–1300.

Robin, A. L. (1998). Training families with AD/HD adolescents. In R. A. Barkley (Ed.), *Attention-Deficit/Hyperactivity Disorder: A handbook for diagnosis and treatment* (pp. 413–457). New York: Guilford Press.

Robins, L. N. (1986). The consequences of Conduct Disorder in girls. In D. Olweus, J. Block, & M. Radke-Yarrow (Eds.), *Development of antisocial and prosocial behavior: Research, theories, and issues* (pp. 385–414). New York: Academic Press.

Robins, L. N. (1991). Conduct Disorder. *Journal of Child Psychology and Psychiatry, 32,* 193–212.

Robins, L. N., Helzer, J. E., Weissman, M. M., Orvaschel, H., Gruenberg, E., Burke, J. D., Jr., & Regier, D. A. (1984). Lifetime prevalence of specific psychiatric disorders in three sites. *Archives of General Psychiatry, 41,* 949–958.

Robins, L. N., Locke, B. Z., & Regier, D. A. (1991). An overview of Psychiatric Disorders in America. In L. N. Robins & D. A. Regier (Eds.), *Psychiatric Disorders in America: The epidemiological catchment area study* (pp. 328–366). New York: Free Press.

Rodin, J., Silberstein, L. R., & Striegel-Moore, R. H. (1985). Women and weight: A normative discontent. In T. B. Sonderegger (Ed.), *Nebraska symposium on motivation: Psychology and Gender, 32* (267–307). Lincoln: University of Nebraska Press.

Rohde, L. A., Biederman, J., Busnello, E. A., Zimmerman, H., Schmitz, M., Martins, S., & Tramontina, S. (1999). AD/HD in a school sample of Brazilian adolescents: A study of prevalence, comorbid conditions, and impairments. *Journal of the American Academy of Child and Adolescent Psychiatry, 38,* 716–722.

Rohde, P., Lewinsohn, P. M., & Seeley, J. R. (1996). Psychiatric comorbidity and problematic alcohol use in high school students. *Journal of the American Academy of Child and Adolescent Psychiatry, 35,* 101–109.

Romano, J. L., & Hage, S. M. (2000). Prevention and counseling psychology: Revitalizing commitments for the 21st century. *Counseling Psychologist, 28,* 733–763.

Root, R. W. & Resnick, R. J. (2003). An update on the diagnosis and treatment of Attention-Deficit/Hyperactivity Disorder. *Professional Psychology: Research and Practice, 34,* 34–41.

Rose, R. J. (1998). A developmental behavior–genetic perspective on alcoholism risk. *Alcohol Health & Research World, 22*(2), 131–143.

Rosenheck, R., & Nathan, P. (1985). Secondary traumatization in children of Vietnam veterans. *Hospital and Community Psychiatry, 36,* 538–539.

Roth, A., & Fonagy, P. (2005). *What works for whom? A critical review of psychotherapy research.* (2nd. ed.). New York: Guilford Press.

Rothbart, M. K., & Bates, J. E. (1998). Temperament. In W. Damon (Series Ed.) & N. Eisenberg (Vol. Ed.), *Handbook of child psychology: Vol. 3. Social, emotional, and personality development* (pp. 105–176). New York: John Wiley & Sons.

Rothbart, M. K., & Mauro, J. A. (1990). Questionnaire measures of infant temperament. In W. J. Fagen & J. Columbo (Eds.), *Individual differences in infancy: Reliability, stability, and prediction* (pp. 411–429). Hillsdale, NJ: Erlbaum.

Routh, D. K., & Schroeder, C. S. (1976). Standardized playroom measures of indices of hyperactivity. *Journal of Abnormal Child Psychology, 4,* 199–207.

Roy-Byrne, P. P., Craske, M. G., & Stein, M. B. (2004). Panic disorder. *The Lancet, 368,* 1023–1032.

Rubin, K. H., Coplan, R. J., Fox, N. A., & Caulkins, S. D. (1995). Emotionality, emotional regulation, and preschoolers' social adaptation. *Development and Psychopathology, 7,* 49–62.

Ruch, L. O., & Chandler, S. M. (1983). Sexual assault trauma during the acute phase: An exploratory model and multivariate analysis. *Journal of Health and Social Behavior, 24,* 184–185.

Ruma, P. R., Burke, R. V., & Thompson, R. W. (1996). Group parent training: Is it effective for children of all ages? *Behavior Therapy, 27,* 159–169.

Rusby, J. C., Estes, A., & Dishion, T. (1991). *The interpersonal process code (IPC).* Unpublished manuscript. Oregon Social Learning Center, Eugene.

Russell, G. (1985). Premenarchal Anorexia Nervosa and its sequelae. *Journal of Psychiatry Research, 19,* 429–448.

Russell, G. (1992). Anorexia Nervosa of early onset and its impact on puberty. In P. Cooper & A. Stein (Eds.), *Feeding problems and Eating Disorders in children and adolescents.* Reading, CT: Harwood Academic Publishers.

Russell, M. (1994). New assessment tools for risk drinking during pregnancy. *Alcohol Health & Research World, 18*(1), 55–61.

Rutter, M. (1995). Routes from research to clinical practice in child psychiatry: Retrospect and prospect. *Journal of Child Psychology and Psychiatry, 39,* 805–816.

Rutter, M., Maughan, B., Mortimer, P., Ouston, J., & Smith, A. (1979). *Fifteen thousand hours: Secondary schools and their effects on children.* Cambridge, MA: Harvard University Press.

Rutter, M., Silberg, J., O'Connor, T., & Simonoff, E. (1999). Genetics and child psychiatry: II Empirical research findings. *Journal of Child Psychology and Psychiatry, 40,* 19–55.

Rutter, M., & Sroufe, L. A. (2000). Developmental psychopathology: Concepts and challenges. *Development and Psychopathology, 12,* 265–296.

Ryan, N. D. (2003). Child and adolescent depression: Short-term treatment effectiveness and long-term opportunities. *International Journal of Methods in Psychiatric Research, 12,* 44–53.

Salaspuro, M. (1994). Biological state markers of alcohol abuse. *Alcohol Health & Research World, 18*(2), 131–135.

Salyers, K. M., Kiwi ie, M. H., Luellen, W. S. & Roseman, C. P. (September 2005). Inclusion of substance abuse training in CACREP-accredited programs. *Counselor Education & Supervision, 45,* 30–42.

Samuda, R. (1998). *Psychological testing of American minorities.* Thousand Oaks, CA: Sage.

Samuel, V. J., Biederman, J., Faraone, S. V., George, P., Mick, E., Thornell, A., Curtis, S., Taylor, B. A., & Brome, D. (1998). Clinical characteristics of Attention-Deficit/Hyperactivity Disorder in African American children. *American Journal of Psychiatry, 155,* 696–698.

Samuel, V. J., George, P., Thornell, A., Curtis, S., Taylor, A., Brome, D., Mick, E., Faraone, S. V., & Biederman, J. (1999). A pilot controlled family study of *DSM-III-R* and *DSM-IV* AD/HD in African American children. *Journal of the American Child and Adolescent Psychiatry, 38,* 34–39.

Sanford, M., Boyle, M. H., Szatmari, P., Offord, D. R., Jamieson, E., & Spinner, M. (1999). Age-of-onset classification of Conduct Disorder: Reliability and validity in a prospective cohort study. *Journal of the American Academy of Child and Adolescent Psychiatry, 38,* 992–999.

Sanford, M., Szatmari, P., Spinner, M., Monroe-Blum, H., Jamieson, E., Walsh, C., & Jones, D. (1995). Predicting the one-year course of adolescent major depression. *Journal of the American Academy of Child and Adolescent Psychiatry, 34,* 1618–1628.

Sanson, A., & Prior, M. (1999). Temperament and behavioral precursors to Oppositional Defiant Disorder and Conduct Disorder. In H. C. Quay & A. F. Hogan (Eds.), *Handbook of disruptive Behavior Disorders* (pp. 397–417). New York: Plenum. CA: Brooks/Cole.

Santrock, J. W. (2002). *Life-span development* (8th ed.). Boston: McGraw Hill.

Sauber, R. S., L'Abate, L., Weeks, G. R., & Buchanan, W. L. (1993). *The dictionary of family psychology and family therapy.* Newbury Park, CA: Sage.

Sayegh, L., & Grizenko, N. (1991). Studies of the effectiveness of day-treatment programs for children. *Canadian Journal of Psychiatry, 36,* 246–253.

Saywitz, K. J., Mannarino, A. P., Berliner, L., & Cohen, J. A. (2000). Treatment of sexually abused children and adolescents. *American Psychologist, 55,* 1040–1049.

Scalf-McIver, L., & Thompson, J. K. (1989). Family correlates of Bulimic characteristics in college females. *Journal of Clinical Psychology, 45,* 457–472.

Scarano, G. M., & Kalodner-Martin, C. R. (1994). A description of the continuum of Eating Disorders: Implications for intervention and research. *Journal of Counseling and Development, 72,* 356–361.

Schaeffer, D., Schwab-Stone, M., Fisher, P., Cohen, P., Piacentini, J., Davies, M., Conners, C. K., & Regier, D. (1993). The diagnostic interview schedule for children—revised edition (DISC-R): I. Preparation, field testing, interrater reliability, and acceptability. *Journal of the American Academy of Child and Adolescent Psychiatry, 32,* 643–650.

Schatzberg, A. F., & Ballenger, J. C. (1991). Descisions for the clinician in the treatment of Panic Disorder: When to treat, which treatment to use, and how long to treat. *Journal of Clinical Psychiatry, 52,* 26–31.

Schaughency, E., McGee, R., Raja, S. N., Feehan, M., & Silva, P. (1994). Self-reported inattention, impulsivity, and hyperactivity in ages 15 and 18 years in the general population. *Journal of the American Academy of Child and Adolescent Psychiatry, 33,* 173–183.

Schneider, J. A., & Agras, W. S. (1987). Bulimia in males: A matched comparison with females. *International Journal of Eating Disorders, 6*, 235–242.

Schultz, D. P., & Schultz, S. E. (2001). *Theories of personality*. Pacific Grove, CA: Brooks/Cole.

Schweibert, K. A., Sealander, K. A., & Dennison, J. L. (2002). Strategies for counselors working with high school students with Attention-Deficit/Hyperactivity Disorder. *Journal of Counseling and Development, 80*, 3–10.

Scott, D. W., (1986). Anorexia Nervosa in the male: A review of the clinical, epidemiological and biological findings. *International Journal of Eating Disorders, 5*, 799–819.

Scott, M. J., & Stradling, S. G. (1992). *Counseling for Post-traumatic Stress Disorder*. Newbury Park, CA: Sage.

Section 504 of the Rehabilitation Act of 1973, 29 U.S.C. Section 794 *et seq.*

Segal, D. L., Hersen, M., & VanHasselt, V. B. (1994). Reliability of the structured clinical interview for *DSM III-R:* An evaluative review. *Comprehensive Psychiatry, 35*, 316–327.

Seidman, L. J., Biederman, J., Monuteaux, M. C., Weber, W., & Faraone, S. V. (2000). Neuropsychological functioning in nonreferred siblings of children with Attention-Deficit/Hyperactivity Disorder. *Journal of Abnormal Psychology, 109*, 252–265.

Seiffge-Krenke, I. (2000). Causal links between stressful events, coping style, and adolescent symptomatology. *Journal of Adolescence, 23*, 675–691.

Seigel, R. K. (March, 1986). Jungle revelers. *Omni*, 71–74, 100.

Seligman, L. (1986). *Diagnosis and treatment planning in counseling*. New York: Human Sciences Press.

Seligman, L. (1990). *Selecting effective treatments: A comprehensive, systematic guide to treating Adult Mental Disorders*. San Francisco: Jossey-Bass.

Seligman, L. (1998). *Selecting effective treatments: A comprehensive, systematic guide to treating mental disorders*. San Francisco: Jossey-Bass.

Seligman, L. (1999). Twenty years of diagnosis and the *DSM. Journal of Mental Health Counseling, 21*, 229–239.

Seligman, L. (2001). *Systems, strategies, and skills of counseling and psychotherapy*. Upper Saddle River, NJ: Merrill/ Prentice Hall.

Sellers, D., & Hall, T. (1998). What a school administrator needs to know about the school counselor's role with multicultural student populations. In C. Dykeman (Ed.), *Maximizing school guidance program effectiveness* (pp. 123–127).

Selvini-Palazzoli, M. (1974). *From individual to family therapy in the treatment of Anorexia Nervosa*. New York: Human Context Books.

Selzer, M. L. (1971). The Michigan Alcoholism Screening Test: The quest for a new diagnostic instrument. *American Journal of Psychiatry, 127*, 1653–1658.

Sexton, T. L., & Whiston, S. C. (1994). The status of the counseling relationship: An empirical review, theoretical implications, and research directions. *Counseling Psychologist, 22*, 6–78.

Shaffer, D. (1974). Suicide in childhood and early adolescence. *Journal of Child Psychology, 15*, 275–291.

Shaffer, D., Fisher, P., Dulcan, M., Davies, M., Piacentini, J., Schwab-Stone, M., Lahey, B. B., Bourdon, K., Jensen, P., Bird, H., Canino, G., & Regier. (1996a). The NIMH diagnostic interview schedule for children (DISC 2.3): Description, acceptability, prevalences, and performance in the MECA study. *Journal of the American Academy of Child and Adolescent Psychiatry, 35*, 865–877.

Shaffer, D., Gould, M. S., Fisher, P., Trautman, P., Moreau, D., Kleinman, M., & Flory, M. (1996b). Psychiatric diagnosis in child and adolescent suicide. *Archives of General Psychiatry, 53*, 339–348.

Shaffi, N., Carrigan, S., Whittinghill, J. R., & Derrick, A. (1985). Psychological autopsy of completed suicide of children and adolescents. *American Journal of Psychiatry, 142*, 1061–1064.

Sharpe, T. M., Killen, J. D., Bryson, S. W., Shisslak, C. M., Estes, L. S., Gray, N., Crago, M., & Taylor, C. B. (1998). Attachment style and weight concerns in preadolescent and adolescent girls. *International Journal of Eating Disorders, 23*, 39–44.

Shaw, P., Lerch, J., Greenstein, D., Sharp, W., Clasen, L., Evans, A., Giedd, J., Castellanos, F. X., & Rapoport, J. (2006). Longitudinal mapping of cortical thickness and clinical outcome in children and adolescents with attention-deficit/hyperactivity disorder. *Archives of General Psychiatry, 63*, 540–549.

Shaywitz, S. E., & Shaywitz, B. A. (1988). Attention-Deficit Disorder: Current perspectives. In J. F. Kavanagh & T. J. Truss, Jr. (Eds.), *Learning disabilities: Proceedings of the national conference* (pp. 369–523). Parkston, MD: York Press.

Shaywitz, S. E., & Shaywitz, B. A. (1991). Introduction to the special series on Attention-Deficit Disorder. *Journal of Learning Disabilities, 24*, 68–71.

Shaywitz, S. E., & Shaywitz, B. A. (1992). *Attention-Deficit Disorder comes of age: Toward the twenty-first century*. Austin, TX: Pro-Ed.

Shick, L. (1998). *Understanding temperament: Strategies for creating family harmony*. Seattle, WA: Parenting Press.

Shiner, R. L., & Marmorstein, N. R. (1998). Family environments of adolescents with lifetime depression: Associations with maternal depression history. *Journal of the American Academy of Child and Adolescent Psychiatry, 37*, 1152–1160.

Shore, R. A., & Porter, J. E. (1990). Normative and reliability data for 11- to 18-year olds on the Eating Disorder Inventory. *International Journal of Eating Disorders, 9* (2), 201–207.

Short, J. F. (1997). *Poverty, ethnicity, and violent crime*. New York: Westview.

Siegel, J. M., Aneshensel, C. S., Taub, B., Cantewell, D., & Driscoll, A. K. (1998). Adolescent depressed mood in a multiethnic sample. *Journal of Youth and Adolescence, 27*, 413–428.

Siegel, K., Raveis, V. H., & Karus, D. (1996). Pattern of communication with children when a parent has cancer. In L. Baider, C. L. Cooper, & A. K. De-Nour (Eds.), *Cancer and the family* (pp. 109–128). Chichester, England: John Wiley & Sons.

Sifneos, P. E. (1972). *Short-term psychotherapy and emotional crisis*. Cambridge, MA: Harvard University Press.

Sink, C. A., & MacDonald, G. (1998). The status of comprehensive guidance and counseling in the United States. *Professional School Counseling, 2*, 88–94.

Skinner, B. F. (1990). Can psychology be a science of mind? *American Psychologist, 45*, 1206–1210.

Slade, P. D., Dewey, M. E., Newton, T., & Brodie, D. A. (1990). Development and preliminary validation of the Body Satisfaction Scale (BSS). *Psychology and Health, 4*, 213–220.

Slone, M., Durrheim, K., & Kaminer, D. (1996). Attention-Deficit/Hyperactivity Disorder: Clinical presentation and correlates in a South African sample. *Professional Psychology: Research and Practice, 27*, 198–201.

Sluzki, C. E. (1998). Migration and the disruption of the social network. In M. McGoldrick (Ed.), *Re-visioning family therapy: Race, culture, and gender in clinical practice* (pp. 360–369). New York: Guilford.

Smart, D. W., & Smart, J. F. (1997). *DSM-IV* and culturally sensitive diagnosis: Some observations for counselors. *Journal of Counseling and Development, 75*, 392–398.

Smith, C., & Carlson, B. E. (1997). Stress, coping, and resilience in children and youth. *Social Service Review, 71,* 231–256.

Smith, K. J., Subich, L. M., & Kalodner, C. (1995). The transtheoretical model's stages and processes of change and their relation to premature termination. *Journal of Counseling Psychology, 45,* 34–39.

Smith, M. L., Glass, G. V., & Miller, T. I. (1980). *The benefits of psychotherapy.* Baltimore: Johns-Hopkins University.

Smith-Stevens, P., & Smith, R. L. (1998). *Substance abuse counseling: Theory and practice.* Upper Saddle River, New Jersey: Merrill Prentice Hall.

Smolack, L., & Levine, M. (1993). Separation-individuation difficulties and the distinction between Bulimia Nervosa and Anorexia Nervosa in college women. *International Journal of Eating Disorders, 14,* 33–41.

Smolak, L., Murnen, S. K., & Thompson, J. K. (2005). Sociocultural influences on muscle building in adolescent boys. *Psychology of Men and Masculinity, 6,* 227–239.

Snyder, B. A. (1996). Counseling children of cultural and diversity orientation. In P. B. Pedersen & D. C. Locke (Eds.), *Cultural and diversity issues in counseling* (pp. 73–75). Greensboro, NC: ERIC/CASS.

Sokol, R. J., Martier, S. S., & Ager, J. W. (1989). The T-ACE questions: Practical prenatal detection of risk drinking. *American Journal of Obstetrics and Gynecology, 160,* 863–870.

Solyom, L., Ledwidge, B., & Solyom, C. (1986). Delineating social phobia. *British Journal of Psychiatry, 149,* 464–470.

Sommers-Flanagan, J., & Sommers-Flanagan, R. (1993). *Foundations of therapeutic interviewing.* Boston: Allyn & Bacon.

Sommers-Flanagan, J., & Sommers-Flanagan, R. (1998). Assessment and diagnosis of Conduct Disorder. *Journal of Counseling and Development, 76,* 189–197.

Son, S. E., & Kirchner, J. T., (2000). Depression in children and adolescents. *American Family Physician, 62,* 2297–2308, 2311–2312.

Southham-Gerow, M. A., Henin, A., Chu, B., Marrs, A., & Kendall, P. C. (1997). Cognitive-Behavioral therapy with children and adolescents. *Child and Adolescent Psychiatric Clinics of North America, 6,* 111–136.

Spann, L., & Fischer, J. L. (1990). Identifying codependency. *The Counselor, 8,* 27.

Speltz, M. L., McClellan, J., DeKlyen, M., & Jones, K. (1999). Preschool boys with Oppositional Defiant Disorder: Clinical presentation and diagnostic change. *Journal of the American Academy of Child and Adolescent Psychiatry, 38,* 838–845.

Spence, S. H., Sheffield, J. K., & Donovan, C. L. (2003). Preventing adolescent depression: An evaluation of the problem solving for life program. *Journal of Consulting and Clinical Psychology, 71,* 3–13.

Spitzer, R., Williams, J., & Gibbon, B. (1987). *Instruction manual for the structured clinical interview for the DSM-III-R.* New York: New York State Psychiatric Institute.

Sroufe, L. A. (1985). Attachment classification from the perspective of infant-caregiver relationships and infant temperament. *Child Development, 56,* 1–14.

Sroufe, L. A. (1997). *Emotional development: The organization of emotional life in the early years.* New York: Cambridge University Press.

Sroufe, L. A., & Rutter, M. (1984). The domain of developmental psychopathology. *Child Development, 55,* 17–29.

Stallard, P., Salter, E., & Velleman, R. (2004). *European Adolescent and Child Psychiatry, 13,* 172–178.

Stark, K. D., Vaughn, C., Doxey, M., & Luss, L. (1999). Depressive Disorders. In R. T. Ammerman, M. Hersen, & C. G. Last (Eds.), *Handbook of prescriptive treatments for children and adolescents* (2nd ed., pp. 114–140). Boston: Allyn & Bacon.

Stead, G. B, (1996). Career development of black South African adolescents: A developmental-contextual perspective. *Journal of Counseling & Development, 74,* 270–275.

Steele, M., & Fisman, S. (1997). Bipolar Disorder in children and adolescents: Current challenges. *Canadian Journal of Psychiatry, 42,* 632–636.

Stefos, G., Bauwens, F., Staner, L., Pardoen, D., & Mendlewicz, J. (1996). Psychosocial predictors of major affective recurrences in Bipolar Disorder: A 4-year longitudinal study of patients on prophylactic treatment. *Acta Psychiatrica Scandinavica, 93,* 420–426.

Steiger, H., & Zanko, M. (1990). Sexual traumata among eating-disordered, psychiatric, and normal female groups. *Journal of Interpersonal Violence, 5,* 74–86.

Stein, M. A., Szumowski, E., & Halperin, J. M. (1994). Using the computer to aid diagnosis: Continuous performance tests. *Attention! The Magazine of Children and Adults with Attention-Deficit Disorders, 2,* 18–20.

Steiner, H., & Lock, J. (1998). Anorexia Nervosa and Bulimia Nervosa in children and adolescents: A review of the past 10 years. *Journal of the American Academy of Child and Adolescent Psychiatry, 37(4),* 352–359.

Steinhausen, H. C., Rauss-Mason, C., & Seidel, R. (1991). Follow-up studies of Anorexia Nervosa: A review of four decades of outcome research. *Psychological Medicine, 21,* 447–451.

Steketee, G., & Foa, E. B. (1987). Rape victims: Post-traumatic stress responses and their treatment: A review of the literature. *Journal of Anxiety Disorders, 1,* 69–86.

Steuer, F. B. (1994). *The psychological development of children.* Pacific Grove, CA: Brooks/Cole.

Stevens-Smith, P., & Smith, R. L. (1998). *Substance abuse counseling: Theory and practice.* Upper Saddle River, New Jersey: Merrill/Prentice Hall.

Stewart, A. J., Steiman, M., & Cauce, A. M. (2004). Victimization and post-traumatic stress disorder among homeless adolescents. *Journal of the American Academy of Child and Adolescent Psychiatry, 43,* 325–331.

Still, G. F. (1902). Some abnormal psychical conditions in children. *Lancet, 1,* 1008–1012, 1077–1082, 1163–1168.

Stowell, R. J. A., & Estroff, T. W. (1992). Psychiatric Disorders in substance-abusing adolescent inpatients: A pilot study. *Journal of the American Academy of Child and Adolescent Psychiatry, 31,* 1036–1040.

Strain, J. J., Newcorn, J., Wolf, D., & Fulop, G. (1994). Adjustment Disorder. In R. E. Hales & S. C. Yudofsky (Eds.) *The American psychiatric press textbook of psychiatry* (2nd ed., pp. 671–680). Washington, DC: American Psychiatric Press.

Strauss, C. C. (1988). Behavioral assessment and treatment of Overanxious Disorder in children and adolescents. *Behavior Modification, 12,* 234–251.

Strauss, C. C. (1993). Developmental differences in expression of Anxiety Disorders in children and adolescents. In C. G. Last (Ed.), *Anxiety across the lifespan: A developmental perspective* (pp. 63–77). New York: Springer.

Striegel-Moore, R. H. (1993). Etiology of binge eating: A developmental perspective. In C. G. Fairburn & G. T. Wilson (Eds.), *Binge eating: Nature, assessment, and treatment* (pp. 144–172). New York: Guilford Press.

Striegel-Moore, R. H., McAvay, G., & Rodin, J. (1986). Psychological and behavioral correlates of feeling fat in women. *International Journal of Eating Disorders, 5,* 935–949.

Striegel-Moore, R. H., Silberstein, L. R., & Rodin, J. (1986). Toward an understanding of the risk factors for Bulimia. *Journal of the American Psychological Association, 41*, 246–263.

Strober, M., Freeman, R., & Morrell, W. (1997). The long-term course of severe Anorexia Nervosa in adolescents: Survival analysis of recovery, relapse, and outcome predictors over 10–15 years in a prospective study. *International Journal of Eating Disorders, 22*, 339–360.

Strober, M., & Humphrey, L. L. (1987). Familial contributions to the etiology and course of Anorexia Nervosa and Bulimia. *Journal of Consulting and Clinical Psychology, 55*, 654–659.

Strober, M., Rao, U., DeAntonio, M., Liston, E., State, M., Amaya-Jackson, L., & Latz, S. (1998). Effects of electroconvulsive therapy in adolescents with severe endogenous depression resistant to pharmacotherapy. *Biological Psychiatry, 43*, 335–338.

Stuber, M. L., & Shemesh, E. (2006). Post-traumatic stress response to life-threatening illnesses in children and parents. *Child and Adolescent Psychiatric Clinics of North America, 15*, 597–609.

Stuber, M. L., Shemesh, E., & Saxe, G. N. (2003). Post-traumatic stress responses in children with life-threatening illnesses. *Child and Adolescent Psychiatric Clinics of North America, 12*, 195–209.

Stunkard, A. J., & Messick, S. (1985). The Three Factor Eating Questionnaire to measure dietary restraint, disinhibition and hunger. *Journal of Psychosomatic Research, 29*, 71–83.

Sue, D. W., Arrendondo, P., & McDaniels, R. J. (1992). Multicultural counseling competencies: A call to the profession. *Journal of Counseling and Development, 70*, 477–486.

Sue, D. W., & Sue, D. (1990). *Counseling the culturally different: Theory and practice* (2nd ed.). Somerset, NJ: John Wiley & Sons.

Sue, D. W., & Sue, D. (2003). *Counseling the culturally diverse: Theory and practice*. New York: John Wiley & Sons.

Sue, D., Sue, D. W., & Sue, S. (2000). *Understanding abnormal behavior*. Boston: Houghton Mifflin.

Sullivan, P. F. (1995). Mortality in Anorexia Nervosa. *American Journal of Psychiatry, 1522*, 1073–1074.

Surgeon General of the United States. (2000). Children and mental health. Retrieved February 21, 2000, from http://www.surgeongeneral.gov/library/mentalhealth/chapter3/rer=f3_3.html.

Swales, T. P. (2001). Diagnostic evaluation of Mental and Emotional Disorders of childhood. In E. R. Welfel & R. E. Ingersoll (Eds.), *The mental health desk reference* (pp. 162–169). New York: John Wiley & Sons.

Swartz-Kulstad, J. L., & Martin, W. E. (1999). Impact of culture and context on psychosocial adaptation: The cultural and contextual guide process. *Journal of Counseling & Development, 77*, 281–293.

Swedo, S. E., & Pekar, M. (2000). PANDAS: A new species of Childhood-onset Obsessive-Compulsive Disorder? In J. L. Rapoport (Ed.), *Childhood-onset of adult psychopathology: Clinical and research advances* (pp.103–119). Washington, DC: American Psychiatric Press.

Sylva, K. (1994). School influences on children's development. *Journal of Child Psychology and Psychiatry, 35*, 135–170.

Szapocznik, J., Kurtines, W., Santisteban, D. A., & Rio, A. T. (1990). Interplay of advances between theory, research, and application in treatment interventions aimed at behavior-problem children and adolescents. *Journal of Consulting and Clinical Psychology, 58*, 696–703.

Szatmari, P. (1992). The epidemiology of Attention-Deficit/Hyperactivity Disorders. In G. Weiss (Ed.), *Child and adolescent psychiatry clinics of North America: Attention-Deficit Disorder* (pp. 361–372). Philadelphia: Saunders.

Szatmari, P., Boyle, M., & Offord, D. R. (1989). AD/HD and Conduct Disorder: Degree of diagnostic overlap and differences among correlates. *Journal of the American Academy of Child and Adolescent Psychiatry, 28*, 865–872.

Tannock, R. (1994). Attention-Deficit Disorders with Anxiety Disorders. In T. E. Brown (Ed.), *Subtypes of Attention-Deficit Disorders in children, adolescents, and adults*. New York: American Psychiatric Publishing.

Target, M., & Fonagy, P. (2005). The psychological treatment of child and adolescent psychiatric disorders. In A. Roth & P. Fonagy (Eds.), *What works for whom? A critical review of psychotherapy research* (pp. 385–424). New York: Guilford Press.

Tarter, R. E., Laird, S. B., Bukstein, O., & Kaminer, Y. (1992). Validation of the adolescent drug use screening inventory: Preliminary findings. *Psychology of Addictive Behaviors, 6*, 322–326.

Task Force on Promotion and Dissemination of Psychological Procedures. (1995). Training in and dissemination of empirically validated psychological treatments: Report and recommendations. *Clinical Psychologist, 48*, 3–23.

Teeter, P. A. (1998). *Interventions for AD/HD: Treatment in developmental context*. New York: Guilford Press.

Teeter, P. A. (2000). *Interventions for AD/HD: Treatment in developmental context*. New York: Guilford Press.

Tems, C. L., Stewart, S. M., Skinner, J. R., Hughes, C. W., & Emslie, G. (1993). Cognitive distortions in depressed children and adolescents: Are they state dependent or traitlike? *Journal of Clinical Child Psychology, 22*, 316–326.

Thapar, A., & McGuffin, P. (1996). The genetic etiology of childhood depressive symptoms. *Development & Psychopathology, 8*, 751–760.

Tharp, R. G. (1991). Cultural diversity and treatment of children. *Journal of Consulting and Clinical Psychology, 59*, 799–812.

Thatcher, R. W. (1994). Psychopathology of early frontal lobe damage: Dependence on cycles of development. *Development and Psychopathology, 6*, 565–596.

Thomas, A., & Chess, S. (1977). *Temperament and development*. New York: Brunner/Mazel.

Thomas, D. W. (1990). *Substance abuse screening protocol for the juvenile courts*. Pittsburgh, PA: National Center for Juvenile Justice.

Thomas, S. C. (1996). A sociological perspective on contextualism. *Journal of Counseling & Development, 74*, 529–536.

Thompson, C. L., & Rudolph, L. B. (2000). *Counseling children* (5th ed.). Pacific Grove, CA: Brooks/Cole.

Thompson, P. M., Giedd, J. N., Woods, R. P., MacDonald, D. E., Alan, C., & Toga, A. W. (2000). Growth patterns in the developing brain detected by using continuum mechanical tensor maps. *Nature, 404*, 190–193.

Thompson, S. J. (2005). Factors, associated with trauma symptoms among runaway/homeless adolescents. *Stress, Trauma, and Crisis, 8*, 143–156.

Thyer, B. A. (1987). *Treating Anxiety Disorders*. Newbury Park, CA: Sage.

Thyer, B. A. (1991). Diagnosis and treatment of child and adolescent anxiety disorders. *Behavior Modification, 15*, 310–325.

Thyer, B. A. (1993). Childhood Separation Anxiety Disorder and Adult-Onset Agoraphobia: Review of evidence. In C. G. Last (Ed.), *Anxiety across the lifespan: A developmental perspective* (pp. 128–147). New York: Springer.

Thyer, B. A., & Himle, J. (1985). Temporal relationship between panic attack onset and avoidance behavior in agoraphobia with panic attacks. *Behaviour Research and Therapy, 23,* 607–608.

Thyer, B. A., Parrish, R. T., Curtis, G. C., Cameron, O. G., & Neese, R. M. (1985). Ages of onset of *DSM-III* Anxiety Disorders. *Comprehensive Psychiatry, 26,* 113–122.

Tranel, D. (1992). Functional neuroanatomy: Neuropsychological correlates of cortical damage and subcortical damage. In S. C. Yudofsky & R. E. Hales (Eds.), *Textbook of neuropsychiatry* (pp. 57–88). Washington, DC: The American Psychiatric Press.

Tufnell, G. (2005). Eye movement desensitization and reprocessing in the treatment of pre-adolescent children with post-traumatic symptoms. *Clinical Child Psychology and Psychiatry, 10,* 587–600.

Turner, R. M. (1987). The effects of Personality Disorder diagnosis on the outcome of social anxiety reduction. *Journal of Personality Disorders, 1,* 136–143.

Turner, S. M., & Beidel, D. C. (1989). Social phobia: Clinical syndrome, diagnosis, and comorbidity. *Clinical Psychology Review, 9,* 3–18.

Turner, S. M., Beidel, D. C., Stanley, M. A., & Jacob, R. B. (1988). A comparison of fluoxetine, flooding, and response prevention in the treatment of Obsessive-Compulsive Disorder. *Journal of Anxiety Disorders, 2,* 219–225.

U.S. Census Bureau. (2001). *Population by race and Hispanic or Latino origin for the United States.* Retrieved from http://www.census.gov

Ullman, R. K., Sleator, E. K., & Sprague, R. L. (1988). *ADD-H: Comprehensive teacher's rating scale (ACTeRs).* Savoy, IL: Institute for Personality and Ability Testing.

Universal Attention Disorders, Inc. (1992). *Test of variables of attention.* Los Alamitos, CA: Author.

Vaillant, G. E. (1977). *Adaptation to life.* Cambridge, MA: Harvard University Press.

van der Ham, T., Meulman, J. J., van Strien, D. C., van Engeland, H. (1996). Empirically based subgrouping of Eating Disorders among adolescents: A longitudinal perspective. *British Journal of Psychiatry, 170,* 363–368.

Van der Kolk, B. A., & Fisler, R. E. (1994). Childhood abuse and neglect and loss of self-regulation. *Bulletin of the Menninger Clinic, 58,* 145–168.

Vandereycken, W. (1990). The addiction model in Eating Disorders: Some critical remarks and a selected bibliography. *International Journal of Eating Disorders, 9,* 95–101.

Vasey, M. W., Dalieden, E. L., Williams, L. L., & Brown, L. M. (1995). Biased attention in childhood Anxiety Disorders: A preliminary study. *Journal of Abnormal Child Psychology, 23,* 267–279.

Verhulst, F. C., & van der Ende, J. (1991). Four-year follow-up of teacher-reported problem behaviors. *Psychological Medicine, 21,* 965–977.

Verhulst, F. C., van der Ende, J., Ferdinand, R. F., & Kasius, M. C. (1997). The prevalence of *DSM-III-R* diagnoses in a national sample of Dutch adolescents. *Archives of General Psychiatry, 54,* 329–336.

Vila, G., Porche, L. M., & Mouren-Simeoni, M. C. (1999). An 18-month longitudinal study of Posttraumatic Disorders in children who were taken hostage in their school. *Psychosomatic Medicine, 61,* 746–754.

Vitiello, B. (2003). Current research on mental health treatments for children and adolescents. *Emotional and Behavioral Disorders in Youth, 3,* 87–88, 99–100.

Vitiello, B., & Stoff, D. M. (1997). Subtypes of aggression and their relevance to child psychiatry. *Journal of the American Academy of Child and Adolescent Psychiatry, 36,* 307–315.

Voelker, S. L., Carter, R. A., Sprague, D. J., Gdowski, C. L., & Lachar, D. (1989). Developmental trends in memory and metamemory in children with Attention-Deficit Disorder. *Journal of Pediatric Psychology, 14,* 75–88.

Vontress, C. E. (1996). A personal retrospective on cross-cultural counseling. *Journal of Multicultural Counseling and Development, 16,* 73–83.

Vostanis, P. (2004). The impact, psychological sequelae and management of trauma affecting children. *Current Opinion in Psychiatry, 17,* 269–285.

Vostanis, P., Feehan, C., & Grattan, E. (1998). Two-year outcome of children treated for depression. *European Child and Adolescent Psychiatry, 7,* 12–18.

Waggoner, R. W. (1992). Peer review of children and adolescents. In M. R. Mattson (Vol. Ed.), *Manual of psychiatric quality assurance: A report of the American Psychiatric Association Committee on Quality Assurance* (pp. 127–131). Washington, DC: American Psychiatric Association.

Wagner, K. D. (2004). Course and treatment of childhood bipolar disorder. *Psychiatric Times, 21,* 34.

Wagner, K. D., Robb, A. S., Findling, R. L., Jin, J., Gutierrez, M. M., & Heydorn, W. E. (2004). A randomized, placebo-controlled trial of citalopram for the treatment of major depression in children and adolescents. *The American Journal of Psychiatry, 161,* 1079–1083.

Waldman, I. D., & Lahey, B. B. (1994). Design of the *DSM-IV* Disruptive Behavior Disorder field trials. *Child and Adolescent Psychiatric Clinics of North America, 3,* 195–208.

Waldman, I. D., Lilienfeld, S. O., & Lahey, B. B. (1995). Toward construct validity in the childhood Disruptive Behavior Disorders. In T. H. Ollendick & R. J. Prinz (Eds.), *Advances in clinical child psychology* (pp. 323–363). New York: Plenum.

Walker, H. M. (1995). *The acting-out child: Coping with classroom disruption* (2nd ed.). Longmont, CO: Sopris West.

Walker, H. M., Colvin, G., & Ramsey, E. (1995). *Antisocial behavior in school: Strategies and best practices.* Pacific Grove, CA: Brooks/Cole.

Waller, M. A. (2001). Resilience in ecosystemic context: Evolution of the concept. *American Journal of Orthopsychiatry, 71,* 290–297.

Walsh, B. T., Hadigan, B. A., Devlin, M. J., Gladis, M., & Roose, S. P. (1991). Long-term outcome of antidepressant treatment for Bulimia Nervosa. *American Journal of Psychiatry, 148,* 1206–1212.

Waters, E., Merrick, S., Treboux, D., Crowell, J., & Albersheim, L. (2000). Attachment security in infancy and early adulthood: A twenty-year longitudinal study. *Child Development, 71,* 684–689.

Watts, S. J., & Markham, R. A. (2005). Etiology of depression in children. *Journal of Instructional Psychology, 32,* 266–270.

Webster-Stratton, C. (1996). Early-onset conduct problems: Does gender make a difference? *Journal of Consulting and Clinical Psychology, 64,* 540–551.

Webster-Stratton, C., & Hammond, M. (1997). Treating children with early-onset conduct problems: A comparison of child and parent training interventions. *Journal of Consulting and Clinical Psychology, 65,* 93–109.

Webster-Stratton, C., & Spitzer, A. (1991). Development, reliability, and validity of the daily telephone discipline interview. *Behavioral Assessment, 13,* 221–239.

Wechsler, D. (1974). *Manual for the Wechsler intelligence scale for children—Revised.* New York: Psychological Corporation.

Wechsler, D. (1989). *Manual for the Wechsler pre-school and primary scale of intelligence—Revised.* New York: Psychological Corporation.

Wechsler, D. (1991). *Manual for the Wechsler intelligence scale for children—Third edition (WISC-III)*. New York: Psychological Corporation.

Weekes, C. (1978). Simple, effective treatment of agoraphobia. *American Journal of Psychotherapy, 32,* 357–369.

Wehr, T. A., Goodwin, F. K., Wirz-Justice, et al. (1982). 48-hour sleep-wake cycles in Manic-Depressive illness. *Archives of General Psychiatry, 39,* 559–565.

Wehrly, B. (1995). *Pathways to multicultural counseling competence: A developmental journey.* Pacific Grove, CA: Brooks/Cole Publishing Company.

Weihs, K., & Reiss, D. (1996). Family reorganization in response to cancer: A developmental perspective. In L. Baider, C. L. Cooper, & A. K. De-Nour (Eds.), *Cancer and the family* (pp. 3–29). Chichester, England: John Wiley & Sons.

Weiner, A. S. (1992). Emotion problems of adolescence: Review of Mood Disorder. In C. E. Walker and M. C. Roberts (Eds.), *Handbook of clinical child psychology* (2nd ed., pp. 565–586). New York: John Wiley & Sons.

Weinert, F. E., & Weinert, S. (1998). History and systems of developmental psychology. In A. Demetriou, W. Doise, & C. F. M. van Lieshout, *Life-span developmental psychology* (pp. 1–33). New York: John Wiley & Sons.

Weiss, G., & Hechtman, L. T. (1993). Hyperactive children grown up *AD/HD in children, adolescents, and adults* (2nd ed.). New York: Guilford Press.

Weiss, J. R., & Hawley, K. M. (2002). Developmental factors in the treatment of adolescents. *Journal of Consulting and Clinical Psychology, 70,* 21–43.

Weiss, L., Katzman, M., & Wolchik, S. (1985). *Treating Bulimics: A psychoeducational approach.* New York: Pergamon Press.

Weissman, M. M., Markowitz, J. C., & Klerman, G. L. (2000). *Comprehensive guide to interpersonal psychotherapy.* New York: Basic Books.

Weist, M. D. (1997). Expanded school mental health services: A national movement in progress. In T. H. Ollendick & R. J. Prinz (Eds.), *Advances in clinical child psychology* (Vol. 19). New York: Plenum.

Weisz, J. R., & Hawley, K. M. (1998). Finding, evaluating, refining, and applying empirically supported treatments for children and adolescents. *Journal of Clinical Child Psychology, 27,* 206–216.

Weisz, J. R., & Hawley, K. M. (2002). Developmental factors in the treatment of adolescents. *Journal of Consulting and Clinical Psychology, 70,* 21–43.

Weisz, J. R., Hensen-Doss, A., & Hawley, K. M. (2006). Evidence-based youth psychotherapies versus usual clinical care: A meta-analysis of direct comparisons. *American Psychologist, 61,* 671–689.

Weisz, J. R., Weiss, B., Alicke, M. D., & Klotz, M. L. (1987). Effectiveness of psychotherapy with children and adolescents: A meta-analysis for clinicians. *Journal of Consulting and Clinical Psychology, 55,* 542–549.

Weisz, J. R., Weiss, B., Han, S. S., Granger, D. A., & Morton, T. (1995). Effects of psychotherapy with children and adolescents revisited: A meta-analysis of treatment outcome studies. *Psychological Bulletin, 117,* 450–468.

Welkowitz, L. A., Papp, L., Martinez, J., Browne, S., & Gorman, J. M. (1999). Instructional set and physiological response to CO_2 inhalation. *American Journal of Psychiatry, 156,* 745–748.

Wellisch, D. K., Hoffman, A., & Gritz, E. (1996). Psychological concerns and care of daughters of breast cancer patients. In L. Baider, C. L. Cooper, & A. K. De-Nour (Eds.), *Cancer and the family* (pp. 289–304). Chichester, England: John Wiley & Sons.

Wells, K. C., Epstein, J. N., Hinshaw, S. P., Conners, C. K., Klaric, J., Abikoff, H. B., et al. (2000a). Parenting and family stress treatment outcomes in Attention-Deficit/Hyperactivity Disorder (AD/HD): An empirical analysis in the MTA study. *Journal of Abnormal Psychology, 28,* 543–553.

Wells, K. C., & Forehand, R. (1985). Conduct and Oppositional Disorders. In P. H. Bornstein & A. Kazdin (Eds.), *Handbook of clinical behavior therapy with children* (pp. 218–265). Homewood, IL: Dorsey.

Wells, K. C., Pelham, W. E., Kotkin, R. A., Hoza, B., Abikoff, H. B., Abramowitz, A., et al. (2000b). Psychosocial treatment strategies in the MTA study: Rationale, methods, and critical issues in design and implementation [1]. *Journal of Abnormal Child Psychology, 28,* 483–505.

Wells, M. E., McQuellon, R. P., & Hinkle, J. S. (1995). Reducing anxiety in newly diagnosed cancer patients with an orientation to oncology clinic service. *Cancer Practice, 3,* 100–104.

Wenar, C. (1994). *Developmental psychopathology: From infancy through adolescence.* New York: McGraw-Hill.

Werner, E. E., & Smith, R. S. (1982). *Vulnerable, but invincible: A longitudinal study of resilient children and youth.* New York: McGraw-Hill.

Werner, E. E., & Smith, R. S. (1992). *Overcoming the odds.* Ithaca, NY: Cornell University Press.

Werry, J. (1995). Q & A: An interview with John Werry, MD. *Attention! The Magazine of Children and Adults with Attention-Deficit Disorders,* 7–31.

Westen, D., & Morrison, K. (2001). A multidimensional meta-analysis of treatments for Depression, Panic, and Generalized Anxiety Disorder: An empirical examination of the status of empirically supported treatments. *Journal of Consulting and Clinical Psychology, 69,* 875–899.

Weyandt, L. L. (2001). *Attention-Deficit/Hyperactivity Disorder: An AD/HD primer.* Boston: Allyn & Bacon.

Whalen, C. K., & Henker, B. (1991). Social impact of stimulant treatment for hyperactive children. *Journal of Learning Disabilities, 24,* 231–241.

Whaley, A. L. (2001). Cultural mistrust and mental health services for African Americans: A review and meta-analysis. *Counseling Psychologist, 29,* 513–531.

Whitaker, A., Johnson, J., Shaffer, D., Rapoport, J. L., Kalikow, K., Walsh, B., Davies, M., Braiman, S., & Dolinsky, A. (1990). Uncommon troubles in young people: Prevalence estimates of selected psychiatric disorders in a nonreferred adolescent population. *Archives of General Psychiatry, 47,* 487–496.

Whiting, B. B., & Edwards, C. P. (1988). *Children of different worlds: The formation of social behavior.* Cambridge, MA: Harvard University Press.

Whitman, F. L. (1983). Culturally invariable properties of male homosexuality: Tentative conclusions form cross-cultural research. *Archives of Sexual Behavior, 12,* 207–226.

Whittal, M. L., Agras, W. S., & Gould, R. A. (1999). Bulimia Nervosa: A meta-analysis of psychosocial and pharmacological treatments. *Behavior Therapy, 30,* 117–135.

Wicks-Nelson, R., & Israel, A. C. (2000). *Behavior Disorders of childhood.* Upper Saddle River, NJ: Merrill Prentice Hall.

Wicks-Nelson, R., & Israel, A. C. (2005). *Behavior disorders of childhood* (6th ed.). Upper Saddle River, NJ: Prentice Hall.

Wiggins, G. (1993). Assessment: Authenticity, context, and validity. *Phi Delta Kappan, 75,* 200–214.

Wilens, T. E., & Biederman, J. (2006). Alcohol, drugs, and attention-deficit/hyperactivity disorder: A model for the study of addictions in youth. *Journal of Psychopharmacology, 20,* 580–589.

Wilens, T. E., Biederman, J., Spencer, T. J., & Frances, R. J. (1994). Comorbidity of Attention-Deficit/Hyperactivity and Psychoactive Substance Use Disorders. *Hospital and Community Psychiatry, 45*, 421–435.

Wilens, T. E., Spencer, T. J., Biederman, J., & Schliefer, D. (1997). Case study: Nafazodone for juvenile Mood Disorders. *Journal of the American Academy of Child and Adolescent Psychiatry, 36*, 481–485.

Willcutt, E. G., Pennington, B. F., Chhabildas, N. A., Friedman, M. C., & Alexander, J. (1999). Psychiatric comorbidity associated with *DSM-IV* ADHD in a nonreferred sample of twins. *Journal of the American Academy of Child and Adolescent Psychiatry, 38*, 1355–1362.

Willcutt, E. G., Pennington, B. F., & DeFries, J. C. (2000). Twin study of the etiology of comorbidity between reading disability and Attention-Deficit/Hyperactivity Disorder. *American Journal of American Genetics, 96*, 293–301.

Williams, S., McGee, R., Anderson, J., & Silva, P. A. (1989). The structure and correlates of self-reported symptoms in 11-year-old children. *Journal of Abnormal Child Psychology, 17*, 55–71.

Williamson, D. E., Birmaher, B., Dahl, R. E., & Ryan, N.D. (2005). Stressful life events in anxious and depressed children. *Journal of Child and Adolescent Psychopharmacology, 15*, 571–580.

Williamson, D., Ryan, N. D., Birmaher, B., Dahl, M. E., Kaufman, J., Rao, U., & Puig-Antich, J. (1995). A case-control family history study of depression in adolescents. *Journal of the American Academy of Child and Adolescent Psychiatry, 34*, 1596–1607.

Williamson, D. E., Birmaher, B., Frank, E., Anderson, B. P., Matty, M. K., & Kupper, D. J. (1998). Nature of life events and difficulties in depressed adolescents. *Journal of the American Academy of Child and Adolescent Psychiatry, 37*, 1049–1057.

Wilson, G. F., & Phillips, K. L. (1992). Residential treatment centers: Quality assurance and utilization review guidelines. In M. R. Mattson (Vol. Ed.), *Manual of psychiatric quality assurance: A report of the American Psychiatric Association Committee on Quality Assurance* (pp. 173–180). Washington, DC: American Psychiatric Association.

Wilson, G. T. (1993). Binge eating and Addictive Disorders. In C. G. Fairburn & G. T. Wilson (Eds.), *Binge eating: Nature, assessment, and treatment.* New York: Guilford Press.

Wilson, S., Becker, L., & Tinker, R. (1995). Eye movement desensitization and reprocessing. *Journal of Consulting and Clinical Psychology, 63*, 928–937.

Windle, M. (1996). Effect of parental drinking on adolescents. *Alcohol Health & Research World, 20*(3), 181–184.

Winters, K. C. (1999). CSAT treatment improvement protocol (TIP) series 31: Screening and assessing adolescents for Substance Use Disorders. (DHHS Publication No.: [SMA] 99-3282). Rockville, MD: U.S. Center for Substance Abuse Treatment.

Wirt, R. D., Lachar, D., Klinedinst, J. K., & Seat, P. S. (1990). *Personality inventory for children—1990 edition.* Los Angeles: Western Psychological Services.

Wirt, R., Lacher, D., Klinedinst, J., & Seat, P. (1977). *Multidimensional description of personality.* Los Angeles: Western Psychological Services.

Witkeiwitz, K., & Marlatt, G. A. (2004). Relapse prevention for alcohol and drug problems: That was zen and this is tao. *American Psychologist, 59*, 224–235.

Wolf, N. (1991) *The beauty myth.* New York: William Morrow.

Wolff, R., & Rapoport, J. (1988). Behavioral treatment of childhood Obsessive-Compulsive Disorder. *Behavior Modification, 12*, 252–266.

Wolfram, S. (2002). *A new kind of science.* Champaign, IL: Wolfram Media.

Wolraich, M. L., Felice, M. E., & Drotar, D. (1996). *The classification of child and adolescent mental diagnoses in primary care: Diagnostic and statistical manual for primary care (DSM-PC) child and adolescent version.* Elk Grove Village, IL: American Academy of Pediatrics.

Wonderlich, S. A., Brewerton, T. D., Jocic, Z., Dansky, B. S., & Abbott, D. W. (1997). Relationship of childhood sexual abuse and Eating Disorders. *Journal of the American Academy of Child & Adolescent Psychiatry, 36*(8), 1107–1114.

Woody, S. R., Detweiler-Bedell, J., Teachman, B. A., & O'Hearn, T. (2003). *Treatment planning in psychotherapy: Taking the guesswork out of clinical care.* New York: Guilford Press.

Woolston, J. L. (1988). Theoretical considerations of the Adjustment Disorders. *Journal of the American Academy of Child and Adolescent Psychiatry, 27*, 280–287.

Wright, E. (1988). *Behavior Disorders identification scale.* Columbia, MO: Hawthorne.

Wright, P. H., & Wright, K. D. (1990). Measuring codependents' close relationships: A preliminary study. *Journal of Substance Abuse, 2*, 335–344.

Wright, R. G., Aneshensel, C. S., Botticello, A. L., & Sepúlveda, J. E. (2005). A multilevel analysis of ethnic variation in depressive symptoms among adolescents in the United States. *Social Science & Medicine, 60*, 2073–2084.

Wu, P., Hoven, C. W., Bird, H. R., Moore, R. E., Cohen, P., Alegria, M., et al. (1999). Depressive and Disruptive Disorders and mental health service utilization in children and adolescents. *Journal of the American Academy of Child and Adolescent Psychiatry, 38*, 1081–1092.

Wu, P., Hoven, C. W., Liu, X., Cohen, P., Fuller, C. J., & Shaffer, D. (2004). Substance use, suicidal ideation and attempts in children and adolescents. *Suicide and Life-Threatening Behavior, 34*, 408–420.

Yalom, I. D. (1995). *The theory and practice of group psychotherapy* (4th ed.). New York: Basic Books.

Yang, K. N., Schaller, J. L., & Parker, R. (2000). Factor structures of Taiwanese teachers' ratings of AD/HD: A comparison with U.S. studies. *Journal of Learning Disabilities, 33*, 72–82.

Young, M. E. (1992). *Counseling methods and techniques: An eclectic approach.* New York: Merrill.

Youngstrom, E. A., & Duax, J. (2005). Evidence-based assessment of pediatric bipolar disorder; part I: Base rate and family history. *Journal of the American Academy of Child & Adolescent Psychiatry, 44*, 712–717.

Youngstrom, E., Meyers, O, Demeter, C., Youndstrom, J., Morello, L., Piiparinen, R., et al. (2005). Comparing diagnostic checklists for pediatric bipolar disorder in academic and community mental health settings. *Bipolar Disorders, 7*, 507–517.

Zahn-Waxler, C., Klimes-Dougan, B., & Slattery, M. J. (2000). Internalizing problems of childhood and adolescence: Prospects, pitfalls, and progress in understanding the development of anxiety and depression. *Development and Psychopathology, 12*, 443–466.

Zemetkin, A. J., & Ernst, M. (1999). Problems in the management of Attention-Deficit/Hyperactivity Disorder. *New England Journal of Medicine, 340*, 40–46.

Zemetkin, A. J., Nordahl, T. E., Gross, M., King, M. C., Semple, W. E., Rumsey, J., Hamburger, S., & Cohen, R. M. (1990). Cerebral glucose metabolism in adults with hyperactivity of childhood onset. *New England Journal of Medicine, 323*, 1361–1367.

Zentall, S. S. (1988). Production deficiencies in elicited language but not in the spontaneous verbalizations of hyperactive children. *Journal of Abnormal Child Psychology, 16,* 657–673.

Zentall, S. S. (1995). Modifying classroom tasks and environments. In S. Goldstein (Ed.), Understanding and managing children's classroom behavior (pp. 356–374). New York: John Wiley & Sons.

Zentall, S. S., & Smith, Y. S. (1993). Mathematical performance and behavior of children with hyperactivity with and without coexisting aggression. *Behaviour Research and Therapy, 31,* 701–710.

Zetin, M., & Kramer, M. A. (1992). Obsessive-Compulsive Disorder. *Hospital and Community Psychiatry, 43,* 689–699.

Ziegler, M. F., Greenwald, M. H., DeGuzman, M. A., & Simon, H. K. (2005). Posttraumatic stress responses in children: Awareness and practice among a sample of pediatric emergency care providers. *Pediatrics, 115,* 1261–1267.

Ziegler, S. (1993). Teacher advisory groups: What, why, how and how successful. *Scope, 8*(1), 10.

Zink, K., & McCain, G. C. (2003). Post-traumatic stress disorder in children and adolescents with motor vehicle–related injuries. *Journal for Specialists in Pediatric Nursing, 8,* 99–106.

Zito, J. M., Safer, D., dos Reis S., & Riddle, M. (1998). Racial disparity in psychotropic medications prescribed for youths with Medicaid insurance in Maryland. *Journal of the American Academy of Child and Adolescent Psychiatry, 37,* 179–184.

Zoccolillo, M. (1992). Co-occurrence of Conduct Disorder and its adult outcomes with Depressive and Anxiety Disorders: A review. *Journal of the American Academy of Child and Adolescent Psychiatry, 31,* 547–556.

Zoccolillo, M. (1993). Gender and the development of Conduct Disorder. *Development and Psychopathology, 5,* 65–78.

Zohar, A. H. (1999). The epidemiology of Obsessive-Compulsive Disorder in children and adolescents. *Child and Adolescent Psychiatric Clinics of North America, 8,* 445–460.

NAME INDEX

SUBJECT INDEX